police hunt
brook Street

sit
...ne
...ang

By Daily Mail Reporte...

THE Commons may ... in the morning s... under Government ... posals for the reform ... Parliament.

At present MPs ... only one morning si... on Fridays. The new ... would add two mo... sessions a week.

Ministers believe tha... hours of business could b... 10.30 a.m. to 9 p.m. T... morning sessions are expe... begin within the ne... months.

Gordon Greig—Page ...

Home buy... are lef... guessin...

THE building societ... day postponed thei... on whether to accep... gage rate freeze.

But their leaders ... would make a defin... at their next me... tember 9.

The Government ... the Building Societ... tion to freeze rat... Prices and Income... ports in mid-Octo... proposal to increas... 6¾ p.c. to 7¼ p.c.

Full story—Pag...

Ban or... de...

LABOUR Minis... Gunter yesterd... ban on a new ... workers of B... which means m... turn for greate...

But Mr. Ja... the company's ... the deal, wh... operation tw... should not be ... wage freeze. ... four unions inv... to discuss Mr. ...

Full Report—...

Close t...

Brian Close, ... shire captain, ... night as Eng... the fifth and ... the West Ind... Oval next T... ceeds Colin ... captain.

Ian Wooldrid...

Ice-...

Walls an... major ice...

AKHTAR HUSSEIN

SCENES OF MURDER THEN AND NOW

The murderer's name was on all our lips in the past few days,
although that of the other young man,
who lost his life when he was doing his duty,
had relatively been forgotten.

THE TIMES, MAY 9, 1959

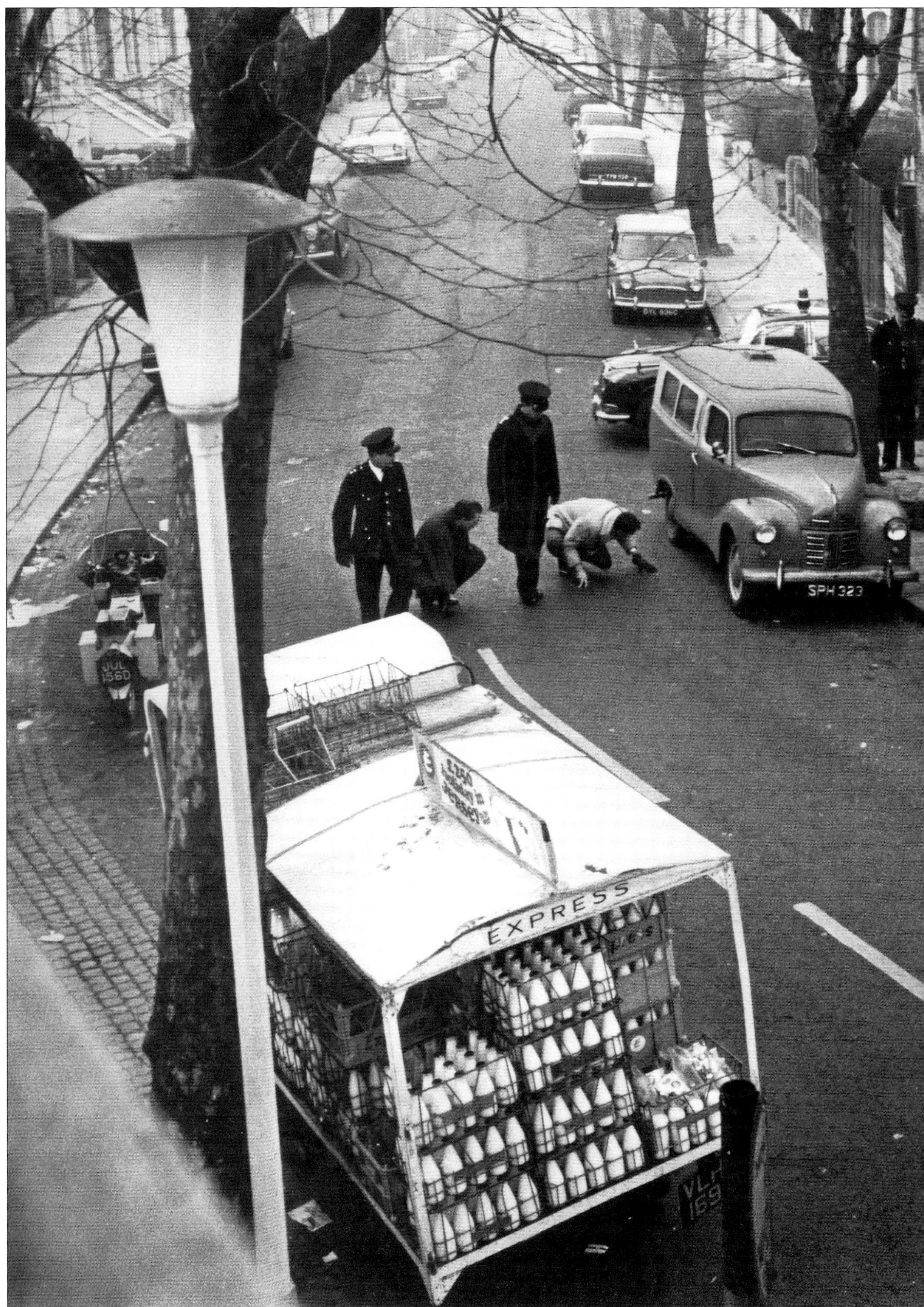
SPH 323
EXPRESS

SCENES OF MURDER THEN AND NOW

Edited by Winston Ramsey

Credits

ISBN: 978-1-870067 75 1

Edited and designed by
Winston Ramsey, Editor-in-Chief

PUBLISHERS
Battle of Britain International Ltd
The Mews, Hobbs Cross House,
Hobbs Cross, Old Harlow, Essex CM17 0NN
Telephone: 01279 41 8833. Fax: 01279 41 9386

PRINTERS
Printed and bound in China by 1010 Printing International Limited.

FRONT COVER
The death of Alec de Antiquis on April 29, 1947 — see page 186. (Geoffrey Harrison)

REAR COVER
If this grave is not that of Belle Elmore, the wife of Dr Hawley Crippen, then whose remains were found at 39 Hilldrop Crescent (see page 38)? And what then happened to Mrs Cora Crippen who was never heard of again after January 31, 1910?

FRONTISPIECE
The scene in Burlington Gardens, Acton, on February 20, 1968 following the shooting of Jorgy Koka (see page 354).

EDITORIAL NOTE
The source is given at the end of each extract in italic. We have largely retained the spelling, capitalisation and punctuation of each individual author to avoid the rigid imposition of an overall house style which would detract from the original reportage. The Editor formally apologises for any errors or omissions while gratefully acknowledging the publishers of the following:

Cherrill of the Yard, Fred Cherrill, George Harrap, 1954.
War on the Underworld, Edward Greeno, John Long Ltd, 1960.
Savage of the Yard, Percy Savage, Hutchinson & Co, 1934.
Forty Years of Murder, Professor Keith Simpson, George Harrap & Co. Ltd., 1978.
The Other Mr Churchill, Macdonald Hastings, George Harrap & Co. Ltd., 1963.
My Sister's Secret Life, Muriel Jakubait, Constable & Robinson, 2005.
The Trial of John George Haigh, Lord Dunboyne, William Hodge & Co. Ltd., 1953.
Mac, I've got a Murder, John McCafferty, Arthur Barker Ltd., 1975.
Bernard Spillsbury — His Life and Cases, Douglas G. Browne and E. V. Tullet, White Lion Publishers Ltd., 1959.
London's Armed Police, Robert W. Gould and Michael J. Waldren, Arms and Armour Press Ltd., 1986.
Executioner Pierrepoint, Albert Pierrepoint, George Harrap & Co. Ltd., 1974.
Country Copper, Superintendent G. H. Totterdell.
Trial of Neville George Clevely Heath, Macdonald Critchley, William Hodge & Co., Ltd., 1951.
Fabian of the Yard, Robert Fabian, Heirloom Modern World Library, 1955.
Francis Camps, Robert Jackson, Hart, Davis, MacGibbon, 1975.
Hume, a Portrait of a Double Murderer, John Williams, William Heinemann, 1960.
10 Rillington Place, Ludovic Kennedy, 1961.
Lifers, Kate Kray, Blake Publishing Ltd., 1994.
Occupied with Crime, Sir Richard Jackson, C.B.E., George Harrap & Co. Ltd., 1967.

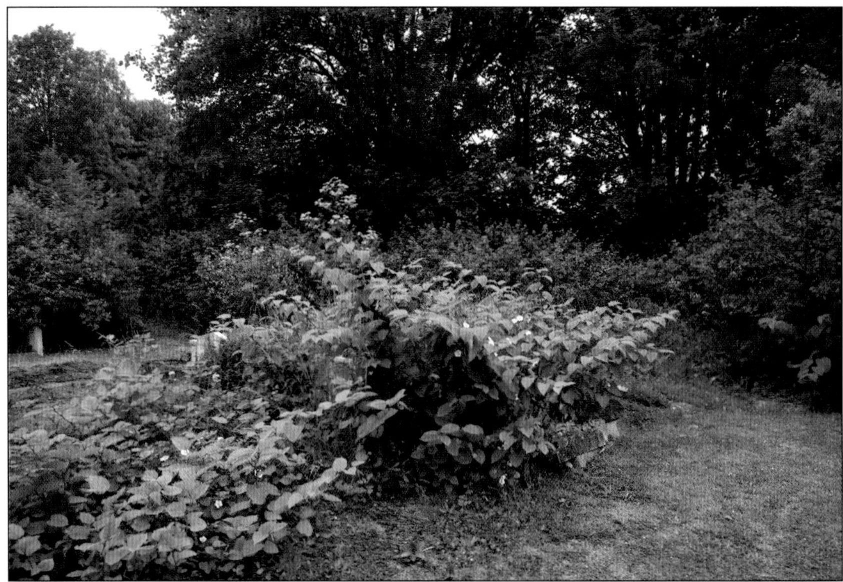

One of our main intentions has been to locate the graves of the victims, not an easy task as people can be buried hundreds of miles from where they were killed. A good example is Margery Gardner, murdered in London but now buried in Sheffield (see page 176). One crime that horrified Britain at the time was the murder of 17-year-old John Beckley in 1953. Teddy Boys with their flick-knives, razors and bicycle chains were a chilling sight on the streets and to read about this boy being dragged from a bus and stabbed to death at Clapham Common in south London horrified the public. Police files included a plan and statements describing exactly what happened, but not where John had been buried. It was not until June 2011 that we finally traced the cemetery where his father Ernest had paid three guineas to bury his son. We first photographed the spot where he died (see page 287) before driving on to Nunhead Cemetery to picture his grave No. 43130 but we were mortified to find that Plot 29 was hopelessly overgrown, a jungle of bushes, trees and shrubbery.

Editor's Appreciation

Producing this book has been a joint effort and first and foremost your Editor is indebted to his wife Gail for spending many hours on extensive background research. Then my thanks are extended to my *After the Battle* team: Rob Green, Jim Stark and Roger Bell. Rob accompanied me on most of the photographic trips, and Jim was indispensable in carrying out research at the National Archives where the majority of the police case files are now deposited. Roger Bell provided much source material from his personal archive and Steve Casely and Kevin Lamberth helped with photography in their areas. Other members of the team who provided invaluable help were George 'Marty' Black, Barry Cheese, Peter Cornwell, Peter Gunn, Roger Morgan and Trevor Popple.

Many other people contributed their time or assistance and the Editor extends his warm appreciation and thanks to the following: Allan Adams, Hugh Alexander (National Archives), Belinda Alley (Land Warfare Centre, Warminster), Sergio Andreanelli, Norman Attwood, Bev Baker (Galleries of Justice), Denis C. Bateman, Saira Bell, Chris Bennett (Croydon Local Studies Library), Reverend Canon Simon Bessant, Eleni Bide (Goldsmiths' Hall), Gordon Blacklock (Norfolk Library), Gary Burks (City of London Cemetery), Roger Carroll, David Church, Michael Collins, Patrick Collins (National Motor Museum), Chris Cooper (HMS *President*), Brian Coulon (*Daily Telegraph* Picture Library), Catherine Coulthard (City of London Police), Nikki Cowland (Epsom and Ewell History Society), Dick Cowley (Northampton Police), Wojtek Deluga (Polish Institute), Anna Derham (Kent Police Museum), Howard Doble (London Metropolitan Archives), Bill Edwards (Guy's Medical Museum), Bryn Elliott, Jonny Epps and Jenny Rawson, Essex Record Office, Jonathan Evans (Royal London Hospital Medical College Archive), Steve Fielding, Carl Forbes (NZK Publishing Ltd), Andrew Frost (John Frost Newspapers), John Gallehawk, Sarah Godfrey (Crawley Library), Sarah Gould (Local Studies Centre, Merton), Lucie Gregory and Jane Speed (Press Association), Jan Hey, Bridget Howlett (City of London Guildhall Archives), Andrew Hudson (Folkestone Library), Mike Jacques, Lynda James and Lisa Lawson (Croydon Cemetery), Lucinda Jones (Wiltshire & Swindon History Centre), Peter Kazmierczak (Bournemouth Library), Mell Knight (Mirrorpix), Ann Laver (Godalming Museum), Professor J. Robert Lilly, Ash Luchmun (Motorsport), Stephanie Maltman (Firemen Remembered), J. W. Marsh, Dipti Masrani (Harrow Cemeteries), Dave McCall (British Film Institute), Stewart McLaughlin (Curator, Wandsworth Prison Museum), Medway Archives and Local Studies Centre, Paul Mepham, Geraldine Middleton-Stewart (Surrey Police), Andrew Mollo, Andrew Muggeridge (Cambridge City Council), James Mullen, Graham Nightingale (Epsom Library), Roger E. Nixon, Barry Noakes, John O'Gorman (Tipperary Library), Anthony Rae (Police Roll of Honour Trust), J. M. Rampton, Anna Renton (London Transport Museum), Richard Riding, Jay Roos (Brompton Cemetery), Andy Saunders, Keith Skinner, Mark Smith (Curator, Royal Artillery Museum), Malcolm Springham (MAG American), Kathy Taylor, Heleni Tepli, Kent Thirley, Alan Tomkins, Wandsworth Library and Heritage Service, Becky Wash (Essex Police), John Weedy, June Wenbom (Ashford Library), Steve Wiltshire (Continental Landscapes Ltd).

WINSTON RAMSEY, EDITOR-IN-CHIEF, *AFTER THE BATTLE*

Contents

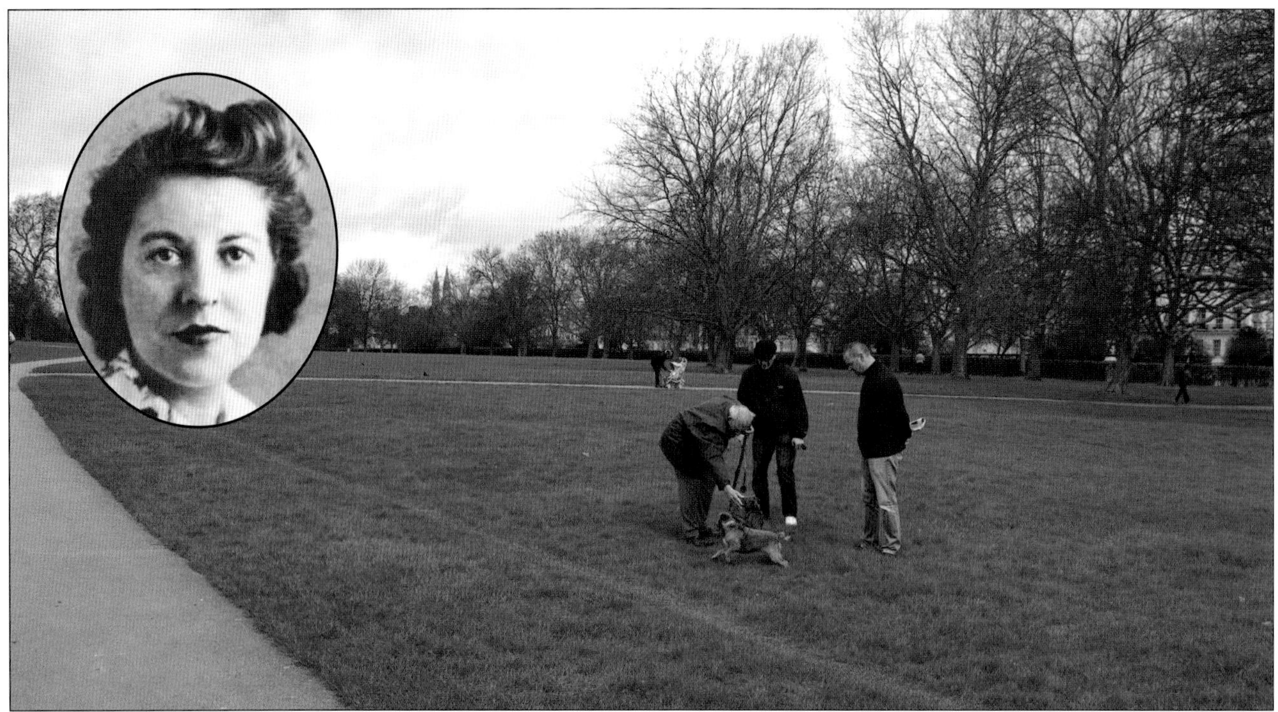

Introduction

Just as during the war when Britain's streets experienced death on every corner, so with murders one can visit the most peaceful of places completely unaware of what has gone before. Gladys Hanrahan died on this exact spot on October 1, 1947.

Murder, the most heinous of crimes, has been the subject of countless books but never before have the scenes of murder been portrayed so comprehensively with 'then and now' comparison photographs which are the theme of all *After the Battle* publications.

Nevertheless we have been very mindful to avoid causing further distress to families that have suffered which is why we have gone to great efforts to seek out the last resting place of the fallen as far too often the spotlight falls on the perpetrator, rather than the victim. We have also deliberately not included any murders more recent than 40 years ago, and none that involve children (apart from Geraldine Evans).

However it would be wrong to sanitise murder and many of the scene of crime photographs taken by the police demonstrate the harsh reality. The more horrific images have not been published and very careful thought has gone behind those that have been included. Television programmes like the CSI series have brought us closer to the forensic aspect of solving crimes which has encouraged us to include first-hand accounts from some of the pathologists involved.

In the first half of the last century there were an average of 150 murders in the UK every year (now there are upwards of 800) so selecting those to be included has not been easy. As the availability of scene of crime photos was an essential pre-requisite, this narrowed the field as quite a number of the crime files which have been released for public inspection no longer include photographs. Also another reason for inclusion is if a particular murder was a milestone legal case, and there were several in the years leading up to the abolition of the death penalty.

Capital punishment finally ceased in Britain with the introduction of the Murder (Abolition of the Death Penalty) Act. The Bill had been promoted by the staunch abolutionist Sidney Silverman, MP, and it received its first reading in Parliament on December 21, 1964 whereupon the Home Secretary Frank Soskice announced that from that date forward, even though the measure had not received the Royal Assent, all convicted murderers would henceforth be reprieved. On November 9, 1965 the Bill became law resulting in 15 men, convicted of murder and under sentence of death, being spared the rope. Thus ended a punishment that had been central to enforcement of the law in Britain since Roman times, if not before.

Up until 1957, the mandatory penalty for murder of any kind or degree was death by hanging but the controversial executions of Derek Bentley in January 1953; the revelation with John Christie's conviction later that year that possibly Timothy Evans was innocent of the crime for which he had been hanged, and Ruth Ellis in July 1955, had led to the introduction of the Homicide Act in March 1957. From that date, the death penalty was limited as a punishment only for the following:

a) Any murder done in the course or furtherance of theft.
b) Any murder done by shooting or explosion.
c) Any murder done in the course or for the purpose of resisting or avoiding or preventing a lawful arrest, or of affecting or assisting an escape or rescue from legal custody.
d) Any murder of a police officer acting in the execution of his duty or of a person assisting a police officer in so acting.
e) In the case of a person who was a prisoner at the time when he did or was a party to a murder, any murder of a prison officer acting in the execution of his duty or of a prison officer so acting.

At the same time, the practice of posting a notice outside the main gate of the prison stating that the execution had been carried out was replaced by the simple placing of an announcement in the Press.

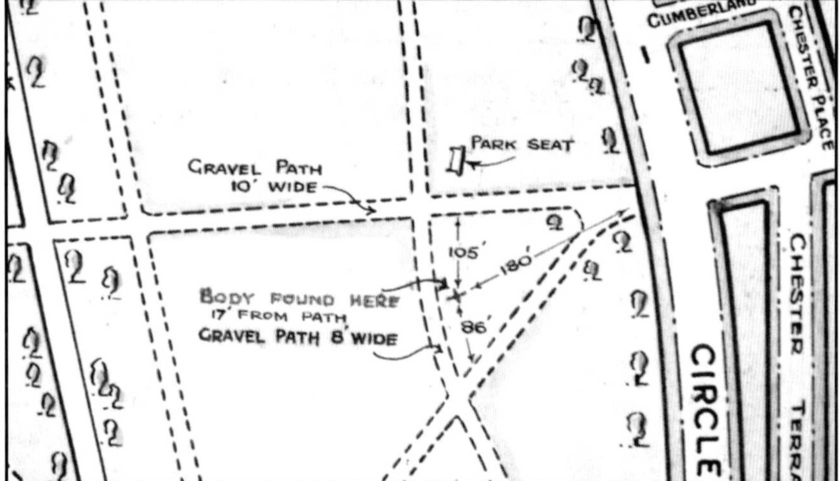

Scene of crime plans pinpoint the exact spot. It was at 10.20 p.m. that day that Gladys was found in Regent's Park by Robert Leslie. A handkerchief had been pushed into her mouth as a gag yet her handbag had been placed under her head for a pillow. Her clothing was not disarranged and there were no visible signs of violence to her body. Death had been caused by suffocation not less than one hour or more than two hours before being discovered. Her killer was never brought to justice.

'The sentence of the Court upon you, is that you be taken to a lawful prison and thence to a place of execution. That you be there hanged by the neck until you be dead, and that your body be buried within the precincts of the prison in which you shall have been last confined before your execution. And may the Lord have mercy upon your soul.' This is the only known photograph of a judge attired with the black cap, pronouncing the sentence of death. In this case Mr Justice Avory, (who sentenced Kennedy and Browne — see page 70) is pictured at Winchester Assizes where Thomas Allaway was found guilty of murdering Irene Wilkins at Bournemouth in December 1921. Executed by John Ellis, he is reported to have made a blunder by not getting Allaway's feet squarely over the drop. When the trapdoor opened, the prisoner swung from side to side instead of hanging straight down. The Governor asked Ellis: 'Was death instantaneous'? The hangman replied: 'Well almost!'

In 1957 there were two executions carried out under the new law, both for deaths caused during the course of theft; five in 1958 including the mass murderer Peter Manuel executed in Glasgow; seven in 1959 of which two — Ronald Marwood (see page 306) and Guenther Podola (page 312) — were for killing police officers; four in 1960; nine in 1961; three in 1962 including James Hanratty (page 328); three in 1963, and the last two, Peter Allen and Gwynne Evans in 1964. Although they were both executed for the same murder, they were hanged in separate prisons, Allen in Liverpool and Evans in Manchester.

Crowds outside prisons on the day of an execution were commonplace, mainly populated by abolutionists protesting against the very principle of the death penalty, regardless of the seriousness of the crime. These were led for many years by Mrs Violet van der Elst, popularly known as 'Sweet Violet' or by the more derogatory 'VD Elsie'.

Born in 1882, Violet Dodge married a Belgian painter, Jean van der Elst, and became a rich businesswoman with the invention of Shavex, the first brush-less shaving cream. In 1935 she purchased Harlaxton Manor in Lincolnshire, renaming it Grantham Castle and turning the estate into an animal sanctuary.

For over 30 years she mounted vociferous campaigns opposing capital punishment, her first major demonstration taking place outside Wandsworth on April 2, 1935 when Leonard Brigstock faced the gallows for murdering Chief Petty Officer Hubert Deggan on board HMS *Marshal Soult*. She organised a 65,000-name petition for a reprieve; employed 50 sandwich-board men and loudspeaker vans outside the prison, while aircraft towed banners overhead proclaiming: 'Stop the Death Sentence'.

Although coming from a humble background, she was a colourful character and would arrive in style outside prisons on the eve of an execution in her Rolls-Royce, and it was not unusual for her to be fined for obstruction or some other public order offence. As part of her on-going protests, she self-published a newspaper in 1935-36; wrote a book *On the Gallows* in 1937 and fought the Central Southwark by-election in 1940.

During the Second World War, the First Airborne Division occupied her estate but by 1948 her fortune had been dissipated through her constant campaigning and she had to sell up and move to London. According to one report, when the contents of the house were auctioned, her late husband's ashes that she kept in an urn in the library, were accidentally knocked down to an unsuspecting bidder and had to be discreetly retrieved! She died penniless in 1966, the year after capital punishment for murder was abolished.

So it came to pass early one bright Sunday morning in 2011 I found myself motoring along the B175 towards Stapleford Abbots, following the same route used by Kennedy and Browne in 1927. Alone with my thoughts I could picture Police Constable Gutteridge slowly walking his beat towards me, taking his last fateful steps on this earth along the narrow lane towards Howe Green. Now the road was wide and the only traffic approaching me were motorcycles, headlamps blazing, the leather-clothed riders hurtling along wrapped in enjoying the speed and power yet risking their lives on every sweeping bend. It seemed so unreal: death in the bright sunshine, then in the dead of night.

Producing this book has brought us face to face with death on every page. It has been hugely absorbing, even if the memories were unpleasant at times, but still a very sobering experience never to be forgotten to have stood by the graves of the fallen . . . and remembered.

WINSTON G. RAMSEY,
NOVEMBER 2011

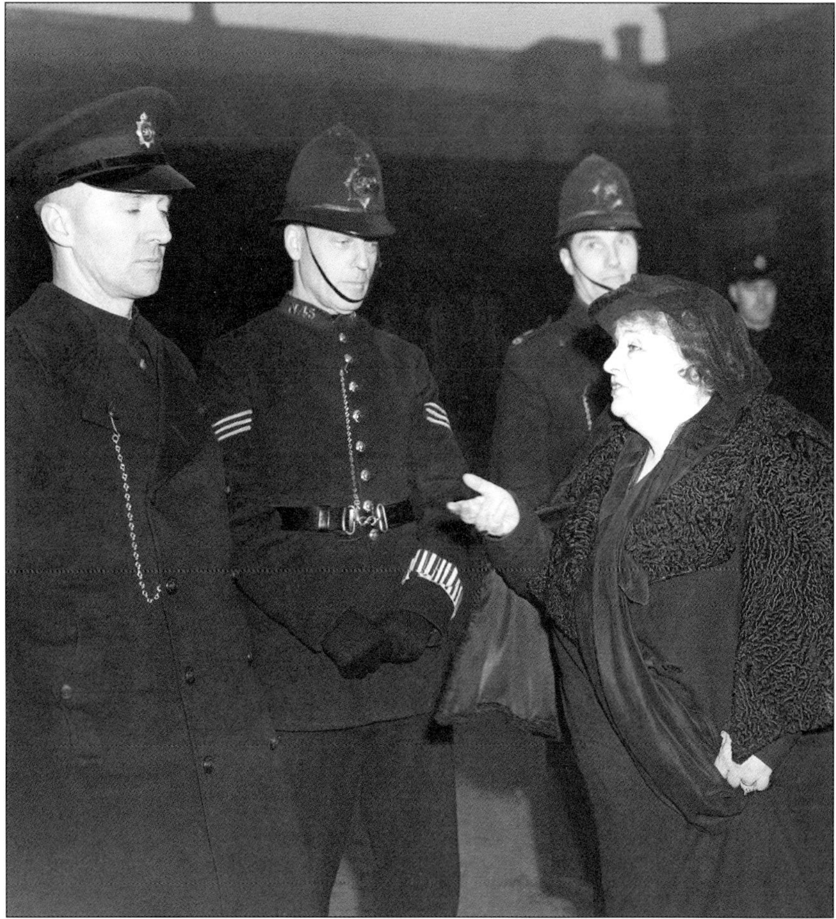

Abolutionist Violet van der Elst in trouble again at the execution of Private Karl Hulten (see also page 165) at Pentonville on March 8, 1945. On this occasion, and watched by a crowd of over 200, she attempted to drive a lorry through the prison gates. It is a sobering thought that between 1965, when capital punishment was abolished, and 2009/10, over 130 individuals convicted of homicide have killed again upon release from prison. And these figures only apply if the second murder took place in England and Wales.

In 1812 Britain suffered its first and only assassination of a Prime Minister in office when John Bellingham *(left)* shot the Rt Hon. Spencer Perceval *(right)* inside the House of Commons. Perceval had entered Parliament in May 1796 and became the First Lord of the Treasury — or Prime Minister — on October 4, 1809. He met his death on Monday, May 11, 1812.

May 11, 1812 — The Death of a Prime Minister

On the 11th of May in the year 1812, an event occurred which excited deep regret in the minds of the whole of the British public — the death of the Right Honourable Spencer Perceval, then Chancellor of the Exchequer.

John Bellingham, the author of this crime, was brought up in a counting-house in London, and afterwards went to Archangel, where he lived during a period of three years in the service of a Russian merchant. Having returned to England, he was married to a Miss Nevill, the daughter of a respectable merchant and shipbroker.

Bellingham, being a person of active habits and of considerable intelligence, was subsequently employed by some merchants in the Russian trade, by whom he was induced

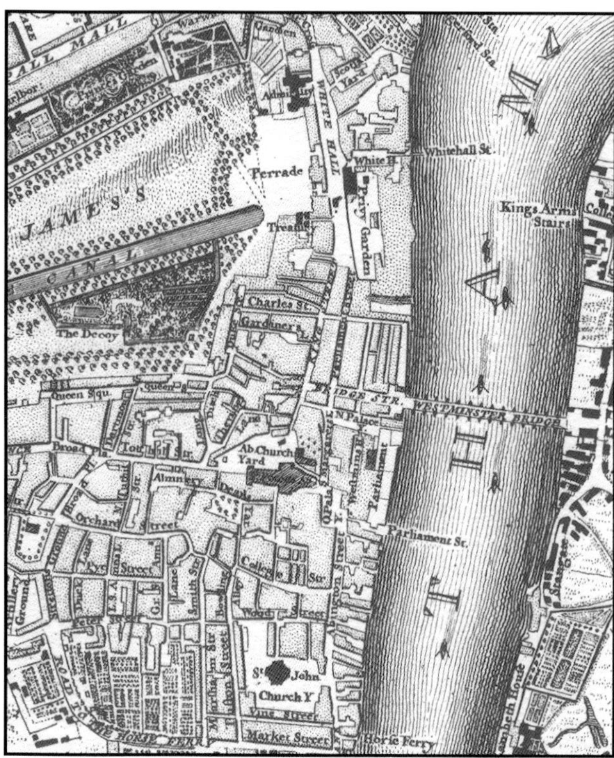

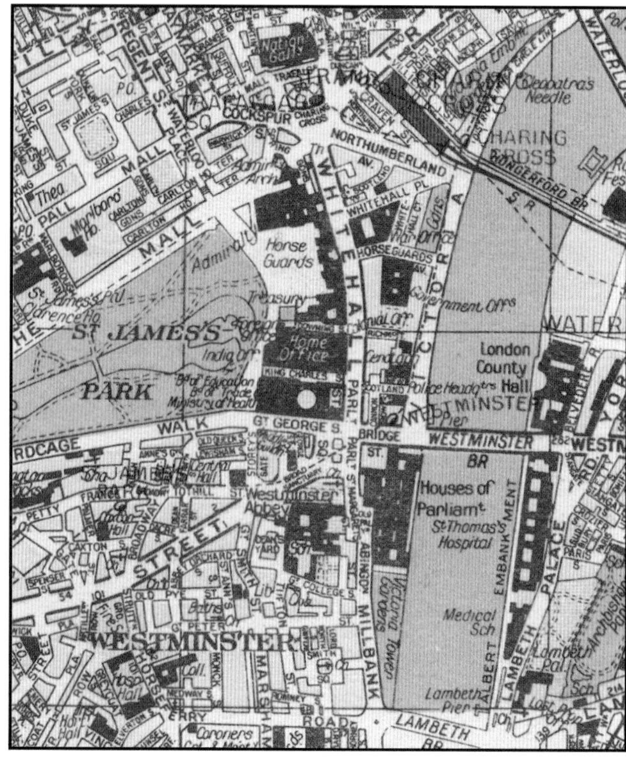

Setting the scene — Westminster then . . . and Westminster now. Although the foundation stone for the present Houses of Parliament was laid in 1840, the building with more than a thousand rooms was not completed for another 12 years.

This original House of Commons had burned down on October 16, 1834. The fire began with two workmen burning handfuls of wooden tally sticks in the coal furnaces. This overheated the flues to such an extent that the copper linings collapsed exposing the brickwork which heated up and, in turn, ignited wooden joists. The blaze was the largest in London since the Great Fire of 1666, destroying most of the palace including the House of Commons chamber which was housed within the former St Stephen's Chapel.

again to visit Archangel, and he in consequence proceeded thither, accompanied by his wife, in the year 1804. His principal dealings were with the firm of Dorbecker & Co. but before twelve months had expired a misunderstanding arose between them, and each party made pecuniary claims upon the other. The subject was referred by the Governor-General to the decision of four merchants, two of whom Bellingham was allowed to select from his countrymen resident on the spot, and by the award of these arbitrators Bellingham was found to be indebted to the house of Dorbecker & Co. in the sum of two thousand roubles but this sum he refused to pay, and appealed to the Senate against the decision.

In the meantime a criminal suit had been instituted against him by the owners of a Russian ship which had been lost in the White Sea. They accused him of having written an anonymous letter to the underwriters in London, stating that the insurances of that ship were fraudulent transactions; in consequence of which the payment for her loss was resisted. No satisfactory proof being adduced, Bellingham was acquitted; but before the termination of the suit he attempted to quit Archangel, and being stopped by the police, whom he resisted, he was taken to prison, but was soon after liberated, through the influence of the British consul, Sir Stephen Shairp, to whom he had made application, requesting to be protected from what he considered the injustice of the Russian authorities.

Soon after this the Senate confirmed the award of the arbitrators, and Bellingham was delivered over to the College of Commerce, a tribunal established, and acknowledged by treaty, for taking cognisance of commercial matters relating to British subjects. He was to remain in custody till he discharged the debt of the two thousand roubles.

Bellingham having, by some means or other, procured his liberation, returned to England in the year 1809, and at Liverpool commenced the business of an insurance broker. It appears, however, that, from a constant recital of the circumstances which had occurred in Russia, his complaints were aggravated in his own mind into grievances, and he at length began to talk of demanding redress from the Government. He eventually wrote to the Marquis Wellesley, setting forth the nature of his case and the grounds upon which he expected that some compensation would be made.

By the noble Marquis he was referred to the Privy Council, and by that body to the Treasury. His efforts being unattended with success in either quarter, he determined to proceed to the Chancellor of the Exchequer [Spencer Perceval] with a view to obtaining his sanction and support for his demand. Mr Perceval however declined to interfere, and Mr Bellingham was then advised by his friends that the only resource left to him was a petition to Parliament. As an inhabitant of Liverpool, he applied to General Gascoyne, then Member for that city, to present a petition to the House of Commons; but that honourable gentleman, having ascertained upon inquiry that the case was unsupported by the Chancellor of the Exchequer, refused to have anything to do with it.

Driven now to pursue a course quite unusual in such cases, he petitioned the Prince Regent; but from him he was referred again to the Treasury, and he again received an intimation that all applications from him must be futile. Three years had now been spent in these constant and fruitless attacks upon the Government, but the unfortunate and misguided gentleman appeared even yet to cherish hopes that his case would be attended to.

It was there that 22 years previously the Prime Minister had been shot and it is said that the site of the murder is where the statue of Edmund Burke now stands, alongside those of other famous statesmen and politicians.

Bellingham purchased a pair of half-inch calibre steel pistols with two-inch barrels — single shot of course — from Messrs W. Beckwith who traded at No. 58 Skinner Street *(above* — see map page 12*)*. He began practising on Hampstead Heath as those were the days when a gentleman could arm himself without any thought of needing a licence. He also had a special pocket sewn on the inside of his coat to conceal the weapons.

On Monday, May 11, Bellingham entered the Parliament building and walked down the corridor to the House of Commons. As the Prime Minister entered the lobby a number of people approached him, none of them noticing the man standing beside the fireplace. Removing a pistol, he walked towards Mr Perceval and fired at close range into his chest. The Prime Minister fell to the ground with the cry: 'I am murdered'.

Once more he applied to the Treasury, and again he was told that he had nothing to expect and, according to his statement, Mr Hill, whom he now saw, told him that he might resort to whatever measures he thought fit. This he declared he considered a *carte blanche* to take justice into his own hands, and he accordingly determined to take such measures of revenge as he madly supposed would effectually secure that attention and consideration for his case which he deemed it had not received, and to which it was in his opinion fully entitled.

This unhappy determination being made, he began to make the necessary preparations for the foul deed which he contemplated. His first step was to make himself acquainted with the persons of those Ministers who had seats in the House of Commons, and for this purpose he nightly visited the House, and there usually took his seat in the gallery appropriated to strangers; and, having obtained a general knowledge of their persons, he afterwards posted himself in the lobby of the House, in order to be able to identify them. He then purchased a pair of pistols, with powder and ball, and had an additional pocket made in his coat for carrying them the more conveniently.

On the evening of the 11th of May, 1812, he took his station behind the folding-doors leading into the body of the House, and at five o'clock, as Mr Perceval advanced up the lobby, he presented one of his pistols and fired. His aim was true, and the ball entered the left breast of his victim and passed through his heart. Mr Perceval reeled a short distance, and exclaiming ' Murder!' in a low tone of voice, fell to the ground.

He was instantly picked up by Mr Smith, Member for Norwich, and another gentleman, and carried into the office of the Speaker's secretary, where he expired almost immediately. Loud cries of 'Shut the door; let no one out!' were heard immediately after the shot was fired, and several persons exclaimed: 'Where's the murderer?'

Bellingham, who still held the pistol in his hand, answered, 'I am the unfortunate man,' and he was immediately seized and searched. Mr V. G. Dowling was among the first who went up to him, and on his examining his person he found in his left-hand trousers-pocket a pistol loaded with ball and primed. There were also found upon him an opera-glass, with which he had been accustomed to examine the persons of the Members of the House while sitting in the gallery, and a number of papers. Upon his being interrogated as to his motives for committing such an act he replied: 'Want of redress, and denial of justice'.

This event excited the greatest sensation in the country. A Cabinet Council was called, and the mails were stopped, until instructions were prepared to secure tranquillity in the districts; for at first it was apprehended that the assassin was instigated by political motives, and that he was connected with some treasonable association.

Bellingham was removed, under a strong military escort, about one o'clock in the morning, to Newgate, and conducted to a room adjoining the chapel. One of the head turnkeys and two other persons sat up with him all night.

On the 15th of May, 1812, four days after the death of Mr Perceval, the trial of the prisoner came on at the Old Bailey. The Attorney-General opened the case for the prosecution and called several witnesses. For Bellingham, witnesses were called who expressed the belief that he was insane. After Lord Chief Justice Mansfield had summed up, the jury retired, and after an absence of

Mortally wounded, Spencer Perceval was carried into the office of the Secretary to the Speaker where he was placed on a table. When the surgeon William Lynn arrived he soon confirmed that the Prime Minister had expired.

At first it was rumoured that Bellingham might be executed in Palace Yard at Westminster as it was thought it would be appropriate that he should be hung close to where the crime had been committed. However, it was at Newgate Prison that he met his end on Monday, May 18, 1812. Although these illustrations date from a later period, they show *(left)* the condemned cell at Newgate and *(right)* the 'Bird-cage Walk' where executed felons were buried beneath the flagstones. (Their remains were disinterred when the prison was demolished in 1904 and reburied in the City of London Cemetery — see page 15.)

fourteen minutes returned a verdict of guilty. The sentence of death was then passed and the prisoner was ordered for execution on the following Monday.

On the Monday morning, at about six o'clock, he rose and dressed himself with great composure, and read for half-an- hour in the Prayer Book. Dr Ford being then announced, the prisoner shook him most cordially by the hand, and left his cell for the room allotted for the condemned criminals. He repeated the declaration which he had frequently before made, that his mind was perfectly calm and composed, and that he was fully prepared to meet his fate with resignation. Just before he left the room to proceed to the place of execution he stooped down his head, and appeared to wipe away a tear. He was then conducted by the Lord Mayor, sheriffs, under-sheriffs and officers (Dr Ford walking with him) from the room in which he had remained from the time his irons were taken off, through the press-yard and the prison to the fatal spot, before the debtors' door at Newgate.

He ascended the scaffold with rather a light step, a cheerful countenance and a confident, calm, but not exulting, air. The fastening on of the cap being accomplished, the executioner retired, and a perfect silence ensued. Dr Ford continued praying for about a minute, while the executioner went below the scaffold, and preparations were made to strike away its supports. The clock struck eight, and while it was striking the seventh time, the clergyman and Bellingham both fervently praying, the supports of the internal part of the scaffold were struck away, and Bellingham dropped out of sight down as far as the knees, his body being in full view, and the clergyman was left standing on the outer frame of the scaffold. The body was afterwards carried in a cart, followed by a crowd of the lower class, to St Bartholomew's Hospital, and privately dissected.

The Complete Newgate Calender, 1926

The young Spencer spent his childhood at Charlton House, south of the Thames, and so it was to St Luke's Charlton that his cortège wended its way from No. 10 Downing Street, across Westminster Bridge, a contingent of the City Light Horse escorting the procession from Newington Butts to Charlton where he was laid to rest in the Perceval family vault.

The Fenian movement was founded in Ireland in the 1860s by John O'Mahony *(left)* and James Stephens *(right)* with the sole aim of freeing their country from British rule. Both were members of the Young Ireland organisation — a serious crime in British eyes — so they fled to France. In 1853 O'Mahony went to America where he became the leader of the Fenian Brotherhood (Fenian coming from the gaelic Fianna), while Stephens formed a Secret Society in Dublin which became known as the Irish Republican Brotherhood. The Fenian organisation recruited both in Ireland and America. An abortive attempt to attack Chester Castle in 1867 led to Thomas Kelly and an accomplice being arrested and taken to Manchester. A rescue, in which a policeman was killed, led to three of the Irishmen being caught and later hanged. To the Fenians they became the 'Manchester Martyrs'. In November that year Richard O'Sullivan-Burke, who had planned the prison van escape, was arrested and imprisoned in the Middlesex House of Detention, located in Clerkenwell.

December 13, 1867 — The Last Public Execution

A crime of unexampled atrocity has been committed in the midst of London. We are not a sanguinary people, and acts of wholesale murder are rare in our annals. Till yesterday we could not have believed that there lived among us men capable of planning such a deed as has just spread destruction over a whole neighbourhood.

The Infernal Machines of 1800 and 1835 have been rivalled by the diabolical device of the Fenian conspirators. In order, as it is supposed, to rescue two of their accomplices who had been remanded by a magistrate and had been placed in the House of Detention at Clerkenwell, it has entered into the minds of the rebels who are planning the overthrow of the Queen's Government in Ireland to destroy the wall of the prison at the moment the prisoners were taking exercise, and to carry them off through the gap which the explosion should create.

So far as regards the effect of the powder, the experiment has been horribly successful. A vast breach has been made in the outer wall; not less than 60 feet have been blown away, and the precincts of the prison are encumbered with the ruins. Never was the tremendous power of gunpowder more clearly shown. The gate of Ghuznee was blown open by a bag of powder hung to it by a nail; a barrel wheeled on a truck and simply placed on the pavement beside the prison wall has sufficed to crush and shatter everything that was exposed to the force of its explosion.

All that is known at present is that yesterday, at about a quarter before four in the afternoon, some persons were seen to wheel a barrel into the thoroughfare called Corporation-lane, one side of which for some

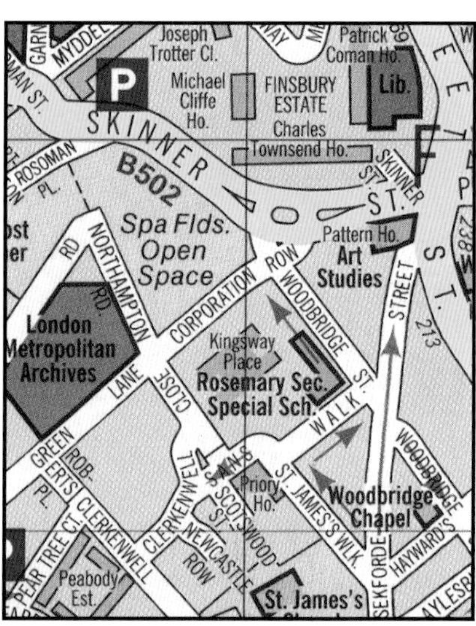

Left: **In 1685 the Middlesex Justices of the Peace built what was then called the New Prison but was a house of detention for prisoners awaiting trial at the Middlesex Sessions who could no longer be accommodated at Newgate Prison. It was rebuilt and enlarged several times between 1774 and 1818, separate cells being introduced in the mid-1840s. It closed in 1886 and Hugh Myddelton School was built on the foundations, preserving the underground cells.** *Right:* **When the school closed in 1971 it became a college of further education until being sold in 1999 for conversion into commercial offices called Kingsway Place.**

Although photography was plentiful in America in the 1860s during the Civil War, at that time images of scenes of crime like this one are extremely rare in Britain. Six people were killed outright and over 50 suffering grevious injuries of which a further six eventually died. The break in the prison wall can be seen on the right.

distance is formed by the prison wall. According to one account a squib was stuck into the barrel, one of the men lighted it, and then the conspirators ran quickly up a court, which leads out of the lane. In another moment the explosion followed. The wall heaved and shook, and then fell inwards with a single crash. Had Burke or Casey been taking exercise in the yard at the time, he might have had little cause to thank those who used so tremendous an instrument of rescue. But at this time the prisoners were within the Prison itself, and as regards them the exploit of the conspirators has been without effect for good or evil.

Not so with the unhappy inhabitants of the neighbouring houses. Corporation-lane is a commonplace street of small tenements, occupied by working people. The houses are neither new nor substantial; but if it were otherwise they could hardly have resisted the violence of the shock. As it is, the devastation has been beyond belief. The whole row opposite to the gap in the prison wall has been wrecked. The house immediately opposite was so completely crushed that there was no alternative but to pull down what remained of the tottering walls, and it is now only a heap of rubbish. On each side, the houses stand windowless and doorless, the cracked brickwork everywhere threatening the bystanders with a speedy collapse. A long way up the neighbouring lanes and courts the glass is broken in the windows, the chimneys have been shaken down, the ceilings have been destroyed. In one case a wall seems to have been not only cracked, but forced out of the perpendicular by the violence of the shock.

The perpetrators of this outrage did not miscalculate the potency of the weapon they used. This new Gunpowder Treason shows what power for mischief is in the hands of any determined ruffians whose fierce passions and seared consciences make them regardless of human life. If the miscreants who have done this deed are capable of remorse, they may well be overcome by the thoughts of their day's work.

The Times, December 14, 1867

FOUR HUNDRED POUNDS REWARD.

Murder and Outrage by Explosion of Gunpowder.—Whereas about 3 45 p.m. on Friday, the 13th inst., the Prison wall of the Middlesex House of Detention, Clerkenwell, was blown down by the explosion of gunpowder, maliciously placed there, and several houses in Corporation-lane were destroyed by the explosion, and divers persons killed and dangerously mutilated thereby, THREE HUNDRED POUNDS REWARD will be paid by Her Majesty's Government to any one who shall give such information as shall lead to the apprehension and conviction of the person or persons who caused the explosion; and the Secretary of State for the Home Department will advise the grant of HER MAJESTY'S gracious PARDON to any accomplice, not being the person who actually set fire to the gunpowder, who shall give such information as shall lead to the same result; a further REWARD of ONE HUNDRED POUNDS will also be paid to any one who shall give such information as shall lead to the apprehension and conviction of any accomplice in the offence, not being one of the persons for whose apprehension and conviction a reward of £300 is offered. The gunpowder, it is believed, was brought in a large cask, on a dark-coloured truck, with low sides.

Information to be given to the Commissioner of Police of the Metropolis, 4, Whitehall-place, London; at the Detective-office, Great Scotland-yard; or at any of the Metropolitan Police Stations.

RICHARD MAYNE, the Commissioner of Police of the Metropolis.

Metropolitan Police-office, 4, Whitehall-place, Dec. 14, 1867.

Then it was Corporation Lane — now it is Corporation Row.

Last evening the Governor of Newgate received an official communication from the Secretary of State for the Home Department respiting for seven days from to-morrow the convict Michael Barrett, now under sentence of death there for the murders caused by the Clerkenwell explosion. Tomorrow had been the day appointed for the execution, and preparations were being made for it. The prisoner, since his conviction, is understood to have behaved with much propriety.

A day or two after sentence the Fenian convicts, Burke and Shaw, were removed from Newgate, to the great relief of those charged with the responsible duty of guarding the prison, but the vigilance of the authorities, instead of being relaxed in consequence, may be said to have been increased, if possible, while Barrett remains there under sentence. Day and night the gaol is surrounded and patrolled, as it has been for months past, by a picked body of the city police, armed with cutlasses and revolvers, no two of whom are ever out of sight of each other, not to mention the special arrangements inside for its greater security.

The Times, May 11, 1868

Newgate Prison on the corner of Newgate Street and Old Bailey as depicted in the 1880s.

Yesterday morning, in the presence o£ a vast concourse of spectators, Michael Barrett, the author of the Clerkenwell Explosion, was hanged in front of Newgate. In its circumstances there was very little to distinguish this from ordinary executions. The crowd was greater, perhaps, and better behaved; still, from the peculiar atrocity of the crime for which Barrett suffered, and from the fact of its being probably the last public execution in England, it deserves more than usual notice.

The execution differed little from other similar exhibitions. On Monday the barriers were put up, and on Monday night a fringe of eager sightseers assembled, mostly sitting beneath the beams, but ready on a moment's notice, to rise and cling to the front places they had so long waited for. There were the usual cat-calls, comic choruses, dances, and even mock hymns, till towards two o'clock, when the gaiety inspired by alcohol faded away as the public houses closed, and popular excitement was not revived till the blackened deal frame which forms the base of the scaffold was drawn out in the dawn, and placed in front of the door from which Barrett was to issue. Its arrival was accompanied with a great cheer, which at once woke up those who had been huddled in doorsteps and under barricades, and who joined in the general acclamation. The arrival of the scaffold did much to increase the interest, and through the dawn people began to flock in, the greater portion of the newcomers being young women and little children. Never were these more numerous than on this occasion, and blue velvet hats and huge white feathers lined the great beams which kept the mass from crushing each other in their eagerness to see a man put to death.

None could look on the scene without a thankful feeling that this was to be the last public execution in England.

Towards seven o'clock the mass of people was immense. A very wide open space was kept round the gallows by the police, but beyond this the concourse was dense, stretching up beyond St Sepulchre's Church, and far back almost into Smithfield.

The convict Barrett had retired to rest about ten the previous evening, and, having spent a somewhat restless night, rose at six, dressed himself, and engaged in prayer. Towards eight o'clock the Sheriffs paid him a visit, accompanied by the Governor, and then retired to a part of the prison leading to the scaffold, where the rest of the authorities and the public representatives had already assembled.

The Sheriffs and Under-Sheriffs, who, with others, stood in a group in a gloomy corridor behind the scaffold, just caught a glimpse of the doomed man as he emerged with his attendants from a dark and narrow passage, and turned a corner leading to the gallows.

He was dressed in the short claret-coloured coat and the grey striped trousers, both well worn, by which he had become familiar to all who were present during his protracted trial. His face had lost the florid hue it then wore, and in other respects he was an altered man.

It was closed in 1902 in preparation for the construction of the Central Criminal Court, seen here in 1905. It is said that the condemned cell was preserved and built into the basement of Lancaster House which borders The Mall.

Executions in the street outside had become huge spectacles until the Capital Punishment Amendment Act of 1868 put an end to public hangings. William Calcroft had been the executioner for the City of London and Middlesex for more than 30 years but his method of a short drop of one or two feet meant that the victim was strangled rather than having died instantly. It was partly due to some of his botched hangings that following Michael Barrett, all executions were performed within prisons in cells specially converted with trapdoors to give a variable drop according to the weight of the person to be hung. The Act also abolished capital punishment for all offences save for treason, piracy, arson in Royal dockyards and murder.

With the first sound of the bells came a great hungry roar from the crowd outside, and a loud, continued shout of 'Hats off!' till the whole dense, bareheaded mass stood white and ghastly-looking in the morning sun. The pressure on the barriers increased so that the girls and women in the front ranks began to scream and struggle to get free.

The Church of the Holy Sepulche on the corner of Giltspur Street still overlooks the execution site.

His clergyman came first. Barrett mounted the steps with the most perfect firmness. This may seem a stereotyped phrase, but it really means more than is generally imagined. To ascend a ladder with one's arms and hands closely pinioned would be at all times difficult, but to climb a ladder to go to certain death might try the nerves of the boldest. Barrett walked up coolly and boldly. His face was as white as marble, but still he bore himself with firmness.

There was a partial burst of cheers, which was instantly accompanied by loud hisses, and so it remained for some seconds till, as the last moment approached, the roars dwindled down to a dead silence. To neither cheers nor hisses did the culprit make the slightest recognition. He seemed only attentive to what the priest was saying to him, and to be engaged in fervent prayer. The hangman instantly put the cap over his face and the rope round his neck. Then Barrett turning spoke through his cap and asked for the rope to be altered which the hangman did. In another moment Barrett was a dead man.

After the bolt was drawn and the drop fell with the loud boom which always echoes from it, Barrett never moved. He died without a struggle. It is worthy of remark that a great cry rose from the crowd as the culprit fell — a cry which was neither an exclamation nor a scream, but it partook in its sound of both.

With the fall of the drop the crowd begun to disperse, but an immense mass waited till the time for cutting down came, and when nine o'clock struck there were loud calls of 'Come on, body snatcher! Take away the man you've killed.' The hangman appeared and cut down the body amid such a storm of yells and execrations as has seldom been heard even from such a crowd. There was nothing more then to be seen so the concourse broke up with its usual concomitants of assault and robbery.

The body on being taken down was placed in a shell and removed to an adjoining building. There the rope having been removed, the surgeon certified that life was extinct. Towards evening the body was buried in the accustomed place within the precincts of the prison, in a grave upwards of five feet deep, in the presence of the Governor and other officers of the gaol.

The Times, May 27, 1868

The 'Newgate Plot' at the City of London Cemetery. When the prison was demolished the remains of the executed dead were moved to Manor Park in east London, including those of Michael Barrett — the last man publicly executed in Britain.

December 1887-September 1889 — 'Jack the Ripper'

The following is a list of the East-end murders:

1. December 1887 — Unknown woman found murdered near Osborn and Wentworth Streets, Whitechapel.
2. August 7th, 1888 — Martha Turner found stabbed in 39 places on a landing of the model dwellings in George Yard Buildings, Whitechapel.
3. August 31st, 1888 — Mary Ann Nichols, murdered and mutilated in Buck's Row, Whitechapel.
4. September 8th, 1888 — Mary Ann Chapman, murdered and mutilated in Hanbury Street, Whitechapel.
5. September 30th, 1888 — Elizabeth Stride, found with her throat cut in Berner Street, St George's.
6. September 30th, 1888 — Mrs May *(sic)* Eddowes, murdered and mutilated in Mitre Square, Aldgate.
7. November 9th, 1888 — Mary Jane Kelly, murdered and mutilated in Dorset Street, Spitalfields.
8. July 17th, 1889 — Alice M'Kenzie, murdered and mutilated in Castle Alley, Whitechapel.
9. The woman whose mutilated body was found on Tuesday morning (10th) in Pinchin Street.

The Times, September 13, 1889

Moving east from Newgate, 20 years after the execution of Barrett, the East End of London was in turmoil as a mass murderer began stalking the cobbled streets around Aldgate. The killings started in December 1887 and reached their crescendo the following autumn. By then the pseudonym 'Jack the Ripper' had been attached to the murderer who had savagely mutilated the victims — all women and mostly of ill repute. This is Whitechapel High Street in the 1800s with our matching view some 200 years later. We are looking towards the City, the church being St Botolph's but now hidden by the bulk of Aldgate House.

Now, the name Whitechapel will forever be linked with the unsolved murders committed in its streets, and one could write a book on the 'Ripper' murders alone. Criminologists, historians, and amateur sleuths, have expended vast amounts of energy trying to put a name to the killer but a hundred years — and dozens of books — later we are really no nearer the truth. Therefore, instead of adding to the speculation with more theories, let us simply go back and recount events as they were reported at the time. Then, *The Times* summarised nine murders in the 'series', but these days 'Ripperologists' only really concentrate on what they call the 'Canonical Five': Nos. 3, 4, 5, 6 and 7 on the list.

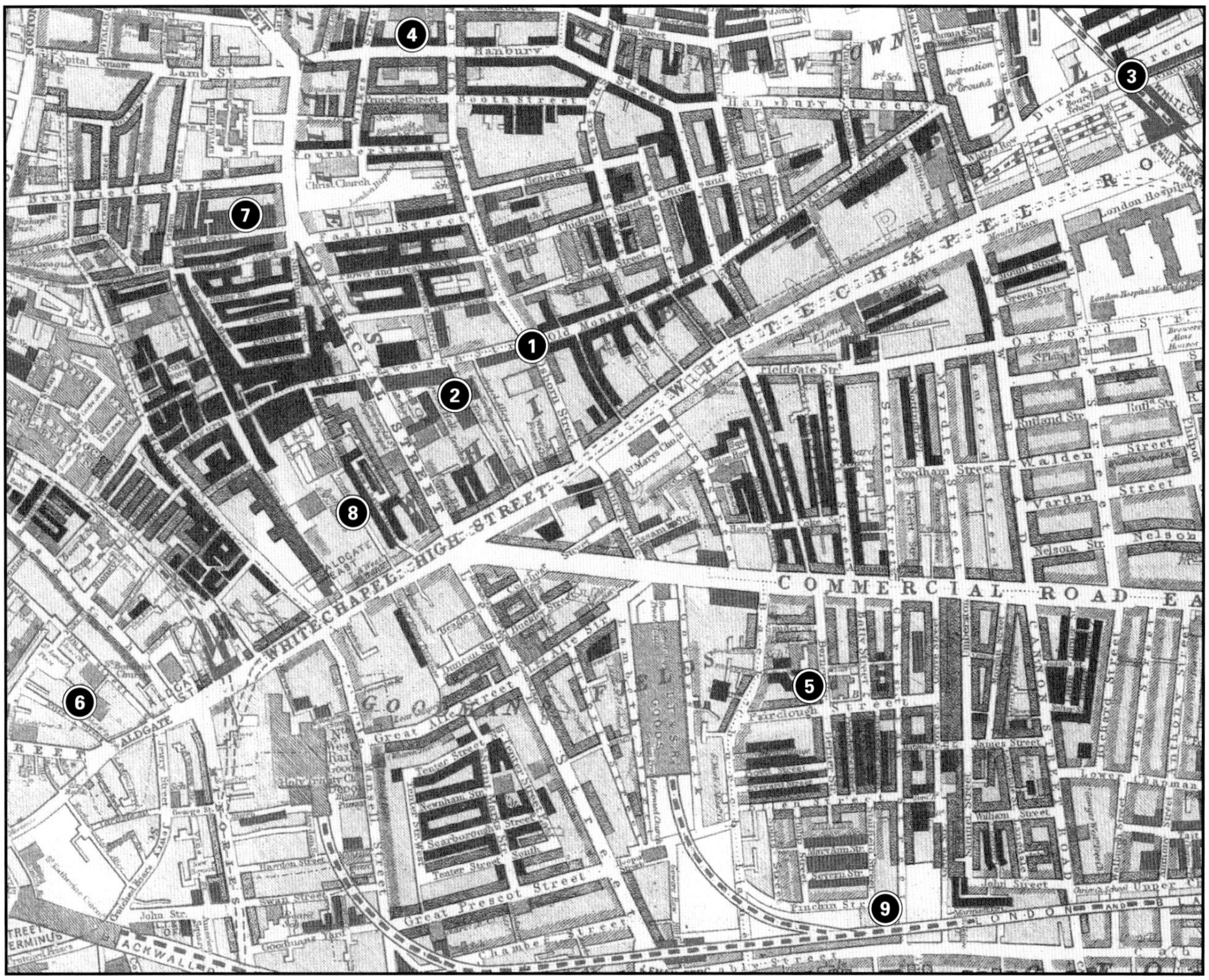

The area involved in the murders covered just under a square mile of the squalid ghetto of the old East End (the numbers on the map *above* refer to *The Times* list of 1889 *opposite*). The streets were dirty and foul-smelling with dark, narrow alleyways, unlit at night. Prostitutes and brothels were commonplace as was violence, drunkenness, and disease. Fights in the street were every day occurrences; thieving and petty crime rife; illegitimacy, infanticide and cruelty to children the norm. By night, the back streets and alleys were the breeding ground of vice as women sought to earn their night's lodging or next day's meal. Those bold enough to venture out after dark took their lives in their hands and could expect little protection from the odd constable equipped with only whistle and truncheon. In *The Nether World* published in 1889, George Gissing described it as 'the city of the damned': 'Over the pest-stricken regions of East London, sweltering in sunshine which served only to reveal the intimacies of abomination; across miles of a city of the damned, such as thought never conceived before this age of ours; above streets swarming with a nameless populace, cruelly exposed by the unwonted light of heaven . . . '.

It was as a direct result of the Ripper murders that the 'light of heaven' shone on the streets of Whitechapel. Pressure was brought to bear on the Board of Works to install gas lighting on street corners to make it safer at night, this picture *(left)* being taken in 1895 on Old Montague Street just 100 yards from where the first murder had taken place. *Above:* Outwardly, Old Montague Street may have changed out of all recognition but, in reality, nothing changes, the 'security' lights of the 1880s just becoming the floodlights and CCTV cameras of today.

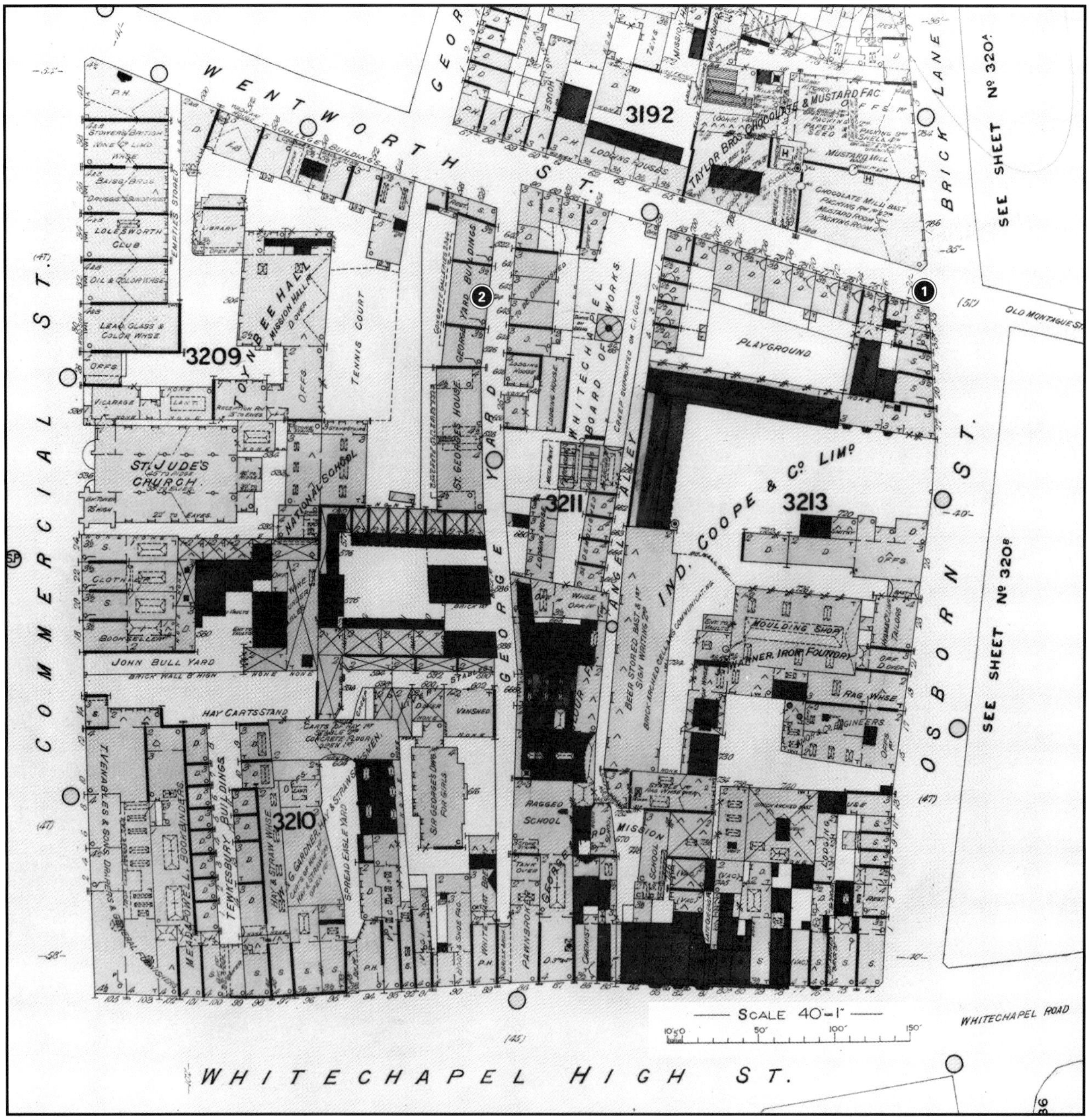

According to *The Times*, the first killing associated with 'the Ripper' (although that nick-name was yet to be seen in print) took place in December 1887 near Osborn and Wentworth Streets. As the map shows, these two streets meet at the crossroads with Old Montague Street and Brick Lane, where Taylor Brothers Chocolate and Mustard factory stood on the north-western corner. Subsequent researchers have failed to put a name to this victim and it may be that the newspaper reporter of the time confused the date with the assault on Emma Smith on the same spot [1] on the night of April 2/3, 1888. The latter woman, believed to have been soliciting, was returning home up Osborn Street after midnight when she was attacked on the corner *(right)* opposite the Mustard factory. She was taken to London Hospital in Whitechapel Road where she died two days later. (All our street plans in this chapter are reproduced from the Goad fire insurance plans of the period which give the detail we require to be able to establish the exact murder sites down to the last yard.)

The second killing took place in George Yard Buildings [2] in the next street to the west. This was a large tenement at the top end of George Yard, since 1912 known as Gunthorpe Street. Mrs Martha Tabram (also sometimes referred to as Martha or Emma Turner after the man she lived with) was stabbed to death on the night of August 6/7, 1888 and found on the first floor landing as depicted here in the Police Budget Edition of *Famous Crimes, Past and Present*. *Above right:* **This picture of the entrance was taken in the 1930s.**

George Yard Buildings — then Charles Booth House, part of Toynbee Hall — were demolished in 1972. The arrow indicates the spot where the entrance lay, the new building, still an extension to Toynbee Hall, now called Sunley House.

Yesterday afternoon Mr G. Collier, Deputy Coroner for the South-Eastern Division of Middlesex, opened an inquiry at the Working Lads' Institute, Whitechapel Road, respecting the death of the woman who was found on Tuesday last, with 39 stabs on her body, at George Yard Buildings, Whitechapel.

Alfred George Crow, cabdriver, 35 George Yard Buildings, deposed that he got home at half past 3 on Tuesday morning. As he was passing the first-floor landing he saw a body lying on the ground. He took no notice, as he was accustomed to seeing people lying about there. He did not then know whether the person was alive or dead.

John S. Reeves, of 37 George Yard Buildings, a waterside labourer, said that on Tuesday morning he left home at a quarter to 5 to seek for work. When he reached the first-floor landing he found the deceased lying on her back in a pool of blood. He was frightened, and did not examine her, but at once gave information to the police. He did not know the deceased. The deceased's clothes were disarranged, as though she had had a struggle with someone. Witness saw no footmarks on the staircase, nor did he find a knife or other weapon.

Police constable Thomas Barrett, 226 H, said that the last witness called his attention to the body of the deceased. He sent for a doctor, who pronounced life extinct.

Dr T. R. Killeen, of 68 Brick Lane, said that he was called to the deceased, and found her dead. She had 39 stabs on the body. She had been dead some three hours. Her age was about 36, and the body was very well nourished. Witness had since made a post-mortem examination of the body. The left lung was penetrated in five places, and the right lung was penetrated in two places. The heart, which was rather fatty, was penetrated in one place, and that would be sufficient to cause death. The liver was healthy, but was penetrated in five places, and the spleen was penetrated in two places, and the stomach, which was perfectly healthy, was penetrated in six places. The witness did not think all the wounds were inflicted with the same instrument. The wounds generally might have been inflicted by a knife, but such an instrument could not have inflicted one of the wounds, which went through the chest-bone. His opinion was that one of the wounds was inflicted by some kind of dagger, and that all of them were caused during life.

The Coroner said he was in hopes that the body would be identified, but three women had identified it under three different names. He therefore proposed to leave that question open until the next occasion. The case would be left in the hands of Detective-Inspector Reid, who would endeavour to discover the perpetrator of this dreadful murder. It was one of the most dreadful murders any one could imagine. The man must have been a perfect savage to inflict such a number of wounds on a defenceless woman in such a way. The inquiry would be adjourned for a fortnight.

The Times, August 10, 1888

But the gate through which the murderer — and his victim — passed still survives. Pictured *(left)* **just before the building was pulled down, your Editor rescued it from the demolition contractor and re-erected it in his garden** *(right)*.

Another murder of the foulest kind was committed in the neighbourhood of Whitechapel in the early hours of yesterday morning, but by whom and with what motive is at present a complete mystery. At a quarter to 4 o'clock Police Constable Neill, 97 J, when in Buck's Row, Whitechapel, came upon the body of a woman lying on a part of the footway, and on stooping to raise her up in the belief that she was drunk he discovered that her throat was cut almost from ear to ear. She was dead but still warm. He procured assistance and at once sent to the station and for a doctor. Dr Llewellyn, of Whitechapel Road, whose surgery is not above 300 yards from the spot where the woman lay, was aroused, and, at the solicitation of a constable, dressed and went at once to the scene. He inspected the body at the place where it was found and pronounced the woman dead. He made a hasty examination and then discovered that, besides the gash across the throat, the woman had terrible wounds in the abdomen. The police ambulance from the Bethnal Green Station having arrived, the body was removed there. A further examination showed the horrible nature of the crime, there being other fearful cuts and gashes, and one of which was sufficient to cause death apart from the wounds across the throat.

After the body was removed to the mortuary of the parish, in Old Montague Street, Whitechapel, steps were taken to secure, if possible, identification, but at first with little prospect of success. The clothing was of a common description, but the skirt of one petticoat and the band of another article bore the stencil stamp of Lambeth Workhouse. The only articles in the pockets were a comb and a piece of looking glass. The latter led the police to conclude that the murdered woman was an inhabitant of the numerous lodging-houses of the neighbourhood, and officers were despatched to make inquiries about, as well as other officers to Lambeth to

Murder No. 3 (and the first of the Ripperologists five 'official' victims) took place at the western end of Buck's Row in the early hours of August 31, 1888. Mary Ann 'Polly' Nichols was on the streets to earn her 4d doss money and was last seen alive at 2.30 a.m. on the corner of Brick Lane and Whitechapel High Street. At approximately 3.40 a.m., her body was found lying in the entrance to a stable yard [3], 70ft to the west of the Board School. *Above left:* **This picture dates from the 1930s while now** *(above right)* **the old Board School, having stood derelict for as long as anyone could remember, has been converted into luxury flats.**

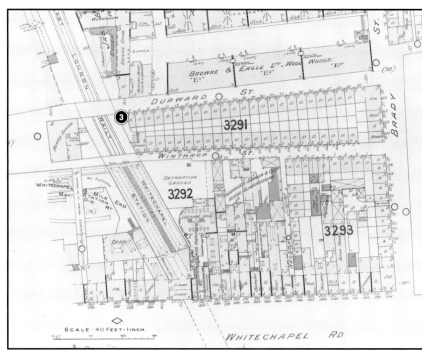

Below left: **When we photographed the street in 1972, the 1880's terrace was still occupied but, after standing empty, it was demolished some ten years later.** *Below right:* **To avoid the notoriety, in October 1892 the road name was changed to Durward Street.**

get the matron of the workhouse to view the body with a view to identification. The latter, however, could not identify, and said that the clothing might have been issued any time during the past two or three years.

As the news of the murder spread, however, first one woman and then another came forward to view the body, and at length it was found that a woman answering the description of the murdered woman had lodged in a common lodging-house, 18 Thrawl Street, Spitalfields. Women from that place were fetched and they identified the deceased as 'Polly', who had shared a room with three other women in the place on the usual terms of such houses — nightly payment of 4d. each, each woman having a separate bed. It was gathered that the deceased had led the life of an 'unfortunate' while lodging in the house, which was only for about three weeks past. Nothing more was known of her by them but that when she presented herself for her lodging on Thursday night she was turned away by the deputy because she had not the money. She was then the worse for drink, but not drunk, and turned away laughing, saying 'I'll soon get my "doss" money; see what a jolly bonnet I've got now'. She was wearing a bonnet which she had not been seen with before, and left the lodging-house door. A woman of the neighbourhood saw her later she told the police — in Whitechapel Road, opposite the church and at the corner of Osborn Street, and at a quarter to 4 she was found within 500 yards of the spot, murdered. The people of the lodging-house knew her as 'Polly', but at about half-past 7 last evening a woman named Mary Ann Monk, at present an inmate of Lambeth Workhouse, was taken to the mortuary and identified the body as that of Mary Ann Nichols, also called 'Polly' Nichols.

The Times, September 1, 1888

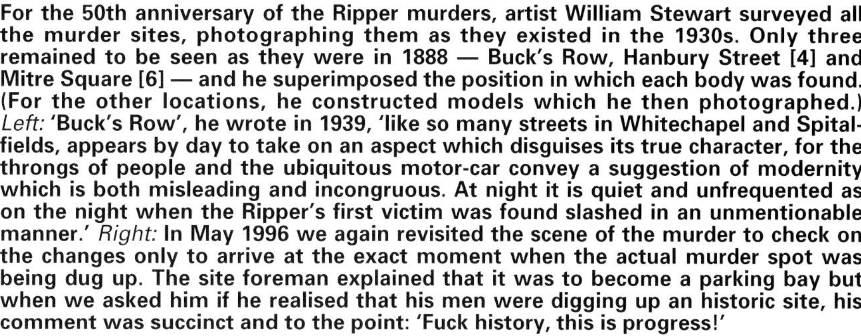

For the 50th anniversary of the Ripper murders, artist William Stewart surveyed all the murder sites, photographing them as they existed in the 1930s. Only three remained to be seen as they were in 1888 — Buck's Row, Hanbury Street [4] and Mitre Square [6] — and he superimposed the position in which each body was found. (For the other locations, he constructed models which he then photographed.) *Left:* **'Buck's Row', he wrote in 1939, 'like so many streets in Whitechapel and Spitalfields, appears by day to take on an aspect which disguises its true character, for the throngs of people and the ubiquitous motor-car convey a suggestion of modernity which is both misleading and incongruous. At night it is quiet and unfrequented as on the night when the Ripper's first victim was found slashed in an unmentionable manner.'** *Right:* **In May 1996 we again revisited the scene of the murder to check on the changes only to arrive at the exact moment when the actual murder spot was being dug up. The site foreman explained that it was to become a parking bay but when we asked him if he realised that his men were digging up an historic site, his comment was succinct and to the point: 'Fuck history, this is progress!'**

'Polly' Nichols, was buried in a common grave (No. 210752) in the City of London (then called Little Ilford) Cemetery at Manor Park. Consulting the cemetery records back in 1996, her grave was pinpointed on the edge of the Memorial Garden.

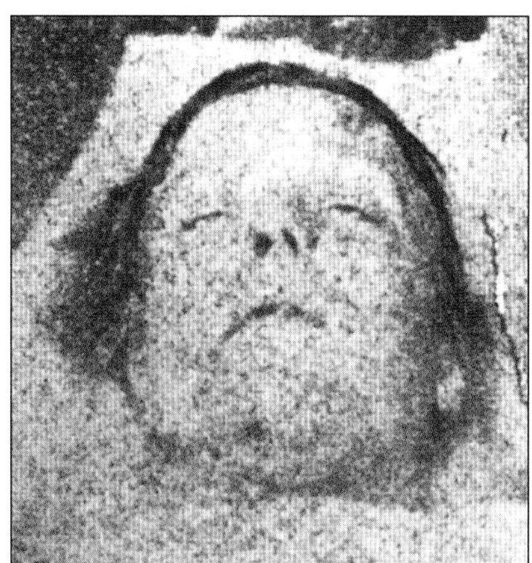

The cemetery administration then decided to mark the spot, the original plaque *(left)* **being replaced in 2004** *(right).*

Left: **William Stewart: 'Hanbury Street runs from Commercial Street to Vallance Road and its postal designation is E.1. It is a typical East End street, containing as it does a preponderance of the foreign element both in its inhabitants and the wares displayed in its shop windows. In the street well-dressed factory girls can be seen during their dinner hour, all hatless, while intense-looking foreigners shuffle along engaged in some occupation which necessitates the carrying of enormous bundles of dresses or dress material. The surrounding locality consists of disreputable thoroughfares with many courts and alleys.'** ***Right:*** **From 1938 . . . to 2011. Wilkes Street on the right is still 'guarded' by the same cast-iron 'cannon' bollards. The facade of the former Truman, Hanbury, Buxton brewery now occupies the whole northern side of Hanbury Street.**

Up to a late hour last evening the police had obtained no clue to the perpetrator of the latest of the three murders which have so recently taken place in Whitechapel, and there is, it must be acknowledged, after their exhaustive investigation of the facts, no ground for blaming the officers in charge should they fail in unravelling the mystery surrounding the crime. The murder, in the early hours of Friday morning last, of the woman now known as Mary Ann Nicholls, has so many points of similarity with the murder of two other women in the same neighbourhood — one Martha Turner, as recently as August 7, and the other less than 12 months previously — that the police admit their belief that the three crimes are the work of one individual.

The Times, September 3, 1888

Whitechapel and the whole of the East of London have again been thrown into a state of intense excitement by the discovery early on Saturday morning of the body of a woman who had been murdered in a similar way to Mary Ann Nichols at Buck's Row on Friday week. In fact the similarity in the two cases is startling, as the victim of the outrage had her head almost severed from her body and was completely disembowelled. This latest crime, however, even surpasses the others in ferocity. The scene of the murder, which makes the fourth in the same neighbourhood within the past few weeks, is at the back of the house, 29 Hanbury Street, Spitalfields. This street runs from Commercial Street to Baker's Row, the end of which is close to Buck's Row. The house, which is rented by a Mrs Emilia Richardson, is let out to various lodgers, all of the poorer class. In consequence, the front door is open both day and night, so that no difficulty would be experienced by anyone in gaining admission to the back portion of the premises.

Shortly before 6 o'clock on Saturday morning, John Davis, who lives with his wife at the top portion of No. 29, and is a porter engaged in Spitalfields Market, went down into the back yard, where a horrible sight presented itself to him. Lying close up against the wall, with her head touching the other side wall, was the body of a woman. Davis could see that her throat was severed in a terrible manner, and that she had other wounds of a nature too shocking to be described. The deceased was lying flat on her back, with her clothes disarranged. Without nearer approaching the body, but telling his wife what he had seen, Davis ran to the Commercial Street Police Station, which is only a short distance away, and gave information to Inspector Chandler, H Division, who was in charge of the station at the time. That officer, having despatched a constable for Dr Baxter Phillips, Spital Square, the divisional surgeon, repaired to the house, accompanied by several other policemen.

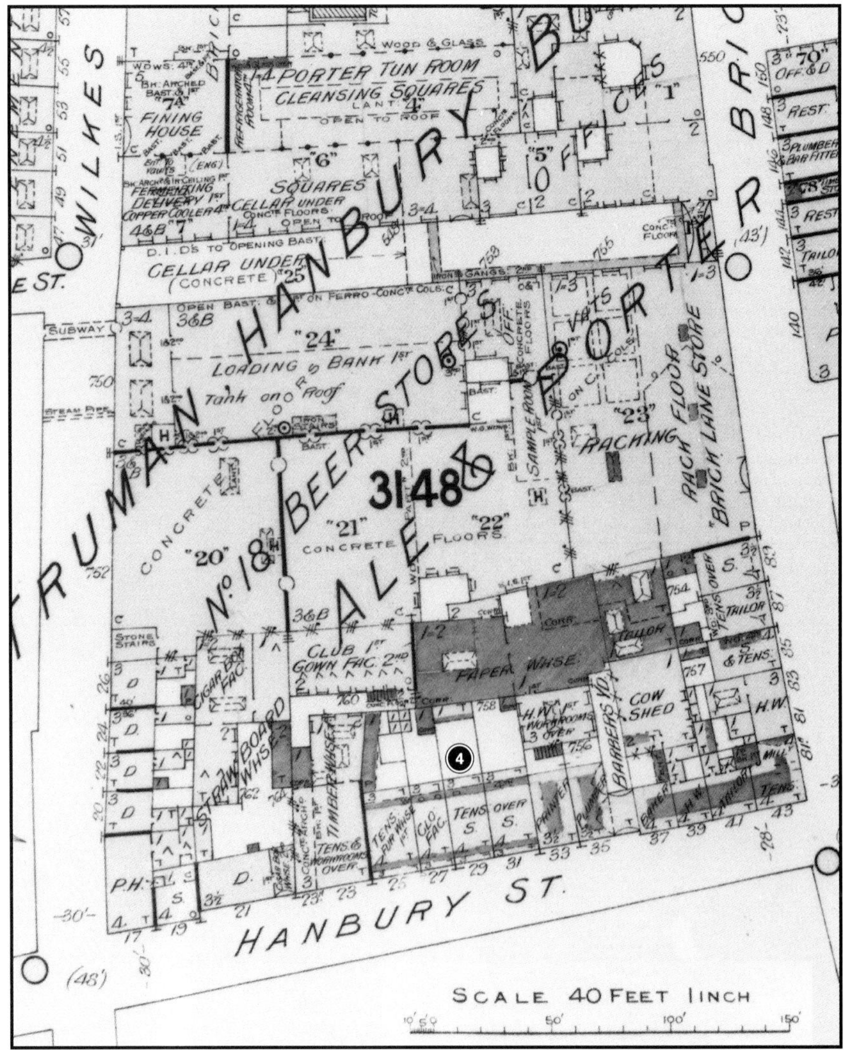

Two days after Mary Nichols had been laid to rest, the body of another woman — horribly mutilated — was found in the back yard of No. 29 Hanbury Street.

The body was discovered early on the morning of September 8. William Stewart described the scene he found in 1939: 'No. 29, in the back-yard of which Annie Chapman was murdered, is practically the same now as it was then. The shop which was then a cats'-meat vendor's is now a barber's establishment and next to the shop entrance is the same door which Annie Chapman went through for the last time on this earth. This door opens on to a dark passage, by which access is gained to the rooms above and to the yard in which Chapman was murdered.'

The body was still in the same position, and there were large clots of blood all round it. It is evident that the murderer thought that he had completely cut the head off, as a handkerchief was found wrapped round the neck, as though to hold it together. There were spots and stains of blood on the wall. One or more rings seem to have been torn from the middle finger of the left hand. After being inspected by Dr Baxter Phillips and his assistant, the remains were removed on an ambulance to the mortuary in Old Montagu Street. By this time the news had quickly spread that another diabolical murder had been committed, and when the police came out of the house with the body, a large crowd, consisting of some hundreds of persons, had assembled. The excitement became very great, and loud were the expressions of terror heard on all sides.

Inquiries were quickly set on foot with a view to having the woman identified, and persons of both sexes were taken out of the neighbouring common lodging-houses, which abound in this district, to the mortuary. Inquiries soon established that the woman's real name was Annie Chapman, and that she was known by the nickname of 'Dark Annie'. She was the widow of a pensioner, and had formerly lived at Windsor. Some few years since she separated from her husband, who made her a weekly allowance of 10s. At his death she had to do the best she could for a living. There were two children — a boy and a girl — of the marriage. The former, who is deformed, is at the present time an inmate of the Cripples' Home, while the girl is away in some institution in France. For some months past the deceased had been living in common lodging-houses in Spitalfields, and when in good health used to frequent the streets of Stratford for a living.

During the whole of Saturday and yesterday a large crowd congregated in front of the house in Hanbury Street, and the neighbours on either side did much business by making a small charge to persons who were willing to pay it to view from windows the yard in which the murder was committed.

Great complaints are made concerning the inadequate police protection at the East-end, and this want is even admitted by the local police authorities themselves, but they are unable to alter the existing state of affairs. Outrages and acts of lawlessness daily occur

We depict the site of the barbarous murder at 29, Hanbury-street, Whitechapel, and the scene in front of the house last Saturday. Succeeding, as it did, several terrible outrages of a similar nature in the same district, this foul assassination of the unfortunate woman, Annie Chapman, alias Sievey, has naturally aroused East London to take sensible precautions to prevent the recurrence of these deplorable murders. A few days after the discovery of the mutilated body of a woman in George-yard last month, a Committee of Safety was formed to assist the Police. Once let every citizen be on the alert to aid the ends of Justice, and such outrages should be stamped out. London needs to be more neighbourly in order to checkmate the criminals in our midst.

SCENE OF THE TERRIBLE MURDER IN HANBURY-STREET, WHITECHAPEL.

By now, all East London was agog with speculation and rumour — and fear — and the news of yet another grisly murder gave the press a field day. This illustration appeared at the time in *The Penny Illustrated Paper*.

Left: **William Stewart's pre-war model of the yard with his own impression of the body superimposed. He wrote that 'the passage [to the yard] was 20ft 9ins long by 3 feet wide and about half way down was a flight of stairs which led to the upper rooms of Number 29. The yard was lower than the level of the passage and access was gained by three stone steps. The door to this yard opened to the left.'** *Above:* **Hanbury Street in 1970, shortly before redevelopment.**

in broad daylight in the principal thoroughfares of the East-end, and the offenders are seldom brought to justice, owing to the inability of the police to properly cover the whole of the ground within their jurisdiction. During Saturday and yesterday several persons were detained at the various police stations in the district, but were liberated after proper inquiries had been made; and up to the present time the police have no clue to the murderer, and lament that they have no good ground to work upon.

The following official notice has been circulated throughout the Metropolitan Police district and all police stations throughout the country: 'Description of a man who entered a passage of the house at which the murder was committed of a prostitute at 2 a.m. on the 8th. — Age 37; height, 5ft. 7in.; rather dark beard and moustache. Dress — shirt, dark jacket, dark vest and trousers, black scarf, and black felt hat. Spoke with a foreign accent.'

Several persons bearing a resemblance to the description of the person in question have been arrested, but, being able to render a satisfactory account of themselves, were allowed to go away. Shortly after 8 o'clock yesterday morning Sergeant Thicke, accompanied by two or three other officers, proceeded to 22 Mulberry Street and knocked at the door. It was opened by a Polish Jew named Pizer, supposed to be 'Leather Apron'. Thicke at once took hold of the man, saying, 'You are just the man I want'. He then charged Pizer with being concerned in the murder of the woman Chapman, and to this he made no reply. The accused man, who is a boot finisher by trade, was then handed over to other officers and the house was searched. Thicke took possession of five sharp long-bladed knives — which, however, are used by men in Pizer's trade — and also several old hats. With reference to the latter, several women who stated they were acquainted with the prisoner, alleged he has been in the habit of wearing different hats. Pizer, who is about 33, was then quietly removed to the Leman Street Police Station, his friends protesting that he knew nothing of the affair, that he had not been out of the house since Thursday night, and is of a very delicate constitution. The friends of the man were subjected to a close questioning by the police. It was still uncertain, late last night, whether this man remained in custody or had been liberated. He strongly denies that he is known by the name of 'Leather Apron'.

Great excitement was caused in the neighbourhood of Commercial Street Police station during the afternoon on account of the arrival from Gravesend of a suspect whose appearance resembled in some respects that of 'Leather Apron'. This man, whose name is William Henry Pigott, was taken into custody on Sunday night at the Pope's Head public house, Gravesend.

The Times, September 10, 1888

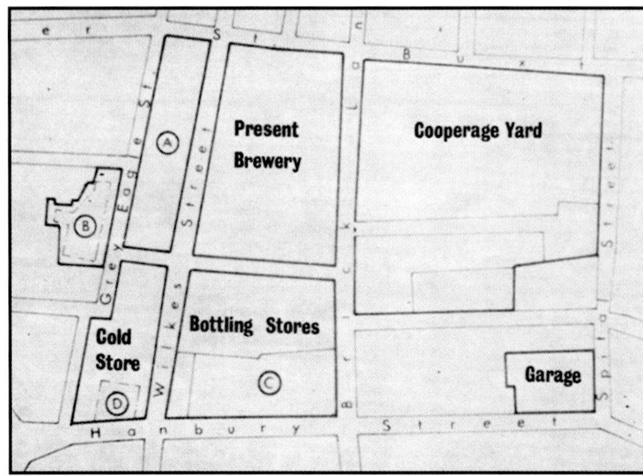

Left: **That year, Trumans began a large-scale modernisation programme for their East London brewery operation. The plan shows the development planned relative to their existing premises. 'A' was to be a complete new brewery including liquor handling, malt storage, brewhouse, and fermenting sections; 'B' a new cold store; 'C' a draught beer production plant and storage area, and 'D' the new main engine room.** *Right:* **Demolition work began in April resulting in the elimination of all the buildings on the northern side of Hanbury Street. No. 29 lay about mid-way along the street.**

Left: **By August 1970, the Hanbury Street site had been cleared and the foundations laid for the steelwork. The mobile generator stands virtually on the murder spot.** *Above:* **Steel-erection was well under way in mid-September.**

The latest reports as to the search for the murderer are not of a hopeful character. On Monday evening it was stated that John Pizer, the man who was detained on suspicion of being concerned in causing the death of the woman Annie Chapman, was still in custody at the Leman Street Police Station. Last night it was decided to release him.

Many reports of a startling character have been circulated; respecting the acts of violence committed by a man wearing a leather apron. No doubt many of the accounts of assaults committed on women in this district have been greatly exaggerated, yet so many versions have been related that the police give credit to at least a portion of them. They have, therefore, been keeping a sharp lookout for 'leather apron', but nothing has been heard of his whereabouts. The friends of Pizer stoutly denied that he was known by that name; but on the other hand Sergeant Thicke, who has an intimate knowledge of the neighbourhood in which the murder was committed, affirms that he knew Pizer well by sight, and always knew him by the nickname spoken of. Sergeant Thicke also knew that he was in the habit of wearing a leather apron after the news of the murder was circulated.

A number of tradesmen in the neighbourhood in which the murder was committed have organised a vigilance committee, and yesterday morning the following notice was published: 'Finding that, in spite of murders being committed in our midst our police force is inadequate to discover the author or authors of the late atrocities, we the undersigned have formed ourselves into a committee and intend offering a substantial reward to any one, citizens or otherwise, who shall give such information as will be the means of bringing the murderer or murderers to justice.'

The Times, September 11, 1888

The police at the Commercial Street Police Station have made another arrest on suspicion in connexion with the recent murders. It appears that among the numerous statements and descriptions of suspected persons are several tallying with that of the man in custody, but beyond this the police know nothing at present against him. His apprehension was of a singular character. Throughout yesterday his movements are stated to have created suspicion among various persons, and last night he was handed over to a uniform constable doing duty in the neighbourhood of Flower and Dean Street on suspicion in connexion with the crime.

Courage, which had taken over Trumans in 1986, closed the brewery and sold the site back in 1991. Five years later, PC Harry Harris, based at the 'nick' in Brick Lane, very kindly made arrangements with the new owners, the E. A. O. O. & J. Zeloof Partnership, to allow us to pinpoint the murder site which we marked in typical scene-of-crime fashion. The building is now used as a garment warehouse.

Regarding the man Pigott, who was captured at Gravesend, nothing whatever has been discovered by the detectives in the course of their inquiries which can in any way connect him with the crime or crimes, and his release, at all events, from the custody of the police is expected shortly.

In connexion with the arrest of a lunatic at Holloway, it appears that he has been missing from his friends for some time now. The detectives have been very active in prosecuting their inquiries concerning him.

The Times, September 15, 1888

On September 14, 1888, Annie Chapman was buried in a common grave (No. 78 in Plot 148) in the burial ground in Sebert Road, Manor Park, which had been established in 1874. Although since buried over again, the original grave site lies somewhere here in the extreme south-eastern corner of the cemetery.

In the early hours of Sunday morning two more horrible murders were committed in the East-end of London, the victim in both cases belonging, it is believed, to the same unfortunate class. No doubt seems to be entertained by the police that these terrible crimes were the work of the same fiendish hands which committed the outrages which had already made Whitechapel so painfully notorious. The scenes of the two murders just brought to light are within a quarter of an hour's walk of each other, the earlier-discovered crime having been committed in a yard in Berner Street, a low thoroughfare out of the Commercial Road, while the second outrage was perpetrated within the city boundary, in Mitre Square, Aldgate.

In the first-mentioned case the body was found in a gateway leading to a factory, and although the murder, compared with the other, may be regarded as of an almost ordinary character — the unfortunate woman only having her throat cut — little doubt is felt, from the position of the corpse, that the assassin had intended to mutilate it. He seems, however, to have been interrupted by the arrival of a cart, which drew up close to the spot, and it is believed to be possible that he may have escaped behind this vehicle. Conflicting statements are made as to the way in which the body was found, but according to one account, a lad first made the discovery and gave information to a man named Costa, who proceeded to the spot, where almost immediately afterwards a constable arrived.

In 1963, the name of the street was changed to Henriques Street in memory of the local benefactor, Sir Basil Lucas Quixano Henriques, who died in 1961.

Three weeks after the Hanbury Street killing came the horrific news of a double murder on the night of September 29/30. The first body was found just inside the narrow entrance to Duffield's Yard in Berner Street. ***Above:*** **This picture was taken in 1909 — the entrance to the yard below the cartwheel still existing, minus only the gates which closed it off in 1888. Then, the corner shop (No. 46) was a beer house and the tall building (No. 40) to the right of the yard entrance the International Working Men's Educational Club. A Socialist discussion meeting was taking place there on the Saturday evening of the murder. In 1939, William Stewart described Berner Street in his book** ***Jack the Ripper,*** **as looking like 'a person half-dressed in a drab garb of the 'eighties while the other half is dressed in that shoddy modernity which is prevalent in other poor quarters and which has been presented to London as the solution to the slum problem.** ***Below:*** **The yard has been demolished and on its site stands a large LCC school [built in 1910].'**

When Mr Wynne Baxter, the Coroner for South-East Middlesex, opened the inquest on Monday morning the first witness called was William West, a printer living at 40 Berner Street. After being sworn in, he said: 'I live on the premises; it is the International Working Men's Educational Club. There are two windows on the ground floor facing the street, and the door opens into the same street. At the side of the house there is a passage into a yard, and there are two wooden gates at the entrance to the yard; they open into the street. The first passage into the club leads into a room, and the door opens out of this passage. The gates are open at all hours of the day, but are mostly closed at night. The door is not closed till the members leave. There is no particular person to look after it. The room contains three doors leading into the yard. There is no other way out of the yard except through the gate. Opposite the gate there is a workshop, which belongs to a sack manufacturer. There is a stable on the left-hand side before you come to the club. In the evening there had been a discussion going on in the large room on the first floor, in which there are two windows looking into the street. About one hundred persons were present on Saturday.' Morris Eagle of 4 New Road, told the Coroner that he was a traveller and a member of the Socialist Club. 'I was at the club on Saturday night,' he said, 'and did not leave till after the discussion. I went through the front door on my way out at a quarter-past twelve, but returned to the club about twenty to one. When I returned the front door was closed, so I went in at the back door in the yard and along the passage into the club. *How wide is the passage?* About nine feet. *When did you hear of the murder?* A member named Gidleman told me there was a dead woman in the yard. I went, and saw a woman lying there in much blood. Her feet were about six feet or seven feet from the gate. *Was she against the club wall?* Yes, sir. *Her head towards the yard?* Yes, her feet to the gate and her head to the yard. I struck a light and saw her covered in blood. I could not look at her long, so I ran for the police. Another man went for them at the same time. We could not find one at first; but when we got to the corner of Grove Street, Commercial Road, I found two constables, and I told them there was a woman murdered in Berner Street. One of them turned his light on down the yard. There were lots of people present in the yard at the time we returned.'

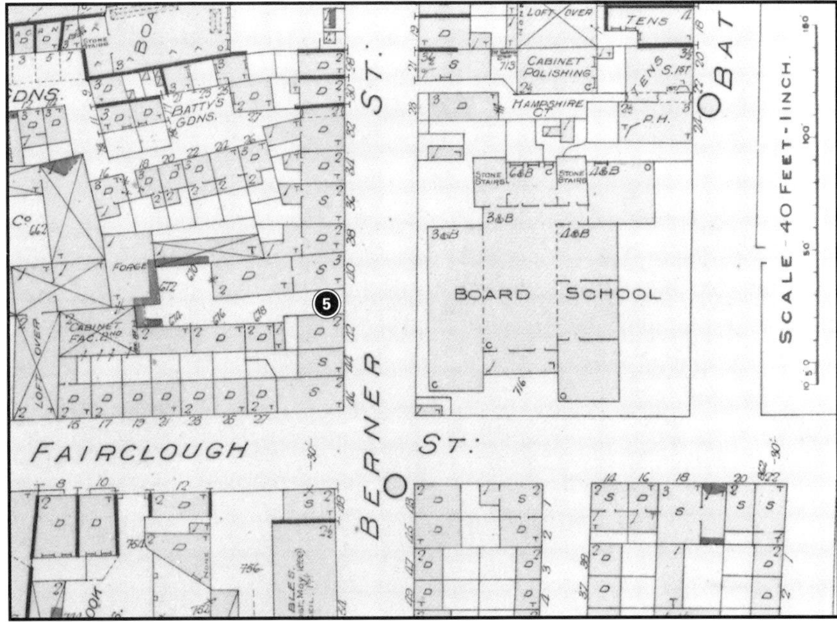

Above left: From the description given by Mr Eagle, it would appear that William Stewart slipped up when he superimposed the outline of the body on his model because her feet should have pointed towards the gate. *Above right:* With the kind permission of what is now Harry Gosling Primary School, one afternoon in September 1996, after the children had left for the day, we plotted the correct spot by measurement and put down our own taped outline the right way round.

Elizabeth Stride was laid to rest in Plot 37 of East London Cemetery. The grave (No. 15509) has now been marked with a simple marble headstone.

THE ILLUSTRATED POLICE NEWS

LAW COURTS AND WEEKLY RECORD.

THE FIFTH VICTIM OF THE WHITECHAPEL FIEND.

FINDING THE MUTILATED BODY IN MITRE SQARE.

When preparing his model of Duffield's Yard, undoubtedly William Stewart referred to the artwork of the time but apparently not to the *Police News* whose illustrator has correctly drawn the body with feet to the gate. The police artist also accurately draws the position of the body of the second victim on Saturday night, that of Catharine Eddowes in Mitre Square *(bottom right)*, which accords to the plan *(opposite)* produced by Frederick Foster for the inquest which opened on October 4. In the case of this murder, the body was discovered by a policeman on his beat, PC Edward Watkins (No. 881) of the City Police. At 1.30 a.m., he had passed through the square, seeing nothing untoward, but, on his return 14 minutes later, discovered the body, dreadfully mutilated, lying in the southwestern corner. Her throat had been cut 'from which blood had flowed in great quantity, staining the pavement for some distance around'.

Mitre Square had three entrances: a roadway for carts from the street to the south-west; Mitre Passage in the northern corner leading to St James' Place (Creechurch Lane) and Church Passage to the east running to Duke's Place.

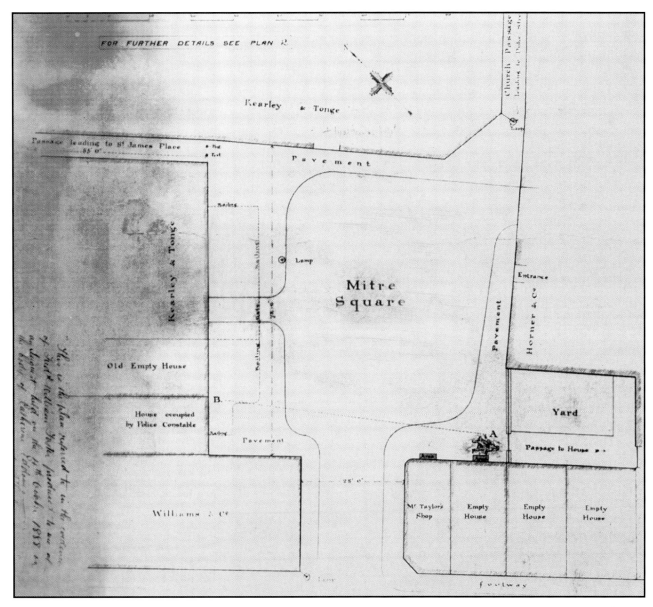

Left: This early — yet unfortunately undated — photograph was taken looking south-west from Church Passage towards the murder site and entrance to Mitre Street. The body lay at the rear of an empty house. *Right:* 'Mitre Square, strictly speaking, is not in the East End, for it lies just within the boundary of the City of London,' explained William Stewart in 1939, 'but here again practically no alteration has taken place since the body of Catharine Eddowes was found in the south-west corner. This spot is still known by the City Police as "Jack the Ripper's Corner" and the same dilapidated building which overlooks the spot stands, as it stood on the night when PC Watkins made his ghastly discovery.'

This time the police sketch *(above)*, drawn by Frederick Foster from position 'B' on the plan on page 29, accords with William Stewart's overlay on his 1930's photograph *(below)*.

The murder in the City was committed in circumstances which show that the assassin, if not suffering from insanity, appears to be free from any fear of interruption while at his dreadful work. Mitre Square is entered from three places — Mitre Street, and passages from Duke Street and St James's Place — through any of which he might have been interrupted by the arrival either of ordinary pedestrians or the police, although the square is lonely at night-time, being occupied chiefly for business purposes. The constable's beat, moreover, is patrolled in between 15 and 20 minutes, and within this short space of time, apparently, the murderer and his victim must have arrived and the crime been committed. The beat is in the charge of a man who is regarded by his superiors as thoroughly trustworthy, who has discharged his duties efficiently for several years, and who reports that when he went through the square at about half-past 1 he noticed nothing unusual and no one about. Plain-clothes constables also occasionally patrol the square, which is a place of irregular form, about 77ft. by 80ft. On two sides of the square are the warehouses of Messrs. Kearley and Tonge, and adjoining them are two old houses, which exactly face the scene of the murder — the wide pavement opposite, where, it is stated, there was some deficiency of light from the gas-lamp.

The square is occupied by business firms, excepting the two old houses already referred to, one of which, curiously enough, is tenanted by a police constable, the other being uninhabited. The corner house of Mitre Square and Mitre Street is held by a picture-frame maker, who, however, does not reside on the premises; and the adjoining three houses in Mitre Street, backing on to the square, are unoccupied.

According to the report of Police Constable Watkins, 881, in passing through the square at a quarter to 2 a.m., he found the murdered woman, lying in the south-western corner, with her throat cut and her intestines protruding.

Crowds of persons on Sunday visited the localities where the murders were committed. The entrances to Mitre Square were, however, closed by order of the police authorities, and a large body of constables, under Inspector Izzard, was kept on the spot to preserve order.

Late on Sunday night the woman murdered in Berner Street was identified by a sister as Elizabeth Stride, who, it seems, had resided latterly in Flower and Dean Street.

At 3 o'clock on Sunday afternoon a meeting of nearly 1,000 persons took place in Victoria Park, under the chairmanship of Mr Edward Barrow, of the Bethnal Green Road. After several speeches upon the conduct of the Home Secretary and Sir Charles Warren, a resolution was unanimously passed that it was high time both officers should resign and make way for some officers who would leave no stone unturned for the purpose of bringing the murderers to justice, instead of allowing them to run riot in a civilized city like London. On Mile End Waste during the day four meetings of the same kind were held and similar resolutions passed.

The Times, October 5, 1888

The square remained just as it was for many years after the Second World War until the City decided to clear the old buildings and erect modern office blocks. Today, all has gone with a brick planter installed on the murder site on 'Ripper corner'. The nick-name for the killer derives from a letter received by the Central News Agency dated September 25, 1888 and signed by 'Jack the Ripper'. It was published in the press the day after the double murder.

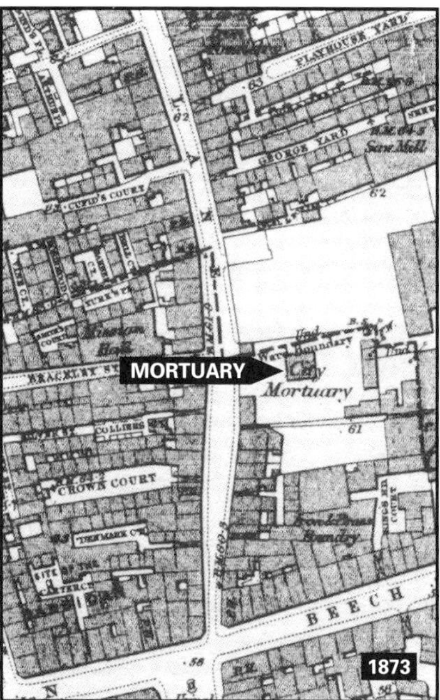

Each victim was photographed by the police, Catharine Eddowes *(left)* being propped up against a wall in the City Mortuary which stood here *(right)* in Golden Lane. The faded photographs are now preserved at the National Archives.

During the three days of the week following the Sunday on which the two murders were committed the following petition to the Queen was freely circulated among the women of the labouring classes of East London through some of the religious agencies and educational centres:

'To our Most Gracious Sovereign Lady Queen Victoria.

'Madam, We, the women of East London, feel horror at the dreadful sins that have been lately committed in our midst and grief because of the shame that has fallen on our neighbourhood.

'By the facts which have come out in the inquests, we have learnt much of the lives of those of our sisters who have lost a firm hold on goodness and who are living sad and degraded lives.

'While each woman of us will do all she can to make men feel with horror the sins of impurity which cause such wicked lives to be led, we would also beg that your Majesty will call on your servants in authority and bid them put the law which already exists in motion to close bad houses within whose walls such wickedness is done and men and women ruined in body and soul.

'We are, Madam, your loyal and humble servants.'

The petition, which received between 4,000 and 5,000 signatures, was presented in due form and the following reply has been received:

Whitehall.

'Madam, I am directed by the Secretary of State to inform you that he has had the honour to lay before the Queen the petition of women inhabitants of Whitechapel praying that steps may be taken with a view to suppress the moral disorders in that neighbourhood, and that Her Majesty has been graciously pleased to receive the same.

'I am to add that the Secretary of State looks with hope to the influence for good that the petitioners can exercise, each in her own neighbourhood, and he is in communication with the Commissioners of Police with a view to taking such action as may be desirable in order to assist the efforts of the petitioners and to mitigate the evils of which they complain.

'I am, Madam, your obedient servant,
Godfrey Lushington.'

The Times, October 26, 1888

The man whose livelihood was to photograph murdered people has died after being knocked down by a lorry in East India Dock Road, E.

He was Mr Joseph Martin, of Canton Street, Poplar, E., who a year ago retired from the position of official photographer to the Metropolitan Police, which he held for half a century.

It was his duty to photograph the bodies of unknown persons in the Metropolitan Police area, and among his 'subjects' were the women killed by Jack the Ripper in the narrow alleys of Whitechapel and Commercial Road, as well as the victims of many other murders.

Daily Herald, December 23, 1933

A macabre letter, reputed to have been written by Jack the Ripper during his campaign of mass murder and mutilation in Victorian London, has been anonymously returned to Scotland Yard after being lost for decades. The letter, written in red ink and sent to a London news agency in September 1888, after the second of five killings of East End prostitutes ascribed to the Ripper, is one of the most important surviving documents of the infamous case.

It was among a bundle of documents sent to the curator of the Yard's Black Museum earlier this year in a plain brown envelope. It had been posted in Croydon but all attempts to identify the sender have failed.

The Daily Telegraph, August 19, 1988

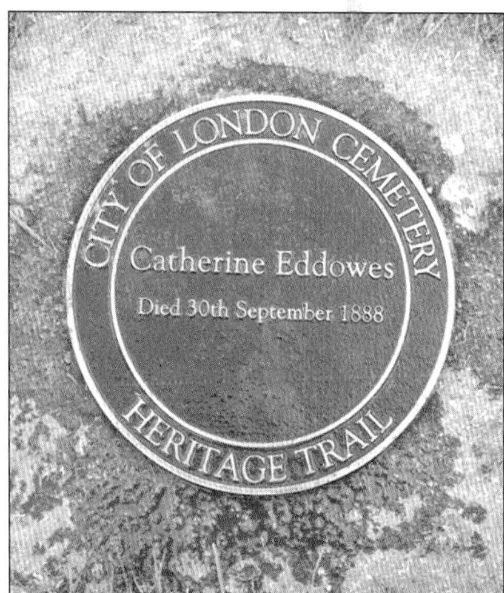

On October 8, she was buried in an unmarked grave (No. 49336) in the City's cemetery at Little Ilford. By now, there were vociferous calls for the resignation of the Metropolitan Police Commissioner, Sir Charles Warren, who was already unpopular for the heavy-handed way he had put down a mass demonstration by the unemployed in Trafalgar Square the previous year by calling in troops. He was also at loggerheads with the Home Office where the Home Secretary, Henry Matthews, was equally being criticised for lack of leadership in the crisis. On Sunday, mass meetings in Victoria Park and Mile End called for both men to resign, and petitions were forwarded to the Queen by the women of the East End. Today, Square 318 has been re-used for part of the memorial gardens for cremated remains, but we established that Catharine lies here, just beside Garden Way in front of Memorial Bed 1849. Late in 1996, the cemetery authorities decided to mark the grave with a plaque (and that of Mary Nichols — see page 21) although with some trepidation knowing that they could be the target of souvenir hunters.

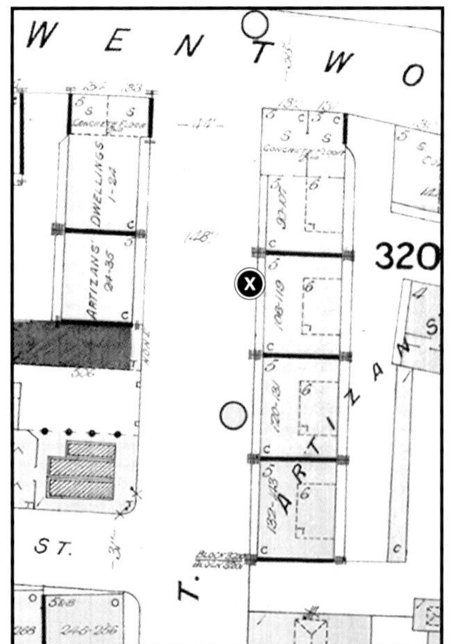

The Ripper letter sent by someone claiming to be the murderer has now been adjudged by most latter-day researchers as a hoax, possibly concocted by a journalist. Another 'clue' which has been the subject of dispute ever since, concerns a chalked message found on the brickwork of Wentworth Model Dwellings which still stand at the top of Goulston Street (see also plan page 35). Inside the doorway (beneath the 'Takeaway' sign) to Nos. 108-119, a bloodstained fragment torn from Catharine Eddowes' apron was found by Police Constable Alfred Long at about 2.55 a.m. on the 30th. Above it was chalked the message: 'The Juwes are the men That Will not be Blamed for nothing'. Although there was no proof that it had been written by the same person who had left the piece of clothing, Long copied the words down, as did Detective Constable Daniel Halse whose version was slightly different: 'The Juwes are not The men That Will be Blamed for nothing'. The building was largely occupied at the time by Jews and, fearing an anti-Semitic backlash if the graffiti was seen by a member of the public, Sir Charles Warren authorised a senior officer to wipe it off which was done around 5.30 a.m. The fact that the City Police were refused permission to photograph it beforehand did not help the subsequent accusations about the destruction of evidence.

During the early hours of Friday morning another murder of a most revolting and fiendish character took place in Spitalfields. This is the seventh which has occurred in this immediate neighbourhood, and the character of the mutilations leaves very little doubt that the murderer in this instance is the same person who has committed the previous ones, with which the public are fully acquainted.

The scene of this last crime is at No. 26, Dorset Street, Spitalfields, which is about 200 yards distant from 35 Hanbury Street, where the unfortunate woman, Mary Ann Nichols, was so foully murdered. Although the victim, whose name is Kelly, resides at the above number, the entrance to the room she occupied is up a narrow court, in which are some half-a-dozen houses, and which is known as Miller's Court; it is entirely separated from the other portion of the house, and has an entrance leading into the court. The room is known by the title of No. 13. The house is rented by John McCarthy, who keeps a small general shop at No. 27 Dorset Street, and the whole of the rooms are let out to tenants of a very poor class. As an instance of the poverty of the neighbourhood, it may be mentioned that nearly the whole of the houses in this street are common lodging-houses, and the one opposite where this murder was enacted has accommodation for some 300 men, and is fully occupied every night.

About 12 months ago Kelly, who was about 24 years of age, and who was considered a good-looking young woman, of fair and fresh-coloured complexion, came to Mr M'Carthy with a man named Joseph Kelly, who she stated was her husband, and who was a porter employed at the Spitalfields Market. They rented a room on the ground floor, the same in which the poor woman was

The title page from *The Penny Illustrated* of November 17, 1888 depicted the next serial killing which took place early on November 9 in a room at the rear of No. 26 Dorset Street.

Dorset Street — sometimes referred to as Dosset Street after the number of lodging houses it contained — was one of the most dangerous streets in the East End. It was renamed Duval Street in 1904, the whole northern side being demolished in 1929 for an extension to Spitalfields Market. ***Left:*** **Unfortunately, the lazy way that Charles E. Goad prepared these plans for the fire insurance companies meant that any alteration to a building was simply drawn separately and pasted over the top with strong glue, thus obliterating the earlier version.**

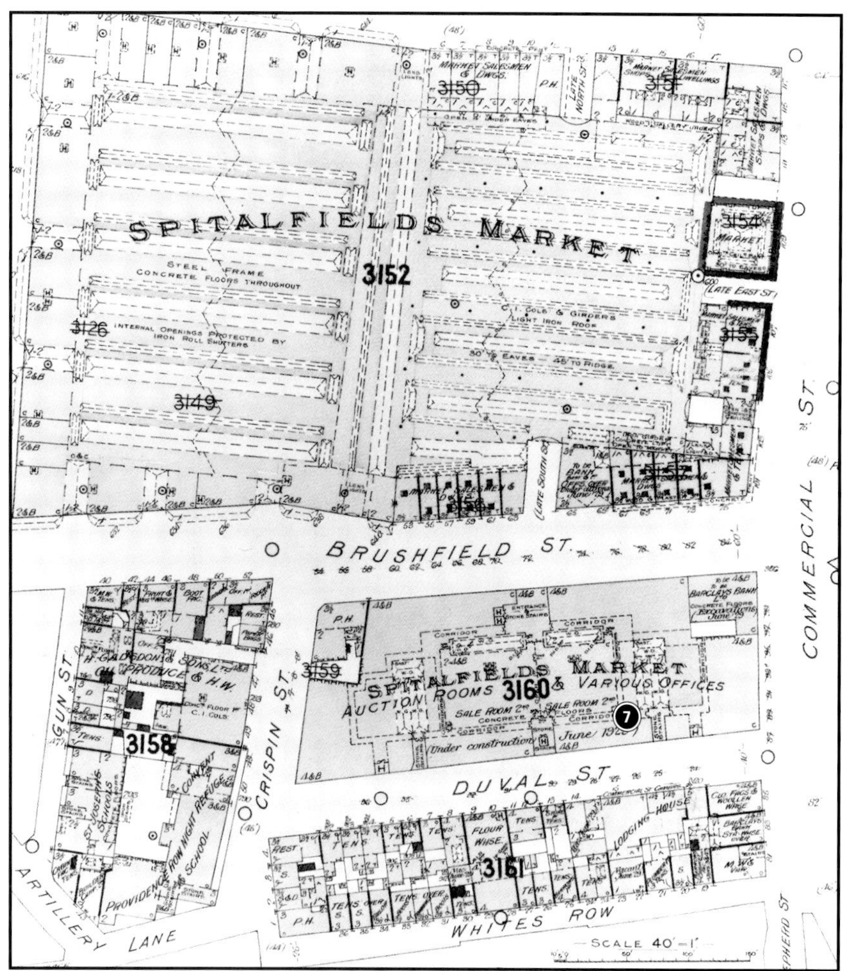

murdered, at a rental of 4s. a week. It had been noticed that the deceased woman was somewhat addicted to drink, but Mr M'Carthy denied having any knowledge that she had been leading a loose or immoral life. That this was so, however, there can be no doubt, for a short time ago she had a quarrel with Kelly, and, after blows had been exchanged, the man left the house, or rather room, and did not return. It has since been ascertained that he went to live at Buller's common lodging-house in Bishopsgate Street. Since then the woman has supported herself as best she could, and the police have ascertained that she has been walking the streets.

None of those living in the court or at 26 Dorset Street saw anything of the unfortunate creature after about 8 o'clock on Thursday evening, but she was seen in Commercial Street shortly before the closing of the public house, and then had the appearance of being the worse for drink. About 1 o'clock on Friday morning a person living in the court opposite to the room occupied by the murdered woman heard her singing the song, *Sweet Violets,* but this person is unable to say whether any one else was with her at that time. Nothing more was seen or heard of her until her dead body was found.

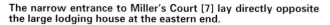

The narrow entrance to Miller's Court [7] lay directly opposite the large lodging house at the eastern end.

In 1996 we plotted the entrance by measurement from Commercial Street whereupon Harry Harris duly took up his station.

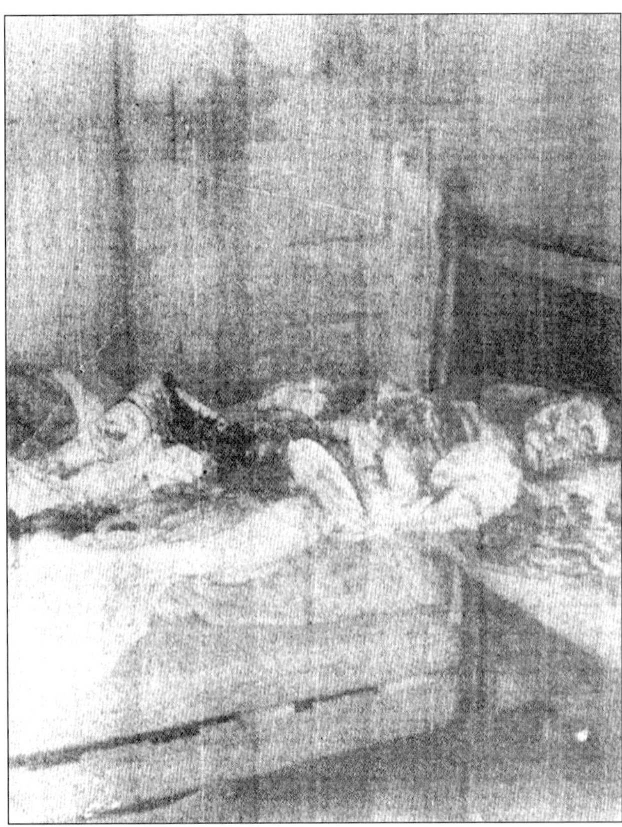

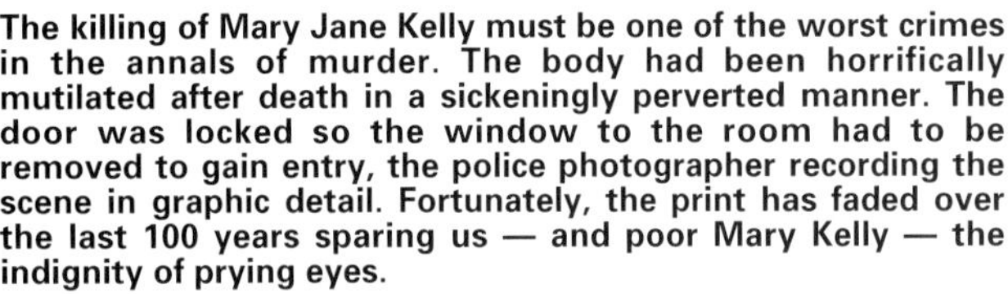

The killing of Mary Jane Kelly must be one of the worst crimes in the annals of murder. The body had been horrifically mutilated after death in a sickeningly perverted manner. The door was locked so the window to the room had to be removed to gain entry, the police photographer recording the scene in graphic detail. Fortunately, the print has faded over the last 100 years sparing us — and poor Mary Kelly — the indignity of prying eyes.

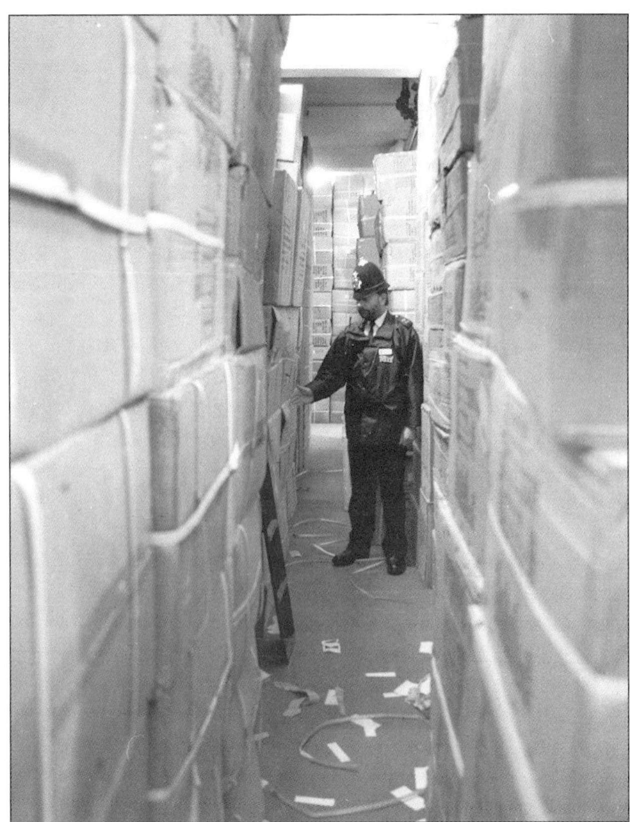

In 1996 the market building was occupied by Deejay Import-Export (London) Limited and David Sadka very kindly allowed us inside. We transposed our measurements made outside along Duval Street (now an unnamed service road) to the interior only to find the spot where Mary Kelly's bed had stood covered with a huge stack of boxes. Your Editor inquired whether they would be shifted in the near future only to receive the fatalistic reply: 'No, sorry, they're dead stock!'

At a quarter to 11 on Friday morning, as the woman was 35s. in arrears with her rent, Mr M'Carthy said to a man employed by him in his shop, John Bowyer, 'Go to No. 13 (meaning the room occupied by Kelly) and try and get some rent'. Bowyer did as he was directed, and on knocking at the door was unable to obtain an answer. He then tried the handle of the door, and found it was locked. On looking through the keyhole he found the key was missing. The left-hand side of the room faced the court, and in it were two large windows. Bowyer, knowing that when the man Kelly and the dead woman had their quarrel a pane of glass in one of the windows was broken, went round to the side in question. He put his hand through the aperture and pulled aside the muslin curtain which covered it. On his looking into the room a shocking sight presented itself. He could see the woman lying on the bed, entirely naked, covered with blood and apparently dead. Without waiting to make a closer examination he ran to his employer and told him he believed the woman Kelly had been murdered. M'Carthy at once went and looked through the broken window, and, satisfying himself that something was wrong, despatched Bowyer to the Commercial Street Police Station, at the same time enjoining him not to tell any of the neighbours what he had discovered.

The Times, November 16, 1888

Mary Kelly was buried in a public grave in St Patrick's Roman Catholic Cemetery in Leytonstone. Her grave, No. 66 in Row 66, was reclaimed with all the other common graves in Plot 10 in the 1950s but the superintendent has since marked the spot with this touching memorial.

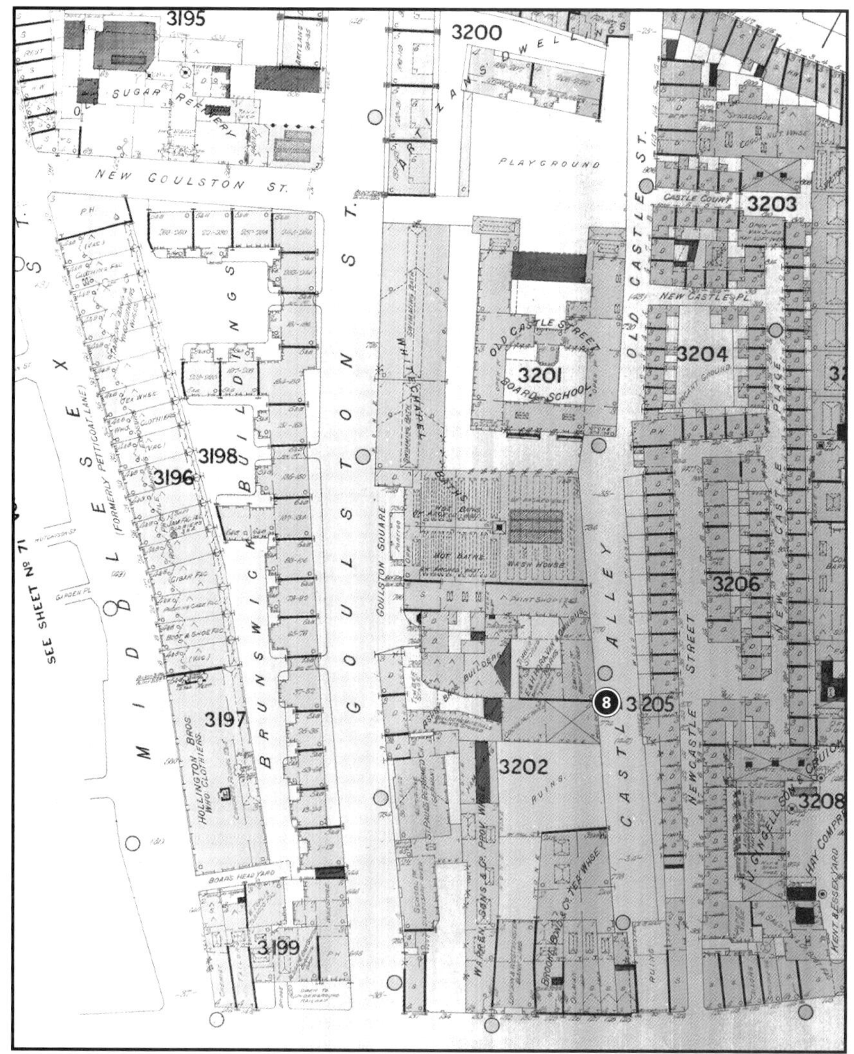

Another poor woman of the same class as the others so shockingly murdered last year in Whitechapel was on Wednesday morning found with her throat cut in a terrible manner and her body mutilated. Although the mutilation was not committed so savagely as in the other cases, it is thought that the murderer would have served this, his latest victim, in similar manner but that he was disturbed by some passer-by in his intention and made good his escape. The place in which the murdered woman was found is known as Castle Alley, High Street, Whitechapel.

The scene of the murder is probably one of the lowest quarters in the whole of East London, and a spot more suitable for the terrible crime could hardly be found, on account of the evil reputation borne by this particular place, and the absence of any inhabitants in the immediate vicinity. Castle Alley, which is within a quarter of a mile of the scenes of the other murders, is principally composed of workshops, and is about 180 yards in length. The thoroughfare itself is blocked up, both day and night, with tradesmen's carts and wagons and costermongers' barrows, while on the opposite side to the workshops or store-houses is a high dead wall, above which, however, are the windows of some dwelling-houses. This alley, which is entered by a passage, not more than a yard in width, between Nos. 124 and 125, Whitechapel Road, is entirely shut off from view of the main road, and would hardly be observed by the ordinary passer-by. At the end of the passage are the Board School and Whitechapel wash-houses, and the thoroughfare, from that end, leads into Newcastle and Wentworth Streets, both of which are principally occupied by foreign Jews and frequenters of common lodging-houses. Although the houses in these two streets are densely populated, the people generally enter them from the Spitalfields end, especially at night time, on account of the dark and lonely nature of Castle Alley, as well as the evil reputation it has always borne among the respectable portion of the inhabitants. The vans and other vehicles which crowd the thoroughfare, notwithstanding the fact that the alley is lighted with three lamps, affords ample cover and secrecy for crime and violence. The exact spot where the body of the unfortunate woman was found was between two wagons, which were fastened together with a chain, outside the premises of Messrs King and Sons, builders. Right against the wagons was a street lamp, and it was against this that the body of the murdered woman was discovered by the police officer.

At about ten minutes to 1 on Wednesday morning, Police Constable Andrews, 272H, while walking round his beat, and passing through the alley, saw a woman lying on the ground about five feet from Messrs King's premises. The officer at first thought the woman was the worse for drink, or one of the many outcasts who nightly frequent the alley to seek a shelter. On turning his light down he was horrified to find a woman lying on her back with a terrible gash in the throat. The skirt and petticoat were turned up and the constable could see that there were gashes about the abdomen, but these did not appear to be very deep. Andrews blew his whistle, and directly afterwards several officers appeared upon the scene. The constables, acting upon instructions, did not shift the body from the position in which it was found until after Dr George Baxter Phillips, divisional surgeon, and Dr Brown had examined it. They, however, felt the face, which was warm, thus proving that the murder had been committed but a very short time before the constable discovered the body.

The doctors, together with several inspectors and detectives attached to the H Division, were quickly on the spot, and the former, having examined the body, pronounced life extinct. They then took minute details of the position of the corpse, which was lying in a pool of blood, and the appearance of the surrounding buildings. The body was then conveyed on a stretcher to the Whitechapel mortuary, in Old Montagu Street.

The Times, July 19, 1889

Alice McKenzie was found close to a lamp-post on the pavement on the western side of Castle Alley [8] just after midnight on July 17, 1889. Partly because of the six-month break in the spate of murders, many Ripper historians do not accept that she was a victim of the same serial killer that had roamed Whitechapel the previous year.

As a consequence of the murder, not only was the southern end of the street widened by demolishing the buildings between Nos. 122 and 125 Whitechapel High Street, but in March 1893 the name was amended to make the bottom end the same as Old Castle Street at the top.

On Wednesday, Mr Wynne E. Baxter, Coroner for the South-Eastern Division of Middlesex, resumed his adjourned inquiry at the Working Lads' Institute, Whitechapel, respecting the death of Alice M'Kenzie, who was found brutally murdered in Castle Alley, Whitechapel, on the early morning of the 17th ult.

The jury, after a short deliberation, returned a verdict of 'Wilful murder against some person or persons unknown', and added a rider endorsing the remarks of the Coroner, and requesting him to forward a recommendation to the County Council and the Whitechapel District Board of Works to open up Castle Alley to the Whitechapel High Street as a thoroughfare.

The Times, August 16, 1889

Early on Tuesday morning a discovery was made which leads to the belief that another horrible murder has been committed in Whitechapel, and that the victim, a woman, belongs to the same class as the eight who have been murdered in the same locality during the last two years. The manner in which the body has been mutilated suggests that the outrage has been committed by the same person.

About half-past 5 o'clock on Tuesday morning Police Constable Pennett, 239H, was passing on his beat by the railway arch in Pinchin Street, St George's, when he noticed something in the arch. The place in question is used as a receptacle for stones belonging to the District Board of Works, and in front of it there is a hoarding. Part of this, however, has been broken down, and the officer, getting through it, was horrified to find the trunk of a woman in a condition which showed it had been hacked about in the most brutal manner. The head had been severed from the body, while both legs were also missing, and from the lower part of the stomach was a deep gash through which the bowels were protruding.

Dr Clarke, who is acting for Dr Phillips, the divisional surgeon, who was away on his holidays, together with Dr Sargeant, who practises in the neighbourhood, was soon at the spot and minutely examined the body. They were of the opinion that death had occurred at least three days previously, as the blood was all dried and signs of decomposition were setting in. Other details having been obtained, a police ambulance was brought and the trunk of the body conveyed on it to St George's Mortuary, where the doctors again examined it. The result of that examination was that the police afterwards issued the following notice: 'Found, at 5.40 this morning, the trunk of a woman under railway arches in Pinchin Street, Whitechapel. Age about 40; height, 5ft 3in.; hair, dark brown; no clothing, except chemise, which is much torn and blood-stained; both elbows discoloured as from habitually leaning on them. Post-mortem marks apparently of a rope having been tied round the waist.'

Dr Sargeant was heard to say that the head had been cut off in a very skilful manner. The medical men were also of the opinion that the cuts were inflicted by a left-handed person, which fact points to the murderer being the same person who killed the eight other poor creatures, as in each instance the cuts are supposed to have been the work of a left-handed person.

The Times, September 13, 1889

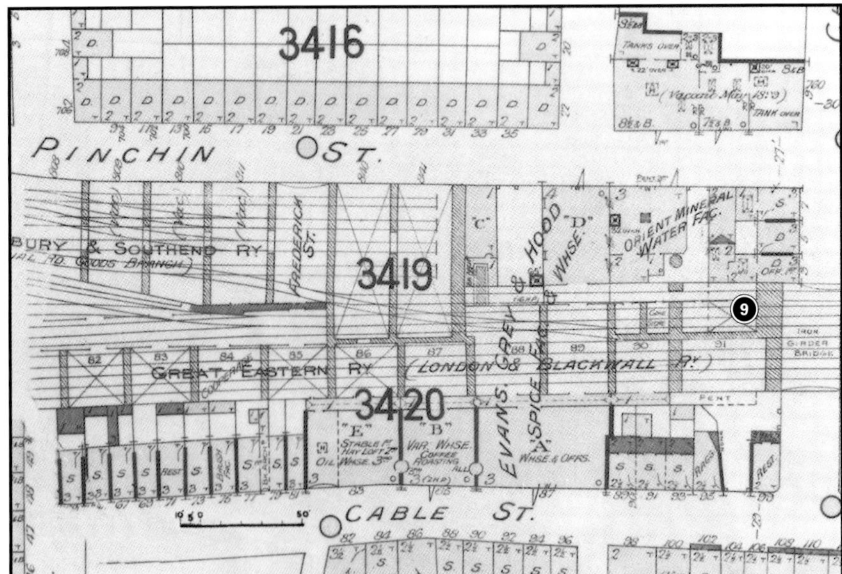

The last victim on *The Times* list [9] was found in a railway arch of the viaduct carrying the Great Eastern line over Christian Street. Police Constable William Pennett discovered the body of a woman, minus the head and legs, lying eight feet inside the last arch in Pinchin Street about a foot from the right-hand wall. She had been dead at least 24 hours and possessed no identification. It was noted that the estimated date of death — September 8 — was the anniversary of the killing of Annie Chapman and one news agency speculated that the body could be that of an East End prostitute, Lydia Hart, who had not been seen around for several days.

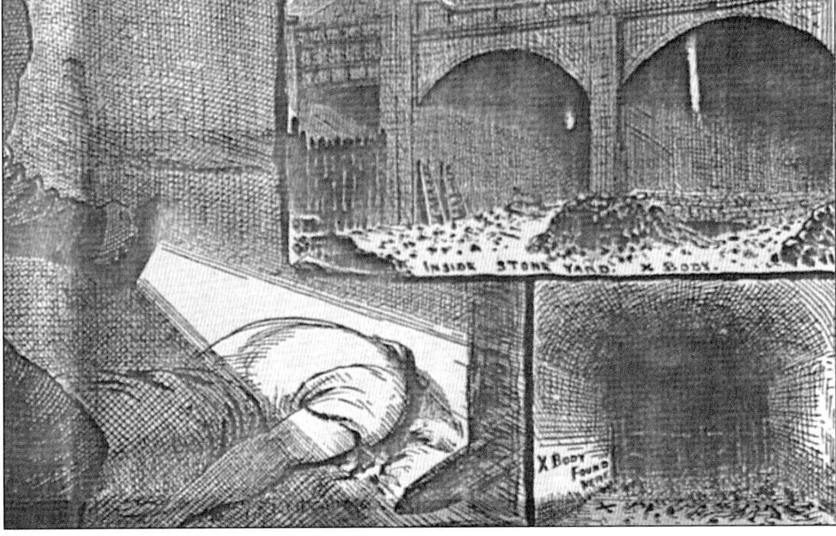

The inquest was held on September 24 in the Vestry Hall in Cable Street (which runs just the other side of the railway line) and where most of the earlier hearings had taken place. No firm conclusions were made and most historians today discount any link with the Ripper murders. ***Right:*** **The body was found in the end arch next to the bridge over Christian Street, behind the Pinchin Street Health Centre.**

The general impression for a long time has been that 'Jack the Ripper' is dead. It was evident that the fiend who committed so many murders in such rapid succession — with such extraordinary daring — with such untiring ferocity — would never cease his bloody work until death or detection. Just three years have now passed away since these murders ceased to take place; and such an interruption in the series of crimes points clearly to the disappearance in some form or other of the man who was guilty of them.

The Sun, February 13, 1894

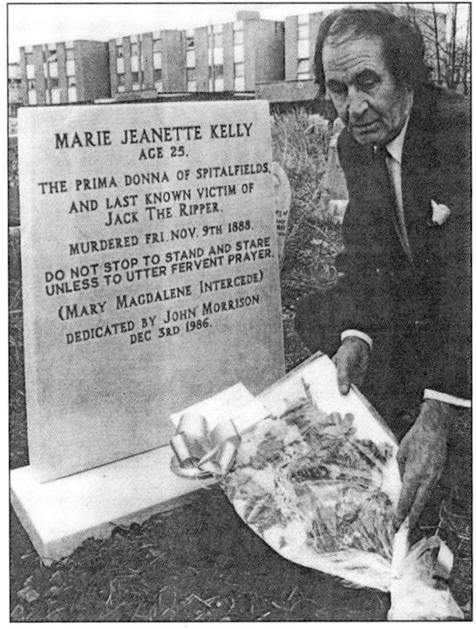

Although Jack the Ripper's head-count pales into insignificance when compared with more recent serial killings, the fascination in his crimes persists, possibly because they remain unsolved in spite of the efforts of dozens of would-be Sherlock Holmes, and, undoubtedly, the East End's reputation throughout the world has been coloured by what took place there over a hundred years ago. ***Left:*** **One tourist attraction is the Ten Bells (contentiously renamed Jack the Ripper for a short period around the 100th anniversary) in Commercial Street where Mary Kelly is supposed to have ordered her last drink on the night she was killed.** ***Right:*** **In 1986, John Morrison achieved considerable publicity for his own theories when he erected this headstone to her in St Patrick's Cemetery, the only problem being that he put it on the wrong grave!**

The controversial Jack the Ripper pub is to change its name — after months of campaigning by women's rights protestors who say it glorifies the horrific spate of murders 100 years ago.

Landlord Ernie Ostrowski says the change is nothing to do with the women's protests — it is part of a major revamp of the pub to be started in the next two months.

But the campaign group Women Against Violence Against Women, and Tower Hamlets Council who backed them, are hailing it as a victory for the dozens of women who picketed the pub in Commercial Street, Spitalfields, last autumn and gathered a 400-signature petition.

'This is a major victory in the women's group's campaign against the glorification of violence against women,' said a council spokesperson.

In the centenary year of the horrific murders of five prostitutes, Tower Hamlets is to ban any filming connected with the Ripper on council property.

But Mr Ostrowski denies that he's cashing in on the anniversary of the still-unsolved murders. 'Whatever the protestors say, the tourist interest in Jack the Ripper in 1988 is going to be fantastic,' he said.

The pub's name was changed from the Ten Bells in 1974 and since then has attracted thousands of tourists to its site, yards from the scene of the last murder. Trumans, the Spitalfields brewery who own the pub, confirmed the name-change was part of discussions going on with Mr Ostrowski about the revamp. 'We obviously listen seriously to what our customers and other people in the local community say,' said a brewery spokesperson.

Hackney Gazette, January 22, 1988

Tower Hamlets Council is considering changing its name to The East End to improve its image.

The Daily Telegraph, October 30, 1993

Jack the Ripper tours in London's East End are to be curbed after residents complained of grisly descriptions and tourists gaping through their windows.

Householders in Whitechapel and Spitalfields, where the notorious killer operated, have complained to Tower Hamlets council about 'voyeuristic' trips which glorify violence against women.

They say that, almost a century after the killing of five women in the area, the Jack the Ripper industry is blighting their neighbourhood. The worst of the estimated 40 official and unofficial tours are accused of relating the multiple injuries suffered by the women in gory detail.

Phoebe Tait, who lives on the well-trodden route, said that some tours stood outside homes most nights until 9.30 p.m. listening to tales of the Ripper's most violent acts. She said that much of the detail was inaccurate and it was unpleasant to be constantly reminded of the murders. Other residents have complained of tourists blocking pavements and peering into their homes.

Up to 100 householders signed a petition calling for action. The Labour-run council is working on a code of conduct to moderate the descriptions used by guides and restrict where tourists stand on pavements. It also wants guides to promote positive features of the area. The council cannot take action under the Environmental Protection Act or public health laws because the tours are not a 'statutory nuisance' or an 'offensive trade'.

The Times, Monday July 22, 1996

In July 1910, Marconi's invention made a deep impression on the general public when wireless telegraphy was used for the first time to catch a murderer who was attempting to escape to the United States aboard this vessel — the SS *Montrose*.

February 1, 1910 — Dr Hawley Crippen

A discovery which was made late last night, after an exhaustive police search, at a large house in Hilldrop-crescent, Kentish Town, N.W., has led to the grave suspicion that a Mrs. Crippen, who was well known in the music-hall profession under the name of Belle Elmore, has been murdered and her body secretly buried.

Mrs. Crippen, a strikingly handsome woman, who was an American by birth, lived at No. 39, Hilldrop-crescent, and up to the time of her disappearance some five months ago was an official of the Music-Hall Artists' Guild.

Daily Mail, July 14, 1910

Though Dr. Crippen, who is wanted in connection with the murder of his wife, the well-known music-hall artist, Belle Elmore, at 39, Hilldrop-crescent, Holloway, has so far eluded capture, there can be very little doubt that the net is gradually closing round him.

Since the body of Mrs. Crippen was discovered buried under the floor of the coal cellar, the police have been searching everywhere for her husband and the young lady typist, Miss Ethel Clara Le Neve, who disappeared with him on Saturday last. Innumerable 'clues' to their whereabouts were forthcoming yesterday, but led to nothing of a tangible character.

Indeed, it may be said that their movements cannot be traced with certainty later than Saturday afternoon. That morning they had left the house in Hilldrop-crescent together and proceeded to the dentistry at Albion House, New Oxford-street, with which Dr. Crippen was associated. There Miss Le Neve had acted for some considerable time as his shorthand-writer and typist.

During the morning the doctor sent out to an outfitter's establishment near by for a boy's suit of clothes. It is suggested that they were intended to be used as a disguise for Miss Le Neve. At 1 o'clock the couple departed.

Centre: **Dr Hawley Crippen, an American dentist born in Michigan, married his second wife Cora Turner** ***(left)*** **in September 1892 after a whirlwind six-week courtship. Mrs Crippen was a music hall artiste performing under the stage name of Belle Elmore, and who fancied herself as an opera singer. They moved to London in 1897 but by the turn of the century the marriage had turned sour and in 1902 Crippen had taken up with his secretary Ethel Le Neve** ***(right)***.

As was reported in yesterday's 'Daily Chronicle,' there is good reason to believe that Dr. Crippen on Thursday visited an office which he had rented for some eighteen months at Craven House, Kingsway. At this office he carried on the business of the Aural Remedies Co., which was conducted almost entirely by correspondence.

Daily Chronicle, July 16, 1910

Dr. Crippen and Miss le Neve were arrested on board the Canadian Pacific Company's liner *Montrose* at 9 o'clock yesterday morning.

Wearing the uniform of a pilot, Inspector Dew, accompanied by four officers of the Canadian Police, boarded the liner about 2 miles from Father Point. Crippen was walking on deck. The Inspector approached him from behind and touched him on the shoulder. He turned round sharply, and there was a mutual recognition between him and the Inspector.

'There's your man!' said Inspector Dew to one of the Canadian officers, and Crippen accompanied his captors to a cabin, where he was formally arrested for the murder of his wife. 'I am rather glad the anxiety is over,' appears to be the only remark he made.

The Inspector then went to Miss le Neve's cabin. She was reading a book and on looking up at her visitors immediatley guessed what their purpose was. She is said to have uttered a piercing scream, then grew suddenly calm and submitted to arrest. Subsequently she collapsed completely.

We have long since grown used to the wonders of telegraphy but 'wireless' is still a miracle to all but the learned in science, and when the clue, unfound on land, leapt suddenly out of the darkness of the night, from an unseen ship far out at sea, it must have seemed to many little short of supernatural.

The Daily Telegraph, August 1, 1910

Crippen and his wife were still living together at No. 39 Hilldrop Crescent in Kentish Town, in North London, and it was here that Cora was last seen alive by two family friends, Mr and Mrs Paul Martinetti, who had been invited to dinner on the evening of Monday, January 31, 1910. The next morning, Crippen sent a message to Ethel at work: 'B. E. has gone to America. Shall be in later when we can arrange for a pleasant little evening'. That night Ethel spent the night at No. 39, moving in on a permanent basis on March 12. On February 20, Ethel had accompanied Crippen to a ball where she was spotted by some of Cora's friends wearing Mrs Crippen's jewellery. The following month Crippen spread the word that his wife was seriously ill, then critically ill, before informing one of her close friends that Cora had died and that she was to be cremated. Her formal obituary then appeared in the theatrical magazine *Era* on March 23 but friends were already suspicious as they had not heard a word from her since she departed. It was also only too obvious that Crippen was now living with a young girl. However it was not until July 8 that the police, in the form of Inspector Walter Dew, called round to interview the doctor. This prompted Crippen to warn Ethel that they would have to go abroad to start a new life so they crossed the Channel the following day. Meanwhile, Inspector Dew issued a description of the missing Mrs Crippen and began a detailed search of the property.

With its notorious past, the owner of No. 39, a Scottish comedian Sandy McNab, wanted to establish a Crippen Museum in the house but ran up against objections from local residents. In the end, the house was destroyed during the Second World War and now a block of flats called the Margaret Bonfield House occupies the site.

Inspector Dew then explained what happened next. 'Next day, Saturday, the 9th July, I circulated a full description of Mrs. Crippen as being a missing person. I sent that description to every police office in London, and I made various inquiries. I did not tell Crippen about that. I continued my inquiries on the 10th, and I went through and considered the statement that had been made. On Monday, the 11th, I went to Albion House [Crippen's place of work], but I did not succeed in seeing Crippen or Miss Le Neve. I ascertained that he was not in the house at the time. I saw two witnesses, Dr Rylance and Mr Long, and they showed me two letters. Not finding Crippen at Albion House I went on to Hilldrop Crescent on the same Monday, and I made a careful search of the house. I dug up portions of the garden, and I also examined the coal cellar. On that day I circulated a description of the prisoner, Crippen, and of Miss Le Neve, and I continued my inquiries. I forwarded the description to various ports in England and abroad. On Tuesday, 12th July, I made a further examination of the house, and also on the 13th, when, amongst other things, I again searched the coal cellar. The coal cellar had a brick floor. There was a very small quantity of coal there, and also a little rubbish, cuttings from small branches of trees, an old chandelier, and such things as that. I went down with Mitchell on to my knees, and probed about with a small poker which I had got out of the kitchen. I found that the poker went in somewhat easily between the crevices of the bricks, and I managed to get one or two up, and then several others came up pretty easily. I then got a spade from the garden and dug the clay that was immediately underneath the bricks. After digging down to about a depth of four spadefuls I came across what appeared to be human remains. After digging further I sent for Dr. Marshall, the divisional surgeon of police in that district, and Sir Melville Macnaughten, chief of the Criminal Investigation Department. Dr. Marshall came between five and six o'clock, and he saw a portion that I had unearthed. After I had procured assistance, we dug further, and Dr. Marshall came back later on. We left the remains where they were that night, without moving them; we covered them up, locked up the house, and left it in charge of two police officers.'

The remains were subsequently buried in this grave (No. 40 in Section RC7) in Islington and St Pancras Cemetery.

Inspector Dew interviewed Dr Crippen at the latter's surgery in Albion House in New Oxford Street. Unfortunately that building has been demolished but Lewis and Burrows chemist shop at No. 110 on the opposite side of the road, where Crippen purchased five grains of hyoscine hydrobromide on January 19, now looks like this. This is the statement verbatim, with its original spellings and punctuation.

I am 48 years of age.

After being questioned by Chief Inspr Dew as to the statements made by me that my wife, known as Belle Elmore, is dead, I desire to make a voluntary statement to clear the whole matter up.

I was born at Cold Water, Michigan, U.S.A., in the year 1862 my father's name being Nyron Augustus Crippen, a dry goods merchant, my mother's name was Ardesee Crippen nèe Škinner.

My mother is now dead but my father lives at Los Angeles, Cal.

I was educated first at Cold Water, Indiana & California, and then attended the University at Michigan until I was about 20 and finished my education at the Hospital College at Cleveland where I took the degree of M.D.

I came over to England in 1883, and attended various Hospitals to see the operations, and returned to the States and was assistant for 5 or 4 months to Dr Porter of Detroit. After that I went to New York and took a degree in special eye and ear work, at the Ophthalmic Hospital. This would be in 1885.

After that I returned to Detroit where I remained about 2 years as assistant to the same Dr. I then went to San Diego, where I practised as an eye & ear specialist for about 2 years.

Before going to this place I was married to a lady named Charlotte Bell of New York, and she accompanied me to San Diego.

We then came to New York. I have had only one child by my first wife. He was born at San Diego about 1887 or 1888 and his name is Otto Hawley Crippen. He is now married and lives at Los Angeles.

My first wife died, so far as I can remember in 1890 or 1891. We were living at Salt Lake City where I was practising as an eye and ear specialist. She was buried at Salt Lake in my name.

After this my son went to live with his grandmother, my mother, until she died.

I then went to New York and went as an assistant to Dr Jeffery of Brooklyn and I lived with him.

About 1895, while with Dr Jeffery, I met Belle Elmore, who was being attended by him. Her name at this time was Cora Turner. I forget where she was living but she was living alone. She was only about 17 years of age, and I, of course, was about 30.

She, at this time, was living under the protection of a man named C. C. Lincoln, a stove manufacturer, of Water St, New York. She had been living with him, but he had given up his house and had taken a room for her and was paying all her expenses.

I took her to several places for some weeks as I was very fond of her, and one day she told me Lincoln wanted her to go away with him. I told her I could not stand that & would marry her right away and a few days after this I married her at a Minister's house at Jersey City, I forget his name or the name of the street.

I had been married to her some little time when she told me her name was not Turner but Kunigunde, Mackamotzhe. She said her mother had been married twice and her name then was Marsingar, and she was living in Brooklyn.

Her mother had been dead some years. My wife told me her father was a Russian Pole and her mother a German.

Her stepfather, so far as I know, is still living and resides at Forest Avenue, Brooklyn.

Her parents were in rather ordinary circumstances, but she had a good education and spoke German well.

After getting married to her, we went to St Louis, where I practised as consulting physician to an optician in, I think, Olive St. His name was Hirsch, I think.

We stayed there about a year, and we returned to New York, where I took a position as consulting physician to the Munyon Co. We lived in the offices at 7 East Fourteenth St.

I was in New York for only a few months when the Co transferred me to Philadelphia.

I was there with my wife about a year and was then transferred to the firm's place at Toronto, where I managed their business. I forget where I lived, but we were there only 6 months and then returned to Philadelphia.

I was there some time and while there about 1899, my wife who had a good voice, went to New York to have her voice trained, as she thought of going in for Grand Opera.

I paid all her expenses, and occasionally visited her at New York, and then in about 1900 I came to England alone, where I was Manager for Munyon's at the offices in Shaftesbury Ave., and I lived in Queens Road, St Johns Wood.

It was in April I came over and she joined me in August, as she wrote and told me she was giving up her lessons in Grand Opera and was going in for Music Hall Sketches. To this I objected and told her to come over here. She came and we went to live at South Crescent.

When she came to England she decided to give Sketches on the Music Hall Stage and adopted the name of 'Macka Motzke', but she did not make anything at it. She gave a sketch at the Old Marylebone Music Hall, but it was a failure, and she gave it up.

After this she did not do anything in it for two or three years until I had to go to America about two years after coming here. My firm sent for me, & I became Manager in Philadelphia.

When I left England my wife and I were living at, I think, 62 Guildford Street, and she remained there while I was away.

I remained in Philadelphia from November till the following June and sent my wife money regularly.

When I returned I found she had been singing at smoking concerts for payment, and that an American Music Hall Artist named Bruce Miller had been a frequent visitor to her at her house.

She told me that this man visited her and had taken her about and was very fond of her, also that she was fond of him. I may say that when she came to England from America her manner towards me was entirely changed and she had cultivated a most ungovernable temper, & seemed to think I was not good enough for her, and boasted of the men of good position travelling on the boat who had made a fuss of her, and, indeed, some of these visited her at South Crescent, but I do not know their names.

I never saw the man Bruce Miller, but he used to call when I was out and used to take her out in the evenings.

When I returned to this Country I did not take up my position to Munyon's but went as Manager to the Sovereign Remedy Co, 13 Newman St.

They failed about 8 months afterwards, and I then went as physician to the Drouet Institute, Regents Park, and afterwards at 10 Marble Arch, and they also failed.

From there I took a position with the Aural Clinic Co, 102 New Oxford Street, where I remained till they failed in about 6 months.

I then went back to Munyon's, 272 Oxford Circus, as Manager and advertising Manager.

I removed to Albion House as Manager about 18 months ago, after which I took it on as an Agency, but as it did not pay, I, in February last, handed it over to the Co again, but for the last two years I had been running the Yale Tooth Specialist Co, with Dr Rylance as partner, and am still doing so.

I ran what I termed the Imperial Press Agency in connection with Munyon's, because by so doing I got their advertisements inserted at a reduction.

At the present time I am interested in a Ear Cure business called the Aural Remedy at Craven House, Kingsway I work at an address in Vine Street.

I did not think anything of Bruce Miller visiting my wife at the time.

After returning from America we went to live at 34 Store Street for about a year. During this time she adopted the stage name of 'Belle Elmore', although she had had it in her mind when she came over, but I persuaded her to use the other name.

She got an engagement at the Town Hall Teddington to sing and then from time to time she got engagments at Music Halls. She went to Oxford as a comedienne and was there about a week. She also went to the Camberwell, and also at a Hall at Balham. She has also sung at the Empire, Northampton, and various towns.

She would probably go away about two weeks and return for about 6 weeks, but used to earn very little.

We remained at Store St for some time and went to 37 same St, for about 2 years, and, about 5 years ago, in, I think, 1905, removed to 39 Hilldrop Crescent, for which I pay £50 a year.

It is quite four years since she ever went out to sing at Halls, and although we apparently lived very happy together, as a matter of fact there were very frequent occasions when she got into most violent tempers and often threatened she would leave me, saying she had a man she could go to and she would end it all.

I have seen letters from Bruce Miller to her which ended 'With love and kisses to Brown eyes'.

About four years ago, in consequence of these frequent outbursts, I discontinued sleeping with her, and have never cohabited with her since.

She did all the work herself with the exception of having a charwoman in occasionally.

About 2 years ago she became Hon Treasurer of the Music Hall Ladies Guild, and was there every Wednesday.

I never interfered with her movements in any way; she went in and out just as she liked, and did what she liked. It was of no interest to me.

As I say she frequently threatened to leave me and said that if she did she would go right out of my life and I should never see or hear from her again.

On the Monday night, the day before I wrote the letter to the Guild, resigning her position as Treasurer, Mr and Mrs Paul Martinetti came to our place to dinner and during the evening Mr Martinetti wanted to go to the lavatory. As he had been to my house several times I did not take the trouble to go and show him where it was.

After they had left my wife blamed me for not taking him to the lavatory, and abused me and said 'This is the finish of it, I won't stand it any longer, I shall leave you tomorrow and you will never hear of me again.'

She had said this so often that I did not take much notice but she did say one thing which she had never said before, viz: I was to arrange to cover up any scandal with our mutual friends and the Guild the best way I could.

Before this she had told me frequently that the man she would go to was better able to support her than I was.

I came to business the next morning and when I went home between 5 and 6 p.m. I found she had gone.

I realised she had gone and I sat down to think it over as to how to cover up her absence without any scandal.

I think the same night or the next morning (Wednesday) I wrote a letter to the Guild saying she had gone away, which I also told several people.

At No. 142 Oxford Street lay the pawnbrokers Jay Richard Attenborough & Co. Ltd, and it was here on February 2 that Dr Crippen pawned a diamond ring and earrings belonging to his wife for £80. He returned on February 9 with six more diamond rings and a diamond brooch for which he received a further £115.

I afterwards realised that this would not be a sufficient explanation for her not coming back and later on I told people that she was ill with bronchitis and pneumonia, and afterwards I told them she was dead from this ailment.

I told them she died in California, but I have no recollection of telling anyone exactly where she died.

Someone afterwards asked me where my son lived and I told them.

I then put an advertisement in the Era that she was dead as I thought this would prevent people asking me a lot of questions.

Whatever I have said to other people in regard to her death is absolutely wrong and I am giving this as the explanation.

So far as I know she did not die and is still alive.

It is not true that she went away on legal business for me, or to see any relatives in America.

I did not receive any cables to say she was ill, and it is not true she was cremated at San Francisco and that the ashes were sent to me, or that she sailed from Havre.

So far as I know she has no claim to any title.

I have no recollection of telling anyone my son was with her when she died.

We had a joint account at the Charing Cross Bank, subject to the signature of either, but it pleased her to think she was signing cheques, and she also did so, and several blank cheques were always already signed by her, and some of these have been changed by me since her departure and there is one here now (produced).

When my wife went away I cannot say if she took anything with her or not, but I believe there is a theatrical travelling basket missing and she might have taken this with some clothes.

She took some of her jewellery I know with her, but she left four rings behind — three single stone (or Solitaire) diamond and a four diamonds and a ruby one, also a diamond brooch.

She had other jewellery and must have taken this with her.

I have never pawned or sold anything belonging to her before or after she left.

Everything I have told you is true.

I do not know what clothes, if any, she took away, she had plenty.

Whenever we quarrelled and she threatened to leave me, she told me she wanted nothing from me.

I have bought all her jewellery and so far as I know, she never had any jewellery presents, and I do not know that she ever had any money sent her except that Bruce Miller used to send her small amounts on her birthday and at Easter and Christmas to purchase a present.

She suffered from bilious attacks and I have given her medicine for that — homeopathic remedies.

It is true that I was at the Benevolent Fund Dinner at the Criterion with Miss Le Neve, and she wore the brooch my wife left behind. She has also worn my wife's furs.

Miss Le Neve has been in my employ and known me through being employed by the firms I have worked for, for the past 8 years, and she is now living with me as my wife at Hilldrop Crescent. I have been intimate with her during the past three years and have frequently stayed with her at Hotels, but never was away from home at night.

After I told people my wife was dead Miss Le Neve and I went to Dieppe for about 5 days, and stayed at an Hotel there. I forget the name, but the proprietors name was Vachen in the name of Mr and Mrs Crippen.

My belief is that my wife has gone to Chicago to join Bruce Miller, whose business on the Music Hall Stage is a Musical Instrument turn, but I think he has now gone into another business and has speculated and made money. Mr Didcot was his agent when he was over here.

I shall, of course, do all I can to get in touch with her so as to clear this matter up.

She has a sister named Louise whose name is Mills, living with her husband, who is a Soap maker, I think living at Brooklyn in fact I know living there. They live with my wife's stepfather Mr Maksangar.

I do not know where any of her other relations live. I cannot tell you how you can find or trace her, except as I have already said.

I will willingly go to my house with you to see if I can find any letters which may throw any light on the matter, and I invite you to look round the house and do whatever you like in the house. This is all I can tell you.

Any notes that I have changed through anyone in this building were in connection with my business.

This statement had been read over to me. It is quite correct and has been made by me quite voluntarily and without any promise or threat having been held out to me.

Hawley Harvey Crippen, July 8, 1910

This was the first message to be sent by Wireless
Form No. 1—100. 19/10/07. Sent date
H. Kendall
The MARCONI INTERNATIONAL MARINE COMMUNICATION COMPANY, Ltd.
WATERGATE HOUSE, YORK BUILDINGS, ADELPHI, LONDON, W.C.

No. 1 OFFICE 190

Prefix: Code Words

CHARGES TO PAY.	
Marconi Charge	
Other Line Charge	
Delivery Charge	
Total	

Office sent to	Time sent	By whom sent

Office of Origin
Service Instructions: Sent to Brookhaven 3.30 pm July 22nd

READ THE CONDITIONS PRINTED ON THE BACK OF THE FORM.

To: Piers Liverpool

3 PM GMT Friday 130 miles West Lizard have strong suspicions that Crippen London Cellar murderer and accomplice are amongst saloon passengers moustache taken off growing beard accomplice dressed as boy voice manner and build

PLEASE ASK FOR OFFICIAL RECEIPT.

Inspector Dew's interview had unnerved Crippen and, after booking in to the hotel on the Continent, he no doubt hoped that the investigation would die down. However, when he read in a newspaper that he was now a wanted man, he hastily booked a passage to Quebec under the guise of John Robinson and his son John Junior. The SS *Montrose* departed from Antwerp on July 20. Although Ethel was disguised as a boy, Captain Henry Kendall *(left)* became suspicious after having read all about the 'North London Cellar Murder'. He recognised the two fugitives from pictures in the newspaper and on July 22, despatched this message to the ship's owner in Liverpool which was to be passed on to Scotland Yard.

I was well posted as to the crime, but I said nothing to the officers till the following morning, when I took my chief officer into my confidence. He then detected the same suspicious circumstances as myself. I warned him that it must be kept absolutely quiet, as it was too good a thing to lose, so we made a lot of them and kept them smiling. During lunch I examined both their hats. Crippen's was stamped ' Jackson, Boulevard le Nord.' Le Neve's hat bore no name, but it was packed round the rim with paper to make it fit. Le Neve has the manner and appearance of a very refined, modest girl. She seems thoroughly under his thumb, and he will not leave her for a moment. Her suit is anything but a good fit. Her trousers are very tight about the hips, and are split a bit down the back and secured with a large safety-pin.

I did not arrest them. The course I am pursuing is the best, as they have no suspicion, and, with so many passengers, it prevents any excitement. They have been under strict observation all the voyage, as if they smelt a rat he might do something rash. I have not noticed a revolver in his hip pocket. He continually shaves his upper lip, and his beard is growing nicely I often see him stroking it and seeming pleased, looking more like a farmer every day The mark on the nose caused through wearing spectacles has not worn off since coming on board.

He sits about on the deck reading, or pretending to read and both seem to be thoroughly enjoying all their meals. They have not been sea-sick, and I have discussed various parts of the world with him. He knows Toronto, Detroit, and California well, and says he is going to take his boy to California, for his health (meaning Miss Le Neve). Has in conversation used several medical terms. Crippen says that when the ship arrives he will go to Detroit by boat, if possible, as he prefers it.

When my suspicions were aroused as to Crippen's identity I quietly collected all the English papers on the ship which mentioned anything of the murder, and I warned the chief officer to collect any he might see. This being done, I considered the road was clear. I told Crippen a story to make him laugh heartily, to see if he would open his mouth wide enough for me to ascertain if he had false teeth. This ruse was successful.

All the 'boy's' manners at table when I was watching 'him' were most lady-like, handling knife and fork, and taking fruit off dishes with two fingers. Crippen kept cracking nuts for her, and giving her half his salad, and was always paying her the most marked attention. During the evening of July 25th, which they spent in the saloon, enjoying songs and music, he was quite interested, and spoke to me next morning, saying how one song, 'We All Walked into the Shop,' had been drumming in his head all night, and how his 'boy' had enjoyed it, and had laughed heartily when they retired to their cabin. In the course of one conversation he spoke about American drinks, and said that Selfridge's was the only decent place in London to get them at.

On two or three occasions when walking on the deck I called after him by his assumed name, Mr. Robinson, and he took no notice. I repeated it, and it was only owing to the presence of mind of Miss Le Neve that he turned round. He apologised for not hearing me, saying that the cold weather had made him deaf. During the day he would often look at the track chart which shows the ship's position, and count the number of days remaining to the end of the passage.

He would often sit on deck and look up aloft at the wireless aerial, and listen to the cracking electric spark messages being sent by the Marconi operator. He said: 'What a wonderful invention it is!'

Though Le Neve does not show signs of distress, and is, perhaps, ignorant of the crime committed, she appears to be a girl with a very weak will. She has to follow him everywhere. If he looks at her she gives him an endearing smile, as though she were under his hypnotic influence.

Crippen was very restless on sighting Belle Isle, and asked where we stopped for the pilot, how he came off, how far from the pilot station to Quebec, and said he would be glad when we arrived, as he was anxious to get to Detroit. I had them both in my room talking over various things connected with the United States, mostly about San Francisco. Crippen says he does not suppose he would know it now, as he had not been there since he was eighteen years of age, but how he loved California, and said he thought of settling down on a nice fruit farm there.

CAPTAIN HENRY KENDALL, JULY 1910

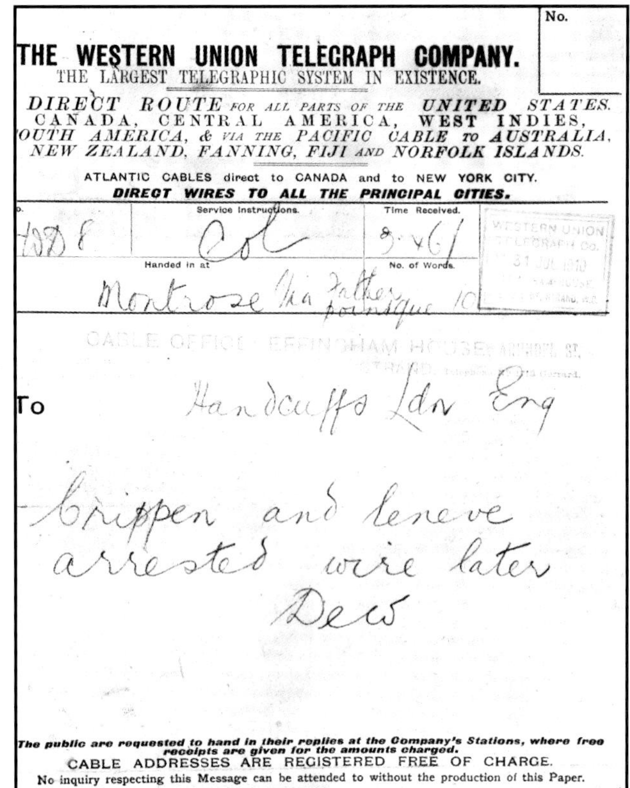

No.

THE WESTERN UNION TELEGRAPH COMPANY.
THE LARGEST TELEGRAPHIC SYSTEM IN EXISTENCE.
DIRECT ROUTE FOR ALL PARTS OF THE **UNITED** *STATES.*
CANADA, CENTRAL AMERICA, WEST INDIES,
OUTH AMERICA, & VIA THE PACIFIC CABLE TO **AUSTRALIA**,
NEW ZEALAND, FANNING, FIJI AND NORFOLK ISLANDS.
ATLANTIC CABLES direct to CANADA and to NEW YORK CITY.
DIRECT WIRES TO ALL THE PRINCIPAL CITIES.

Service Instructions. | Time Received.
4088 Col 8.v6/
Handed in at | No. of Words.
Montrose Via Father Pointque 10

WESTERN UNION TELEGRAPH Co. 31 JUL 1910

CABLE OFFICE: EFFINGHAM HOUSE, ARUNDEL ST, STRAND.

To Handcuffs Ldn Eng

Crippen and leneve arrested wire later Dew

The public are requested to hand in their replies at the Company's Stations, where free receipts are given for the amounts charged.
CABLE ADDRESSES ARE REGISTERED FREE OF CHARGE.
No inquiry respecting this Message can be attended to without the production of this Paper.

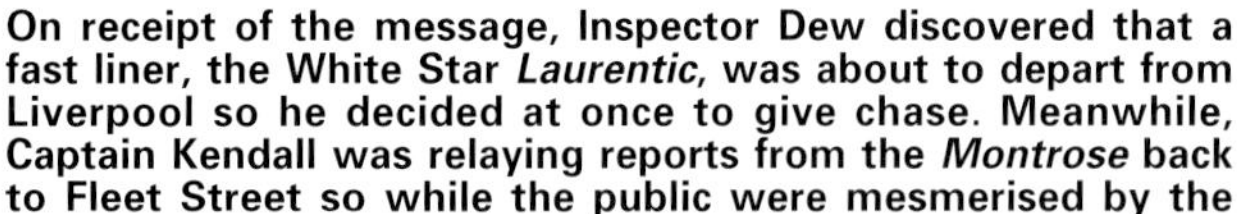

On receipt of the message, Inspector Dew discovered that a fast liner, the White Star *Laurentic*, was about to depart from Liverpool so he decided at once to give chase. Meanwhile, Captain Kendall was relaying reports from the *Montrose* back to Fleet Street so while the public were mesmerised by the chase, Crippen was totally unaware that he had been rumbled. On July 27 the *Laurentic* overtook the *Montrose* and Dew arrested Crippen and Le Neve in Canadian waters. Within three weeks Crippen and his lover had been extradited and were on their way back to Britain to stand trial.

Inspector Dew in bowler hat escorts Dr Crippen, his face hidden with a scarf, from the *Montrose* after it docked at Liverpool on August 28.

Photography during court proceedings has been banned in Britain since the introduction of the Criminal Law Act in 1925 but before that photographs, like this one of Dr Crippen and Miss Le Neve in the dock at Bow Street Magistrates Court, were commonplace. Crippen always protested his innocence and today questions have been raised as to whether his execution was a miscarriage of justice. David Foran of the University of Michigan has conducted geneaology research and checked the DNA of a tissue sample still held by Scotland Yard. He claims that not only does it not match that of Cora's relatives but that it comes from a man! The Criminal Cases Review Commission has been examining the evidence on behalf of Patrick Crippen, a relative of the doctor, who has also asked for the body to be exhumed from Pentonville and repatriated to the Crippen family plot in the United States.

In 2005 the court was sold to an Irish property developer. It concluded its last case on July 14, 2006 but we were priveleged to picture the old No. 1 Court in 2011.

Ethel Le Neve was cleared of any complicity — here she is pictured leaving the court. Crippen saw her for the last time at Pentonville prison on the day before his execution, having declared his love for her in his 'farewell letter to the world': 'Written as I face eternity, I say that Ethel Le Neve has loved me as few women love men, and that her innocence of any crime, save that of yielding to the dictates of the heart, is absolute. To her I pay this last tribute. It is of her that my last thoughts have been. My last prayer will be that God may protect her and keep her safe from harm and allow her to join me in eternity. I make this defence and this acknowledgment that the love of Ethel Le Neve has been the best thing in my life — my only happiness — and that in return for that great gift I have been inspired with a greater kindness towards my fellow-beings, and with a greater desire to do good. We were as man and wife together, with an absolute communion of spirit. Perhaps God will pardon us because we were like two children in the great unkind world, who clung to one another and gave each other courage.' On November 23 as he stood on the gallows with executioners John Ellis and William Willis, she was boarding a liner bound for New York. She returned to England a few years later under the name of Ethel Nelson and married a Stanley Smith who had no idea of her earlier relationship. That was only revealed to author Ursula Bloom in 1954. Ethel died in 1967.

To put the dramatic events of 1910-11 into proper perspective, we must first set the scene in East London. Then, the word 'anarchists' was on everyone's lips; somewhat of an old-fashioned term with not quite the same meaning as the terrorist of today. The anarchists sought to bring about political change and the overthrow of orderly government more by way of social agitation and strikes rather than violence yet, as far as the East End was concerned, their actions ended in open gun battles and violent death. By the turn of the century, London — and the East End in particular — had become a second home for dozens of political refugees deported from eastern Europe, particularly Russia, Germany, and France from where some 7,000 insurrectionists were deported after the French civil war in 1871. The rising of the workers against the French government from March to May that year — dubbed the Commune of Paris — became a symbol of the social revolution preached by the German socialist writer Karl Marx. Marx himself *(left)* became a refugee in London, other transients being *(L-R)* Lenin, Stalin and Trotsky. At the time of the Ripper murders, the so called 'Anarchists' Club' operated under the guise of the International Working Men's Educational Club in Berner Street — we saw it next to Duffield's yard on page 26.

December 16, 1910 — The Houndsditch Murders

At 10.45 p.m. on the 16th December,' Police Constable 344 'C' Piper was informed by a resident that he had heard an unusual noise at the rear of a jeweller's shop at 118 [*sic*] Houndsditch. The Constable arranged for P.C. Ernest Woodhams to keep observation in Exchange Buildings at the rear of Houndsditch, and for P.C. Walter Choat in Houndsditch, and went to pass word for the Sergeant to attend to the matter.

He shortly afterwards saw Sergeant Robert Bentley who, leaving Piper at the front of the premises, went with Sergeants Charles Tucker and William Bryant, and two Constables who had arrived on the scene, to 10 Exchange Buildings, where some foreigners were known to be residing, with a view of ascertaining the cause of the noise. Sergeant Bentley knocked on the door, which was opened by a man whom Bentley asked if anyone was working there, but the man did not appear to understand English, and Bentley asked if there was anyone there who could understand English, and stepped inside the doorway.

The man apparently went a little way up stairs and another rushed from the back of the room, and fired a revolver at Sergeant Bentley who fell wounded in the doorway. The men then came out of the house firing revolvers and shot Sergeants Bryant and Tucker, and Constables Woodhams and Choat. The wounded officers were all removed to Hospital.'

Sergeant Tucker was found to be dead on arrival at the Hospital having been shot through the heart. Constable Choat was found to be wounded in five places, and was operated upon owing to wounds in the abdomen. He died at 6 a.m. 17th instant.

Sergeant Bentley was wounded in the right shoulder and right side of neck and died at 8 p.m. 17th instant. Sergeant Bryant was shot in the chest and left arm. Constable Woodhams was shot in the left thigh which is badly fractured, and in the right calf. Bryant and Woodhams are progressing favourably .

The Criminals escaped and enquiry showed that they had taken two houses, Nos 9 and 11 in Exchange Buildings, some three weeks ago, paying rent in advance, but the landlord did not know where they came from or anything about them.

Chief Superintendent, City Police Office, December 20, 1910

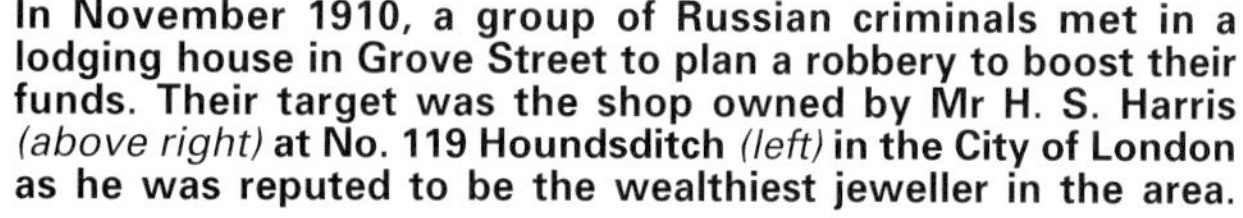
In November 1910, a group of Russian criminals met in a lodging house in Grove Street to plan a robbery to boost their funds. Their target was the shop owned by Mr H. S. Harris *(above right)* at No. 119 Houndsditch *(left)* in the City of London as he was reputed to be the wealthiest jeweller in the area.

For security reasons his safe was positioned facing the front window so that it was clearly visible to a policeman on his beat. *Right:* When redeveloped, the site became the Sir John Cass School of Navigation but today the shop has a far more mundane use.

Behind the shop lay Exchange Buildings, the row of lock up premises on the left in this picture looking towards Cutler Street.

The yard still remains yet the exit to Cutler Street has shrunk to a narrow opening in the new office block.

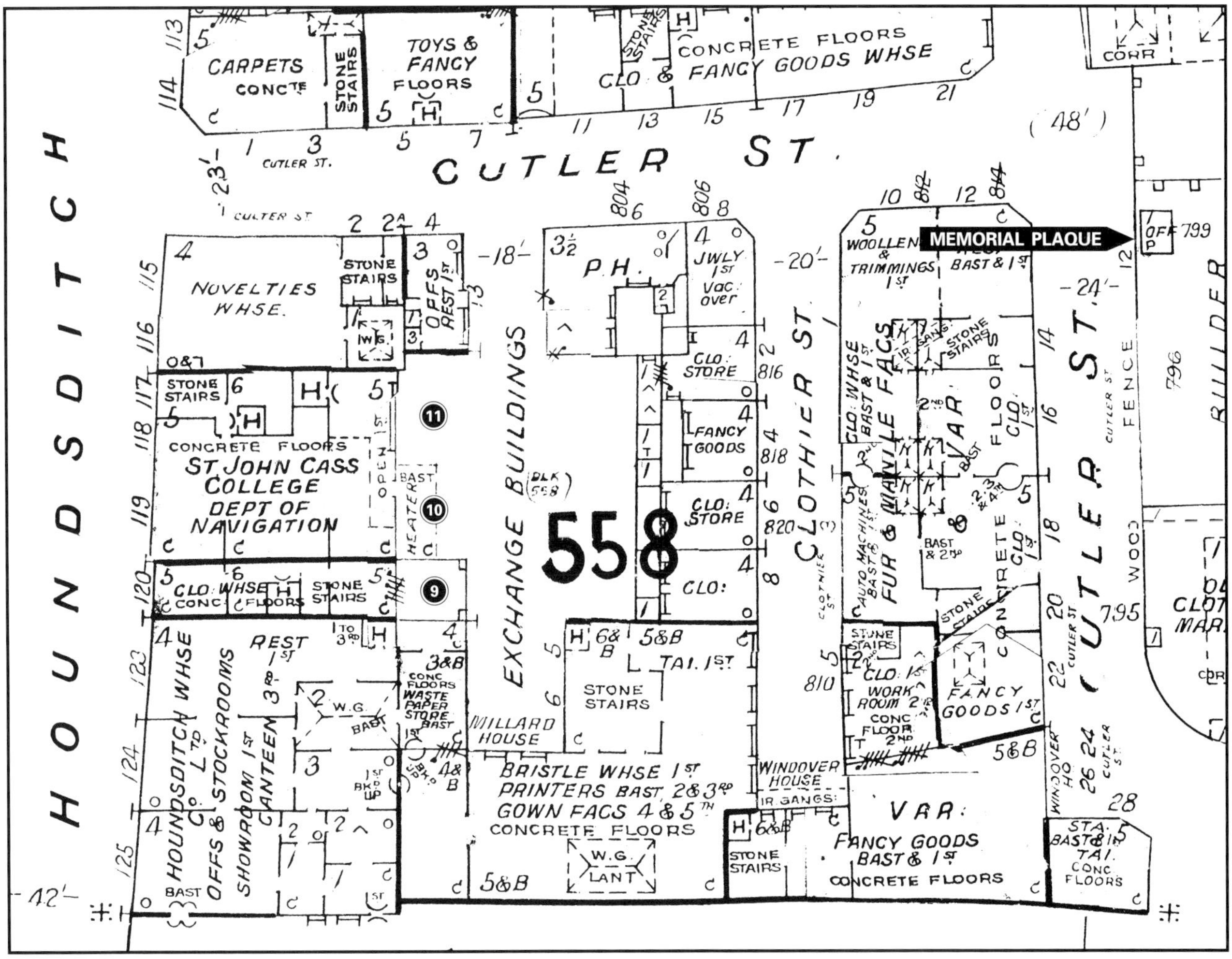

The plan shows the layout subsequent to the demolition of Exchange Buildings. We have indicated the relevant doorways.

Inquest by the City Coroner on the policemen shot at Exchange Buildings, Houndsditch, in the City of London.

Gentlemen, this long and difficult, enquiry has been held, as by law directed, to ascertain how, when, and where Police Sergeant Robert Bentley, an officer of the City of London Police Force, came by his death on the 17th December 1910. His death was one link in a chain of a complicated series of events which have attracted a considerable amount of public attention. I must ask you, however, in arriving at your Verdict, to dismiss from your minds any facts or statements within your knowledge other than those that have been laid before you by witnesses in this Coroner's Court. This is all the more important inasmuch there appear to be a number of persons implicated in the affair which culminated in the shooting of Sergeant Bentley and others in the blind alley known as Exchange Buildings, Houndsditch, within the precincts of the City of London.

The evidence shows that Sergeant Bentley, the deceased officer, was shot in the house No. 11 Exchange Buildings at or about 11.30 on the night of Friday, December 16th. He and other officers had been called to the house by Police Constable Piper. Bentley, who was in uniform, obtained admission but almost immediately shots were heard and deceased fell over the threshold with his head on the footway. What followed afterwards is not quite clear, but, as the result of further shooting, five Police Officers in all were shot, three of them died of their wounds, and one has fortunately recovered but the other is likely to be invalided for a long time. The names of the dead officers were Sergeant Bentley, Sergeant Tucker, Constable Choat, and of those who recovered, Sergeant (now Sub-Inspector) Bryant and Constable (now Sergeant) Woodhams.

Another death appears to have occurred in connection with the affray, namely that of a Russian known as Gardstein who was seen on the premises and whose body has been identified as the man who opened the door of No. 11 on the night of the 16th. He, and at least one other man, possibly or probably with several other persons, were on the premises at the time of the shooting. Gardstein was seen by Police Constable Strongman to leave No. 11, but there is no other testimony before us as to anyone else having been seen to leave that house at or after the affray.

At this point it may be best to give a short account of the locality. Exchange Buildings is a cul-de-sac some forty or fifty yards in length opening off Cutler Street, which runs right and left leading on the left-hand into Houndsditch. Exchange Buildings comprises 12 small dwelling houses, three rooms in each, some of which are used as workshops. At the north-east corner stands a public house, the Cutler's Arms, the side entrance of which opens into the Buildings. The inhabitants are mainly of the Hebrew race. We may safely assume that the two houses, Nos. 9 and 11, were in common possession of Gardstein and others concerned with him, while No. 10 was empty, having been cleared of certain goods stored therein on the evening shortly before the shooting occurred. It has been shown by the evidence of the police that with little difficulty it was possible to get from Nos. 9 to 11 by climbing over out-houses which were the party boundaries of the narrow passage at the back of each house.

For the purposes of this enquiry we may safely assume, on the evidence before us, that the purpose of the occupants of Nos. 9 and 11 on the night of the 16th of December was to break into the premises of a jeweller, Mr Henry Samuel Harris of 119 Houndsditch, the back of whose premises abut on No. 9. A space of about two feet square of the brick wall of the out-house of No. 9 was broken almost through and at one small point the breach had actually exposed the match-boarding on Mr Harris's side of the wall. Implements such as those used by burglars were found both in Nos. 9 and 11. We have it on the evidence of Detective Superintendent Ottaway that amongst these were found in No. 9 a cylinder of oxygen gas and sixty-three feet of india-rubber tubing, with an oxyhydrogen blow-pipe. The length of this pipe was more than enough to reach from the gas pipe in the ground floor of No. 9 through the breach in the wall to the back of the safe in Mr Harris's premises. On the strength of such evidence it may be assumed that a carefully planned attempt was made on the night of the 16th of December to break through the party wall between No. 9 Exchange Buildings and the lock-up shop of Mr Harris. Further, that the oxyhydrogen apparatus was for the purpose of penetrating the metal of the safe in which property belonging to Mr Harris was contained to the value of £7,000. This safe was placed against a wall at the back of the shop facing Houndsditch in such a position and so lighted that it could be seen through the window by the policemen on beat at all times of the night. The only way for a thief to get at the contents of the safe without being seen from the street was by breaking through that portion of the wall against which it rested.

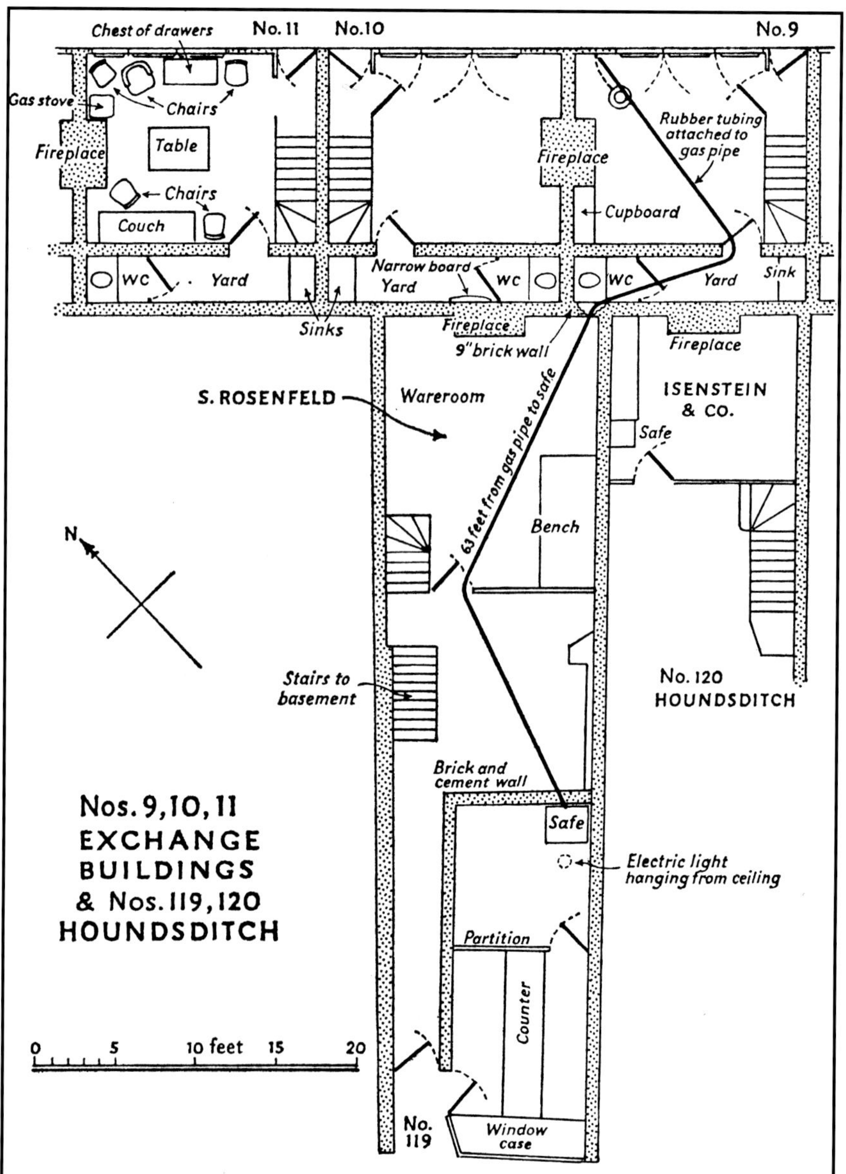

Going back to the commencement of the plot, we have heard that No. 11 was entered on November 30th by a foreigner who gave the name of Levi and four or five days later another foreigner, who gave the name of Goldstein, entered No. 9. Some furniture was put into No. 11 and certain chairs placed therein were afterwards found to match a suite found at No. 59 Grove Street, the house in which Gardstein died. The tools and appliances above-mentioned were found distributed between the two houses. The intention clearly was to enter the back part of Mr Harris's premises and then to break through that portion of the wall which lay behind the safe in the shop.

The room which the thieves would first enter was in the occupation of a sub-tenant of Mr Harris together with the rest of the building except the shop. The safe itself was to be attacked by the oxyhydrogen blow-pipe flame whereby the steel would be softened so that it could be penetrated by cutting instruments. The necessary hydrogen was to be brought by india-rubber tubing from a gas pipe in the front of the ground floor of No. 9 to the blow-pipe and cylinder of oxygen, both of which would be placed in position close to the safe.

The plans being thus deliberately and skillfully laid, the work of breaking through the party wall was commenced some time on the night of the 16th. The piercing and removal of the bricks naturally made a good deal of

Left: **No. 9 Exchange Buildings was used by the gang to break through the adjoining wall into Mr Harris's shop.**

Right: **Nos. 10 and 11. The former premises were vacant and it was in the doorway of No. 11 that the murders took place.**

noise in spite of every precaution. This did not matter in the case of Mr Harris's house, as the shop was shut up on Friday evening at seven o'clock and not opened until ten on Sunday morning. Mr Harris was away from Houndsditch and no one else was sleeping in the house. In the house next to Mr Harris's shop, however, it so happened that the occupants lived over their business premises. The householder, Mr Max Weil, told us that on the night of the 16th the maid-servant was in the counting house on the ground floor at a quarter to ten when her attention was drawn to certain noises proceeding from the back of the premises. She informed her mistress and on Mr Weil's return shortly afterwards he heard the noises and informed Police Constable Piper.

After surveying the premises and listening to the noises, the constable went round to No. 11 where the door was opened to him by a foreigner who he identified in this Court by means of a photograph as that of a man named Gardstein, whom he had seen lying dead the next day in the first floor front room of No. 59 Grove Street. Piper's suspicions being aroused, he placed Constables Woodhams, Smoothy and Choat to watch while he fetched Sergeant Bentley. Both of them went to Mr Weil's house and listened to the noise.

We have police evidence to show that Piper was left at Mr Harris's. Sergeant Bentley and plain clothes Constables Martin and Strongman went to No. 11, meeting on the way Sergeant Tucker and Sergeant Bryant. When these five were near the house, other constables near were Choat opposite the Cutler's Arms and Woodhams a little higher up in Exchange Buildings. Constable Martin stood behind Sergeant Bentley while the latter knocked. The door was opened about six inches by a man whom Martin testified to have been identical with Gardstein, subsequently found dead at No. 59 Grove Street and whose body Martin saw at the London Hospital. The Sergeant asked if any work was going on inside. No answer was made but the door was nearly closed and the man recognised as Gardstein then apparently went upstairs. Bentley then pushed the door open and stood inside in a doorway between the lobby and the room. Directly afterwards a shot was fired, according to Martin from the back of the room, and he saw a man's arm and hand holding a revolver. Martin and Sergeant Bryant rushed to the door and a second shot was fired from the stairs a few paces away from and facing the front door. Bentley fell backwards through the doorway, and the hand with the revolver fired up and down Exchange Buildings. Martin tripped and fell into the carriageway. On rising he saw Sergeant Bryant leaning against the wall bleeding from the hand while Bentley, Woodhams and Choat were on the ground. Martin saw no one leave No. 11 or No. 9.

Sub-Inspector Bryant, who has happily recovered from his wounds, has given most important evidence as to the identity of the man who fired the shot that proved fatal to Sergeant Bentley. He told us that he stepped into the passage after Sergeant Bentley and saw a man coming from the back door of the room with a pistol in his hand with which he fired at Bentley. This man Bryant identifies as Gardstein.

The medical evidence shows conclusively the fact that deceased died as the result of an injury to the spinal cord caused by a pistol bullet. The evidence of Dr Biggar, the House-Surgeon at St Bartholomew's, was to the effect that the deceased was brought to the hospital shortly after midnight on the 16th of December. He was semi-conscious although unable to make any statement. His death took place on the following evening at 6.45, and before that event he was able to answer questions but made no statement as to the cause of his injuries. The post-mortem examination was performed at the hospital by the Surgical-Registrar Mr Elmslie in the presence of Dr Biggar who testified to the following facts. There were two wounds in the body of deceased, one at the front of the right shoulder joint and the other at the root of the neck. The only one that need concern us is the latter, which entered the neck an inch above the inner end of the right collarbone. The bullet then passed to the right of the windpipe and pierced the spinal column severing the spinal cord almost completely in its course, and was found lodged beneath the skin of the back. This was the wound that proved fatal. Both bullets were found in the body. The medical evidence to the effect that death resulted from paralysis of respiration due to the bullet wound of the spinal cord is clear beyond all doubt and I will ask you to find your verdict in accordance with the facts that have been laid before you.

George Gardstein who fired the first shots was himself hit by another assailant. Police found him expired at No. 59 Grove Street which no longer stands today.

It has been shown in evidence that shots were fired from the staircase as well as from the back of the room. It is possible that the exact details of the affair will never be ascertained. You will probably agree with me, however, that there is no doubt from the evidence we have heard about the main fact that a carefully contrived shop-breaking was attempted by certain persons whom we know were at least two in number, and who in all probability had many confederates. Five policemen were shot, three of whom were killed by the persons engaged in carrying out the actual breaking into of Mr Harris's shop. The actual shots that killed the deceased, Sergeant Bentley, if we believe the evidence of Bryant, were fired by Gardstein.

Some important evidence has been given by Mr Goodwin, an expert in firearms. He identified the two bullets found in Sergeant Bentley's body as coming from a Dreyse pistol or a modern automatic magazine weapon of similar type. On each bullet he found four marks caused by the rifling of a barrel thereby showing that the bullets had been fired from a Dreyse pistol. The last link in this chain of circumstantial evidence is the fact that a Dreyse pistol was found under the pillow of the dead body of Gardstein at Grove Street. On this evidence I shall ask you to say whether in your opinion Gardstein fired the two bullets which we have been told by the medical witness caused the death of Sergeant Bentley.

Sub-Inspector Bryant, who was wounded, explained to the Coroner what happened: 'As the door was opened Sergeant Bentley stepped inside the passage and I saw the lower part of a man standing on the staircase in the inside of the room, which was lighted. Bentley said to him on the stairs, "Is anyone working at the back?" The man replied "No." Bentley said "Can we have a look out at the back?" and the man replied "Yes." Thereupon Bentley said, "Then show us the way." Soon afterwards the man put his hand over the door of the entrance to the next room and said, "In there." Bentley took a step to the right into the doorway of the room indicated, and immediately a man came from the back door of the room between Bentley and the table. "That man," continued Inspector Bryant, "I have since identified as Gardstein. I noticed that this man as he appeared in the room had a pistol in his hand. He twice misfired towards Bentley's right shoulder. I then heard three or four shots fired rapidly. I at once put my hands up and a bullet made my left hand fall as he commenced to fire. I fell on the footpath, and Bentley staggered back against the doorpost of the door opening into the room. I staggered along towards Cutler Street, but I must have been dazed because I lost recollection of what had happened. When I recovered I found myself standing against the wall of No. 10."' Sergeant Robert Bentley *(left)* **was mortally wounded and died in St Bartholomew's Hospital. Sergeant Charles Tucker** *(centre)* **was killed on the spot and Police Constable Walter Choat** *(right)* **was wounded and died later in the London Hospital, Whitechapel.**

The evidence renders it not impossible that Bentley was exposed to a cross-fire from both stairs and room. In any case it is my duty to tell you that it makes no difference in the eye of the law. Any person engaged in the conspiracy to steal Mr Harris's jewels becomes responsible for a murder committed in the course of their common purpose. An accessory before the act, even though he was a long distance away from the scene of the felony at the time of the attempted commission of the murder, would become responsible for that crime. To quote the words of a modern writer on the law of evidence: 'Persons who are guilty of illegally conspiring together or of committing jointly any criminal offence are deemed to be mutual agents or confederates for the purpose only of the execution of the joint purpose. Accordingly any act done by any one of them in the execution of the common purpose is deemed the act of the others also, and is consequently admissible as evidence against them'.

With this principle of law clearly in view, I will ask you, Gentlemen, to say whether in your opinion the deceased Robert Bentley met with his death as the result of bullet wounds inflicted on the night of December 16th by the deceased man Gardstein; also whether in your opinion the man Gardstein was aided and abetted in the attempted shop-breaking by one or more confederates, and if such persons were legally responsible for the death of Sergeant Bentley.

In accordance with the traditional usages of the Coroner's Court, you, Gentlemen of the Jury, may consider it your duty to comment upon the issues raised by circumstances attending the death of the deceased. In other words, the special value of the Coroner's Court so far as it is concerned with criminal acts, is not so much from the number of crimes detected as from the number of those prevented. The special features likely to demand your attention are suggested by the fact that the attempted shop-breaking which resulted in the death of Sergeant Bentley and others was the work of aliens; secondly, that the police who tried to arrest the thieves were unarmed. You may therefore wish to express an opinion as to the control of aliens, especially of criminal aliens, with a view of preventing such outrages in the future, and as to the further question of arming the police.

With regard to the arming of the police, it is a matter of common information that arms are available for their use under exceptional circumstances. Such weapons, however, are of an old-fashioned pattern, not at all approaching those used by Gardstein as regards range, rapidity of fire, and general handliness. The matter of arming the police, however, involves many considerations of a constitutional nature and I imagine you will agree with me that they may safely be left in the hands of the proper authorities. At the same time you may think fit to forward some note of opinion as to the desirability of providing weapons of modern type for use by the City Police under exceptional circumstances.

The funeral of the murdered officers took place on Thursday, December 22. Here the cortege halts for the service in St Paul's Cathedral.

Sergeants Bentley and Tucker were buried side by side in the City of London's own Cemetery at Manor Park but Police Constable Choat was taken to St Mary's Church at Byfleet in Surrey.

As regards the control of alien criminals, I will ask you to consider various points that may perhaps strengthen to some extent the hands of the authorities. Speaking generally, it seems hardly possible to frame any measure for the exclusion of criminals short of preventing the entry of all foreigners since aliens and alien criminals come from all parts of the world. It must be conceded that the present Aliens Act (1905) fails absolutely so far as the exclusion of criminal aliens is concerned. A money test is imposed and that obviously fails to keep out the criminal, who as a rule is well provided with money, and who after admission usually settles down to some occupation and lives outwardly the life of a law-abiding citizen.

It is a self-evident fact that the present system has not succeeded in excluding those aliens engaged in the Houndsditch crime. Expulsion is wisdom after the event and a remedy applicable only when the criminal stands revealed. All punitive criminal law, however, is subject to similar criticism, for crime cannot be dealt with from that standpoint until it arises. Were there some system of international police control of criminal aliens founded on the scientific method of fingerprint identification, it would probably to a large extent do away with the necessity of an Aliens Act. The weak point in that direction lies in the fact that the system has not yet been adopted or at any rate systematically applied for a sufficient length of time in all countries.

The first logical step in obtaining control of domiciled aliens appears to lie almost necessarily in their registration and subsequent supervision for a certain number of years after arrival in this country. A proper system of registration, fingerprint identification, and systematic compulsory personal report at intervals during, say, a period of half a dozen years, would lay the foundation of a system of efficient control over alien criminals. Failure to comply with these regulations should be a punishable offence, and, if repeated, should constitute a liability to deportation.

As regards the carrying of arms by aliens, it is at once evident that the Pistols Act (1903) does not exercise any efficient control over them in that particular direction. For that matter the Act does not in practice prevent criminals of any nationality from carrying arms. So far as the safety of the British subject is concerned, it seems desirable to devise some plan for the repression of the armed criminal no matter whether he comes from home or abroad. For that purpose I will ask you to consider whether it would be desirable to institute a special penalty for all persons found in possession of deadly weapons when engaged in the commission of a serious or indictable crime. The mere fact of a man who commits, or attempts to commit, a crime being in possession of such weapons implies an intent to resort to their use if necessary for his purpose or to effect his subsequent escape. The possession of arms under such circumstances might be rendered an offence punishable by flogging.The principle of flogging for violence used in the commission of an indictable offence is recognised in the Garrotters Act (1863) but there is no legislation of the kind applicable to indictable offences generally than those against the crime of robbery from the person with violence.

In 2010 it was planned to dedicate a memorial plaque to be unveiled on the 100th anniversary. However, the private companies which now surround the murder spot would not give permission so instead it had to be erected on a wall owned by the Corporation of the City of London (see plan page 47) merely stating 'near this spot'.

January 1, 1911 — The Murder of Leon Beron

East London has been excited this week by another sensational murder. The New Year had just been ushered in when under the cover of darkness, a man was brutally done to death on Clapham Common.

The man's surname is understood to be Beron (another report gives the name as Leon Rason), and he had been living in Jubilee Street, Mile End.

The crime was committed at a lonely spot on the west side of the common, not more than fifty yards from the road.

From the bandstand in the centre of the common, narrow pathways radiate in all directions, and it was on one of these that the murderer's attack was made.

The pathway is bounded on one side only by an iron railing, the other side being unfenced, and skirted by grass.

The tragic discovery was made on Sunday morning. A constable, whilst on duty, was passing along this pathway when he noticed a splash of blood on the railings. He thereupon looked round, and found the body of an elderly man. The head was terribly battered, and the face and hands were mud-stained, showing that the body had been dragged along the ground.

His face was so battered as to be almost beyond identification, and, but for the documents found on him, his identity would probably have remained a mystery.

He was an alien Jew without doubt, and resembled so many of the men seen daily in the East End that it would have been difficult to trace him but for the papers found in his possession.

The hair and moustache were iron grey, the complexion sallow. From the appearance of the remains, the man seemed well-to-do. He wore a dark suit and Melton overcoat with astrakhan collar. He had a bowler hat and patent leather boots. The hat was found several feet away from the body, and bore the name of an East End firm. It was this fact that assisted the police in establishing the identity of the man.

Dr. Joseph Needham, who was called by the police when the body was discovered, said death was due to concussion of the brain from fracture of the skull, due to wounds inflicted over the right side of the forehead. There were also some dagger or knife wounds in the body, both the liver and stomach being injured. A letter 'S' was cut on both sides of the face, a circumstance which has given rise to the suggestion that it is a murder of revenge as well as robbery.

East London Advertiser, January 7, 1911

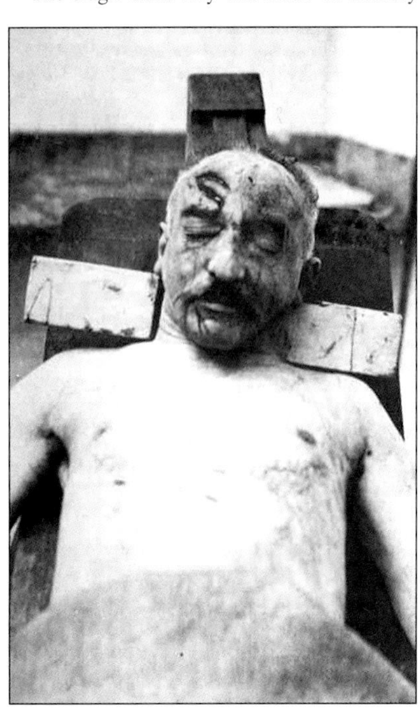

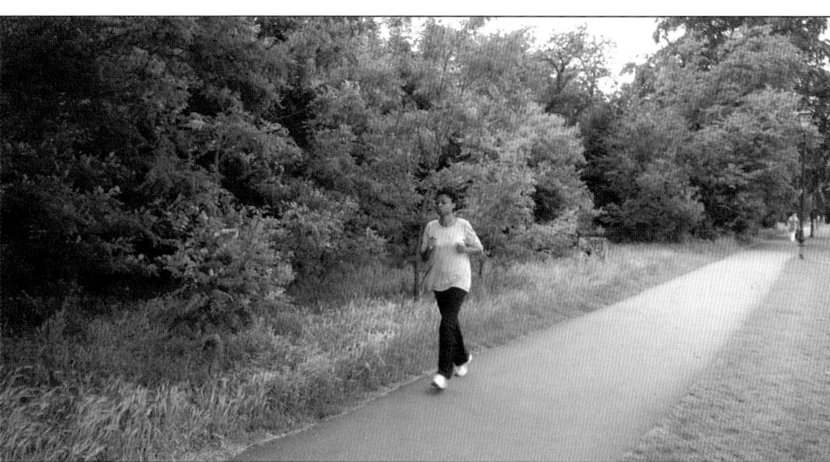

Left: **It was the letter 'S' cut on Leon Beron's forehead — possibly standing for the initial letter of the Russian word for traitor — which led to speculation that this was a revenge killing for betraying the anarchists involved in the Houndsditch murders.** *Above:* **His body was found in this copse on the western side of Clapham Common on New Year's Day 1911. (An ex-convict, Steine Morrison was later arrested as he had been seen in the company of Beron on New Year's Eve. However, the evidence presented at his trial was weak and, although found guilty, he was reprieved.) In any case, the police were now hard on the heels of the Houndsditch killers and by midnight on January 2/3 were planning to surround No. 100 Sidney Street in Whitechapel.**

Having managed to surreptitiously evacuate the tenement, save for the room occupied by the two suspects, at 7.30 a.m. several police officers approached the front door and threw pebbles up at the second floor window. This action heralded a fusillade of shots, wounding Sergeant Leeson. The ten-shot Mauser semi-automatic pistols in the hands of the anarchists meant that the police were totally out-gunned and ill-equipped to deal with armed terrorists. As a result, an urgent request was made to the Tower of London to despatch guardsmen with .303 Service rifles. A contingent of 70 men and NCOs from the 1st Battalion, Scots Guards, arrived, seen here kneeling on newspaper placards at the northern end of the street.

The oldest inhabitants of East London cannot remember scenes such as were witnessed on Tuesday. Dense crowds flocked into the Mile End Road from the City and suburbs, all bound for the one centre of interest — Sidney Street. This thoroughfare was unknown outside the Borough of Stepney a week ago, and was not regarded with particular interest by East Enders themselves.

Quite suddenly, however, Sidney Street has become one of the most notorious thoroughfares in Europe. Here was waged on Tuesday the most remarkable duel ever recorded in the long history of civilisation — two men against a thousand. But the men were desperate criminals implicated in the sensational Houndsditch murders of a few weeks ago. They had taken refuge in a house in Martin's Mansions, Sidney Street, and it was the efforts of the police to effect their arrest which led to the scenes to which we have referred.

The bulk of the crowd stood in Mile End Road, near Mile End Gate, a solid row of uniformed men preventing the people from passing to Sidney Street. Here they stood from hour to hour discussing the events which were taking place. Mixing among them one could not but be impressed with the facts that they were wholly in sympathy with the police, and even the foreign element expressed the hope that the desperadoes would be captured.

Inside the police cordon the scene was sufficiently thrilling. Police and soldiers with rifles, shot guns and revolvers were waging an intermittent battle with the occupants of the house, 100 Sidney Street. The 'ping ping' of the shots rang out at frequent intervals, the soldiers kneeling or lying prone to take aim, and the police standing with guns ready in case the desperate men should attempt to make a rush for it.

East London Advertiser, January 7, 1911

Left: **The only life lost, apart from the two anarchists, was that of District Officer Charles Rearson of the London Fire Brigade who died six months later from injuries received when part of the building collapsed on him.** *Right:* **A memorial plaque was unveiled on Wexford House, which now stands on the site of No. 100, in January 2011.**

By midday the police were planning to storm the building but at 1.30 p.m. a wisp of smoke from the upper windows quickly led to the whole house catching fire. Not wanting to risk the lives of firemen, the Home Secretary Winston Churchill, who had arrived on the scene during the morning, gave instructions to let the house burn down. Two bodies, charred beyond recognition, were later recovered from the ruin and buried in an unmarked grave at the City of London Cemetery, the burial register simply recording the names of 'Fritz' and 'Joseph'. (For a detailed account of the siege, see *The East End Then and Now*.)

This is Woodcote Park Convalescent Camp at Epsom in Surrey. In the aftermath of the First World War, troops from the Empire were anxious to return home, none more so than the hundreds of Canadian soldiers kicking their heels in frustration at still being confined to the camp more than six months after the Armistice had been signed.

June 17, 1919 — Riot by Canadian Troops at Epsom

At Bow-street Police Court yesterday, before Sir John Dickinson, the eight Canadian soldiers who are alleged to have taken part in the fatal disturbance at Epsom Police Station on June 17 were charged on remand with being concerned in the manslaughter of Station-sergeant Thomas Green, of the Epsom police. The defendants are: Pte. Allen McMaster, aged 30, of the 3rd Canadian Reserve; Pte. Frank Harold Wilkie, 21, 102nd Battalion, Canadians; Gunner Herbert Tait, 29, 11th Canadian Division; Pte. Gervas Porrier, 24, C.A.M.C.; Pte. Alphonse Masse, 27, C.A.M.C.; Pte. Robert Alexander McAllan, 45, C.A.M.C.; Pte. James Connors, 19, 13th Canadian Highlanders; and Pte. David Yerex, Canadian Forestry Corps.

Sir Richard Muir and Mr. William Lewis conducted the case on behalf of the Director of Public Prosecutions; Mr. Bernard Abinger defended.

Sir Richard Muir said that at 9.45 p.m. on June 17 two Canadian soldiers in a convalescent camp at Epsom were taken to the local police station for disorderly conduct, and in the ordinary course they would have been handed over to the military police. The same night a number of men in the convalescent camp made up their minds to rescue their comrades from custody. Officers and N.C.O.'s did their best to dissuade the men, but without avail. The police station was surrounded and attacked in front by the soldiers. Inspector Pawley, who was in charge of the station, wisely decided to surrender the two men to Major Ross, who was there trying to restore order. But neither the police nor the military officers were able to dissuade the men from violence. Missiles were thrown, the police station was partly wrecked, and some of the men got into the cell passage through a window and forced one of the cell doors open with a crowbar. The police then made a charge from the rear of the station. Sergeant Green, who was in front of the charge, was struck down beside another officer, who had to fight his way back to the police station. Ultimately the two men in custody were released and the rioters decided to return to camp. Sergeant Green was taken to an adjoining house where his skull was found to be smashed, and he died shortly afterwards.

Major Sandys Bird, adjutant of Woodcote Park Camp, said that he remained at the camp in telephonic communication with Headquarters during the disturbances. He did not put any of the men under arrest when they returned, as he feared a further disturbance.

Major James Ross, who was officer of the day at the camp, said that after the men had left camp he overtook them and urged them

The site of the camp is now occupied by the prestigious Royal Automobile Club's golf course.

On the evening of Tuesday, June 17, 1919, two Canadians were arrested by the local police for disorderly conduct and taken to Epsom Police Station *(left)*. Under normal circumstances, they would have been released to the custody of the Military Police but, before that happened, the soldiers at Woodcote Park decided to take matters into their own hands. They marched on the police station and forced their way inside causing much damage. During the riot Police Sergeant Thomas Green was struck violently on the head, dying from the wound within a few minutes. *Right:* The station stood here on Ashley Road.

to keep order. On arriving at the police station he went inside and presently came out and told the men that Inspector Pawley was going to hand over his two prisoners to him. He then returned to the cells and while the prisoners were being released many missiles came hurtling through the windows.

Police-constable Rose said that he saw Sergeant Green struck down with a piece of fence-rail about six or seven feet long. The witness identified Connors as one of the men who attempted to strike Sergeant Green with a piece of railing, but he did not think he actually struck him.

The Times, June 20, 1919

The funeral took place at Epsom yesterday of Police-sergeant Green, who died from injuries received during the raid by Canadian soldiers on Epsom Police Station last Tuesday. The procession extended over half a mile and about a thousand persons took part, of whom some hundreds were members of the Metropolitan Force of various divisions. There were also special constables, members of local bodies, Epsom magistrates, discharged soldiers, fire brigade, postmen, wounded soldiers, Major-General Horwood, Assistant Police Commissioner, Major Maxwell, P.M., Major Cornwallie-West, A.P.M., and Colonel Guest. Commandant of the Canadian Convalescent Camp, Epsom.

The service was held at the Wesleyan Church, and the interment took place in Epsom Cemetery in the presence of a large crowd. The widow, who is in a London hospital, sent a wreath. Her right hand is paralysed and she had inscribed with her left, 'In deep love to my dear, noble husband, who was killed doing his duty. From his broken-hearted wife.'

The Times, June 24, 1919

This plaque was mounted on the house which now occupies the site on the 90th anniversary of the riot.

Six days later Sergeant Green was buried in Epsom Cemetery.

In January 1919, Sinn Fein (Ourselves Alone) and the Irish Republican Army (IRA) — the successor to the Irish Volunteers who had fought the British in Dublin in 1916 — began a new campaign of guerilla warfare. Ambushes, assassinations, reprisals and counter-reprisals followed as the hated 'Black and Tans' and the Auxiliary Division Royal Irish Constabulary clashed with the IRA led by Michael Collins, Eamon De Valera and Arthur Griffith. In the end, after the British had lost over 500 men killed and the IRA some 200, a cease-fire was agreed on July 11, 1921. The Anglo-Irish Treaty, negotiated at 22 Hans Place *(left)* was signed on December 6, 1921, leading to the creation of the Irish Free State the following December.

June 22, 1922 — The Assassination of Sir Henry Wilson

Field-Marshal Sir Henry Wilson, M.P. was assassinated yesterday afternoon on his doorstep in Eaton Place S.W.

His murderers were two members of the Irish Republican Army named John O'Brien and James Connolly. They were arrested after a sensational pursuit and struggle, in which they shot and wounded a policeman, a detective and a chauffeur.

In Dublin murderers have often quelled a crowd with their pistols. The terrorist's task is not so easy in London.

Sir Henry had just returned from unveiling a war memorial at Liverpool Street Station. His last words spoken in public were 'It is a lovely and honourable thing to die for one's country.' The last music he heard was the notes of the 'Last Post.'

Shots were fired at him at point-blank range as he stepped from a taxicab. His assassins commandeered a Victoria in their attempt to escape, and fired further shots to intimidate the people who followed them. They were roughly handled and almost lynched by the infuriated crowd when they had been cornered and caught.

Daily Express, June 23, 1922

In February 1918, General Sir Henry Wilson was appointed Chief of the Imperial General Staff and was the principal military advisor to Prime MInister Lloyd George. However, as an Ulsterman, in 1914 he had surreptitiously supported British Army officers who refused to conduct operations against Ulster Unionists opposed to Irish Home Rule in an incident known as the Curragh Mutiny. Promoted to Field-Marshal in 1919, he left the army because he disagreed with the government's policies towards Ireland, and entered the House of Commons as a member for the Ulster constituency of North Down in February 1922. Winston Churchill wrote that 'in Sir Henry Wilson the War Cabinet found for the first time an expert advisor of superior intellect, who could explain lucidly and forcefully the whole situation and give reasons for the adoption or rejection of any course.'

The following month he was invited to become the Northern Ireland Government's adviser on security making him a target for the IRA. On the morning of Thursday, June 22, he was at Liverpool Street Station in London to unveil the impressive memorial to employees of the Great Eastern Railway who had lost their lives in the Great War . . .

. . . but little could Sir Henry have known that his own memorial would later be added to it *(right)*.

Taking a taxi to his home at 36 Eaton Place, Belgravia, he had just paid the driver and was feeling for his keys when two men approached and opened fire. The press coverage of the day graphically illustrated the assassination with artist's impressions.

Above: **This drawing appeared in the *Daily Telegraph* and that** *(below)* **in the *Daily Mail*. Sir Henry attempted to draw his sword to defend himself, history having now recounted that he is the only Field-Marshal to have died with his sword in his hand.**

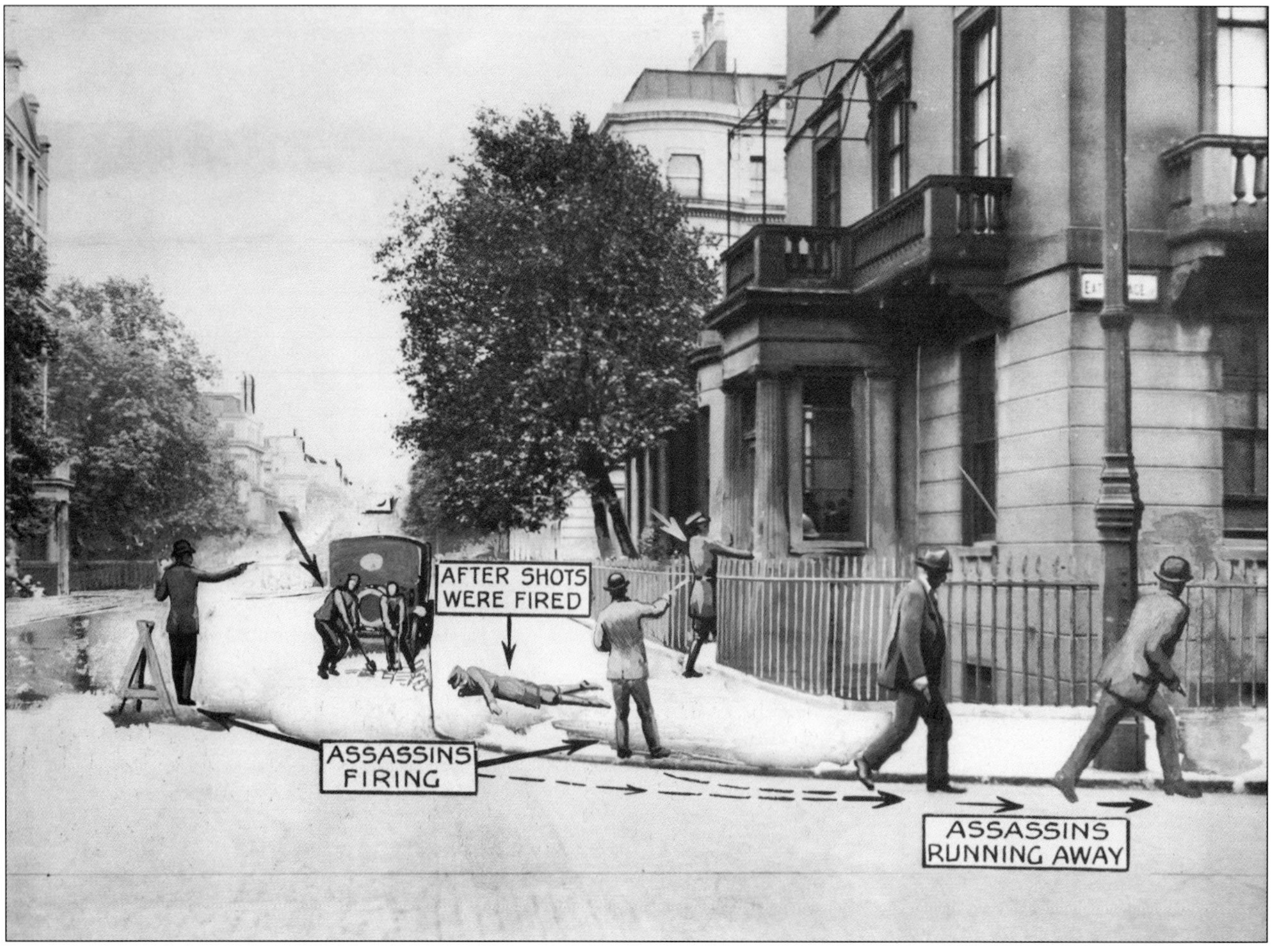

The pistols used by the assassins were later sent to David Lloyd George and Winston Churchill. Sitting in the Cabinet Room at 10 Downing Street: 'There was no Henry Wilson. The Prime Minister and I faced each other, and on the table between us lay the pistols which an hour before had taken this loyal man's life. The House of Commons was immediately adjourned as a mark of respect and King George V sent his equerry, Colonel Arthur Erskine, to Eaton Place to convey the royal sympathy to Lady Wilson.

The body of the Field-Marshal had been laid on a couch in a darkened study, and Spilsbury's examination was carried out by electric light. Wilson, known throughout the Army as 'Ugly,' from his puckish mobile face, was fifty-eight, and almost as tall as Spilsbury. He had been shot in the left forearm, twice in the right arm, twice in the left shoulder, in both armpits, and twice in the right leg. The armpit wounds were fatal, piercing the lungs. In his notes he wrote: 'Wilson was not shot after he had fallen. All nine wounds were inflicted when he was erect or slightly stooping, as he would be when tugging at his sword-hilt. The chest injuries were from shots fired at two different angles — one from the right to left and the other from left to right. Either would have proved fatal and produced death inside ten minutes. The bullet through the right leg passed forwards and downwards, and therefore the shot came from directly behind. That in the top left shoulder had been fired from the left side and rather behind, and the downward direction proved that the arm was in a raised position as the bullet entered. The wounds in the forearms were inflicted from behind whilst the arms were still at the side of the body.'

Douglas G. Browne and E. V. Tullet, Bernard Spilsbury — His Life and Cases, 1951

The original entrance in 1922 to Sir Henry's home lay on the left in Belgrave Place, as can be seen surrounded by bystanders in the top photograph, but when the building was remodelled it was moved round the corner into Eaton Place. This has confused many tourists into believing that Sir Henry was killed near the present-day steps on the right, next door to the Italian Consulate-General at No. 38. (Leasehold flats in No. 36 now change hands for in excess of £1,500,000.)

The escape route taken by the assasins.

The assassins were Reginald Dunn and Joseph O'Sullivan, both aged 24, and each armed with a Webley .380-calibre revolver. The cab-man, who had witnessed the shooting, was obviously a practising non-interventionist, for he immediately drove away and was not interviewed by police until 24 hours later. Both ambushers made off, reloading as they went, shouting to some road-menders who gave chase to 'keep back'. Dunn had a wooden leg and was not able to run in the accepted sense of the word. At this point they attempted to board a passing van, but were foiled by the driver who was struck in the face by a revolver butt during the struggle. The two murderers then turned right into Lowndes Place [1] where they tried to engage a taxi, but a passing lorry driver, who was also an eyewitness, shouted a warning to the cabby who slammed the passenger door and escaped.

After turning into Chesham Place [2] and thence into Chesham Street [3], Dunn and O'Sullivan commandeered a one-horse open brougham, driven by a coachman in full livery, and standing on the carriage steps fired several shots at their pursuers. The two men left the brougham at the end of Chesham Street and entered West Eaton Place [4] on foot. Here the chauffeur of a private motor car swerved his vehicle towards the fugitives but one of them fired and punctured the offside rear tyre; the car hit a kerb and stopped.

Meanwhile several policemen had joined the hue and cry and the sound of police whistles and gun-fire had attracted others. One of these was P.C. 411B Walter March who ran along West Eaton Terrace [5] and confronted the two gunmen as they came towards him. Despite the fact that they were armed, March immediately tackled O'Sullivan, but was then shot in the groin at point-blank range by Dunn. As O'Sullivan and March both fell to the pavement, Alexander Clark, the chauffeur of the damaged car, jumped out of his vehicle to help and was shot in the right thigh, the bullet passing through his leg.

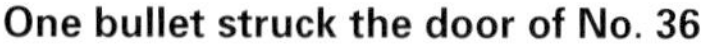
One bullet struck the door of No. 36.

Leaving March on the ground in a pool of blood, O'Sullivan got to his feet and he and Dunn turned into Chester Row [6] and then turned right into South Eaton Place [7]. This was a mistake, as their route took them past the mouth of Gerald Road which housed a police station with single mens' accommodation. All the available duty men who could be spared, plus eleven off-duty constables, who were mostly in shirt sleeves, turned out and some had the foresight to draw a pistol and ammunition. The gunmen hurried towards Ebury Street firing more shots to deter their pursuers and although no one was hit, a bullet passed through the rolled-up left sleeve of one of the off-duty men, P.C. 202B Duff.

Since the armed officers were at the back of the crowd and unable to shoot, the murderers' fire was answered with successive volleys of truncheons and the odd milk bottle. These all missed, but the truncheons were retrieved for future use as the posse moved forward. Another off-duty man, P.C. 519B Skilton, stopped a cab and asked the driver to pass as close as possible to the two fugitives so that he could lean out and hit one with his truncheon. Unfortunately, as the taxi drew abreast of the two men, they both opened fire and Skilton was obliged to duck; he threw his truncheon, which missed. As there were now several bullet holes in the cab, Skilton decided to return to Gerald Road Police Station for a pistol, a decision of which the taxi-driver undoubtedly approved.

Turning left into Ebury Street [8], the gunmen tried to climb onto a small green van, but the driver accelerated and they fell off. They now walked backwards threatening with their weapons the hostile crowd pressing towards them. More shots were fired, one of which hit Detective Constable Sayers in the right leg from a distance of about ten yards. The shots drew more flying truncheons and on this occasion one struck O'Sullivan on the head. P.C. 510B Walter Bush took advantage of the distraction to rush O'Sullivan and knock him to the ground. As they wrestled he tore a revolver (later found to contain four live and two

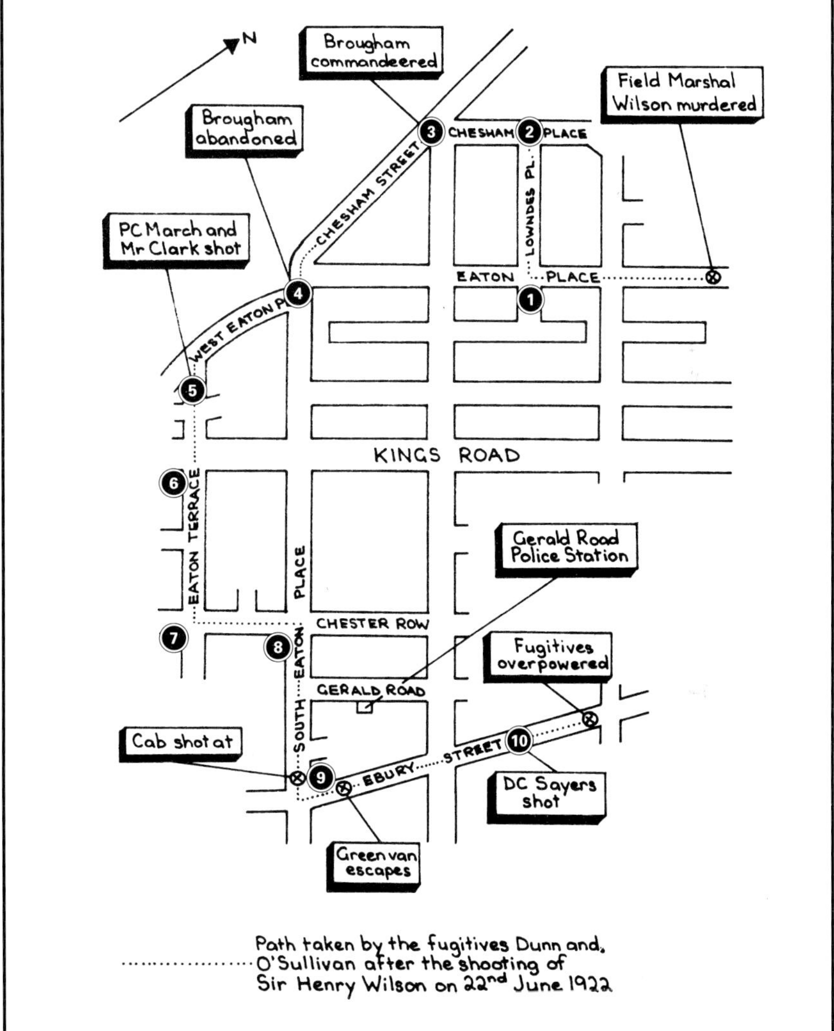

expended rounds) from the Irishman's hand. During this encounter, Dunn took deliberate aim at the policeman's head, but his gun misfired and before he could again squeeze the trigger he in turn was overpowered by P.C. Duff (still in his bullet-holed shirt sleeves).

The prisoners were taken to Gerald Road Police Station where Dunn gave his name as O'Brien and O'Sullivan identified himself as James Connolly. Their true names were only established after police notices had been circulated to other forces and the Press. Both men were sentenced to death at the Old Bailey on 18 July and their appeals were dismissed on 3 August.

Robert W. Gould and Michale J. Waldren, London's Armed Police, 1986

Irishmen and Irishwomen knelt and prayed outside both Wandsworth and Pentonville Prisons yesterday morning while Joseph O'Sullivan and Reginald Dunn, the assassins of Field-Marshal Sir Henry Wilson, were executed.

The two men were kept in Pentonville Prison until a few days ago, when they were taken to Wandsworth and the execution took place there. The fact that they had been moved was not announced, and a crowd of about 200 persons assembled outside Pentonville in the belief that the execution was to take place there. As eight o'clock approached they knelt in the street, sang hymns, and recited prayers. It was not until half an hour later that they were told that the men had been executed at Wandsworth.

Relatives of O'Sullivan and Dunn were aware of the place of execution, and members of both families, with many other Irish persons, were outside Wandsworth Prison long before eight o'clock. O'Sullivan's brother and three sisters, and two of Dunn's brothers and two sisters, were there, but went away before the hour of death arrived. The crowd numbered hundreds, and many wore the Irish Republican colours. A woman held a Republican flag.

The two men were finally overpowered in Ebury Street and taken to Gerald Road Police Station (which no longer exists). With their conviction and their appeal dismissed, the *Daily Herald* mounted a campaign for clemency, stating that the men should be treated as prisoners of war. The execution was fixed for August 10 but the particular prison was not announced for fear of an armed rescue attempt. In the end large crowds gathered outside both Pentonville and Wandsworth, both men being executed at the latter prison by John Ellis assisted by Edward Taylor and Seth Mills. Following the ending of capital punishment, their remains were exhumed and reburied in Ireland on July 6, 1967. (The identification of O'Sullivan was made easier as his artificial limb was discovered during the exhumation. He had lost his lower right leg during the First World War whilst serving in the British Army.)

For an hour before eight o'clock men and women, led by a lay preacher named O'Leary, who wore cassock and surplice sang hymns and recited the Catholic rosary. O'Leary held a lighted candle in his hand. The brothers and sisters of the condemned men took part in the prayers.

The tolling of the prison bell shortly before eight suddenly thrilled the crowd. Men and women sank to their knees, and prayed for the souls of the men who were about to die. The bell ceased for a time. Then it tolled again. The execution was over. The prayers came to an end, men and women sang the Irish song, 'Wrap the old green flag around me.'

Daily Express, August 11, 1922

Joseph O'Sullivan alias James Connolly.

John O'Brien who was identified as Reginald Dunn.

St Paul's Cathedral, June 26, 1922. The 12 pall-bearers at the funeral were Field-Marshals Lord Grenfell, Lord Methuen, the Earl of Ypres, Earl Haig and Sir W. R. Robertson, Admiral-of-the-Fleet Earl Beatty, Air Chief Marshal Sir H. M. Trenchard, Generals Sir J. Wilcocks, A. F. Gatliff (Royal Marines), Sir C. C. Monro, Bt., and Sir C. F. N. Macready, and Lieutenant-General Sir A. S. Cobbe, V.C. Earl Beatty can be seen in the background to the left of the coffin, and Earl Haig in the background on the right, with Sir Hugh Trenchard (in RAF hat) in front of him. Sir William Robertson is the third from the front on the left. The coffin was covered with the Union Jack, and on it rested the late Field-Marshal's plumed hat and his baton. Lady Wilson's wreath of roses and laurel was at the head, and at the other end of the flag wrought in flowers. The Prime Minister and all the members of the Cabinet were present.

Left: Sir Henry Wilson was interred in the Crypt between the tombs of Viscount Wolseley and Field-Marshal Lord Roberts of Kandahar. Ironically, Sir Henry had been present when Lord Roberts died at Saint-Omer in France in November 1914, and was an Insignia Bearer at his funeral. He had also attended Lord Wolseley's burial at the cathedral three years earlier. Two months later another impressive funeral was held in another cathedral . . . but this time in Ireland in the Pro-Cathedral in Dublin. Michael Collins, one of the two main signatories of the Anglo-Irish Treaty was ambushed and killed by anti-treaty Republicans just ten days after the Irish President Arthur Griffith had collapsed and died. Collins was the only fatality in the 20-minute gun-battle at the village of Béal na mBláth (The Mouth of Flowers). His body was driven to Cork before being transferred to Dublin. There it lay in state in the City Hall for three days, his funeral taking place on August 28 and was attended by half a million people — at the time a fifth of the country's population.

Left: **No. 41 Kensington Gardens in Ilford, Essex, was the centre of a huge national debate in 1922 for it all began here — the affair between Mrs Edith Thompson and her lodger, Frederick Bywaters.** *Right:* **At first Percy Thompson, reading the newspaper, appeared to be oblivious of the secret liaison which began when Bywaters accompanied the Thompsons on holiday to the Isle of Wight in June 1921, but when Percy realised that something was up, he kicked him out for getting too friendly with his wife. However, the relationship continued with the couple booking into hotels under false names.**

October 4, 1922 — The Bywaters/Thompson Affair

I beg to report that at 12.40 a.m., on the 4th October 1922, a telephone message was received at Ilford Police Station from Doctor Maudsley of 62, Courtland Avenue, Ilford, asking for the ambulance to be sent to Belgrave Road, where a man was lying who had died from haemorrhage. P.Cs 515 'K' Pearcey and 1148 'K' Geal, were directed to take the ambulance there, and on arrival found the dead body of Percy Thompson, age 32, of 41, Kensington Gardens, Ilford, in a sitting position on the pavement with his back to the wall.

At this moment P.S. Walter Mew 149 'K' arrived on the scene, where he saw Dr. Maudsley and Mrs. Edith Thompson. When asked by the Officer what had occurred, the Doctor replied, 'A case of sudden death; haemorrhage from the mouth'. The body was placed on the ambulance and taken to the Mortuary, High Road, Ilford.

P. S. Mew then escorted Mrs Thompson to her house, 41, Kensington Gardens, Ilford. On the way she said 'Will he come back'. The officer replied 'Yes'. Mrs. Thompson then said 'They will blame me for this'.

The Officer then went to the Mortuary and examined the body. He found a cut about 1½ inches along on the back of the neck, slightly on the right side; a cut about an inch long on the right side of the neck; a cut about two inches long on the inside of right forearm, near the joint, and a cut about one inch long at the back of the neck, slightly below the first cut described.

The Officer reported his discovery to the Station Officer and returned to the scene of the occurrence. He there found a large quanitity of blood on the pavement for a distance of about 40 feet, and made a search for the weapon, but was unsuccessful. He then again went to the residence of Mrs Thompson. He said to her 'Can you account for the cuts on your husband's neck' and she replied 'No; we were walking and my husband said 'Oh'! I said 'Bear up' thinking he had one of his attacks. He then fell against the wall and then to the ground'. The Officer then said to her, 'Did he have a knife or anything'.

The Officer returned to the Mortuary and examined deceased's clothes. He found on his waistcoat a cut on the left shoulder: a cut on the right side of neck, 2 cuts right side of shoulder. On the jacket he found a cut on the left lapel. 2 cuts on left shoulder, 4 cuts on right collar, 2 cuts on right sleeve; there were also three cuts on his white linen collar, and one cut on tie, all various dimensions, and apparently done with a sharp instrument.

I was informed shortly afterwards and in conjunction with other Officers, proceeded with the investigation.

On the afternoon of October 3, 1922, the couple met at Fullers' Tea Shop at No. 42 Aldersgate. Edith worked across the road at No. 168 as a book-keeper for Carlton & Prior and two doors away Messrs Osborne & Co. sold knives exactly similar to the one used in the murder. *Left:* **The street suffered severely in the Blitz leading to wholesale reconstruction after the war** *(right).*

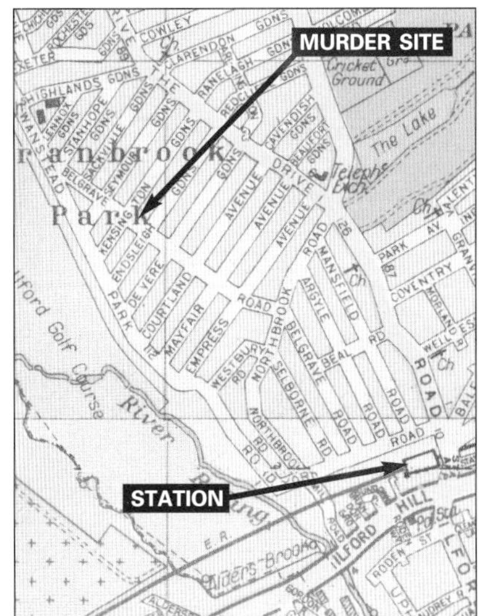

That evening Percy Thompson took his wife to the Criterion theatre on Piccadilly Circus to see a farce called *The Dippers*. Travelling back to Ilford by train, they emerged from the station by its rear entrance *(right)* which cut out a much longer walk around the corner to Belgrave Road. From here it was about a 15-minute walk to their home, the police in their investigation into the murder actually going to the trouble of measuring the distance as 1,400 yards.

At 11 a.m., 4th October 1922, I went to 41, Kensington Gardens, Ilford, where I saw Mrs. Thompson. I told her I was an Inspector of Police and that I was satisified that her husband had been assaulted and stabbed several times, in Belgrave Road, earlier in the morning. She said that she and her husband were going home along the Belgrave Road, and when near Endsleigh Gardens, he said 'Oh!' and fell against her. She put her arm to save him, and found that he was bleeding: she thought from the mouth. She tried to hold him but he fell down by the wall, and did not speak. She felt him and found his clothing was wet with blood. She then ran for a Doctor, and appealed to a lady and gentleman who were passing for assistance. She further stated that she did not see anybody about at the time, and that she and her husband were quite happy together, and were talking about going to a dance.

In view of this extraordinary and improbable statement, I asked her to come to Ilford Police Station, which she did, and where she was placed in the Matron's room.

Mr Richard Halliday Thompson, of 49, Seymour Gardens, Ilford, was then interviewed and from him certain information was received respecting a man named Frederick Bywaters, age 20, a Ship's writer, of 11, Westow Street, Upper Norwood. I gave directions for Officers to go to 231 Shakespeare Crescent, Manor Park, and if Bywaters was there, to bring him to the station. The Officers were successful and brought Bywaters to me. I said to him 'I am a Police Inspector and shall detain you, and retain possession of your overcoat'. He said 'Why? I know nothing about it', and commenced making a statement. I said 'If you wish to make a statement, it would be better to put it in writing'. I cautioned him, and he then

Around midnight, walking on the pavement on the right-hand side of Belgrave Road *(above left)*, the couple first passed Beal Road *(above right)*, crossed over Northbrook Road, and past several side turnings — Empress *(below left)*, where a memorial stands to PC Phillip Walters, shot on this spot on April 18, 1995, Mayfair and Courtland Avenues and De Vere Gardens *(below right)*.

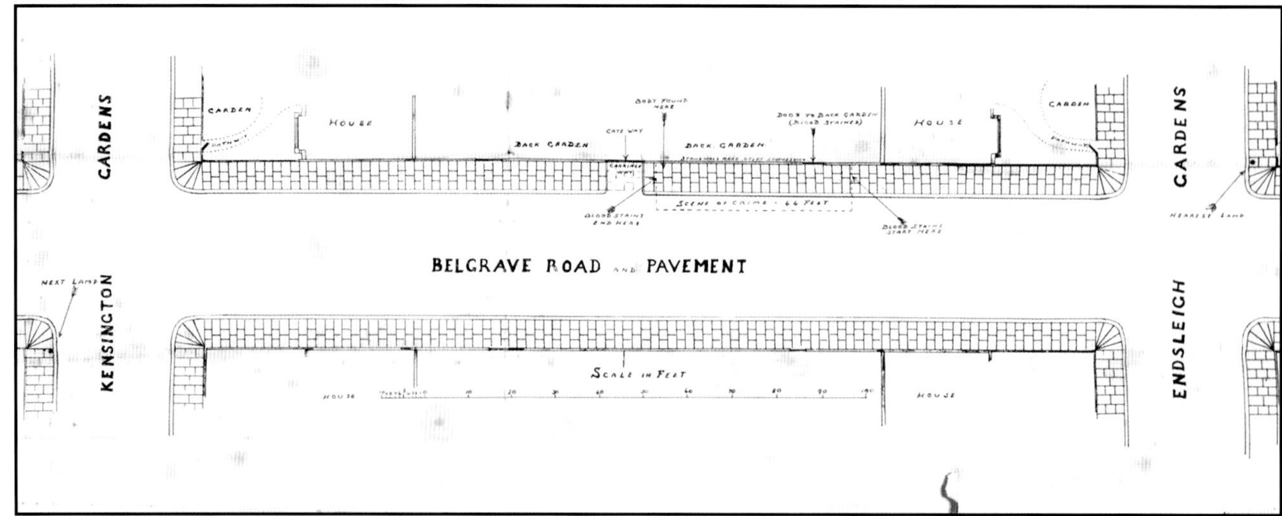

made a statement. In it he said that he had known Mr. Thompson for four years, and Mrs Thompson for seven years. He had stayed with them as a guest for a week, and later as a boarder, paying 25/- per week. He had seen Mr and Mrs Thompson quarrel, and had interfered on her behalf with the consequence that Mr. Thompson asked him to leave, which he did.

On the 7th September, 1921, he went to sea, but returned to England in October 1921. Shortly afterwards he called upon Mr and Mrs Thompson. She received him quite friendly but he a little coldly, but they all parted as friends. He last saw Mr Thompson in June last. This statement Bywaters signed, but I was convinced he was withholding important information. In the meantime his coat was examined by Doctor Drought. Divisional Surgeon, and on it were found several slight bloodstains.

Acting upon the instructions of Superintendent Wensley, Detective Inspector Page, C.O., went to Bywaters address at Norwood, and made a search of his belongings. He there found a number of letters written by Mrs Thompson, couched in extravagantly affectionate language.

Just after they crossed Endsleigh Gardens, a man jumped out and stabbed Percy several times. Edith is reputed to have cried out 'Don't! Don't!' as Bywaters fled the scene. However, by the time Mrs Thompson was questioned by the police, she had recovered her composure and said that she did not recognise the assailant. On this plan, the police have indicated where bloodstains were found and where Percy Thompson was lying (see enlargement *below*).

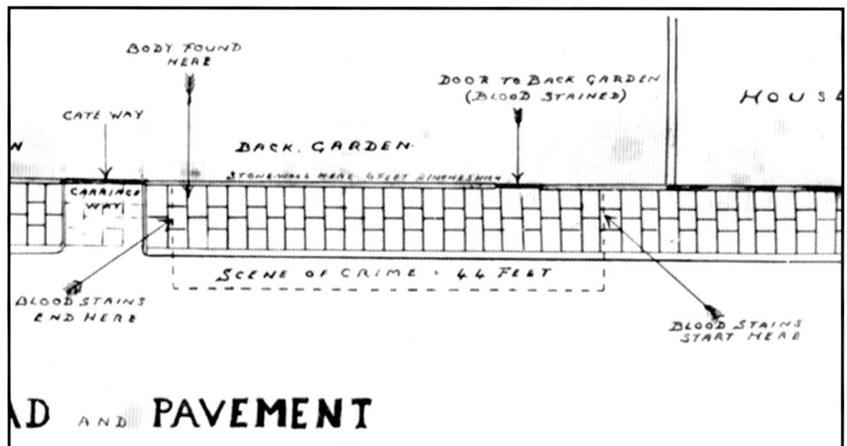

This is the same stretch of pavement with your Editor standing where Percy was lying.

Edith's screams had been heard by a passer-by who called Dr Noel Maudsley who lived at No. 41 on the corner of Courtland Road. We were amazed to find that it is still a doctor's surgery today!

Acting on information received, police went to 231 Shakespeare Crescent at Manor Park where they found Bywaters.

On the afternoon of the 5th October, I again saw Mrs Thompson, and asked her if she could give any further information as to her husband's assailant. She said 'I will tell you all I possibly can' and then made a statement, in which she stated that her husband was employed as a shipping clerk by Messrs C. J. Parker & Co., Peel House, 20, Eastcheap, E.C. — that she herself was employed as a book-keeper by Messrs. Carlton & Prior, Millinery Manufacturers, 168, Aldersgate Street, E.C. They had been married for 6 years, but without issue. She said that on the morning of the 3rd October, she and her husband left home and went to their respective places of business. At 5.45 p.m. she met her husband, and together they went to the 'Criterion Theatre', where they met her aunt and uncle, a Mrs. and Mr. J. Laxton, of 5, Rostrever Avenue, South Tottenham. The party left the Theatre at about 11 p.m., and all four then went to the Piccadilly Circus Tube, where they separated. She and her husband then went to Liverpool Street Railway Station, and caught the 11.30 p.m. train for Ilford, where they arrived about 12 night. They then proceeded to their residence, 41, Kensington Gardens, Ilford, and when approaching Endsleigh Gardens, her husband suddenly went into the roadway. She went after him, and he fell up against her and cried 'Oh!'. He was staggering and bleeding, and she thought he was bleeding from the mouth. He stood for a minute or two: she assisted him to the wall, where he collapsed. She then went for Dr. Maudsley, who came and said that her husband was dead. She further stated that she had known Bywaters for seven years. He had been on visiting terms with her family and on one occasion when visiting them, he witnessed a quarrel between her and her husband, in which he interfered on her behalf. She admitted that she was in the habit of corresponding with him in affectionate terms, also that she had been in the habit of going out with him, without her husband's knowledge.

At the conclusion of this statement, I accompanied her to the Matron's room, and in passing the room where Bywaters was detained, she saw him at the window. She then said, 'Oh God! Oh God! What can I do? Why did he do it? I didn't want him to do it'. She further said, 'I must tell the truth. When we got near Endlsleigh Gardens, a man rushed from the garden and knocked me away, pushed me away from my husband;

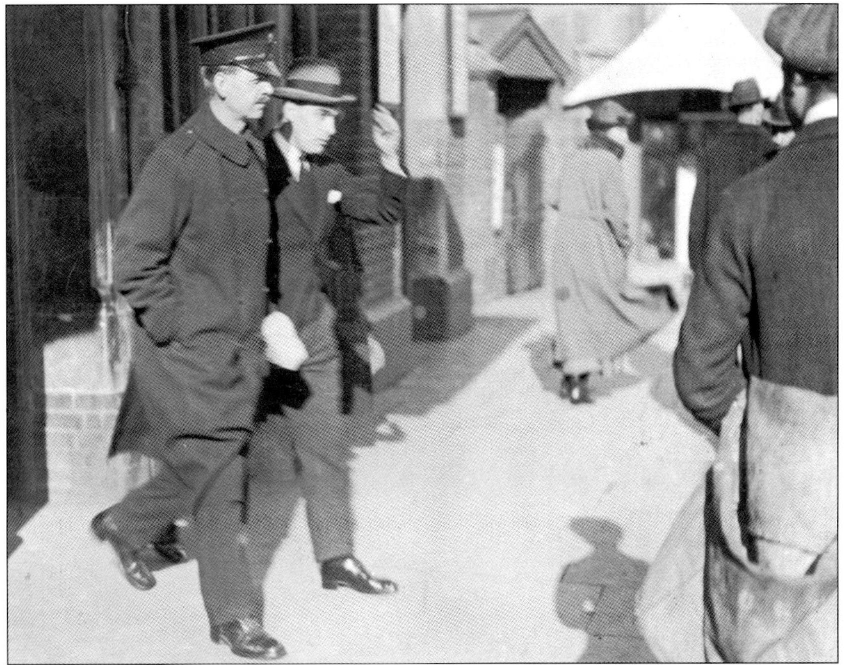

Ironically following in the Thompson's footsteps that fatal evening, Bywaters is escorted from Ilford railway station although this is the main entrance on Cranbrook Road.

Edith was also arrested soon afterwards and charged with murder or with being an accessory to murder. She did not know that Bywaters had been arrested but saw him in the police station later and exclaimed: 'Oh God! Why did he do it?', continuing 'I didn't want him to do it.' Bywaters insisted that he had acted alone in the crime and stated that 'I waited for Mrs Thompson and her husband. I pushed her to one side, also pushing him into the street. We struggled. I took my knife from my pocket and we fought and he got the worst of it. The reason I fought with Thompson was because he never acted like a man to his wife. He always seemed several degrees lower than a snake. I loved her and I could not go on seeing her leading that life. I did not intend to kill him. I only meant to injure him. I gave him the opportunity of standing up to me like a man but he wouldn't.' Edith had written no less than 62 intimate letters to Bywaters and stupidly he had kept them. in these, she referred to Bywaters as 'Darlingest and Darlint' and some described how she had tried to murder Percy on several occasions. In one referring, apparently, to an attempt to poison him, she wrote, 'You said it was enough for an elephant. Perhaps it was. But you don't allow for the taste making it possible for only a small quantity to be taken.' She had also tried broken glass, and told Bywaters that she had made three attempts but that Percy had discovered some in his food so she had had to stop. Edith also had sent Bywaters press cuttings describing murders by poisoning and had told Bywaters that she had aborted herself after becoming pregnant by him. The existence of the love letters was first raised at Coroner's inquest at Ilford when Detective-Inspector Hall said that on October 5 a number of letters were handed to him by Inspector Page of Scotland Yard as having been found at Bywaters' address. Written in violet ink, they were identified as being in Mrs Thompson's handwriting. However, Mr Stern, when he appeared for Mrs Thompson, objected to the letters. He said he was going to make serious objection to these letters being put in because he contended they were not evidence against his client. The law, he said, was on his side. The charge against his client was one of the wilful murder of her husband and, until a prima facie had been made out, he submitted they could not put in some letters to show, which he presumed they did show, some expression of animosity against the dead man.

I was dazed for a moment. When I recovered I saw my husband scuffling with a man. The man whom I knew as Freddie Bywaters was running away. He was wearing a blue overcoat and a grey hat. I knew it was him although I did not see his face'. This statement I wrote down and Mrs Thompson signed it.

On the evening of the 5th October, I went to Bywaters and said to him 'I am going to charge you and Mrs Thompson with the wilful murder of Percy Thompson'. He said 'But why her? Mrs. Thompson was not aware of my movements'. I said 'If you wish to say anything I will take it down in writing'. I again cautioned him, and he made a statement which he signed.

In it he states that Mrs Thompson was not aware of his movements on the night of the murder. He left Manor Park at 11 p.m., and went to Ilford. He waited for the Thompsons near Endsleigh Gardens, and when they arrived he pushed her on one side, and him (Thompson) further up the street. He said to Mr. Thompson 'You have got to separate from your wife'. He said 'No!'. Bywaters said 'You will have to'. They then struggled together and Bywaters took a knife from his pocket and fought with it. He then ran from the scene of the crime, and went to his home at Norwood, arriving there about 3 a.m.

He further stated that his reason for fighting with Thompson was because he failed to act like a man to his wife. He (Bywaters) loved her himself. He did not intend to kill him, but only meant to injure him. The knife was a sheath knife. This he threw down a drain as he was running away.

Later, both Mrs. Thompson and Bywaters were charged with being concerned together in the wilful murder of Percy Thompson. Mrs. Thompson made no reply. Bywaters said 'It's wrong! It's wrong'.

On the 6th October they both appeared at Stratford Petty Sessions, and after I had given evidence of arrest, they were remanded until 10 am. Wednesday.

Police Report, October 8, 1922

Dr. Maudsley said:- 'At 12.30 this morning a woman called here and told my wife that a doctor was wanted. In Belgrave Road I saw a man on the pavement. His hat was off, and his head had fallen forward. Blood was flowing from his mouth. He was dead. His wife, standing near, appeared to be hysterical, and could give me no clear account of what had happened. About 3 o'clock this morning the police called me on the telephone.

Daily Express, October 5, 1922

Wilful murder was the verdict returned by the Ilford Coroner's jury today against Frederick Edward Bywaters, 21, of Westow Street, Upper Norwood, S.E. accused of killing Mr. Percy Thompson, at Ilford in the early hours of October 4.

The jury made no mention in their verdict of Mrs. Edith Thompson, 28, widow of the murdered man, who is also charged with the murder.

The Evening News, October 23, 1922

The trial opened at the Old Bailey on December 6, 1922. Bywaters refused to incriminate Edith and when cross-examined told the prosecution that he did not believe that Edith had actually attempted to poison Percy but instead had a rather vivid imagination and a passion for reading sensational novels that extended to her imagining herself as one of the characters. Edith had been advised against going into the witness box by her solicitor but decided to do so and promptly incriminated herself by being asked what she had meant when she had written to Bywaters asking him to send her 'something to give her husband.' The judge in his summing up described Edith's letters as 'full of the outpourings of a silly but at the same time, a wicked affection.' The summing up was fair in law but the judge made much of the adultery, Mr Justice Shearman being a very Victorian gentleman with high moral principles. He instructed the jury that 'You will not convict her unless you are satisfied that she and he agreed that this man should be murdered when he could be, and she knew that he was going to do it, and directed him to do it, and by arrangement between them he was doing it.' The jury were not convinced with the case of the defence and took just over two hours to find them both guilty of murder.

Although Bywaters had done the deed, the incriminating letters sealed Edith's fate and both were sentenced to death. At 9 a.m. on Tuesday, January 9, 1923, Frederick Bywaters was hanged by William Willis and Seth Mills (not as quoted in the press report below) at Pentonville. We are told that he met his end bravely but down at Holloway Edith had to be carried unconscious onto the drop to be held on the trap by the executioners: John Ellis, Robert Baxter and Thomas Phillips. Although the authorities claimed that nothing untoward happened, it leaked out that a considerable amount of blood had run from her after the hanging. Bernard Spilsbury, who carried out the autopsy, claimed it was caused by a miscarriage although had Edith admitted she was pregnant, there would have been a stay of execution until the baby had been born. And then she would have almost certainly have been reprieved. Another theory which has been put forward is that she may have aborted herself during the three months in prison and in so doing, damaged her uterus so it inverted with the shock of the drop. (As a result, females due to be hanged in future had to wear canvas knickers.) The experience unnerved the executioner, and after the botched hanging of another woman in October when Susan Newell freed her arms and pulled the white hood from her head, Ellis resigned.

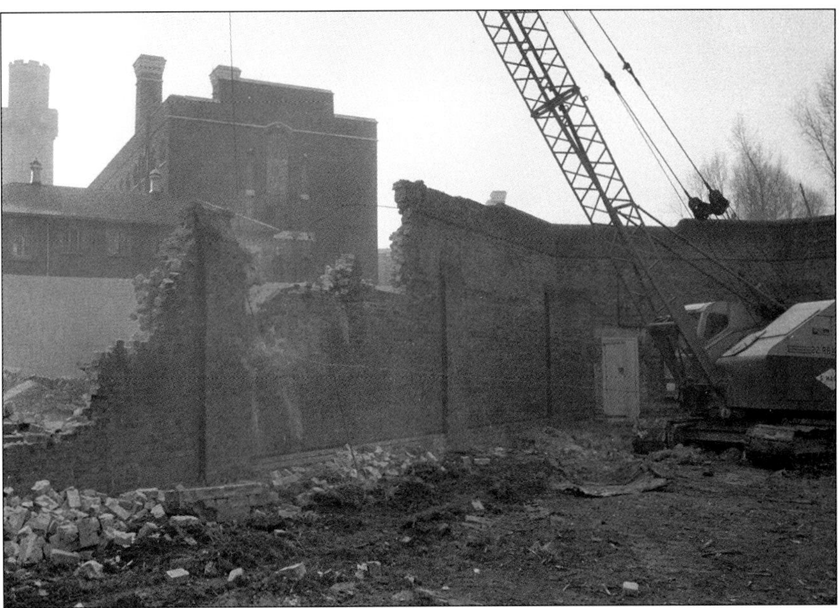

Holloway had been opened in 1852 but by 1968 it was decided to demolish it in stages while a new prison was built with accommodation for 500 women. As five bodies of executed dead (Amelia Sach and Anne Walters hanged February 3, 1903; Edith Thompson; Styllou Christofi, executed December 15, 1954, and Ruth Ellis, hanged July 13, 1955 — see page 288) still remained buried within the precinct, the bodies were exhumed for reburial elsewhere.

The Home Office made the following announcement yesterday:-

The Secretary of State, after careful consideration of all the circumstances, is unable to advise interference with the due course of the law in the case of Frederick Edward Francis Bywaters and Edith Jessie Thompson, convicted of the murder of Percy Thompson.

The executions have been fixed to take place at nine o'clock on Tuesday morning. The arrangements are in the hands of the Under-Sheriff for Essex.

Mrs Thompson will be exectued at Holloway Gaol and Bywaters in Pentonville.

Daily Express, January 6, 1923

Mrs Edith Thompson will die on the scaffold in Holloway Prison at nine o'clock this morning. The dramatic final effort made by Mr. F. A. S. Stern, her solicitor to save her has failed.

Daily Express, January 9, 1923

Mrs Edith Thompson and Frederick Edward Francis Bywaters, her lover, convicted of the murder of the woman's husband at Ilford in October 1922 were hanged at nine o'clock yesterday morning.

Willis and Pierrepoint carried out the execution of Bywaters in Pentonville. Ellis and Pierrepoint jun. executed Mrs. Thompson in Holloway Prison.

'It is learned,' states the Central News Agency, 'that Mrs. Thompson was prostrate nearly all night and was continually under the doctor's care. At five o'clock she was unconscious, and when the hour for the execution arrived she was in a dazed state, only partially conscious and unable to walk, so that she had to be carried. The doctor was in attendance almost up to the time of the execution.'

'It is understood,' states the Exchange Telegraph Company, 'that Mrs. Thompson was in a state of collapse. In moments of consciousness she asked for Bywaters.'

The *Daily Express* has received corroboration of these distressing accounts from reliable sources.

Daily Express, January 10, 1923

A formal submission is to be made to legal experts to clear the name of Edith Thompson, who was hanged for murder in 1923.

The fight to clear Edith's name is being spearheaded by her biographer Dr Rene Weis. He said: 'I have just had the papers from the Criminal Cases Review Commission.'

He is considering making the formal submission on January 9 — the anniversary of Edith's death and to shadow the publicity generated from a forthcoming film about her death.

The submission is being prepared by legal experts at University College London where Dr Weis is a professor of English literature.

He added: 'We should be able to draft something watertight. The truth of course, is that it shouldn't need to be like that.

'In recent months I have read through acres of secondary literature again and I am truly astonished to find that almost none of the lawyers dispassionately writing about the case thought she was guilty.'

The planned submission has delighted Charles Buhler, 80, of Custom House, whose grandfather Carl was one of the Old Bailey jurors who convicted Edith.

Mr Buhler said: 'I was about 14 when my grandfather first talked to us about the case. He believed that Edith was only guilty of adultery and should not have suffered the ultimate penalty.

'This really troubled him throughout the rest of his life and left a scar on his conscience.

'I think the jury were more or less directed by the judge towards the verdicts they should bring in. It altered my grandfather's view on capital punishment and for this reason I have always been opposed to the death penalty.'

Ilford Recorder, November 2, 2000

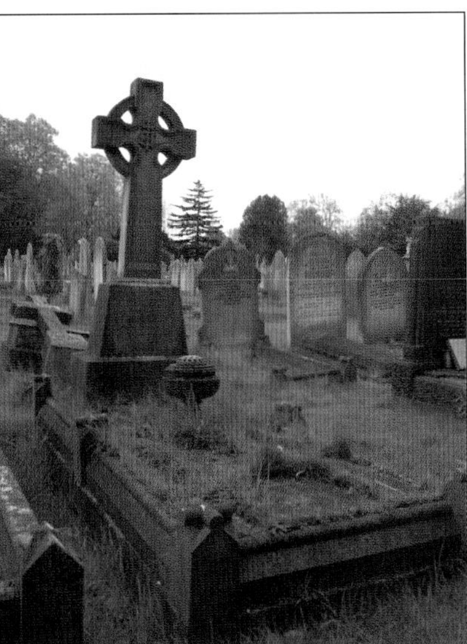

Percy Thompson was laid to rest in the City of London Cemetery at Manor Park (Plot 192, Grave 9386). Other family members are now buried with him.

Edith Thompson (with Sach, Walters and Chrisofi) were reinterred in Plot 117 in a remote corner of Brookwood Cemetery in Surrey and marked with this simple slab.

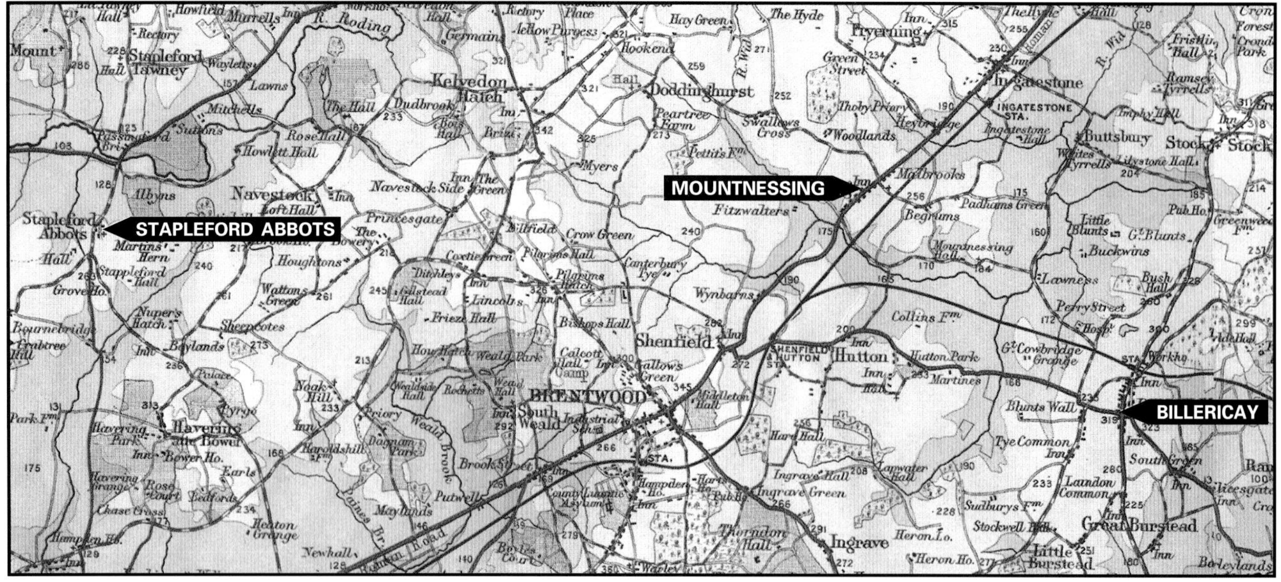

September 27, 1927 — Police Constable George Gutteridge

Epping police were last night searching for a 'grey-capped man' in connection with the murder of Police Constable G. W. Gutteridge early yesterday.

Police Constable Gutteridge was on duty about six miles from Romford and was only 300 yards from his home at Stapleford Abbots when he met his death, being shot four times. Last night it was revealed that two shots were fired with the revolver held against his head. Few people use this road at night.

Who the murderer was is as great a mystery as the reason for his action. By the dead man's side was his notebook and from this the police believe that he was interrogating someone, possibly criminals in a motor-car who became alarmed when stopped for some trivial motoring offence.

The only real clue the police have is that the bullets are of the calibre used in Army revolvers.

All shopkeepers, licensees and hotel-keepers in the neighbourhood have been asked if they have seen a man answering the following description: —

Height 5ft., complexion dark; wearing dark suit with neckerchief; grey cap.

Every available policeman in the Epping area is taking part in the search for Constable Gutteridge's murderer — or murderers.

There are two theories on which investigations are being based. These, briefly are: —

That Constable Gutteridge stopped a suspicious character — probably a burglar — and was shot by him.

That criminals in a motor-car, stopped for some trivial offence, became alarmed and murdered the policeman rather than have the number of their car taken.

The latter theory is held to be the more probable. It would explain the fact that Gutteridge had taken out his pencil and notebook, a thing he would hardly have done while questioning a man on foot.

A high-powered car was heard at the time of the tragedy by Gertrude Lady Decies, who lives nearby. About the same time she heard a loud noise which she now believes to have been a revolver shot.

At first it was believed that he had attempted to write a message before he died, but medical examination proved that death must have been almost instantaneous.

Police Constable Gutteridge was lying on his back and, it would seem, not in a position a man would involuntarily sink into if shot. It rather looked as though he had been dragged to the side of the road.

There were four wounds in the neck and head, it is stated, two of them apparently having been fired from a distance and two with the revolver held against the constable's head. Apparently the first two had not killed Gutteridge and the murderer had fired two more as he lay on the ground.

Police Constable George Gutteridge joined the Essex County Constabulary in April 1910 and, after service in the First World War, rejoined the force, being posted to the Epping Division.

Left: **He was based at Stapleford Abbots and lived at No. 2 Townley Cottages.** *Right:* **The same cottages albeit modernised, still stand on Tysea Hill.**

On September 26, 1927, PC Gutteridge (left) left his home at 11 p.m. to meet his opposite number Constable Sydney Taylor (right) who covered Lambourne End.

The planned conference point was here on the B175 Romford to Chipping Ongar Road beside Grove House. This road has been considerably altered since 1927.

The body was discovered at six o'clock this morning by Mr. Alex Ward, of Brentwood, Essex, the driver of a mail van from Abridge.

'I saw someone lying on the side of the road, and I stopped the van. I found it was Police Constable Gutteridge. I said: "What's the matter, Bill?" and then I realised that he was dead.'

In his right hand Constable Gutteridge held a pencil, and by his side lay his helmet and his open notebook, as if he had been murdered when about to make a note.

One of the first persons on the scene of the tragedy was Mr A. Parrott, an insurance agent, who lives in a cottage 100 yards away. He and his wife were awakened at six o'clock by the mail-van driver.

'I hurried out, but there was nothing I could do for Gutteridge. Then a motor-cyclist came along and he stayed by the body while the driver rang up the police.'

Police officials hurried to the spot, and after a short consultation decided that Scotland Yard's aid must be called in. This was done, and a little later Chief Inspector Berrett was on his way here accompanied by Detective Sergeant Harris.

The last person, apart from the murderer, to see him alive was Police Constable Taylor, of Lambourne End, who spoke to him at 3.30 this morning, 500 yards from the spot where the body was found. Gutteridge's last words were: 'Good night, see you tomorrow', and then the two parted. Taylor going in the direction of Lambourne End and Gutteridge towards Stapleford Abbots.

Daily Mirror, September 28, 1927

Dramatic developments occurred yesterday in the hunt for the murderer of Police Constable Gutteridge at Stapleford Abbots, Essex.

Scotland Yard last night issued photographs of a handkerchief, bearing a name in which was wrapped revolver ammunition, a tin cake box, a cardboard carton, and a number of cartridges, all found behind a fence at Brook Green, Hammersmith.

A fifth photograph is of a revolver discovered on the Thames foreshore below Hammersmith Bridge.

Earlier in the day a woman visited Scotland Yard on her own initiative and was questioned at a conference of C.I.D. chiefs. Detectives later began a new 'comb-out' in the South of London.

Five photographs were issued by Scotland Yard last night.

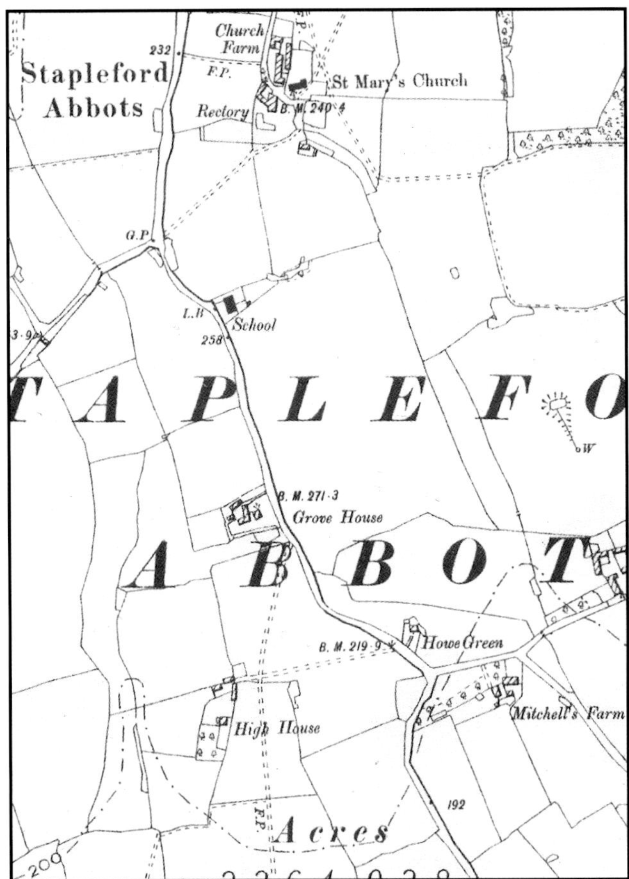

Although the carriageway has been widened and straightened, fortunately the bend at Howe Green (now named Gutteridge Lane) has been bypassed, leaving it virtually the same as it was over 80 years ago. After meeting with PC Taylor, Constable Gutteridge turned around to continue his beat and eventually make his way home.

Meanwhile, two car thieves had travelled to Essex from South London. Leo Brown (or Frederick Guy Browne as he is more generally known) had a long record of convictions stretching back to 1911 when he received two months' hard labour for stealing a bicycle in Oxford. A burglary in 1912 led to 12 months' hard labour with a similar sentence the following year for theft. He enlisted in the Royal Engineers in May 1916 but was discharged for an offence in November 1918. Three concurrent sentences of 10 months' hard labour were given to him by the Hampshire Assizes for stealing a motor cycle the same month. Browne was then convicted at the Central Criminal Court for conspiracy to defraud and forgery, serving four years' penal servitude from February 1923 to April 1927. Before being apprehended for the murder of PC Gutteridge, a further string of offences took place between October and January 1928, mainly the stealing of motor cars but it was the theft of a Vauxhall from Mrs Hulton at Tooting on November 12/13, 1927 which ultimately led to his arrest.

The most important is that of a man's white cambric handkerchief with the letter 'M' worked in white in one corner and 'A. H. Miller' in black marking ink in another corner.

The other photographs are of a Service revolver, a tin cake box, a cardboard box, a cardboard carton and a number of cartridges.

With the photographs Scotland Yard issued the following statement:—

'At 11.30 a.m. on September 27 there was found behind a fence on some waste ground at Brook Green, Hammersmith, a round tin cake box 6in. in diameter and 2in. in depth, with "Caledonia Oat Cakes" in large lettering on lid, containing:—

101 rounds .455 revolver ball ammunition marked on base R L II., wrapped in a man's white cambric pocket handkerchief, 27in. square narrow hemstitch, letter "M" worked in white in one corner and "A. H. Miller" in black marking ink in another corner (a piece of brown wool is sewn in the handkerchief under the name, apparently to serve as a personal identification mark).

'And there was also found a brown cardboard carton, 4½in by 3¼in. by 1¼in., metal corners containing twelve rounds .303 Service rifle ball ammunition C K II. on base; three blank ditto.; and one musketry dummy ditto. (on the lid of this box is pencilled writing which as far as decipherable, reads "March 14, Sinclair)."

'Shortly after noon on September 28 a Mark VI Webley Service revolver No. 286165, 1917 issue, was found on the Thames foreshore, on the Hammersmith side, immediately below Hammersmith Bridge.

'The cartridge case that was found in the car abandoned at Brixton which had been stolen from Billericay, could have been fired from this revolver.

'Police are anxious to establish the identity of the owner of the two boxes, cartridges, revolver and handkerchief. All these can be seen at New Scotland Yard any day between 10 a.m. and 6 p.m.'

Daily Mirror, September 30, 1927

I was conveying mails from Romford to Abridge and picked up at Romford at 5.35 a.m., today. My first call in my car (a touring car) was at Havering. I handed one bag in there and my next stop was at Stapleford Abbotts where I also left one bag. I went then on my way to Stapleford Tawney and on going round the bend at Howe Green I saw a form which looked like a bundle at first, but on approaching I saw two legs in the road. I came to the conclusion that something was wrong and pulled up and saw it was P.C. Gutteridge, whom I knew. I said, 'Is that you Bill?' and shouted out louder 'What is wrong Bill?' As I got no answer I took hold of his hand and found it was cold. There was a lot of blood under his head and across the road. His legs were straight across the road — open — but his head and shoulders were just at the bank (the bottom where it joins the road). His pocket book and helmet were on his right hand side slightly up the hill about a yard away. The helmet was farthest from the body. His left hand was raised and is the one I took hold of. I saw no marks of any vehicle.

I went along and called at Mr. Perritt's cottage and while I was waiting for him, I met a bus driver on his motor cycle. I told the driver what I had found and asked if he would come along with me and help. Just then Mr. Perritt came along and we satisfied ourselves that he was dead.

I asked the bus driver to let the policeman at Havering know and also told Perritt that I would go on with my mails and telephone Romford Police as to what we had found. At Stapleford Tawney I got through to Romford Police and they said they would see to the matter at once. I delivered my mail at Abridge and returned to the scene of the occurrence. I found then that his feet had been moved into the side of the road and he was covered over.

I did not see anything that attracted my attention on my journey from Romford beyond a young man on a motor cycle, and I

Patrick Michael William or Willie Henry Kennedy served in the Loyal North Lancashire Regiment from 1903 to 1911. In May that year he received two months' hard labour for indecent exposure and four months in October for theft. He served further sentences for thieving, being drunk and disorderly, more indecent exposures and was even given one day's imprisonment for loitering! Three years penal servitude followed in October 1913. On his release he enlisted again but deserted in August 1916. He then fraudulently joined up again the same month in Dublin but was convicted of theft. A string of crimes followed including more indecent exposure, theft and housebreaking, leading to three years penal servitude in June 1924 for armed robbery. Around June 1927 he went to work with Browne in his garage at No. 7a Northcote Road at Clapham in south London. There, stolen cars were transformed and given new identities before being sold on, a Singer stolen at Tooting and a Buick taken from Harringay being found by police at the garage on Browne's arrest.

At around 6.30 p.m. on September 27, 1927, the pair left the garage and caught a train from Liverpool Street for Billericay in Essex where Kennedy had designs on a Raleigh car at Bell House in the High Street. However, when they arrived there, a dog started barking so Browne told Kennedy that they would have to try somewhere else. They walked through the village and arrived at Dr Edward Lovell's house *(above)* located at the junction with the Mountnessing Road. Waiting until all the lights went out, Kennedy forced the doors to the garage. The car was a blue Morris Cowley TW 6120 and inside it were three cases containing the doctor's surgical instruments and drugs.

Early on the morning of September 27, 1927, Police Constable Gutteridge, of the Essex Constabulary, was found lying dead on the roadside at Stapleford Abbots. There were two bullet wounds in his left cheek and both his eyes had been shot out. His notebook was on the ground, and his lead pencil was clutched in his right hand. On the near side of the road was a motor tyre mark close to the bank, and a trail of blood as if he had staggered backwards after being shot and had fallen against the side of the road. Soon after this discovery was made, Dr Lovell reported that his motor car had been stolen from the garage of his house at Billericay during the night, and there seemed to be no doubt then that the thieves who stole this car were the murderers of Police Constable Gutteridge. Captain Unett, Chief Constable of Essex, telephoned to Scotland Yard and asked for the assistance of an experienced officer, and Chief Inspector Berrett was deputed to take charge of the inquiry.

At 7.30 the same morning, Dr Lovell's car was found abandoned in a cul-de-sac off a road in Brixton, but unfortunately it was not until about twelve hours later that the police were informed of this important fact. The car was removed to Brixton station, and spots of blood were found on the off-side running board, while on the floor of the car was the shell of a spent cartridge which had been fired from a Service revolver.

think I meet him every morning, but this was not the actual road of the occurrence, but at Havering.

I have spoken to Mr. Gutteridge on many occasions while conveying mails, but have never had long conversations with him. I used to call him Bill but did not know if this was his name. I know nothing of his private affairs or if anyone has a grudge against him.

I have been conveying mails on that road for about four or five years, but have never had any untoward incident.

(Signed) W. A. Ward.

Statement of William Alec Ward, Warley Road Garage, Brentwood, Essex, Motor Engineer. Taken down, read over by Police Sergeant Harris and signature witnessed by me at Romford Police Station on 27.9.27.

(Signed) J. Berrett — Chief Inspector

During the time I was Superintendent of the Central Office, New Scotland Yard, there were many occasions when I felt proud of the really brilliant work done by officers of the Criminal Investigation Department, but perhaps the proudest moment of all was when, sitting in my room, I received the news that Frederick Guy Browne had been unmasked as one of the two men who had murdered Police Constable Gutteridge in a lonely Essex lane four months before.

I knew Browne very well. Indeed, one of my officers, Inspector Lawrence, arrested him at Southend only five years previously for committing a series of motor-car insurance swindles, and on that occasion he boasted that he would never be captured alive again, and that he would shoot the next police officer who tried to arrest him. He was on that occasion sentenced to four years' penal servitude and, as a consequence of his violent conduct in prison, he had to serve every day of his sentence. Bearing in mind these facts, I took especial interest in the prolonged hunt for the murderers of Gutteridge, and when at last the moment came for definite action to be taken, I was careful to suggest the exercise of the greatest caution in making the arrest. Before, however, coming to the climax, I will relate the facts of the murder.

Dr Lovell's house named Shirley lay on what was then known as Oak Tree Corner, although both the house, garage and the oak trees have long gone.

Checking that the tank had plenty of petrol, they pushed the Morris some 100 yards along the Mountnessing Road before climbing aboard. Thomas Wilson was awakened at 2.30 a.m. by the unusual sound of a car starting up outside his house Ridgeways. He said that the car then drove off towards Mountnessing. A neighbour further down the road even recognised the noise as it passed by as that of Dr Lovell's car.

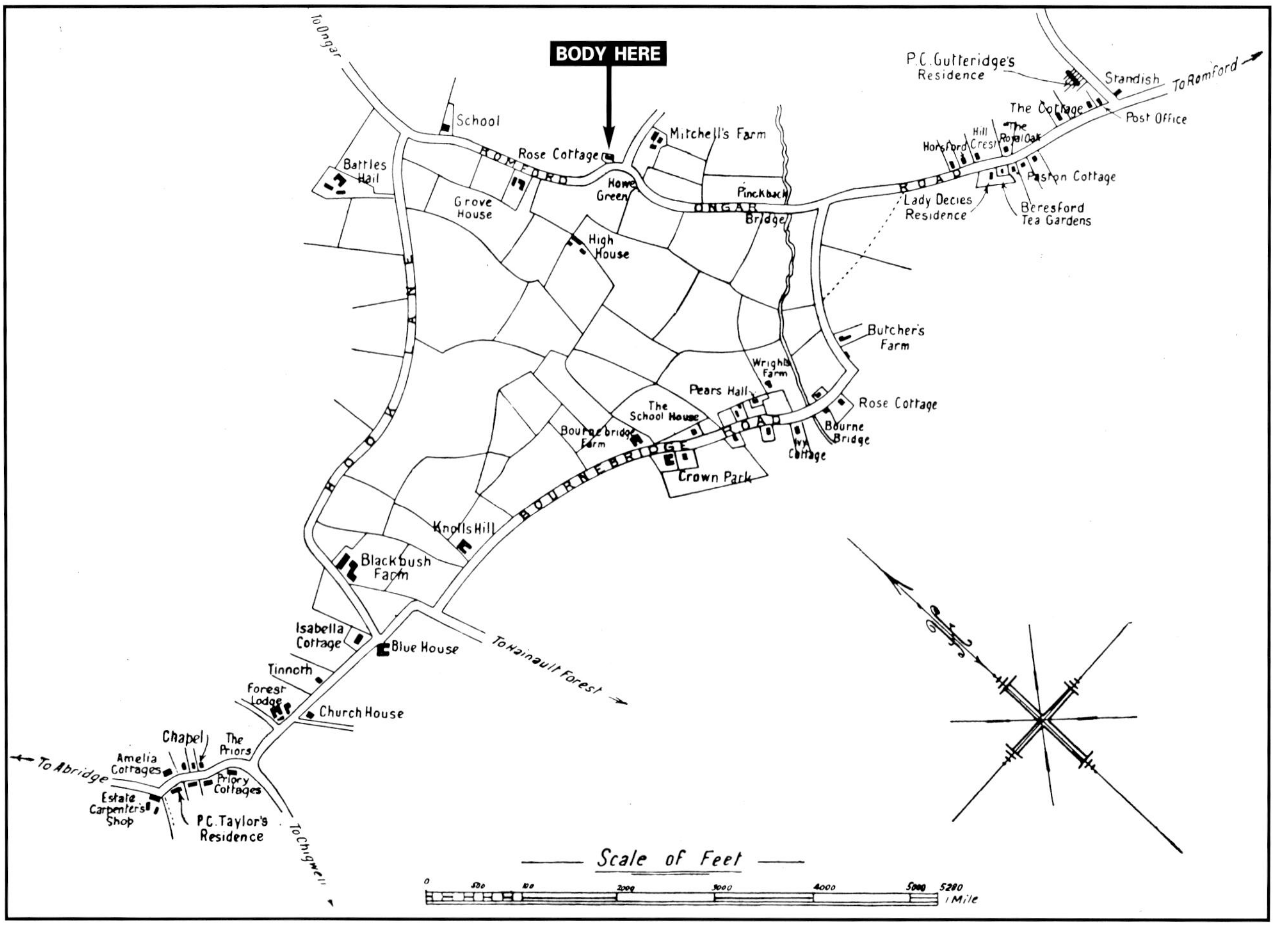

Frederick Masters: 'I am a police constable and am accustomed to preparing plans. I prepared Exhibit No. 46, which is a plan showing a portion of the road between Romford and Ongar. I was shown a spot on the road marked in the upper section of that plan as the spot where the body was found. From that spot to the conference point at Grove House is a distance of 638 yards. From that spot to P.C. Gutteridge's house is a distance of 1,680 yards. From the conference point to Police Constable Taylor's house is a distance of 1 mile and 1,533 yards.'

Eustace Wyrall: 'I am a photographer, and I live at Ilford. On the 27th of September last I went to the spot on the Romford-Ongar road, where there was blood on the roadway, and I took a photograph of the road looking in the direction of Romford. It was looking downhill. The white line across the road is the carbolic powder, which was sprinkled on the line of the trail of blood from the pool of blood to the side of the road.'

Mr Wyrall's second shot was taken closer to the bloodstains which had been highlighted by the carbolic powder. This view looks towards Romford.

Many weeks of anxious inquiries followed in the effort to trace the criminals. Browne was always a suspect because of his black record and the threats he had uttered, and it was also known that he was armed and if cornered would not hesitate to shoot. We were, however, unable to find him, because he had not been released on ticket of leave, and therefore had been under no obligation to notify his address to the police. Then one day an accident happened in Sheffield. A large motor car which was being driven in a reckless manner came into collision with a van, the driver of which took the number of the car and reported the occurrence to a constable. He took out a summons against the driver of the car, and it was sent to London for service at the address given on the licence. It was then found that the licence had been issued to a person who was not the driver of the car. Eventually, it was discovered that the car had been stolen from a private garage at Tooting, that the driver was Frederick Guy Browne, and that he had a garage at Battersea. With him at the time of the accident was an ex-convict who had known Browne at Dartmoor, and it was he who came forward with the information that Browne was one of the men who had murdered Gutteridge.

When this news was received at Scotland Yard, I realised the necessity of taking every possible precaution. Detective Inspector Barker, Detective Sergeant Miller and other officers kept day and night watch on Browne's garage, and when on the evening of January 20 Browne drove up in the stolen car, he was immediately seized and closely guarded. In the pocket at the right hand of the driver's seat was a fully loaded Webley revolver, and in his hip pocket were twelve cartridges. A stockinet mask, with holes for the eyes and nose, was also found upon him. In his house were two other revolvers, and in a secret cupboard behind the driver's seat was found another Service revolver. 'If you had stopped me while I was in the car,' said Browne, 'I should have shot five of you and kept the other for myself. From what I can see of it, I shall have to make a machine gun for you boys next time.'

At this stage of the inquiry there was really no direct evidence proving Browne's connection with the murder, nor did we know anything about the whereabouts of Kennedy. A day or two later we heard that Kennedy had left London, and I sent Inspector Kirchner and Sergeant Duncan to trail him. They traced him to Liverpool where he had just been married. They at once went there and, with the aid of the Liverpool police, found the house where he was staying. At 11.45 at night Kennedy left his lodgings. The collar of his coat was turned up, the brim of his hat was pulled down, and he covered his face with his left hand. He was hurrying down the street when Detective Sergeant Mattinson, of the Liverpool force, who knew him well, called out: 'Now then, come on, Bill.'

Kennedy swerved round, facing the detective. 'Stand back, or I'll shoot,' he exclaimed. He drew an automatic pistol from his pocket, thrust it against the detective's ribs, and pressed the trigger. There was a click, but happily the safety catch was on and, although the weapon was fully loaded, it did not go off. Mattinson stuck to his prisoner, twisted his arm into the air, and wrenched the pistol from his grasp. Then this brave officer almost collapsed, but the Scotland Yard men and others rushed up and secured their man. He was taken to the station, where he remarked to Mattinson: 'You ought to be in heaven by this time.' Later he was taken to London, and his wife was given permission to travel in the same compartment with him.

On arriving at Scotland Yard he was seen by Chief Inspector Berrett who asked him if he could give any information about the murder of Police Constable Gutteridge. 'I may be able to tell you something,' he replied, 'but let me think a while.' After a pause he asked if he could see his wife. When she entered the room, he said: 'Well, my dear, after I was arrested at Liverpool, I told you there was something more serious at the back of it. Well, there is. These officers are making inquiries about the policeman who was murdered in Essex.'

'You did not murder him?' Mrs Kennedy asked. 'No, I did not,' he replied, 'but I was there, and I know who did. If I am charged with the murder and found guilty, I shall be hanged and you will be a widow. On the other hand, if I am charged and found guilty of being an accessory after the fact, I shall receive a severe sentence of penal servitude and be a long time from you. Will you wait for me?' She said: 'Yes, love, I will wait for you. Tell the gentlemen the truth of what took place.' 'All right', said Kennedy, 'I will. Take down what I say and I will sign it.'

Kennedy then told his story. He said that in the previous June or July he was working on a farm in Cheshire when he received a letter from Browne stating that he had started a garage at Battersea and asking him to act as manager. He accepted the offer. On September 26 Browne suggested that they should go to Billericay and steal a car. They went by train from Liverpool Street, and late at night Browne entered the grounds of a house, opened a garage door with a key, examined a car, and then hid in the grounds until the owner of the car went to bed. Then he went back to the garage, but just then a dog barked, and Browne left and rejoined Kennedy. 'It's no good here,' he said. 'We cannot get back by train, so we will try somewhere else.'

The aspect of this end of the bypassed bend at Howe Green has been altered — the main road runs just beyond the sign.

Alfred Perritt, when later questioned in court, stated that 'I am an insurance agent, and I live at Rose Cottage, Howe Green. On the morning of the 27th September last, about six o'clock, I was wakened by Mr Ward knocking at the door. I at once dressed, and, in consequence of what he told me, I went out with him in the direction of Romford about 250 yards from my house. It is downhill. As we went along, I saw the body of P.C. Gutteridge. He was lying on his back with his head downhill. I moved the body; I got hold of his ankles and lifted his feet towards the hedge to prevent any vehicles going over them. His head was lying near to the hedge. After I had moved the body the legs were slightly uphill and the head rather downhill. I saw no signs of struggling on the road. I saw a large splash of blood in the centre of the road, but that was not the only blood I observed; there were splashes of blood across to where the body was lying in a pool of blood. When I first came up to the body the shoulders, I believe, were lying on the bank, which would make it look as if it was in a semi-sitting position.'

From the spot where Police Constable Gutteridge was killed, there is about a 1 in 30 gradient in the direction of Ongar. Rose Cottage still lies behind the hedge at the top of the bend.

This section of the road is still 17 feet 6 inches wide, as measured by the police in 1927, and still has a bank on the right foreground where the body once lay.

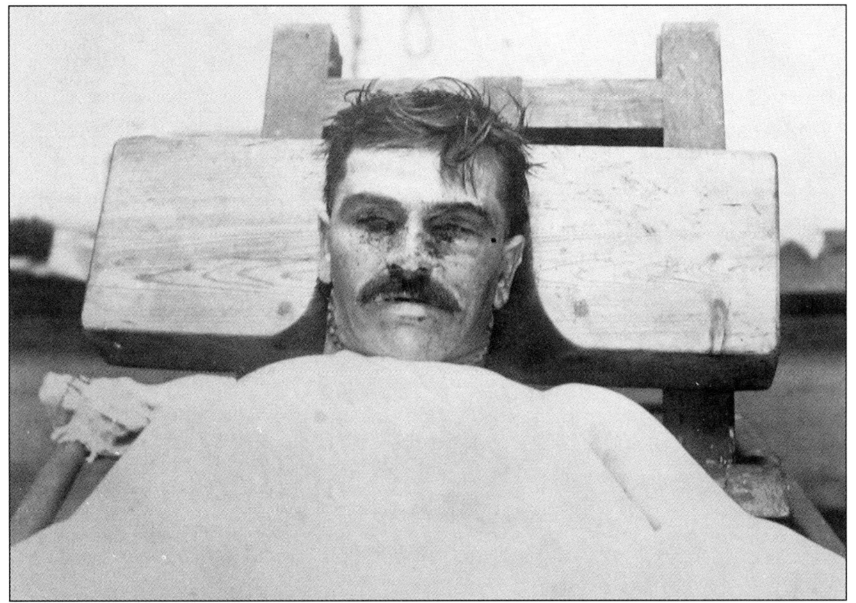

John Crockford explained that he was a Detective Inspector in the Essex Constabulary stationed at Romford. 'At about 7.45 in the early morning of 27th September I left my station in a car and went to the spot where I found P.C. Gutteridge's body. When I reached the body it was lying by the side of the road. I noticed a notebook lying close to the body. A little farther up the hill his helmet was lying in the road. I noticed blood on the road. The blood started 6 feet from the near side of the road as you go uphill till you came to the deceased's head. It was a continuous trail of blood. At the place where the head itself lay there was a pool of blood. There is no entry in the pocket book relating to this charge. The constable was wearing his cape. I examined the body. The two buttons of his tunic were undone, and his whistle was hanging from his pocket on his chain. His pencil was in his right hand between his thumb and finger. The whistle is generally carried in the pocket. His truncheon was in his truncheon pocket on his right-hand side. His torch was also in his pocket. I found there was a ragged cut on the right-hand side of the collar of his tunic, immediately on the numbers. There was also a tear on the back of his cape at the back slightly on the right-hand side. I sent for a doctor and Dr Woodhouse arrived at nine o'clock. The body was then removed to the cart-shed at the Royal Oak *(right)* public-house, and the next day it was removed to Romford mortuary.'

They walked through the village and stopped outside Dr Lovell's house. Browne waited for the lights in the house to be put out, and then he forced open the garage door, pushed the car into the road, and about a hundred yards farther on started the engine. 'We will go by the by-ways and escape the main roads,' Browne explained as they both got into the car and drove away. They went a circuitous route and eventually got on the main Ongar road. There, said Kennedy, somebody flashed his lamp as a signal to stop.

'We drove on ahead, and I heard a police whistle,' Kennedy continued. 'I told Browne to stop. He did so, and when the person came up we saw he was a policeman. Browne was driving, and I was sitting on his left in front. The policeman came up close to the car and asked him where he was going, and where he came from. Browne told him we had come from Lea Bridge Road garage and had been out to do some repairs. The policeman asked him if he had a licence, and I said the car was mine, and he then flashed his light in both our faces. He was now standing close to the running-board on the off-side. He asked me if I knew the number of the car, and Browne said: 'You can see it on the front of the car.' The policeman said: 'I know the number. Do you?' I said I knew the number, and the policeman then pulled out his note-book and was in the act of writing when I heard a shot, quickly followed by another. Then I saw Browne had a large Webley in his hand. He said: 'Get out, quick.' I got out and went to the policeman, who was lying on his back. Browne came over and said: 'I'll finish him.' I said: 'For God's sake don't shoot any more. The man's dying. He's groaning.' The policeman's eyes were open, and Browne, addressing him, said: 'What are you looking at me like that for?' and stooping down he shot him at close range through the eyes.

Then Browne said: 'Let's get back into the car.' He gave me the revolver, and as we drove on he told me to load it. I loaded it and in my excitement I dropped an empty shell in the car. I threw the other three away into the road. We got to Brixton at 5.30 and left the car in a cul-de-sac. We took a tramcar back to the garage, taking with us two cases containing the doctor's instruments. I then suggested that we had better go away, and Browne said that if I left him he would blow my brains out. 'If anybody comes here there will be a shooting match,' he said. 'I went to Liverpool on January 21.'

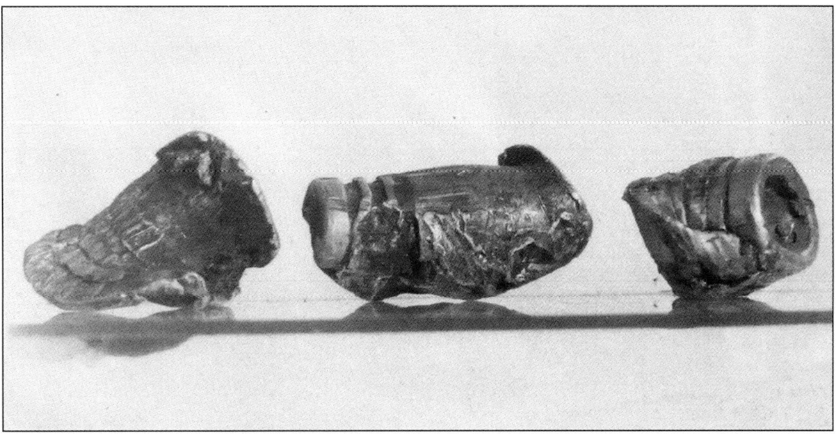

'After the body had been removed I went back to the spot where I found the constable, and I saw Detective Norman, and he handed me two bullets. I handed them to Chief Inspector Berrett *(left)*. There is always a police officer on duty at night at Brentwood on the London-Chelmsford road.' The aspect of the murder which so shocked the nation was that the constable's eyes had been shot out by the murderer in the belief that the last image seen before a person died would still remain on the eyes to identify him. The two .45 bullets retrieved from the road are left and right.

Rather than be found with the doctor's car in Browne's garage, it was abandoned in an alleyway *(left)* beside No. 21 Foxley Road quite near to the Kennington Oval. Albert McDougall *(right)* described how he found it. 'I leave home in the mornings about half-past seven. I go out of our back door which leads into a little passageway where there are two iron gates before you get to the road. I left on the 27th September as usual by that door. As I came out of my door I found a Morris-Cowley car drawn up within about 4 to 6 inches of my house wall, and within 5 to 6 feet from the gates at the end of the passage. On account of my disability I put my hand on the radiator to get round the car. It was very warm. When I arrived home that evening between a quarter to six and six o'clock the car was still there. I took the number when I came home. It was TW 6120. I gave the car a rough examination in the evening. I noticed that the near side front mudguard was sheered off from the running board. I reported the matter to a policeman on duty in Brixton Road.'

I have quoted freely from Kennedy's vivid description of this ghastly murder, because later, when Browne and he were brought up at the police court charged with murder, he, through his counsel, pleaded that his statement was inadmissible, that it had been pumped out of him by promises and threats, and that he had been kept without food. As I have explained, I was Superintendent of the Central Office at the time, and Kennedy suggested that I was the evil genius who had by some subtle art played upon his delicate feelings to such an extent that he was persuaded against his better judgment to make his confession and put the entire blame for the murder on Browne. By doing this, he declared, he was led to believe that he would be regarded only as an accessory to the crime and would escape with something less than hanging. His allegations were disproved, and I was particularly interested in the fact that at the trial before Mr Justice Avory they were not repeated.

Kennedy's statement was not admissible as evidence against Browne, but the certain proof of Browne's participation in the crime was forthcoming in a dramatic manner. You will remember that an empty shell was found on the floor of Dr Lovell's car when four months before it was abandoned at Brixton. That shell was submitted to Mr Robert Churchill, the well-known gunmaker, who has given expert evidence at many trials. He told us that if we could find the revolver he would be able to prove it was the weapon used by the murderer. When Browne was arrested at his garage on a charge of car stealing, the revolvers which were seized by Inspector Barker and other officers were taken to Mr Churchill. He stated definitely that the Webley revolver found in the pocket on the off-side of the car driven by Browne on the day of his arrest was the one which had fired the cartridge picked up on the floor of the stolen car abandoned at Brixton.

Mr Churchill explained that the breech shield of a revolver was filed by hand in its finishing process, and no two workmen or files could make absolutely identical marks. When a revolver was fired, the indentations on the breech shield produced corresponding marks on the cartridge, and a microscopical examination enabled him to say that the empty cartridge case was fired from Browne's revolver and none other because the marks on the two were precisely the same. War Office experts also gave similar evidence, and enlarged photographs were produced showing clearly the various similarities, just as is the case with two identical sets of fingerprints.

Browne went into the witness box and declared that he had never fired a single shot from any of the revolvers, and that Kennedy's statement was a fairy story from beginning to end. Kennedy preferred to read his defence from the dock. So far from

Eighty years later, we found the same alleyway virtually unchanged, save for the more modern motor car!

Sergeant Charles Hearn came to inspect the car. He said that 'I examined it carefully. I found that the near side mudguard was damaged and bent inwards. I examined the dumb irons, the front springs. I noticed on the nuts of the dumb irons there was some substance which had the appearance of bark of a tree. I scraped some of it off after I drove the car to the police station. At the station we examined it in the light of a torch and Detective Hawkyard found an empty cartride case by the front seat on the near side, next the driver. The cartridge case was marked on the cap. "R.L.IV." I handed it to Detective Inspector Jones, and saw it placed in the safe at the police station. The next day I saw it handed to Chief Inspector Berrett.'

making any complaint against me or anyone else of the circumstances in which his statement was made, he excused himself for not having previously told the police of the murder on the ground that he was terrified. 'I thought,' he said, 'that if it were known that I was present at the time of the murder I should have been accused of it, although I was completely innocent. I can only express my deep regret to Mrs. Gutteridge that I was in the car at the time of the murder.'

It was feared that Browne would make a savage attack on Kennedy in the dock, and six hefty prison officers stood close up to the prisoners when the jury returned into court with the verdict of guilty. Both Browne and Kennedy heard their fate without moving an eyelash, and when asked whether they had anything to say why judgment of death should not be passed, their replies were more in the nature of a vote of thanks to everybody concerned in the case. 'I will admit,' said Browne with a smile, 'that the counsel have acted very fairly as far as I am concerned. I admit that I would not wish to be tried by a better judge, but the jury have had stuff given to them which is not genuine. It will come out later that I had nothing to do with it, but I am not going to argue the point. I am quite content. My conscience is clear.'

The police station at Brixton, where the car was photographed, was demolished in 1959, although rebuilt on the same corner of the High Road at Canterbury Crescent and Gresham Road. However, the Media and Communication Manager of the Metropolitan Police Service for the Lambeth area refused permission for us to take a comparison photograph in the yard at the rear of the building.

In 1939 the Morris Owners Club tried to trace the car but discovered that TW 6120 had been entered as a 'dead number' by the Essex Taxation Office .

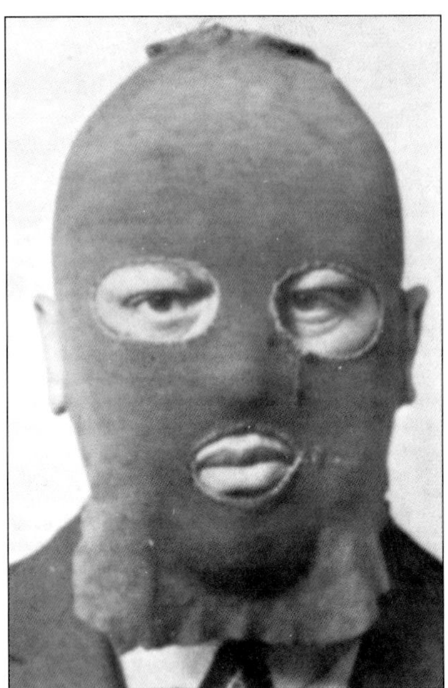

Above left: **On January 20, 1928, officers went to the Globe Garage where they found Browne in this room behind the workshop. Detective Inspector William Barker arrested him, initially on a charge of stealing the Vauxhall from Franciscan Road, Tooting, the previous November. On searching the premises, some of the doctor's implements were found together with a fully-loaded revolver and cartridges and a stocking mask** ***(left)*** **(being worn here for the cameraman by a member of the CID at New Scotland Yard).** *Above right:* **Detectives then went to Browne's house at 33a Sisters Avenue where another revolver and cartridges was found and more incriminating medical supplies.**

Then Kennedy, speaking in soft, well-regulated tones, also acknowledged the fairness with which he had been treated, and attributed the verdict to 'Fate'. 'I am not afraid of death,' he added. 'I shall die willingly, because I have a certain knowledge that in the hereafter I shall be united in all eternity to the one darling girl who has stuck to me through all this ordeal.'

When the two men left the dock after being sentenced to death I felt relieved that the world would never be troubled again with the two worst criminals I have ever known. Browne was not only a great scoundrel, but, like so many other confirmed criminals, a great fool. It was his folly that brought him to the scaffold. He was always a rebel against authority and law and order. Even while in the condemned cell he tried to defeat justice. One night, he cut the veins in one of his arms with a portion of a safety razor which he had mysteriously and cunningly concealed about him. Fortunately, the prison officers in the cell saw the attempt in time to save his life—for the hangman.

As for Kennedy, he was a fit companion of Browne, a vicious criminal who, like his partner in crime, was determined on shooting anybody who stood in his way. I have always believed that it was he, and not Browne, who shot poor Gutteridge through the eyes.

Superintendent Percy Savage,
Savage of Scotland Yard, 1934

Today, the Globe Garage in Northcote Road has ceased to exist. These pictures show the site after demolition ***(below left)*** **and as it is today** ***(below right)*****.**

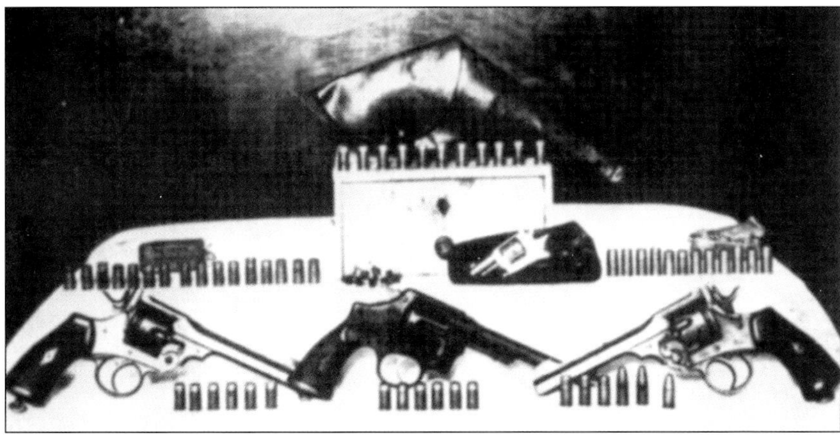

The armoury as revealed by the police. The Gutteridge murder was the first major case in which firearms evidence helped secure a conviction.

The solution of the crime is generally regarded as one of the greatest achievements of Scotland Yard. Robert Churchill, gunmaker in business at 32 Orange Street in the West End of London, had a very important part in it.

Initially Churchill began by saving the police a lot of trouble. Within a few days of the start of the hue and cry, he was shown a Webley service revolver which had been found on the foreshore of the Thames at Hammersmith. Gutteridge had been shot with Webley revolver bullets but Churchill proved that it was not the wanted weapon. Then a parcel containing both rifle and revolver ammunition was uncovered in the Thames mud. He again showed that it was the wrong ammunition. The lead bullets removed from the constable's body were too deformed for Churchill to identify them conclusively with a particular weapon but the prints left by the rifling were sufficient to enable him to define the make of revolver from which they had been fired and to disassociate them from other revolvers even of the same make. It was a useful, even if negative, contribution to the early enquiries.

It's said that ten thousand policemen were finally alerted in the quest for the murderers of their comrade. It was four months before two men named Browne and Kennedy were charged. Chief Inspector Berrett of Scotland Yard was in charge of the case. It was notable for the pertinacity of the police in reconstructing the crime, and for the fact that the decisive evidence of guilt at the trial was given by the firearms experts. Churchill was one of four who were called. The others were from the Royal Arsenal at Woolwich and the Royal Small Arms Factory at Enfield Lock.

Suspicion had been awakened only because on the floor of the car there was a fired cartridge marked on the base 'R.L.IV'. When it was shown to Major-General Sir Wyndham Childs, then chief of the C.I.D., he recognised it immediately as a Mark IV made at the Royal Laboratory, Woolwich Arsenal.

It was a flat-nosed type of revolver ammunition which had been issued when the B.E.F. left for France in 1914. As a soldier, Sir Wyndham remembered that although it was manufactured in accordance with the Hague Convention, the Germans claimed that it was an expanding bullet which violated the agreement. As a consequence, they themselves cut the tops of their nickel-coated ammunition into 'dum-dums' until the Mark IV was withdrawn. At least one of the bullets in Gutteridge's head was a Mark IV.

When he examined the bottom of the case more closely under a microscope, Sir Wyndham discovered that what had appeared to the naked eye as a little blister was actually an elevation of copper above the normal level of the cap. It was a fault of high significance because it meant that the odd mark on the base of the cartridge had printed there, under about five tons pressure on discharge, an impression which would show on the breech shield of the weapon which had fired it. He guessed, as it turned out correctly, that the punch-holes in the breach shield had been caused by somebody cleaning the barrel of the revolver with an improvised steel rod.

Sir Wyndham had noticed the deformation on the base of the cartridge picked up in the stolen car. Churchill subsequently called it 'the jockey's cap'. When McBride came to photograph the pistols found in Browne's possession, he records that 'I thought I detected in the Webley a small flaw in the breech-block and, on examining the weapon more closely, noticed that it seemed to have a defective striker. Either a minute piece was missing, or a small dent had been made. When I looked again at the base of the cartridge case we had found in the doctor's car, the marks compared. I photographed both, enlarging them seven diameters in the camera.'

Churchill then examined the exhibits again under the comparison microscope. He himself photographed the breech-block of the revolver and the cartridge case microscopically to see whether his own tests corresponded with McBride's. He tested fifty other Webleys for comparison with Browne's. None produced the same mark on the cartridge case. Subsequently the revolver and cartridge were sent to Enfield Small Arms Factory where they were examined and photographed microscopically again. The police were taking no chances. The firearms evidence against Browne and Kennedy was tested past all possibility of a flaw.

At the trial before Mr Justice Avory, Churchill produced a target of pigskin on which he had tested the exhibit revolvers at distances of 3 inches, 6 inches, and 12 inches from the target. He said that three of the cartridges which killed Gutteridge were loaded with cordite and one with black powder. If so, they matched with the ammunition in Browne's possession, too.

That both Browne and Kennedy were equally implicated there is no doubt but who fired the four shots, whether both did or one, was never established. Sir Wyndham took the view that Browne fired the first shot which killed the constable, and that Kennedy subsequently blew his eyes out. Berrett was sure that Kennedy shot the policeman from the passenger seat while Browne was talking to Gutteridge, and that Browne then got out of the car to settle the matter. Churchill thought that Browne probably fired the lot.

By way of a postscript, Major Gerald Burrard gave his own opinion. 'This was the first occasion on which the task of identifying individual firearms by means of fired cartridge cases or bullets was attempted in this country, and the Home Office very wisely sought the help of the War Office. The result was that the technical staff at Woolwich and Enfield conclusively proved that the fired cartridge case found in the abandoned car had beyond doubt been fired by Browne's revolver, and that was that, except that it has never been generally realised that this work of identification was carried out by the War Office, and not by the Home Office or Police experts.'

Macdonald Hastings,
The Other Mr Churchill, 1963

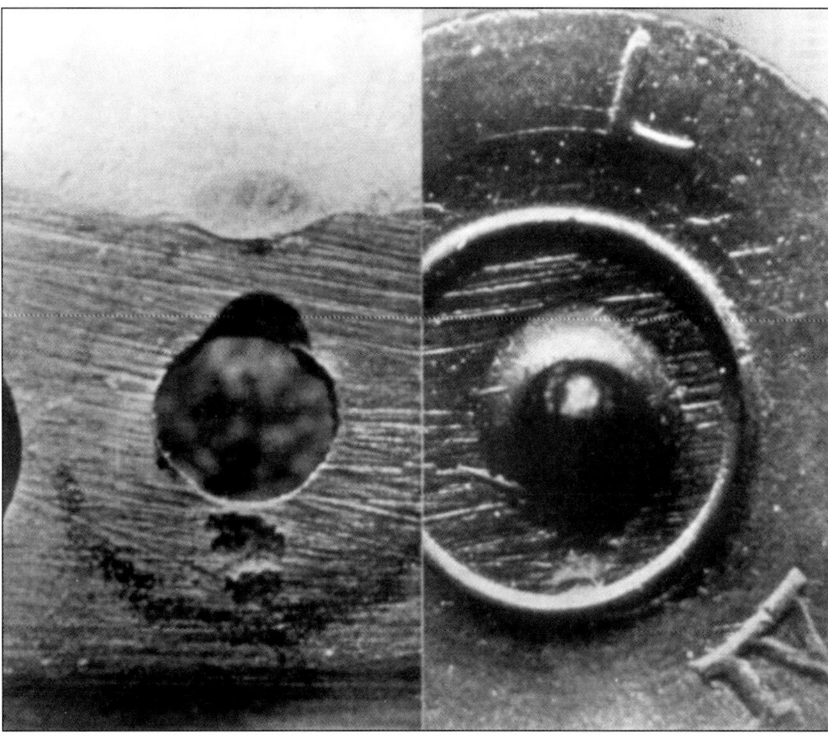

The left-hand photograph shows a portion of the breech shield of Browne's revolver and on the right the base of the fired cartridge case.

The funeral of PC George Gutteridge took place on October 1, 1927 in pouring rain, the cortege wending its way up Warley Hill in Brentwood to his final resting place in Lorne Road Cemetery ***(opposite).***

On April 27, 1928, the jury returned with the verdict of guilty. Mr Justice Avory then pronounced the sentence.

Frederick Guy Browne and William Henry Kennedy, the jury have found you both guilty of murder. The sentence of the Court upon each of you is that you be taken to a lawful prison and thence to a place of execution. That you be there each of you hanged by the neck until you be dead and that your bodies respectively be buried within the precincts of the prison in which you shall have been last confined before your execution. And may the Lord have mercy upon your souls.'

Mr Justice Avory, April 27, 1928

Frederick Guy Browne and William Henry Kennedy were hanged yesterday — Browne at Pentonville and Kennedy at Wandsworth — for the murder of Police Constable Gutteridge, eight months ago.

Crowds waited outside both prisons as the hour of execution drew near. Mrs Kennedy arrived outside Wandsworth Prison in a taxi-cab, in which she sat sobbing until the notice of her husband's execution was posted on the gate.

Daily Express, June 1, 1928

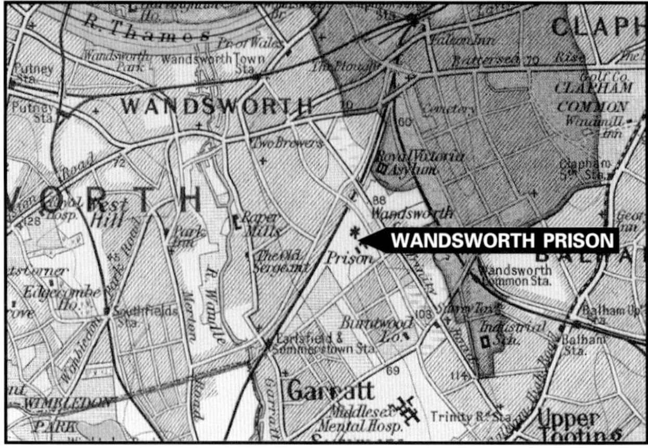

As we have seen on page 13, once Newgate as a site of execution was no more, alternative prisons had to have gallows installed. The task of executing the condemned was then split between Pentonville ***(left)*** **for crimes committed north of the River Thames and Wandsworth** ***(right)*** **for those on the southern side. Unusually, Kennedy suffered death at the latter prison, hanged by Thomas Pierrepoint and Robert Wilson, although the murder took place in Essex. Browne was executed by Robert Baxter and Henry Pollard at Pentonville. Holloway was reserved for female executions.**

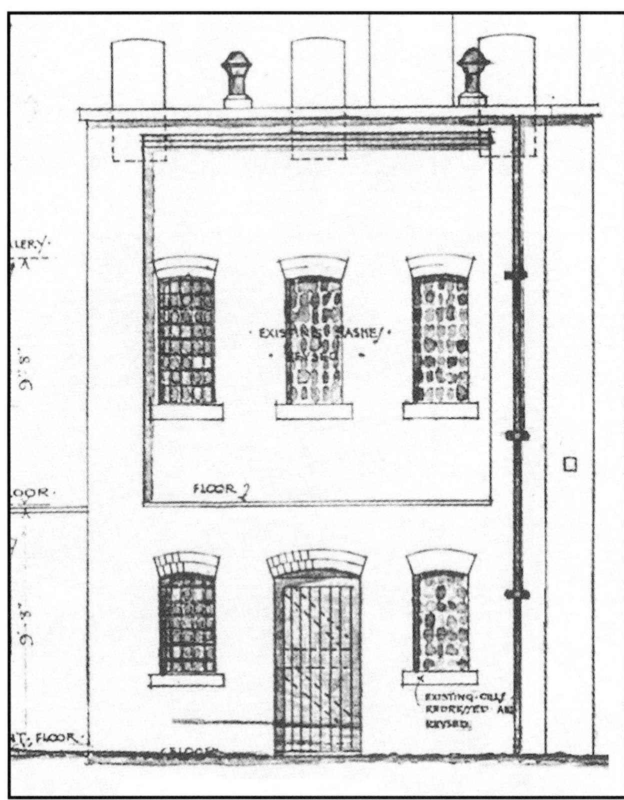

At first a free-standing shed was provided at Wandsworth for executions but this was superceded in 1911 with this two-storey annexe *(left)* built against the exterior of F Wing and this is where Kennedy met his end. *Right:* The discoloured brickwork still shows where the building stood. In 1937 it was replaced by a purpose-built execution suite — see pages 92-93.

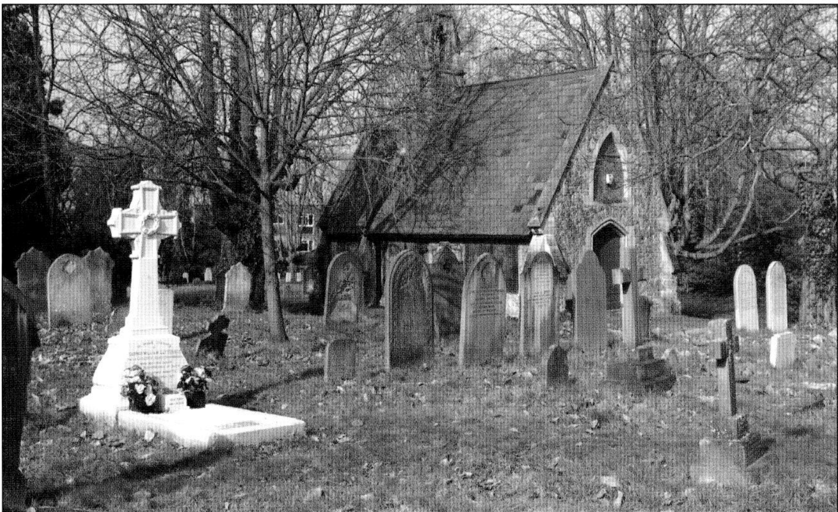

A memorial is to be sited on the roadside at Stapleford Abbotts where a police constable was shot dead while on duty almost 63 years ago.

Essex PC George Gutteridge is to be remembered on a granite stone and a bronze plaque at the spot on the main road where he was gunned down.

Local beat officer Mr Gutteridge was based at Abridge, then Lambourne End, when he tried to arrest two car thieves on September 27, 1927.

Chief Inspector Ian Cotgrove, of Epping and Ongar sub-division, said: 'It was a particularly horrendous death. He was arresting some car thieves when he was shot in the face. The bullet went in one cheek and out the other. He was then shot at point-blank range, once through each eye.'

Two people were later arrested and hanged.

The memorial is the idea of officers in the Epping and Ongar sub-division as a gesture to mark the 150th anniversary of the Essex police force. Once the stone and plaque has been laid it will be maintained by local police in their own time.'

Mr Gutteridge is the only police constable to have been killed on duty in this area.

The cost of the memorial is £750 and so far about half the total has been raised.

Contributions have been received from Epping Forest Council, Stapleford Abbotts Parish Council and Lambourne Parish Council, but individuals are also invited to make a donation.

Anyone who would like to contribute should contact Epping or Ongar police stations. All those who make a contribution will be invited to the unveiling of the memorial.

Added Mr Cotgrove: 'I feel officers who put their lives on the line should not be forgotten. There should be a permanent reminder that police officers do sometimes suffer the ultimate penalty themselves.

Epping Guardian and Gazette, July 13, 1990

In 1990 moves were made by the Epping and Ongar Sub-Division, as a gesture to mark the 150th anniversary of the Essex Police Force, to place a memorial on the B175 close by the entrance to the bypassed loop at Howe Green, officially called Gutteridge Lane, some ten miles from where he lies buried.

Alfred Arthur Rouse was born in 1894 and sent to live with an aunt on the separation of his parents in 1900. On August 8, 1914 — four days after Great Britain declared war on Germany — Rouse enlisted and was drafted into the 24th Battalion, The London Regiment (The Queens). He married Lily Watkins before he was sent to France in March 1915 but two months later was wounded by the explosion of a shell, shrapnel cutting his head so badly that he was unable to wear any kind of headgear. He also suffered a severe wound above his left knee. The head injury caused him dizzyness and some loss of memory and, as a result, he was invalided out of the army on February 11, 1916. In 1920 he began a liaison with Helen Campbell who he bigamously married in 1924. She had two children by him although the first died when just five weeks old. He then sired a child with Nellie Tucker in 1928 and a second had just been born on October 29, 1930 in City Road Maternity House in London. *Right:* Nice wedding photo . . . but which one?

November 6, 1930 — The Strange Case of Alfred Rouse

When two Hardingstone men were returning home about two o'clock this morning (Thursday), they were met, on the lane leading from the main road to the village, with the astonishing sight of a small motor-car enveloped by flames. They were unable to get near the car, and summoned police aid.

When the fire died down a charred body was found inside the car. It could not be definitely established at the moment whether the body was that of a male or female, although circumstances were strongly in favour of it being that of a woman.

The identification plate bore the registration number MU 1468 and upon this the police at once started investigations in the hope of establishing identification.

Kettering Evening Telegraph, November 6, 1930

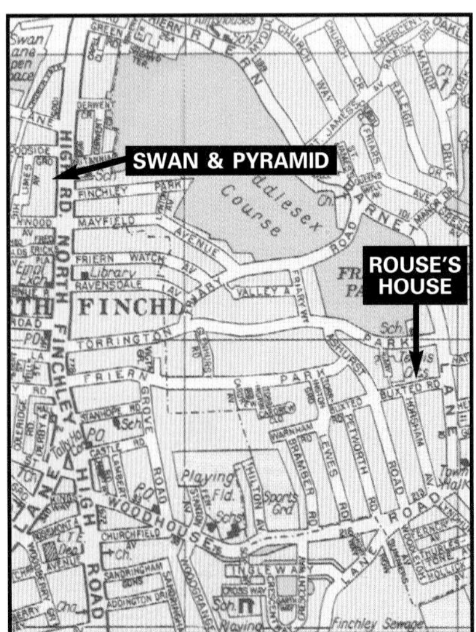

Rouse still lived with his legal wife at 14 Buxted Road, Friern Barnet (on the northern outskirts of London), Mrs Rouse having agreed on certain conditions to bring up Helen Campbell's boy. However, Nellie believed Rouse was a single man who lived at Gillingham Street, Victoria, but yet another young girl, Ivy Jenkins, also believed she was his wife. She was presently lying seriously ill at her parents house in Monmouthshire and she too was expecting his child. Rouse had told her he had bought them a house at Kingston. All this was pure fiction but, if his personal problems were not complicated enough, he had invited Ivy's sister Phyllis to come and stay with them. We are told that there were even further women in his life at Birmingham, Southampton and elsewhere, a child of his in Paris and another in an English county! So quite simply by November 1930 Rouse was in deep trouble both morally and financially. Why Arthur Rouse would further want to complicate his life by murdering a total stranger is something that even the trial could not fathom. He told lie after lie in court to try to wriggle free, one remarkable aspect being that the Crown Prosecutor, Norman Birkett, withdrew all the evidence of Rouse's immoral character to cut short the need for discussion as to whether it was admissible. Only Nellie Tucker was called to the stand and she just gave her address — 49 Hendon Way, Hendon — and that she last saw him from 7.10 p.m. to 8 p.m. on November 5.

It was only after Rouse had been executed in Bedford prison by Tom Pierrepoint and Tom Phillips on March 10, 1931 that his confession as to what had really taken place was published in the *Daily Sketch*. *Left:* The story began when he picked up a man he said he knew, although not by name, at the Swan and Pyramid pub in Whetstone High Street, not far from his home (see map opposite). *Right:* No longer standing, the site of the pub at 975 High Road is now occupied by the Safari Bar Indian restaurant.

The mystery of the finding of a body in a blazing saloon car on the road to Hardington, a vlllage near Northampton, was still unsolved this morning.

It was shortly before midnight that the announcement was made that a post-mortem examination of the remains had revealed the fact that the body was that of a man.

The burnt-out car was a small saloon with a registration number which showed that it was owned by Mr Alfred Rouse, of Buxted Road, North Finchley, Middlesex.

There is still no sign of the mystery man for whom the police are appealing, and who was seen a few hundred yards away from the blazing car. The police have issued the following description of him.

'Five feet ten inches, heavily built, dark curly hair, clean shaven, with good-looking stern features, between 30 and 40 years of age.'

Yet another mystery in connection with the case is whether Mr Rouse was driving the car at the time of the tragedy or not as, of course, there is the possibility of it having been stolen. A further complication is added by the finding of a pair of heels from a woman's shoes in the wreckage of the car.

Kettering Evening Telegraph, November 1930

It was the Agnes Kesson case at Epsom in June which first set me thinking. It showed that it was possible to beat the police if you were careful enough.

Since I read about that case I kept thinking of various plans. I tried to hit on something new. I did not want to do murder just for the sake of it.

I was in a tangle in various ways. Nellie Tucker was expecting another child of which I would be the father and I was expecting to hear from 'Paddy' Jenkins similar news. There were other difficulties and I was fed up. I wanted to start afresh.

I let the matter drop from my mind for a while, but in the autumn of last year something happened which made me think again.

A man spoke to me near the Swan and Pyramid public-house in Whetstone High Road. He was a down-and-out, and told the usual hard-luck story. I took him into the public-house and he had some beer. I had lemonade. Of course, I paid for the drinks.

He told me he usually hung about there. I met him once again and stood him a couple of drinks. He did not tell me his name, but he did say that he had no relations, and was looking for work. He said he had been to Peterborough, Norwich, Hull, and other places trying to get work, and that he was in the habit of getting lifts on lorries.

He was the sort of man no one would miss, and I thought he would suit the plan I had in mind. I worked out the whole thing in my mind and, as it was then early in November, I suddenly realised that I should do it on November 5, which was Bonfire Night, when a fire would not be noticed so much.

I think it was on November 2 or 3 that I searched out the man He was having a drink of beer and we talked. When I said that I intended to go to Leicester on the Wednesday night he said he would be glad of a lift up there. This was what I thought he would say.

I made an appointment with him for the Wednesday night for about eight o'clock. I met him outside the Swan and Pyramid, and we went into the bar. He had more beer, and again I had lemonade.

I asked him if he would like something to drink on the journey, and he said he would. I bought a bottle of whisky. Then we both got into the car which was outside the public-house.

We drove first of all to my house in Buxted Road. I got out, leaving the man in the car. My wife was in. She had seen me draw up near the house and she asked me who it was I had in the car. I said it was a man I knew but she suspected that it was a woman.

I said, 'All right. I'll drive close up in front of the house, as I am turning round, to let you see that it is a man.' I did so, as I drove out of Buxted Road so that my wife could see for herself and would have no grounds for jealousy.

So far as I remember, it was about 8.30 when I started off for the north with a man in the car, though I might be mistaken about the time. I drove slowly because I wanted it to be late when I did what I had in mind. I don't think I travelled more than fifteen miles an hour.

I stopped at St Albans partly for a rest and partly to fill in the time. The man, switched

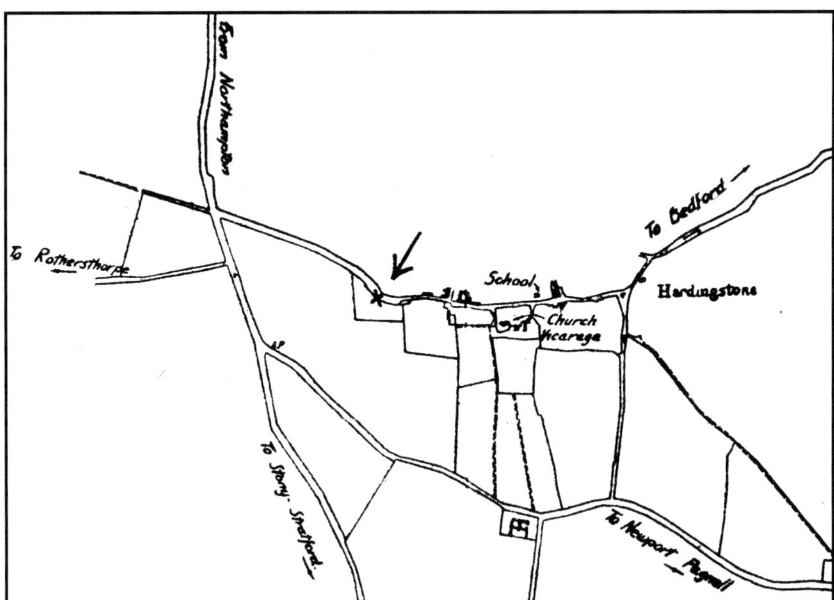

His burning Morris was first spotted in Hardingstone, a small village near Northampton, by Alf Brown and his cousin Bill Bailey as they returned home along Hardingstone Lane from a dance around 1.45 a.m on Thursday, November 6. Mr Brown told the court that 'it was a bright moonlit night. We were walking on the footpath on the left-hand side of the Northampton Road. When we got to the junction with Hardingstone Lane I saw a glare in the direction of Hardingstone. I could not judge how far it was away.I saw a man coming out of the ditch there. I noticed that he was wearing a light mackintosh and had no hat on. He was carrying an attaché case in his hand. Mr Bailey and I walked a few yards, and as we saw that the blaze appeared to be getting brighter we ran down towards Hardingstone. The man whom I saw climbing out of the ditch walked on towards the main road. We passed him. He did not say anything to us as he passed and we did not say anything to him. We ran up the lane.' This is the original scene of crime plan produced in court.

out the lights by mistake and a policeman spoke to me.

During the journey the man drank the whisky neat from the bottle and was getting quite fuzzled. We talked a lot, but he did not tell me who he actually was. I did not care.

I turned into the Hardingstone Lane because it was quiet and near a main road where I could get a lift from a lorry afterwards. I pulled the car up.

The man was half dozing — the effect of the whisky. I looked at him and then gripped him by the throat with my right hand. I pressed his head against the back of the seat. He slid down, his hat falling off. I saw he had a bald patch on the crown of his head.

He just gurgled. I pressed his throat hard. My grip is very strong

I used my right hand only because it is very powerful. People have always said that I have a terrific grip. He did not resist. It was all very sudden. The man did not realise what was happening. I pushed his face back. After making a peculiar noise, the man was silent and I thought he was dead or unconscious.

Then I got out of the car, taking my attache case, the can of petrol, and the mallet with me. I walked about ten yards in front of the car and opened the can, using the mallet to do so. I threw the mallet away and made a trail of petrol to the car. I took the mallet away with one purpose in view.

Also, I poured petrol over the man and loosened the petrol union joint and took the top off the carburettor. I put the petrol can in the back of the car. I ran to the beginning of the petrol trail and put a match to it. The flame rushed to the car which caught fire at once.

Petrol was leaking from the bottom of the car. That was the petrol I had poured over the man and the petrol that was dripping from the union joint and carburettor.

The photographs of the burned out car were taken by Arthur Ashford, a commercial photographer who had heard about the incident and was planning to send them to the London press. When he reached the spot at about 11 a.m. there was no police present, only a couple of onlookers.

The first police officer on the scene was PC Harry Copping who arrived around 2 a.m. in response to Alf Brown's message. He could see that there was a body in the car lying across the front seats. Calling for buckets of water from the village, the flames were doused. At that point, Inspector James Lawrence arrived to what was initially thought to be some sort of accident. The number plate was still readable so the owner was easily traced and Mrs Rouse was summoned to Northampton where she was shown some buckles which she said might have belonged to her husband. Meanwhile, Rouse was in south Wales but when he read the next morning's edition of the *Daily Sketch* containing a photo of the car and description of himself, he returned to London and at 9.30 p.m. on November 7 was detained at Hammersmith Police Station. The next day he was taken to Northampton and charged with murder.

On November 6, 1980 — the 50th anniversary of the murder — the *Northampton Chronicle & Echo* tracked down Alf Brown, then at 70 still an usher at the Magistrates Court, and took him back to the exact spot where he had seen the car on fire.

The fire was very quick and the whole thing was a mass of flames in a few seconds. I ran away. I was running when I came near the two men, but I started to walk then. It is not true that I came out of the ditch when the men saw me. I was on the grass verge. I did shout to them that there must be 'a bonfire over there'.

I did not expect to see anyone in the lane at that time of night. It surprised me and I decided to change my plans.

I had intended to walk through Northampton and to get a train to Scotland. But when the men saw me I hesitated and went the other way. The men were right when they said they saw me hesitate.

I left my hat in the car. When I was driving, I nearly always did so with my hat off. I forgot in the excitement to take it out of the car.

I went to Wales because I had to go somewhere and I did not know what to do. I did not think there would be much fuss in the papers about the thing, but pictures of the car with long accounts were published, and I left Wales.

I was not going to Scotland, as I said. I just went back to London because I thought it was the best thing to do. London is big.

In my attache case was my identity disc which the police still have. I intended to put it on the man in the car so that people would think it was me. I forgot to do so.

I knew that no one would find out that the man had been strangled because the fire would be so fierce that no traces of that would be left.

I am not able to give any more help regarding the man who was burned in the car. I never asked him his name. There was no reason why I should do so.

Daily Sketch, March 11, 1931

Behind Hardingstone Church is a well-kept grave with a cross on which is written 'An unknown man, 6th November 1930'.

Mr G. J. Norris was in the village in 1930 and still lives in the same house. 'I made that cross,' he says.

Kettering Evening Telegraph, November 7, 1987

Twenty years on, we asked Kevin Lamberth to investigate. He found Hardingstone Lane unchanged . . .

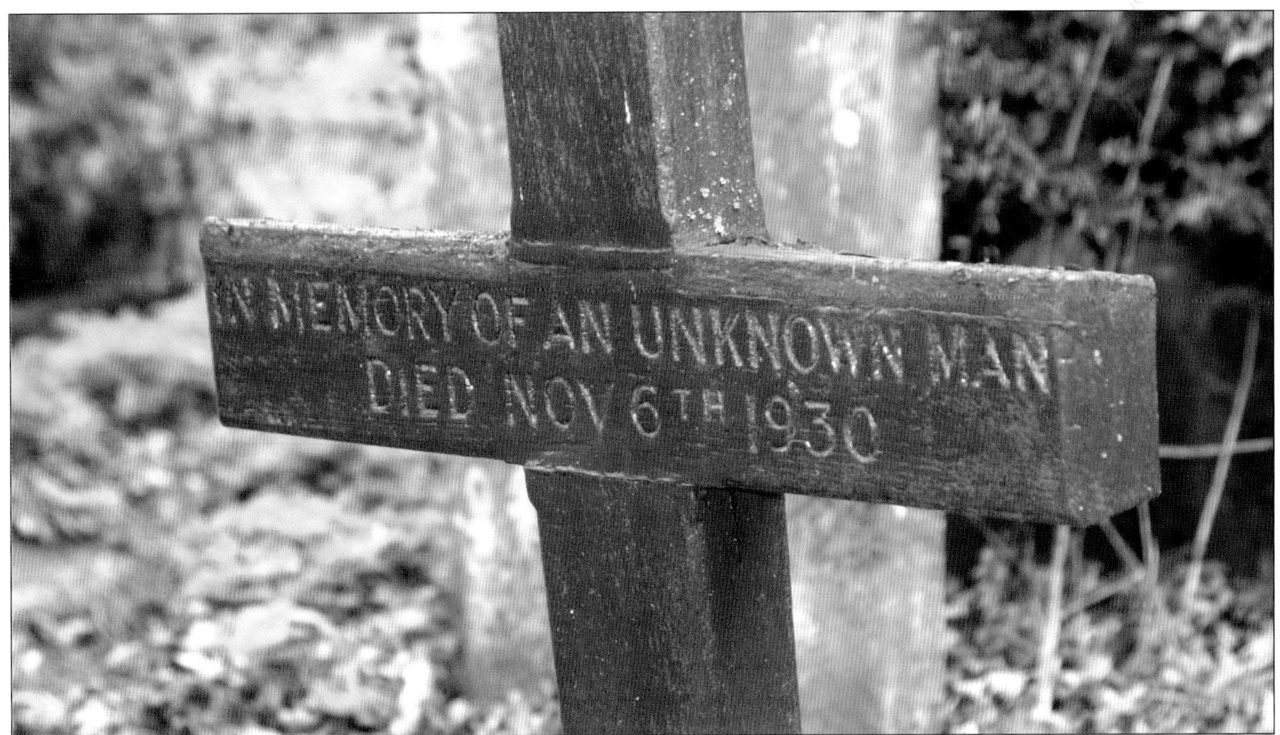

. . . and then Kevin made a pilgrimage to the churchyard. Who the man in the grave is we will never know.

August 7, 1934 — Death at the Palace Cinema

Mr. Dudley Hoard, aged about 40, manager of the Palace Cinema, Bow Road, E., and his wife were found yesterday morning with serious head injuries. The former was in the balcony of the picture house, and the latter on the bed in her room. Mr. Hoard died yesterday afternoon.

The discovery was made by a woman cleaner, who sent for the police, and later the injured couple were removed to St Andrew's Hospital, Bow. Examination of a safe by detectives showed that takings, amounting to over £100, were missing. Mr. Hoard took over the managership of the cinema only a few months ago, and he and his wife occupied a flat upstairs at the back of the balcony.

The Times, August 8, 1934

Important discoveries were made yesterday by the many detectives engaged on the investigation of the attack on Mr. Dudley Hoard, aged 35, the manager of the Palace Cinema,in Bow Road, E., who died on Tuesday from his injuries and his wife who is in St Andrew's Hospital, Bow, with serious head wounds. Although Mrs. Hoard was still suffering from her injuries and shock, it was stated that she would probably recover.

Mr. and Mrs. Hoard were asleep early on Tuesday morning in their flat, which is situated behind the balcony of the cinema, when they were awakened by a noise. Mr. Hoard put on his trousers and went to investigate. Mrs. Hoard followed and saw her husband struggling with a man. She ran towards them and received a blow on the head and lost consciousness. Later Mr. Hoard was found on the balcony of the cinema and Mrs. Hoard upon her bed.

Among the articles found is a hammer, which a police search revealed in a yard near the cinema. They have no doubt that it had been thrown there, and they think that it may have been used by the man who attacked Mr. and Mrs. Hoard. They also discovered finger prints and the imprint of a man's hand on the wall of the cinema, and part of the wall was removed intact for microscopic examination by experts at Scotland Yard.

The police lost no time after the discovery in the cinema in organizing a hunt for the person responsible, and yesterday the already large force of detectives concentrated on the case was supplemented by

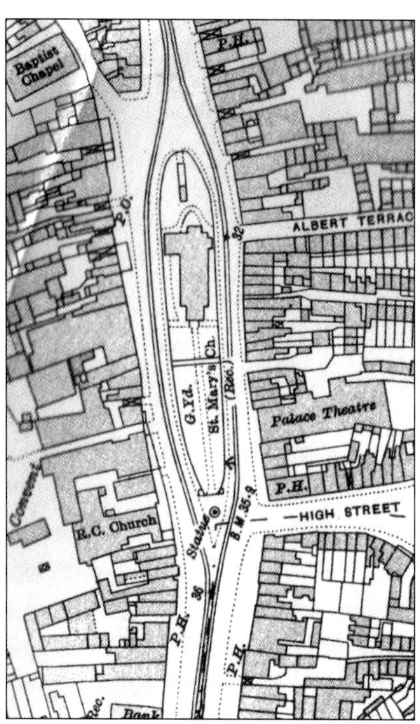

Top: **The Palace (on the extreme right) at 156-158 Bow Road originally opened as Marlows Palace of Varieties in July 1892, later becoming the Eastern Empire with an audience capacity of just under 1,000. Cinematograph shows began in 1906. It was rebuilt as the Bow Palace in 1922-23 solely for cinema use, the pit having a full orchestra and organ to provide the background music for silent films. Rebuilt yet again in 1935 soon after the murder of the manager Dudley Hoard, it was closed during the Second World War due to bomb damage. It reopened in 1947 but closed in 1958 and was demolished for the site to be redeveloped** *(above).*

others with a special knowledge of underworld haunts.

A valuable statement was made to the police by a man, who said that he had seen a man answering to the official description running from the alleyway leading to the back of the cinema at about 3 o'clock on the morning of the attack. Further inquiries showed that the fugitive was seen to enter a taxicab shortly afterwards in Campbell Road, near by.

Early yesterday Scotland Yard issued a description of a man whom they would like to interview regarding the crime. Their statement was as follows:

'The man, who is described as being 22 years of age, 5ft 10in. or over in height, complexion pale, clean shaven, long dark hair, dressed in a dark suit and no hat, is believed to have left the cinema by an exit door at the rear about 4.30 a.m. on August 7. It is possible that he hired a taxicab near the scene of the crime. His clothing is probably considerably bloodstained. The police will be glad of any information from the public which is likely to assist in the inquiries.'

The Times, August 9, 1934

Mr. John Harris, at the Thames Police Court yesterday, committed John Frederick Stockwell, aged 19, cinema attendant, for trial on the charge of murdering Mr. Dudley Hoard, manager of the Eastern Palace Cinema, Bow, on the night of August 6-7, and robbing him of approximately £90. Mr. Gwatkin appeared for the Director of Public Prosecutions, and Mr. Frederick Levy (instructed by Mr. E. Fail) defended. At the conclusion of the evidence for the prosecution Mr. Gwatkin asked that Stockwell should be committed not only on the charge of murdering and robbing Mr. Hoard but also for the attempted murder of Mrs. Hoard. Mr. Levy objected. He contended that there was no proof that Mrs. Hoard (who is still in hospital) would be able to give evidence, and that there was not sufficient evidence to commit on the charge of attempted murder. The Magistrate overruled the objection, and committed Stockwell for trial at the Central Criminal Court on the three charges. Stockwell pleaded 'Not Guilty,' and reserved his defence.

The Times, September 19, 1934

John Frederick Stockwell, 19, was executed at Pentonville Prison yesterday for the murder of Mr. Dudley Hoard, manager of the Palace Cinema Bow, E.

The Times, November 15, 1934

Steve Fielding decribes how the murderer was caught in *The Hangman's Record, Volume Three*: 'A list of current and former employees contained the name of John Stockwell who was found to be missing from his lodgings. A letter bearing a Lowestoft postmark reached detectives which suggested that Stockwell had committed suicide by drowning. Unfortunately for Stockwell, his clothes were discovered on the beach before the letter reached the police and, to add to his misfortune, he signed the hotel register in his hideaway as "J. F. Smith, Luton, Hertfordshire". The manager, who was suspicious of the young man, knew that Luton was in Bedfordshire and informed the police that one of his guests might be the wanted murderer. Stockwell was arrested in his hotel room and on the journey back to London he made a full confession. He pleaded guilty at his trial before Mr Justice Goddard at the Old Bailey on October 22. Prior to his execution Stockwell said to his girlfriend: "I can't imagine what made me do it except that I wanted money to get on in the world." Stockwell was hanged by Robert Baxter and Robert Wilson.'

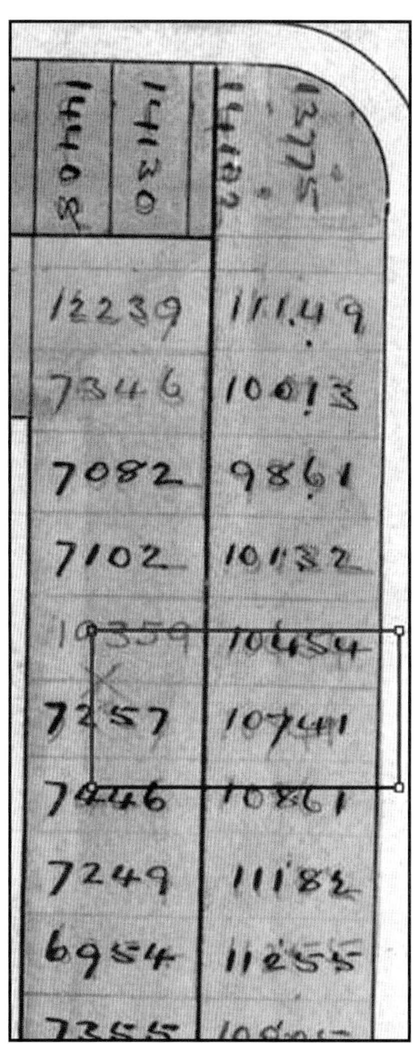

It has been so sad to find the graves of so many murder victims unmarked and Dudley Hoard was no exception. His grave in Croydon Cemetery in Mitcham Road, Croydon, also contains Oscar Lister who died in June 1919, Dudley, and his wife Jane who joined her husband in January 1947. Also Mary White who passed away in 1965. With nothing to identify its precise position, we had to resort to the cemetery plan *(left)* to pinpoint Grave No. 10741 in Plot J.

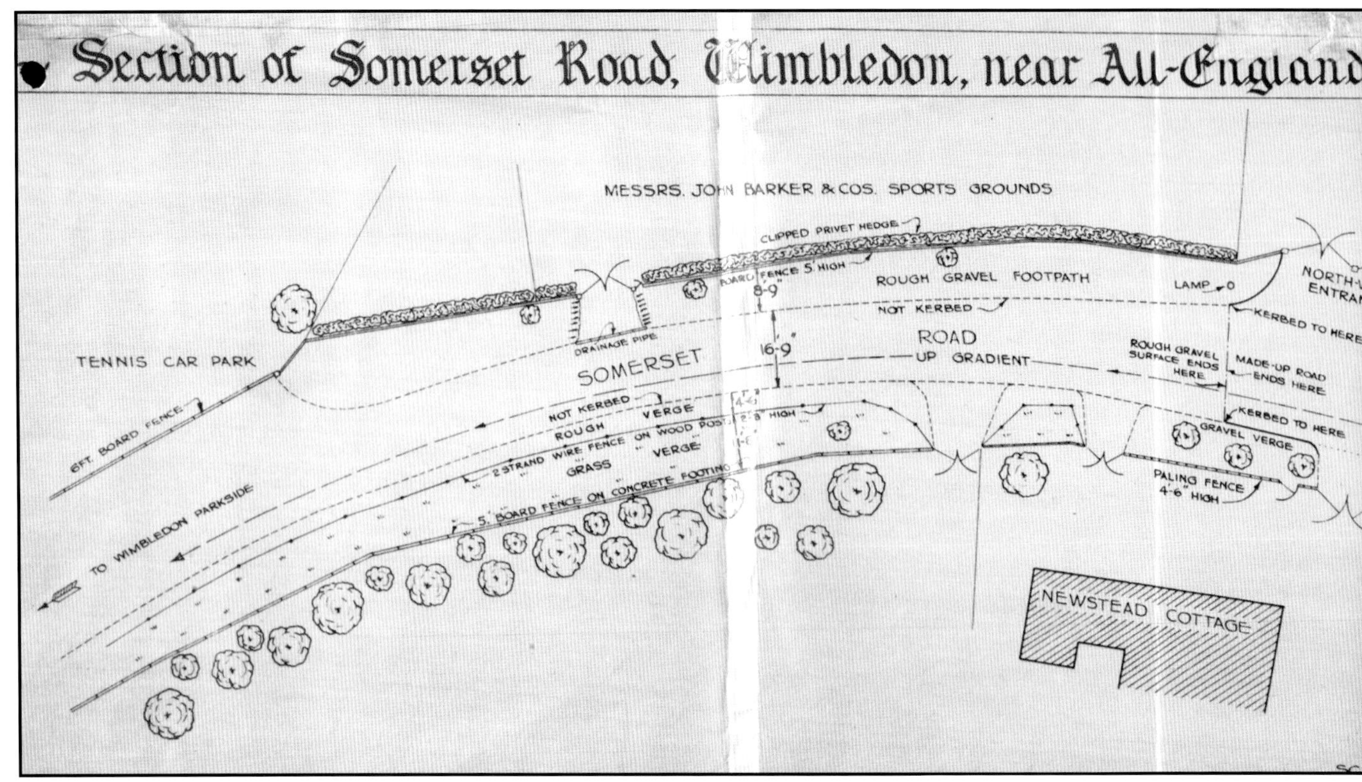

July 14, 1938 — The 'Lovers' Lane' Murder

George Brain, appeared at Wimbledon Police Court yesterday on the 'Lovers' Lane' murder charge. He was remanded for a week after evidence about his arrest had been given.

Brain, twenty-seven-year-old van driver, was silent when the charge was read to him: 'That you did wilfully and feloniously murder Rose Muriel Atkins, aged thirty, between 11.30 p.m. on July 13 and 12.10 a.m. on July 14, at Somerset-road, Wimbledon.'

Divisional Detective Inspector John Henry said that at 1 a.m. on July 14 he went with Detective Inspector Philpott to Somerset-road and in the roadway saw the body of a woman since identified as Rose Muriel Atkins.

The officer continued: 'I caused certain extensive inquiries to be made and as a result at 7.30 p.m. yesterday, with Inspector Philpott and Detective Sergeant McGrath I saw the prisoner detained at the police station, Sheerness, Kent.

When he was cautioned Brain said "Yes I understand. I will speak the truth. It's the best way.' He then made a statement under a written caution.

Daily Express, July 27, 1938

I wish to tell the truth as to what happened. I met the girl several months ago. I have seen her about four times altogether.

On Wednesday night I picked up with her at the corner of the road. I had the firm's van with me. The question of money was not raised, but she got into the van.

She said, 'I am in financial difficulties and want some money.' I told her, 'You will not get much out of me'. She said she would report me about having the firm's van out late at night if I did not give her money.

I said 'Don't be silly.' I struck her with my hand. She started to scream and then everything went blank. I hit her with the starting handle which I kept in the van. When I came to there was her body in the van.

I turned down the road and left her body on the side of the road. I then drove home. The next morning I gave the van a good wash. There were some rags in the van and I poured petrol on them and burned them.

I found the girl's handbag and I opened it. There was about four shillings in it. I took it out and hid the handbag behind some boards in the washhouse. I had a knife, and this I hid on an iron beam.

I later drove the van to Frost's house. I went to Camberwell Green, walked through to Sheerness and have since been sleeping on the cliff until I was picked up by the police.

Daily Express, August 2, 1935

Metropolitan Police, Station 'V' Division, July 28, 1938: 'The deceased woman was Rose Muriel Atkins, neé Rose Miriam Burden. Formerly a domestic servant, she married George Robert Atkins, an ex-soldier, on 7th April, 1928, at the Clapham Junction Register Office. They lived at various addresses in Lambeth, Peckham and Tooting and there are two children of the union, a boy — Cecil George — born on 17th May, 1929, and a girl — Rose Lavinia — born in October 1931. Mrs. Atkins was employed as a counter-hand at Lyons Corner House, Coventry Street, London, and for a time the family was a happy one. Then the deceased commenced to stay out at nights and her husband suspected her of going with men. This was in the beginning of January, 1934. Trouble ensued between them. A climax was reached in July 1934 when Mrs. Atkins left her husband and children. This was whilst they were living at Albert Mansions, Rosetta Street, South Lambeth. A month after she had left her husband, Mrs. Atkins broke into his flat and took their marriage and the children's birth certificates. Mr. Atkins saw his wife once only after her departure. This was some two years ago in Long Road, Clapham Common. She was joined by a man who stated he was living with her. (This was Frank Saich, Criminal Record Office No. 6382/32.). Her husband saw no more of her until he identified her dead body on Saturday, 16th July, 1938, at the Wimbledon Mortuary. In the meantime, Mrs. Atkins led the life of a prostitute. She lived with many men — some who appeared to have lived on her earnings — and took on several names and sobriquets. She became known as Mrs. Mullens, Barton, Saish, Moore and Brown. To her associates she was known familiarly as 'Irish Rose' and 'Pat'. She resorted to soliciting motorists in the vicinity of Parkside, Wimbledon, and at the time she met her death she was living with William Brown, C.R.O. No. 16834/32, known as 'Frank'. They were known as Mr. and Mrs. Frank Brown and had a flat at 196, Putney Bridge Road, S.W.15. Such was the sordid life of Rose Muriel Atkins. Despite her shocking mode of living, her death was a cruel one.'

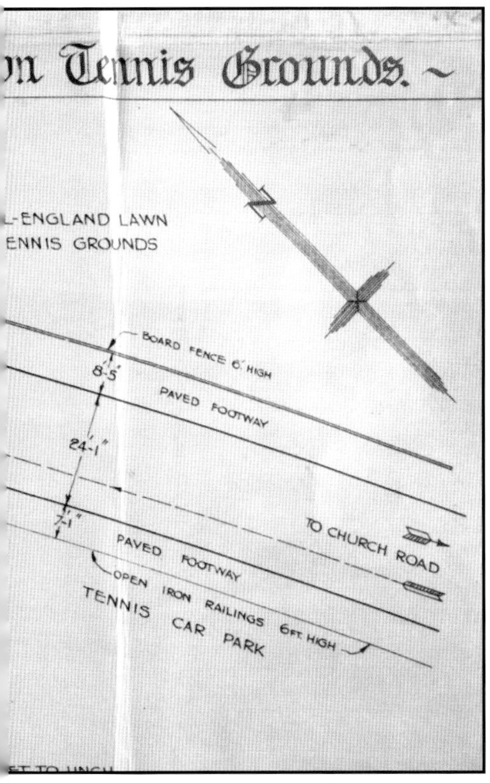

This is Hart's delivery van in which Rose Atkins was battered to death. George Brain was allowed to use it for travelling from his home in Richmond to his place of work in the West End. On the evening of July 13, 1938 he drove two workmates to their homes in Richmond. The following day Brain picked up Bill Frost from Twickenham who noticed that the inside of the van had been washed and the same day Brain was seen burning something in a dustbin. The next day he told Frost he was going to clear out and when he failed to turn up for work, Hart's got in touch with the police.

At 2.40 a.m. on the 14th. July, 1938, I attended Somerset Road, Wimbledon, where I saw the dead body of Rose Muriel Atkins. She was lying on the west side of the road. Her head was on the grass verge and her feet towards the centre of the road. The body was lying due East and West. On instructions I have prepared a scale plan twenty feet to the inch, shewing a section of Somerset Road where the body was lying.

Charles Deighton, PC 646, August 9, 1938

Brain had bludgeoned Rose to death with the starting handle and then ran over her body to make it look as if she was the victim of a road accident. ***Above:*** **Police described Somerset Road as the local 'Lovers Lane' a quiet road which runs from Church Road, Wimbledon Park through and up past the south-east side of the All England Lawn Tennis Club — as it still does today** ***(right)*** **— but then it was bounded mostly by fields. The scene of the murder was at the foot of a sharp incline and it was reported that this was the spot where she usually took her clients for sexual intercourse.**

As Rose had been seen climbing into a green van, and the tyre marks on her legs matched those on Austins and Morrises, the police began contacting the owners of all similar vehicles. Hart's responded and told police that two days after the murder, their van had disappeared along with the driver George Brain who lived at 18 St James Cottages at Richmond. Ten days later the vehicle was located containing Rose's handbag and bloodstains indicated that she had been killed inside. Two weeks later Brain was recognised and arrested at Sheerness in Kent. He was executed by Tom Pierrepoint and Stanley Cross.

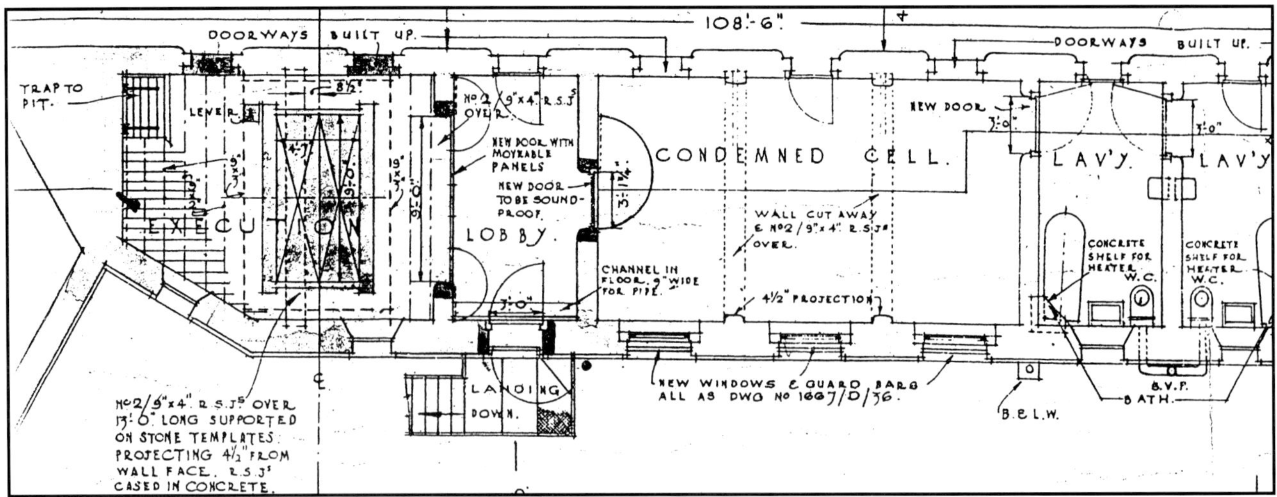

And this is where Brain met his end . . . Wandsworth Prison in South London. In 1937 there were no executions so the opportunity was taken to install a purpose-built execution suite at the end of E Wing to replace that of 1911 (see page 83). The new arrangement occupied three floors and one entire landing on E2 *(above)*. **A man under sentence of death would be brought to the condemned cell via an outer metal staircase. On entering the prison he would turn right into the large condemned cell [1] which had been created by knocking three cells into one. This is the sealed up doorway [2] The cell with the gallows [4] was hidden by a partition made of removable panels** *(below left)* **fitted with coat hooks disguising the lobby [3] as a cloakroom. There was a second condemned cell alongside the first and visiting facilities on the same floor. Under the trapdoors was the pit on level E1 into which the man dropped and which was accessible by the stairway seen in the corner of the photo** *(below right)*.

At an execution officers would stand on scaffold boards placed on either side of the prisoner in case he needed supporting. Hand ropes were supplied to help steady the officers.

The apparatus for lengthening or shortening the drop, designed to snap, not strangle, the person's neck, was via a chain fitted to a supporting beam which was accessed on level E3.

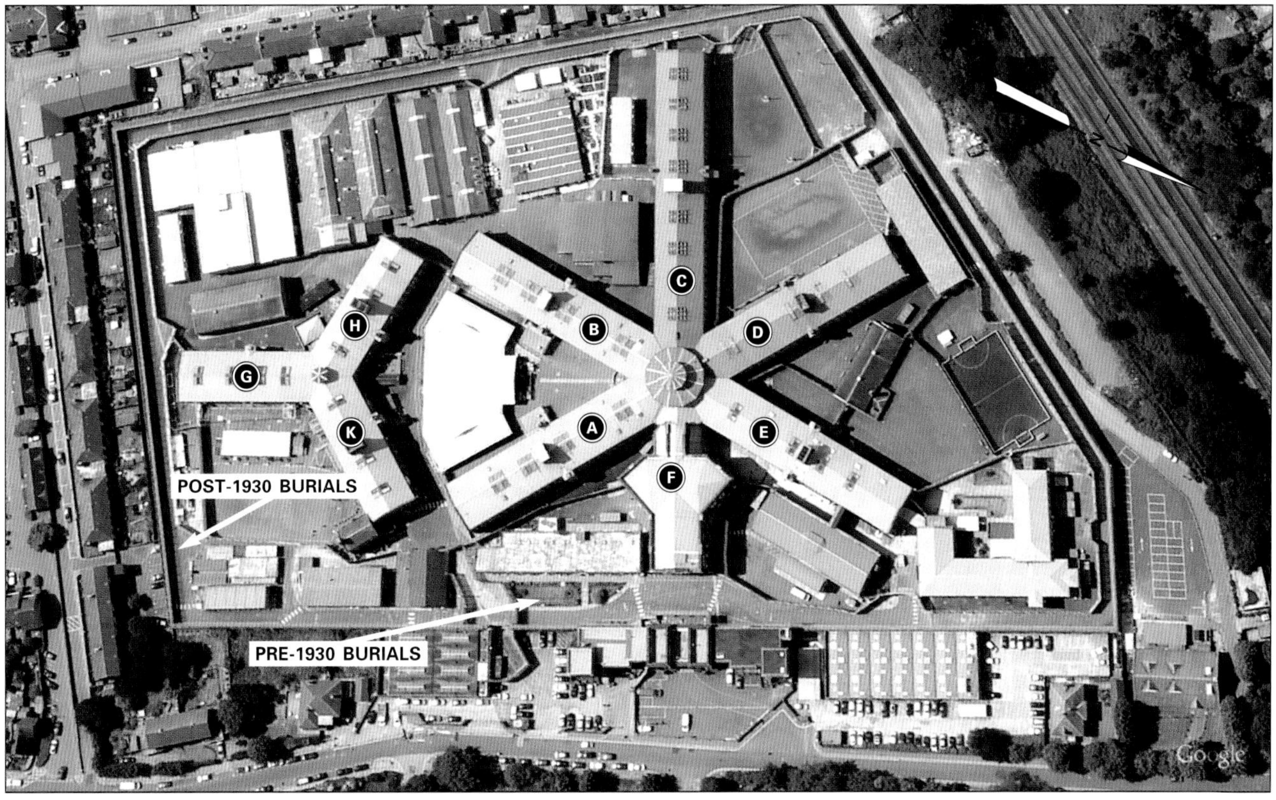

The prison was built in 1851, initially as the Surrey House of Correction, like Pentonville (see pages 114-115) on the principle of several wings radiating from a central control point.

Executed prisoners were buried within the prison although since the ending of capital punishment several have been exhumed for reburial like O'Sullivan and Dunn (see page 62).

Although the abolition of the Death Penalty Act in 1965 ended hanging for murder, the gallows were still maintained as arson in Royal Navy dockyards, piracy and high treason still remained capital offences. Further debate on the reintroduction of the death penalty took place in Parliament in 1988 although the measure was defeated by 341 votes to 218. Two years later it was put to the vote again, the Commons rejecting restoration by 350 votes to 215. In 1998 the death penalty was abolished for crimes committed under military jurisdiction and in July that year treason and piracy ceased to be capital crimes. The execution suite at Wandsworth had already been dismantled in 1992. The condemned cell was converted into a staff rest room (see page 279), the lobby and gallows into an office and a stationery store. The trapdoors and lever have been preserved at the Galleries of Justice in Nottingham and officer Stewart McLaughlin has set up a small museum alongside the prison. Here he demonstrates one of the restraining straps and an execution box containing the ropes and other impedimenta used to carry out an execution.

March 13, 1940 — The Shooting of Sir Michael O'Dwyer

Sir Michael O'Dwyer, Governor of the Punjab at the time of the Amritsar 'massacre' in 1919 was shot dead in full view of 180 people in London yesterday afternoon.

Just as a lecture in Caxton Hall, S.W., held by the East India Association and the Royal Central Asian Society, was about to end, six reports startled the audience. Sir Michael fell dead, with two bullets through his heart.

The Marquis of Zetland, Secretary of State for India, who was presiding toppled from his chair, wounded in the ribs; Lord Lamington, seventy-nine-year-old ex-Governor of Bombay, had part of his right hand shattered; and Sir Louis Dane, eighty-four-years-old, whom Sir Michael succeeded in the Governorship of the Punjab, was shot in the arm.

The meeting had been called to hear an address on Afghanistan by Brig.-General Sir Percy Sykes. It was held in the oak-panelled Tudor room of Caxton Hall, on the first floor, in which distinguished people are married.

On a three-foot high platform was a small table at which sat Lord Zetland and Lord Lamington. Sir Michael and Sir Louis were in the front row of seats in the body of the hall.

Suddenly, above the clatter of the people pushing their chairs aside as the meeting ended at 4.30 came the rattle of the shots in quick succession. They were fired at point-blank range, some five or six feet from the side of the room close to the Press table.

For the few moments that Sir Michael lived after the bullets struck him, a woman, who declined to give her name, bent over and comforted him.

Lord Zetland, grazed by one of the bullets, fell from the platform to the floor. Colonel Reinhold, a retired member of the Indian Medical Service ran to help him, Lord Lamington and Sir Louis Dane.

Daily Express, March 14, 1940

Caxton Hall, Westminster, is better known to the public as the venue for celebrity weddings like that of Diana Dors on July 3, 1951. She was just 19 and already a film star, and in 1956 portrayed Ruth Ellis (see page 288) in *Yield to the Night*. Yet Caxton Hall had been a location for numerous political meetings going right back to the first by the Suffragette Movement in 1906. When it originally opened in 1883 it was as Westminster Town Hall and the Ministry of Information used the building during the Second World War, Winston Churchill holding press conferences there. Today the Grade II listed building has been converted into residential apartments,

Michael Francis O'Dwyer was the sixth son of a family of 14 children and was born in County Tipperary in Ireland. He passed an entrance examination to the Indian Civil Service in 1882; joined the service in India in 1885, and served in various positions until Lord Curzon selected him for a prominent post in the organisation of the new North-West Frontier Province and its separation from Punjab. Appointed Lieutenant Governor of Punjab in 1913 when he was created Knight Commander of the Star of India, Sir Michael was cautioned that the province would require very careful handling as it was a powderkeg waiting to explode. Riots broke out in April 1919 after Sir Michael expelled two Indian nationalists following the murder of several English residents. Banks and public buildings were set on fire and looted. Having imposed martial law, troops under Brigadier-General Reginald Dyer were despatched to Amritsar to restore order. On April 13, confronting a crowd of some 20,000 assembled on the Jallianwalla Bagh public square, Dyer ordered his men to open fire. The British reported that 379 civilians had been killed although other sources say the casualties could have totalled 1,500. One of those killed was the brother of Udham Singh — the man who sought vengeance eleven years later at Caxton Hall. Sir Michael defended the action of Dyer but he could not avoid responsibility for sending an aircraft to bomb and strafe civilians rioting at Gujranwala when at least a dozen people were killed. After the Punjab killings, Sir Michael was relieved of his office and later condemned at an official enquiry in 1920. Brigadier Dyer was also forced to retire and return to Britain.

I am the Secretary of State for India.

On Wednesday, 13th March, 1940, I attended the meeting of The East India Association held in conjunction with the Royal Central Asian Society at Caxton Hall, Westminster. The purpose of the meeting was to listen to a lecture on Afghanistan by Sir Percy Sykes. I took the Chair at the meeting which commenced at 3 p.m. and finished at approximately 4.30 p.m.

Amongst those present were Sir Michael O'Dwyer; Lord Lamington; Sir Louis Dane and Sir Frank Brown, the Secretary of the East India Association. Apart from the lecturer and myself the only speakers were Sir Michael O'Dwyer; Mrs. Malam; Sir Louis Dane and Lord Lamington.

At the conclusion of the meeting I was walking with Sir Frank Brown across the platform. I had just reached the edge of the platform when there was a flash and a report of a pistol quite close to me and I felt a blow on my left side. I staggered back to the chair on the platform and whilst doing so heard further shots. I could not see what happened for I was immediately helped into a recumbent position on the floor by some of those present and shortly afterwards I was carried out and conveyed to St. George's Hospital where the wound in my left side was dressed. I was also X-rayed and a bullet was found in my clothing and this was handed to me by one of the hospital attendants.

I did not see the person who fired the shot which caused my injuries. At the time of the explosion I was in conversation with Sir Frank Brown and I must have been standing quite close to the person who actually fired the shot.

It was the first shot which struck me and I saw nothing of the results of the further shots which I heard. I think I must have been dazed after the bullet struck me.

I can only add that during the meeting I noticed a tall man with a swarthy complexion standing against the wall on my left and at a distance of five or six yards from the platform. It was from the direction of where I had seen this man standing that I saw the flash and then felt the blow, but I cannot say if it was this man who fired the shot. I think I might recognise this man if I saw him again.

Statement by The Marquess of Zetland, March 13, 1940.

The House will be aware from the reports which have appeared in the Press that at the conclusion of a meeting held yesterday afternoon at the Caxton Hall under the auspices of the East India Association and the Royal Central Asian Society, several shots were fired by a man in the audience with the result that Sir Michael O'Dwyer was killed and the Secretary of State for India, Lord Lamington and Sir Louis Dane were wounded. An Indian named Udham Singh, who is believed to have been responsible for the outrage, was seized by members of the audience and handed over to the police and he has this morning been brought before the magistrate at Bow Street Police Court on a charge of

Also wounded by the gunman were the 2nd Marquess of Zetland *(left)*, the Secretary of State for India since 1935; Sir Louis Dane *(centre)*, Sir Michael's predecessor as Governor of Punjab 1908-13; and Lord Lamington, a previous Governor of Bombay.

murder. In these circumstances it would not be proper for me to make any comment on the facts of the case. I know however, that the House will wish to join me in expresing our deep sense of sympathy with Lady O'Dwyer and her family in the sudden and tragic loss which they have suffered. The House will also desire to extend to those who were wounded their good wishes for a rapid recovery. I understand that their injuries, happily, were not grave, and that all are making satisfactory progress.

Rt Hon Neville Chamberlain, March 14, 1940

At the end of a public meeting in connection with Indian affairs, held at Caxton Hall, Westminster, on March 13, an Indian who was present went berserk with a revolver among the big-wigs on the platform. He fired six times; twice at Sir Michael O'Dwyer, a former Lieutenant-Governor of the Punjab, twice at Lord Zetland, then Secretary of State for India; once each at Lord Lamington and Sir Louis Dane. Every bullet found its mark. Sir Michael O'Dwyer fell dead with two bullets in his back. The remaining three, like survivors in a game of Russian roulette, were astonished to find that, although they had all been hit and hurt, the bullets had bounced ineffectively off their bodies. Two men held down the lunatic who did it until the police arrived.

Robert Churchill's first thought was that the powder charge in the cartridges might have been deliberately reduced, perhaps by as much as three-quarters, to diminish the penetration force of the bullets. It would have suited the case for the defence, which was that the accused man only fired to make a demonstration. In the police court Churchill agreed that powder charges were often reduced 'for duelling purposes.' But it wasn't the answer in R. *v.* Udham Singh.

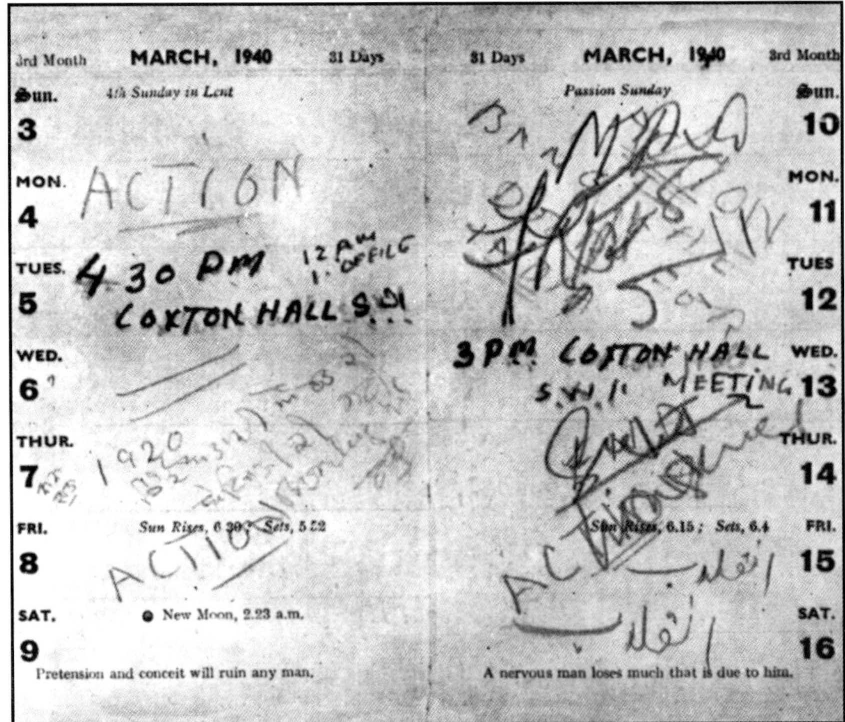

Sir Michael's diary entry for his meeting, the one at 3 p.m. on Wednesday 13th.

Neither was it the accused man's real name. Like so many of the prisoners in the Lahore Conspiracy Trial, the true identity of the man who brought drama to the staid surroundings of the Tudor Room at Caxton Hall remained as mysterious as his reasons for it.

He was arrested under the name of Singh Azad, he was tried as Udham Singh, and he was executed protesting that he was neither. His false names were part Sikh, part Moslem, part Hindu. His true identity was never discovered.

It was said in court that he had been involved in the Amritsar Riots in the Punjab in 1919, when his victim, Sir Michael

The police photograph of the chaos in the Tudor Room after the shooting. Unfortunately, the conversion of Caxton Hall into apartments by Southern Land resulted in this room being demolished with none of the panelling retained.

Singh Azad aka Udham Singh is escorted from the Tudor Room. He was executed at Pentonville on July 31 by Stanley Cross and Albert Pierrepoint.

The expertise of Robert Churchill was once again brought to bear at Singh's trial at which he demonstrated how unlucky Sir Michael had been to be killed by a shot from this particular pistol as it had been loaded with ammunition some 30 years old and of the wrong calibre.

O'Dwyer, was Lieutenant-Governor. But, as he gave his age as thirty-seven in 1940, it seems unlikely that he can have played a prominent part. His mental condition can be assessed from the disjointed statement he made during four hours' interrogation by the police when he was charged:

'I did it because I had a grudge against him. He deserved it. I don't belong to any society or anything else. I don't care. I don't mind dying. What is the use of waiting until you get old? That is no good. You want to die when you are young. That is good. That is what I am doing. I am dying for my country. Is Zetland dead? He ought to be. I put two into him. I bought the revolver from a soldier in a public house. My parents died when I was four or five. I had property which I sold. I had over £200 when I came to England. Only one dead, eh? I thought I could get more. I must have been too slow. There was a lot of womans about.'

When he was hanged at Pentonville on July 31, 1940, too much else was happening in the world for it to be noticed. There was scarcely enough space left in the newspapers to report why his gun behaved as it did. It was Hitler's summer. The case was a mere incident in the surge of world-shattering events.

Yet once again Churchill's evidence in the magistrates' court and the Old Bailey was memorable. He solved how the 'impossible' had occurred. The weapon, he said, was a six-chambered American Smith and Wesson, .455 calibre, made for the British Government in the First World War. It was a relic of which thousands had got into private hands. It was in working order; but the ammunition which Udham Singh used was of a smaller size than the barrel of the gun. It was .40 ammunition, uncommon in England, loaded with black powder and a pure lead bullet, and 'quite thirty years old.'

He explained that the cartridges were such a loose fit in the chamber of the revolver, and the bullet such a loose fit in the barrel of the gun, that when it was fired the bullet wobbled out without engaging the rifling grooves. The escape of the propellent gases around both the cases and the bullets was such that, with every round, accuracy and penetration were quite unpredictable.

One bullet, which had hit Lord Zetland over the heart, appeared to have cartwheeled through the air, penetrating ten thicknesses of handkerchief in his breast-pocket, 'key-holing' his shirt and under-vest with a sideways hit, and then dropped to the ground. Somebody picked it up afterwards. Sir Louis Dane's jacket had a bullet-hole in the right sleeve, but the projectile only penetrated the cloth. Yet the shots were all fired within eighteen inches.

When the trial was over Churchill told Mr R. L. Jackson who was briefed for the prosecution, that it was 'just rank bad luck that Sir Michael O'Dwyer caught one which flew straight and hard.' He might equally well have said that the other three could count their lucky stars. It's not often that a well-aimed bullet at close range has failed to hole the target.

Oddly enough, at the time Udham Singh murdered Sir Michael O'Dwyer one of our Intelligence Departments which included on its staff some of the toughest agents and some of the most miraculous pistol-shots in the world, was situated almost next door to Caxton Hall. The James Bonds there all regretted a missed opportunity!

Macdonald Hastings,
The Other Mr Churchill, 1963

On Saturday, March 16, 1940, Sir Michael was laid to rest in Brookwood Cemetery in Surrey (Plot 123, Row B, Grave 16), joined in November 1956 by his wife Dame Una.

Gordon Cummins was born in York on February 18, 1914 and enlisted in the RAF in November 1935. As AC2 Cummins, 525987, he was posted to No. 3 School of Technical Training (Men) in January 1936 and in March to No. 2 Technical Wing at the Home Aircraft Depot at Henlow Camp in Buckinghamshire. Before the war, his forte would appear to have been with the Marine Aircraft Experimental Establishment at Felixstowe (where he was promoted to AC1) and at Helensburgh. Having been raised to Leading Aircraftman on March 1, 1940, he was posted to Catterick to join No. 600 'City of London' Squadron in February 1941. When he was earmarked for pilot training, he was sent to be processed through the Air Crew Reception Centre based in Abbey Lodge *(right)*, St John's Wood, London on February 2, 1942.

February 1942 — The 'Black-out Ripper'

In the pitch-like darkness of the black-out which enveloped London in February 1942, terror stalked through the blitz-shattered streets of our city. It was not just the terror that rained from the sky as Hitler's Luftwaffe flew overhead to wreak his mission of hate upon Britain. It was the terror created by a ghoulish slayer who within four days strangled and mutilated four hapless women and attempted to murder two others.

Not since those panic-ridden days in 1888, when Jack the Ripper was abroad in the East End, had London known such a reign of terror as that which existed in that war-time February, when, night after night, death—fiendish, revolting, and gruesome, came to four unsuspecting women in the heart of the Metropolis.

There was no inkling of the orgy of murder which was to follow when, in the early hours of February 9, 1942, the body of Miss Evelyn Hamilton, a woman of irreproachable character, was found strangled in an air-raid shelter in Montagu Place, Marylebone. It was one of those ordinary surface shelters which lined the streets in those days, brick-built, with a seat along one side. The dead woman was a chemist's assistant who had not long before resigned her post as manageress of a shop at Hornchurch, Essex, and had come to stay in the Marylebone area of London.

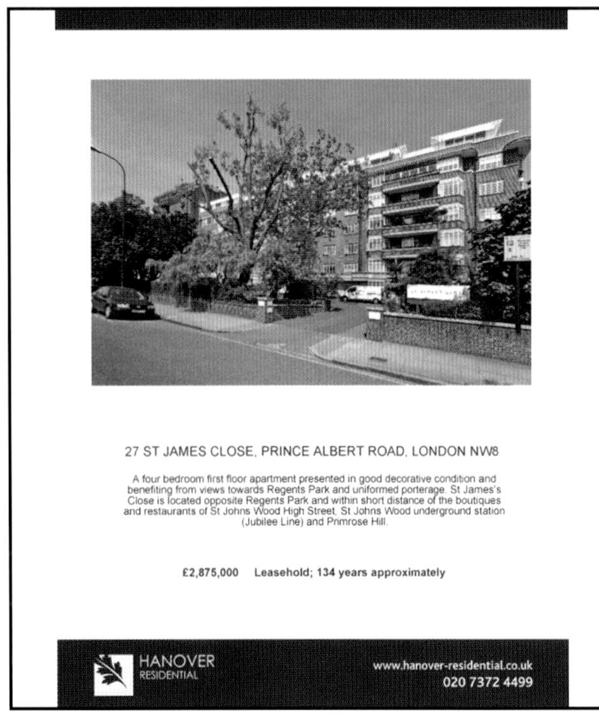

27 ST JAMES CLOSE, PRINCE ALBERT ROAD, LONDON NW8
A four bedroom first floor apartment presented in good decorative condition and benefiting from views towards Regents Park and uniformed porterage. St James's Close is located opposite Regents Park and within short distance of the boutiques and restaurants of St Johns Wood High Street, St Johns Wood underground station (Jubilee Line) and Primrose Hill.
£2,875,000 Leasehold; 134 years approximately
HANOVER
RESIDENTIAL
www.hanover-residential.co.uk
020 7372 4499

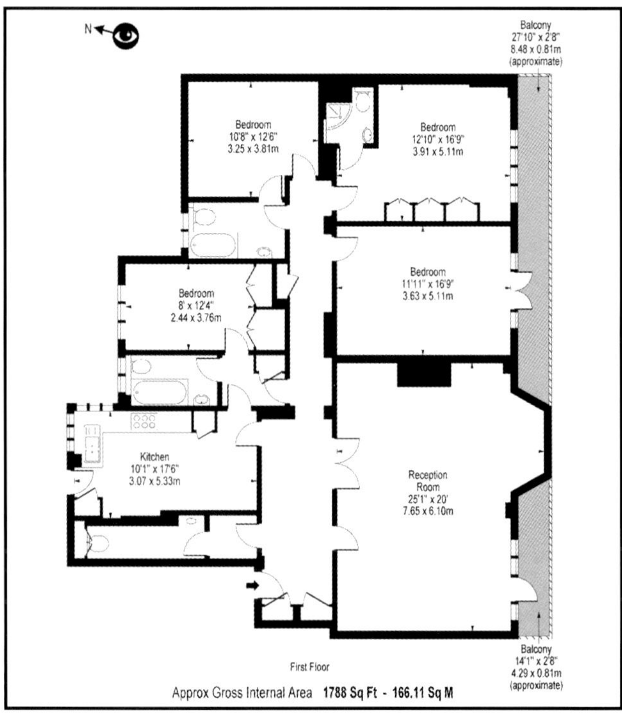

Cummins was quartered in a nearby block of flats at St James's Close and when we went to take the photo, one can imagine our amazement when his particular billet — No. 27 — which he shared with five other airmen, was up for sale!

The lure of London's West End and the fleshpots of Soho were a magnet and much use was made of the fire escape to return to the billet unseen by the Orderly Sergeant following after hours nefarious activities by all the cadets.

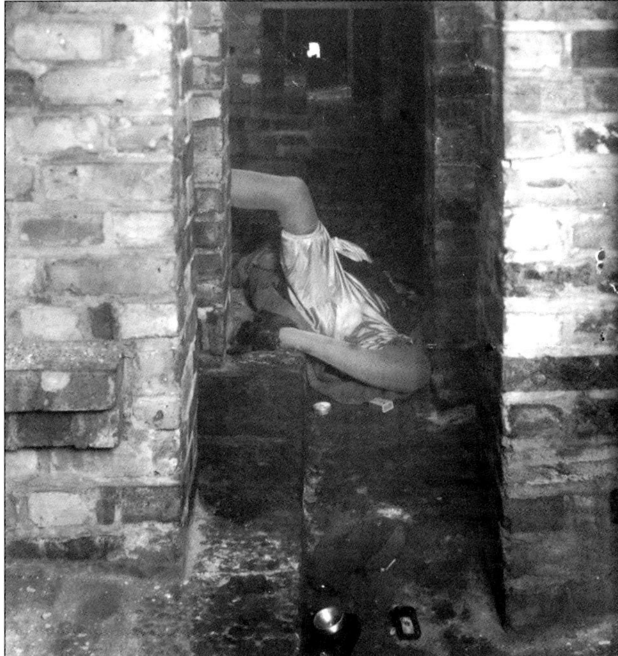

Evelyn Hamilton had been employed as a chemist's assistant in Hornchurch but on Sunday, February 8 she left with the intention of travelling to Grimsby the following day. Around 10.30 p.m. she booked a room for the night at 76 Gloucester Place but went out almost at once for something to eat at the Lyons Corner House at Marble Arch. She failed to return and just after 8.30 a.m. her dead body was discovered in an air raid shelter near to where she was staying. Divisional Detective Inspector Leonard Clare was on the scene at 8.55 a.m. together with Detective Inspector Fleshney. PC 185 Knowles and 437 Miles were already present at the shelter with the 5D Area Car.

When I arrived at Montagu Place it looked to me as though the body had been hurriedly pushed through the narrow door of the shelter after strangulation. It lay upon the floor against the seat, face upward. Round the mouth and nose the murderer had wound tightly the woman's own silk scarf as a gag. Her clothes were disarranged and a hat lay near by. At her side were a matchbox and a powder-compact, which had been turned out of her handbag. A foot or two away was an electric torch which she doubtless carried to light her on her way through the black-out.

What interested me most, however, were marks on the victim's throat. In the dim light of the shelter they appeared to have been made by the fingers of the murderer. From their position I rapidly made another deduction, and said to myself: 'This seems to have been a left-handed job'.

Under a powerful light and with the aid of my hand-lens I made a close and minute examination of the marks in the hope that the murderer might have left some trace of his fingers — no matter how small — that would assist in deciding whose hands had choked the life out of this poor victim.

Luck was against me in this respect for the marks were only bruises, but they enabled me to confirm my first impression that they had been made by the left hand of the strangler, whoever he might be. I was no more fortunate with the handbag and its contents, for the only finger-marks upon them were those of the dead woman.

'Inside the centre shelter *(below left)*, at the entrance nearest Gloucester Place, I saw the body of a woman lying on her back in the gutter of the roadway which runs through the shelter. Her feet were pointing in the direction of Gloucester Place. Her right leg was raised, resting on some brickwork in the corner of the shelter and her left leg was lying on the ground in the entrance. Her head was turned slightly to the left and a scarf was lying loosely over her face.'

The shelter stood here on the southern side of Montagu Place between Gloucester Place and Gloucester Place Mews. There were three separate shelters, built partly on the footpath and partly on the road. Rob Green stands in front of the centre shelter (B.147) where Miss Hamilton's body was found.

Setting the scene in Soho. Although this picture was taken in 1947, we are in Wardour Street, just a few yards from where the next murder took place. The pub on the corner of Peter Street is the Intrepid Fox, occupying Nos. 97 to 99. Evelyn Oatley's room was located on the same side of the road but further along at No. 153.

Evelyn earned her living by prostitution using the name Lila or Nita Ward. She was last seen alive about 11.10 p.m. on Monday, February 9. She occupied the front room on the first floor of No. 153 Wardour Street and her body was found there the following morning by two men who arrived to check the electric meter. In this case it was Detective Inspector Clarence Jeffery who arrived on the scene at 9 a.m. 'I saw the body of a woman lying across a divan bed. A cushion was on the floor beneath her head. There was a severe wound in the right side of her throat and signs of severe bleeding. She was almost nude but was wearing a vest and nightdress which had been rolled up over her breasts, the lower parts of which were just shewing. Doctor Baldie, Divisional Surgeon, was present. The black-out blinds, which had been drawn, were opened to show light for the benefit of the Divisional Surgeon. I immediately caused a message to be sent to Superintendent Cherrill, Finger Print Department, and Detective Inspector Percy Law, Photographic Section.'

I had only just reached my office at the Yard the next morning, February 10, when a message came over the 'phone asking me to go at once to a flat in Wardour Street, where a Mrs Evelyn Oatley (also known at Nita Ward) had been found murdered.

On my arrival I entered the bedroom. Lying across a bed, consisting of nothing but a flock mattress, with not even a sheet as covering, was the almost nude body of a woman. She was a ghastly sight as she had been the victim of a sadistic attack of the most horrible and revolting nature.

There were scarcely any signs of disorder in the room itself, articles on a table beside the bed being undisturbed. Some stockings hung upon a rail at the head of the bed, and, but for the still, dead figure of the murdered woman, there was little to show that anything untoward had taken place in that room. Near the body of the dead woman lay a pair of curling-tongs and a blood-stained tin-opener. The latter was evidently the weapon with which the murderer had so wantonly mutilated his victim. At one side of the room was a couch, on which I found a woman's handbag. It was open, as if the contents had fallen out, but inside was a piece of mirror.

After a minute examination of the room and its contents I took possession of the tin-opener and the piece of mirror. To me these were very interesting exhibits, for upon that bit of looking-glass, into which the dead woman had doubtless looked a hundred times in the process of beautifying herself, I detected what I knew to be a thumbprint. I soon ascertained that it had not been made by the dead woman, and I assumed that it had been made by the murderer when he was turning out the handbag.

On the handle of the tin-opener I also discovered faint impressions of fingers. They had been made by a left hand, and were not in such a position that they could have come there by the innocent use of this utensil. Indeed, they were so arranged that I decided this improvised weapon had been grasped in the left hand of the murderer during his attack on the woman. Moreover, certain aspects of the print on the mirror indicated to me that it had been made by a left thumb.

Were there any records in our files of corresponding prints?' If so, it need be a matter only of minutes, perhaps, before a nationwide search for the man who had made it could be set in motion. Alas, once more the fates were against us. The killer of Mrs Oatley had no criminal record. He had never been in the hands of the police.

No. 153 Wardour Street has since been demolished to be replaced by this ubiquitous office block.

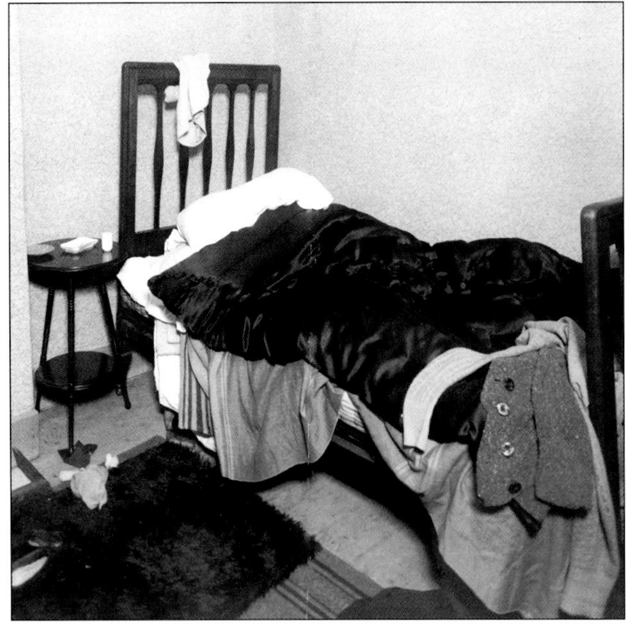

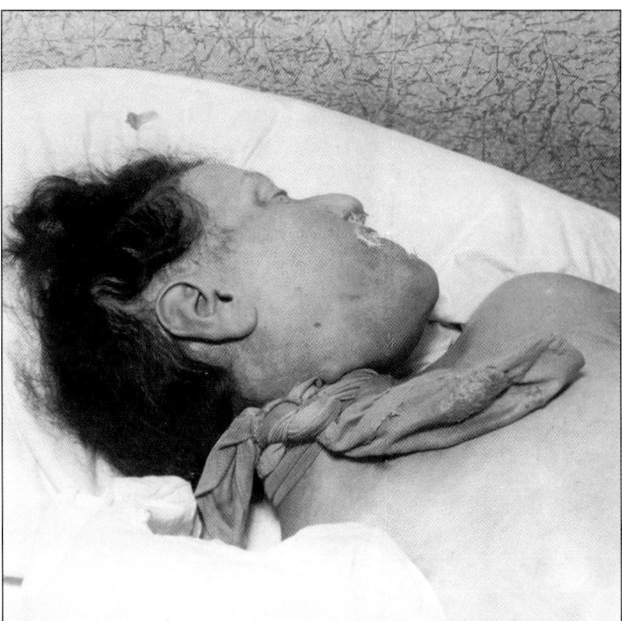

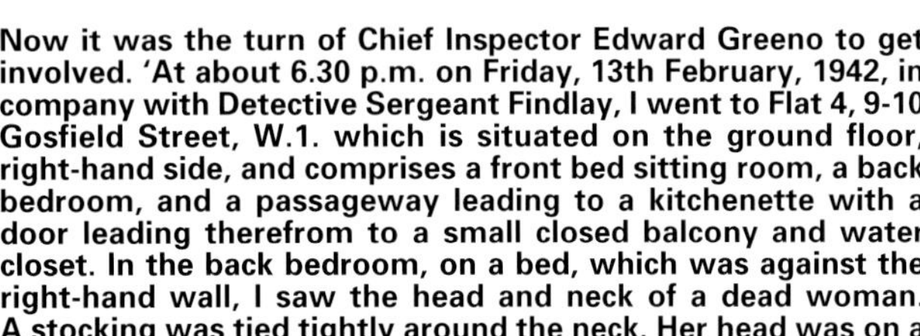

Now it was the turn of Chief Inspector Edward Greeno to get involved. 'At about 6.30 p.m. on Friday, 13th February, 1942, in company with Detective Sergeant Findlay, I went to Flat 4, 9-10 Gosfield Street, W.1. which is situated on the ground floor, right-hand side, and comprises a front bed sitting room, a back bedroom, and a passageway leading to a kitchenette with a door leading therefrom to a small closed balcony and water closet. In the back bedroom, on a bed, which was against the right-hand wall, I saw the head and neck of a dead woman. A stocking was tied tightly around the neck. Her head was on a pillow and turned to the left. A fair amount of foam was adhering to the nostrils and mouth and there was also a little blood present in the foam. The face was livid and death by strangulation was apparent. The knot of the ligature around the neck was on the right side under the angle of the right jaw. The body was covered with bedclothes consisting of an eiderdown bedspread, three blankets and one sheet. I turned back the top bed clothes and found the body of a female, I now know to be that of Margaret Florence Lowe. The body was lying on its back and was naked.'

Two days went by — two days during which Yard men followed up every slender clue in their possession in an effort to find the strangler of Evelyn Hamilton and the sadistic 'ripper' who had murdered Mrs Oatley.

The husband of the latter was traced to Blackpool and was able to prove that he and his wife had separated by mutual agreement some time before, and were living apart. A woman in the next room to Mrs Oatley described how she saw the latter enter the house with a man about 11.15 p.m., and heard voices and the wireless.

Evelyn Oatley had once been a promising young actress on the London stage, but, with the outbreak of war, engagements became few, and she drifted into the life which was destined to end in tragedy. Already the reports of these two crimes, coming so quickly one upon the other, had aroused a feeling of alarm among the people of London. As women passed through the lightless streets at nights on the way to their regular air raid shelters, they looked apprehensively around them, wondering whether the silent and elusive murderer might be lurking in some door or alleyway ready to pounce upon another victim.

Nor was this alarm lessened when the evening papers of February 13 came out with the startling news that another woman had been found strangled and mutilated in a flat at Gosfield Street, just off the Tottenham Court Road.

The discovery was made by a neighbour of the dead woman. The victim was Mrs Margaret Lowe, a handsome and finely built woman who was known locally as 'Pearl'. The neighbour noticed that a parcel lying outside the door of the flat had not been taken in and therefore notified the police. The door of the flat was forced and the tragedy revealed in all its stark and vivid horror. In a scantily-furnished room, almost bare except for a single bed set lengthwise against a wall, an occasional table, a small carpet, a rug, and a chair or two, death had come to Margaret Lowe.

At first sight on entering the room there was no sign of the gruesome work which had been carried out by the sex-mad murderer. On the black eiderdown near the foot of the bed lay a woman's coat, skirt, and jumper, where they had been hurriedly flung down by their owner. Lying on the floor was a gay little hat with a feather, while on the mantelpiece stood a glass candlestick and a tumbler containing a liquid which looked like beer.

A sinister hump in the eiderdown gave an inkling of what lay beneath. There was an unnatural stillness about it. When the bedclothes were pulled back the nude dead body of Margaret Lowe was revealed. Round her neck was tightly knotted a much-darned silk stocking but it was not these things which attracted my eye so much as the vicious mutilations which had been wreaked upon the dead woman, and which were even more shocking than those inflicted upon Mrs Oatley. This, and the small armoury of weapons with which the mutilations had been inflicted.

A rapid survey of the room showed me that a candle had been wrenched from the glass candlestick on the mantelpiece. This candle appeared incongruous against the collection of sinister-looking implements surrounding the body. Yet that innocent-looking object was destined to lead to the identification of the murderer of Mrs Lowe for it directed my attention to the candlestick from which it had been torn. There were finger-impressions upon the base of it.

After examining the room where the body lay I went to the kitchen at the rear of the premises, where I found a bottle of stout. Some of the contents had been drunk. There were fingermarks on the bottle, and I came to the conclusion that the beer in the glass on the bedroom mantelpiece had been poured from this bottle.

As he describes in this chapter, Scotland Yard's fingerprint expert, Chief Superintendent Fred Cherrill was now amassing evidence to track down the killer.

I took possession of the glass candlestick, together with the tumbler and bottle. The marks on the candlestick were of particular interest to me as they were prints of the fingers of a right hand. By means of a rapidly conducted experiment, placing myself in the position of the murderer, I was satisfied that a *right*-handed person, in snatching the candle from the candlestick, would naturally place his *left* hand on the base, using his right hand to grasp the candle. The process would be reversed in the case of a *left-handed* person, so that once more it appeared that a left-handed person had been at work.

If this deduction proved correct, in view of the similarity in the mode of killing and the nature of the injuries inflicted, it appeared likely — in fact, almost certain — that the two murders, those of Mrs Oatley and Mrs Lowe, were the work of one and the same left-handed man. It also struck me at this time that the same person might have strangled Miss Evelyn Hamilton, the victim of the air raid shelter crime on whose throat I had detected the finger-marks of a left hand.

In view of these premises, it may appear something of a paradox that I should make another check-up on the newly discovered prints, for were not the impressions found in the flat of Mrs Oatley available for comparison with those which I had now obtained from articles in Mrs Lowe's flat? Would not such a comparison either confirm or disprove my suspicions? They might do, but, on the other hand, they might not. A comparison of the prints in both places would not settle the matter one way or the other, for the simple reason that although they might well be the prints of the same man, they might be the marks of *different fingers*.

That is why I carried out a further search in our records for any prints corresponding to those found in Mrs Lowe's flat only to come up against the same apparently impenetrable barrier. The search proved negative.

It now seemed pretty certain that a killer was abroad who murdered not only for gain - — in each case the handbags of the murdered women had been rifled — but in order to indulge a wicked and insensate lust to perpetrate the most diabolical injuries upon the women he killed.

It was at 6.30 on the evening of February 13 that I went to Mrs Lowe's flat in Gosfield Street, the murder having actually taken place on the 12th. Having completed my fingerprint investigations there I returned to the Yard. The time was then about 10.30 p.m., and I was just preparing to go home when the telephone-bell in my office rang again.

I lifted the receiver. 'Fingerprint Office', I said, in what sounded to me a rather tired voice. And then came this: 'Will you go at once to Sussex Gardens, Paddington? Another woman has been found murdered.'

It only needs a message like this to snap one out of all sense of weariness. In a matter of minutes I was on my way to carry out a second murder investigation, within a few hours of the other, and both on the same day.

The victim was a Mrs Doris Jouannet, the wife of a London hotel manager. He usually slept at the hotel but saw his wife daily at their flat in Sussex Gardens. On the night of the tragedy he had supper with his wife and she accompanied him to Paddington Station. But let Mr Jouannet tell his own story.

'She wished me good-night very sweetly, and her last words to me were "Don't be late to-morrow, darling". I returned to the flat at seven o'clock on Friday night and was surprised to see that the milk had not been taken in. When I got into the flat I shouted out "Doris" but there was no reply. On going into the sitting-room I found that the supper things from the night before were still on the table, and the curtains had not been drawn. I was worried, and when I found the bedroom door locked I knew something was amiss. I could not get any reply, so I went to the housekeeper, and we sent for the police.'

Mr Jouannet described how the police burst open the door, and how a kindly constable held him back from entering the room of death with a gentle 'Don't go in, Sir' and then broke the news that his wife was dead. Thus it was only an hour or two after the body of Doris Jouannet was discovered that I was in the flat where she lay.

One glance was sufficient to tell me that the strangling 'ripper' had struck again. There was no doubt about it. He had left his signature to the atrocities as surely as if he had written his name. Around the neck of the woman was a tightly knotted stocking. Her body, clad only in a dressing-gown,

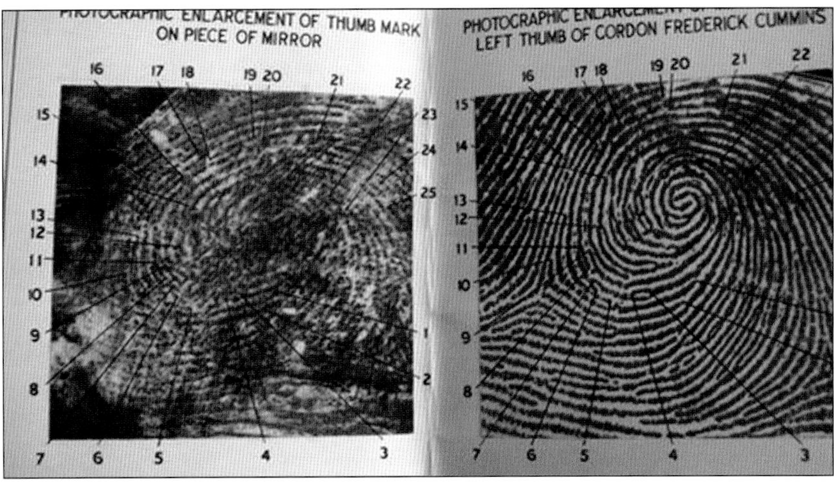

From Evelyn Oatley's room he obtained a print from a piece of mirror *(above)* **and from Margaret Lowe's candlestick** *(below)*.

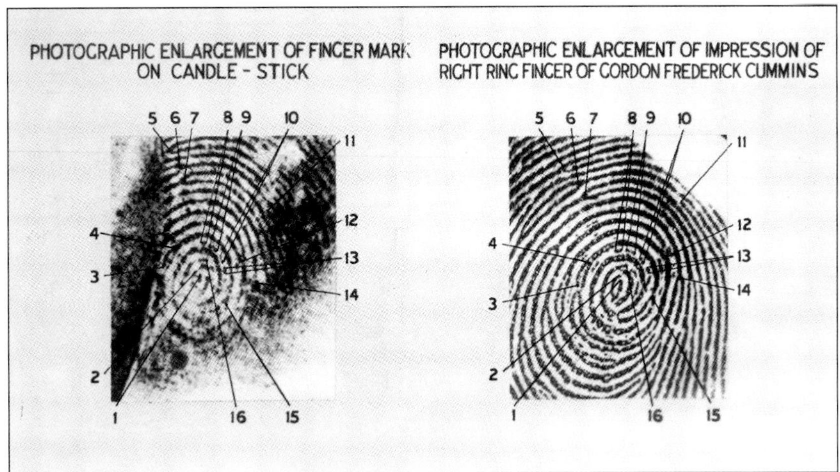

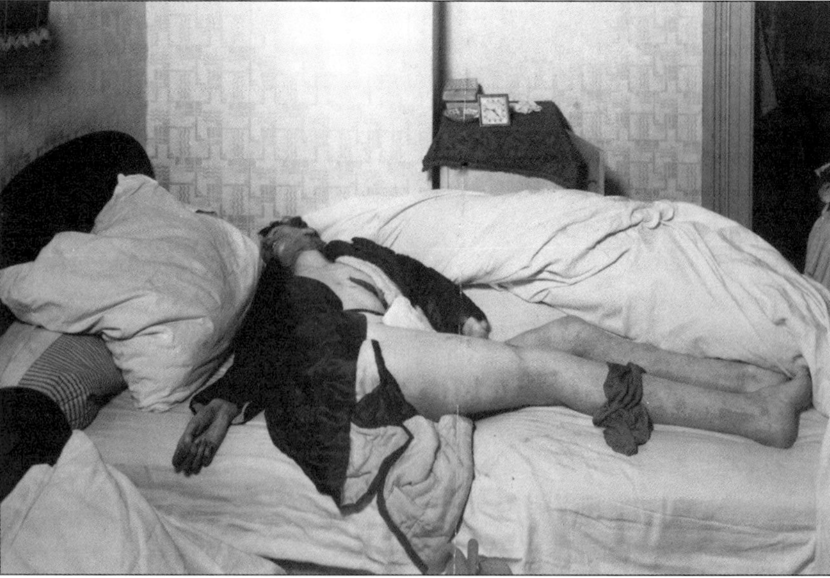

The next victim was Doris Jouannet who worked as a prostitute while her husband was occupied elsewhere managing a hotel. He had first met her in 1935 when she was soliciting in Oxford Street. On the evening of February 12 his wife walked with him to Paddington Underground Station from where he was to return to his hotel, following which Mrs Jouannet began to walk the streets. The next evening Mr Jouannet returned home to find his wife murdered. Detective Inspector Clare was on the scene in Sussex Gardens by 8 p.m. 'This address is a self-contained ground floor flat. Entrance to the flat is gained by a street door. There is no rear door to the premises and access to the rooms on the first floor and basement at No. 187 Sussex Gardens is gained from No. 189 Sussex Gardens. It will thus be seen that the ground floor flat at No. 187, is completely isolated from any other floor at the address. The premises consist of a front room, which is used as a dining room; a bedroom; lavatory; bathroom; kitchen and spare room. A passageway leads from the street door, to the rear of the premises and the rooms in the above order are on the right side of the passage. The door of the bedroom had to be forced.'

which had been dragged open in the frenzied lust of the murderer, was lying across a bed, the clothes of which had been flung back in haste by the killer after he had completed his crime. The body had been savagely slashed.

There had been no struggle. The murderer had worked swiftly and surely. The woman's clothes lay in a heap on a chair at the foot of the bed. A clock standing on a bedside table had stopped. It registered the time: 4.45.

I made an intensive search for fingerprints. On the door of a cupboard close to the bed I found several. I detected others on a hand-mirror lying on the dressing-table. From the dust on the latter I could see that some articles had recently been removed from it. On the door of the bedroom itself I found other impressions. I took possession of the mirror, and had the cupboard and bedroom doors removed and brought to the Yard for a more detailed and exhaustive examination. This time, however, the murderer had left behind no fingerprints of any value. All those which were identifiable belonged to the dead woman.

Such was the position on February 14 when the whole resources of Scotland Yard were mobilised to run this wholesale murderer to earth. At that time we were not absolutely certain that Evelyn Hamilton had met her death at the hands of the same person, although, as you will remember, I was convinced that her strangler was left-handed.

Women police in ordinary clothes — always under the alert and watchful eyes of Yard men — strolled about the streets of the West End in the hope of being accosted by the unknown killer. So great was the terror which swept like a wave over the square mile in which these crimes had been committed that the regular street-walkers who haunted the area were too scared to venture out. Small wonder, for nobody knew when or where the killer would strike next. That he would strike again seemed certain for the lust of killing appeared to have seized him in a merciless grip. And he did strike again though not with such fatal results.

On the night of February 12, within a few hours of the murders of Mrs Lowe and Mrs Jouannet, Mrs Greta Heywood was having a quiet drink in a public-house near Piccadilly when an air force cadet entered. He got into conversation with her, flourishing a wad of Treasury notes and made a certain suggestion which she rejected.

When she left he followed her into the darkened street, and, having caught up with her, pushed her into a doorway. 'You must let me kiss you good-night,' he said. He placed his gas-respirator on the ground and made as though to put his arm round her. Instead he seized her by the throat, maintaining his grip until she lost consciousness. One can only imagine what might then have happened but for the approach of a passer-by, who heard scuffling and saw a man disappear into the shadows. He then noticed Mrs Heywood lying on the ground. She was just regaining her senses. The stranger helped her to her feet and, when she gasped out the story of the attack upon her, he escorted her to the police station.

Chief Inspector Greeno described what they found: 'In the bedroom I saw two single beds to the left of the door, and on a bed nearest the left wall I saw the dead body of a woman I now know to be that of Doris Jouannet. The body was naked except for a black dressing gown, the front of which was open exposing the chest, stomach and legs. The bed clothing had been rolled back towards the wall. I examined the body and found that a silk texture lady's stocking was tied tightly round the neck, forming a ligature. The knot of the ligature was in the front slightly to the left of the point of the chin.'

On the evening of Saturday, February 12, an airman with a flash in his cap denoting he was aircrew under training, was having a drink at Piccadilly with Greta Heywood. He was pressing her for sex saying, 'All right, if you don't want to I can't make you but you are a nice girl and I do fancy you. I have been watching you and I like everything about you and I really do want you'. Greta replied: 'I'm sorry, it's no use. I don't do that sort of thing'. Greta later told police that 'We then left the Trocadero [1], the airman having picked up his gas mask which he carried in his hand until we got into the street, when he slung it over his left shoulder. It was then about 8.45 p.m. and he said, "I'll see you back to the Brasserie. We'll go in the Jermyn Street entrance". It was very dark and I took my torch from my handbag and switched it on but the airman said, "You don't want to use the torch" and took it from me and switched it off. We then went by way of Windmill Street across Piccadilly *(above left)*, along the west side of Haymarket *(below left)*, then turned right along the south side of Jermyn Street *(below right)*. I said, "You are taking me the wrong way round", and he said, "I want to kiss you Good Night. Aren't there any air raid shelters around here?". I said, "I don't know of any and in any case I wouldn't go in one with you".' *Above right:* Eros, boarded up during the war, was moved a few yards to the south to avoid sightseers risking their lives dodging the traffic to reach the Island.

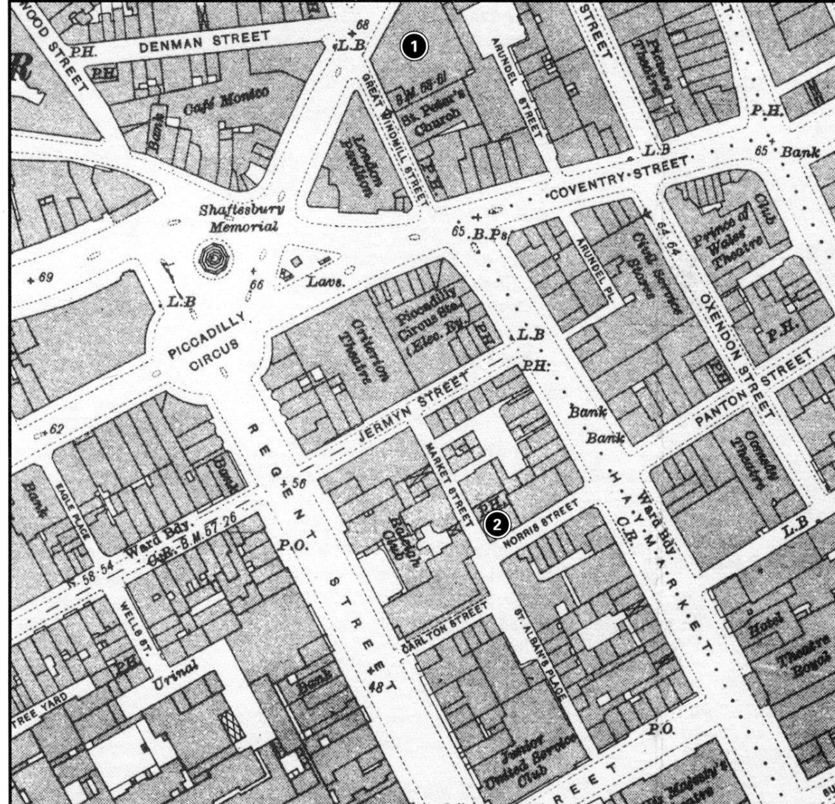

'We next turned left into St. Alban's Street and came to a doorway alongside the Captain's Cabin [2] *(right)* and he steered me into the doorway. I think he placed his gas mask down in the doorway. We stood in the doorway and he embraced me and we kissed. He then tried to pull up my skirt with both hands. I said, "You mustn't do that", and I tried to push his hands away. He then placed one hand on either side of my face and went to kiss me but suddenly shifted his hands on to my throat and commenced to press. I tried to get his hands away but the pressure increased and I felt myself passing out. I remembered him uttering something which sounded like, "You won't, you won't". When I regained consciousness I was lying on the ground and a young man in civilian clothes was asking me what was wrong with me. I tried to answer him but found my voice had gone. He assisted me to my feet and suggested that he should take me to the police station.' That young man was a night porter, John Shine.

'At about 9.45 p.m.' said John Shine in his statement to the police, 'I was walking through St. James's Market, Haymarket, S.W.1, in the direction of Regent Street. I saw a light which appeared to be coming from an electric torch in the doorway of St. James's Restaurant, St. James's Market. As I got nearer I heard a shuffling noise and the light had gone out. I got near the doorway and the light again came on and I noticed the legs of a woman who was lying on the ground and I heard something drop onto the ground. The person holding the light walked round the corner to St. Alban's Street. I could not see who it was owing to the pitch-black darkness. I struck a match and saw a woman lying with her head in the doorway with her feet towards the kerb. I said, "What is wrong?". The woman was groaning and said something which I could not understand. I noticed that her skirt was pulled up, shewing the tops of her stockings and the clips of her suspenders. One or two of the buttons of her dress were undone and appeared to be missing. Her face was dirty and had some blood on it. I called for assistance and a lady came forward with a torch. She said, "I have seen this woman in a pub. She has been drinking with an airman", and she immediately went away. I lifted the woman on to her feet and propped her against the wall. I said, "Are you all right?", and she said, "Oh, my bag, what has he done?", and started to cry. I then saw a gas respirator and a pair of lady's gloves lying in the doorway near where her head had been. She was in a very distressed condition and I suggested that I should take her to hospital and she agreed to go with me. We both started to walk towards Haymarket. I retained the gas respirator and gloves. We then met my workmate, Joseph Nash, and I asked him if he had a torch. He said, "No, perhaps the lady's got one". I felt in her pocket and there was a small electric torch there which I took out and we used. On reaching the junction of Haymarket and Piccadilly I saw a policeman and told him what I knew.'

At once police officers went to the scene of the attack. There they found the woman's handbag rifled of its contents, while in the doorway lay the respirator belonging to her assailant.

Meanwhile the young airman had happened on another woman, Mrs Catherine Mulcahy. The lust for blood must still have been upon him for he persuaded her to enter a taxi-cab with him, and together they drove to her flat in Southwick Street, Paddington, less than a stone's throw from Sussex Gardens, where lay the undiscovered body of Doris Jouannet (for it was not till the following day, February 13, that her husband returned to the flat to find her dead).

While the airman was in the room with Mrs Mulcahy the electric light failed, and it was at this propitious moment that her companion seized her by the throat and tried to strangle her. The frightened woman fought and kicked with such violence, however, that she managed to free herself from the hand that was choking her and gave vent to piercing screams which aroused the household. Her would-be murderer fled the scene but in his anxiety to get away left behind the belt belonging to his uniform.

So within the space of forty-eight hours the mysterious murderer had slain and mutilated two women and had attempted to murder another two. He had gone straight from one crime to another almost without pause. I still felt that he was the man who had also killed Miss Hamilton.

But now he was no longer a mystery man. There was a definite clue to his identity — the respirator which he had left in the doorway when interrupted in his attack upon Mrs Heywood. On this respirator was his air force number, 525987, and to trace its owner was just a matter of routine inquiry. A scrutiny of RAF records was sufficient to establish that the owner of the gas-mask and also the belt was a 28-year-old RAF cadet Gordon Frederick Cummins. He was soon tracked down at his billet in north London and put up for identification by the two women whom he had tried to strangle.

Mrs Heywood had no difficulty in picking him out as the man who had attacked her, but Mrs Mulcahy could only say that his eyes were the same as those of her assailant, who was in RAF uniform. Cummins was charged with the murders of Mrs Oatley, Mrs Lowe, and Mrs Jouannet, and with the attempted murder of Mrs Heywood and Mrs Mulcahy. At that time there was not sufficient evidence on which to charge him with the murder of Miss Hamilton although there was now little doubt that the accused was responsible for her death.

The final attack took place the same night in Southwick Street, a turning off Sussex Gardens. It appears that after escaping into the black-out, having failed to get his way with Greta Heywood, the killer was propositioned by Catherine Mulcahy, although it appears that her 'business' name was Kathleen King! She was picked up at about 8.30 p.m in Piccadilly when she told the man she would charge him £2 but they would have to take a taxi to her room at No. 29 Southwick Street (the white door just behind the cab). Having both removed their clothing, the electric light suddenly failed whereupon the man tried to strangle her. She managed to kick him in the stomach as she still had her shoes on which caused him to make a quick exit, giving Catherine/Kathleen £10 for her trouble!

At West End Central police station, John handed over the service-pattern gas mask that he had picked up which bore the number '525987'. The time was now 10 p.m. but by midnight police had determined from the RAF that the number belonged to LAC Gordon Cummins who was billeted at Flat 27, St. James's Close, and also that he was absent. The RAF police were asked to contact West End Central as soon as Cummins returned and at 4.30 a.m. on Sunday morning, the sentry saw an airman trying to slip into the drive. He was challenged and asked for his identification card which was that of LAC Cummins. He was taken to the guardroom and told by the Orderly Sergeant, that he was to wait in his room — behind these windows on the first floor — for the arrival of the civil police who wanted to interview him as his respirator had been found at the scene of a crime. He was carrying a gas mask and said that he must have picked it up by mistake saying that he had been to a party. When the police arrived they were annoyed to find that Cummins had not been held under guard.

On his arrest he made a statement. In it he described how, on the night of February 9 — the night of the Hamilton murder — he and another cadet named Johnson spent the evening in the West End visiting various bars. About 11 p.m. they met two women and separated, arranging to meet later. Cummins insisted that they did meet and that they were so drunk when they reached their billet that other airmen had to put them to bed.

When Johnson was interviewed he stated that after waiting for some time at the appointed rendezvous, and Cummins not putting in an appearance, he (Johnson) went off with another woman and did not return to the billet until 6 a.m. when he found Cummins in bed. So the latter's story of his movements on that fatal night was obviously false.

When Cummins was brought up at Bow Street Police Court and formally charged I took his fingerprints. As is usual on these occasions, he was asked to sign the fingerprint form. He made no demur and signed with his left hand.

Meanwhile his respirator had been minutely examined. Adhering to the fabric were found particles of dust. On comparison with dust taken from the air raid shelter where Miss Hamilton's body was found, these particles were found to be identical in colour and in form with mortar-dust taken from the shelter. Thus was forged the first direct link in the chain connecting Cummins with the murder of Evelyn Hamilton.

There was another link for when his billet was searched a fountain-pen which had belonged to the dead woman was discovered among his possessions, together with a cigarette-case which was subsequently identified as the property of Mrs Lowe.

The strands of evidence connecting Cummins with the crimes which had created a reign of terror throughout the West End of London were gradually being woven into a noose. But still the final strand had yet to be included which would place that noose around the neck of this multi-murderer.

During the search of Cummins at West End Central, Chief Inspector 'Ted' Greeno, right (seen here with Detective Superintendent Bert Sparks), who had been put in charge of the murder investigation, found items later identified as belonging to Doris Jouannet and Margaret Lowe, and a search of his billet revealed further personal possessions of Evelyn Oatley and Evelyn Hamilton.

I was not idle after taking the accused man's fingerprints at Bow Street Police Court. On comparing these prints with those on the tin-opener found on the bed where lay the body of Mrs Oatley I was able to establish that the clearest mark was made by the left little finger of the accused, while the print on the mirror taken from the handbag of the dead woman was that of his left thumb. So much for Mrs Oatley.

The finger-marks on the base of the candlestick taken from the flat of Mrs Lowe were made by the fingers of the right hand of Cummins. Those on the tumbler and beer bottle found in the flat of Mrs Lowe were also made by the same hand. The accused had been in that flat and had undoubtedly joined his victim in her last drink on earth before killing and mutilating her.

As I have already stated, there were no prints of any value in connexion with the murder of Mrs Jouannet and, apart from the left-hand marks on the throat of Evelyn Hamilton, none that helped in the inquiries into the deaths of these two women.

Cummins was brought to trial at the Old Bailey in April 1942. And it was there, while I was in the witness-box giving fingerprint evidence, that I was instrumental in stopping a trial for murder, a dramatic and almost unheard-of thing.

I should explain that Cummins was tried on one charge of murder only, that of Mrs Evelyn Oatley. This is the usual practice when a person has been committed for trial on more than one murder charge and is an example of the scrupulous fairness with which justice is administered in our criminal courts. During my evidence I had just reached the point where I was about to

Gordon Cummins was formally arrested on February 16 — four days after the last killing and brought to trial on April 27 solely for murder of Evelyn Oatley *(right)*. (No doubt had he not been found guilty of her murder, the police would have pressed on the other three cases.) As it was, the trial lasted only two days, the jury needing only 35 minutes to reach a verdict of guilty.

describe to the jury how I had come to my conclusions regarding the print on the tin-opener and the mark on the bit of mirror when the fingerprint exhibits were put in. These were photographic enlargements of the marks on the articles side by side with the corresponding prints taken by me from Cummins, and copies were handed to the jury, so that they could follow what I was about to say. Mr G. B. McClure, counsel for the Crown, was just about to ask me to describe the similarities when, out of the corner of my eye, I observed that the jury had been handed copies of the fingerprints in another case on which Cummins had been indicted but was not being tried.

Even from that distance, between witness-box and the box where the jury sat, just to my right, I could detect the difference in the prints before me and those they were gazing at. I stood for a moment, not a little perplexed. I realised that somehow a mistake had been made and I had to think quickly. There was only one course to take. I turned to Mr Justice Asquith, the presiding judge. 'I think the jury has been handed a wrong exhibit,' I said quietly.

Puzzled looks appeared on the faces of the jurors, and the copies with which they had been provided were hastily recovered. However the damage had been done, and the whole essence of that justice to which I have referred would have been vitiated if those same jurors had been allowed to continue the hearing of the case.

They were asked to retire while the legal position was discussed. On their return Mr Justice Asquith discharged them, explaining that 'It is possible, and very probable, that from the exhibit before you that you might have drawn certain inferences which would have made it impossible for you to try this action properly. I know I can rely on you not to mention anything that has come to your knowledge from this exhibit.'

The judge also appealed to the Press to 'treat this with every discretion' adding: 'The full truth will be published later but not until this trial is over.'

It was the first time in the history of the Old Bailey that a trial had ever been stopped for such a reason.

On the following Monday the trial was reopened with another jury and Cummins was found guilty and sentenced to death.

Cummins appealed, and while seated between two warders in the dock at the Court of Criminal Appeal, he laughed and appeared to be joking with his guardians. Now and again he looked across the court and smiled at his wife.

Mr Justice Humphreys concluded his reference to the fingerprint evidence by pointing out that no witness had been called to combat my evidence, which he described as being 'this peculiar but singularly conclusive form of evidence, because it was claimed nearly 600,000 persons have been identified without any error being known to have been made, and in no case have two people been found to have fingers or thumbs which make identical marks.'

The appeal was dismissed and on the morning of June 25, 1942, Cummins went to his death at the hands of the hangman.

Chief Superintendent Fred Cherrill,
Cherrill of the Yard, 1954

Having been charged, tried, convicted and sentenced to death, Cummins still protested his innocence. His wife, Marjorie, who he had married in December 1935, refused to accept he could possibly be the killer, telling the *News of the World*: 'I know the world believes him guilty, but until I die I will never believe he was capable of the revolting murders.' Her father believed her implicitly and fought right to the last to prove his son-in-law was innocent.

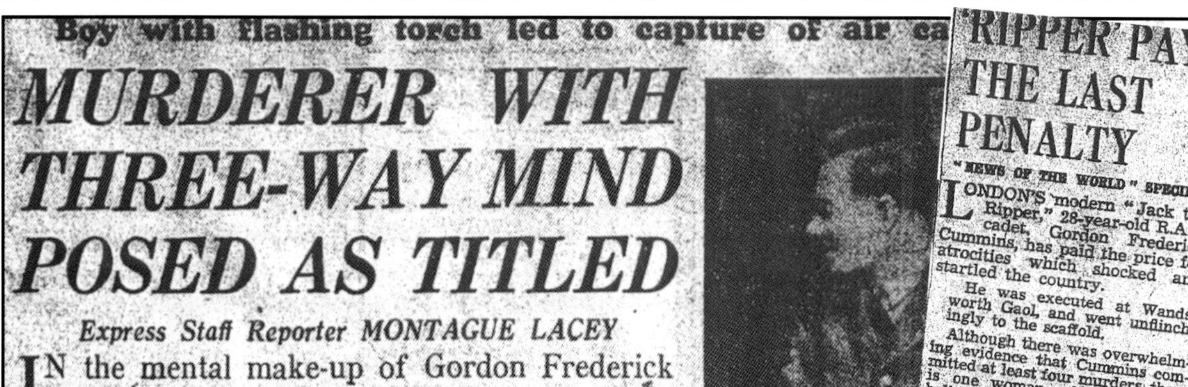

Boy with flashing torch led to capture of air ca

MURDERER WITH THREE-WAY MIND POSED AS TITLED

Express Staff Reporter MONTAGUE LACEY

IN the mental make-up of Gordon Frederick Cummins, 28-year-old married air cadet, sentenced to death at the Old Bailey yesterday

'RIPPER' PAYS THE LAST PENALTY

"NEWS OF THE WORLD" SPECIAL

LONDON'S modern "Jack the Ripper," 28-year-old R.A.F. cadet, Gordon Frederick Cummins, has paid the price for atrocities which shocked and startled the country.

He was executed at Wandsworth Gaol, and went unflinchingly to the scaffold.

Although there was overwhelming evidence that Cummins committed at least four murders, there is one woman who will never believe in his guilt.

She is his wife—secretary to a famous London theatre manager—who told a "News of the World"

Prisoner 1644 G.F. Cummins
H.M. Prison, Wandsworth.

29.4.42.

Dear Dot and Laurie,

By this time you will, of course, have seen the news. The past few days have been a dreadful ordeal, and I am glad it is all over. Now that I am here my father and our legal advisers are, I hope, redoubling their efforts to find the guilty man, and prove my innocence before it is too late.

You will know, of course, that I was only tried on one case, obviously the one in which the prosecution thought they had the most evidence. Although John Flowers, my Counsel, put up a magnificent fight, it was no good. I am convicted on several so-called 'facts', which are ridiculous. (I hope I'm not boring you.) In the first place, parts of my original statement to the police are inaccurate as to time — quite naturally, seeing that I was extremely drunk on the evening in question. To my horror the prosecution took the line, which was accepted by the judge, that the time errors were really an attempt to establish an alibi!

I was last seen on the evening in question by a woman at about 12.30 when I was making my way back to the billet. As, of course, there was no one who saw me after that it is concluded that I murdered this woman then! There were, in her flat, two fingerprints that Scotland Yard say are mine. Well, I don't know how they identify these things, but for every similarity, we could show at least two dissimilarities.

These dissimilarities were brushed aside by Cherrill, the 'expert'. Those prints cannot have been mine, yet the jury accepted the police evidence.

Another 'fact' was that a cigarette case, without a doubt belonging to the woman, was found near my bedroom, four days after my arrest, although the police searched the place the day after my arrest. It was obviously planted by the guilty man!

When two of the murders happened (although it couldn't be mentioned at the trial) it was proved that I was in bed at the time, feeling unwell from the after effects of inoculation. There again articles belonging to the dead women were found near my room.

With all these facts in mind, and with the knowledge that the police were unable to find any bloodstains on my clothing, my legal advisers were convinced of my innocence weeks ago, and they rightly thought that the culprit must be another cadet, and they started investigating. They found the man! There was, to their minds, overwhelming proof of his guilt, so last week they laid their information before Scotland Yard. The Police refused to act on it!

The facts we knew against this man did not consist of proof, so nothing could be said about it at the trial. However, now that I am sentenced to death, I think my father is going to the Home Office to get things moving.

Incidentally, nothing could he said at the trial about my character which might have helped, because our dear friend Gwen had taken out a Summons against me. Thank her, will you?

Two Days Later.

My solicitor has just been to see me and I am appealing. Also he is hot on the trail of this other cadet.

Jerry seems to have made a mess of Bath, doesn't he? I wonder if the Christopher has been touched. Or the Hole in the Wall? Perhaps not — dens of iniquity nearly always escape unscathed! I'll bet Colerie was fog bound that night.

Give my regards to any of the lads who may still think well of me and of course to Bailleaw, Beattie, Dessy Farmer, John Owen, and Nelson. Tell them that I'm eating well and being fattened up. Robinson or Morris never came to see me at Brixton; but I received a strange and illegible communication containing the Gospel according to St. John from 'the boys', who ever they may be.

My love to you, Dot, and to niece Sally. If there's any justice in this world I'll be seeing you all again. If not, tell Gwen I'll come and haunt her!

I'll write again sometime and let you know how things are going on.

Yours optimistically,

Gordon.

Darling Marjorie,

Your letter came this morning and I have read it for perhaps the hundredth time. It is heartening to know that you believe in me. I am given confidence in the outcome of all this sordid business.

I do hope that D. N. Pritt has this case at his fingertips. Mr. Kenwright seems to have confidence in him — but he also had confidence in Flowers! If there is failure, it will be a case of 'Mors acerba, fama perpetua, stabit vetuo memoria facti'.

I have made myself beautiful for a possible visit and jump every time a key grates in the lock. So far — nothing doing, but there's still time. I sent the orders out yesterday. One each to Father, Mary, and the R.A.F. padre.

Dot's letter was short but nice. Evidently she has not been influenced by the News of the World! You must meet her and niece Sally someday. Both of you have something in common — erratic husbands, the source of many a headache! Laurie was perhaps one of the most drunken fellows it is possible to meet, due, I think, to the fact that he worked in a bank. Also all members of his family are noted for their eccentricity. Less kind people would say madness, of course.

Our new flat. In which district are we to settle this time? Hampstead or Curzon Street? Bermondsey or Whitechapel? There is much to be said for Tooting Bec — and of course Wandsworth would be a good spot — it would serve as a perpetual reminder and a strong deterrent!

Or perhaps the bridal suite at Keith Gibsons' place the Spread Eagle would be more in our line? I could imagine his leers coupled with the presentation of such a gift as we received from him six years ago!

No visit yet. And its nearing tea time. I have a sort of empty and lost feeling as though everyone has said 'Oh to hell with him'. I know that is not so, of course — the slips cannot have been received. So I must wait until to-morrow. And I'm used to waiting by now!

When I don't feel like reading or writing I play chess with one of the two officers who are always with me. Perhaps it is significant of my mental condition that I fail to see even the simplest of moves, leaving myself open to attack from all quarters. (In fact, on reflection, I think that has been characteristic of me all through this business.) I try to concentrate, with the unfortunate result that I only see vaguely some black and white pieces with absolutely no relation to one another.

By now I am convinced that there is no justice in this country. I, who am completely innocent, am sitting here — waiting. And yet there was a certain man in Brixton with me on the same charge — murder. He admitted his guilt to us, and yet he was acquitted! There was also a few months ago a man who was found with a companion, in a house, with a murdered woman. They were both dead drunk and their pockets were filled with her jewellery. One was acquitted and nulli casus brought against the other!! Of course all these men were Canadian. Then there is the young Canadian soldier who shot two policeman. He was as sane as you or I — he goes to Broadmoor, to work on a farm. Do you call that justice? A modern trial has developed into a lot of legal mumbo-jumbo with a jury composed of self-opinionated grocers. Incidentally the jury system as first conceived was to have twelve men who <u>knew</u> both the plaintiff and defendant. These men were in a position to know small facts which might escape counsel.

But looking at my jury — did you ever see such a collection of dimwits'? Why, they couldn't even read properly! And, of course, even if they had wished to be fair, nothing in the world could shake their preformed opinion as culled from the Press.

But that's enough of that. The evil is done, and we must look forward, not back.

<u>Wednesday.</u>

I didn't feel I could write another word yesterday so I lost myself in a book — Hugh Walpole's Roman Fountain. Once more I don my smart grey suit by Moss Bros and await the representatives of the outside world. Who will come, I wonder? Yours is the only visit that I await with eagerness, darling. I listen each morning and evening to the trains roaring by and think to myself 'Marjorie may be on that.' I love you dearly, and I know that God (if there is one) cannot separate us for much longer. I have been punished enough for my wayward habits — and I daren't think of the appeal — I 'come all over pessimistic'.

See you on Saturday, honey,

Your adoring,

Gordon.

P.S. Give my regards to Ethel and Stanley. Your other letter has just come. Looking forward to seeing Freda. I love you.

To Mrs M. Cummins
'Uplands'
Maybury Hll,
Woking
Surrey.

Wandsworth Prison, 2.5.42

My Darling Marjorie,

Your visit has given me renewed hope and courage and I love you more than ever. Darling, this gross injustice cannot be allowed to stand. Something must be done. It is dreadful to sit here just waiting, — knowing full well that I am completely innocent of the whole affair. I <u>have</u> been foolish, but <u>never</u> a murderer:

You are very brave, my Sweet, and I am very proud of you; have no fear, everything will work out alright in the end, I hope.

I'd like to know who the devil told the newspapers of our little joke — the Earl of Buchan etc. It's not much use pointing out to people now my peculiar sense of humour!

<u>Wednesday</u>

Three letters have just arrived — one from, Mary, one from Mother, and yours. They give me great comfort — it <u>is</u> comforting to know that there are some who believe in me!

I am treated here with every consideration; there is a greater degree of comfort than at Brixton — and that's saying something! I have plenty of good books from the prison library, cards, dominoes, draughts, etc, and an issue of 15 cigarettes a day. My food is better, I think, than any I have tasted in the R.A.F.

Of course it is very difficult to settle down quietly under the present circumstances, as there is always at the back of my mind the distressing thought that my appeal may fail! In that event, the person to see would be the Home Secretary himself. For I have an objection to being punished for something I haven't done — and I hate to think that the guilty man remains unpunished. It would be no use dragging a confession from him if I were one of the minor angels!

I do <u>not</u> wear night clothes when being visited, Mother. The neat and fashionable garb in which I was nearly lost is a <u>prison suit</u>; which garments have been worn by all the best people from time to time. A great friend of mine in Brixton, first cousin to a well-known Peer, took a pride in these clothes!

I'm rather tired, so I think I'll pop into bed. Don't forget Saturday — or before then.

All my love,

Gordon.

To the Home Secretary
The Right Hon Herbert Morrison
Lambeth Palace, S.E.

June 15, 1942.

My dear Morrison,

<u>Frederick Gordon Cummins.</u>

I hope you will forgive me for writing to you about this case of conviction for murder. There are two points which I wish to put before you. Naturally I do not myself enter for a single moment into an estimate of the actual evidence or the conduct of the case, but the two points are these:

(1) A number of people, well known in their neighbourhood, who watched the case closely, were disturbed and dismayed by the verdict and by the decision of the Court of Appeal. To them it seemed, rightly or wrongly, that the evidence was extremely precarious and that the arguments advanced to shake it were brushed aside too lightly.

(2) I know that people whose judgement deserves respect regard the alleged crime as utterly incompatible with the known character of the accused person; so that if in fact it was committed by him, it must be a medical rather than a strictly criminal case.

I confine myself to these points which I think that I am entitled to bring before you as a plea for a very serious consideration of the main arguments in favour of reprieve or commutation that will be advanced by others.

Yours sincerely,

William Cantuar.

Archbishop of Canterbury

P. S. m.	Unit From	Unit To	Reason	Checkd.	Appd.	Date of Movmnt.	Cas. Form confirming Arrival.
		T Dept Sqd				11.11.35.	
9/36	T Dept Sqdn	3S.OF T.T.(M)	H.	[illegible]	[illegible]	17.1.36	11/36
49/36	3S of T.T.(M)	2(T) Wing H.A.D.	H.	8.	[illegible]	13.3.36	10/36
61/36	2 Wing Henlow	MAEE Felixstowe	[illegible]	[illegible]	[illegible]	20.11.36	95/36
32/38	M.A.E.E. Felixstowe	2 Wing, Henlow (a)	H	[illegible]	[illegible]	29.4.38	
	2 Wing Henlow (A)	M.A.E.E. Felixstowe				26.7.38	57/38
205/39	M.A.E.E.	Calshot (A)				28.8.39	
	Calshot (A)	M.A.E.E.				29.8.39	206/39
124/39	MAEE	240 Sqdn. (A)				2.9.39	
	240 Sqdn (A)	MAEE				13.10.39	30/10/39
384/39	MAEE Felixstowe	MAEE Helensburgh				24.10.39	21/10/39
		600 Sqd	BX [illegible]			19/3/41	14/41
20/41		Stn. Catterick (A)				14.3.41	
		600 Sqdn				26.4.41	24/41
		ACRC	H.	[illegible]		2/2/42	
		Discharge				19.6.42	

On April 20, Chief Inspector Greeno was informed by Cummins Commanding Officer at the ACRC, Group Captain Alfred Gilligan, that Mr John Cummins, Senior, had been to see him. He had told him that he believed another cadet, a Raymond Beetham, with four previous convictions to his name and currently in jail for larceny, was absent from the ACRC at the time of the murders. Following the dismissal of Cummins's appeal against the conviction on June 9, Greeno was summoned to the Home Office to be given detailed arguments from Marjorie Cummins, John Cummins and Messrs Harold Kenwright and Cox, their solicitors. As a result the Inspector had to burn the midnight oil, responding to all the points raised, his report running to 12 pages being sent to the Home Office on June 17. Two days after it was received by the Home Office, LAC Gordon Cummins was dismissed from the Royal Air Force.

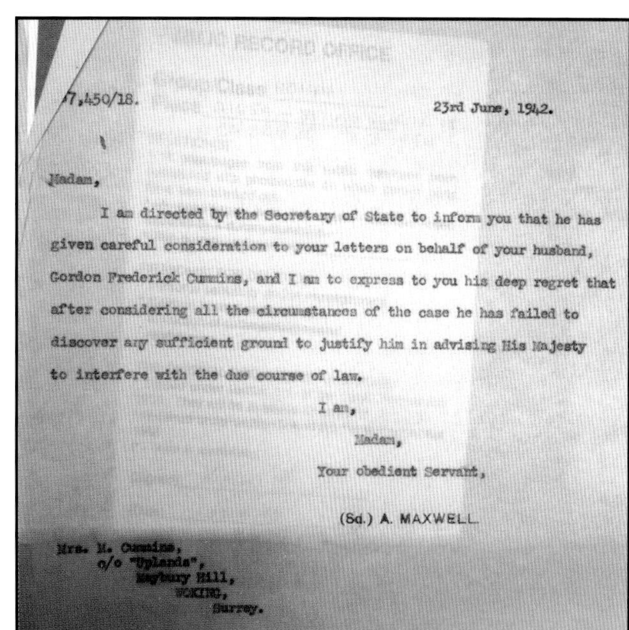

7,450/18.

23rd June, 1942.

Madam,

I am directed by the Secretary of State to inform you that he has given careful consideration to your letters on behalf of your husband, Gordon Frederick Cummins, and I am to express to you his deep regret that after considering all the circumstances of the case he has failed to discover any sufficient ground to justify him in advising His Majesty to interfere with the due course of law.

I am,
Madam,
Your obedient Servant,

(Sd.) A. MAXWELL.

Mrs. M. Cummins,
c/o "Uplands",
Mayberry Hill,
WOKING,
Surrey.

Marjorie had moved from Barnes to be with her father in Woking and it was there that she received this letter just two days before her husband's execution, carried out by Albert Pierrepoint assisted by Harry Kirk. Having been discharged, he met his death as a civilian, to be buried in unconsecrated ground in the prison yard (see also pages 356-359). Greeno wrote in his memoirs. 'Meanwhile, Cummins went on denying his guilt, and the night before he hanged *[sic]* I did not see my bed because an organisation got up a petition claiming that Cummins's story was true and that somebody else — the man who "mixed" the gas-masks at the Trocadero — had done the murders. I worked all night preparing a report which thoroughly answered the charges in the petition and just after 8 a.m. in Wandsworth jail [on June 25] I testified before a coroner that the man "of whose body I have had the view" was in fact Gordon Frederick Cummins, mass murderer.'

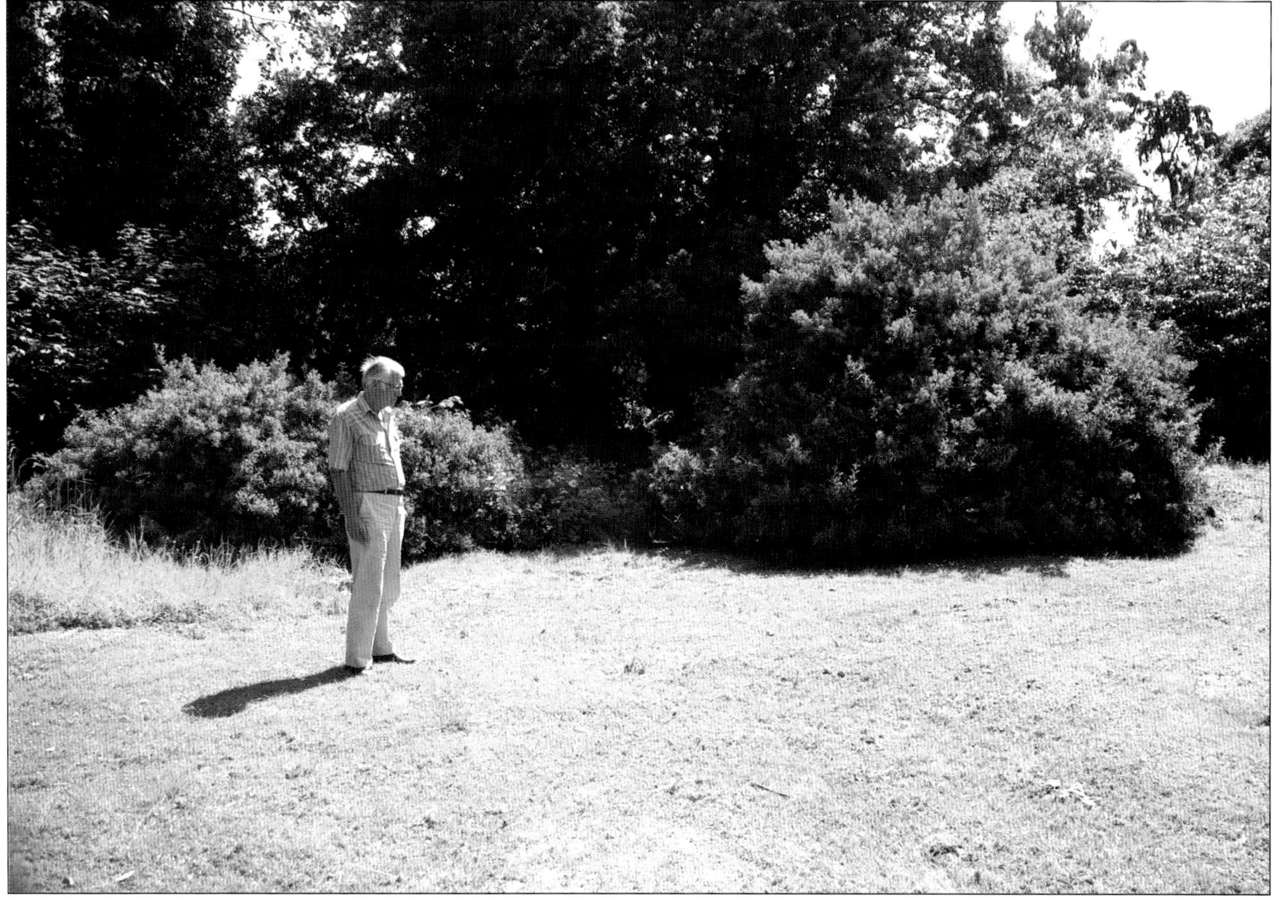

Unmarked yet not forgotten. Evelyn Hamilton and Margaret Lowe lie here in a common grave (B19) at East Finchley Cemetery.

A peaceful recreation ground in the heart of the East End of London belies its past for here a 71-year-old pawnbroker, Leonard Moules, met his end at the hands of two incorrigible criminals with a record of theft and violence.

April 30, 1942 – Double Execution for Murder

George William Silverosa, C.R.O. 27067-36, age 23, a wood machinist of no fixed abode, and Samuel Sidney Dashwood, alias Glen, C.R.O. No. 28693-39, age 22, a motor driver of no fixed abode, were on the 16th May, 1942, charged at this Station as follows: 'Did, on 9th May, 1942, wilfully murder Leonard Moules'. Apprehended in the Parish of Pitsea.

On 18th May, 1942, the accused appeared before D. Roland Thomas Esq., Magistrate, at Old Street Police Court, and were remanded in custody under the powers of the Defence Regulations without evidence until 10.30 a.m., 1st June, 1942.

The facts are as follows:

Leonard Moules, age 71 years, a pawnbroker of 226 Hoe St. Walthamstow, also proprietor of 299 Hackney Road, Shoreditch, was brutally assaulted in his shop at 299 Hackney Road, on 30th April 1942, sometime between 12.50 p.m., and 10.30 p.m. On the 9th May 1942, at 10 a.m., Mr Moules succumbed at Bethnal Green Hospital due to injuries to his face and internal complications resulting from the assault on the 30th April, 1942.

The premises at 299 Hackney Road, a lock-up pawnbrokers shop, consisted of shop, back room on ground floor, a basement consisting of two rooms with two vaults. There are two floors above the shop which are used as a storage of pledged clothing, and there is also a yard at the rear which has an outdoor lavatory.

The entrances leading to these premises are by the front door, leading from Hackney Road into the shop, and three doors leading from a passage-way known as Essex Place. The first door in the passage-way leads into the pledging section of the shop; the second door giving access to the private part, and the third into the enclosed yard at the rear. The second and third doors have not been opened for a considerable period. The two doors which have been in constant use are the front door and the first passage door.

At the rear of the premises there is a wall enclosing the yard which has been severely damaged by enemy action. There is also a door leading from the yard into a passage at the rear of the premises. The interior of the shop discloses a shop front for the display of jewellery and other articles, it has a glass frame partition. There is a counter which runs the whole length of the shop. The shop itself is divided by a partition, this allowing it to be used partly for ordinary sales and partly for pledging purposes. The first mentioned door in the passage is a double one, one door opening to the left, and the other to the right. The door opening to the right fits back into the partition, parting the shop from the pledging section.

Leading from the rear of the counter is a passage and stairway to the basement. Facing the exit door at the rear of the counter is a door leading to the back ground floor room. Inside this room there are three safes, a large one, medium and small, a table and a washhand stand. The basement consists of two rooms and two vaults, but there is nothing of any consequence kept in these rooms. It appears that Mr Moules utilised the front room basement to have his meals. The two floors above the shop consist of store rooms as previously described.

Mr Moules, for many years, has conducted a pawnbrokers business at 299 Hackney Road assisted by a sales manager, Walter John Cullen. On Thursday, 30th April, 1942,

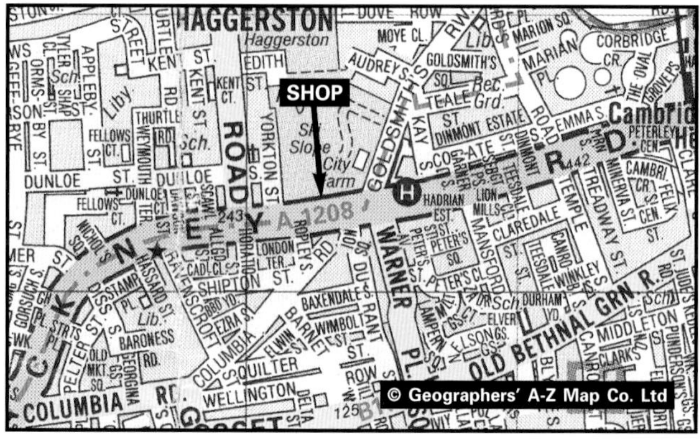

Mr Moules's shop lay at No. 299 Hackney Road. It was there in the basement that he was discovered severely beaten around the head on April 30, 1942. Poor Moules lingered in hospital for eight days and died on May 9 without having been able to tell the police anything about his attackers. The picture *(top)* was taken from the mouth of Columbia Road with Tuilerie Street on the left.

Mr Cullen arrived at the shop at 9.30 a.m. and he opened up in the usual way with the keys he had in his possession. At 10.30 a.m., Mr Moules arrived. The two men continued to conduct the business of the shop until 12.40 p.m., when Cullen closed the door leading from the pledge office into Essex Place. Mr Cullen put the shutters up to the front shop window, returned to the shop, put his clothes on, and said 'Good afternoon' to Mr Moules who replied in a like manner, leaving Mr Moules and an Airedale dog in the shop. The front door was left open with a view to Mr Moules conducting any business that came in until he made his mind up to close the shop.

Thursday in this area is a half-day closing, and it is usual for the shop to be closed at 1 p.m.

Mr Cullen states that it was 12.50 p.m. when he left the shop and on returning to the shop on the morning on the 1st May, 1942, he was notified by Police that Mr Moules had been severely assaulted.

Albert Ernest Norris, War Reserve Police Constable 557 'G' Division, observed a light shining through the fan-light over the front door of the shop at 299 Hackney Road at 10.15 p.m. on the 30th April, 1942. The Officer knocked on the front door and failing to get a reply, he entered Essex Place and knocked on the first side door. As he knocked, a slight push opened the door. He entered and called out, 'Is there anyone at home?'. Getting no answer, he looked around and saw the shop was in disorder. The Officer at once suspected thieves had broken into the shop and immediately communicated with New Scotland Yard for assistance.

Stewart Allen, Police Sergeant 22 'G' Division, with other Officers, arrived on the scene shortly after 10.20 p.m., 30th April 1942. The officers entered and searched the premises and P.C. 193 'G' Clement Aprille found a man, now known to be deceased, Leonard Moules, in the basement back room, standing on his feet, bent over, arms rested to a wall and his head hanging limply. The exact position where Moules was found was inside the first back room basement just by the door leading into the vault on the right. P.C. Aprille spoke to Mr Moules and he mumbled something unintelligible. Mr Moules appeared to be semi-conscious.

P.C. 123 'G' John Calder conveyed Mr Moules by ambulance to Bethnal Green Hospital. P.C. Calder and P.S. Allen, prior to leaving the shop, questioned Mr Moules as to his name and asked him how he came by his injuries, and indistinctly Moules said, 'Leonard Davis, 226 Hoe Street.'

Mr Moules was seen by Dr Worrell who, after examination, stated he was of the opinion that Moules was suffering from a fractured base of the skull and ordered him to be detained in D.2. ward. At this stage, Mr Moules was totally unconscious. Arrangements were made for a C.I.D. officer to continuously remain at the bed-side to obtain any statement that he might make should he regain consciousness, but at no time did Moules become conscious. He remained in this condition until 10 a.m. 9th May, 1942, when he died.

At 12.15 a.m., 1st May 1942, Detective Inspector Withers, 'G' Division, attended 299 Hackney Road, and upon making a cursory examination saw just behind the counter, a large pool of blood. Near it was a top denture plate, a coat button with strands of black cotton attached but, owing to the inadequate 'black-out', caused the premises to be closed and a police officer posted outside for a more convenient examination in daylight. Prior to the premises being closed, Superintendent Cherrill of Fingerprint Department arrived and made a brief examination.

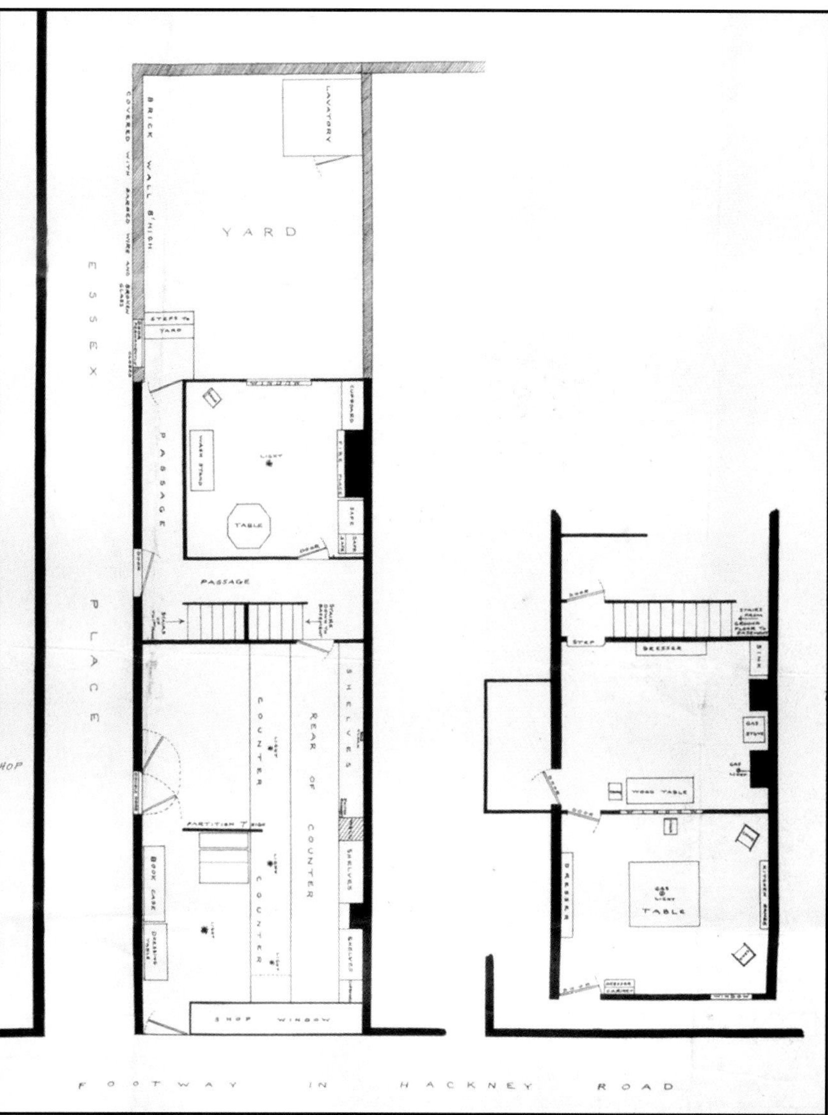

A search was made in the basement and in the centre of the rear room where Mr Moules was found by Police, a set of ten keys on a ring was lying. These keys are a complete set which fit the safes in the room.

Superintendent Cherrill made a thorough examination of the premises for fingerprints with the result that he found a palm impression of a left hand inside the medium safe as shown in the photograph. He also discovered a very poor finger impression on the woodwork of the window frame fitted to the back of the window from where the glass found on the floor by the counter had been broken. Superintendent Cherrill also found a finger impression upon the milk bottle. I would here mention that the palm print of Silverosa's left hand is identical with that impression left on the medium safe.

On 9th May, 1942, a post-mortem was held on the body of Leonard Moules by Dr. C. Keith Simpson, pathologist, at Shoreditch Mortuary and I was present with Detective Inspector Withers and W. H. Heddy Esq., Coroner. Dr Keith Simpson discovered (1) five blunt injuries to the top of the head which he states were consistent with five successive blows with a blunt instrument of moderate weight; (2) group of injuries to the front of the neck consistent with having been gripped very tightly by a left hand from the front; (3) broad crushing injury across the entire left side of the face, stating this could have been caused by a fall.

Police report, City Road Station, 'G' Division, May 21, 1942

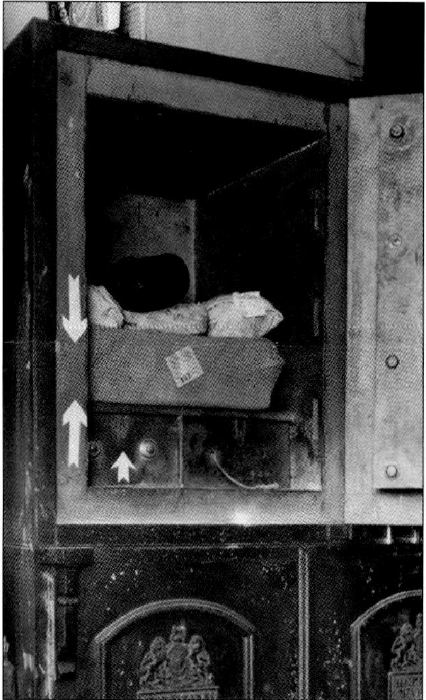

This is the photograph mentioned in the text of the safe where Superintendent Cherrill found a palm-print — the first time such evidence had been successfully used to secure a conviction.

Pentonville on the Caledonian Road was the prison used for executions for crimes committed in London north of the River Thames after Newgate closed in 1902 (see page 13). In fact the same gallows was dismantled and transferred to Pentonville.

His scalp had been split by five successive blows with a blunt instrument of moderate weight. Four of the injuries were set close together and parallel to one another: this suggested to me that these blows had been struck when the old man was already incapable of resisting or moving, or perhaps when his head was being held steady for the purpose; and deep bruising of the neck muscles did, in fact, indicate that the neck had at some point been gripped strongly by a left hand. The fifth injury lay apart, being set in a different place and at a different angle. It was distinctly heavier than the others and I thought it would have been sufficient to disable the victim although not, perhaps, to knock him out completely. It could well have been delivered as Moules approached with his head slightly bent forward, and I thought it quite likely that this disabling injury had been the first. If I was right, Old Moules had been knocked out and then deliberately and cold-bloodedly battered to death.

Professor Keith Simpson, Forty Years of Murder, 1978

Inspector Keen decided that the murderers would be found somewhere in the maze of streets within the radius of Hackney Road, Kingsland Road, and Bethnal Green Road. But days went by, and it was not until May 15 that a soldier was heard to remark in a Bethnal Green cafe that round about the time of the crime he had seen two men, whom he referred to as 'George and Sam,' examining a revolver in another cafe in the district.

Further inquiries sent Keen post-haste to an address in Pitsea, where he found a twenty-three-year-old machinist named George Silverosa, who made a statement. In it he related how on the day of the murder he and another man were walking along the Hackney Road when his companion showed him a revolver, remarking that 'the gun was enough to frighten anyone.'

They happened to be passing the pawnbroker's shop, when, said Silverosa, 'I told him it was an old boy, and he said, 'We will do this if you are game.' I said, 'All right, but no violence.''

He went on to describe how they saw the old man putting up the shutters, and walked into the shop after him. The statement then went on:

'The man who was with me, whose name I now know is Sam Dashwood or Glen, went in first, and I followed him. I closed the shop door, and as I turned round I saw the old man falling down. I didn't see Sam strike him, but I surmised what he had done. I gave Sammy £20. Sammy kept the rings, which he sold, and I had my wages left out of it — about £50 or £60.'

Dashwood also made a statement on being arrested. His statement ran as follows:

'George went in first. There was a man and a dog there. There was a scuffle, and the dog started barking. George and the old man were scuffling, and the old man went down. He tried to get up, and we both pushed him down again.'

When he saw Moules about to blow a whistle, Dashwood continued, 'I picked up my revolver, and when Moules put his arm round my neck and tried to pull himself up I hit him on top of the head.'

The subsequent trial of these two men was marked by a dramatic incident such as I do not remember ever having witnessed in any other murder trial during my long experience.

Opened in 1842, Pentonville was designed as a model for British prisons which were needed because of the ending of capital punishment for lesser crimes and the reduction in transportation to the colonies.

The design was based on the Eastern State Penitentiary in Philadelphia where separate wings radiated from a central hub so that officers could keep an eye on all the wings from one point. The first execution shed was situated at the end of B Wing but this necessitated a long walk for the condemned from their cell. Therefore in 1928 a purpose-built 'suite' was built at the end of A Wing. Comprising three levels, the upper room contained the beam and chain to which the noose was attached; the centre the chamber with double-leaf trapdoors, and the lower level the pit into which the condemned would drop.

Both Silverosa and Dashwood refrained from going into the witness-box to give evidence on their own behalf, doubtless to avoid cross-examination which would have been levelled against them by counsel for the Crown.

The most sensational moment was, however, when Dashwood, after the opening of the trial, abandoned the services of the two eminent counsel who had been appointed to defend him after he had asked for legal aid. These were that grand old legal warrior — now retired from the Bar — Serjeant Sullivan and Mr Fordham. It was a tense and dramatic moment, relieved only by the immediate response of Mr Fordham, who illustrated how careful is British justice to watch over the interests of a prisoner, even though he himself has objected to its representations on his behalf.

Mr Fordham said, 'Serjeant Sullivan and I will be glad to render any assistance we can. Our view is that there is certain evidence which ought to be placed before the court, and if at any time we can be of any use to Dashwood we shall be glad to be so. One of us will remain in court all day. I shall take no part in the trial except to remain here.'

'I object to them saying anything in my defence,' said Dashwood.

A little later the tall, bearded figure of Serjeant Sullivan entered the court, and the judge, Mr Justice Wrottesley, explained what had happened. The Serjeant stated that he had undertaken the defence, and even if he had to do it through the prosecution there were matters to be considered to which he had given careful thought. In case he could be of assistance, he proposed to remain at the disposal of the judge.

'I cannot force legal assistance upon him,' said Mr Justice Wrottesley.

'Unless he is unfit to plead,' suggested the Serjeant.

'He seems perfectly sane,' commented the judge.

And so the trial went on. I testified that the palm-print on the inside of the safe was made by Silverosa. This was not contested by the defence. Dashwood did not ask a single question throughout the entire hearing, and the only defence raised by Mr Hector Hughes, K.C., on behalf of Silverosa was that, while the prisoner pleaded guilty to robbery, he did not plead guilty to murder. He argued that there was no common design to kill, and that the only common design was to rob.

'Only one man used violence,' concluded counsel, 'and that man was not Silverosa.'

Five stalwart warders were in the dock, and others were near at hand when the prisoners were ushered in to hear the verdict of the jury. It was feared that there might be a scene such as took place in an Old Bailey dock in 1896, when Millsom and Fowler flew at each other like tigers as sentence of death was passed.

There was, however, nothing like this. Both men remained calm and unruffled as they heard their doom from the lips of the judge. In fact, Dashwood almost swaggered from the dock as he cried to someone, 'Don't worry,' while Silverosa waved to a woman who shouted from the back of the court, 'Hard luck, George.'

There was a sequel in Pentonville Gaol a few days before the execution. Silverosa, in the condemned cell, asked permission to burn two letters in the incinerator. He was granted permission, but suddenly, while the letters were burning, he snatched up a poker and attacked the two warders in charge of him, causing them severe injuries. He was eventually overpowered and taken back to his cell, where he remained until his execution on the following Thursday morning.

Superintendent Fred Cherrill,
Cherrill of the Yard

The last execution at Pentonville took place on July 6, 1961, by which time 120 men had been hung, including several German spies and prisoners of war convicted of murder. So far in this account we have seen Hawley Crippen, Frederick Bywaters, Frederick Browne, John Stockwell and Udham Singh meet their end here; now it was the turn of Samuel Dashwood *(left)* and George Silverosa, despatched by Albert Pierrepoint and Herbert Morris assisted by Stephen Wade and Harry Kirk on September 10, 1942.

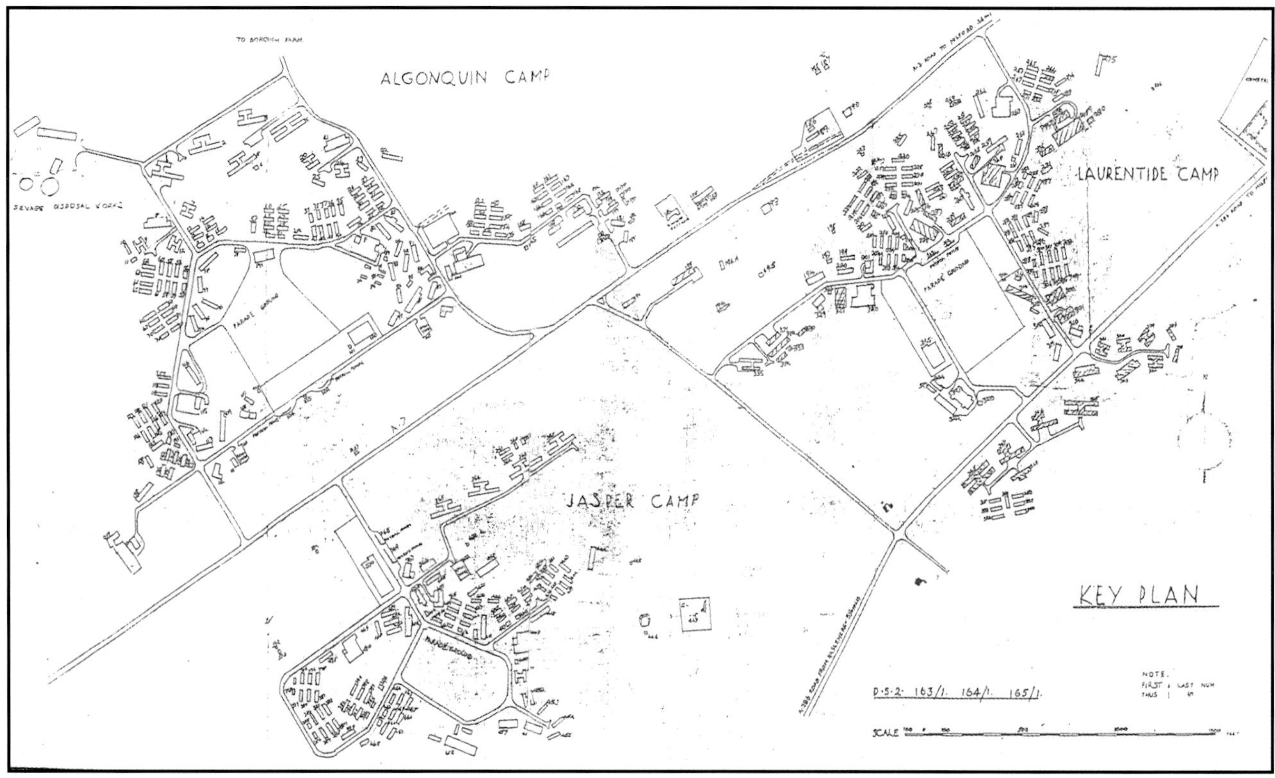

October 7, 1942 – The 'Wigwam' Murder

Up to yesterday the police, although in possession of tangible information, were not in a position definitely to establish the identity of a woman whose body, almost completely covered with sandy soil, was found on Hankley Common, Thursley, on Wednesday last week.

The cause of death also has not yet been determined owing to the body being in an advanced stage of decomposition.

The Surrey police and Scotland Yard detectives, who are closely collaborating in efforts to solve the mystery of what is in the light of certain facts appears to have been a murder, have satisfied themselves that the woman did not belong to the district and that she is one of a number who have from time to time been temporarily staying in the neighbourhood.

The Surrey Advertiser, October 17, 1942

Surrey has always had a long history of military activity and training and Witley Common was the location of a Canadian Army camp in both world wars. Between 30,000 and 60,000 troops were camped there and serious rioting broke out in 1918 and 1919 for similar delays in demobilisation as occured at Epsom (see page 54) when the greater part of the camp was burned down.

The Canadians returned during the Second World War when Camp Witley was one of three facilities in the Aldershot Command, the other two being at Bordon and Bramshott. Today the area occupied by the Witley camps — Algonquin, Jasper and Laurentide has totally returned to nature. This is exactly the same area, now crossed by the upgraded A3 dual carriageway.

The mystery of the death of 19-years-old Joan Pearl Wolfe, whose partly-buried body was found at the Thursley end of Hankley Common over a fortnight ago, is still engaging the close attention of the Godalming police and Scotland Yard detectives.

The police are not yet acquainted with the actual cause of death. The body was decomposed, and chiefly on that account pathologists have been unable to submit their final report. No date has yet been fixed for the inquest.

The Surrey Advertiser, October 24, 1942

Scotland Yard and the Surrey police are still investigating the death of 19-years-old Joan Pearl Wolfe.

The police have not given up their search of the commons in the Thursley, Elstead and Witley districts and inquiries are being continued over a wide area.

The Surrey Advertiser, October 31, 1942

The former training ground is now a heather-covered plateau. Although we were armed with the scene of crime photographs, and plans from the Surrey Constabulary, we still had to make two visits to confirm we had the right location and even then matching up photographs in a natural environment after nearly 70-odd years was not a simple matter. Nevertheless it was a beautiful day with the sound of automatic gun-fire emanating from the nearby Army ranges.

On October 7, 1942, Royal Marines were camped at Houndown, some two miles west of the Canadian camp, and were engaged in exercises on Hankley Common. At around 10.30 a.m., Marine William Moore of 'F' Battery, Royal Marines (H.A.A.) Regiment was passing a line of earthworks on the top of the plateau when he noticed a human hand and arm protruding from one of the mounds. He called the attention of Sergeant Withington who in turn reported the discovery to Lieutenant McLeod. Later that afternoon the lieutenant notified the civil police at Hindhead whereupon Superintendent Webb of the Godalming Division arrived at the scene with Inspector Head.

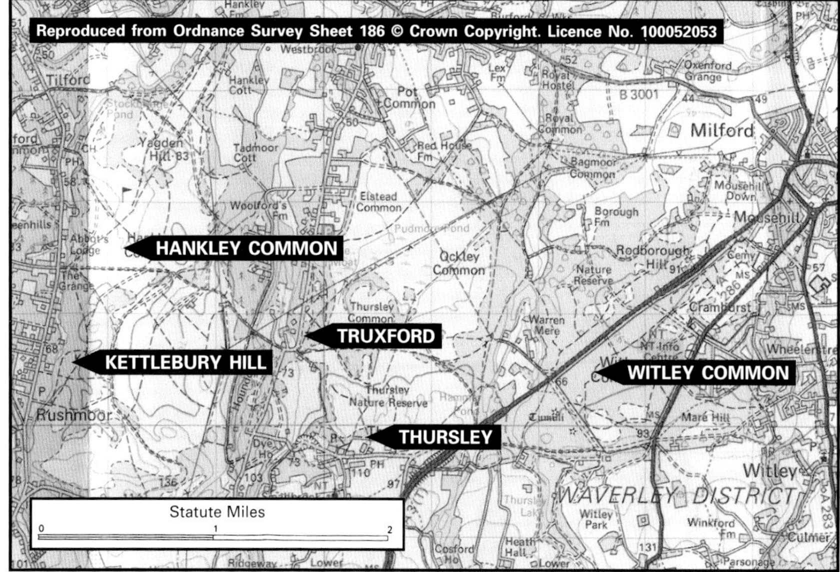

There are still mounds of earth on Hankley Common but all are now covered with heather.

On October 7, 1942, Dr. Keith Simpson received a telephone call from the Surrey police. A body had been found buried on Hankley Common, near Godalming. Would Dr. Simpson come at once?

We arrived at the common to find a party of policemen headed by the Chief Constable of Surrey, and including Dr. Eric Gardner, the pathologist. Greetings were exchanged and we climbed a windy ridge, rain-swept and dismal. I have often thought it odd how it nearly always began to rain when Dr. Simpson and I reached the scene of a crime. Until our arrival it had been quite bright and sunny. As we struggled up the ridge, Superintendent Roberts told us that on the previous day two marines had discovered an arm sticking from a mound of earth on top of the ridge and had reported it to the police. The body had been left buried until the pathologists arrived.

We reached the mound and stood looking at the arm. We shivered a little in the wet wind, and tried to warm ourselves with cigarettes. Below us, soldiers were at mortar practice, and their shells whirled and whined over our heads.

The two pathologiests took shovels and began carefully uncovering the body, until the sprawling corpse of a girl in her teens lay exposed.

The arm and leg can be seen protruding from the mound of earth as first photographed by the police.

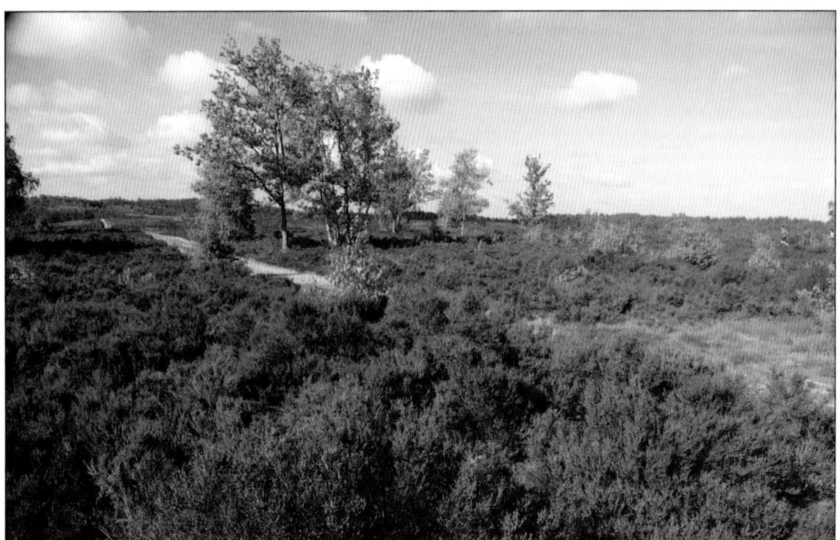

She was clothed in a green and white summer dress, light summer underwear, woollen ankle-socks, and a headscarf, which lay loosely round the neck. The head had been battered by a heavy, blunt implement.

It was decided to move the body to Dr. Simpson's laboratory at Guy's Hospital, where 'C. K. S.,' as we called Dr. Simpson, had it placed in a large carbolic tank. He wanted to study it in his 'spare time.'

Molly Lefebure, Illustrated, December 4, 1954

On 7th October 1942 a party of Marines was exercising in the sand dunes high up on Hankley Common, near Godalming, when one of them caught sight of a dried brown hand sticking out from a mound of earth. He looked more closely and saw, also shrivelled and discoloured, part of a leg.

The Surrey police were called in by field telephone, and when Superintendent Webb saw the hand and leg he decided it was a case for experts and simply posted a guard and covered the mound with a mackintosh sheet. By noon next day we were all there: Major Nicholson, the Chief Constable, and Detective Superintendent Roberts, head of the Surrey CID; sundry other police officers, including the photographer; my old friend Dr Eric Gardner, instructed by the Coroner, and I as medico-legal adviser to the Surrey Police. The famous Dectective Inspector Ted Greeno was on his way from Scotland Yard.

Roberts saw the area cordoned off and the photographer started taking pictures. I collected samples of the soil and examined the remains of the hand. The thumb and first two fingers had been bitten away close to their roots, as by rats. Both the hand and the leg were becoming mummified, so death had occurred at least a few weeks before.

I said Gardner and I had better do the digging, as the body was fragile, and we pulled away the turves and soil with gloved hands. 'Buried five or six weeks ago,' Gardner said confidently after turning over a sod of earth that had been lying upside down; the heather growing on it was still green and had already flowered, and Gardner knew his Surrey heaths. 'Heather finishes flowering about the beginning of September in these parts,' he explained. This observation initially 'timed' the murder for the police.

It was a very shallow burial and the body was disintegrating so we scooped more than we dug as we wondered what was going to

The Surrey Constabulary immediately called in one of the leading forensic pathologists of the day, Dr Keith Simpson. Together with Dr Eric Gardner, they carefully scraped away the soil to reveal a woman's body lying face down.

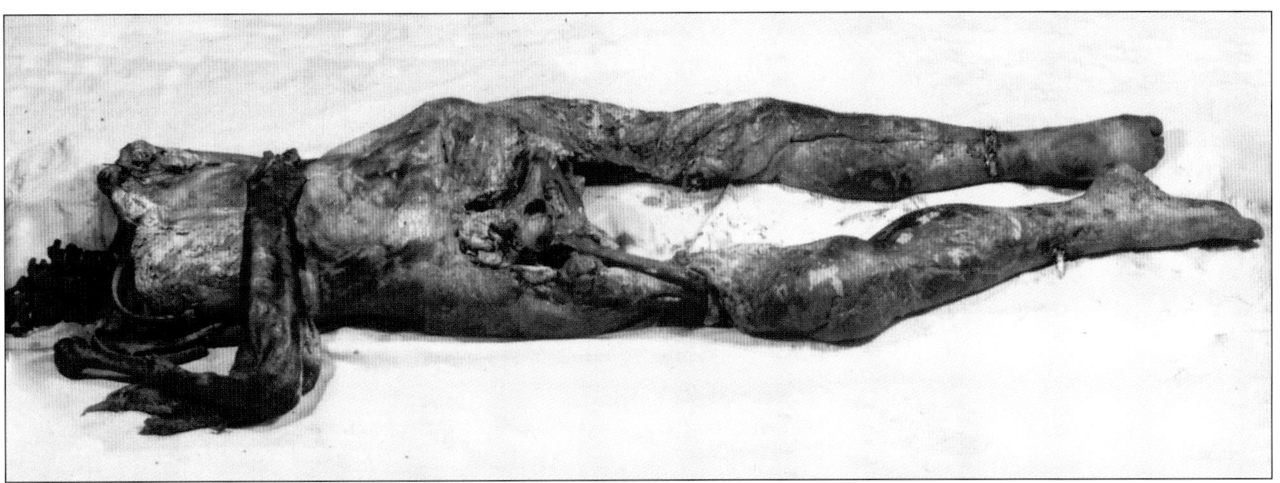

As the body was in such an advanced state of decomposition, Dr Simpson decided to have it taken back to his laboratory at Guy's Hospital in London where he could immerse it in a carbolic bath to kill off the maggots.

emerge. A ritual burial on a hilltop? A sex assault and strangling? Concealment after a stabbing in London, or an abortion death in some near-by city? It could well be any of these.

The clothing was female: a soiled and rather tatty green and white summer frock with a lace collar, held round the waist by a string; a slip, a vest, a brassiere and french panties. All the underclothes were shabby but not disarranged, and her legs were only slightly apart. A head scarf was tied loosely round her neck, knotted in front, but the loop was much too slack for strangling. She lay face downward with her right arm outstretched. The back of her skull was smashed in, and as a result of vermin action her head was falling to pieces. 'A heavy blunt instrument,' I told the police. 'Perhaps an iron bar, or a wooden pole or stake.' She wore socks but no shoes. I saw one sock was torn, and found lacerations above and below the ankle with soil ground deeply into both. A short graze led down into each wound, and a third graze ran out of the lower wound towards the toes. 'I think she was dragged here, head first, probably by her right arm. I suppose her shoes fell off on the way.'

My secretary, Molly Lefebure, later recalled shivering in a cold wind on that unsheltered moor, but I only remember taking off my jacket because of the heat. The stench of putrefaction was strong, the air was buzzing with flies, and the remains of the body were crawling with maggots. It must have been exposed to the air before burial long enough for the blowflies to settle and propagate. 'Possibly even for one or two days,' I told the police. I thought there might have been two, less probably three, successive egg layings. 'The body could have been incompletely covered, perhaps by loose leaves or a cloth or blanket.'

Chief Inspector Greeno arrived and organized a search for the murder weapon and shoes, coat and handbag. The masses of blowfly larvae made it difficult for us to find out much more at the time. I could see there was some kind of wound in the right forearm, but the maggots obscured it. It would need a day or two in a Lysol bath to kill them off, and we probably had a week's work in the lab ahead of us, piecing the shattered skull together. I proposed to Gardner that we should ask the Coroner, Dr Wills Taylor, to let us take the body to Guy's to finish the job.

The Coroner agreed, and we carefully rolled the disintegrating body into the waterproof sheet. Maggots seethed out of the chest and the abdominal cavity when the body was moved, and by teatime thousands more were struggling for life in a carbolic bath in the Guy's Hospital mortuary.

When the maggots had died off Superintendent Webb came to Guy's and watched me remove the clothes. He thought he might have seen the frock before. The woman's features were unrecognisable but I could build up some kind of description of her. Her teeth and bone X- rays put her age between nineteen and twenty. She was 5 feet 4 inches in height, with small hands and feet. Her hair was sandy brown, fine, bobbed, and had been bleached some weeks before death. Her two upper central teeth had been knocked out but I could see they had been very prominent, with sufficient overlap to be remarked on.

At first I thought she had been dead five, six, or seven weeks. Parts of her breasts and thighs had been converted to the white substance, foul-smelling and unctuous to the touch, called adipocere. This stiffening and swelling of the body fats usually takes at least five or six weeks in a temperate climate; but maggots generate heat. The heavy infestation could have raised the temperature of the tissues sufficiently for the formation of adipocere within a month.

Her skull had been shattered by a single blow, very violent and certainly lethal. There were thirty-eight major pieces, and Gardner worked all one Sunday and two evenings in my laboratory, sorting, drilling, wiring, and riveting them together until we had the cranium intact except for a gap at the back which had evidently been occupied by the smaller fragments we had left over. The blow must have caused immediate unconsciousness and death very shortly, perhaps within a few minutes.

Professor Keith Simpson,
Forty Years of Murder, 1978

The skull had fallen to pieces when the body was moved so Dr Gardner spent some hours wiring it back together again. It then became clear that the back of the girl's head had been stoved in. Produced as evidence in court, the skull remains an exhibit in the Gordon Medical Museum at Guy's Hospital.

Meanwhile police continued to comb the common for clues. In this photo taken on October 15, the car indicates the position of the cart track; the man on the horizon to the left of the fir tree standing roughly where the body was found, with the detective on the right on the spot where various personal items were discovered.

Our car stands on the same track although a forest has now grown up to mask the view.

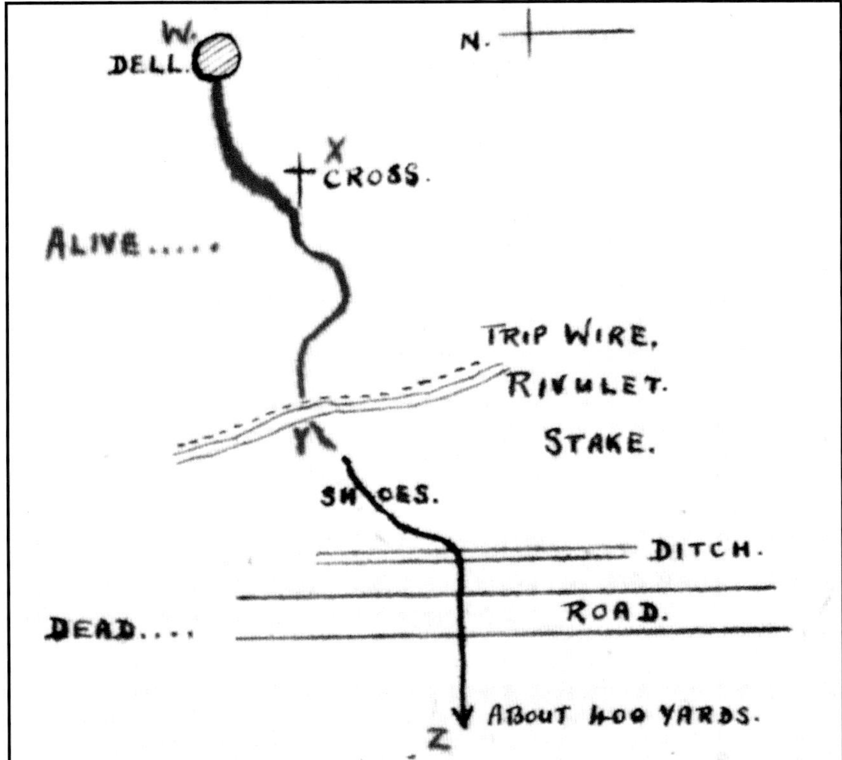

I have attempted to reconstruct the crime from information available to me, from what I saw on Thursley Common on 8th October, from what was shown me there on 18th October by Chief Inspector Greeno, and from what I found in my examinaiton of the body of the deceased.

Presumably there was a quarrel and an attack made on the girl, when she was struck on the top of the head by some pointed instrument which may well have been the jack-knife. In this attack she apparently raised her arms in front of her to protect herself, and received a wound on the front of the right arm, and in the palm of the right hand as she lowered it, and from both of these wounds tendons were dragged out, it is suggested by the turned point of the knife already described.

I suggest this attack was begun in the bothy near the top of a steep bank some distance to the east of the 'grave', and that as a result of it the deceased ran away down a track that eventually crosses a stream at the bottom of the slope nearly 400 yards from the bothy. If this were so, she would be running in a direct line for the 'grave' which would be several hundred yards directly in front of her.

It is possible that in the attack the chain of her crucifix was broken, and that when she ran down the slope it fell; anyhow it was found just off the track as it runs downhill.

Just before the stream is reached, and actually on its bank, is a trip wire; if she fell over this she would fall with her face on the opposite bank which is hard. It is possible if the fall were a heavy one her projecting front teeth were broken, or they may equally well have been broken from a blow from a fist delivered during the attack.

Somewhere about this stage I presume the final blow with the stake to have been given. It was found on the direct line between the bothy and the 'grave', a line continuing the course of the track down the slope; on the ground some few yards beyond the stream, and between it and the stream was one of her shoes and a little beyond it the other one.

She may have been struck as she was lying after tripping over the wire (if she did actually do so) or she may have got up, run a little way and then fallen, but I think it is certain that when she was struck she was lying on her face, for on the opposite side of the head to the injury on the back of it, and more especially opposite that part of this injury to the left of the middle line where the intensity of the blow was greatest, is the right cheek bone; this was completely detached. In my opinion this was due to heavy contact with the ground when her face was lying on it and the opposite pole of her head was heavily struck.

After death the body was left lying possibly somewhere near, possibly carried back to the bothy, but certainly for some days exposed to the attacks of rats and infestation by flies. It was then presumably dragged by one arm up the hill to the 'grave', when the grazes on the right foot were sustained and a fragment of the skull fell out.

It was laid at the foot of the mound already mentioned and the soil lightly scraped over it, and this was probably done after dark or the tell-tale hand would never have been left exposed.

Dr Eric Gardner, November 1, 1942

The most prominent feature in Dr Gardner's report, which still remains as it was in 1942, is the rivulet.

Early on Chief Inspector Ted Greeno was called in from Scotland Yard and the identity of the victim was soon established. PC Tim Halloran, stationed at Godalming, remembered a girl who looked as if she was living rough back in July. He had taken her in to the police station for questioning together with her boyfriend. The policeman had noted her name and including in his description that she was 5ft 4in with big breasts and big uneven teeth. Although dressed like a tramp she spoke nicely and wore a crucifix. She was Joan Pearl Wolfe *(left)*, born March 11, 1923, but was estranged from her mother who lived at Tunbridge Wells following the breaking off of an engagement. Relocating to the Aldershot area, she can best be described by using that old-fashioned term: 'camp follower'. She had spent time in hospital for treatment for a miscarriage and VD. She had been living wild in the forest in wigwams which had been built for her by her Canadian Indian boyfriend Private August Sangret *(right)*, who was stationed at Jasper Camp.

At Jasper Camp his commanding officer told me more about Sangret. The major did know a girl who looked as though she lived rough — so rough that he had given her a pound for food and shelter. He said that Sangret did more than know her; he had lived with her right on the camp site in wigwams that he built, Red Indian style, by binding down a growing sapling to make a frame which he thatched with heather and bracken. Sangret had been arrested for so doing.

The girl's name? Joan Pearl Wolfe. The major knew it because Sangret had talked of marrying her, though he had never gone as far as to ask for official permission and the subject had not been mentioned again. Lately Joan Pearl Wolfe did not seem to have been seen around, either. Now the case was moving. In three weeks, or maybe even in two if I was lucky, I would have enough to confront Sangret, but his course at Jasper Camp was ending and he qualified for a fortnight's leave, starting the next Monday. We had kept details of the murder quiet, but if they came out Sangret might never return and I just could not question Sangret yet. Could the major postpone the man's leave to give me time to marshal facts for that crucial meeting? He thought he could, and meanwhile he would ask Sangret if he still thought of marrying Joan Pearl Wolfe.

They had their talk on Saturday. The girl had gone away, Sangret didn't know where and he didn't seem to care. All the time our questioning and searching went on. At nine o'clock on Monday morning the major came to Godalming police station to tell me that he was sorry, but he could not postpone Sangret's leave after all and that an appeal to a higher officer wouldn't help either.

'Major,' I said, 'do you understand the nature of my enquiries? This is a murder case, you know.'

Yes, he appreciated that, and he was sorry, but in two hours there would be a pay parade. Sangret had asked for a warrant to Glasgow and there was no way in which the major could stop him. 'Very well,' I said, 'I'll have to see him today. I didn't want to, but I must.'

While the men paraded for pay I waited in the major's office with Sergeant Hodge and the local superintendent, Webb. Nobody else knew we were there except the provost sergeant, a wily old warrior called Wade who had been in the Coldstreams in World War One, and who figured that Scotland Yard wouldn't be there unless something serious was afoot. When Sangret had checked in his kit and blankets with the quartermaster, drawn his pay and his warrants and was heading for the camp gate, one of Wade's men called him back. 'Hey, soldier, you're wanted in the guardroom.'

'What for?'

Nobody could answer that except with the well-known army advice, go and find out. He went. And he waited. And he waited. He started asking Ralph Stiles, a provost corporal: 'How long does this go on? How long are they going to keep me here?' He was getting jittery, Stiles noticed. He roamed around the guardroom; he drummed on tables, getting really impatient — or was he nervous?

He went to the shower-room at the back to wash his hands, but the water was cut off. He stayed there four or five minutes and came out again. Of course, nobody searched him on the way in or out. If he had been a prisoner he would have been searched, but he wasn't a prisoner; he was just a soldier somebody wanted to see. But who? He kept asking and nobody could tell him.

Just before eleven-thirty they brought him into the major's office, and a handsome brute he was — stocky, not more than 5 feet 7 or 8 in., with a deep chest and massive shoulders tapering on to a ballet dancer's waist. His hair was oily black and his face lean and swarthy. He was unmistakably Red Indian, but did he have that 'streak of savagery'?

Maybe it was just the waiting that had made him jittery because he was calm now and certainly unawed by the news that we were from Scotland Yard. I told him that we wanted to know about his friendship with Joan Pearl Wolfe, but I did not say that she was dead. In fact, at that stage we still did not know if the body on the common was Joan Wolfe's.

When I said that it would be more convenient to talk in the police station he simply replied, 'That's all right.' He came willingly and at half past two he started to talk. Then more news came through from the dragnet on the common. They had found the girl's shoes, trashy things with high wedge heels and coloured cord lace-ups that she had bought secondhand for five shillings, in the heather thirty yards apart and three-quarters of a mile from where the body had been found. One had the sole torn loose as though she had been dragged along, feet trailing, before the shoe fell off.

Among the thousands of twigs and trunks and fallen branches in Houndown Wood that skirted the common a stick had been found — a stick different from all the others because hairs were found sticking to it. They were hairs from the head of an Eton-cropped bleached blonde and when they were mounted on microscope slides they matched with hairs from the grave.

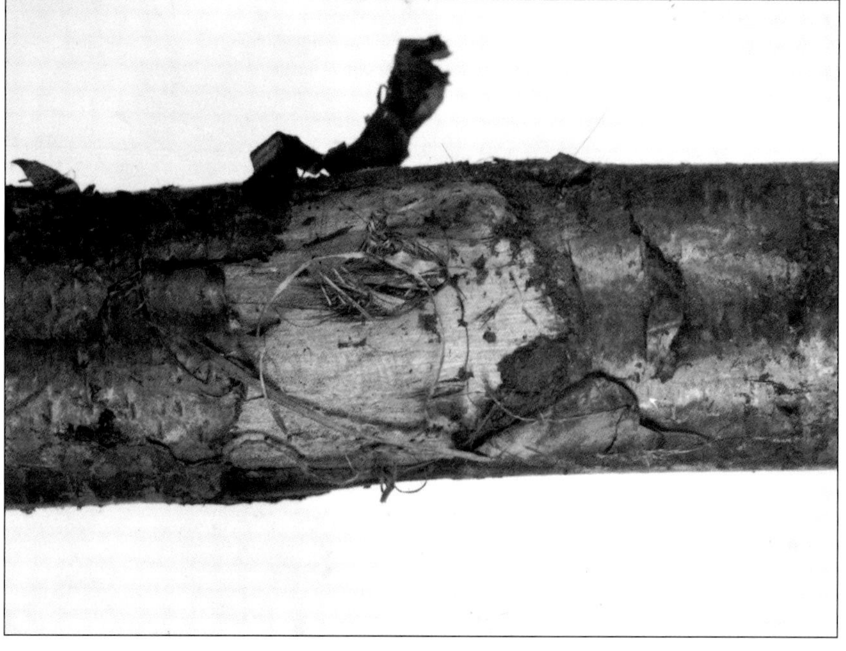

Section of birch stake upon which hairs were adhering and from which hairs were taken for examination.

The stick — a birch stake thirty-eight and half inches long and an inch and a half thick — was put beside the skull Dr. Gardner had built up. The thickness of it fitted exactly into that smashed-in cavity at the back.

But the girl was dying — or dead — before that blow. The stick was not the instrument of death. What we were looking for was something sharp and curiously hooked. She had put her hands up to protect her face and the murder weapon had stabbed her in the arm, dragging the tendons with it as it came out. There was also a strange wound right on top of the skull that could cause death; it was round like a hole made with a drill, and bevelled as though it had been finished with a brace and bit. What weapon made wounds like that?

At seven-thirty Sangret was still talking and Sergeant Hodge was still writing it all down in longhand. Sangret had a soft voice and he spoke slowly, but he was never lost for words, and his memory was phenomenal. He could remember dates and fit the days to them and when we checked with the calendar they were always right. He remembered the days and dates of his arrival in England, of his posting to Jasper Camp, and of his first meeting with Joan Pearl Wolfe. He remembered the things they said and the spot where they made love within three hours of meeting.

We took a break and Sangret and I went for a walk, and he remembered every foot of ground where he used to stroll with Joan. He took me to a house he called 'the old lady's cottage' where Joan had once spent a night — that was the night before they met. He stormed up hills and pointed out the whole panorama of the plain, pitted with tank traps and pimpled with those man-made mounds. He showed me where he built wigwams in which the two of them had lived, first behind the officers' lines at Jasper Camp and then behind the sergeants' lines. He took me to the burned-out shell of a cricket pavilion at Thursley into which they had moved after they were warned off the wigwams.

Suddenly I said, 'Let's go over there,' pointing to where we had found the body. He was sullen and answered, 'No, I don't want to go there.' I pointed to the woods where the stick had been found a few hours earlier and he repeated, 'I don't want to go there.'

We went back to the police station and at three-thirty in the morning he was still talking — and Hodge was still writing. We made Sangret a bed in the police station and next morning he went on talking. Meanwhile we took his kit out of the quartermaster's store to inspect his blankets. One had been washed recently, but there was still a suspicion of blood in three places — not enough for Dr. Roche Lynch, the analyst, to swear that it was blood, but enough to convince him that it could be. Furthermore, the stains were just where they would be if a girl of five-foot-four were stabbed and then wrapped in the blanket.

To check this further we took a policewoman who was the same size as the dead girl and marked her in the places where the girl was wounded. Then we wrapped her in that same ghastly blanket — and the markings tallied.

Sangret went on talking. He slept that night again at the police station, and on Wednesday, Sir Norman Kendal rang me up from Scotland Yard.

'Where have you got this fellow?' he asked, and I replied, 'He's still lodging with us.'

'I suppose you know what you are doing?' he said. The Assistant Commissioner was worried and, frankly, so was I.

The law of this land says that you cannot detain a person more than twenty-four hours without charging him before a court. Defence counsel could get very nasty about this if we ever got into court. If we couldn't go to court and we had kept this man for days without charging him, some M.P. might get even nastier. But I had to go on. This was murder, and it had to be proved.

The 3ft length of birch now preserved at Guy's Hospital.

The dragnet was still out; behind the burned-out cricket pavilion was found a pair of girl's stockings and a black elastic garter, a knitting-book and four pieces of sacking which had been her furniture when the pavilion was her home.

The cricket ground at Thursley with the pavilion on the far side as pictured *(above)* by the police in 1942 and *(below)* by *After the Battle* in 2011.

When interviewed, Arthur Robinson, a road-worker employed by Thursley Council said that on September 2 he had started working on Dye House Hill near where the fire-damaged cricket pavilion stood on the pre-war pitch. Just before 7 a.m. on September 7 or 8, he walked across to the pavilion and looked inside to find a female lying on the floor. She wore a grey check-pattern coat and had a blanket over her legs. Robinson asked her what she was doing there and she replied: 'I must sleep somewhere. I cannot sleep outside'. Then Police Constable Brian Gunning reported that 'On the 13th October, whilst searching among gorse bushes at the rear of the cricket pavilion, Thursley, Surrey, I found a pair of lady's fawn coloured stockings, a knitting instruction book and four pieces of sacking. These articles were hidden under a thick gorse bush about 12 yards from the rear of the cricket pavilion. I could not find any knitting. On the 16th October, I found a black elastic garter in the copse at Houndown Bottom, Thursley. I handed these articles over to Superintendent Webb.'

On Thursday while Sangret was still at the police station the finds were more dramatic, and not a little pathetic. These were a little white elephant charm and a letter which Joan Pearl Wolfe had written to August Sangret after the police had sent her into the public ward of a hospital. We found also an identity card and a National Health card, mildewed and illegible — until Scotland Yard laboratories deciphered the name: Joan Pearl Wolfe. Something else was found — the crucifix P.C. Halloran remembered her wearing. A straggling branch had torn her neck as she raced through the woods in terror just before the murderer caught up and smashed her skull with that last mighty blow.

It was now beyond doubt that the dead girl was Joan Pearl Wolfe but to make even more certain I went to Tunbridge Wells, and found the girl's mother whom she had last visited the previous March. I showed her the white elephant. She remembered bringing the charm home from Hastings two years before for Joan.

We still had no proof that Sangret was the man who killed her. We had the stick with which she was hit, but we wanted the weapon with which she was stabbed. If we could find that and trace it back to him.

Sangret was still talking and still remembering many things with amazing clarity. From his statement we began to see almost three-dimensionally this pathetic little tramp who was all a bad girl is supposed to be — her own mother suspected that she was diseased. She could not live without sex, but she could be unshakably faithful to one man while romance lasted. She allowed herself to be ordered about like a dog, to be left shut in a shack all day till her master returned at night. Yet she had a strong streak of religion and wrote beautiful things on the wall of the shack.

They had first met the day after one lover — she called him Francis, but Sangret did not know whether that was his Christian name or surname — was posted back to Canada. She was distraught when Sangret spoke to her in the pub opposite a cinema in Godalming about 8 p.m. on Friday, July 17. He was then on his second pint and she was drinking a lemonade, because she neither drank nor smoked. She wasn't looking for men. She had been looking for a job. She was bedraggled and dirty, but before eleven she had let Sangret take the place of Francis — 'I asked her if she would go with me, and she did not refuse.' They parted unlingeringly to meet again by accident four days later outside a fish-and-chip shop, and later they made love.

Three days afterwards Sangret received a letter from her, and asked a friend to read it because he could neither read nor write. This was the letter we had found in which she said she was in hospital. She had fainted in the street, and she thought she was pregnant. A week later she was out of hospital and Sangret built a love-nest for them — that Red Indian wigwam behind the officers' lines at his camp — and they lived together until the military police found them there on August 20.

There were some gloriously hot days in August 1942 and some passionately hot nights. Sangret remembered that at 10 p.m. he used to return to the camp for roll call and then go back to the wigwam and Joan Pearl.

Sangret and Joan Pearl first met at the The Richmond Arms pub at the top of the High Street in Godalming.

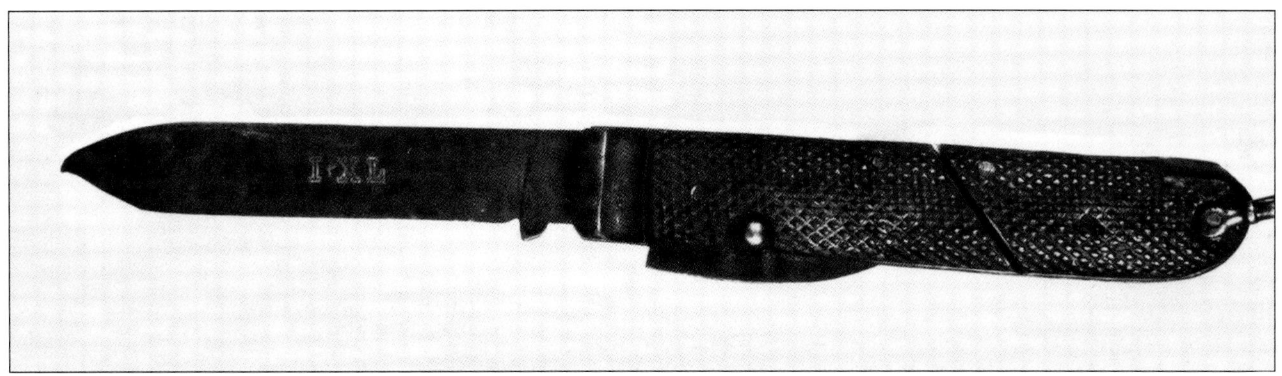

Above: **The knife with the hooked blade is also preserved at Guy's Hospital as one of the exhibits retained by Dr Simpson.**

Below: **Photographs showing the wounds caused in right forearm and top of the head.**

After their second wigwam was found (and Sangret spent the night in the guardroom as a result) Joan was again taken to hospital, dirty and verminous. She took her leave three days later and spent the first night in the station at Godalming. On the next night, Wednesday, September 2, they moved into the wreck of the cricket pavilion at Thursley. Sangret said that an air-raid warden had ordered them to leave, but he relented when Joan Pearl pleaded and they stayed there another week, until Monday, September 14. The last time he saw her, he continued, was when he went to camp that morning, because when he waited at their trysting place in the evening she did not turn up.

Where had she gone? 'Maybe,' said Sangret, 'with a German soldier' — actually a Sudeten Czech in the Canadian Army — or with an American soldier he accused of trying to talk her into bed, or with her previous boy-friend, Francis.

That was the end of Sangret's statement, which was the longest I remember in a murder hunt; fifty-eight pages of Hodge's handwriting and 17,000 words. It boiled down to this, boy meets girl, true love runs unsmooth and suddenly girl vanishes, leaving boy sorrowing. But Sangret was lying somewhere. The air-raid warden Sangret mentioned told me that he not only ordered them out of the pavilion, but that he made them go, so they must have lived somewhere else, probably in another wigwam for their last week together. I was certain that they did not arrange to meet on the Monday night because Joan was dead before Monday dawn.

Hodge read the long statement through to Sangret and I showed him the crucifix we had found on the common. I showed him some cheap red-and-blue ringed socks she used to wear, a piece cut from her dress, her stockings and her shoes — one with the wedge sole still hanging off.

Shivering, he sat head in hands for a moment, and then he spoke. 'I guess you have found her. Everything points to me. I guess I shall get the blame.'

I said, 'Yes, she is dead.'

'She might have killed herself,' he said.

I took him back to his commanding officer at the camp. His leave was overdue and there was a girl in Glasgow waiting for him. He had written her passionate letters, through the same soldier who wrote and read his correspondence with Joan. We could not stop him going. If only we could have found that murder weapon with the strangely hooked end!

Sangret went to Glasgow and the next day for me seemed like disaster. First I found that a reporter had caused hell's delight by pretending to be me. Everywhere I went these reporters swarmed — they were not the experienced murder gangs with whom I had worked for years, but newcomers — and when they followed me to my lunch table, I said, 'Look, leave me alone now and I'll give you a statement later.'

Two were named to take the statement which I gave to them, simply, 'Tell your editors to withdraw the war reserves and send me some regulars.'

After that I felt a little better, but there was worse to come. A rumour reached me that eight days earlier, on the first Sunday of our search, one of the dragnet policemen had found a jack-knife. He had tried to clean it up to use as a gardening knife, but as he couldn't get the rust off he threw it away, sure it had nothing to do with our case. But the knife had a white handle, like the one Joan Pearl Wolfe used to hack at her chunks of bread. It could be the murder weapon. Where was it now?

I questioned all sixty of the dragnet policemen and one of them admitted to finding the knife. He had found a ration bag containing a piece of soap and a rosary — Joan Pearl Wolfe's rosary — and had thrown that away as well. This constable and I scoured the common. We found the ration bag, but not the knife. One of the half-tracks must have ploughed it back into the earth.

That night Sir Norman Kendal asked me on the telephone, 'What are we going to do about this constable?'

'Nothing,' I answered.

'That's a very charitable view. But why?'

'He has been truthful,' I said. 'If he had lied, as some men would have done, that would really have complicated the case.'

'I suppose that's one way of looking at it.'

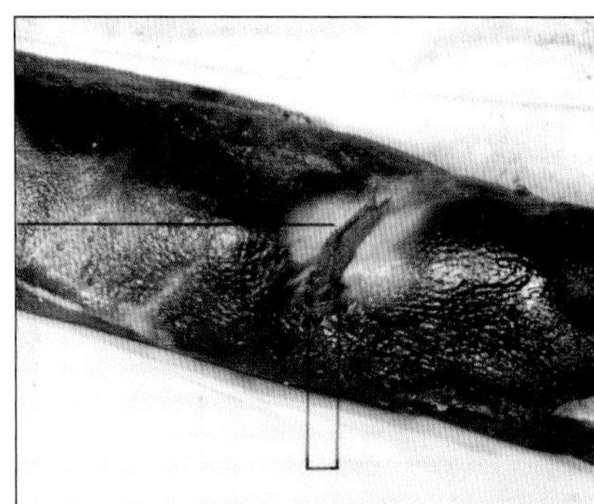

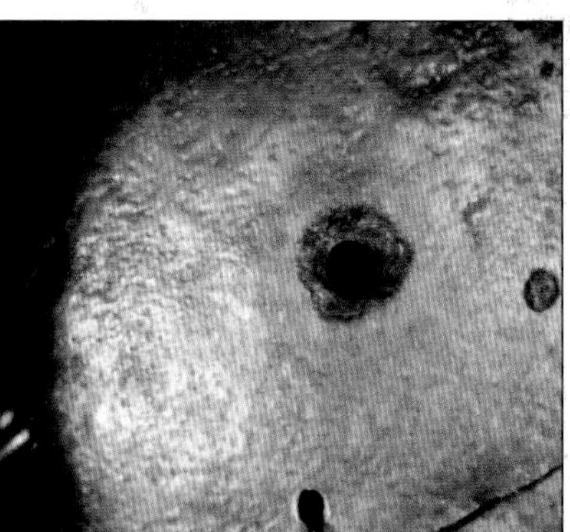

On the morning of November 27, the U-bend on the six-inch drain in the lavatory and shower room of the guardhouse at Jasper Camp showed signs of being blocked. As it was being cleared, a black Army jack-knife, fitted with one blade and a tin opener, was found. The tip of the blade had broken away leaving a hook like a parrot's beak.

Unlike the Americans who reserved the right to try their own servicemen under the Visiting Forces Act, the Canadian government placed no such restriction so Sangret was tried in a British court. This was held in the Surrey Winter Assizes in the County Hall at Kingston upon Thames on February 22, 1943. On Tuesday, March 2, the jury took only two hours to bring in a verdict of guilty.

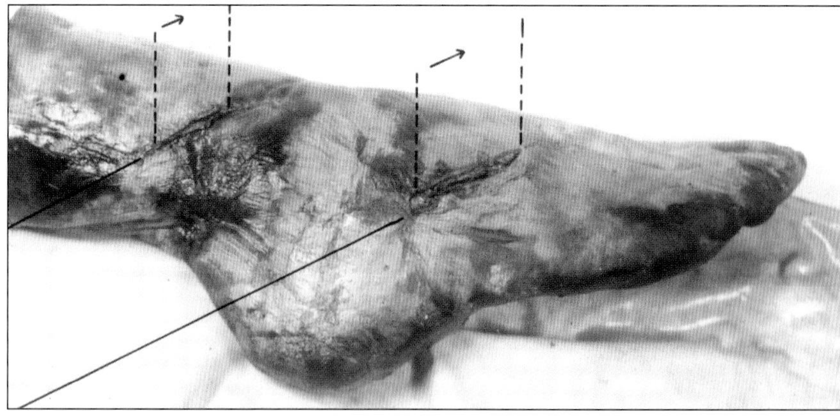

Evidence in court. Dragging wounds across the right ankle and foot.

'It's the only way,' I commented, and we went on searching.

We discovered one very odd fact. Sangret had been a silent man. He had scarcely mentioned Joan to anybody, but after Sunday September 13 — the night on which I was sure she died — he had suddenly become talkative. He told one soldier that Joan had gone to hospital again but that he didn't know why. He told another that he had sent her home because he didn't like the way she dressed. To a third he said simply, 'She's left me' — and this to a man he had told two days earlier, 'I'm not fussy about getting married, but I suppose it's the only thing I can do.'

To the man who wrote his letters for him, Sangret said Joan was 'off on a three weeks' "scheme"' — though what civilians were doing on schemes he never explained. Then he started dictating a letter to 'my dear sweetheart' in Glasgow. The soldier asked, 'What if Joan finds out?' and Sangret replied, 'She will never find out.' To another soldier he said simply, 'She is crazy enough to kill herself.'

All that week Sangret went through a pantomime exactly like a man trying to build up an alibi. A soldier mentioned that he was going into Hindhead, so Sangret said, 'See if you can see Joan there.' He went up to the 'old lady's cottage' — though he had never been there before and Joan had stayed only one night at the cottage — to ask if she was there. He kept nipping out of a pub 'to see if I can see Joan', and, when he met a twelve-year-old girl who had vainly helped Joan to seek rooms after they were ordered out of the cricket pavilion, he said: 'Have you seen that girl I was with last week? I haven't met her since.'

We reached the seventh week of the case. Suddenly on Monday, November 27, there was a phone call from Provost Sergeant Wade at Jasper Camp, 'I've got something interesting to show you.' It was a jack-knife with a strangely hooked end. Somebody had snapped off the tip and ground it again so that the end was now shaped like a parrot's beak.

I took the knife to Dr. Gardner and said to him, This is what we've been looking for ever since the case started — the knife that killed Joan Pearl Wolfe.' It fitted exactly into the wounds in the skull, but the doctor put his finger on that curious countersunk hole in the skull and asked, 'How do you make it do this?'

'Like this,' I replied. 'He has already stabbed her several times with the knife. He stabs her on the head for the third time. She's dizzy and she spins round. If he had twisted the knife in the wound you would get the countersinking, and by having the wound twist under the knife you get the same countersinking.'

'That's right,' said Dr. Gardner.

How had the knife come to light? Somebody had put it down the waste pipe in the shower behind the guardroom at Jasper Camp — but whoever it was did not know the pipe was blocked. That person had not been in the shower-room long enough to find out. Who could that be? Sangret, on the morning I waited for him in the major's office.

Could anybody swear it was Sangret's knife? Yes, a military policeman who discovered him and Joan in their wigwam on August 20 and who saw the knife sticking in a tree there. And a provost corporal swore that when Sangret was released from the guardroom the corporal handed the knife back to him.

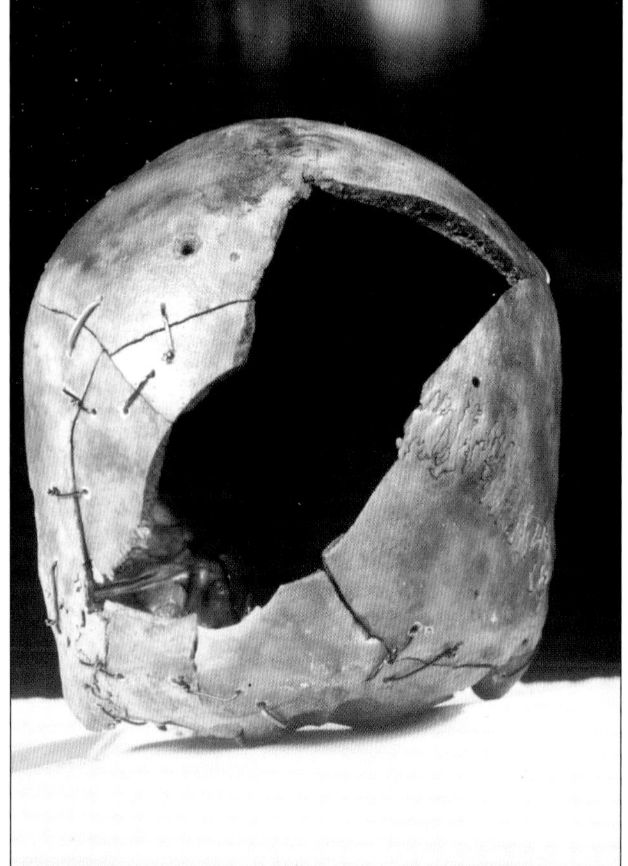

Conclusive proof of the weapon which was used to smash her skull to pieces.

The little girl remembered that, and she also remembered that at the first meeting Sangret had said, 'I don't care if she doesn't get rooms; I'm going back to camp.' The girl's brother-in-law had cycled in search of Joan Pearl Wolfe to offer her a room, but he never found her.

I traced the former boy-friend, Francis, back to Canada and found he had been there long before the murder. I found 'the German soldier', who was also in the clear, and I went through thousands of photographs at U.S. headquarters to find the G.I. Sangret had tried to implicate. We had no name for him, but I traced him to Ireland and fetched him back. He admitted telling Joan three times to leave Sangret, he admitted asking Sangret to stop treating her like a squaw — but he was posted out of England before she was murdered.

Now Joan Pearl Wolfe's last night could be reconstructed. It was Sunday and the two of them were sitting in Houndown Wood probably talking about marriage, as she did too often for a man who had a girlfriend in Glasgow and another back in Canada.

They quarrelled and she got up. So did he, and punched her face. She ran but he caught up quickly and slashed at her face with his knife. She shielded herself with her hands and he kept on slashing. That 'streak of the savage' was out all right.

He stabbed her seven times in the hand and arm, three times in the head. Reeling in terror, she ran downhill out of the woods. She got a hundred yards before she fell over a booby trap, a trip-wire, and sprawled on her face. He grabbed a birch stake and smashed at the back of the skull so viciously that it caved in, and her cheek bone was crushed against the ground.

Then he dragged her back into the wood. One shoe came off; the other one almost parted from its sole before it too came off. She was dead now. He wrapped her in the blanket and left her. She lay in the wood for days before Sangret had an idea. He and Joan used to gather blackberries in a two-gallon billy-can and sell them for seven or eight shillings to the sergeants' mess. So he almost filled the billy-can before begging the afternoon off because, he told his instructor, he had been asked to gather more blackberries for the sergeants.

He went into the wood and buried the girl, and then topped up the billy to look as though he had spent the whole afternoon blackberrying. He went to the sergeants' mess, but they did not want his blackberries.

Joan's father, Charles Wolfe, died in April, 1930, and was buried on the 26th in Tonbridge Cemetery. At first, we thought she would have been buried with him . . .

That was the case against August Sangret. He had been posted to Aldershot and I went there, but no Sangret. 'God!' I thought. 'After all this he's skipped.' But no, he was in sick bay with some trivial illness and I returned a fortnight later. This time he had tripped and hurt his face and was in sick bay again, so on December 6 I paid my third visit to fetch him back to Thursley. We walked over Hankley Common again, looking at things in more detail this time, and again when I pointed to the spot where Joan Pearl Wolfe had died he said, 'I don't want to go there.'

At 4 p.m. he was charged with murder. 'I didn't do it,' he said. 'No, sir. Someone did, but I'll have to take the rap.'

At the first hearing in Godalming court I found a girl slipping him sweets. At the assize when I was asked how long he had been kept at the police station to make his statement, the judge repeated my words after me, 'A week!'

'Now it comes,' I thought. 'Trouble!' But no, the defence counsel said how pleased he was with the meticulous care I had taken. 'It has helped the defence considerably.'

However, it didn't help Sangret to escape the gallows. I had interviewed thousands of people in this case and seventy-four of them went into the witness-box. The case was so watertight that, as Sir Norman Kendal said later, Sangret's appeal against the death sentence 'was almost a farce'.

One small doubt remained. Sangret murdered the girl because she was expecting his child — but was she? Was she expecting anybody's child?

The doctors didn't think so on the occasion that the police sent her to hospital, and when her body was found it was too late to tell.

But this is certain: Sangret did murder her. He confessed before he died, and this is where I quarrel with the rules. It is never announced when a murderer confesses. But why not? There are always cranks and crackpots to argue that some wicked policeman has framed some poor fellow. So why make an official secret of the fact that the policeman did his job?

Ex-Detective Chief Superintendent Edward Greeno,
War on the Underworld, 1960

. . . **but sadly Joan Pearl Wolfe appears to have been given an anonymous burial. The final ignominy is that the name of the perpetrator has been commemorated on the Memorial to the Missing at Brookwood, in spite of the fact that he is not missing but buried in the confines of Wandsworth Prison (see pages 356-359).**

Albert Pierrepoint, assisted by Henry Critchell, carried out the execution on March 2, 1943, but because the War Office failed to give Sangret a dishonourable discharge beforehand, his name was put forward after the war to be inscribed on Panel 23 of the memorial, merely because he died while still in service!

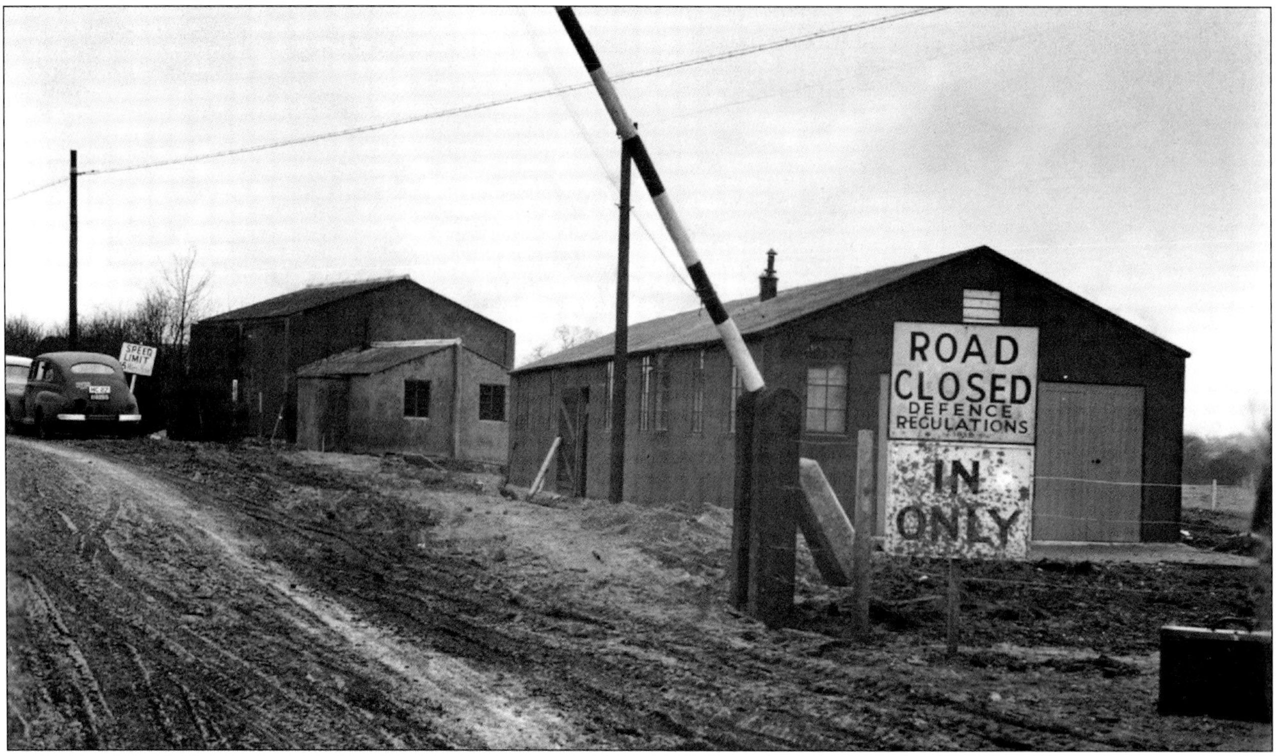

In 1942 this was the Ordnance Depot of the US 827th Engineer Battalion (Aviation) at Desborough, Northamptonshire.

December 27, 1942 – The First American Execution in Britain

A negro private in the U.S. Army, David Cobb, faces the death penalty before an American court-martial, held in East Anglia today.

He is charged 'with malice aforethought wilfully, deliberately, feloniously, unlawfully and with premeditation killing Second-Lieutenant Robert J. Cobner, shooting him with a rifle.'

Cobb pleaded not guilty.

Lieutenant David J. Pinsky, assisted by Lieutenant Reed, prosecuted and Captain Tracey appeared for the defence.

Corporal Willie Mason, a negro, said that on December 27 he was acting as sergeant of the guard at a U.S. camp. Private Cobb was one of the guard and Lieutenant Cobner as officer of the day.

While outside the guard-house Cobb told Cobner 'that he wasn't staying at his post no longer.' The lieutenant then told another guard to arrest the man, but Cobb pointed his rifle at him and told him to halt.

Witness was next told to arrest Cobb, who at once aimed his rifle at him and told him also to halt.

Lieutenant Cobner then started towards Cobb as if to grab his gun, but before he could do so Cobb pulled the trigger. The lieutenant fell to the ground, and Cobb keeping several other soldiers covered, told them to cart the lieutenant away in a jeep.

Medical evidence was given that Cobner had a bullet wound through his chest..

Cobner's clothing was produced in court and showed that the bullet had gone right through his body.

Kettering Evening Telegraph, December 1942.

The camp was located on the Arthingworth road (mis-spelt on the plan opposite). Kevin Lamberth pictured the scene in 2011.

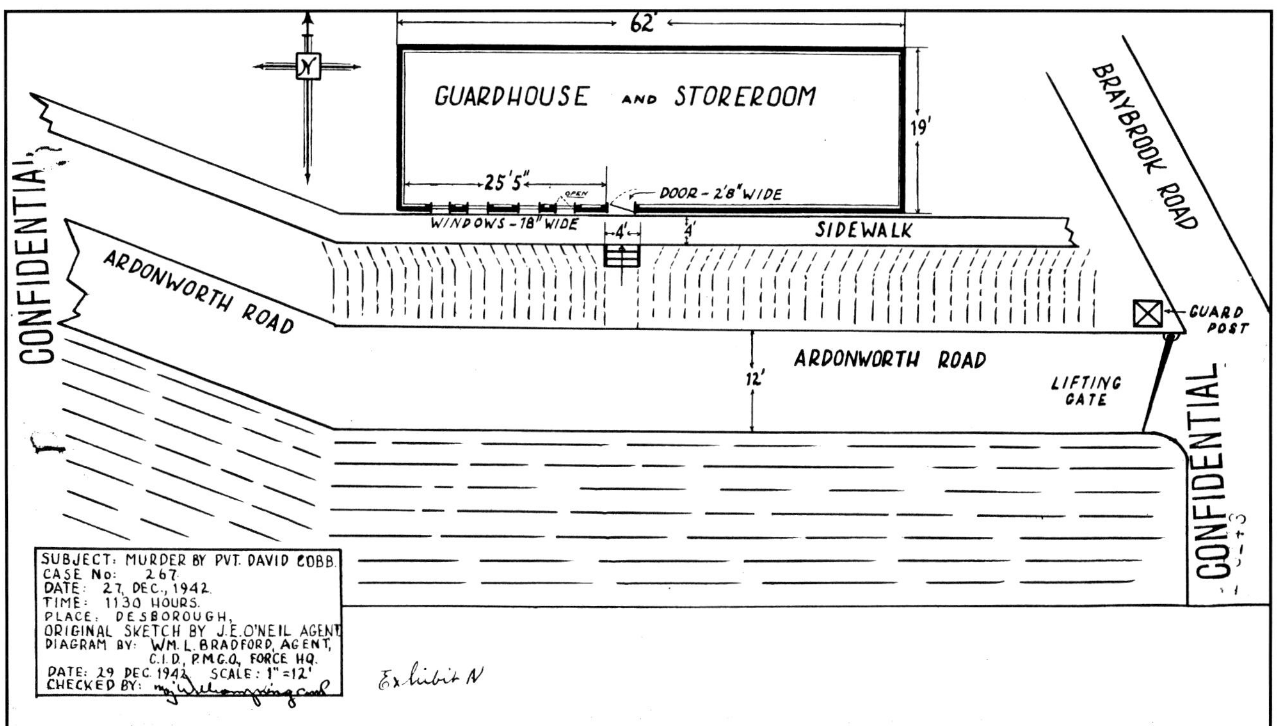

Between 1000 and 1100 hours, 27 December 1942, Lieutenant Cobner came to the guard-house to have some beds moved and to have the premises policed. The accused told him that he was not going to stand post any longer for the reason that he had been on duty for four hours. While talking to the officer, the accused was carrying his rifle across his shoulder in an improper manner.

The deceased told him to act like a soldier, and while addressing an officer, to stand at attention. The accused replied that he did not care as he had been restricted for six months. The deceased called a guard to arrest accused and to put him in the guard-house. When the guard walked towards Cobb, the accused brought his gun down to his waist, pointed it at the guard and halted him. The Sergeant of the Guard was then directed by the deceased to arrest accused, who pointed the gun at him and ordered him to halt. The accused said that he would not give his gun to anyone until he was properly relieved. When the Sergeant of the Guard failed to take the piece, deceased started towards Cobb to take the gun, and when within two or three steps, the accused shot him. The deceased fell to the ground and death was almost instantaneous due to the fact that the bullet penetrated the heart.

After the shot was fired, accused pointed the rifle at the Sergeant of the Guard and the others standing nearby and directed them to place the body of deceased in a jeep and take him to headquarters. After the shooting, accused addressed the group and asked if there was anyone who didn't like what he had done.

The testimony of the accused is substantially as follows. He had been in the Army for one year, and had been taught that the proper way to relieve a guard was for the Sergeant or Corporal of the Guard to bring a relief. That he went on duty at midnight, 26 December 1942 and stood his post for five hours; he was relieved and again went on duty at 1000 hours the following day. That his post was at the guard-house.

Lieutenant Cobner and the Sergeant of the Guard came to the guard-house at about 1130 hours. Accused asked the Sergeant of the Guard when he could get a relief so that he would not have to walk his post for so long and not receiving an answer, inquired of the deceased if there would be any possibility

A set of steps led down to the guardroom and, although the camp has been completely demolished, amazingly Kevin found that the steps still remain, albeit somewhat overgrown.

According to his only brother Richard, who was himself a Second World War Third Army volunteer infantryman, David Cobb *(left)* was 'wayward and mischievous'. He was the second son of the mild-mannered and upwardly mobile Revd. Howard Cobb and his devoted wife Addie Mae who lived in Dothan, Alabama. He is remembered for his inclination to drink beer and his fondness for playing pool, although much to the consternation of his parents. Richard, his older brother, often took care of David, particularly on Saturday nights after he had drunk 'too many beers and got in his last shot [of pool]'. It was Richard who made sure that David always made it safely home. As Richard and David grew older, Revd. Cobb gave them an ultimatum: go to school or go to work! Richard continued with school and enrolled in the famous Tuskegee Institute before he entered the service. David opted for the latter choice. While in either the 7th or 8th grade he dropped out of the segregated school that both he and Richard attended to work as a driver on a paper delivery truck. He also continued his habit of night-time imbibing and, on some mornings after a night of drinking, it was brother Richard who came again to the rescue and made the delivery rounds at David's request. In 1938, at the age of 17, David married a young local woman from a respected family. Her name was Cornelia Dozier. They lived with the Revd. and Mrs. Cobb and Cornelia gave birth to two children. Howard and Christine. After some marital difficulties, David and Cornelia parted ways. She took their children and went to live with her parents. However, the children preferred the home of their paternal grandparents and spent much of their time with David's parents. Inducted as a volunteer on January 8, 1942, Private David Cobb departed the US from Fort Dix, New Jersey, on December 5 that year and arrived in England on the 16th. Before leaving he had been assigned to a new unit, Company C. 827th Engineers. The crime of which David was accused was committed on Sunday, December 27, 1942, just eleven days after his arrival in the UK.

of being relieved from the post so as to go and eat before going on his next post.

Lieutenant Cobner replied that it did not make any difference to him whether he got relieved or not, and that it was not his fault he had to walk guard around that post but that it was the fault of the men inside. Lieutenant Cobner then told the Sergeant of the Guard to take accused's rifle and put him in the guard-house. Cobb further testified that when the Sergeant of the Guard attempted to take his rifle, he halted him and stated: 'You can't give me an order where you can take that gun on this post, remember I am on guard.' That the lieutenant then made a fast step towards him and he attempted to halt him. The last words of the deceased were: 'Soldier, give me that gun!' The accused testified that when deceased reached for the gun he shot him; he did not know Lieutenant Cobner was the Officer of the Day. The accused was relieved of his post about fifteen minutes after the shooting.

He further testified that he had been on guard duty about twelve times. In answer to a question by the court, he testified that if he had known that Lieutenant Cobner was Officer of the Day he would have obeyed his order. The accused denied that Private Jacobs made any effort to take his gun or that he ever pointed the gun at him; he further denied that the deceased told him to carry his gun like a soldier. The accused admitted, however, that he knew that Corporal William Mason, Jr., was the Sergeant of the Guard.

With reference to the shooting, accused stated that he tried to hit deceased in the hip in order to stop him. Upon inquiry by a member of the court as to why he did not give the Sergeant of the Guard his piece, he replied that he was supposed to be properly relieved. Later he testified that he was afraid to give it to him. He further stated that at no time did he ask the Sergeant or Corporal of the Guard to get the Officer of the Day. The accused, while on the witness stand, was unable to quote or give the substance of any of the General Orders.

Report of Trial by General Court-martial

Two days after Christmas Day, Private Cobb was on guard duty at the main gate. US military police restaged the scene although the Officer of the Day, Lieutenant Cobner, was hardly likely to have worn a trilby!

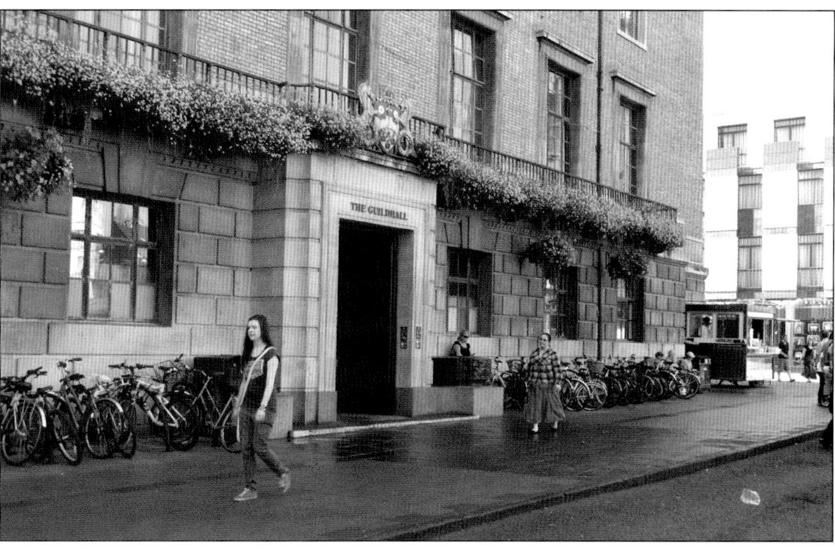

Left: **Cobb's General Court-Martial was held in the Court of Quarter Sessions in the Guildhall in Cambridge.** *Centre:* **This courtroom was frequently used during the war by the US Advocate General for the trial of American servicemen when it temporarily became an extension of United States territory.** *Bottom:* **It closed in 2004 and has since been opened as a tourist attraction.**

David Cobb, a Negro private in the United States Army, who while on guard duty shot and killed an officer, was sentenced at an American court-martial in East Anglia yesterday to be hanged.

Cobb was found guilty by secret ballot after he had told the court he had been taught not to give up his rifle to anyone till he had been properly relieved from guard duty. He said that until that time he had never fired a rifle and had not received instruction in the use of the type of rifle he had.

Kettering Evening Telegraph, January 7, 1943

Professor Robert Lilly, Adjunct Professor of Law at the Salman P. Chase College of Law of the University of Northern Kentucky has studied this case in detail (see *After the Battle* No. 90) and comments that 'while there is no doubt Cobb shot Lieutenant Cobner, there is considerable evidence which indicates that he believed he was acting appropriately according to his training. Cobb had already been on guard duty from midnight until 0530 hours and, after serving a further four hours, he asked Cobner if he could be relieved. Lieutenant Cobner said he could not do anything for him, and he berated Cobb for his appearance and ordered him to shape up. The lieutenant did not like Cobb's response and ordered him to give him his rifle. Cobb testified that he had been taught that to be relieved from guard duty required a specific procedure which Lieutenant Cobner was not following; for instance, did not first remove Cobb from his post to his barracks, and then take his weapon. Nor did Cobner identify himself as the Officer of the Day; neither did he have with him Cobb's replacement. Cobner, according to witnesses, 'crowded' Cobb and backed him up against a truck, while Cobb continually kept saying 'Halt!' Lieutenant Cobner's behaviour confused Cobb, who according to his own testimony, had been taught by a previous commanding officer that while on guard duty not to allow anyone within five paces of his gun.

Cobb also testified that he had been trained with a bolt-action Springfield rifle, and did not know how to handle the MI [Garand semi-automatic rifle] given to him for guard duty. In fact, he testified that he did not know how to load the rifle, a task completed by another trooper in his barracks. The previous day he had been a truck driver. The defence attorney, a captain, did very little to help Cobb. He did not develop a 'theory of defence' which might have elaborated or demonstrated that Cobb's testimony had merit. On two occasions during the one-day trial, the defence attorney referred to the shooting as an 'accident', a term suggesting an occurrence far less serious that one meriting a death sentence. Six days after the conviction, Cobb's attorney wrote to the Commanding General requesting that a plea of clemency be considered. In it, he reasoned that Cobb believed that he was fulfilling his duty as a guard by not relinquishing his rifle until he was properly relieved.

The American military prison was at Shepton Mallet, and they were allowed most of the American customs except the actual method of execution: no standard drop, no hangman's knot, but a variable drop on a modern noose suspended from a British gallows and designed to impart instantaneous death.

The timing of the execution was American-style. It was generally carried out at about one o'clock in the morning. Another custom which was strange to me was the practice of laying on a mighty feast before the execution. We were eating badly in this country at that time, but at an American execution you could be sure of the best running buffet and unlimited canned beer The part of the routine which I found it hardest to acclimatise myself to was the, to me, sickening interval between my introduction to the prisoner and his death. Under British custom I was working to the sort of timing where the drop fell between eight and twenty seconds after I had entered the condemned cell. Under the American system, after I had pinioned the prisoner, he had to stand on the drop for perhaps six minutes while his charge sheet was read out, sentence spelt out, he was asked if he had anything to say and after that I was instructed to get on with the job.

Even a few seconds can be a long time when a man is waiting to die. On my first execution in Shepton Mallet, long before the drop fell, the officer of the escorting party surrounding the scaffold was flat on the floor in collapse. Afterwards, at the continuation of the feast, a soldier said to me of the fainting officer: 'Just imagine a man like that leading you into battle!' I did not think his scorn was justified. A man can fight like a hero, and still be unable to face the death of a comrade in cold blood.

Albert Pierrepoint,
Executioner Pierrepoint, 1974

Shepton Mallet is Britain's oldest-serving prison, having been built in 1625-27 at a cost of £300. When the prison population declined after the First World War, the prison was closed but kept in good repair for possible future use. With the outbreak of hostilities, the military authorities had the need for additional 'glasshouses' and the buildings were transferred to the Army in October 1939. It was soon filled to capacity, some 300 prisoners occupying the 162 cells, and overflow facilities had to be provided by Nissan huts built within the walls. When the Americans arrived in Europe their first military offenders were held in Holywood in Northern Ireland but in mid-1942 an American advance party of an officer and two enlisted men arrived to begin the American take-over of Shepton Mallet which became officially Disciplinary Training Center No. 1 under Lieutenant Colonel T. W. Gillard. Over the next three weeks all the British prisoners were transferred elsewhere and a period of three months was then spent in getting everything ready for the new inmates.

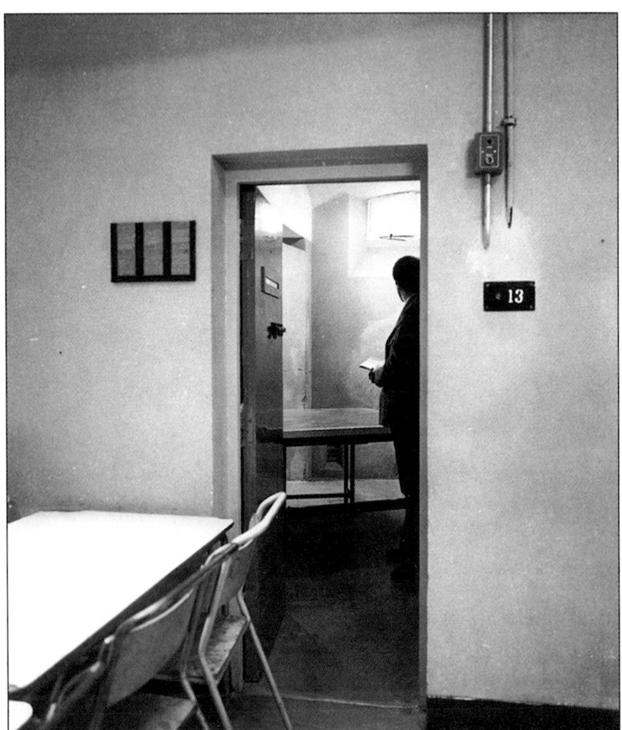

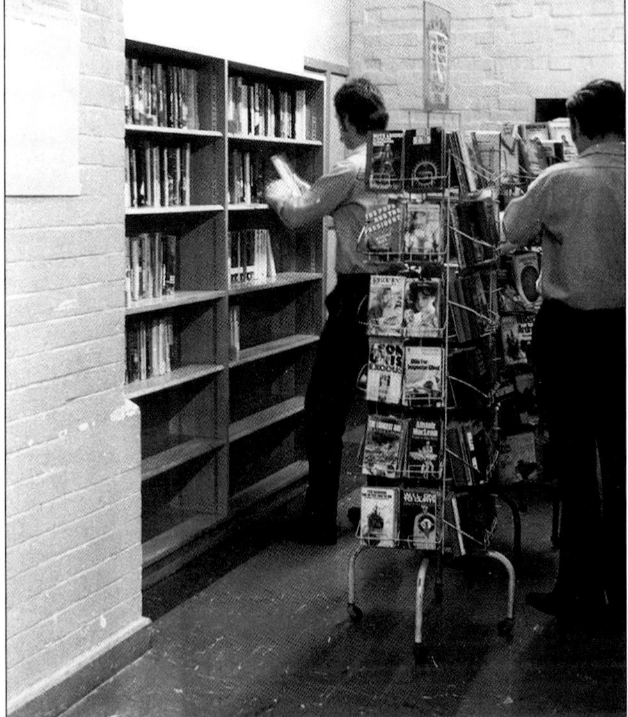

Shepton Mallet had been used for civilian executions between 1889 and 1926 but the gallows had fallen into disrepair by the time the Americans wanted to use it and the room filled with ARP equipment, Wellington boots and buckets of sand. Early in 1943 Bill Pyle, the civilian works foreman, was asked to get the trapdoor working as there was going to be a 'necktie' party. Although no expert in scaffold construction. Bill obtained a lever and installed this on the right-hand side and, with the help of two stokers, tested its operation. The sound of the doors banging open was loud enough to be heard outside the walls and a guard came in to ask if the noise could stop as it was disturbing the occupant of the cell next door who was waiting to be hung! This must have been Private Cobb as his was the first US execution in Britain. Today the room has been divided in half: one part being used as a warder's rest room the other for the prison library. 'When I took this photograph in 1978,' recalls your Editor, 'and I moved the rack of paperbacks standing where the trapdoor once lay, I couldn't help smiling at the title of one book prominently displayed at the front: *Heaven Next Stop*. I somehow thought that Private Cobb might have gone to the other place!'

CONFIDENTIAL

HEADQUARTERS
EUROPEAN THEATER OF OPERATIONS
UNITED STATES ARMY.

Copy

In the foregoing case of:

Private DAVID COBB (34165248)

Company C, 827th Engineer Battalion

(Aviation).

the sentence is confirmed and will be carried into execution on Friday, *12* March 1943, at DISCIPLINARY TRAINING CENTER, NO. 1, Shepton Mallet, Somerset, England. The act of execution will be under the direction of the Commanding Officer of DISCIPLINARY TRAINING CENTER, NO. 1.

(ETO 255).

Sgd F. M. Andrews
Lieutenant-General
United States Army
Commanding.

1 March ~~February~~, 1943.

Eight days before the execution by Tom and Albert Pierrepoint, Cobb was informed in the company of five witnesses that the order for his death had been approved. The next day, March 5, 1943, the Judge Advocate General's office outlined the rituals of Cobb's execution in two pages of instructions containing five separate procedures. The first addressed 'Preliminary Arrangements', including the opportunity for Cobb to have 'consolation and ministration' of the chaplain or clergy of his choice. Two days later, the instructions were modified and extended. The procession along the corridor *(above)* from Cobb's cell to the death chamber required the military to lead and religion to accompany. Lieutenant Colonel Gillard, took the lead with Captain J. O'Brien, chaplain, on his left. In addition to Cobb, 21 people were present including 12 commissioned officers, six non-commissioned officers, one private and two civilians. Thirteen of the 21 were witnesses.

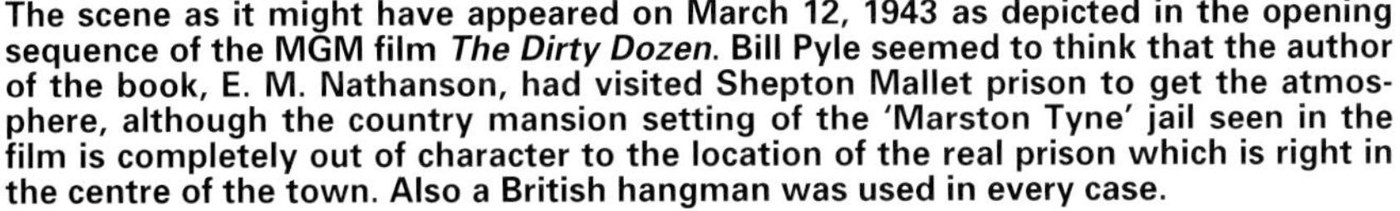

The scene as it might have appeared on March 12, 1943 as depicted in the opening sequence of the MGM film *The Dirty Dozen*. Bill Pyle seemed to think that the author of the book, E. M. Nathanson, had visited Shepton Mallet prison to get the atmosphere, although the country mansion setting of the 'Marston Tyne' jail seen in the film is completely out of character to the location of the real prison which is right in the centre of the town. Also a British hangman was used in every case.

After Cobb spoke his last words to the chaplain, 'Just pray for my soul as I asked before', he was executed at 0103 hours. He was left hanging until 0208 when he was declared dead by three medical officers.

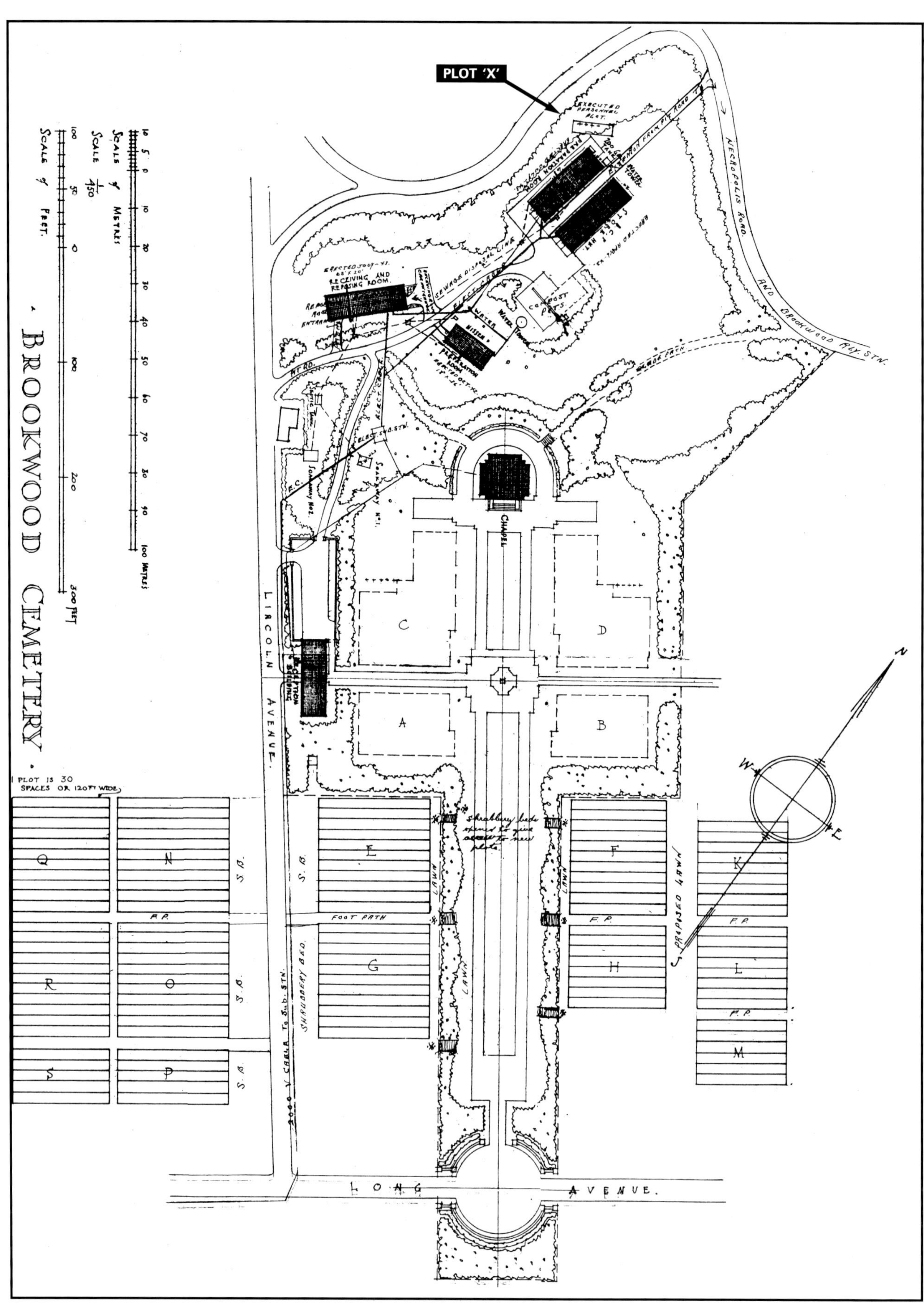

On March 12, 1st Lieutenant W. Brooks Bradley of the US Army Graves Registration Service signed a receipt for the body of Private Cobb. It was taken to Brookwood Cemetery in Surrey where the Americans were establishing a temporary burial ground alongside their permanent First World War cemetery comprising Plots A, B C and D *(above)*, the Second World War plots being labelled E to S. However, as the US military wanted to avoid any stigma being attached to their honourable dead, and to prevent any publicity that might be given to those who had been executed for the committing of heinous crimes, a special Plot 'X' for the executed dead was established hidden away behind the service area (see also page 148).

Left: Cobb's victim, 1st Lieutenant Cobner, was buried with full military honours in Plot E (Grave 15 in Row 8) — the First World War pavilion can be seen peeping through the trees in the background. After the war this temporary cemetery was cleared for the building of the Commonwealth War Graves Commission Memorial to the Missing where the names of Sangret (page 127) and Kemp (page 157) are commemorated. Sixty per cent of the American war dead were repatriated to family graves in the United States, the remainder being interred in the permanent cemetery established by the American Battle Monuments Commission in Britain at Madingley near Cambridge. *Right:* Lieutenant Cobner now lies there in Plot D, Row 3, Grave 50.

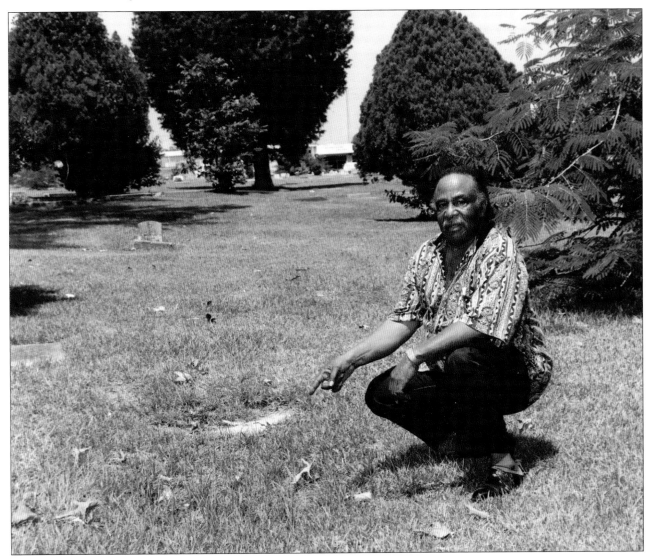

On March 23, 1942, only a few days after the execution, Cobb's mother, by telegram from Dothan to the US Judge Advocate General, requested that his body be returned to Alabama. The request was filed and in September 1948 Cobb's wife Cornelia, who was his rightful next of kin, confirmed the request and Cobb's coffin arrived at Hawk's Funeral Home the following April. Here David Cobb's son Howard indicates the unmarked grave in North Highland Street Cemetery.

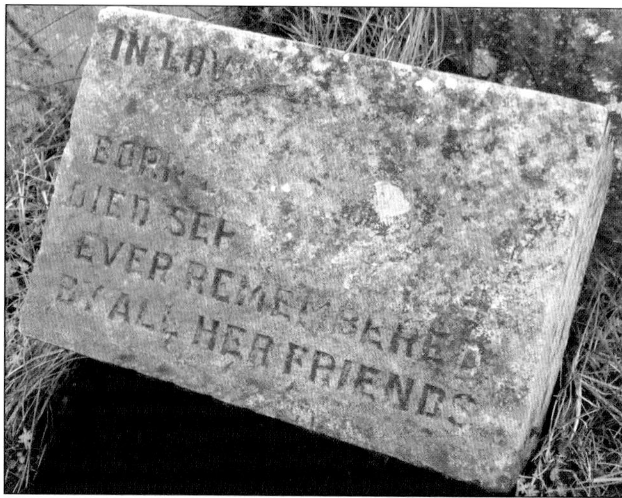

'In loving memory of June Lay, born July 11th, 1924, died Sept. 28th 1943. Ever remembered by all her friends.' *Left:* So read the inscription on this small marker in the cemetery at Marlborough in Wiltshire when we found it in 1978, although sadly it had been defaced and placed on the wrong grave when Steve Casely pictured it *(right)* in 2011. The story behind the events of that Tuesday over 60 years ago is horrific. Muriel Fawden, a nurse at Savernake Hospital, had gone to the pictures in the town and on leaving the cinema *(below right)* around 7.15 p.m. she met another nurse, June Lay. No doubt they chatted about the following week's film — Spencer Tracy in *Keeper of the Flame* — as they walked back to the hospital.

'We got half-way up the hill to the hospital,' testified Miss Fawden at the General Court-Martial, 'and a coloured American soldier came up from behind and spoke to us. He said, 'How far are you going?' We both answered, 'We are going to the hospital.' He said, 'How far is that?' and I said, 'Just up there,' and with that he dropped behind us again. A few minutes afterwards I heard a voice behind us say "Stand still, or I'll shoot" or words to that effect I can't really remember the exact words. We both turned round, hardly believing our ears, and we saw a coloured American soldier standing levelling a rifle at us. He told us to get over the other side of the road, into the bushes. We sort of went towards that side of the road, and tried to stall him.'

September 28, 1943 – Rape and Murder at Marlborough

Marlborough has been shocked by a very painful tragedy. About 8.30 p.m. on Tuesday night, on the London Road close to the railway bridge not far from Savernake Hospital, the dead body of a girl named June Lay, who had received bullet wounds, was found by a lorry driver proceeding in the direction of the town. The local police were at once notified, as well as the Matron of the Hospital where the girl had been employed as assistant cook.

But this was not the whole of the tragedy for it was known that Miss Lay had been accompanied by Miss Muriel Fawden, assistant to Mr G. V. Mathews, secretary-accountant at the Hospital. So a search was made, and this continued for some hours. It was nearly midnight when she was seen making her way to the Hospital in a very distressed condition.

There have been many stories circulating as to how it all happened, and it would appear that the two girls had attended the Marlborough Cinema, and that while they were returning they were accosted by a soldier. They started to run and Miss Lay fell, wounded in the head. It is presumed that following this, Miss Fawden was pursued and threatened.

We are informed that in connection with this sad affair, a man has been handed over to the United States military authorities, and that the inquest concerning Miss Lay will be opened by the Wiltshire Coroner in the near future.

We cannot too strongly point out that two more respectable young girls it would be hard to find and that many stories published have been exaggerated in the extreme.

Mr Robert Freeman, of St Paul Street, Chippenham, and Mr Beasley of Deansway, Chippenham, were the lorry drivers who found the dead body of Miss Lay. They drive milk tankers from Wiltshire to London, and they are employed by the Bulwark Transport Company. Mr Freeman said to a reporter that they reached the hill leading to the Hospital about 8.15 p.m., and they noticed that a lorry that had passed swerved suddenly and started to pull up. Then he saw the body in the road and his vehicle stopped alongside it. He could see that the girl had severe head injuries. Mr Beasley went for the police and he stayed at the spot, and gave what aid he could. Later, the girl was recognised by two girls who came from the Hospital.

Marlborough Times, October 1, 1943

THE CINEMA
MARLBOROUGH 'Phone Marlborough 21

Times of Shows— 5-15 & 8-0 p.m. MATINEE, Sat., at 2 p.m.

This Hall is thoroughly ventilated, the atmosphere being changed every few minutes.

Sunday, Sept. 26 Doors open 6-0 *No Children admitted to Sunday shows*

Jean Hersholt & Anne Bennett in **They Meet Again**
and SCATTERGOOD MEETS BROADWAY

Commencing Mon., Sept. 27 (A.)
CARY GRANT
in
ONCE UPON A HONEYMOON
with
GINGER ROGERS

Commencing Thurs., Se[illegible] (U.)
ARTHUR ASKEY
in
Miss London Ltd.
with
EVELYN DALL

WITH FULL SUPPORTING PROGRAMMES. Deaf aid services free

Prices ... ... Week Days: 3/6 2/9 2/3 1/9 & 1od.. including tax
Sundays ... ... 1/9 & 1od. „ „

The old cinema is now a supermarket.

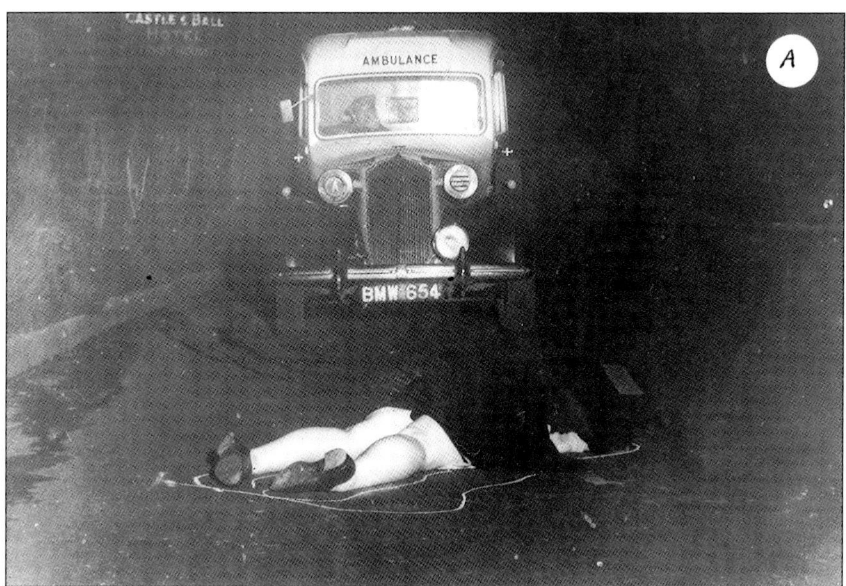

'We said we could not get into the bushes because there was barbed wire there, which was a lie — we were trying to stall him.'

The trial by General Court Martial of Private Lee A. Davis, 22, charged with the murder of Miss Cynthia June Lay, 19, who was a cook at Savernake Hospital and a daughter of Mr E. R. Lay, a bus inspector, of Union Street, Aldershot, and with a criminal assault on Miss Muriel Joyce Rosaline Fawden, 22, daughter of Mr and Mrs. F. T. Fawden, of Castle Carey, Somerset, opened near Marlborough on Wednesday.

After formal evidence had been given by Harold R. Grow, registrar of births and deaths, Detective Sergeant R. T. Butler, in the photographic branch of the Wilts Constabulary at Devizes, said he was called upon to visit the scene, where he took photographs, including one of the body facing towards Marlborough and another facing towards the forest. He also took a photograph of a part of the fence on the side of the road, and one of three gulleys. There was, in addition, a photograph showing haystacks and the railway bridge over which, it was alleged, one of girls was taken.

Sergt. W. J. Willis, of Marlborough police station, said that on Sept. 28th, at 8.20 p.m., he was on duty at the station when he received information that there had been what appeared to have been an accident on the London Road. He was directed by his superior officer to go to the scene and report to him. He went to the spot in a police car with another police officer. At a point 200 yards above the railway bridge, he saw the body of a woman lying in a prone position on the near side of the road, facing Marlborough. Her head was in the direction of Marlborough. As a result of what he heard there, he went to the Hospital and established that the person was a girl named June Lay, and it was believed that another girl named Muriel Fawden was in her company. He telephoned to the doctor and to the Superintendent and returned to the scene. He conferred with Dr. Tim Maurice, and as a result of what the doctor told him he returned to Marlborough police station and spoke to the Superintendent, who made a request that a photographer should be sent for. He went back to the scene, with other police officers and comenced to search the immediate locality. At that stage of the proceedings his superior officer took charge of the case, and he continued enquiries under his direction.

George Edward Browning, aged 15, of South View, Marlborough, said he was on the railway bridge on 28th September, just after 8 o'clock at night, when he heard two shots in quick succession, a scream and a scuffle. When he got to the spot whence the sounds came, he saw that a lorry had stopped, and that a woman was lying on the ground. The girl was alive at the time. A few days later, he found a cartridge case, 65 yards away from the spot. He handed this to the Head Porter at the Hospital. The cartridge case was quite near to the kerb.

Superintendent W. H. Gibson, of Marlborough said that at 8.30 p.,m. on 28th September, he received information that the dead body of a girl was lying in the road at a place known as London Hill, Marlborough, and also that the body had been identified as that of a girl named June Lay, who had been employed as Assistant Cook at Savernake Hospital. At the same time, he received information that a girl named Fawden, who was employed as Assistant Secretary at the Hospital, had been in the company of the dead girl, and that she was missing from the Hospital. He immediately, in company with Detective-Sergeant Hill and Detective-Sergeant Vincent, went to the scene, where he saw the body of a girl. She was lying face downwards in a pool of blood, on the near side of the road facing towards Marlborough. He gave instructions to Detective-Sergeant Vincent to take necessary particulars. He also gave instructions for photographs to be taken of the body. In addition, instructions were given to make a search for the missing girl, and, of course, for the assailant of the dead woman. After he had seen to this, he went with other Police Officers in the ambulance containing the dead woman to the Hospital.

At 11.30 p.m. on the same day, he went to a camp, and at 11.55 p.m. he was handed an American Army cap by Inspector Keiller, of the Wilts Special Constabulary. Enquiries were made and it was ascertained that this cap belonged to someone in the Quartermaster's branch. He found the letter 'W' and the figures '8470'. He took possession of the cap, and at 1.45 a.m. Lieutenant Mothershed showed him a pair of American khaki trousers. On examining them he found what appeared to be a patch of blood on the seat of the trousers. In one of the pockets of the trousers he saw a blood-stained handkerchief. In the same pocket, he found a pair of pigskin gloves, with initials marked in red cotton. In the pocket, too, was another kind of handkerchief, and there was a Service tie. In the right-hand pocket he found a .30 live carbine bullet. About 4 a.m. he went to a hut, where he saw the accused. He saw him in the presence of Colonel Meeks and other officers of the American Army, and also in the presence of Police Officers. He told Davis that he was the Superintendent of the Police from Marlborough, and that he was going to ask him some questions. He then showed the accused the trousers, and asked him if they belonged to him. He said that they did belong to him. He then showed him a blood-stained handkerchief, and asked him if it belonged to him. After looking at it, he said that it belonged to him. He was then shown the Service cap which had been handed to him. He pointed out the number to him and asked him if he knew who the cap belonged to. He said it belonged to Private Wheeler. He (the Superintendent) then said: 'Were you wearing that cap to-night?' Accused replied: 'I was wearing the cap last night (meaning the previous night.) Accused was also shown a pair of gloves, and the initials were pointed out so him. He asked Davis to whom they belonged and he replied: 'They are mine.' He (the Superintendent) asked him where he got the gloves from and he said: 'He gave them to me.' He (the Superintendent) said: 'Who is "he"?' Davis replied: 'I don't know who he is, but he gave them to me to-night.' After that evidence he (the Superintendent) saw Colonel Meeks, and requested him to place accused under arrest, and to notify the Special Investigation Branch of the U.S. Army.

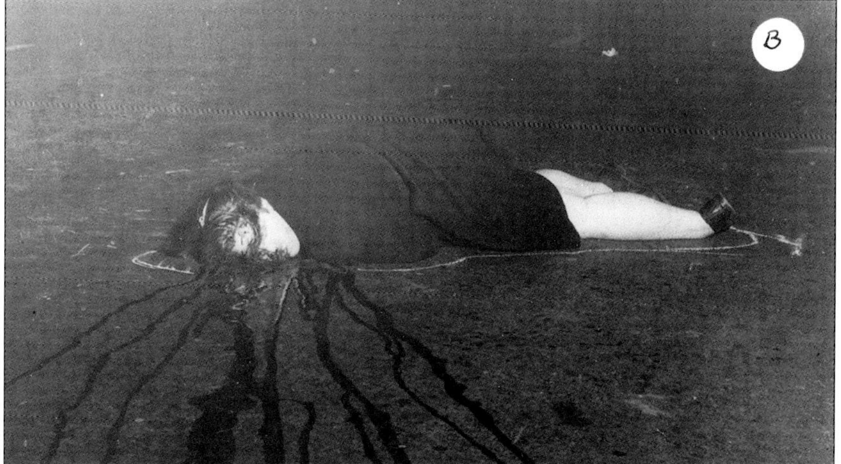

'We said it was much better further down the road, so we walked backwards, facing him, down the road, and he still leveled the rifle at us. Then June said to me "Run, Muriel!" We both started to run, and then I heard shots. I was in front I was leading June behind and I looked round and June was still running, and I heard more shots, and I turned round and June threw up her arms and screamed, and rolled over in the road.'

'Well, I then turned my back and started running hard, and I could hear more shots, and had the impression of bullets whistling past me, so I stopped dead in my tracks, because I thought the next one would go in my back. I didn't turn round. I just stayed there as I was, with my back towards him. Then after a few seconds he caught me up and caught hold of my arm and pulled me through the barbed wire at least, he ordered me to get through the barbed wire and we crouched there for a few minutes listening. I had a white mackintosh on, and he stood over me with the gun and said "Take your white coat off. When we run it will show up." I could not take my mackintosh off without taking my gloves off, which I did, and for some reason or other I sort of handed them to him, I mean I don't know why I did it, but I did, and he took them from me, and then I took my mac off and just left it where we were crouching. Then we went further up into the forest, up on the hill into the grass, and stayed there a few minutes listening, and I heard a lorry come down the hill and stop, and I knew June had been found, and I knew that people would start searching for me. Then he stood over me with the gun, and he said "Either you do what I want you to do or you die. I am going to count ten." So he started to count ten. I did not want to die, so I had no option but to give in to him.' Detective Sergeant Reginald Butler took the scene of crime photographs, exhibits 'A' and 'B' being the two pictures of June Lay lying in the road at 12.30 a.m. Exhibit 'C' ***(opposite)*** **and Exhibit 'E'** ***(above)*** **were taken on October 1. To indicate where certain articles of clothing had been found, one of the search party, Albert Smith, marked this photograph in court with a 'Y' where he found a scarf; Constable Bowyer added an 'X' to indicate the spot where he found a US forage cap, and Sergeant Gale a 'Z' for the position of Muriel's mackintosh.**

Police Constable A. E. Bowyer stated that he was on duty at Marlborough police station on the night of September 28th when a lorry driver came and reported that he had found the body of a woman lying on the road on the London Hill. He went to the scene and remained on duty there until 11.20 p.m. when Special Constable Smith came and said, 'I have something to show you.' He accompanied Special Constable Smith to a barbed wire fence on the near side, facing Marlborough, and there found a brown, woollen ladies scarf. It was lying on the grass close to the wire fence. In company with Special Constable Smith, he continued the search and about eight yards inside the undergrowth, and close to the fence, he found an American soldier's cap. At 12.10 a.m. he heard awful screams by a woman, these coming from the direction of Savernake Forest. He searched the forest and eventually found Miss Fawden. She was in a very hysterical distressed condition. He said, 'I am a police officer. Don't worry.' Miss Fawden then got hold of him and made a certain remark concerning an assault made upon her. Miss Fawden also said, 'He fired two shots at June and marched me off to some haystacks in the forest, pointing a rifle in my ribs.'

The young woman was in a very weak state and he had to assist her. She was taken in a police car to the Hospital. He had to carry her into the Hospital at the end of the journey.

Special Constable A. Colvin Smith said that shortly after 11 o'clock on the night of September 28th, when he was on duty in the neighbourhood of the scene of the tragedy, he heard a girl say, 'My God, where am I ?'

Special Sergeant J. W. Gale said he was one of a party in search of Miss Fawden. The search commenced at 10 p.m., and at 10.15 p.m. he found a lady's mackintosh at a spot about ten yards from the wire fence. It was on the ground near some bushes.

Detective Sergeant Hill gave evidence as to going to the spot where Miss Lay was found and to being present when Superintendent Gibson interviewed accused. At 4.30 a.m. on September 29th he saw bloodstains on some of accused's underclothing. He asked accused to take off his under-garments, saying he would require these for scientific examination. He took possession of the garments and at 4.45 a.m. he examined accused's hands. He saw a small stain of blood on the middle finger of the left hand. He assisted Detective-Sergeant Vincent to take scrapings from underneath accused's fingernails on each hand.

At 7.15 a.m. on September 29, he was searching the scene of the crime when he found a .30 carbine rifle cartridge case. This was 14ft from where the head of the deceased had been, in the direction of Marlborough, and was 2ft from the kerb. Directly opposite the cartridge case, and on the kerb, were splashes of blood. At 9 a.m., in consequence of information received, he visited the camp and took possession of a carbine rifle, a greatcoat, and a shirt, also a magazine containing a carbine cartridge. The greatcoat had a stain of blood on the inside. All these exhibits were taken to the Marlborough Police Station by him and locked in a separate room until they were handed to the Investigation Branch.

Wilts Berks & Hants County Paper, October 8, 1943

There were three cases in the UK during the war in which American servicemen paid the supreme penalty for the double crime of murder-rape: Corporal Ernest Clark and Private Augustine Guerra at Ashford, Kent (see page 158); Private William Harrison, Stewartstown, County Tyrone; and here at Marlborough, Wiltshire. If indeed such horrific crimes can be compared, the latter by Private Lee Davis might be considered the most depraved for having shot June Lay through the back and head, he left her dying in the road while he dragged her friend away at gunpoint. Although June was found just after 8.00 p.m. it was not until after midnight that Muriel escaped from her ordeal. Davis was executed by Tom Pierrepoint and Alex Riley at Shepton Mallet on December 14, 1943.

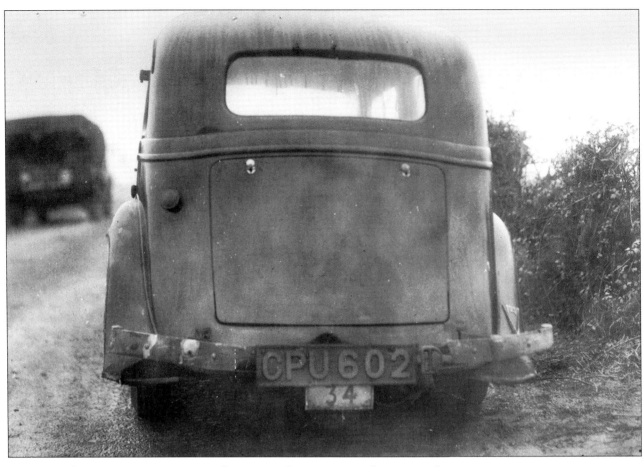

December 8, 1943 – The Birch Taxi-cab Murder

At 10 p.m on Wednesday, December 8, 1943, I received a telephone message from the police at Clacton-on-Sea to say that a Vauxhall taxicab, CPU 602, had been found abandoned by Police Constable 505 McCormack, in Haynes Green Lane, Layer Marney, containing a jacket and blood-stained mackintosh. With Detective Inspector Draper I went at once to Copford Police Station, where I conferred with Sergeant Garrett, who had been to Haynes Green Lane and brought back the clothes with him.

I examined them and found that the sleeves of the jacket were turned inside out and looped together as if the garment had been pulled off the wearer from behind. There was what appeared to be blood-stains on the back of the mackintosh near the collar. Neither of the garments were torn and the mackintosh appeared to be new.

In the pockets I found a motor driving licence in the name of Henry Claude Hailstone and a taxicab driver's plate No. 842. From the address we found on the licence, 127 Maldon Road, Colchester, we interviewed Hailstone's landlady, Mrs Pearce, and she identified the clothing as her lodger's. She said that she had last seen him at ten minutes past eleven on the night of December 7. He had called to say that he would not be ready for his supper for at least half an hour as he had two fares to take to the American camp at Birch. He told her that both were American coloured soldiers, one an officer and the other a private.

With Inspector Draper I then set off for Haynes Green Lane to inspect the cab. Having arrived there, I found the windows closed, and the headlight and rear-lights still switched on. The gears were in 'neutral' and the hand-brake hard on. The ignition had been switched off, and the tank contained about a gallon of petrol. The radiator was cold and the engine in running order. The only external damage was to the near-side rear bumper which had a bolt missing and was hanging down, and the rear-plate was slightly cracked in two places. Though the car was on the wrong side of the road, it appeared to have stopped naturally. There were no signs of a struggle on the road or the grass verge, but I found a sixpence wedged between the offside running-board and the body of the car.

However the interior of the cab showed clear evidence of a struggle having taken place. Personal papers belonging to Hailstone were strewn about the floor. The leather upholstery was badly scratched. One piece near the driver's seat was hanging down, together with the telephone flex that ran along the roof to the rear of the car, and a string parcel-net had been torn down. Hailstone's empty wallet, his brown leather gloves, and another sixpenny piece were on

On the evening of Wednesday, December 8, 1943, a taxi was found abandoned on Haynes Green Lane just 50 yards off the Colchester-Malden road. Foul play was suspected as bloodstained clothing was found inside. Also the fact that the vehicle was parked on the right-hand side of the road could indicate that it was driven there by an American serviceman, many thousands of whom were then stationed in that part of Essex.

the floor. On the rear seat there was a clot of blood and on the inside of the offside window a number of small blood spots.

There seemed to my mind very little doubt that Hailstone had been attacked from the rear while on his journey from Colchester and that his assailant had afterwards driven his cab to where it had been abandoned. That the cab had been drawn up on the right side of the road seemed to indicate that his passenger could have been an American. It, moreover, appeared probable that after the attack Hailstone's body had been lifted out of the driver's seat and placed in the rear seat where we had found the clot of blood.

Photographs of the exterior and interior of the cab were taken and a search made for fingerprints. The only ones discovered were useless to us. The rear seat was sent to Hendon Police Laboratory for examination.

A search in the immediate vicinity was made for Hailstone's body. We found no trace of it. A wide and systematic search was then made, concentrating on the road leading to the five American Army camps, which included many coloured troops, in the neighbourhood of Birch. The Garrison adjutant at Colchester was contacted, and he brought eighteen of his men to assist us. Later two members of the Investigation Staff of the American Forces at Ipswich arrived to assist in the inquiry.

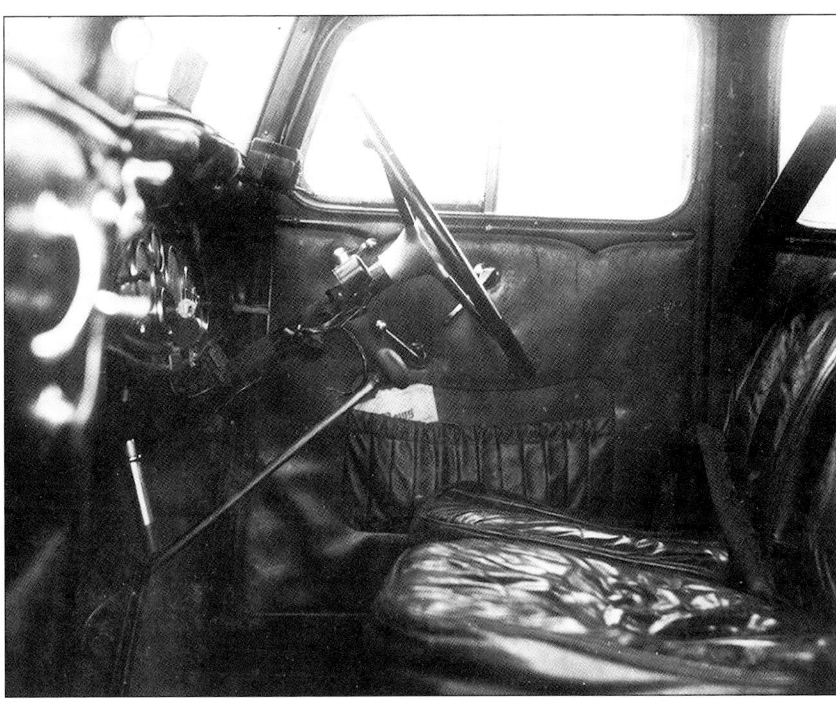

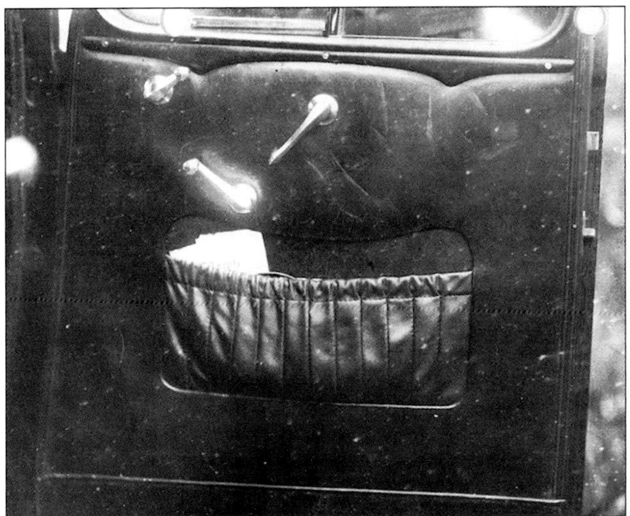

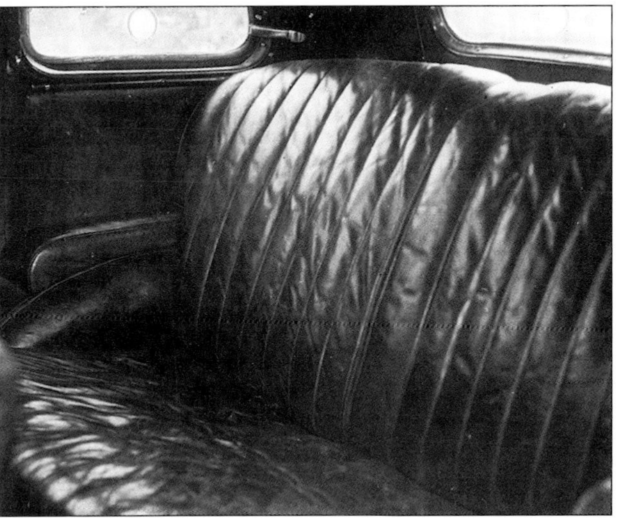

The broken telephone lead between the driver and passenger compartment and torn parcel net, coupled with spots of blood on a window, all indicated that a struggle must have taken place in the cab.

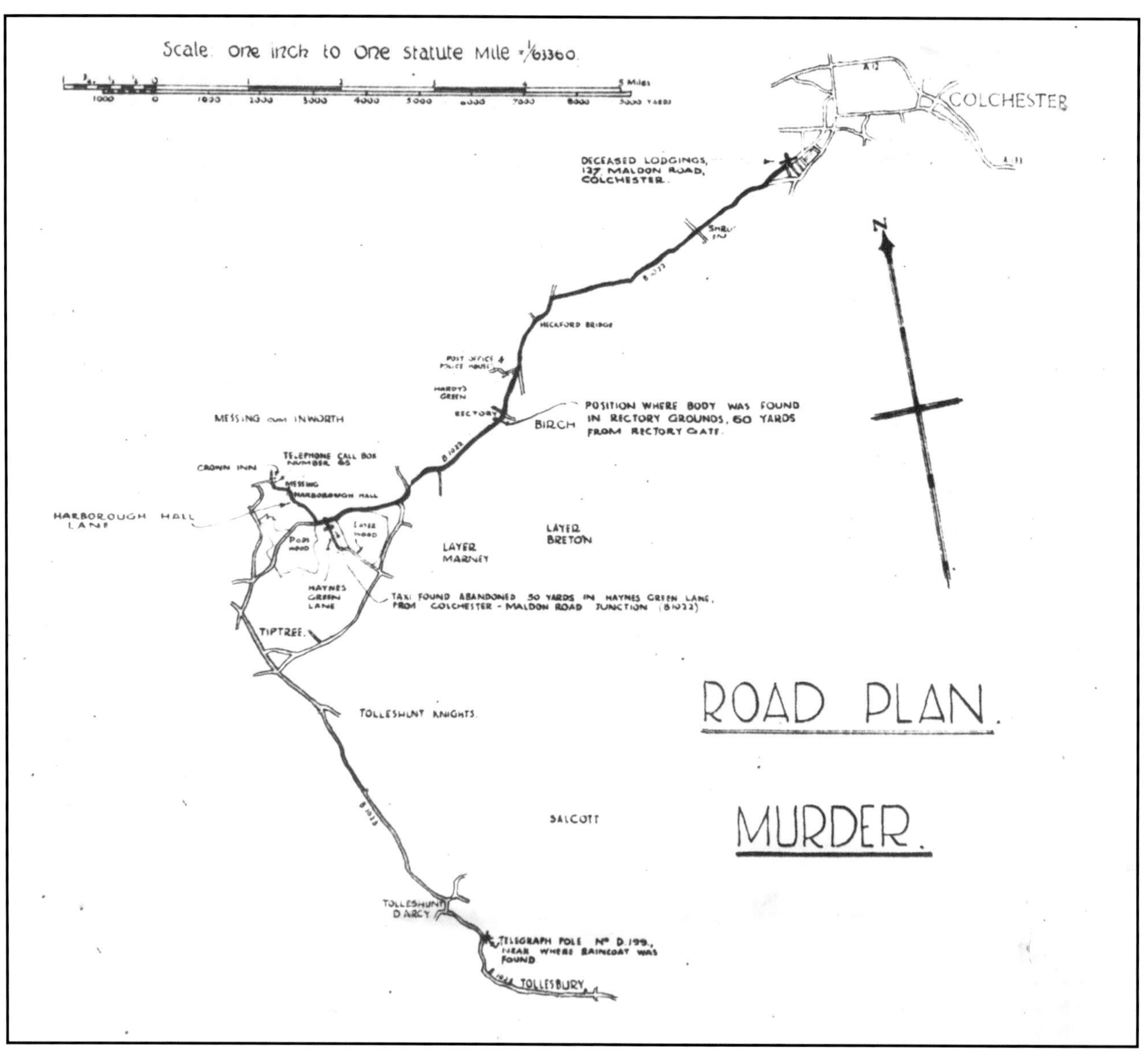

Private John C. Leatherberry and Private George Fowler were stationed with the 356th Engineer General Service Regiment at Birch near Colchester where an airfield was being constructed for the United States Army Air Forces. On Sunday evening, December 5, 1943, they decided to go AWOL to London, not returning until Tuesday evening after having spent almost all their money.

On December 8 a civilian-pattern mackintosh, considerably bloodstained down the front, with the words 'Captain J. J. Weber' written near the collar-band, was found lying in the gutter of the main road to Maldon, near Tollesbury. In one of the outside pockets was a new cloth American Service emblem and on the inside of the coat a Canadian maker's label. The coat was found six miles farther along the Maldon Road from Haynes Green Lane, where the taxi was first discovered.

We got in touch with Canadian Army Headquarters in London in order to ascertain if any officer of the name of Weber was serving in this country. At first we drew a blank but later information came through that an officer, J. J. Weber, was attached to the Canadian General Hospital at Cuckfield in Sussex. He was interviewed by the Sussex C.I.D. and made a statement.

On December 5 he had been stationed at 18th Canadian General Hospital, Cherry Tree Camp, at Colchester, completing a course. On returning to camp from London he had met a coloured sergeant of the American Forces at Liverpool Street Station, and they had struck up an acquaintance. Arriving at Colchester, he had invited the sergeant back to his mess for a drink. During his temporary absence from his room the American had absconded, with a bottle of whisky and his mackintosh (the one in question). In the pockets of the latter were five pounds in notes, a Rolex wrist-watch, a torch, and a pair of gloves. Captain Weber was asked to come to Chelmsford to help us in our inquiries.

At 12.55 midday on Thursday, December 9, Police Constable Snowling of Copford, who was one of the search-party, found the dead body of Hailstone. The body was lying on the side of a bank in the grounds of Birch Rectory, which forms the boundary between the Maldon Road going from Colchester in the direction of the American camps and the Rectory. I went immediately to the place.

The dead man was fully clad with the exception of hat, jacket, and overcoat. The left-hand pocket was turned inside out. The head was pointing towards Maldon with the left of the face badly injured and the features covered with blood. The body was invisible from the road. Two strands of barbed wire ran along the top of the bank. The bottom strand opposite to where the body was found was partly bloodstained. There were no signs nearby of a struggle or footprints or the impression of tyres.

I was not of the opinion that Hailstone had been killed at this spot, and, since he weighed between eleven and twelve stone, it seemed reasonable to assume that more than one person had been needed to deposit the body. I was of the opinion that it had been lifted on to the top of the bank from the road, pushed over, and then allowed to roll down the far side till it was stopped by the brambles at the foot.

A post-mortem was carried out by Dr Camps, who found death was due to manual strangulation. There was bruising on the face from at least three heavy blows, and marks on the neck indicated that they had been made by somebody with a strong left hand.

Every effort was made to trace the car's movements and the telephone call, but to no purpose. The following morning I went to the 18th Canadian General Hospital in Colchester to check Captain Weber's statement.

The mess orderly, Private Clifford Hall, remembered the incident of December 5 when Captain Weber had arrived back to camp with a coloured American soldier. The latter had left his gas-mask behind. It was the usual standard Service issue in a canvas case, and written inside the flap was the name 'J. Hill' and at the bottom of the case the letter 'H' followed by the figures '1031'.

I took possession of the gas-mask and after inquiries, found the owner of the name on the flap was stationed at Birch and was in

E Company of the 356th Engineers Regiment, American Forces. He was interviewed and stated that the gas-mask was his property but that on December 1 he had lent it to another coloured soldier of the same regiment by the name of Fowler. He had not seen it since.

Private George E. Fowler of E Company was then interviewed He admitted borrowing the gas-mask on December 1 when he went on leave to London. He was asked to account for it. He had of course no idea that it was now in our possession. In a long and rambling statement he gave the following facts.

He had gone to London on a day-pass on December 1, having borrowed Hill's gas-mask in the morning. He had booked in at the Liberty Club in Euston Square and left the gas-mask there. An account of his traffickings with women followed. On the evening of December 5 he went on a pub-crawl with another woman with whom he spent the night. He did the same on December 7. He could not remember how he got back to camp at 9.45 on December 8. Some of the whisky he had drunk in company with his lady-friends must have been doped. When he came round in camp he found he was wearing a sergeant's blouse. He had no idea how he had got hold of it. He had not seen his gas-mask since he had left it in the Liberty Club.

The discrepancy with Captain Weber's statement — in that they had met on the way back to Colchester on December 5 and that on that night he had slept in London — the constant insistence on his absence from Colchester on the night of the murder, December 7, and the flagrant falsehood in relation to the disposal of the gas-mask was more than ample justification for detaining Private George Fowler on suspicion. We transferred him to Colchester Police Station and locked him up.

We searched his hut. Hanging over his bed was a soldier's blouse bearing sergeant's stripes. There appeared to be traces of blood on it. In his kit-bag we found an envelope containing several papers and a pawn-ticket issued by W. P. Hyde, 117 Cannon Street Road, London, E.1. for a Rolex wrist-watch, dated December 6, 1943, to the value of £3. On the back of the envelope was the name Charlie Huntly, C.O.F. 356 Engineers Regiment, A.P.O. 563, G.P.M.

The next move was to trace and interview Charlie Huntly of 'F' Company of the 356th Engineers Regiment. He too was a coloured soldier who admitted that he had been in London on December 6 and had met a Private Leatherberry who was with another coloured American whom he called 'George'. They had met in the West Indies Club, and George had given him a watch and asked him where he could pawn it. Huntly had pawned the watch for £3 and when the pawnbroker handed him the ticket it was in a sealed envelope. Huntly had written his own name on the back of it before he had passed over the envelope to 'George'.

I sent an officer to Cannon Street Road to recover the watch. It was identified by Captain Weber as his.

Fowler was again questioned. His confidence in himself appeared to be shaken. His third statement was illuminating, to say the least of it. The differences between this and his former statements were apparent. The strain of a guilty conscience was beginning to tell.

He now admitted that he had left London on December 5. He went to Liverpool Street Station to get a train for Colchester. In the buffet bar he met a British Army captain. They got into conversation and stood each other drinks and together caught the 2.15 from Liverpool Street. Arrived at Colchester, the captain persuaded him to come to his camp and they left by taxi just after 4.30. In the officer's hut they continued their drinking.

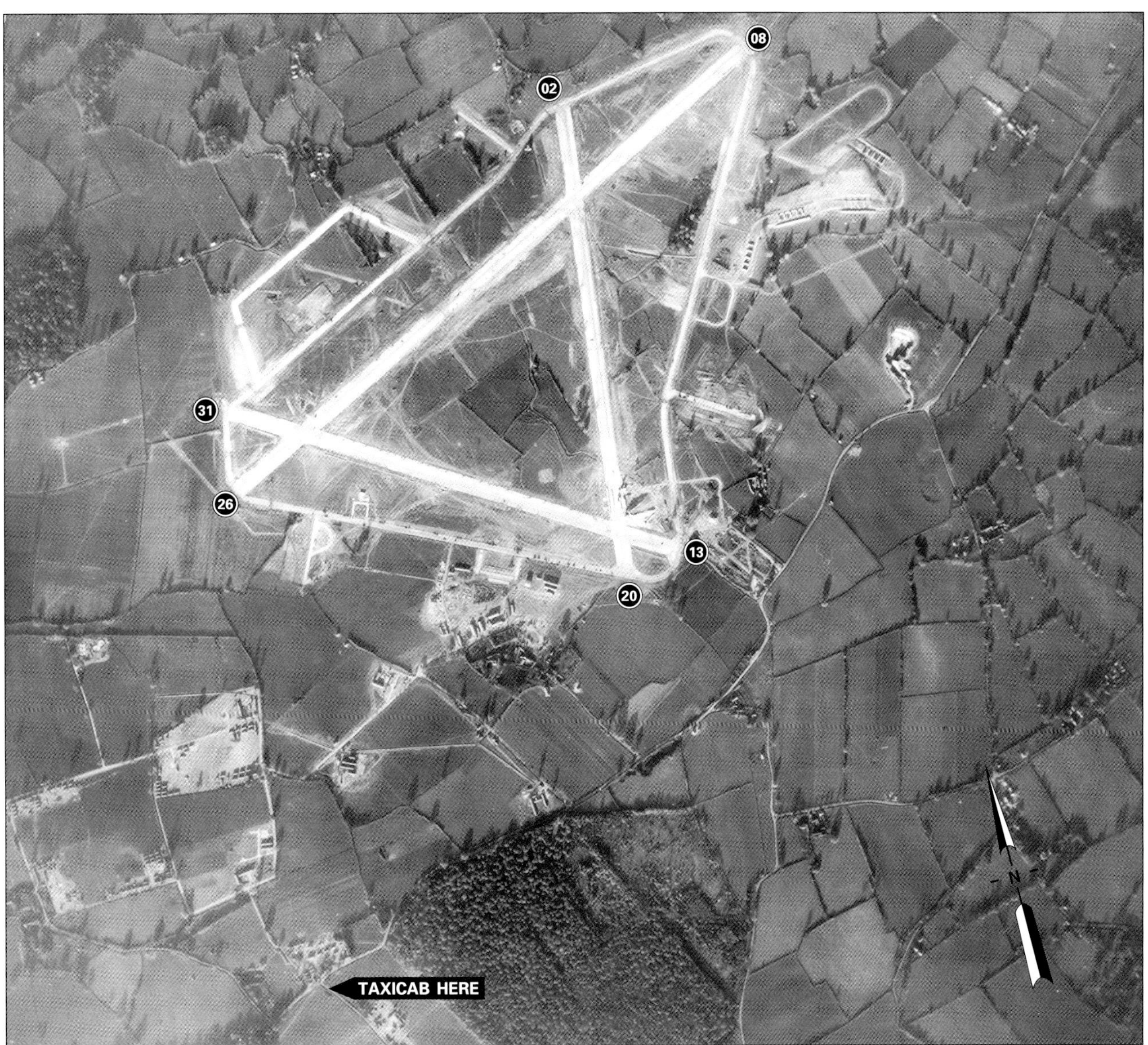

Leatherberry proposed to Fowler the idea of taking a cab at Colchester and robbing the driver on the way back to their camp at Birch airfield. The unfortunate driver waiting in his Vauxhall outside the station was 28-year-old Henry 'Harry' Hailstone. During the journey of just over seven miles, Fowler asked the driver to stop so that he could relieve himself and at his court-martial he maintained that it was while he was out of the taxi that Leatherberry killed the driver.

Fowler *(left)* **helped Leatherberry carry the body across the road where they rolled it under the fence surrounding Birch Rectory.** *Right:* **The position where Hailstone was discovered two days later is marked in this scene-of-crime photo with an 'X'.**

He then caught a bus at the gate of Cherry Tree Camp and left for his own camp. There were friends of his, soldiers from his own unit, on the bus, and before reaching camp thev got off at the White Horse public house. One of the soldiers called Leatherberry said that he too was in the 356th Engineers Company. They decided to return to London, though he told Leatherberry he had already outstayed his pass by two days, but he was eventually persuaded. They went to London and slept the night there. The next day he had become short of money, so he went to the Rainbow Club and borrowed ten shillings, and then went to some pubs in the West End by himself. He never went near any pawn-shop. He met Leatherberry at the West Indies Club about 8.30 that evening. That was when he had picked up the envelope with the pawn-ticket inside.

On December 7 they returned to Colchester. They had been drinking heavily but were not drunk. On the way down on the train Leatherberry suggested that they should hire a taxi when they arrived and rob the driver on the way back to camp. They reached Colchester at 10.45 and hired a cab. The driver stopped at his lodgings and Leatherberry said that he'd gone in to get a gun.

Four miles on the way back to camp the driver stopped the taxi and he himself got out to make water. Leatherberry remained inside the taxi. Then Fowler heard Leatherberry calling for him, and when he reached the cab the two men were struggling together. Leatherberry kept on asking him to help him overpower the driver as 'I was in it just as much as he was'. Leatherberry was standing on the floor of the back of the cab holding the driver in the front seat with his left hand and punching him in the face with his right. When he himself managed to get back into the taxi the driver was limp, and Leatherberry was hauling him out of the front seat into the back.

We searched Leatherberry's hut on the camp and found a bloodstained shirt, pants, and vest. He was arrested on suspicion and taken to Colchester Police Station. On December 14 his fingerprints were taken and he was closely interrogated on his statement for a considerable time. He remained obdurate. He had, he said, spoken the truth and it was down in writing. He had absolutely nothing more to say. He wasn't talking any more and all our efforts to shake him were fruitless. Nothing could induce him to alter one word.

On the same day an identification parade was held at his Regimental Headquarters at Birch. He was picked out by Fowler as the soldier who was with him on the night of December 7 and had assisted in the murder of the driver of the taxi.

On December 19 both suspects were handed over into the custody of the Commanding Officer of 356th Engineers Regiment and copies of all statements, documents, and exhibits submitted to him for charges to be listed against Fowler for murder, robbery, and larceny, and against Leatherberry for murder and robbery.

The trial of both men opened before a General Court Martial at the Town Hall, Ipswich, on Wednesday, January 19, 1944. Both trials took place simultaneously in the same building. Fowler in his defence repeated the facts as given in his former statement, while attempting all the time to put the blame of the actual murder onto Leatherberry. He was found guilty and sentenced to life imprisonment. He was then called as witness in Leatherberry's court martial.

Leatherberry in the main stuck to his story. He stated that he had been in London at the time of the murder, though medical evidence proved that from the scrapings found beneath his nails his hands at one time had been 'steeped in blood'. He attempted to prove that any bloodstains found on his clothing had arisen through a fight or sexual intercourse. He failed to convince the court and was sentenced to death.

Leatherberry was hanged at Shepton Mallet in Somerset, on Tuesday, May 16, 1944. I received an invitation to be present at his execution. I declined.

Superintendent G.H. Totterdell,
Country Copper

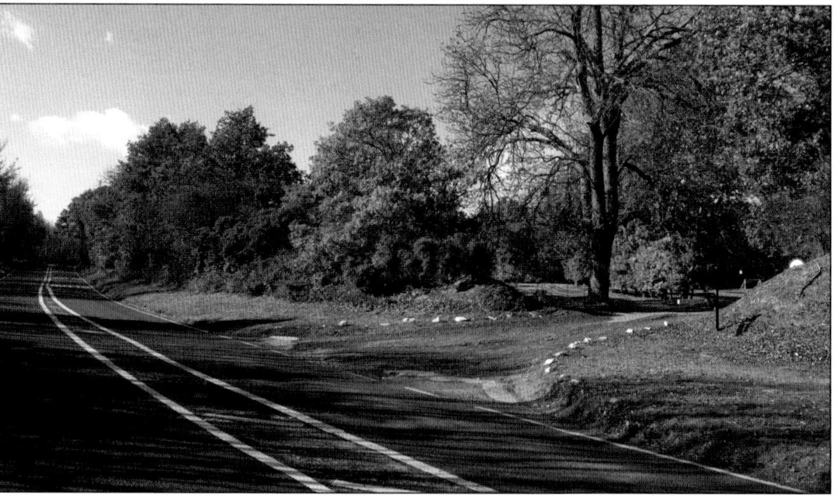

The body was lying six feet from the road and 60 yards from the entrance to the Rectory, which has since been demolished, the grounds now occupied by the Essex Care Consortium. Dr Francis Camps performed the post-mortem and told the court-martial that 'there were very severe bruises on the outer side of the left eyebrow, in the region of the mouth and jaw, and one in the scalp which must have been caused by something from above or behind. There were several marks on the neck, one of which was typical of a thumb mark and which clearly indicated that the attack was accomplished with the left hand and from behind. An internal examination disclosed a fracture of the thyroid cartilage which was typical of manual strangulation, and there was evidence of congestion of the windpipe. Haemorrhages of the eyelids and whites of the eyes were typical of constriciton of the neck. There were old adhesions in the lungs which were deeply congested and also haemorrhages on the surface of the heart. These conditions were absolutely typical of an asphyxial death.'

Harry Hailstone had been buried in Colchester Cemetery on December 16 but when we visited his grave (No. 91 in Section X7) we found it unmarked and most probably untended for over 50 years. It feels disrespectful just to walk away so in October 2011, Rob Green set off to redress the balance to ensure that Harry will no longer be forgotten.

Leatherberry had been inducted at Camp Shelby, Mississippi, on October 16, 1942 and had one previous conviction for being absent without leave. Harry Hailstone had the rare blood group 'AB', (found in only five per cent of the population) and this matched the blood found on Leatherberry. He was hanged by Tom and Albert Pierrepoint at Shepton Mallet on May 16, 1944.

In preparation for the invasion of Normandy, thousands of American servicemen were camped in the west of England, the 42nd Field Artillery Battalion being stationed in Broomhill Camp in Honiton, Devon. *Left:* Steve Parsons indicates the entrance opposite Bramble House. *Right:* On the evening of March 5, police spotted a soldier in the doorway of No. 186 High Street. Steve found the shopfront had been modernised, losing the recessed doorway and Steve Casely took the picture.

March 5, 1944 – Execution by Firing Squad

The evidence for the prosecution shows in substance that at about 12.15 a.m. 5 March 1944, Special Sergeant William J. Durbin of the Devonshire Division police, together with a Constable North brought accused [Private Alex F. Miranda, 39297382] to the police station because of a certain incident (urinating on the street). Accused's speech was thick, his breath smelled of alcohol and he was 'nasty, abusive in general.' In Durbin's opinion he was drunk but not so drunk that he did not know what he was doing.

Accused remained at the police station about 15 minutes and was driven to camp by Technician 5th Grade James W. Wesley and Corporal Joel R. Wehking, Battery C and Headquarters Battery respectively, 42nd Field Artillery Battalion. He was taken to the guardhouse and released about 12.30 a.m.

Shortly after midnight on 5 March, accused entered the hut in a noisy, boisterous manner and said a few curse words against the first sergeant who was asleep. He said he had been picked up in town by the military police for urinating in the street and appeared to be 'quite disturbed' about the incident and that 'the 1st Sergeant would ride him for it'.

Sergeant Bill Durbin and Constable Henry North were on patrol that night when they noticed a stream of urine coming from the shop entrance, Constable North said he flashed his torch and saw a US soldier crouching in the doorway. He asked him what he was doing and the American replied that he was waiting for someone. The policeman accused him of having urinated in the street and, as he also appeared to be drunk, they took him to the police station situated beside the Volunteer pub *(above right)*. At the station, Private Alex Miranda said: 'I was not pissing in the street. Your are lying. I will rip your guts out.' Contact was made with the camp and a Jeep was sent with Technician 5th Grade James Wesley and Corporal Joel Wehking to escort him to the guardhouse. As Miranda could still walk without stumbling, he was released around 12.30 a.m. to return to his hut. *Right:* The police station has now been replaced by a modern building.

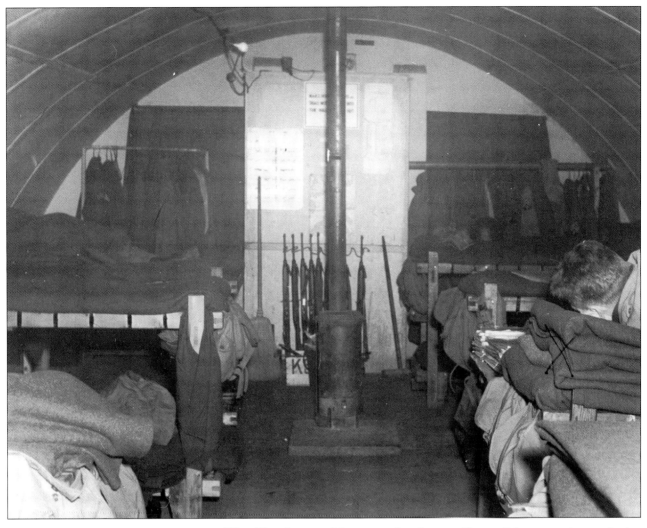

Corporal Walter F. Cooney saw him go over to the left side of deceased's bunk and bend over him. 'It looked like he had his hands raised and was looking straight into his face.

When Miranda entered the quonset hut, Sergeant Thomas Evison was asleep on the top bunk in the left-hand corner (where the soldier is reclining). Miranda's bunk was the one marked with the 'X' in the right foreground. The black-out curtain covers the door. The M1 Carbine used to shoot the sergeant was taken from the rack behind the stove. Photo taken by Corporal Frederick Kimbrough, the 4th Infantry Division photographer.

This is the site of Broomhill Camp today. The huts ran in rows along the length of the field.

When found guilty of murder at his General Court-Martial on March 20, it was really an open and shut case. There were no mitigating circumstances in what was adjudged a premeditated cold-blooded killing and unusually, and for the first time in the United Kingdom, the US court sentenced Miranda 'to be shot to death by musketry'. He faced the firing squad here in the yard of Shepton Mallet prison (see page 132) on May 30, 1944.

Deceased suddenly awakened and asked in a surprised manner 'What's the matter — What's going on?'. Accused said 'You are snoring too loud, making too much noise'. Deceased said 'go back to bed and do your own snoring', turned over on his left side and began to snore again. Accused returned to his bunk and stood smoking a cigarette for some length of time.

Accused laid his blanket on top of his bunk, left the hut and then returned to his bunk where he appeared to be fumbling with his musette bag. He then went toward the door near deceased's bunk. There was an 'explosion or a shot' and accused, who was laughing hysterically, said 'Your worries are over now, boys. I have shot the 1st Sergeant and I will turn on the lights so I can show you'.

He turned on the lights and was seen standing beyond the stove about two feet from deceased's bed, between the bed and the door. He was armed with a carbine which he carried at 'port arms'.

US Judge Advocate General, May 18, 1944

After his execution, the body was taken to Brookwood Cemetery in Surrey to be buried in the 'dishonoured Plot X' located behind the US First World War Cemetery (see plan page 134). When it was decided after the war to establish the permanent American World War II cemetery in the British Isles at Cambridge, exhumations from the main burial area at Brookwood commenced early in 1948, being completed by the end of May. At a conference of the American Graves Registration Command held in AGRC HQ in Paris on March 16, 1948, it was instructed that 'all exhumations [were] to include those from the general prisoner plot . . . the excavations to be well back-filled by AGRC and tamped in order to minimize future settlement.' The graves were opened on May 26 and by July the whole of the temporary cemetery at Brookwood had been evacuated, and the ground smoothed off. This is where the American executed dead, including Miranda, were once buried.

Left: The following year those American servicemen who had been executed in the European Theater of Operations, and not repatriated, were gathered from all over Europe and interred in a special 'dishonoured' plot with just numbered graves in a walled-off area of the First World War cemetery at Oise-Aisne in France. *Right:* In 1990, the Pentagon agreed to let Miranda's nephew, Louis Martinez, have the body exhumed for reburial in Santa Ana Cemetery in California.

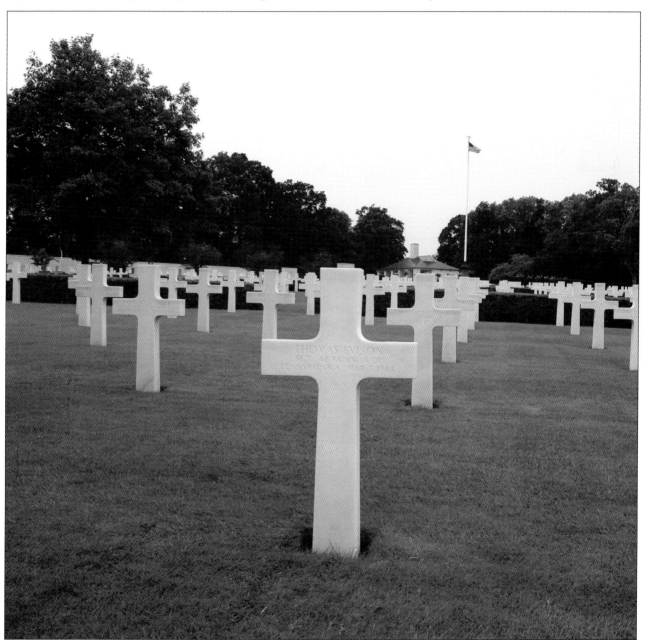

The next of kin of American service personnel were given the option of having their loved ones interred in permanent military cemeteries overseas or repatriated to the United States. First Sergeant Thomas Evison had initially been buried at Brookwood in Plot O, Row 9, Grave 1 (see again plan on page 134), and his family chose to have his remains re-interred in the United Kingdom. He now lies buried at Cambridge American Military Cemetery at Madingley, in Plot C, Row 5, Grave 42.

Twenty-one-years-old Miriam Iris Deeley had joined the Women's Auxiliary Air Force on August 7, 1942, being sent to No. 2 Radio Direction Finding School on September 24.

After training as a radar operator she received her first posting to RAF Folly in south-western Wales on November 5, one of the Chain Home stations overlooking St Bride's Bay.

February 14, 1944 – The 'Cabbage Patch' Murder

The body of Iris Deeley, aged 21, a member of the W.A.A.F. stationed in the locality, was discovered on an allotment off Sherard Road, Eltham, S.E., yesterday. She had been strangled. Her body was partly clothed. Her home was at Wanstead. It is believed the murder was committed on Sunday night a short distance from where the body was found.

The Times, February 15, 1944

Iris Miriam Deeley was a pretty WAAF of 21 — even after she was dead, strangled with her own scarf and lying naked in a cabbage patch with her greatcoat and tunic thrown over her so that she could scarcely be seen from the road. Her body was spotted by a special constable going to his allotment at Eltham at 8.35 a.m. on Monday morning, February 14, 1944. She had been there six or seven hours, but she had died a couple of dozen yards away, suddenly and in great terror. Her murderer had dragged her across the allotments, and I followed the furrows of her trailing feet in the soft earth. I measured the prints of his feet too — size 11.

Among the cabbages he had stripped and robbed the body. He had thrown her identity discs into a ditch leaving beside her the book she had been reading: *War and Peace*. Carelessly the murderer had left his own glove, snagged in a thorn bush. It was a soldier's khaki glove, largest size.

In 1943 she became romantically attached to one of the station's radar mechanics Aircraftman William Quill, their engagement being announced ten days before Bill received his commission as a Pilot Officer on February 3, 1944. Six days later he was posted for a conversion course to No. 7 Radio School located in the Science Museum in South Kensington, having arranged to be billeted with Miriam's parents at No. 29 Blake Hall Road, Wanstead. It was an ideal situation as his fiancée had just been transferred to No. 1 Balloon Centre at RAF Kidbrooke *(left)* in south-east London. *Right:* The camp was demolished in the late 1960s.

But for the book Iris Deeley might not have died. She left home in Wanstead on Sunday night to return to Kidbrooke where she had been stationed for a fortnight. She was engaged to a pilot officer and, although they had to shelter from an air raid on the way, he saw her off at Bow Road station in good time to reach Charing Cross for the eleven-one, the last train to Kidbrooke.

People saw her on Charing Cross station long before the eleven-one came in yet she missed it. Why? Was she engrossed in the book or had she already met the killer? It was even money that the killer saw her on the train, a hundred-to-one on that he spoke to her as she left it. But which train? Where did she get off? Did anybody else see her — or him?

It was Monday afternoon before we knew who she was. A schoolboy found her identity discs. It was Tuesday, with the post-mortem already done, before her father identified the body. We had not been wasting time. I had made Eltham police station my headquarters and an army of policemen was questioning people arriving on evening trains at every station from Charing Cross to the ends of Kent. Did you travel this way on Sunday night? Did you see a WAAF with very dark eyebrows? Did you see a soldier acting strangely?

On the weekend following Bill's promotion, Miriam managed to obtain a two-day pass so the couple were able to spend a pre-Valentine's Day weekend together at Wanstead. As Miriam had to be back at camp Sunday night, at around 8.30 p.m. that evening Bill set out to escort her to Charing Cross so she could catch the 10 p.m. train to Kidbrooke. They left her parents' house *(left)* and walked to the Green Man pub to catch a bus but when it reached Bow Road station, an air raid warning sounded and all the passengers had to get off. This is where they said their last goodbye.

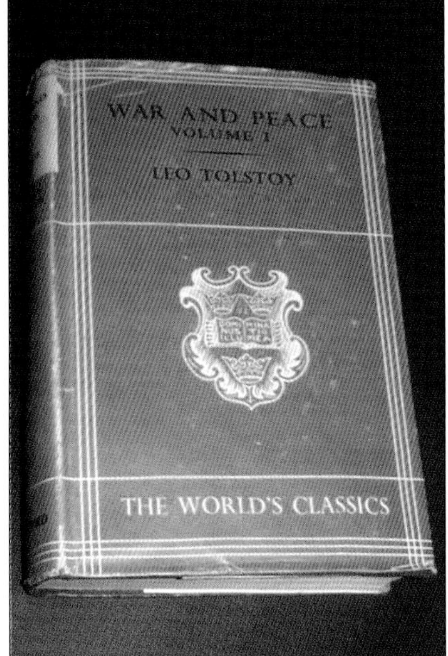

SERVICES CLOTHING BOOK

M4/88

You will insert your name, rank and Military Identification Card or Official Number in ink before using this book.

DO NOT INDICATE YOUR UNIT

Name .... QUILL

Rank .... F/O.

Military Identification Card or Official Number 170512

SEE INSTRUCTIONS WITHIN

As Detective Chief Superintendent Greeno surmises, had Miriam not been absorbed in her book — *War and Peace* by Tolstoy — she might never have missed her connecting train at Charing Cross. At the same time, it was another of her possessions that helped convict her killer as Bill had given her a book of his clothing coupons.

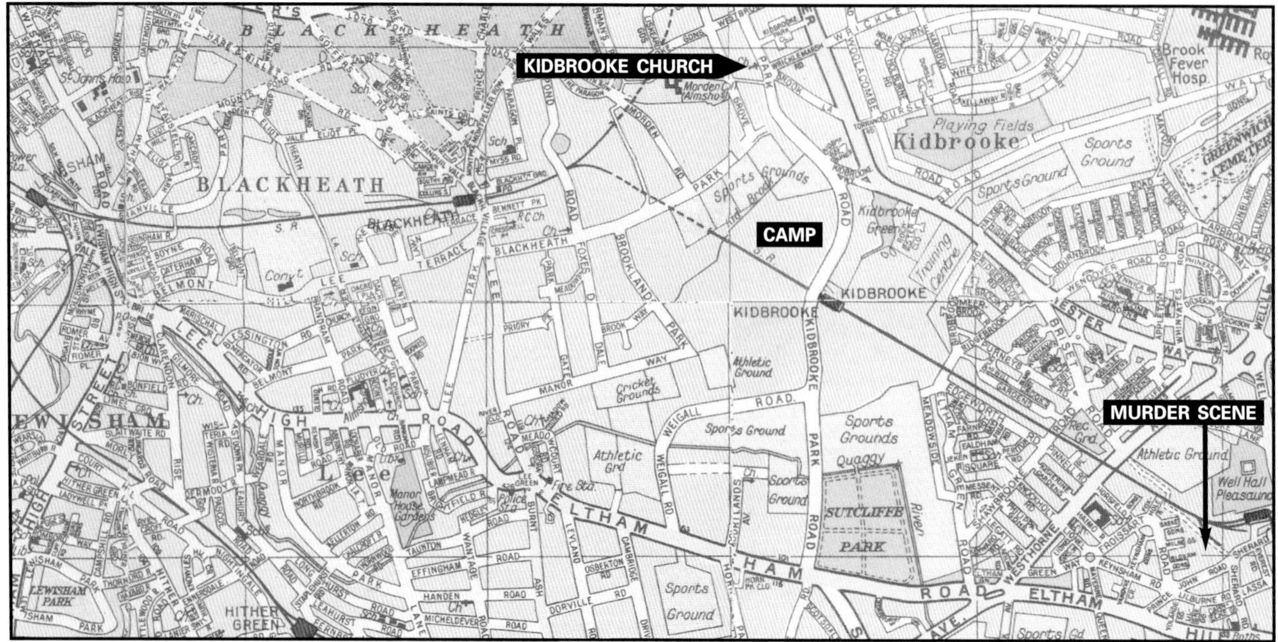

Miriam's arrival at Charing Cross station was confirmed by ACW2 Winifred Allen, who was also stationed at Kidbrooke, as she recalled seeing Miriam engrossed in a book in the YMCA canteen at around 10.35 p.m. Then a Mrs Margaret McGregor came forward to say she remembered getting off the 11.25 train to Lewisham at 11.40 and saw an attractive WAAF carrying a book under her arm. In the company of her brother-in-law, she said she walked with the WAAF and a soldier who joined them. They all walked up Belmont Hill and along Blackheath Park to Kidbrooke Church which was only 400 yards from the RAF camp.

We knew the murderer was a big man from his footprints and his gloves. I reckoned he must know this district to have found these allotments and from the timing he was either an absentee, a deserter or a soldier on late pass. There could be millions in those three categories as the south of England was full of soldiers. This one might even be anywhere by now. There comes a time in every murder hunt when everything looks hopeless — and this was it.

We pressed on. We interviewed hundreds of soldiers billeted in the area and we asked about thousands more. Who was missing? Who was out on Sunday night? Who was too glib with his alibi? Every available policeman in the Division was on this hunt. Throughout Britain local police enquired at local camps. The result was still stalemate.

A mysterious telephone caller said, 'If you want to find the murderer go to the Union Jack Club at Waterloo.' We went expecting a hoax, and that's what it was. There was another phone call from a police station this time. 'American soldier, very dishevelled, left Well Hall, S.E.9, on the two-twenty train due in Charing Cross at two-fifty. Can you contact?' That seemed more promising and my men were there when the train arrived. We took a man off the train. He looked like a murderer, but he wasn't and we let him go.

There were more false alarms. There always are and they are not always malicious in intent. When people think they know something the police ought to be informed; one in ten thousand may be right, so the police would be fools if they didn't listen to the 9,999 first.

Margaret Mary McGregor might have been one of the 9,999. Her husband thought she was, when she said she thought she had seen Iris Deeley and the man who killed her that night — and not only seen them but walked and talked with them. Her husband said, 'Fancy wasting the time of the police with your stories.' She sat back abashed, the way a woman would, but after a day or two she said to hell with it, or whatever a housewife says in such circumstances, and she telephoned me at Eltham.

That started the case moving. Mrs McGregor remembered getting off the eleven-twenty-five train at Lewisham at twenty minutes to midnight on Sunday, and she remembered a well-spoken WAAF who wanted to go to Kidbrooke. This girl had rung her camp to report that she had missed the eleven-one. Mrs McGregor remembered she had a thick book under her arm. This was Iris Deeley all right.

So what about the soldier? Mrs McGregor was able to describe him. It was the first and only description we ever had: a rough-tough individual with a light blond moustache and an amazing paraphernalia of regimental flashes and glider pilot's wings, four medals, sergeant's stripes and a gymnast's badge.

Mrs McGregor, her brother-in-law, Iris Deeley and the soldier, began to walk towards Kidbrooke. The soldier was talking to the brother-in-law but pretty soon he arranged it so that he and the WAAF dropped behind together. Mrs McGregor shouted, 'Step it out, the army!' and he answered, 'I'm trying to keep in step with Snow White here.'

Mrs McGregor remembered his talking about that night's air raid, bragging that he

Left: **Reaching the church, Mrs McGregor and her brother-in-law crossed the road to reach their home in Broad Walk, having directed the WAAF to walk straight ahead down Kidbrooke Park Road to the camp. However, she never arrived.** *Right:* **The police box and wartime air raid siren have both disappeared, the junction with Brook Lane also having been realigned.**

had found some American soldiers cowering in a shelter and had ordered them out at pistol point' only Mrs McGregor was sure that he had no pistol. He talked a lot about Americans. He hated them. He said that it was a good job his sister hadn't brought an American home at Christmas. 'My father's a copper and there would have been murder.'

Obviously a braggart who talked rubbish, he made one remark more significant than he would ever know. As they neared the church at Kidbrooke he said, 'I've walked this way a few times.' I was right: it was a local man. We were learning fast.

From her father we knew that Iris had been robbed. A wallet containing £11, a long heavy silver cigarette case which he had given her, and a book of clothing coupons in her fiancé's name were missing. I sent a message to all pawnbrokers in Britain warning them to watch for the cigarette case, but a reporter discovered this and now I knew we would never find the case. Once the murderer read about the cigarette case there was one thing he would do: throw it away. Fortunately nothing was printed about the clothing coupons.

I notified the police throughout Britain about the soldier's medals and flashes and at 5 a.m. on Monday the 21st, exactly a week after Iris Deeley's murder, old Charles Memory, who had been a railway police sergeant for thirty years, saw a soldier and a WAAF cuddling on the platform at St Pancras. In those days of wartime farewells, railway police learned to look away from platform wooings, but Memory had also been a soldier and he recognised the medals this fellow wore. Apart from the Military Medal, which was rare enough for a lad who looked about twenty, he had the North-West Frontier, Afghanistan and Palestine medals, and these were old soldier's decorations.

After the young man had seen his WAAF to the train, Memory looked closer. The soldier was wearing American army trousers and was carrying an American officer's valise. Memory questioned him. The valise, he answered, he had found in Euston Road but there is such a thing as 'stealing by finding' so Memory was well within his rights in arresting him there and then. At Albany Street police station they found he had a wallet, a Waterman pen and a book of clothing coupons with the front page missing. He also had a left-luggage ticket for a kitbag at Waterloo station.

He was very cocky when I got there so I stayed just long enough to take his name and details: Gunner — despite his three stripes — Ernest James Harman Kemp of the Royal Artillery. I left him guessing and went off to find out more about him. He had been an absentee for a fortnight but how he had walked freely about his home area without being picked up by the military police I did not know. Four hours later I went back and

Gunner Ernest Kemp had been detained at Woolwich Barracks awaiting a court-martial for desertion but had absconded from the Dental Centre at Charlton on February 8. However, now the police had Mrs McGregor's description, early on February 21 Kemp was spotted at St Pancras Station. Having now bedecked himself with medals and flashes to which no young soldier would be entitled, this immediately aroused the suspicions of a railway policeman and Kemp was detained. He told Greeno that he had convinced the WAAF that he knew a short-cut to the camp but in fact was deliberately leading her to an allotment beside the railway sidings at Eltham, over a mile away, which he must have been familiar with. ***Above left:*** **The scene of crime plan shows where Kemp took Miriam through the opening in the sleeper fence, seen on the right, and through the cabbage patch.** ***Right:*** **This is the same Foxhole Path today.**

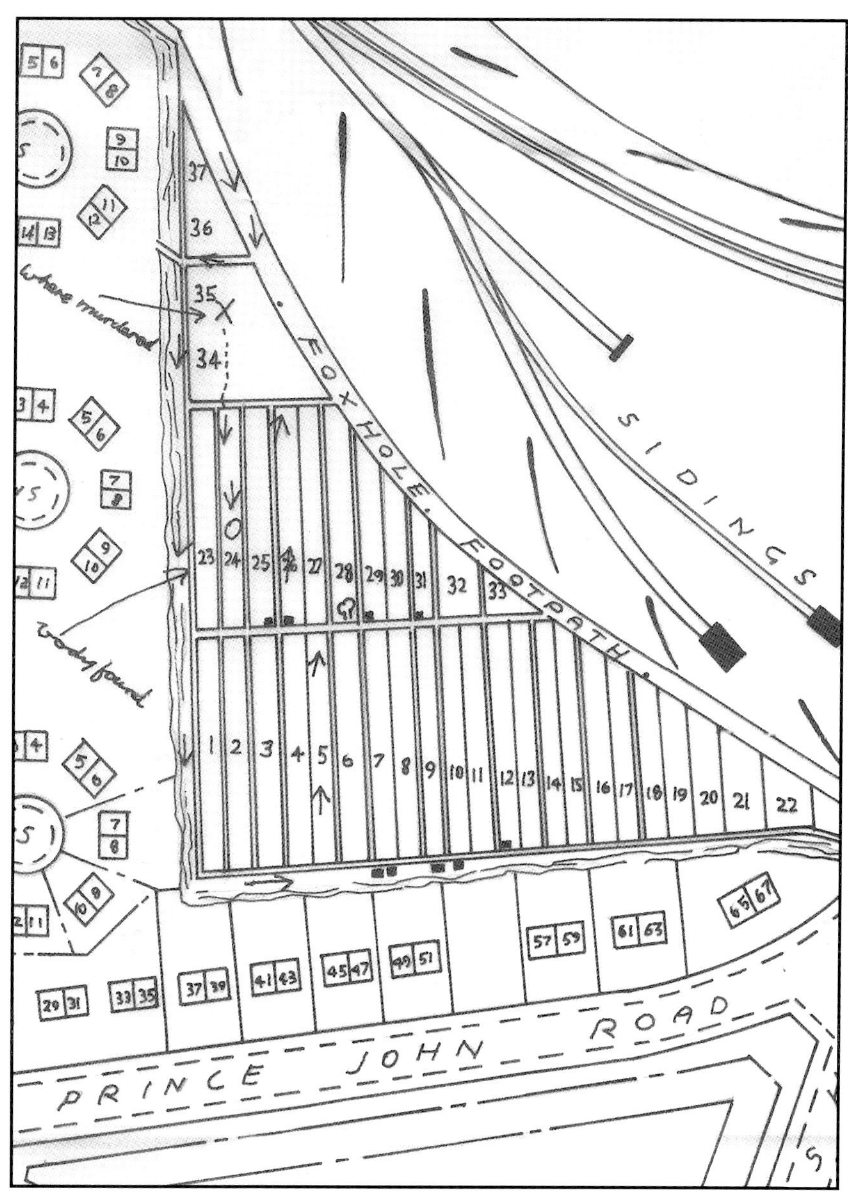

Miriam was murdered at the spot where the two policemen are standing just inside the sleeper fence but was then dragged away from the path to the roughed up area in the foreground. Her cap and book were found lying beside the drag route.

this time I told him I was on a murder hunt and asked him if he would like to account for his movements.

'Certainly,' he replied, and while he talked I produced the wallet. He said he had had that for two years. The coupons? Oh, they were issued to him. The pen? He bought that near the Marquis of Granby at Lewisham.

There was just one thing he didn't know. We had got his kitbag from Waterloo and in the field-dressing pocket of some trousers we had found the front page torn from a ration book. There was a name on it — the name of Iris Deeley's fiancé.

Kemp was most explicit about the night Iris was murdered. He made a statement starting with his getting up at 6.30–6.45 on Sunday morning and going right through his day until he met the 'WAAF with a book under her arm'. Mrs McGregor and her brother-in-law had walked to Kidbrooke church with them. He said that he and the WAAF walked on to a railway bridge near her camp and that he left her there before catching a 46 tram to Woolwich.

It was all very detailed. He remembered the kind of coat Mrs McGregor was wearing and the case her brother-in-law was carrying. Probably all of it was very true — except for the last part. He was still cocky. 'If I can help you I will be very pleased.'

'Yes,' I said, 'I shall be pleased, too' and I left the police station. At 8.15 that night I went back and I looked him up and down anew. He was a big powerful chap all right in just the way I had imagined. I looked at his boots, size 11, and asked, 'Are those proper service boots?'

'Yes. Why?'

'Take them off.'

'Whaffor?'

'Just take them off,' I said.

He looked at me blankly. He probably guessed that we would measure them against footprints on the cabbage patch. He was right; we would but my need was more immediate. If he got rough when he heard what I had to say next, I didn't want any kicks from a fellow his build, wearing size 11 boots!

I told him that I knew he had lied about his movements and that I was going to detain him in connection with the murder of Iris Deeley. Later Kemp made this statement:

'I have not told you the truth about what happened when I was with the W.A.A.F., but all this is true.

'When I was walking with the W.A.A.F. and we got to the end of the footpath running alongside the railway I think a man said "Halt." I did not say anything to him and he said no more to me. He shone his lighted torch on the W.A.A.F. and me. Just at that time an R.A.F. car did come along. I walked with the W.A.A.F. under the arch and into a second passageway alongside the rail road on the left and some allotments on the right. We walked alongside the passageway, and I saw a wooden gateway on the right. I tried the gate and found it shut but it moved. I put my hand on the inside of the gate and found a button and opened the gate. I walked through with the W.A.A.F. and shut the gate behind me.

'We walked straight across the path to the back of some houses, along another path to the top of the allotments, along another path to the centre and down another path to the middle of the allotments.

'Whilst we were walking along I put my hand on her breasts on the outside of her coat. She kept smacking my hand away and said "Don't do it."

'I could see she was frightened. We walked along until we came to some soft earth towards the bottom of the allotments about a dozen yeards or so away from the wooden gate. I put my right arm behind her and placed my right hand over her mouth and pulled her down to the ground. She tried to struggle, but she had no chance. I laid her on the ground, undid her coat at the neck, and noticed she was wearing a scarf folded across her tunic. I held her head down on the ground with my hand over her mouth. She still tried to struggle.

'I twisted the scarf round her neck and pulled it too tight. She went out and I felt her heart and found she was gone. I took her coat off while she was there. I got the wind up being near the footpath and dragged her up near the cabbages and left her.

The allotments disappeared many years ago, the site now occupied by the Tattersall flats. Your Editor stands where Miriam was murdered. The railway embankment is now hidden by trees but the concrete posts supporting the chain-link fence, seen behind the garage on the right, still form the connection between then and now.

After his dastardly act, at least Kemp had the decency to cover her naked body with her greatcoat.

'I don't know what made me do it, but I undressed her. I took all her clothes off, but did not interfere with her [*not strictly true as traces of semen were found on her body by the pathologist Arthur Davies — Ed*]. After I had taken off her clothes I saw her naked body, and thinking someone might see it whilst going along the pathway I put her tunic over the top part of the body and placed the overcoat over the lower part of the body.

Before I had covered her over I searched the pockets of her clothing and found a wallet in her tunic pocket. There was also a long silver cigarette case in the pocket. I took these and put them in my pocket. I also took a fountain pen from her pocket. I tore the pocket from her skirt. I then covered her over as I have said.

'I left the allotments by the same gate and walked back along the footpath to the tramlines. Whilst I was walking along I looked in the torn out pocket and found an identity disc and some small coins. I threw the pocket and the identity disc over the railings alongside the railway and put the coins in my pocket. I then looked at the cigarette case, it was no good to me as I don't smoke so I dropped it inside the railings, pushed it in the soil and covered it over with my boot. I then caught a tram as I have previously said and when on the tram near my barracks I looked inside the wallet and found eleven one pound notes and some clothing coupons. There were forty coupons, and I think the name on the front of the book was Quill. I have used some of the front sheet of coupons to buy a shirt, two handkerchiefs, and a pair of gauntlet gloves at Hopes near Charing Cross.'

Detective Chief Superintendent
Edward Greeno,
War on the Underworld, 1960

Investigation having been completed, Miriam is carried from the field of battle.

Left: **The police stretcher-bearers emerge from Foxhole Path.** *Right:* **The concrete fence post is still there!**

Sentence of death was passed at the Central Criminal Court yesterday on Ernest James Harman Kemp, 21, a gunner in the Royal Artillery, who was found guilty of the murder of Iris Miriam Deeley, 21, a member of the W.A.A.F., who was found strangled with a scarf tied tightly round her neck on an allotment at Kidbrooke at daybreak on February 14. The jury added to their verdict a recommendation to mercy, which Mr. Justice Cassels said would be forwarded to the proper quarter.

The Times, April 19, 1944

The court dismissed the appeal against his conviction of Ernest James Harman Kemp, aged 21, a gunner in the Royal Artillery, who was convicted before Mr. Justice Cassels at the Central Criminal Court on April 18 last of the murder of Iris Miriam Deeley, 21 years old, a member of the W.A.A.F., whose body was found on an allotment at Kidbrooke on February 14, death having been caused by strangulation. The jury recommended Kemp to mercy.

The only ground of appeal relied on was that the trial Judge misdirected the jury as to the meaning and nature of the presumption that a person intends the natural consequences of his own acts, and that, in so doing, he told them in effect, that they were not to consider the defence put forward on behalf of the appellant that he had no intention to kill and that he had no intention to commit a felony.

They mourn a daughter, sister, and fiancée — the Deeley family with Bill Quill.

Leading Aircraftwoman Miriam Iris Deeley, 2130707, is laid to rest with full military honours, February 18, 1944.

Mr. F. H. Lawton appeared for the appellant: Mr. L. A. Byrne for the Crown.

Mr. Lawton said that his submission at the trial was that in making a sexual assault, the appellant's intention in pulling the girl's scarf round her neck was to keep her from struggling or screaming, and that he had no intention of causing grevious bodily harm.

Counsel objected that, in his summing-up the Judge said, in effect, that the presumption in law with regard to the natural consequences of a man's act was an irrebuttable presumption, and that because it was an irrebuttable presumption, the appellant could not, through his counsel, say that he never intended to cause grievious bodily harm.

The Lord Chief Justice giving the judgement of the Court, said that the Judge had accurately stated the law to the jury and properly left the question of the appellant's guilt to them. If a person intentionally did an act likely to kill another, or caused that other person grievious bodily harm and death resulted in consequence, that was murder.

The facts were plain and undisputed: there was no ground on which the direction could be assailed, and the Court saw no reason at all to interfere with the verdict.

The appeal would be dismissed.

The Times, May 23, 1944

Gunner Ernest James Harman Kemp, aged 21, Royal Artillery, whose appeal was dismissed against sentence of death for the murder of 21-year-old Leading-Aircraftwoman Iris Miriam Deeley, of Wanstead, London, was executed today at Wandsworth Prison.

Evening Despatch, June 6, 1944

'In proud and loving memory of "Cis" our precious daughter.' An inscription in stone but how can one adequately convey the tragedy of Miriam's death in words. They laid her to rest in a shady corner of the City of London Cemetery at Manor Park, the grave (number 111455 in square 261) now marked by the Commonwealth War Graves Commission.

DISGRACEFUL DEATH

DEATHS 1939 - 46 (ENTRY FORM) FORM RH

REGT OR CORPS TO WHICH THE PERSON BELONGED AT TIME OF DEATH) ....

Part I	Army No (1)	Rank (2)	Name in full (Surname first) (3)	Age (4)	Country of birth (5)	Date of death (6)	Place of death (7)	Cause of death (8)
	6105471	GNR	KEMP ERNEST JAMES	20	ENGLAND	6.6.44	WANDSWORTH PRISON	JUDICIAL HANGING

Part 1 DECORATIONS - ENTER one in each space

Left: **This poor newspaper picture of Kemp shows him sporting the cap badge of the Army Physical Training Corps, instead of the muzzle-loading gun insignia of the Royal Regiment of Artillery, and wings and medal ribbons to which he was not entitled (see page 153). Kemp was sent for trial at the Central Criminal Court yet the jury only required a recess of 15 minutes before returning with a unaminous verdict of guilty. On June 6, 1944, Gunner Kemp became Britain's most ignominious casualty of D-Day . . . yet after the war his name was still forwarded for commemoration on the Memorial to the Missing at Brookwood Cemetery** ***(right).*** **Unlike Fred Cummins (see page 111), where the Royal Air Force dismissed the convicted murderer from the service before he was executed, thus eliminating the obligation for any commemoration as a wartime casualty, due to a total act of administrative incompetence by the War Office, Kemp was never discharged from the Army before being hanged by Albert Pierrepoint and Herbert Morris at Wandsworth prison, where his body lies buried in Grave No. 58. (See pages 356-359 and also** ***After the Battle*** **No. 45.)**

This is the scene photographed by police from the bridge crossing New Town Road in Ashford, Kent, on the morning of August 23, 1944. The police car stands at the end of the Black Path which leads back beside the old cricket field to the Smiths Arms. Betty Green's home lies a few hundred yards up New Town Road to the left, but instead of reaching it she lies (circled) where two American servicemen left her for dead, close to the fence to the right of the gates.

August 22, 1944 – The Killing of Betty Green

Brutally strangled, Betty Green, of New Town, Ashford, was found lying huddled behind the sleeper fence at the Black Path, near Hastings Bridge, early on Wednesday morning.

A workman walking along the railway shouted down to a man in the road, 'Look there's a girl in that field.'

Closer enquiries revealed that she was dead, circumstances pointing to murder, and the police were informed immediately.

Det. Supt. Smeed of Maidstone, well-known in police circles for his success in these cases, visited the scene with Supt. Broughton, of Ashford. Photographs were taken and the matter appeared well in hand. Late on Wednesday night, though, Supt. Smeed admitted that there was 'a wide field of suspects.'

Mr. and Mrs. William Green, the girl's parents, thought that Betty had gone to a cinema with her friend Peggy Blaskett of Francis Road. Instead of this they had gone to the fair in the town, and there had met three soldiers. One soon left but the others stayed with the girls for a couple of hours.

Peggy said on Wednesday night: 'About half-past nine we said goodbye and started on our way home. The soldiers persisted in following us although we told them to go away. When we got near home they seemed to have disappeared. Outside my house I said goodbye to Betty and she went towards her home. I never saw her again.'

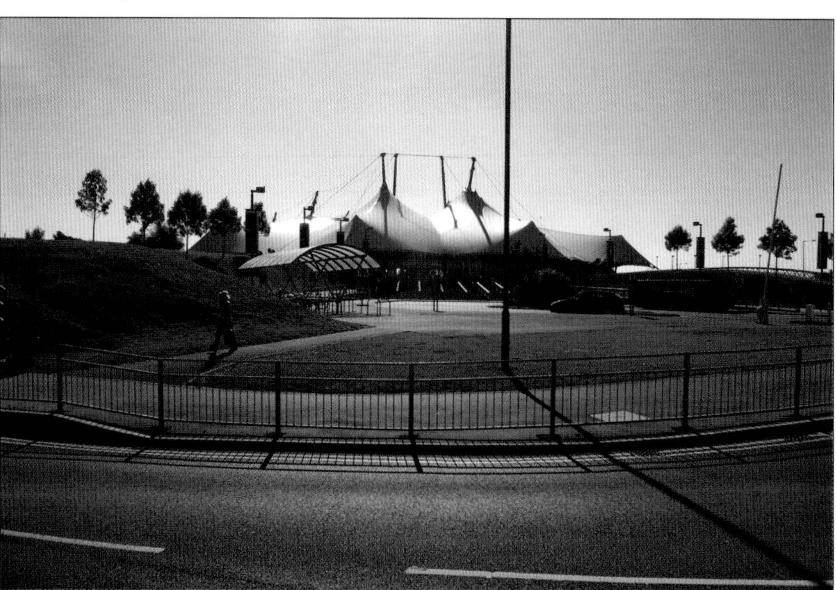

Top: **At 7.15 a.m. that morning, a railway worker on the Hastings line bridge 'noticed something lying like a body' in the old cricket field which was separated from the bridge by the Black Path. Together with another railway employee he went into the overgrown field where they found the body of a girl lying close to the fence.** *Above:* **In September 2011 a lady walks down the only section of Black Path that still remains as the Ashford Designer Outlet has since expunged the rest from the map.**

Dr Keith Simpson, the pathologist at Guy's Hospital, was summoned from London. He found parts of her clothing disarranged, the skirt being lifted so the lower hem was above the knees. The left shoe was lying beside the body. Certain hairs and fibres were removed from various parts of the body. Later at the mortuary, he removed the clothing and examined the body in detail. The injuries to the neck were as follows: 'There was a single deep-seated bruise on the right side of the neck, the deceased's right side. It lay immediately under the angle of the jaw on the side and there was also near to it a number of scratches or other marks. On the opposite side of the neck I found four rounded or oval bruises, the whole group being, in my view, very much in keeping with the tight application of a right hand from in front. The voice box was not fractured but some bruising was present behind it as a result of it being pressed against the spine. Intense asphyxial changes were developed in the lungs and the heart, but, in keeping with death, asphyxia due to manual strangulation by the hand [with] the same condition of asphyxia present of head and neck.'

CHARGE: Violation of the Ninety-second Article of War.

Specification 1: In that Corporal Ernest Lee Clark, 306th Fighter Control Squadron, IX Air Defense Command, did, in conjunction with Private Augustine M. Guerra, at Ashford, Kent, England, on or about 22 August 1944, with malice aforethought, wilfully, deliberately, feloniously, unlawfully and with premeditation kill one Betty Dorian Pearl Green.

Specification 2: In that Corporal Ernest Lee Clark did, in conjunction with Private Augustine M. Guerra, at Ashford, Kent, England, on or about 22 August 1944, forcibly and feloniously, against her will, have carnal knowledge of Betty Dorian Pearl Green, a female child below the age of sixteen years, the said Corporal Ernest Lee Clark penetrating the sexual organs of the said Betty Dorian Pearl Green with his penis, being aided and abetted therein by the said Private Augustine M. Guerra who held and subdued the said Betty Dorian Pearl Green during such action.

Specification 3: In that Private Augustine M. Guerra did, in conjunction with Corporal Ernest Lee Clark, at Ashford, Kent, England, on or about 22 August 1944, forcibly and feloniously, against her will, have carnal knowledge of Betty Dorian Pearl Green, a female child below the age of sixteen years, the said Private Augustine M. Guerra penetrating the sexual organs of the said Betty Dorian Pearl Green with his penis, being aided and abetted therein by the said Corporal Ernest Lee Clark during such action.

Officer of the Judge Advocate General, European Theater of Operations, Ashford, Kent, October 1944.

Mr. Green, after attending the post mortem examination, said 'I think it reveals that the manner of her death, following a struggle, shows that what many people may be thinking is not true.

'Betty was a vivacious girl, but a good girl. God bless her. She made friends too easily and I had warned her about mixing too readily with strangers.'

On their evening stroll Mr. and Mrs. Green passed the scene of the crime a short while before Betty met her death.

The last person apparently to see Betty alive must have been Mr. Harry Champion, when standing on the railway embankment at 10.20 p.m., shouted to the girl, 'Goodnight, Betty,' and she replied 'Goodnight, Harry.' Then she was running along towards her house and singing.

At a Press interview late on Wednesday night Supt. Smeed denied that there had been any struggle or that Betty had been raped, although her clothes were definitely disarranged.

Kentish Express, August 25, 1944

Further light has been thrown on the mystery of the murder of Betty Dorian Pearl Green, of New Town, Ashford, as the result of intensive enquiries.

Two American soldiers have been arrested and are awaiting court-martial. It is understood that both have made extremely important statements bearing upon the matter. The case is now being dealt with entirely by the American authorities and names will not be released.

The court-martial will take place in approximately three weeks time.

Kentish Express, September 1, 1944

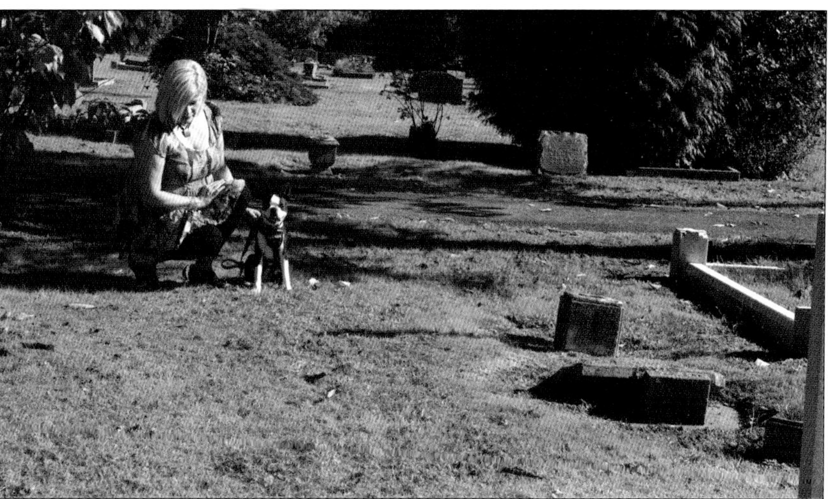

Meanwhile the girl had been identified as Betty Green by her father. He had been at the Smiths Arms — some 200 yards from the murder spot — and he recalled that two Americans had been at the pub the previous evening. They had left just before him and as he walked behind them he saw them turn towards the Black Path. Later at an identification parade he picked out the men he had seen. Betty Green's clothing and the hair samples had been sent to the Metropolitan Police Laboratory at Hendon where they were examined by Dr Henry Walls. The clothing of the two men identified by Mr Green — Private Augustine Guerra and Corporal Ernest Clark — was also examined and hair samples compared to those found on the dead girl. Faced with damning forensic evidence, both confessed that they had met a girl. Clark admitted that he had approached her and asked her to go for a walk. When he picked her up to carry her into the field she had started to scream and Guerra put his hand over her mouth. They then admitted that they had laid her gainst the fence and taken turns in raping her. On returning to camp Guerra had asked Clark if there was anything wrong with the girl after he left her lying on the ground. Clark told him he didn't think so as her heart was still beating. He thought she had fainted and after a rest she would be all right again. ***Above:*** **Gail Ramsey pays her respects at Betty's unmarked grave in Willesborough Cemetery. Private Guerra and Corporal Clark were executed by Tom and Albert Pierrepoint at Shepton Mallet on January 8, 1945.**

In 1944, Elizabeth Jones — who preferred to be called 'Betty' — had already spent time at an approved school and had proved to be a troublesome teenager to her parents in Neath, in Wales. After her husband Stan was called up, she gravitated to London to seek work — any work — be it a waitress, cinema usherette or barmaid. She rented a room above a shop at 311 King Street, Hammersmith and when we visited it in 2011 it was selling beauty treatment with the door to the flat on the left.

October 7, 1944 – US Deserter tried in a British Court

Private Karl Gustav Hulten, an American paratrooper, 22, of Boston, Mass., and Elizabeth Marina Jones, 18, dancer, of King Street, Hammersmith, appeared at the Feltham (Middlesex) magistrates' court yesterday charged with being concerned together in the murder of George Heath, 35, a taxicab driver, of Kennington, who had been described as the man with the cleft chin. They were remanded until Wednesday, December 6, when they will be committed for trial to the Central Criminal Court. They pleaded 'Not Guilty' and reserved their defence.

Heath was found dead with a bullet through his back in a ditch at Knowle Green, near Staines, in October.

Mr. H. A. K. Morgan represented the Director of Public Prosecutions. Mr. T. K. Edie appeared for Hulten, and Mrs. Lloyd Lane for Jones. Mr. Morgan, opening the prosecution's case, said that Hulten was a private in the American forces and in the ordinary course, under the Visiting Forces Act, he would have been tried by an American court-martial. The American authorities made representations to our Government that this was a case which should be properly dealt with in the criminal courts of this country.

Mr. Morgan went on: Jones describes herself as a 'strip-tease artist' at a night club. She is a married woman, her husband serving abroad.

'Any' work led to her becoming a hostess at the Panama Club at 23/24 Cromwell Place, Kensington. *Left:* Today Alfred House has a more mundane purpose as commercial offices but back in those days this is where Betty also performed strip-tease. *Right:* We don't claim that this is her but it is nevertheless a genuine wartime performance which was too tempting to omit!

Private Karl 'Ricky' Hulten was a paratrooper with the American forces in Britain who had gone absent from his unit for several weeks, this photograph *(left)* being taken in the US before he was sent overseas. Early in October 1944, he had met up with Betty, boasting that he was a gunman from Chicago now leading a gang in London. Betty was impressed with the brash American and they quickly became lovers. On Friday, October 6, 1944 they did not get up until just before 3 p.m., Hulten going out about 4.30 saying he would call back for her at 6 o'clock. Betty said later in court that she stayed in waiting until she heard their pre-arranged whistle from the street around 11.30 p.m. 'He came indoors,' she said to police, 'and then said: "Come on, let's go and get a taxi." I knew the meaning behind his words and that he wanted me to go with him to rob a taxi-cab driver.' That unlucky driver was George Heath *(right)* and the interior of his taxi was later photographed by police *(below)*.

The case for the prosecution is that the killing of Heath was a deliberate, cold-blooded act by Hulten, and even if Jones did not know that Hulten intended to kill Heath, she certainly knew that Hulten was armed and that he intended to use violence if necessary to attain their joint purpose, which was robbery. Before the occurrence Hulten had been absent without leave for about six weeks, and was frequenting the Hammersmith district, where Jones had a room.

According to a statement by Jones, she and Hulten left her room on the evening of October 6 with the avowed intention of stopping a taxicab and robbing the driver. They walked towards Kensington, and opposite Cadby Hall Jones stopped a car driven by Heath. He agreed to drive them to the end of King's Road, Hammersmith, for 10s. Hulten and Jones got into the car, and at the end of Chiswick Road, Hulten told him to stop. Heath stopped and leant over from his seat to open the rear door for the girl. As he was in that position he was shot through the back: the bullet then struck the door and ricocheted on to the dashboard.

The Times, November 28, 1944

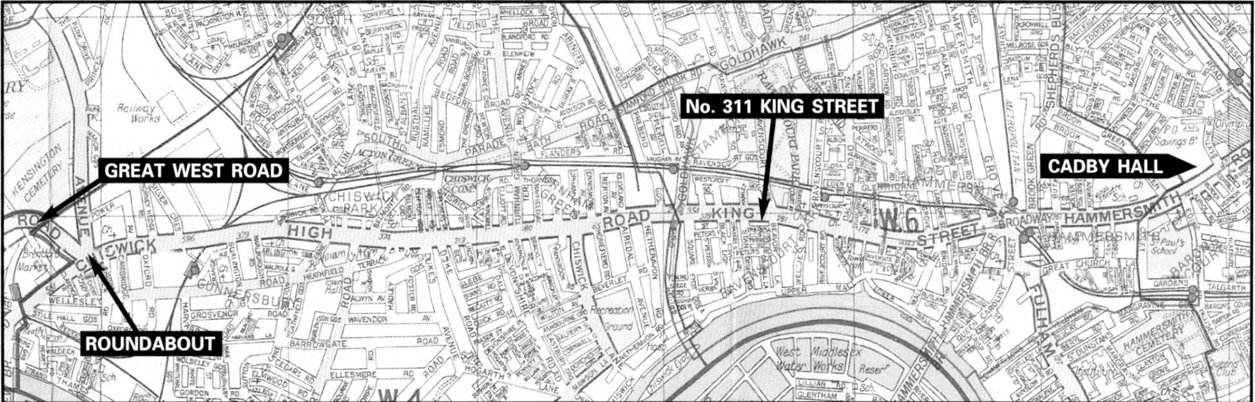

Betty Jones: 'We walked along Hammersmith Road and stood in a shop doorway opposite Cadby Hall. After about ten minutes a grey Ford car approached us very slowly like a taxi-cab, it was coming from the direction of Hammersmith Broadway. I yelled "Taxi" and it stopped. Ricky thought it was a Naval car and Ricky stopped in the shop doorway while I went over to speak to the driver. I said "Are you a taxi?" and he said "Private hire, where do you want to go?" I replied "Wait a minute," and went back to Ricky. I told him it was a private car and he asked how many men were in it. I told him only the driver so we went across to the car and Ricky asked the driver to take us to the top of King Street. He told Ricky that the fare would be 10/- and Ricky said, "That's all right". I know that Ricky had 19/- in his pockets and I had 10/3d. We got into the car and drove down King Street. After a while Heath said, "We've passed King Street where do you want to go?" Ricky said, "It's farther on, I don't mind paying more". Heath seemed cross, but drove on and when we came to the roundabout, Heath said: "This is the Great West Road". Ricky and I were sitting in the back seat of the saloon car and as we got into the Great West Road, Ricky told Heath to drive slowly and when we had travelled about 300 yards before reaching a bridge, Ricky said to Heath, "We'll get out here" and Heath stopped. Just as we were passing the roundabout I heard a click and saw that Ricky had his automatic in his right hand. I realised that Ricky was going to frighten the driver with the gun and take his money because we had passed my house on the way.'

Although an enlarged roundabout still exists at what was in 1944 the beginning of the Great West Road, today the junction has been changed with a ramp to the M4. *Left:* We drove the route taken by George Heath and it was probably about this spot *(right)* that he was shot. Betty Jones describes exactly what happened: 'Heath leaned over from his seat towards the middle of the car with the obvious intention of opening the nearside back door for me to get out. Ricky was sitting to my right and as Heath was leaning over I saw a flash and heard a bang. I was surprised that there was not a loud bang because Ricky had told me it would make a big noise when it went off. I was deafened in my right ear by the bang. Heath moaned slightly and turned a little towards his front. Ricky said to him, "Move over or I'll give you another dose of the same". I saw that he still had the automatic in his hand. Heath seemed to understand what Ricky said because he moved further over to the left-hand side of the front seat until his shoulder was almost touching the nearside door. I heard him breathing very heavily and his head slumped on to his chest. The next I realised was that Ricky was in the driving seat and the car was moving. As we went over the bridge nearby, Ricky told me to tear down the back window blind to see if any one was following us. I tore the right corner down, looked out and told Ricky no one was following. Ricky then told me to go through Heath's pockets. I leaned over and I heard his breath coming in short gasps. Ricky told me to look for his wallet in the breast pocket of his jacket. I felt in that pocket, but did not find the wallet. I found it instead in the left-hand outside pocket of his overcoat. It was a small folding wallet with a photograph inside and four £1 notes in it. I put the wallet on the back seat. Then I removed papers and a white book from his pockets. Among these were his identity card from which I learned his name and address, a cheque book with a blue cover, a driving licence, a blue card, some petrol coupons, and some photographs and letters. I also put this stuff on the seat by my side. From his trousers pocket I took a pound in silver and a few pennies which I put into my pocket. From other pockets I took a big brown fountain pen, a silver pencil, a long silver cigarette case which had a funny sliding action to open, it had 119, Regent Street, W.1. printed on the bottom inside, and an expensive looking cigarette lighter with a snap down action. I put all these things in my pocket. Ricky then asked me if Heath had a watch and I found a wrist watch on Heath's left wrist and I gave it to Ricky. I think I took everything from his pockets. All this time Ricky was driving fast along the road and I sat back examining the things I had taken from Heath's pockets. Ricky told me to put all the valuable things which I thought he would want to keep in my pockets and put the other stuff on the back seat. I did this and he then told me to look on the floor of the car with a torch for the bullet. I did this but did not find the bullet.'

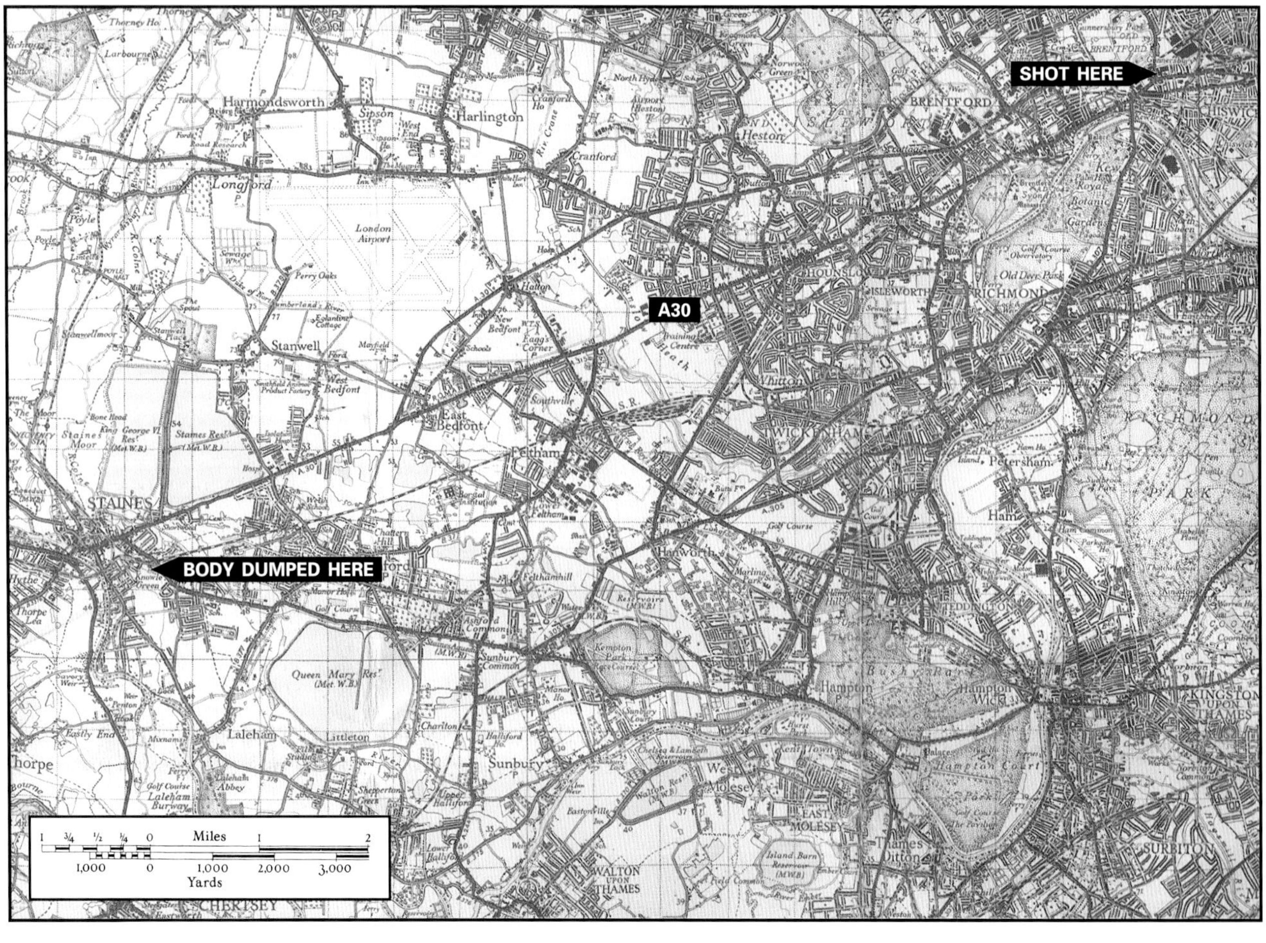

SHOT HERE

A30

BODY DUMPED HERE

At 11.30 a.m. on 7th October, 1944, I went to Knowle Green, Staines, where I saw Divisional Detective Inspector Tarr and Detective Inspector Tansill. Acting on their instructions I took measurements of a section of the road and certain marks which I saw on either side of the road. I later prepared a plan of Knowle Green and this section of roadway, correctly down to scale, which I produce.

Knowle Green is a small area of common land, adjoining Kingston Road, Staines, bounded on the south by the River Ash, on the east by an aqueduct, on the north by the Southern Railway, and on the west by Kingston Road. There is only one entry for normal traffic, by way of a narrow unnamed road leading from Kingston Road. After a few yards this road branches into two, one road leading to Manor Place, a cul-de-sac, and the other going across Knowle Green until it reaches a level crossing of the Southern Railway. (This road is marked 'A' on the plan.)

At a point along this road, about 440 yards from Kingston Road, I saw the body of a man lying face down in the ditch between two trees (marked 'A' and 'B' in the lower plan) with the head towards the west or Kingston Road. This ditch is dry and at the point where the body was lying, is 11 ft wide and 3 ft. 4 ins. deep. It is 26 feet from the edge of the ditch to the road.

I also saw marks on the ground on both sides of the road. On the north side, commencing at the edge of the road, were two straight parallel marks going diagonally towards the ditch. They were 4 ft. 10 ins. apart measured from the centre of each mark and the one nearest the ditch was 36 ft. long, finishing 9 ft. from the edge of the ditch. The mark nearest the road was 26 ft. 9 ins. long. These two marks were only just discernable.

Commencing from the termination of these marks were two parallel marks going in a curve to the edge of the road. The curved mark nearest the ditch was 19 ft. 6 ins. long, finishing 19 ft. from the commencement of the first straight mark. The second curved mark was 15 ft. long, commencing at a point 11 ft. 6 ins. from the edge of the road. These marks were very distinct, as the grass was torn away in places, exposing the soil.

P.C. Thomas Walton, October 19, 1944

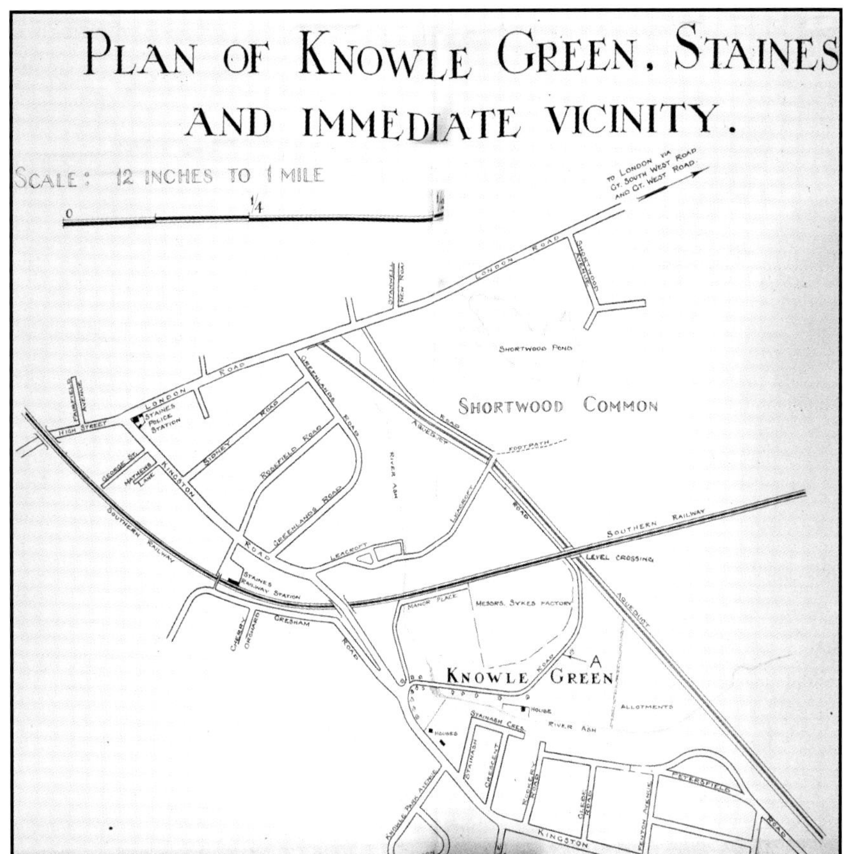

Betty Jones: 'Ricky drove on until he turned off the main road on to a sort of common. He drove on to the grass and stopped 2 or 3 yards from the ditch. He got out and dragged Heath's body from the car and rolled it into the ditch. He said there was blood on his hands and I gave him Heath's handkerchief to wipe it off. He then told me to pick up the papers and get into the front seat quickly. He told me to be careful of fingerprints at the same time. He turned the car right round and drove over the grass and eventually on the road again. When the car went over the grass it was very bumpy. After we got off the grass he told me to look for the bullet again with the aid of Heath's torch. I found a bronze coloured bullet on the floor by the nearside door and gave it to Ricky. After I found the bullet Ricky told me to take over the wheel and said he wanted to look at the things I had taken from Heath's pockets. I drove along and I noticed that there was no window in the offside door of the car near the driving seat.'

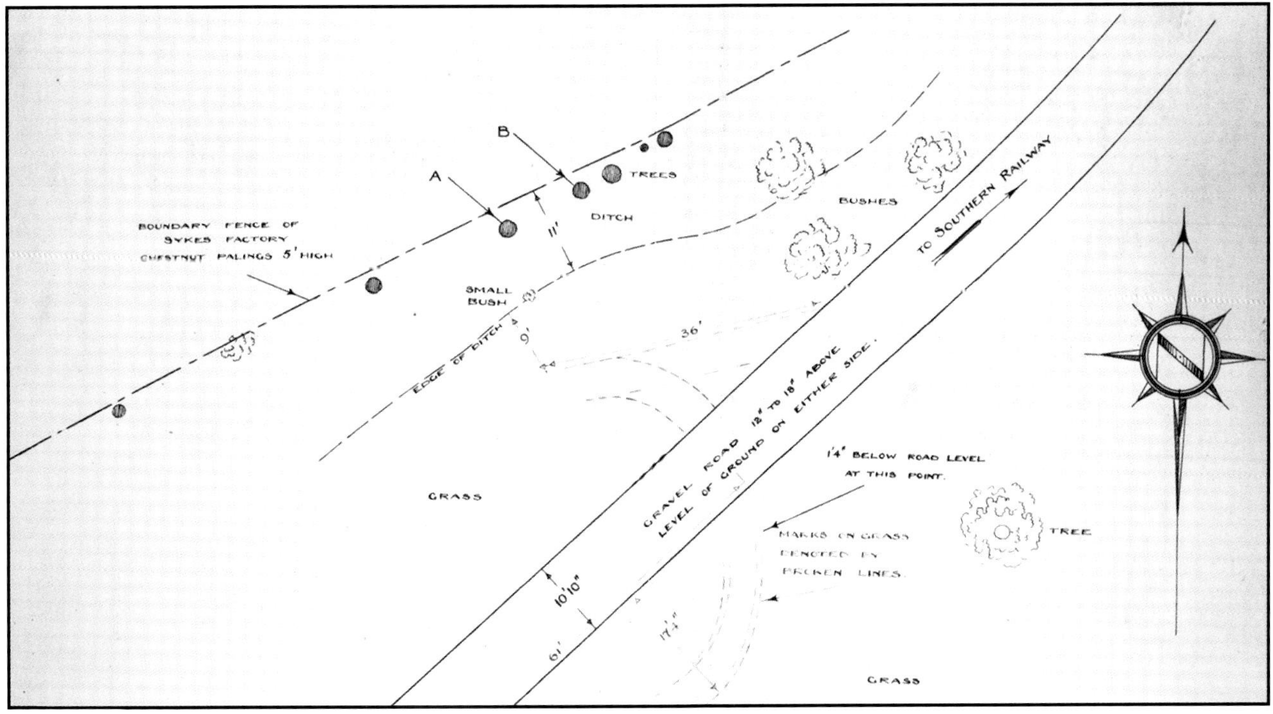

Scene of crime plans drawn by Police Constable Thomas Walton.

Having driven a distance of ten miles from London, Hulten pulled up on this gravel track to dump George's body. We had to carefully map read to find it in broad daylight so one can only assume that he was familiar with the area to have found it at night in the dark. A forest has since grown up on the left where the body was found.

At 7.30 p.m., 9th October 1944, whilst working my beat, I walked through Lurgan Avenue, Hammersmith. No cars or other vehicles were in the Avenue. I continued my patrol to Barons Court and returned to Lurgan Avenue at 8.10 p.m. when I saw a Ford V-8 trailer car, grey saloon, RD 8955, stationary, which had been previously circulated. The car lights were on. It was facing east away from the main road.

I notified Hammersmith and as the result of instructions received from Detective Inspector Read, I kept observation on the car. At about 9 p.m. I saw an American soldier leave a house in Lurgan Avenue and enter the car by the offside door, which was unlocked, and sit in the driver's seat as though he was the owner of the car.

PC William Waters, October 9, 1944.

At about 8.15 p.m. on 9th October 1944, in consequence of a telephone message received from P.C. 579 'F' Waters, I went with other officers to Lurgan Avenue, Hammersmith. There I saw a Ford V-8 motor car, index No. RD 8955, facing away from the main road. It was stationary and the lights were on.

I decided to keep observation and at about 9 p.m. the door of No. 159, Fulham Palace Road, Hammersmith, W., which is situated in Lurgan Avenue, was opened and a figure came out and crossed to the stationary car.

At the same time a police car which had been concealed across Fulham Palace Road but facing Lurgan Avenue, was driven into the cul-de-sac with its lights full on illuminating the car. We rushed up to the Ford V-8 car immediately. P.C. Waters, who had been keeping observation on the car from the far end, shouted out, and spoke to the man.

I noticed that a man was sitting in the driver's seat of the motor car and he was wearing American military uniform. We pulled him out of the car, pinioned his arms and faced him against the wall and at the same time I searched him. In his left hip pocket I found a 'Remington' make automatic pistol with six bullets in the magazine, one in the breach and the hammer was back with the safety catch off. I said to him, 'Is this your car?' He replied, 'No.' I told him that I would take him to Hammersmith Police Station for enquiries. He made no reply.

At the Station I noticed he was wearing the gold bar of an American Second Lieutenant. He then gave his name as Richard John Allen, aged 22, No. 0/1283187, 501 Parachute Infantry, U.S. Army. I would add that when searching him in the street in his left hand trousers pocket I found a spare magazine which contained six bullets. He was detained.

Detective Inspector Percy Read, 'F' Division, October 9, 1944.

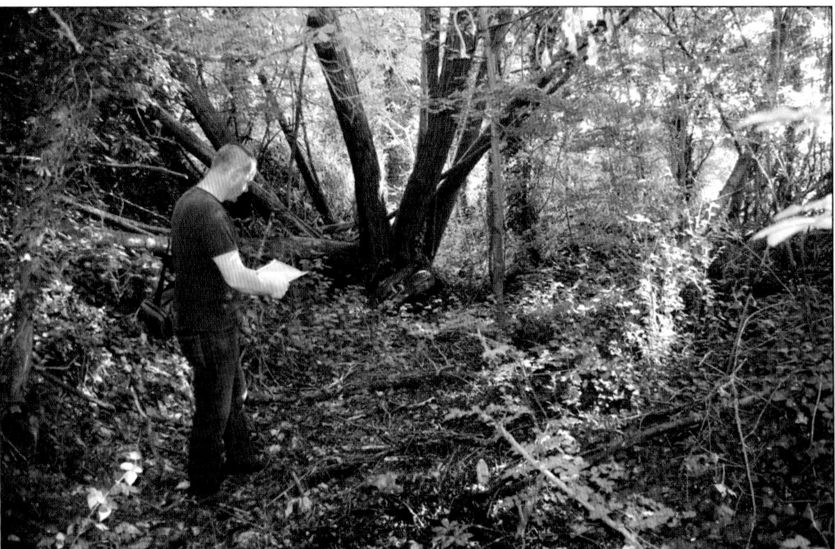

Robert Balding found the body here in the wide ditch: 'I live at 24 Gordon Close, Staines, and am an Auxiliary Fireman attached to the National Fire Service at the Ship Garage, London Road. I came off duty at 9 a.m. on Saturday the 7th October. To get home I walked across Knowle Green. To take a short cut I left the roadway and passed close to the ditch on my right-hand side. In the ditch I noticed what I thought was a man lying asleep. I went to him. He was lying on his right side with his left shoulder over and his head down. He was wearing a blue overcoat with the collar pulled up over his head hiding his face. I shook him. I looked at his face and then realised he was dead. I at once fetched the police.'

Left: **The Ford V8 was found abandoned back in Hammersmith at the side of Lurgan Avenue but unfortunately this road has since been swallowed up in the enlargement of Charing Cross Hospital.** *Right:* **In this picture, Lurgan Avenue began on the far side of the busy Fulham Palace Road, almost directly opposite Rosedew Road in the foreground.**

WESTERN UNION

CABLEGRAM

1945 Mar 1 PM 10

728 BOSTON MASS 76 1

RLT HON JOHN G WINANT
US AMBASSADOR LONDON
1 GROSVENOR SQ.

UNITED STATES ARMY HAS AGREED TO TRANSPORT BY AIR APPEAL FOR CLEMENCY TO HOME SECRETARY IN CASE OF PRIVATE HULTEN WHICH I AM FILING ON BEHALF OF HIS MOTHER AND WIFE RESPECTFULLY REQUEST YOU PRESENT APPEAL AND NOTIFY HOME SECRETARY IN ADVANCE THAT APPEAL IS FORTHCOMING AT EARLIEST POSSIBLE MOMENT AND ASK HIM TO STAY EXECUTION IF NECESSARY UNTIL APPEAL ARRIVES

SENATOR CHARLES J INNIS STATE HOUSE BOSTON

As this was the first case of an American serviceman tried in a British court for a capital offence, pressure was brought to bear on the Home Secretary by Senator Innis on behalf of Hulten's mother Signe and his wife Rita. Some files on the murder are still closed, possibly due to political sensitivities over the execution.

Five days before Hulten was due to be executed, Rita made efforts to talk with him by transatlantic telephone, obviously oblivious as to the fact that a person under sentence of death in Britain would be held incommunicado in the condemned cell. No doubt this photo was staged by the press in America.

Mr. J. D. Casswell, K.C., for Jones, said he had seen a copy of a letter which Hulten had referred to in his evidence and the Judge ruled that the letter should be read in Court. Mr. Casswell said the letter was written by Jones from Holloway and dated December 9, 1944. In it she said:

'Dear Ricky. I arrived back to Holloway about 7 p.m. on Monday night. My people were in Court and I was talking to them after Court was over. They were so very worried. Mum was breaking her heart over me. If I get sent to prison, convicted, it will kill her. So you see Ricky why you must tell the truth. If I lost my mother I would go mad. You must tell the truth. Ricky. Don't you think I've suffered enough being in Holloway on remand only? 'You promised me in Court you would tell the whole truth. Do not go back on your word. Ricky. What the police have against me is going through the man's pockets. Had you not ordered me to do so I would never have done it. But as my own life was in danger I did so. I could not believe you had done it. Ricky. You know the condition I was in. For hours afterwards I was dazed and still you threatened me, even when you knew I was too scared to go to the police. And there is another thing. You must tell the police as you promised the truth about the body. I did not help you to carry him to the ditch. You know that Ricky, for God's sake tell the truth. You and God are the only two who know of my innocence.

Half of this case is fresh to me. The gun, for instance — I did not know it was stolen. I did not know your real name, your age, your right rank. You were posing as an officer. I did not know you were married and had a child. I did not know you had deserted the Army. Why did you do it, Ricky, and why have you got me into this? You are making me pay for a nightmare which I can't believe has really happened. I beg of you to tell the truth, Ricky. If you have any respect, any honour or pride left you will speak the truth, Ricky. Sincerely, Georgie.'

The Times, January 23, 1945

Gustav Hulten, the 22-year-old American soldier who was sentenced to death with Elizabeth Maud Jones, since reprieved, for the murder of George Edward Heath, was hanged at Pentonville Prison yesterday.

At the inquest on his body conducted by Mr Bentley Purchase, Sir Bernard Spilsbury stated that Hulten's injuries conformed with instantaneous death. Two American officers, one of them a surgeon, represented the American Army and saw the jury sign the declaration testifying to Hulten's death. Dr. H. T. P. Young, medical officer of Pentonville Prison, said the execution had been carried out humanely.

Shortly before the execution was due to take place, there was a demonstration outside the prison in which, among others, Mrs Violet van der Elst was involved. Later Mrs Van der Elst and a man described as Charles Francis Smith, 28, slaughterer and motor driver, were charged at Clerkenwell with being concerned in causing grievous bodily harm to a policeman. They were remanded on bail of £50 each until March 26.

The Times, March 9, 1945

Both Hulten and Jones were sentenced to death, although the jury recommended Jones to mercy. Even though she had written to Hulten back in December appealing to him to come clean, as she was taken down she shrieked 'Oh! Why didn't he tell the truth?' A crowd of more than 200 gathered outside Pentonville on March 8, 1945, including the redoubtable Mrs van der Elst (see page 7), as Albert Pierrepoint and Henry Critchell carried out the execution. Although this case has gone down in history simply as 'the Cleft-Chin Murder', the victim — as in so many cases — has been overshadowed by the perpetrator. After much searching, we found George's grave (No. 40803 in Square 14B) in Streatham Park Cemetery in Rowan Road, sadly unmarked and forgotten. So we felt we could not walk away without leaving an appropriate marker.

putana. *Address*: Narendranagar, Tehri-Garhwal State, U.P. Agra and Oudh, India. *T.A.*: Vishalesh, Narendranagar.

TEICHMAN, Sir Eric, K.C.M.G., *cr.* 1933; C.M.G. 1927; C.I.E. 1919; Counsellor of Embassy, Chungking, since 1942; *b.* 16 Jan. 1884; *s.* of E. Teichman, Chislehurst, Kent; *m.* 1921, Ellen Cecilia, *widow* of Major D. S. Niven, O.B.E., I.A., *d.* of M. J. Teesdale, Walton-on-the-Hill, Surrey. *Educ.*: Charterhouse; Caius College, Cambridge (B.A.). Entered H.M. Consular Service in China 1907; attached to the Legation at Peking, 1907-17; on special service, 1917-19; assistant Chinese Secretary to H.M. Legation at Peking, 1919-20; employed in Foreign Office, 1921-22; Chinese Secretary at Peking, 1922-36; given local rank of Second Secretary in Diplomatic Service, 1920, First Secretary, 1924, and Counsellor, 1927; retired, 1936; awarded Murchison Grant Royal Geographical Society, 1925. *Publications*: Travels of a Consular Officer in North-West China, 1921; Travels of a Consular Officer in Eastern Tibet, 1922; Journey to Turkistan, 1937; Affairs of China, 1938. *Recreation*: shooting. *Address*: British Embassy, Chungking, China; Honingham Hall, Norfolk. *Clubs*: United University; Norfolk, Norwich.

TEICHMAN, Major Oskar, D.S.O. 1918; M.C. 1917; T.D.; late R.A.M.C.; Sub-County Army Welfare Officer, Wilts.; *b.*

It was somewhat ironic that with Sir Eric Teichman's entry in the 1943 edition of *Who's Who* giving his recreation as shooting, that this is how he should have met his death on his estate at Honingham Hall, in Norfolk.

December 3, 1944 – The Murder of Sir Eric Teichman

Sir Eric Teichman, noted traveller, diplomat, and expert on Chinese affairs, was found shot dead early yesterday in a wood near his home, Honingham Hall.

It appears that about 2 o'clock on Sunday afternoon while in the Hall he heard a shot fired on the estate. Having been troubled a good deal of late by poachers he went outside to investigate but took no weapon.

Some time passed and he did not return. Eventually search parties including a number of U.S.A.A.F. men went over the estate without success and at 9 p.m. owing to darkness, they were called off.

Lady Teichman, unable to rest, made a later search, accompanied by the district nurse, Miss V. Childerhouse. Shortly after midnight they found the body of Sir Eric about 500 yards from the Hall. It was in a wood, with considerable undergrowth, and death had evidently occurred some hours before.

There was a bullet wound in his cheek and later it was found that the bullet had penetrated to the shoulder from which it was removed. It is believed that death was instantaneous.

Eastern Daily Press, December 5, 1944

The Honingham estate was sold and broken up in 1936, being purchased by Sir Eric in 1937 when he retired as Governor of Hong Kong. He lived at the Hall alone with his wife until the day he was shot by an American airman stationed at the nearby airfield of Attlebridge. At the time of the murder, Station 120 was the home of the 466th Bombardment Group of the US Eighth Air Force which had arrived at the base with their B-24 Liberators in March 1944. It was handed back to the RAF in July 1945 and sold off during 1959-62, being purchased by Bernard Matthews Ltd for the rearing of turkeys in the buildings which now line the old runways.

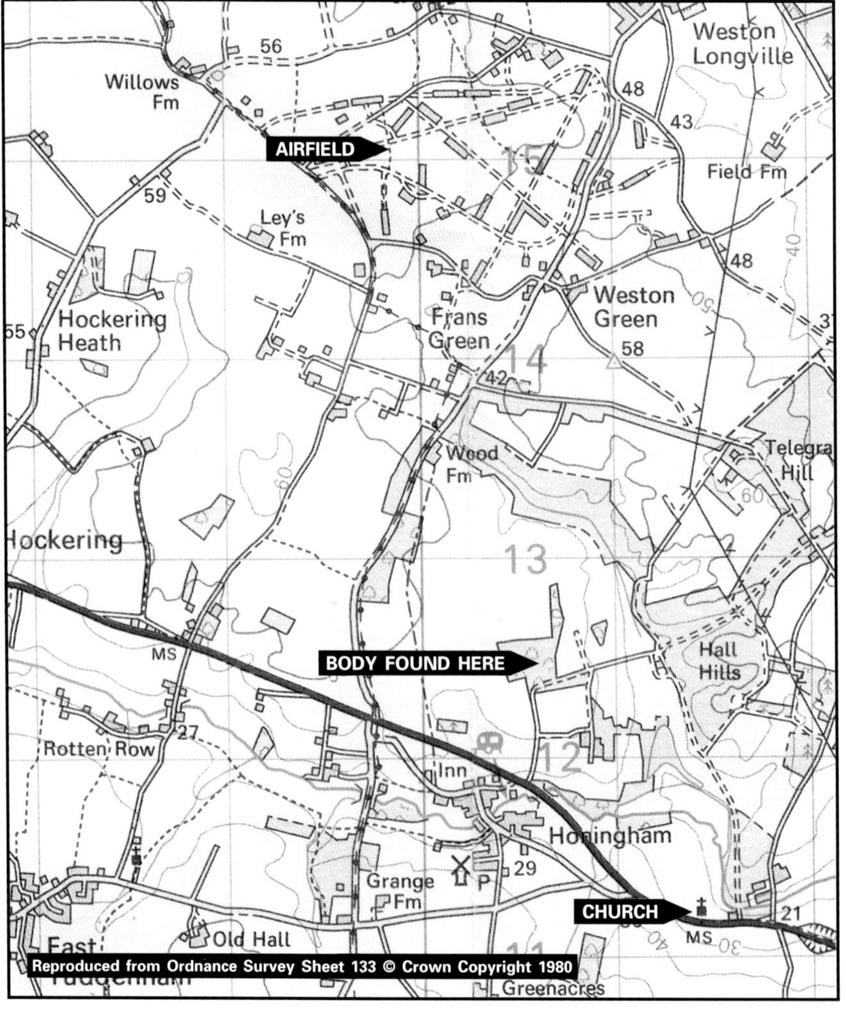

Reproduced from Ordnance Survey Sheet 133 © Crown Copyright 1980

Left: **After Sir Eric died, the Hall was given to Dr Barnardos Homes for 25 years to be used by orphan boys. When Mr J. M. Rampton purchased the estate in 1964, he told Barnardos they could stay on rent free but they decided to move elsewhere.**

The cost of renovation was put at £60-70,000 with extensive repairs required to the roof but, following a Public Enquiry to establish whether it was worth preserving, Honingham Hall was demolished. Only the coach house now survives.

I had called on Sir Eric Teichman and asked about pheasant shooting on the estate. He said an invitation would be sent to the Base CO inviting two American officers to the next shoot. Naturally, I was designated to represent the USAAF.

The first time, I wore old clothes like we do in the US when we go hunting. All the British gentry wore Norfolk jackets and breeches — rather dressed up for a social occasion. That first time was a disaster as my 12-gauge automatic jammed after the first shot. So I ate my lunch and drank Sir Eric's beer in disgust.

I was invited to hunt the following week for a pheasant shoot. This time I wore my Class 'A' uniform and took a sergeant and a staff car with driver and two shot-guns. The local gentry had two double-barrel shot-guns and a loader to carry and load the second gun. I had a slight advantage. I had my 12-gauge automatic and my sergeant loader with the second gun.

The beaters again beat the birds out. The shooters lined up and fired overhead at the flying birds. I suggested to Sir Eric that I go with the beaters through the bracken. He agreed so I was able to make the shots I knew best. I got 16 pheasants and two woodcocks on the first pass.

At the end of the day I had shot 26 pheasants out of the total of 100 bagged by 12 guns. Each gun got a brace of birds (two) that were worth about 10 shillings each on the free market. As I left, the old boy put his arm around me and the old boy said to come back the next week.

George Parker, 472nd Sub-Depot, 466th Bomb Group

At 1800 hours on 3 December, Colonel Joseph H. West, phoned, asking if we had seen Sir Eric Teichman anywhere in the squadron area during the past few hours. It seems that Lady Teichman had called the Colonel as she was greatly concerned because her husband had not returned after leaving the house at 1600 hours. It was unusual for him not to return before dark. We were ordered to get out all the men we could for a search for him. At the same time, the military police were sent by car to Honingham Hall.

About 30 men gathered at the Hall and an organized search was made, fanning out in the area surrounding the Lodge. The local constables joined the search parties. The search continued until about 2330 hours.

Early in the morning it was learned the body of Sir Eric was found by Lady Teich-

Private George E. Smith, accompanied by Private Leonard S. Wojtacha, had gone onto the Honingham estate to hunt for squirrels with .30-calibre M1 Carbines. Wojtacha told his court-martial, held in the Protestant Chapel on the New Communal Site on the airfield, that 'After passing Sir Eric Teichman's house, we both fired at a squirrel which jumped from tree to tree. I stood one side of a tree, and Smith on the other side. Then Smith told me there was a man behind me. I saw an old man coming up. I started to walk towards Smith and glanced over my shoulder at the old man, who was hunched over and was about 15 feet behind me. The man said, "Wait a minute. What are your names?" The next thing I knew a gun was fired and I saw the old man lying on his arm. Smith said, "Let's get out of here."' After they had walked a few yards they saw an old man with a dog. Wojtacha told the court that he said 'There's the old man again.' Smith replied: 'I must have missed him. I should have shot him again.'

man about 500 yards from the house (¾ of a mile from Site 1). There was heavy underbrush there but the family dog had found him. Sir Eric had been shot in the head.

Upon receiving word of the killing, the base was sealed with no one allowed to leave. An examination of the spent slug found in Sir Eric's clothes showed it to be from a 30-caliber carbine, the kind issued to all ground men on the base.

Orders were issued to interview every man in the 784th Bomb Squadron to ascertain their whereabouts between the hours of 4 and 6 p.m. on Sunday, 3 December. Also each man was required to bring his carbine with him so that the serial number could be checked against the records.

On 5 December, officers of the Army's Criminal Investigation Division arrived to assist in the questioning. When it became known that CID men were on the base, one of the kitchen helpers came to the Orderly Room to tell the 1st Sergeant that he had information that might bear on the Teichman killing, provided his name could be kept out of it. We couldn't promise but Sergeant Rowe told Robert Griffin he would try. Our informant told us he had seen Private George E. Smith, Jr. and a boy from another squadron, Private Leonard S. Wojtacha, leave Smith's barracks with carbines in their hands on Sunday afternoon.

Next morning two Scotland Yard men arrived. The carbines of both men were taken from the Supply Room for examination. It was clear that Smith's gun had been recently fired. Both guns were taken to the firing range and fired into a bucket. The recovered slugs were placed in envelopes with statements of the witnesses and attached to the respective guns.

Meanwhile, the CID men, working with Wojtacha, promised he would be treated lightly if he told all he knew about the incident. He finally broke down and told what he knew. With this information they confronted Smith and he confessed to the crime.

Smith related that Private Wojtacha had asked him 'to go hunt a little'. He had some extra ammunition he wanted to shoot up. Though it was against the regulation to go into the woods, or hunt, or even carry firearms, they shot up approximately 100 rounds between them.

Sir Eric heard the shooting and told his wife he was going to put a stop to the shooting so near to the house. Sir Eric came upon the men as they treed a squirrel. Wojtacha started to walk away when Sir Eric said, 'Wait a minute young man, what is your name?' Smith was facing in their direction and holding his carbine at his side with his finger on the trigger. When Sir Eric was about 30 feet away, Smith said, 'Old Man. Don't come any closer'. Sir Eric didn't stop and Smith fired from his side, not lifting the weapon. Sir Eric was killed instantly, the bullet entering his jaw and coming out the back of his neck.

1st Sergeant Leonard Rowe and Wallace Wessels of the 784th Bomb Squadron, 466th Bomb Group

Uncle Joe West sent me over to make peace with Lady Teichman. Joe and I went to the services at a small church. Sir Eric's body was conveyed from the Hall to the church by a black, horse drawn, hearse, circa 1890, and was buried in a wooden coffin in the churchyard.

George Parker, 472nd Sub-Depot, 466th Bomb Group

When the news first broke I was visited by a CID representative. It was a typical cold, English day. I suggested that we go to the kitchen, get a cup of coffee and discuss things at a table near the kitchen where it was warm and where we could have complete privacy.

We went into the mess hall, over to where the coffee pot was and then to the table. In so doing we passed by Smith who was sitting at the table next to us with a butcher knife in his hand. Later when confessing, he stated that he had thought that the CID investigator and myself had come for him. He had been prepared to first stab me and then the CID man.

Floyd Cooper, 784th Executive Officer

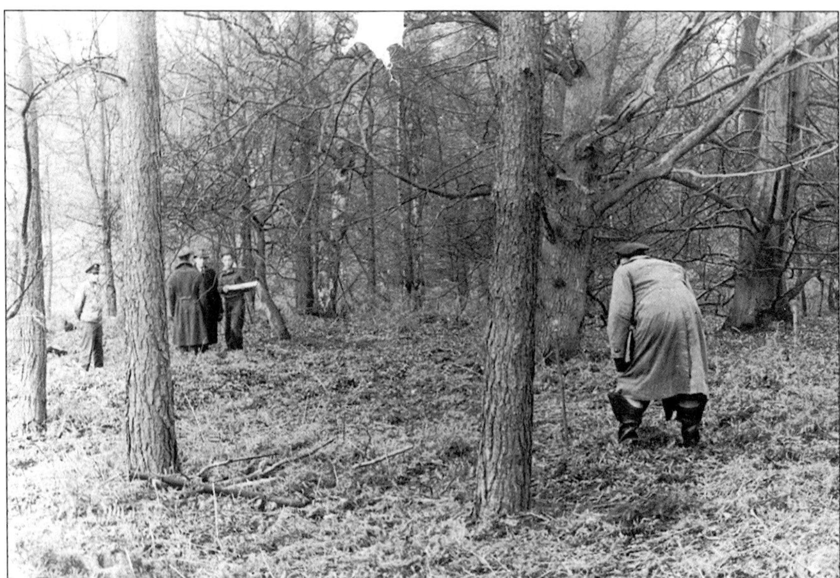

Major Tyler M. Birch, the Provost Marshal, then explained to the court how he accompanied Smith and Wojtacha over the route taken in their hunting trip from the camp on December 3rd. They found empty cartridge cases and they saw a metal drum with bullet holes in it. The men went on to the spot in the woods where the body had been found and with the aid of Smith and Wojtacha they reconstructed the scene at the time of the shooting. Smith stood in the spot where he said he was at the time the shot was fired and Wojtacha stood opposite him on the other side of a tree. 'I stood in the position where they said the old man was standing', added the Major. It was the exact spot where he saw the body in the early hours of December 4th. The carbine with which Smith was alleged to have fired the fatal shot was also produced as an exhibit. Although the scene of crime photographs were introduced without protest by the defence, the legal authorities were in conflict as to the admissability of re-enactment photographs, so the scenario was then acted out in court.

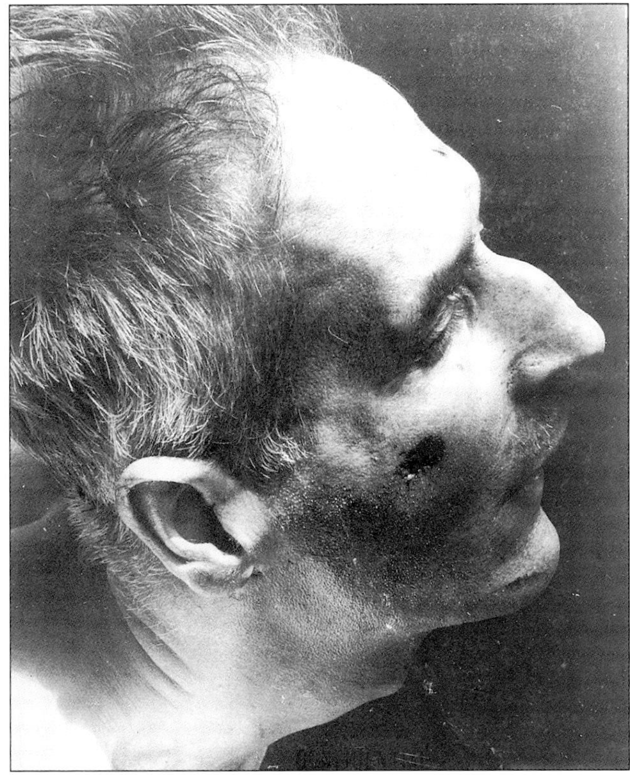

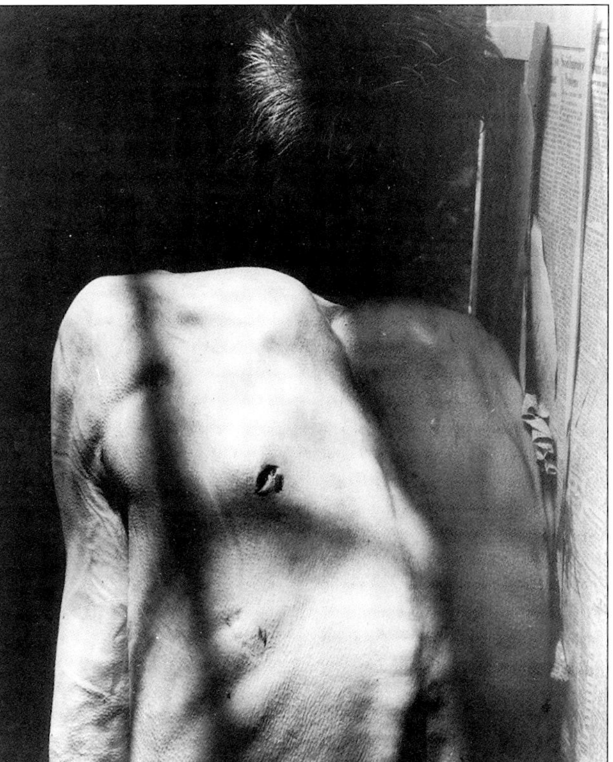

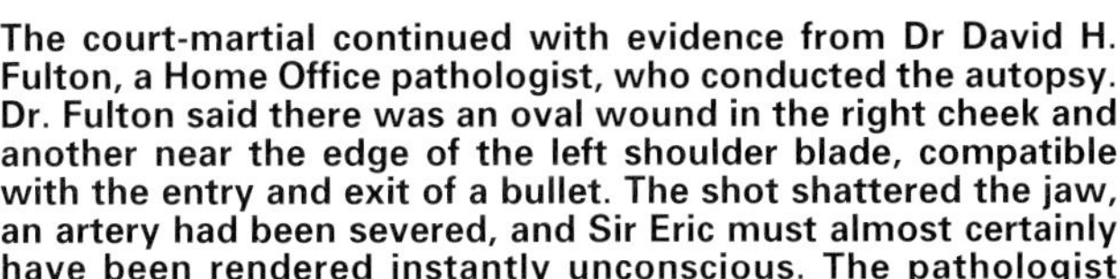

The court-martial continued with evidence from Dr David H. Fulton, a Home Office pathologist, who conducted the autopsy. Dr. Fulton said there was an oval wound in the right cheek and another near the edge of the left shoulder blade, compatible with the entry and exit of a bullet. The shot shattered the jaw, an artery had been severed, and Sir Eric must almost certainly have been rendered instantly unconscious. The pathologist told the court that there was no scorching of the face and the bullet was fired from at least six feet away or possibly much more. Detective Constable Barker of the Norfolk County Police identified a spent bullet which he found between the wound in Sir Eric's back and his vest. George Smith had the dubious privilege of being a casualty on VE-Day when he was executed by Tom Pierrepoint assisted by Herbert Morris.

Betraying no apparent emotion, Pvt. George E. Smith, Jr., yesterday heard the President of the U.S. court-martial at Attlebridge sentence him to death by hanging for the murder of Sir Eric Teichman by shooting him with a carbine in the woods at Honingham on December 3rd.

The unanimous verdict of 'Guilty' by the eleven officers comprising the court came late in the afternoon of the fifth day of the trial following a retirement of about eighty minutes. Before leaving the court, handcuffed to one of the guards, Smith bade a warm farewell to his counsel, Lieut. Max Sokarl, and he left the building with a half smile on his features.

In his attempt to show the defendant as being mentally defective and therefore not responsible for his actions, his counsel reported to the court that Smith, in the *2½* years he had spent in the Army had been court-martialled eight times and that he had served 18 months in the Huntington Reformatory in Pennsylvania after being convicted of the theft of an automobile. In continuing the insanity defense, Sokarl had Smith disrobe for the court and display his 17 tattoos. To no avail.

Eastern Daily Press, January 13, 1945

I participated in the review of the General Court-Martial of Smith. I remember we discussed the case at length and the contents of the review. Also I clearly remember carrying the written review from our office to General Kepner and discussing the review of the case with him. He asked me many questions about it, particularly about the question of insanity. He finally picked up his pen and signed the order for execution of the sentence saying, 'May God have mercy on his soul'. Just at that time the sun was setting and shadows were creeping into the room.

Lady Teichman appealed to our headquarters to spare Smith's life. She also appealed to General Eisenhower who also denied the request. Finally she appealed to U.S. Ambassador Winant but all of her gallant efforts failed.

Major C. Douglas Smith, Assistant Judge Advocate General for the 2nd Air Division

Pvt. George E. Smith, Jr. (28), a member of the U.S. Army, of Pittsburgh, Penn. sentenced to death by a U.S. court-martial for the murder of Sir Eric Teichman, the former British Diplomat, was hanged at a U.S. Army Disciplinary Training Centre on Tuesday (8 May).

Eastern Daily Press, May 11, 1945

Sir Eric's grave lies in the shadow of Honingham Church.

March 1943: the Duchess of Kent, Commandant of the Women's Royal Naval Service, arrives for an inspection of HMS *President*. On the extreme left an officer who was to pay the supreme sacrifice . . . but not on the battlefield — Captain Ralph Binney.

December 8, 1944 – Captain Ralph Binney, R.N.

A naval officer who made a gallant attempt to stop smash and grab raiders in the City yesterday afternoon was dragged for half a mile underneath the thieves' car. He received injuries from which he died in Guy's Hospital last night.

The naval officer was Captain Ralph Douglas Binney. C.B.E., R.N. (retd.), Chief-of Staff to the Flag Officer in Command, London, was aged 56. He retired at his own request in 1934 with the rank of captain, but resumed service with the Royal Navy at the outbreak of war and was on the staff of the Rear-Admiral at Alexandria until November 1942.

The smash and grab raiders made off in a dark coloured saloon car with jewels stated to be worth £3,500 from Thomas Wordley Limited in Birchin Lane. E.C. Captain Binney jumped on to the running-board as the car, making a getaway, swerved out of Lombard Street and then turned into King William Street towards London Bridge. The car was found abandoned in Tooley Street, S.E.

The Times, December 9, 1944

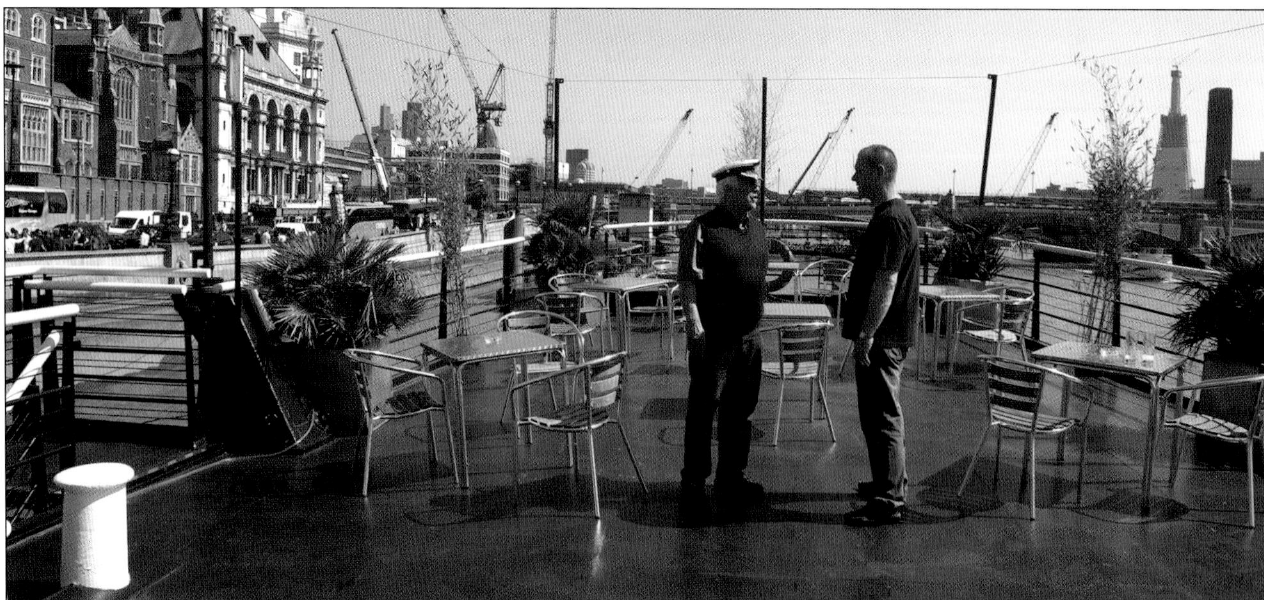

The ship was built in 1918 as an Anchusa-class corvette originally named HMS *Saxifrage* and commandeered as a 'Q' ship — a vessel disguised as a merchant ship to protect convoys. In 1922 she was renamed HMS *President* on becoming the shore station for the Royal Naval Volunteer Reserve and moored on the Thames near Tower Bridge. She remained in RN hands until purchased commercially in 2006 as a venue for conferences and functions under Captain Chris Cooper (left).

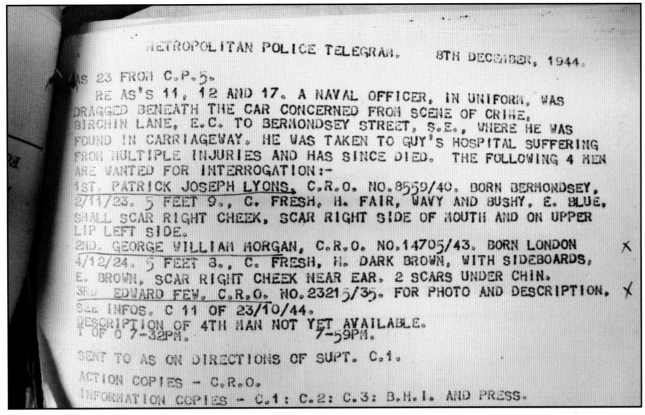

METROPOLITAN POLICE TELEGRAM. 8TH DECEMBER, 1944.
AS 23 FROM C.P.5.
RE AS'S 11, 12 AND 17. A NAVAL OFFICER, IN UNIFORM, WAS DRAGGED BENEATH THE CAR CONCERNED FROM SCENE OF CRIME, BIRCHIN LANE, E.C. TO BERMONDSEY STREET, S.E., WHERE HE WAS FOUND IN CARRIAGEWAY. HE WAS TAKEN TO GUY'S HOSPITAL SUFFERING FROM MULTIPLE INJURIES AND HAS SINCE DIED. THE FOLLOWING 4 MEN ARE WANTED FOR INTERROGATION:-
1ST. PATRICK JOSEPH LYONS, C.R.O. NO.8559/40. BORN BERMONDSEY, 2/11/23. 5 FEET 9., C. FRESH, H. FAIR, WAVY AND BUSHY, E. BLUE, SMALL SCAR RIGHT CHEEK, SCAR RIGHT SIDE OF MOUTH AND ON UPPER LIP LEFT SIDE.
2ND. GEORGE WILLIAM MORGAN, C.R.O. NO.14705/43. BORN LONDON 4/12/24. 5 FEET 8., C. FRESH, H. DARK BROWN, WITH SIDEBOARDS, E. BROWN, SCAR RIGHT CHEEK NEAR EAR. 2 SCARS UNDER CHIN.
3RD. EDWARD FEW, C.R.O. NO.23215/35. FOR PHOTO AND DESCRIPTION, SEE INFOS. C 11 OF 23/10/44.
DESCRIPTION OF 4TH MAN NOT YET AVAILABLE.
T OF O 7-32PM. 7-59PM.
SENT TO AS ON DIRECTIONS OF SUPT. C.1.
ACTION COPIES - C.R.O.
INFORMATION COPIES - C.1: C.2: C.3: B.H.I. AND PRESS.

Ralph Douglas Binney was born on October 14, 1888 in Cookham, Berkshire, and joined the Royal Navy in 1903 as a Midshipman. Promoted to a Sub-Lieutenant in 1907, he served in the First World War and later in HMS *Royal Sovereign* in the Mediterranian before taking command of HMS *Marshal Soult*. He retired in 1934 with the rank of Captain. He then served in the Colombian Navy and was instrumental in setting up their naval cadet and officer training scheme (the Escuela Naval Almirante Padila still has a 'Binney' Class). On the outbreak of war in 1939, he was recalled to the colours and had a series of staff appointments, most notably as Flag Captain at HMS *Nile*, the naval base at Alexandria. In January 1943, he was back in the UK serving as Chief-of-Staff to the Flag Officer in Command of the London Area.

At the Mansion House yesterday, Thomas James Jenkins, 24, a welder, of Aylton Estate, Rotherhithe, and Ronald Hedley, 26, a labourer, of no fixed abode, were charged on remand with being concerned with other men in breaking and entering, on the afternoon of December 8 last, the shop occupied by Thomas Wordley in Birchin Lane and stealing a pearl necklace and 19 rings of the value of £3,795. Of this property, five rings, worth together £1,232, have been recovered by the police.

Detective-inspector T. Gankerseer, City Police, said that Jenkins was arrested on December 23, and Hedley on December 27. In the course of identification parades at Cloak Lane police-station both were picked out by witnesses. They were then told that they would be charged with being concerned in a 'smash and grab raid' at Birchin Lane in the course of which a man (Captain R. D. Binney, R.N.) was knocked down and killed by a car in which the alleged thieves were making their escape.

Mr. Lawson Walton said this case was now in the hands of the Director of Public Prosecutions, on whose behalf he appeared. It was obvious that the matter was a very serious one, and the police had not completed their investigations. It was apparent that a much graver charge would be preferred when the case was opened at the next hearing.

The Lord Mayor remanded the accused in custody to January 12.

The Times, January 5, 1944

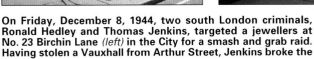

On Friday, December 8, 1944, two south London criminals, Ronald Hedley and Thomas Jenkins, targeted a jewellers at No. 23 Birchin Lane *(left)* in the City for a smash and grab raid. Having stolen a Vauxhall from Arthur Street, Jenkins broke the front window of Thomas Wordley Ltd, and grabbed a tray of jewels. Jumping in the getaway car, Hedley carried on down the narrow road *(right)*, barely the width of the vehicle, towards Lombard Street.

Above left: **As the car reached the corner with Lombard Street, Captain Binney stepped out in front of it with arms raised but Hedley did not hesitate in knocking him down. Witnesses said that the car then stopped and reversed before driving forward again with the naval officer caught up underneath.** *Above right:* **The car then turned down Lombard Street.**

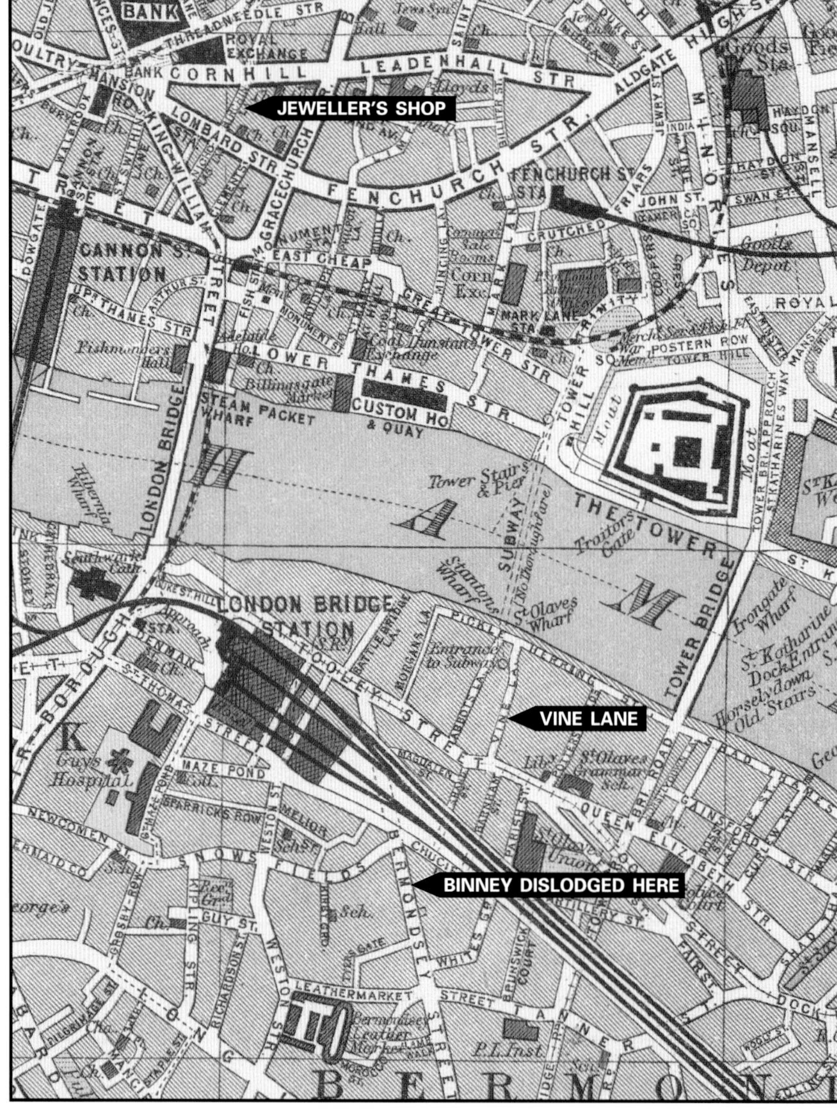

A charge of murdering Captain Ralph Douglas Binney, R.N., who was killed in trying to stop a car used in a smash-and-grab raid, was preferred at the Mansion House yesterday against Thomas James Jenkins, 34, welder, of Aylton Estate, Rotherhithe, and Ronald Hedley, 26, labourer, of no fixed address. Captain Binney was Chief of Staff to the Flag Officer in Command, London.

Jenkins and Hedley were also charged with shop-breaking at a jeweller's in Birchin Lane, E.C., on December 8, and stealing jewelry worth £3,795. Mr. Lawson Walton, for the prosecution, said that after the jeweller's window had been smashed a waiting motor-car was driven towards Lombard Street. At the corner of Lombard Street Captain Binney was seen with both arms out trying to stop the car. It was going slowly, and went straight into Captain Binney. and a wheel went over him. The car then stopped. reversed several yards, and with Captain Binney underneath it went forward again. It was alleged that Hedley was driving and Jenkins was sitting beside him.

A motorist. sounding his klaxon horn all the way, followed the car along Lombard Street, King William Street, across Cannon Street, over London Bridge into St. Thomas's Street to Bermondsey Street where Captain Binney rolled from underneath. He had been dragged underneath the car for more than a mile during part of which time he was heard shouting 'Help, help.' He died in Guy's Hospital about three hours later.

Mr Denis Allen gave chase through the streets leading to London Bridge *(below left)*, **Captain Binney finally becoming dislodged at this spot in Bermondsey Street** *(below right)*.

Captain Binney, said Mr. Walton, was killed 'while doing his duty as a brave citizen should.' The car was found abandoned a short distance from Bermondsey Street. One of three bank employees who gave evidence, George William Townsend, of New Cross, a messenger, said there were cries of 'Stop thief' in Birchin Lane as the car moved away. 'After knocking down the officer the car was driven forward about two yards, leaving the body clear of the car,' he said. 'The car stopped, although there was nothing to prevent it going straight along Lombard Street. It then backed until it went over the body again. This time the body was not left in the road, but was carried away underneath the car.

The Times, January 13, 1945

After a trial lasting six days, Ronald Hedley, 26, was found guilty at the Central Criminal Court yesterday of the murder of Captain Ralph Douglas Binney, R.N., and he was sentenced to death. His accomplice, Thomas James Jenkins, 25, was found guilty of manslaughter, and he was sentenced to eight years' penal servitude.

Mr Justice MacNaghten said the jury had taken a merciful view of Jenkins's case. The circumstances were such that the jury might properly have found him also guilty of murder. They had taken the view that he might be regarded as having had no desire in common with Hedley to resist arrest at all costs, and in his case had returned a verdict of manslaughter.

The Times, March 13, 1945

Mr Allen lost sight of the car in Tower Bridge Road and at 2.22 p.m. the vehicle, registration mark EDU 617, was found abandoned in Vine Lane Buildings off Tooley Street (seen in the background). This whole area has since been redeveloped but this is what is left of Vine Lane today.

The Home Secretary has recommended the reprieve of Ronald Hedley, 26, labourer, who was sentenced to death at the Central Criminal Court on March 12 for the murder of Captain R. D. Binney of the Royal Navy after a City 'smash and grab' raid. Hedley was to have been executed at Pentonville tomorrow.

The Times, April 27, 1945

'All the persons concerned in this and in the subsequent Antiquis case were associates and lived in the Bermondsey district. After the result of the case against Hedley and Thomas James Jenkins they became actively engaged in crime. Some of them were arrested and sentenced to varying terms of imprisonment, but still they continued living their life of crime.

Fabian of the Yard, Robert Fabian, 1955

Captain Binney was rushed to Guy's Hospital but he could not be saved, his dying words: 'I tried to stop some thieves and was dragged under the car'. *Left:* Cremated at Golders Green, his name now appears on the Commonwealth War Graves Commission memorial located in the grounds. Writing in *The Times* of January 4, 1945, Admiral Sir Martin Dunbar-Nasmith, V.C., the Flag Officer-in-Charge, London, said that, 'The very gallant action by which he met his death is in keeping with his conduct throughout his life and was in accord with his sense of duty as a naval officer. I trust his family will find comfort in the remembrance that, in a busy London street of today, there was one who remembered Lord Nelson's signal before Trafalgar and acted upon it'. In 1946, the Binney Memorial Fund was founded by fellow naval officers to provide the annual award of the Binney Medal to members of the public who, at great risk to themselves, have attempted to intervene in violent crimes in the City of London and Metropolitan Police areas. The first award was made in 1948 to Thomas Beall, 24, from Surrey who assisted police during the arrest of a criminal armed with a sawn-off shotgun. Goldsmiths' Hall still provide funds to ensure that such civilian bravery is honoured today. *Right:* Professor Alistair McDonald received his award for saving a young woman from a knife-wielding attacker in south London in 2001.

Neville Heath was born in Ilford, Essex, in 1917. On leaving school in 1935 he enlisted in the Artists' Rifles and in February 1936 obtained a short-service commission in the Royal Air Force. However, between March and July 1937 he went absent without leave having taken a motor car without consent and committed other offences. Following his court-martial in August, he was dismissed from the service. Two years probation followed as a result of further misdemeanours including fraud, motor offences and masquerading as 'Lord Dudley'. In July 1938 he was sentenced to three years' Borstal training for housebreaking, theft and forgery. Released early due to the outbreak of war, he enlisted in the Royal Army Service Corps in October 1939, being posted to the Middle East where he was soon in trouble for writing cheques which were dishonoured and obtaining a second pay book. He was court-martialled and dismissed for a second time but en route for the UK, he jumped ship in Durban and enlisted in the South African Air Force under a false name. It was only a question of time before his past caught up with him but, in view of his then good conduct, he was given a second chance and even promoted to captain. In February 1944 he was seconded to the RAF and served with No. 180 Squadron undertaking just one operational trip. Earlier in February 1942 Heath had married Elizabeth Pitt-Rivers from one of Britain's leading families, and their son was born later that year. Heath returned to South Africa early in 1945, only to be arrested on fraud charges. As a result Elizabeth divorced him in October 1945. In December, he was court-martialled yet again, this time for 'conduct prejudicial to good order and military discipline' and for wearing decorations to which he was not entitled. Consequently he was dismissed from the services for a third time, arriving back in Britain on February 5, 1946. On the 23rd he booked into the Strand Palace Hotel with a woman using the name Captain James Cadogan Armstrong of the South African Air Force. When screams were heard, the manager was called to the room to find him beating the woman with a cane. The young lady did not want to bring charges and the couple reportedly checked out on good terms. Her identity is believed to be that of Margery Gardner.

June 21, 1946 – Wanted for Murder: Neville Heath

The story opens in London on Thursday, 20th June, 1946, when a good-looking man of 29 years, Neville Heath, drank and danced at the Panama Club, South Kensington. He was in the company of a Mrs. Margery Gardner, a woman of 32 of somewhat bohemian ways.

Somewhere around midnight they left the club and took a passing taxi-cab to the Pembridge Court Hotel, Notting Hill. It is possible that Mrs. Gardner was a little the worse for drink. Heath was known at the hotel, having stayed there before. He had booked a double room some days previously and had been given a front-door key. Consequently no person saw them enter. No one seemed to be stirring in Heath's room later that morning so that at 2 o'clock in the afternoon the maid knocked on the door. Getting no answer, she looked inside. The blinds were down. Heath had gone. Lying in one of the beds, naked but under the bedclothes, was the dead body of Mrs. Gardner.

The weals of 17 lashes were found across the body, front and back, and on her face. Her nipples had been practically bitten off. Her ankles were fastened together, her right arm lay under the body and had obviously been pinioned. Marks were present high upon the neck and under the chin. Blood had oozed from the private parts, due, it subsequently was proved, to an extensive laceration of the passage leading to the womb.

The manageress was called and she instantly notified the police. With the help of photographers and police surgeons, the usual steps were taken to secure all the necessary factual information. It became obvious the victim had died from suffocation, probably after being gagged. The internal injury had been due to some large implement being forced up her vagina shortly before death, and then rotated. The assault upon the nipples had also been made before death, and the lashing too had taken place while the victim was still alive. Close scrutiny of the marks of the lash showed a criss-cross suffusion, suggesting the plaited thong of a whip with a metal tip.

In June 1946, Mrs Margery Gardner was living at No. 24 Bramham Gardens *(left)*, just off the Old Brompton Road in South Kensington. She had moved to London after leaving her husband and baby daughter in Sheffield, living, so we are told, with the more seedy aspects of life in the early post-war years with few qualms as to how she earned her bed and board.

On the evening of Thursday, June 20, she was with Heath at the nearby Panama Club at 23-24 Cromwell Place (the same club where Betty Jones had worked — see page 160) close to South Kensington underground station. *Left:* The building still stands although the interior has since been gutted and converted into modern offices.

Right: Around 12.15 a.m., Harold Harter was driving his taxi along Old Brompton Road when he was hailed outside the club by a man and a woman. 'I stopped in the middle of the road and they walked across to me. The man asked to go to Pembridge Gardens at Notting Hill.' The taxi fare cost Heath 1s. 9d (say 9p) — your Editor's charge in 2011 was £11!

Many bloodstains were seen in the bedroom, especially upon the sheets of the other twin bed. A linear smear upon the pillow-slip showed the same interlacing type of markings suggesting that the bloodstained whip had lain there. A tiny bloodstain was also seen in the wash-basin. There was blood in the victim's nostrils and over the cheeks, but it was obvious that the face had been washed. The handkerchief which bound the victim's ankles was embroidered with the letter 'K' and was marked 'L. Kearns.' This clue proved to be misleading.

DATE	NAME IN FULL	ADDRESS	
15th June	Jessie C A Traill	Shipley Alnwick	British
16th June	Mr & Mrs A. Thomas	4, Angel St. Bridgend Glam.	British
16th "	[illegible] Heath.	Black Hill Cottage [illegible]	British
17th "	[illegible]	[illegible]	"
[illegible]	[illegible]	[illegible]	

Heath was already registered at the Pembridge Court Hotel having stayed there the previous weekend with his girlfriend Yvonne Symonds calling himself 'Lieutenant-Colonel N. G. C. Heath'. Having a night key, he let himself in and escorted Margery to his room No. 4 on the first floor. *Above left:* In 2005 the hotel at No. 34 Pembridge Gardens changed its name to the Lennox, described on a website as being 'managed by the vivacious Nicola Green, but supervised by Churchill, a vast and presidential ginger cat. The Lennox Hotel (formerly known as Pembridge Court) is a 19th century London town house guarded by bay trees and just far enough removed from the bustle, buses and tubes of Notting Hill to be quiet. Long-established and much loved by its regular guests, many from the worlds of music, motor racing and antiques, the hotel is very much treated as a home from home. One faithful guest actually went so far as to buy it! Rooms vary in size and cost, but unusually for a small hotel, those advertised as large are exactly that: substantial enough for a business meeting or a small party if you feel like it, and certainly smart enough and well-equipped enough for either. The smallest room is also honestly described: it is called The Last Resort. On the ground floor is a comfortably furnished sitting room, dressed in yellow and blue, which can also be borrowed for private meetings. Hung everywhere in frames are Victorian lace gloves, fans, beadwork and other fascinating but less instantly recognizable items of millinery. Downstairs the bar and restaurant have now been converted into a breakfast room. A long-time fixture in our London hotel selections.' *Right:* One wonders how many guests walked down these steps not knowing that once a sadistic killer came that way. In 2008 the hotel closed, the property being converted into private residential accommodation.

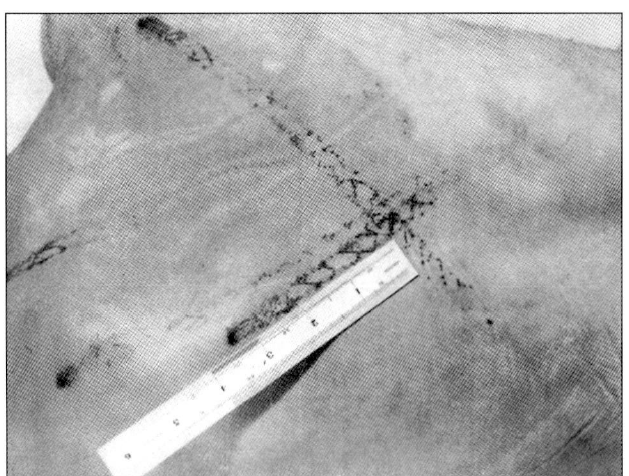

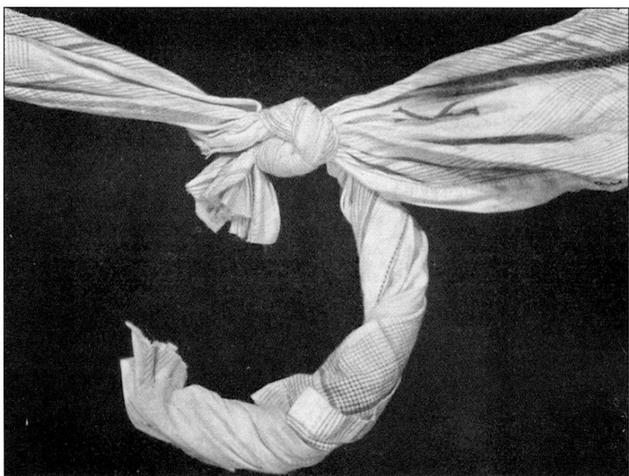

Dr Keith Simpson: 'I found a number of injuries. There were 17 lash blows as from a woven or similarly patterned thong or whip with a ferrule-like tip. Nine of these lay over the back between the shoulder blades, over the small of the back and the buttocks and six lay over the front of the right side of the body injuring the breast, the chest and abdomen. The remaining two were to the head. There were two injuries to the face from a fist. The nipples had been virtually bitten off. The ankles were tightly bound together with a handkerchief. I found a seven-inch-long tear of the interior of the vagina running four inches up its right wall and a further three inches across its back wall, consistent, in my view, with a tearing instrument being thrust into the vagina and rotated. In the absence of any strangling marks or any other cause for blocking the air passages, I attributed suffocation by the closing of the nostrils and mouth by something soft like a pillow.'

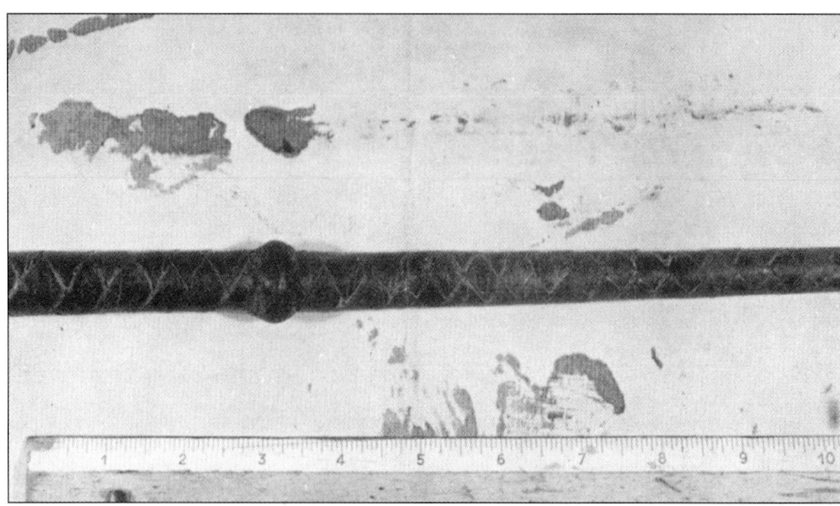

When Heath's riding crop was found later, it matched bloodstains on the adjacent bed.

Margery's parents, Mr & Mrs Gilbert Wheat, made a specific request to the police for her body to be released to enable her to be buried in Sheffield, having already instructed agents to carry this out. However, for some reason, instead she was interred in St Marylebone Cemetery (now called East Finchley).

Left: On August 12, 1947 she was exhumed and the following day reburied in Eccleshall Churchyard in Ringinglow Road, Sheffield. (Her husband Peter joined her on June 20, 1946.) *Right:* Rob Green found that her former grave (No. 136 in Plot Y5) in East Finchley has since been re-used.

OCEAN HOTEL

"A SUN TRAP ON THE SEA FRONT"

The Brightest Hotel in Worthing

Unrivalled position, Facing Sea, yet centrally situated for Shops and Cinemas

World Famous Cuisine
45 Superb Bedrooms
Central Heating. Dictograph Service

Telephones and Gas Fires in every Bedroom.

LICENSED. GARAGE.

PHONE : **6300** (3 lines)
TELEGRAMS : "OCEAN, WORTHING"

DANCING TO BOB CROWDER IN THE NEW MAPLE BALLROOM

The movements of the missing Neville Heath came to light only after his subsequent arrest. It transpires that on the morning in question he went from London to Brighton and thence to Worthing, where he made contact with a young lady he had met at a W.R.N.S. dance some days before. Under promise of marriage, this girl had spent the night of 16th June with Heath also at the Pembridge Court Hotel, where they had checked in under the names of Mr. and Mrs. Armstrong. No violence whatever had occurred during this intimacy. Returning to Worthing the next day, this young lady, Miss Yvonne Symonds, had had various telephone conversations with Heath.

On Friday, 21st June, Heath, having arrived in Worthing, 'phoned Miss Symonds and invited her to lunch, having meantime put up at the Ocean Hotel. On the Saturday morning, 22nd June, they met again. 'Lt.-Col. Heath,' as he called himself, brought up the news, which had by now appeared in the papers, that a dead body had been found in the Pembridge Court Hotel in the bedroom which they had recently shared. He went on to assert that he himself had been associated with this event and that he would tell her more about it in due course. Later that morning Miss Symonds introduced Heath to her parents, for she regarded herself at the time as his fiancée.

Although Heath had only met Yvonne at a dance on Saturday, June 15 at Chelsea, he had followed his usual practice of taking the girl on to the Panama Club. On Sunday morning, he telephoned her to ask if they could spend the day together and by evening he had proposed! As a result, Yvonne had spent the night with Heath in Room No. 4 — the murder room at the Pembridge — although nothing untoward took place. As soon as he arrived in Worthing he telephoned her and they had lunch together, meeting again on Saturday morning when Heath casually asked Yvonne if she had seen an account of a murder at the Pembridge, to which she said she had not.

After Heath walked out the front door of the Pembridge Court Hotel in the early hours of Friday morning, he caught a train to the south coast resort of Brighton from where he went to Worthing where Yvonne Symonds lived. There he booked into the Ocean Hotel at 77-79 Marine Parade as Lieutenant Colonel Heath *(below)*.

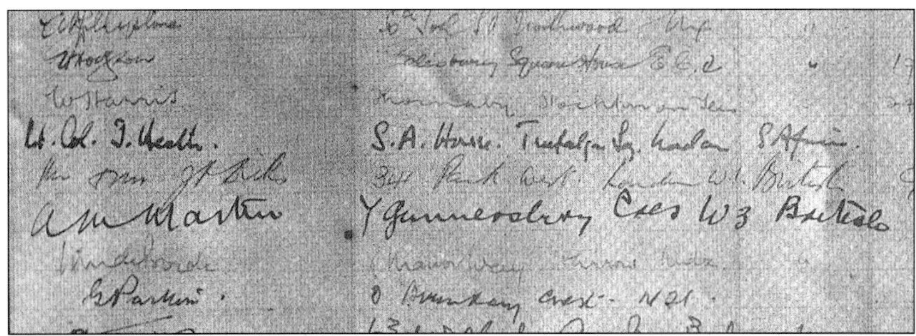

Lt. Col. J. Heath. S.A. House. Trafalgar Sq. London S.Africa.

The hotel is no more having been converted into apartments.

After lunch on Saturday, Yvonne *(left)* introduced Heath to her parents after which they dined at the Blue Peter Club at Angmering. The club was a well known fashionable watering hole on the south coast, the Lido alongside being considered unique with tea room and an upper tea deck, a dance lounge, and terrace overlooking the sea. *Right:* Unfortunately neither has stood the test of time, the Bella Vista restaurant now occupying the site. Over dinner Yvonne brought up the topic of the murder. It had already been reported in the London evening paper *The Star*, stating that police were looking for a Neville George Clevely Heath to help them with their enquiries. Although Yvonne had not seen the report, Heath admitted that he was closely involved in the murder as he had met Margery Gardner in the company of another man and lent him his key to Room 4. He also told Yvonne that he had seen the body 'a very gruesome sight' and that 'a poker had been stuck up her'. Heath had dropped Yvonne back at home that night and, apart from a telephone call on Sunday at which she expressed that her parents were worried after reading their newspaper, Yvonne never saw Heath again until she faced him in court. It was a very odd — yet amazing — interlude between two horrific murders and we will never know why Heath spared Yvonne from an awful death.

That evening they dined and danced at the Blue Peter Club in Angmering, and there Heath, upon her prompting, discussed once again this crime, and went on to tell a curious story. He said that the murder had taken place in the very bedroom that he had booked, but that he had given the key to a man and a woman for immoral purposes and that he had slept elsewhere. Furthermore, he said that 'Inspector' Barratt of Scotland Yard had made contact with him and had taken him to see the body, 'a gruesome sight.' He stated that a poker had been stuck up the victim and that this deed had probably killed her, but that Mr. Barratt, on the other hand, thought she had been suffocated. (As a matter of fact, Superintendent Barratt had had no dealings with Heath at this time, nor had any other police officer.) Heath expressed the view that the crime had been the work of a sexual maniac.

Next morning Miss Symonds herself read an account of the murder in the Sunday papers and spoke about it to her parents, for Heath's name was mentioned. She then telephoned Heath at the Ocean Hotel saying that her father and mother were concerned. Heath replied he was going to London by car and that he would 'phone her later. Fortunately, however, this was the last that Miss Symonds had to do with Neville Heath.

To Chief Inspector Barratt, Scotland Yard

Sir,

I feel it to be my duty to inform you of certain facts in connection with the death of Mrs. Gardner at Notting Hill Gate. I booked in at the hotel last Sunday, but not with Mrs. Gardner, whom I met for the first time during the week. I had drinks with her on Friday evening, and whilst I was with her she met an acquaintance with whom she was obliged to sleep. The reasons, as I understand them, were mainly financial. It was then that Mrs. Gardner asked if she could use my hotel room until two o'clock and intimated that if I returned after that, I might spend the remainder of the night with her. I gave her my keys and told her to leave the hotel door open. It must have been almost 3 a.m. when I returned to the hotel and found her in the condition of which you are aware. I realized that I was in an invidious position, and rather than notify the police, I packed my belongings and left.

Since then I have been in several minds whether to come forward or not, but in view of the circumstances I have been afraid to. I can give you a description of the man. He was aged approx 30, dark hair (black), with small moustache. Height about 5' 9" slim build. His name was Jack and I gathered he was a friend of Mrs. Gardner of some long standing. I have the instrument with which Mrs. Gardner was beaten and am forwarding this to you to-day. You will find my fingerprints on it, but you should also find others as well.

N. G. G. HEATH, WORTHING, JUNE 23, 1946

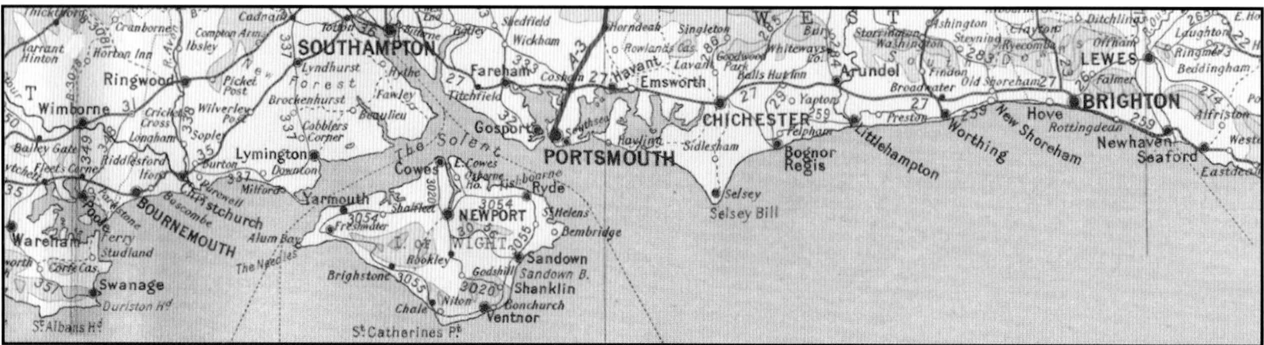

Although Heath told Yvonne that he was going to London, instead he travelled west to Bournemouth. Before leaving he sent a letter (post-dated 5.45 p.m. on June 23) to 'Chief Inspector' Barratt at Scotland Yard although, despite the assertion contained in the last two sentences, Heath did not forward the instrument to Barratt.

For more than half a century the Tollard Royal had been one of Bournemouth's foremost sea-front hotels, this picture dating from 1907. Heath booked in here on Sunday (June 23) under the guise of Group Captain Rupert Brooke, no doubt in an endeavour to cover his tracks. Now he was on the lookout for his next conquest . . . or was it his next victim?

Leaving Worthing, Heath journeyed not to London but to Bournemouth, where he put up at the Tollard Royal Hotel, calling himself — of all names — Group Captain Rupert Brooke, though not wearing uniform. During the following eleven days, 23rd June to 3rd July, he lived at the hotel, mixing with other guests, chatting in a rather over-familiar way with the head porter. Only his dress was informal, for he wore constantly a sports coat and flannels. It is doubtful whether he brought any luggage with him to the hotel.

On 3rd July he made the acquaintance of a Miss Doreen Marshall, recently in the W.R.N.S. and convalescent from influenza, who was staying alone in the Norfolk Hotel. He took her to tea at the Tollard Royal Hotel, and again that same evening to dinner. Afterwards they sat in the lounge until just after midnight. Heath was perhaps a little drunk and Miss Marshall appeared tired, pale, and distressed. She begged another hotel resident to order her a taxi. A little later Heath cancelled this, saying Miss Marshall would walk home. On the way out he told the porter he would be back in half an hour. 'No, in a quarter of an hour,' Miss Marshall corrected.

Yet another of Heath's hotels has been converted into private apartments, although in this case the Tollard Court was in the news via the Channel 4 *Grand Designs* television programme which featured the addition of a penthouse on the roof with a very distinctive copper-clad domed solarium.

Twenty-one-year-old Doreen Marshall (on the left) was about to be demobilised from the Women's Royal Naval Service and had come to Bournemouth for a holiday. She came from a good class family and was used to staying at top class hotels so had booked into the Norfolk Hotel on Richmond Hill. Just over a week after he had arrived, Heath said that he saw Doreen and a friend walking along the Promenade near the Tollard Royal on July 3 — a Wednesday. He quickly made a date with Doreen for that afternoon for tea at his hotel, and also for dinner that evening. The Norfolk was closed in 1985 for total restoration to reflect its original Edwardian grandeur and it was re-opened with the addition of the title 'Royale' by the Duke of Norfolk whose family had used it as a summer residence back as far as 1840.

In the lounge of the Tollard, the couple were joined by three fellow guests, a young lady and a Mr and Mrs Phillips. Heath had noticeably imbibed so Doreen asked Mr Phillips if he would call her a taxi. He did as she asked but Heath cancelled the cab saying that he would walk Doreen back to her hotel. *Left:* On returning to the Tollard, instead of entering via the reception, Heath scaled the builders' ladder which fortunately gave him access to the balcony outside his room — No. 81 on the second floor (marked X). *Right:* Now converted into separate flats, Heath's room overlooks West Hill Road — not the seafront. Next morning, Heath actually joked about his questionable method of entry with the manager, passing it off as a joke.

They then left together, and some time later Heath returned to his own hotel. We do not know the exact hour of his return because he did not pass the night porter in the front hall, but slipped round the back and scaled a ladder, entering his bedroom by way of the window. Wondering whether Group Captain Brooke were in or not, the night porter peeped into the bedroom at 4.30 a.m. and found him soundly asleep. The porter noticed that Heath's shoes, which had not been put out for cleaning, were caked with sand. The next morning Heath disclosed to the head porter his unconventional method of entry, saying that he had done it as a joke.

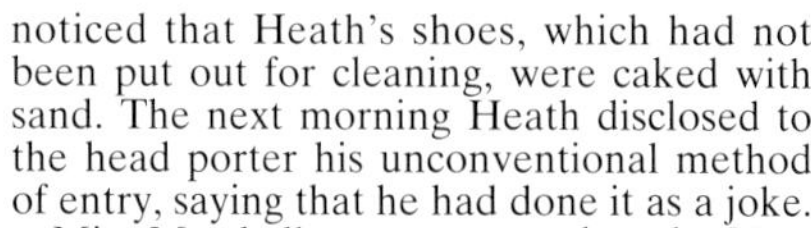

Miss Marshall never returned to the Norfolk Hotel. When her absence was noted — not until Friday, 5th July — the manager of the Norfolk Hotel notified the police. He also telephoned his colleague at the Tollard Royal Hotel, saying that he believed Miss Marshall might have taken dinner there on the evening of the 3rd. The manager questioned Heath as to whether his guest had been a Miss Marshall of Pinner. Heath laughed the matter away, saying that his companion had been known to him for a number of years and that she certainly did not live in Pinner. The manager nevertheless advised Heath to get in touch with the police.

In Heath's statement to the police this was his explanation of the events that evening: 'Conversation continued general until approximately 11.30 p.m. At 11 p.m. (approx) Miss Marshall suggested going away but I persuaded her to stay a little longer. At about 11.30 p.m. the weather was clear and we left the hotel and sat on a seat near the hotel overlooking the sea. We must have talked for at least an hour, probably longer, and then we walked down the slope towards the Pavilion. Miss Marshall did not wish me to accompany her but I insisted upon doing so — at least some of the way. I left her at the Pier *(left)* and watched her cross the road and enter the gardens *(right)*. Before leaving her I asked her if she would come round the following day, but she said she would be busy for the next few days, but would telephone me on Sunday if she could manage it. I have not seen her to speak to since then although I thought I saw her entering Bobby's Ltd., on Thursday morning. After leaving Miss Marshall I walked along the seafront in a westerly direction and up the path from Durley Chine and to the cliff top and so back to the hotel, whereupon I went to bed. It rained heavily before I reached the hotel.'

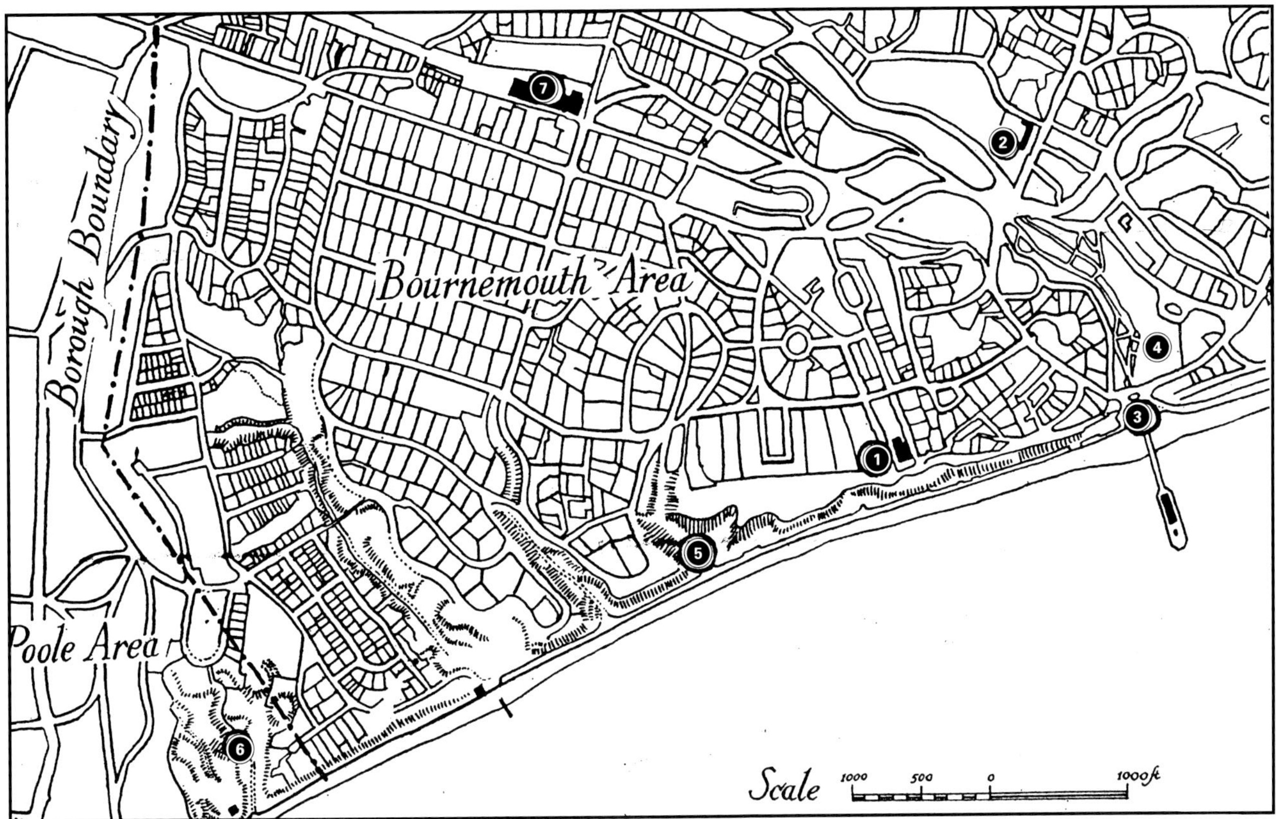

We must now look at the map (bearing in mind that this is Bournemouth in 1946, not today), to see just how implausible Heath's statement was. [1] is the Tollard Royal Hotel and [2] the Norfolk Hotel. Heath claimed that he walked with Doreen to the pier [3] from where she turned north through the Lower Gardens [4]. Having left her, he said he returned to the Norfolk via a roundabout route up Durley Chine [5]. However, Doreen's body was found over four miles away on Branksome Dene Chine [6].

We will never know what really happened . . . how he managed to persuade Doreen to take a four-mile walk away from her hotel after midnight when she was already tired and wanting to leave. *Above left:* This is the Promenade on the cliff-top just west of the Tollard. Branksome Dene Chine is at the end of the beach in the far distance. *Above right:* Their most probable route led down the cliff via the nearby Zig-Zag-Path and then along the beach *(below left)* to the chine *(below right)*. This journey is a good 30-40 mintues walk. Also remember that the chine was then still sealed off with wartime anti-invasion dragon's teeth.

Ignore the tarmac . . . ignore the yellow lines . . . this is where Doreen's body was found. On Sunday afternoon Miss Kathleen Evans who lived close to the chine, was walking her dog when she saw a swarm of flies over a bush. The next day she told her father what she had seen and the whole Evans family went down the chine to investigate. When they spotted what appeared to be a bundle of clothing under a rhododendron bush, they looked no further and informed the police.

On the evening of Monday, 8th July, the dead body of Miss Marshall was found in a lonely part of Branksome Chine not far from the centre of Bournemouth. A passer-by with a dog had noticed a swarm of flies. This lady told her father and, mindful of the missing girl, the two of them returned later to the spot. Under some rhododendron bushes the body was found. The corpse was naked except for the left shoe, but it was covered by the discarded clothing — underclothes, a black frock turned inside out, and a yellow swagger coat — and also by some boughs. There were signs that the body had been moved a short distance into this place of greater concealment, and some distance away there was a compact and stockings which had belonged to the deceased. Twenty-seven artificial pearls lay on the ground near by, due to her necklace having broken. Her empty handbag was found the next morning at the bottom of the chine.

Examination of the body showed abrasions on the face and back, bruises upon the arm, the region of the collarbone, and the wrists, but the cause of death was a deep cut of the throat. The fingers of both hands had been severely cut as if the victim had seized the blade of a sharp knife. There were injuries to some ribs, one of which had splintered and pierced the underlying lung. After death a number of mutilations had been perpetrated. The right nipple had been bitten clean away, the left one also having been severely torn. A long and deep cut had been made, starting in the thigh and passing upwards alongside the pudenda and the abdominal wall, up so as to meet a second slash which had connected the two breasts. There had been four knife-strokes in all, and the interior of the private parts had been savagely wounded from the violent insertion of some implement. No knife could be found.

Let us now return to Neville Heath himself and especially to the period between 3rd July when he (in the guise of Group Captain Brooke) had dined with Miss Marshall at his hotel and 8th July when Miss Marshall's dead body was found. It will be recalled that on Monday, 24th June, Superintendent Barratt had received the astonishing letter from Heath. The writer's whereabouts were unknown and the police circulated a description and a photograph of Heath, which they obtained from his home, as a wanted man.

On Thursday, 4th July, Heath was observed by other residents at the hotel to have a couple of scratch marks on his neck. He was wearing for the first time a scarf. Also for the first time he had ready cash with which to pay for his drinks. On Friday, 5th July, Heath stepped into the net by telephoning a Bournemouth police station. He volunteered information about his Wednesday dinner guest, for the missing Miss Marshall had not yet been traced to the Tollard Royal Hotel. On Saturday, 6th July, he went again, and was shown a photograph of Miss Marshall. It was, of course, impossible to deny further that he was the friend of the missing girl. During this police station interview, a detective-constable noted the likeness of Group Captain Brooke to the wanted Heath and taxed him with being one and the same. This Heath denied.

At this point he was detained pending further enquiries. He complained of feeling chilly, for he was wearing a sports shirt and no jacket. The police collected this coat from the head porter of his hotel, and in the pocket they found a cloakroom ticket issued at Bournemouth West Station on 23rd June. With this ticket they recovered a suitcase which when opened was seen to contain, amongst other articles, a blood-stained scarf and a leather riding-whip with a plaited thong. There was no metal tip, it was true, but the leather at the end had worn away, exposing

Police investigations continued today into the disappearance of Miss Doreen Margaret Marshall, an attractive 21-year-old girl from Pinner, Middlesex, who was staying on holiday at a Bournemouth hotel, following demobilisation from the W.R.N.S.

Miss Marshall is five feet three inches in height, of medium build, dark brown hair with light coloured streak in front. She was wearing a black dinner gown, black sandals with open heels and toes, pearl ear-rings and necklace, lemon-coloured full swagger coat, with possibly a glass ball type fob watch in lapel, and also a three-stone diamond ring.

Bournemouth police ask that Miss Marshall or any person who can give information as to her whereabouts, should communicate with telephone Bournemouth 6666 or any police station.

BOURNEMOUTH ECHO, JULY 8, 1946

'I, Neville George Clevely Heath, lately residing at the Tollard Royal Hotel, Bournemouth, hereby state:

'On Wednesday, 3rd July, during the morning I was seated on the Promenade on West Cliff when I saw two young ladies walking along the front. One of these two was a casual acquaintance whom I had met at a dance at the Pavilion during the latter half of the preceding week (Her Christian name was Peggy but I was unaware of her surname). Although I was not formally introduced to the other I gathered that her name was 'Doo' or something similar. The girl Peggy left after about half an hour and I walked along the front with the other girl whom I now know to be Miss Marshall. I invited her to have tea with me in the afternoon and she accepted.

'I met her along the promenade about 2.45 p.m. in the afternoon and after a short stroll we went to the Tollard Royal for tea at about 3.45. The conversation was fairly general and covered the fact that she had served in the W.R.N.S. She mentioned the fact that she had been ill and was down in Bournemouth to recuperate.

'She left the hotel at about 5.45 after accepting my invitation to Dinner in the evening.

These are two of the police photographs. 'The body was found on Monday, July 8. It was some way from the beach up that chine, up a sort of subsidiary chine to the left going from the sea. It was naked except for the left shoe. The body was covered with clothing and some effort had been made to conceal it with fir boughs. There were various things belonging to the deceased such as stockings and a compact within a space of about 20 feet from the body. Doreen's handbag was found behind one of the beach huts.'

bare filaments of wire. Yet another vital piece of evidence was found in a pocket of Heath's sports jacket, namely the return half of a first-class railway ticket from Bournemouth to London — a ticket which was later proved to have belonged to Miss Marshall. Furthermore, in the pocket was a single artificial pearl which matched the twenty-seven others found near Doreen Marshall's body. In the dressing-table drawer in room 81 was a soiled blood-stained handkerchief, tightly knotted; a few hairs, avulsed from the scalp and identical with those of Doreen Marshall, were entangled in the knot.

At 9.45 p.m. Detective-Inspector Gates told the questionee that he was satisfied that he was Neville Heath and that he was going to detain him pending the arrival of officers of the Metropolitan Police, who wanted to see him in connection with the murder of Margery Gardner in London on the night of 20th/21st June. To this Heath replied, 'Oh, all right.'

It was also discovered that on Friday, 5th July, Neville Heath had pawned a ring belonging to Miss Marshall, and later a crystal fob watch of hers. Heath then volunteered to give a written statement after he had had some sleep. Being provided with materials, he wrote from 11.30 p.m. to 2.45 a.m. an account of the latter part of his stay in Bournemouth.

Dr Crichton McGaffney reported that Doreen's throat had been cut through severing her windpipe which he thought had occurred before death. There were abrasions on her back caused by her being dragged naked to be hidden beneath this bush *(right)*. He thought that marks on her wrists indicated that she had been tied up before she died. She had a compound fracture of her ribs, possibly caused by the murderer kneeling on her chest. The nipple of the right breast had been bitten off with slashes to the left breast and front of her body. A knife had also been used on her private parts.

What is described as 'a very gruesome murder' was revealed today following the discovery in Branksome Dene Chine of the body of a young woman which the police state they believe it to be that of Miss Doreen Marshall, aged 21, of Pinner, Middlesex, who was spending a holiday at Bournemouth.

She had been missing since Wednesday night and an intensive search by the Bournemouth police over all the cliff area of the Dorset boundary had proved fruitless. A clue was later forthcoming from what a young woman had noticed in the thickly wooded and secluded Branksome Dene Chine just within the Dorset area.

Signs of a struggle were found and after a four-hour examination today by Dr. McGaffney, the pathologist, and police experts, Police Superintendent Carter, of Poole stated: 'It is a very gruesome murder.'

The body was found 10 yards off the narrow path leading from the beach and about 100 yards from the shore, almost concealed in the wild undergrowth.

The main entrance to the Chine from Pinewood Road was immediately closed to the public and a guard placed upon it. Today there is a police barrier outside and an officer on duty barring the public from entering.

Bournemouth police are still co-operating in seeking to trace the movements of the man by whom Miss Marshall is believed to have been accompanied last Wednesday evening.

BOURNEMOUTH DAILY ECHO, JULY 9, 1946

'At approximately 7.15 I was standing outside the hotel when I saw Miss Marshall approaching the hotel on foot down West Hill Road. I entered the hotel, went to my room to get some tobacco and came downstairs again just as she was entering the lounge. We dined at about 8.15 p.m. and sat talking in the lounge after dinner, moving into the writing room at about 10 p.m. The conversation was again general but she told me she was considering cutting short her holiday in Bournemouth and returning home on Friday instead of Monday. She mentioned an American staying in the hotel (her hotel) and told me that he had taken her for car rides into the country and to Poole.

'She also mentioned an invitation to go with him to Exeter but I gathered, although she did not actually say so, that she did not intend to go.

'Another American was mentioned — I believe his name was Pat — to whom I believe she was unofficially engaged some while ago.

'The next I heard about this matter was on the morning of Saturday, 6th July, at about 10.30 a.m. when the hotel manager asked me jokingly if I had seen the lady with whom I had dinner on Wednesday evening. I told him that I thought I had seen her on Thursday morning, and he then told me that someone had left the Norfolk Hotel on Wednesday evening in a taxi for the Tollard Royal and had not been seen since. He said that this particular lady's father and the manager of the Norfolk Hotel had been on the telephone to him and as there were so few guests for dinner in the hotel that night, he wondered if the missing lady was my guest. I said I didn't think it would be.

'During the morning I thought more about it and wondered whether perhaps the missing girl might be Miss Marshall. I telephoned the Police Station and asked to speak to the officer in charge of the case but he was out. I asked if a photograph was available but was informed that none was, at the present. I left a message to say that I would 'phone again at 3.30 in the afternoon.

'I telephoned the Police Station in the afternoon and spoke to Det/Const. Suter.

'He informed me that a photograph was now available and offered to come round and show it to me. I offered to visit the Police

POLICE GAZETTE

PUBLISHED BY AUTHORITY.

NEW SERIES. TUESDAY, JUNE 25, 1946. No. 147. VOL. XXXIII.

Manuscript for publication should be addressed "THE COMMISSIONER OF POLICE, NEW SCOTLAND YARD, S.W.1." with "**C.R.O. (P.G.)**" in top left corner.

HAROLD SCOTT
The Commissioner of Police of the Metropolis.

Special Notice

MURDER

M.P. (FH).—It is desired to trace the after-described for interview respecting the death of MARGERY GARDNER, during the night of 20th-21st inst.—NEVILLE GEORGE CLEVELY HEATH, alias **ARMSTRONG, BLYTH, DENVERS** and **GRAHAM, C.R.O. No. 28142-37**, b. 1917, 5ft. 11½in., c. **fresh**, e. **blue**, believed small fair moustache, h. and eyebrows **fair**, square face, broad forehead and nose, firm chin, good teeth, military gait; dress, lt. **grey d.b.** suit with pin stripe, dk. **brown trilby**, brown suede shoes, cream shirt with **collar attached** or fawn and white check **sports jacket** and grey flannel trousers. **Nat. Reg. No. CNP 2147191.**

Has recent conviction for posing as Lt.-Col. of South African Air Force. A pilot and believed to possess an "A" licence, has stated his intention of going abroad and may endeavour to secure passage on ship or plane as passenger or pilot. May stay at hotels accompanied by woman.

Enquiries are also requested to trace the owner of gent's white handkerchief with brown check border, bearing "L. Kearns" in black ink on hem and stitched with large "K" in blue cotton in centre.

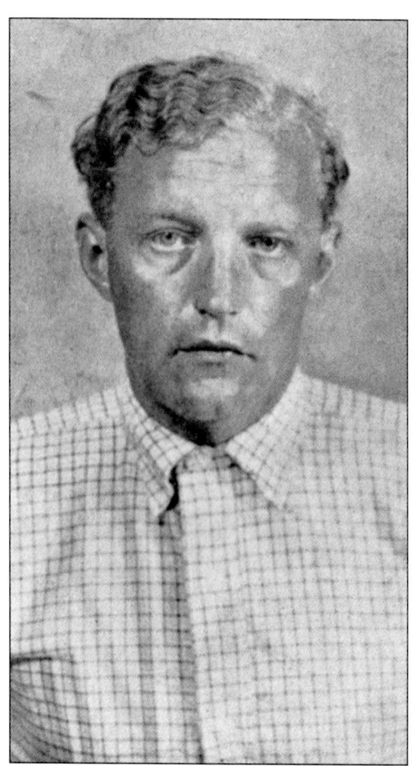

New Scotland Yard had already issued a wanted notice for Heath following the discovery of Margery Gardner in London; now it was the turn of the Bournemouth Constabulary — and also the Poole police as Doreen's body was discovered in their patch — to apprehend the killer. The case against him was overwhelming and Detective Inspector Reginald Spooner travelled down to Bournemouth where the riding crop had been found in Heath's suitcase which he had deposited in the left luggage office of the town's West Riding railway station ([7] on the map on page 181). Heath had also pawned a ring and broach identified as belonging to Doreen. *Left:* This picture was taken of Heath on his visit to Bournemouth Police Station.

The body of the dead girl was identified late yesterday afternoon by her father, who had travelled to Poole from London accompanied by his wife and his other daughter, Mrs Joan Cruikshank. They were all dressed in black.

It took Mr Marshall only a minute to satisfy himself that the body was that of his daughter.

Superintendent F. W. Carter of Poole announced yesterday that the police were searching for a sharp cutting instrument which had been used to inflict wounds upon the girl but a close search of the chine in the vicinity of the spot where the body was found failed yesterday to disclose any fresh discovery.

So dense are the shrubberies in the chine, particularly the rhododendron bushes around the scene of the search, that today special implements had to be obtained for cutting down the jungle-like tangle to facilitate the search for the missing instrument and other articles. The endeavours of the police were rewarded by the find of a short end of lipstick. This followed the discovery of a powder compact near where the body was found and which, it was thought, might reveal finger prints.

BOURNEMOUTH DAILY ECHO, JULY 10, 1946

Station at 5.30 p.m. and see if I could identify it. The arrangement suited him well.

'At 5.30 p.m. I visited the Police Station and identified the photograph shown to me by Mr. Suter as being the girl with whom I dined on Wednesday. I told him as much as I could remember, but I believe I told him I met her on the afternoon of 3rd July instead of in the morning as was the case.

'During our conversation Mr. Suter identified me as the person wanted for questioning by the Metropolitan Police and I have since been detained.

'On the evening of 3rd July Miss Marshall was dressed in a dark frock and wore a yellow camel-haired coat. She carried a dark handbag and wore a single rope of pearls. She also had in her possession a powder compact with a cracked mirror. I remember this because she explained that she was always breaking things. She wore no hat. When I left Miss Marshall and saw her enter the gardens, I was standing on the West side of the Pier near the commencement of the Undercliff and Overcliff drives.

'The Night Porter at the hotel served us with drinks in the writing room and let us out when we left the hotel. I had always been on friendly terms with the Night Porter and often stayed up late to talk to him. I guessed that he would be waiting for me to come in and as a ladder had that day been placed up against my window, I decided to practise a small deception on him, and entered my hotel bedroom via the ladder, knowing well that in the morning he would wonder how I managed to enter the hotel. This, in fact, he did, and although I told the Manager and several others of the staff about my method of entry, the next morning, I left the Night Porter guessing until the following night.

'I wish to make two points quite clear.

(1) The times I have given are only very approximate.

(2) Knowing full well that every Police Station in the country had my description, I came quite voluntary to give what information I could.

Signed. N. G. C. Heath. 0245 hrs. 7/7/46."

Neville Heath leaves West London Police Court. Found guilty at the Old Bailey on September 26, 1946 for murdering Margery Gardner, his counsel's plea of insanity was rejected and Heath was executed at Pentonville by Albert Pierrepoint and Harry Kirk on October 16. We are told he asked for a double whisky before being led to the gallows.

In the early hours of the morning of 8th July, Detective-Inspector Spooner of 'F' Division confronted Heath in the Bournemouth Police Station, who admitted his own identity. When challenged, he offered to make a statement about the Pembridge Court murder, admitting that he was there but not that he had done it. In conversation with the Inspector, Heath stated that the switch found in the suitcase was the one he had referred to in his letter to Superintendent Barratt. Next day Heath was recognized on an identification parade both by the receptionist at the Panama Club and by the taxi-driver who had taken him to the Pembridge Court Hotel. When charged with the murder of Margery Gardner, Heath replied that he had nothing to say at the moment.

Heath was charged with the two murders at the West London Police Court in August before Mr. J. L. Pratt. Mr. H. A. K. Morgan appeared for the Director of Public Prosecutions; the accused was defended by Mr. Anthony Jessel. He made three appearances, having pleaded not guilty and reserving his defence. He was committed for trial at the Central Criminal Court.

Neville Heath came up for trial at the Old Bailey, London, on 24th September, 1946, before Mr. Justice Morris. Instructed by the Director of Public Prosecutions, Mr. Anthony Hawke and Mr. Henry Elam appeared for the Crown. Heath was defended by Mr. J. D. Casswell, K. C., Mr. E. A. Jessel, and Mr. J. MacGillivray Asher. To the charge of the murder of Margery Gardner on 21st June, the prisoner pleaded not guilty. A charge of murder against Doreen Marshall was not proffered.

Macdonald Critchley,
Trial of Neville George Clevely Heath, 1951

Gail found Doreen's last resting place in Pinner New Cemetery, Harrow, Middlesex. She had been laid to rest by her father in Grave 54 in Section F6 on July 13, 1946. William Marshall, his heart broken, died eight years later aged 54. He lies in a nearby section H3, Grave 152.

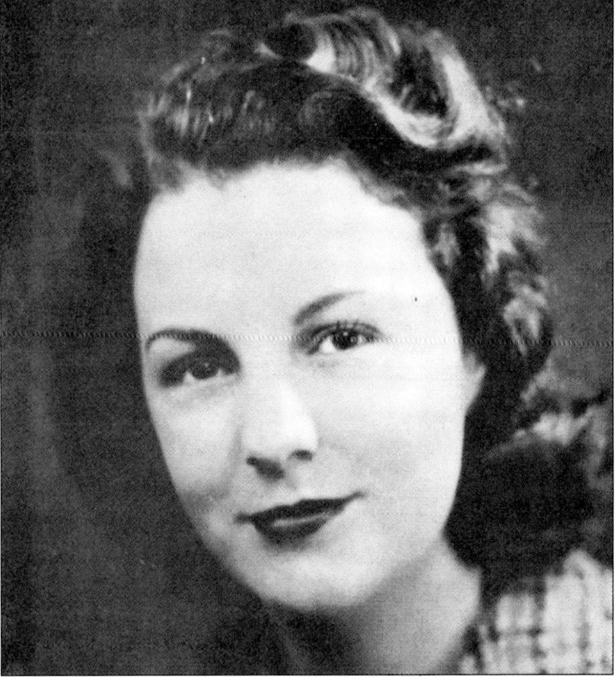

As we believed that Doreen had died while still in service, we approached the Commonwealth War Graves Commission for her name to be commemorated, and in September 2011 the Naval Historical Branch gave authorisation for her name to be included in the CWGC Debt of Honour (see also page 368).

On Saturday, April 26, 1947, a gunsmith shop at 10 Union Street, Bermondsey, was broken into and three shotguns and several revolvers were stolen. The thieves remained on the warehouse premises of Frank Dyke & Co. overnight, emerging at noon on Sunday. *Left:* The old four-storey premises managed by Ernest Reeve is now no more, having been replaced by offices for Price Waterhouse Coopers . . . yet Frank Dyke's lives on in West Norwood *(right).*

April 29, 1947 – The Killing of Alec de Antiquis

When Chief Superintendent Tom Barratt went on holiday with his wife in April 1947 I was put in charge of No. 1 District of the Metropolitan Force — the entire West End of London. I carried my fountain pen and little brown brief-case up to the second floor of Great Scotland Yard, sat down in his padded chair in his roomy office, lit my pipe and began to sift through the heap of routine documents Tom had left for me, scratching signatures on a dozen regulation forms.

After a while I decided to go for lunch. It was after two o'clock, and peaceful in the quiet office with the glint of fragile April sunshine outside. I did not know that a citizen of London was even at that moment sprawled dying from a gunman's bullet upon the grey pavements of Charlotte Street.

I strolled to lunch at the Colonial Club, where I got a phone call from Detective Inspector Higgins: 'A nasty job at Charlotte Street, Sir! Some young fellows with guns held up Jay's, the jewellers. Battle in the shop and a man shot outside, trying to stop 'em as they ran away. He's in hospital — going to die!'

I forgot my lunch. 'Get the Yard photographic department out Bob', I said to Higgins. 'Phone the fingerprint people — Superintendent Cherrill or Syd Birch — then the divisional surgeon. See if the forensic laboratory can help. Phone for my car and send it down to Jay's for me. I'll come in by taxi!'

This is what happened. Three young masked men with loaded guns had rushed into Jay's just after lunch, one of them jumping the counter. The 60-year-old director of the firm, Alfred Ernest Stock, heaved the big safe door shut, but the gunman chucked a pistol at his head and, leaping upon him, hammered him with the barrel of another gun until he fell bleeding to the floor. The gunmen demanded the safe keys from 70-year-old manager Bertram Thomas Keates, who threw a heavy wooden stool. A gun boomed and its bullet thudded into the shop wall. More assistants appeared, the gunmen fled outside where their car waited. But a lorry blocked the way so they abandoned the car, ran down Charlotte Street, eyes wild above their scarf masks, guns clutched in white-knuckled fists. People on the pavement scattered.

Then a motor-cyclist drove around from behind the lorry and, with quick decision, seeing the running gunmen, switched off his engine and skidded the heavy bike into their path. They shot him through the skull and he fell, the motorbike toppling across his limp body. The gunmen ran on into the busy traffic of Tottenham Court Road. Alec de Antiquis, father of six children, was left dying in the gutter.

When I reached the scene, Alec de Antiquis had been tenderly covered by the jacket of a police officer and carried to hospital. As he was lifted into the ambulance his blood- blackened lips stirred. 'I'm all right . . . stop them . . . I did my best.' They were his last words.

There seemed plenty to work on: a stolen motor-car; a bullet in the shop woodwork; a bullet in Alec de Antiquis's left temple, just between ear and eyebrow; an abandoned revolver. Also 27 men and women who had been on Charlotte Street when the murder shot was fired.

First discouraging report was from burly Superintendent Fred Cherrill of the Fingerprint Department. 'Nothing on the car to help you, Bob', he said. 'Nothing in the shop, either.' Next came Detective Inspector Higgins who had the task of taking those 27 statements from witnesses.

Now well armed, on Tuesday, April 29, the Bermondsey gang left their homes preparing to rob a jewellery shop in the West End. *Left:* Henry Jenkins departed through this doorway from No. 21 Weller House at Dockhead, while Tony Rolt exited from 28 St John's Estate *(centre)* in Bermondsey. *Right:* The third member, Christopher Geraghty, lived north of the river at 23 Liverpool Road, his house having now been replaced by the Finsbury branch of Sainsbury's.

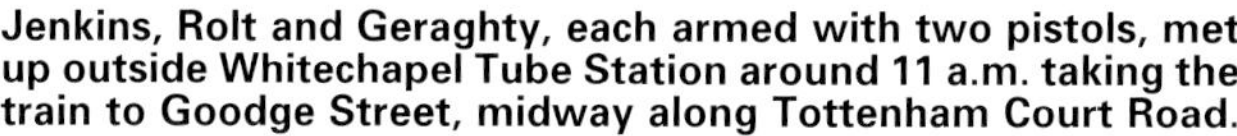

Jenkins, Rolt and Geraghty, each armed with two pistols, met up outside Whitechapel Tube Station around 11 a.m. taking the train to Goodge Street, midway along Tottenham Court Road.

From there they split up, Jenkins and Rolt going off to steal their getaway car while Geraghty went to case the shop they had chosen to rob — Jay's jewellers and pawnbrokers.

'Well, Chief, I've got the descriptions,' he said. But his eyes were mournful. 'They're all different!' I glanced over the stack of descriptions, each in the witness's own words: 'Three enormous men' . . . 'Three dodgy little fellows' . . . 'I think one was lame' . . . 'They all ran like blazes' . . . 'All wearing raincoats' . . . 'They wore battledress jackets' . . . 'Definitely foreigners, swarthy' . . . 'They were blond and wore no hats' . . . 'Caps pulled down over their eyes.'

My phone rang — the Forensic Science Laboratories at Hendon. 'Mr. Fabian? We've examined that stolen Vauxhall 14 saloon, registration KPK 524, put a micro-camera over the upholstery and so on. There isn't a shred of a clue.'

We took the 27 witnesses into Scotland Yard's Criminal Record Office to inspect photographs of known criminals likely to use guns. It went on until late evening but it was completely unsuccessful. Next day the late Sir Bernard Spilsbury was called in and held a post-mortem. Antiquis had certainly died from the bullet but Spilsbury could help no further. In his ballistics laboratory, Britain's foremost firearms expert, Robert Churchill, examined the murder bullet and decided it had been fired by a .320 calibre, centre-fire revolver.

Then, just as I sat sipping a cup of brackish cold coffee and realising I had not slept for three days, 55 hours after brave and quick-thinking Alec de Antiquis had given his life in London's gutters, a Mr Albert Victor Grubb walked into Tottenham Court Road Police Station. Rain glistened on his dark leather taxi-driver's coat. 'Do you want to know anything about two young fellows I saw disappear into a building off the Tottenham Court Road just after the murder?' he asked. 'They had handkerchiefs knotted round their chins.'

I was alert, listening to Mr. Grubb's story. A young man with a handkerchief knotted under his chin had jumped on the running-

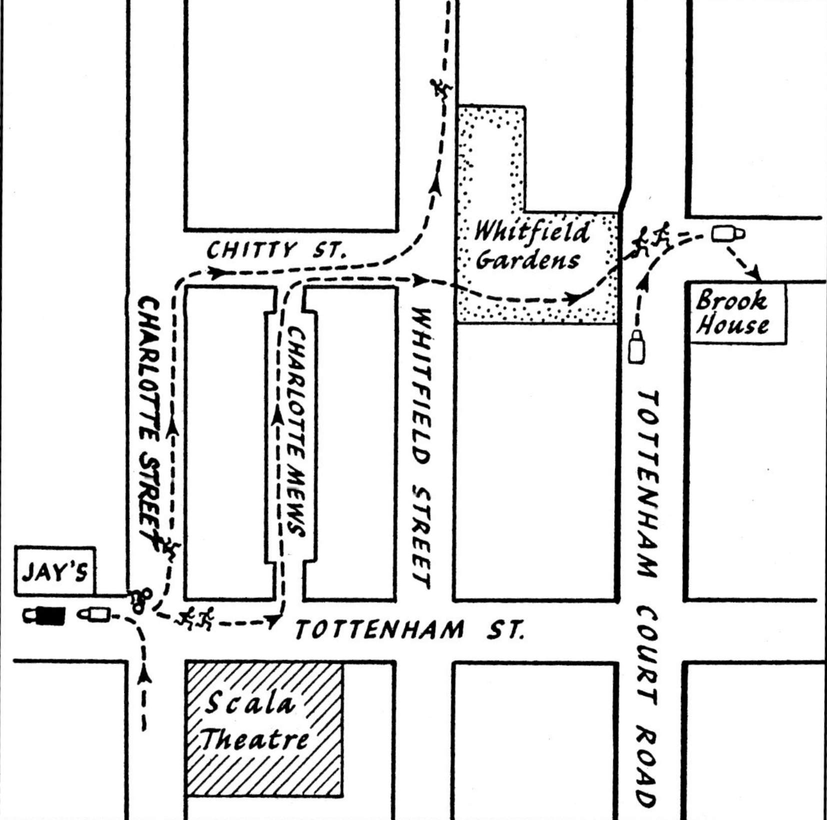

Jay's on the corner of Tottenham Street and Charlotte Street was a single storey jewellers and pawn shop. There were two entrances: the door on Tottenham Street led into the pledge department which was divided into three booths for privacy, while the sales department was accessed via a gate to the side yard. There is no scene of crime plan in the police file — this one being drawn up in 1964 for David Cargill and Julian Holland's book *Scenes of Murder — a London Guide*.

Clad in trench coats with flat caps pulled down and cowboy-style scarves over their faces, the gang prepared to strike. The car stolen from nearby Whitfield Street was parked at the kerbside while two gunmen entered the front door to the pledge department while the third came in the rear sales door. All were waving revolvers, one jumping on the counter announcing — just like in the movies — 'It's a hold-up!' The 70-year-old manager, Bertram Keates, was pushed aside but pressed the alarm. The 17-year-old sales assistant Leslie Grout threw a stool and Alfred Stock bravely tried to knock the pistol out of the hand of the nearest robber. For this, the second gunman hit him over the head with the butt of his gun. At this point the third man entered from the rear, firing a warning shot. With the whole robbery having gone wrong, the three men fled empty-handed to the car.

board of his cab. Mr Grubb, already carrying a fare, had brushed him off. The young man then ran across the road, where another young man was at the door of Brook House, No. 191, Tottenham Court Road. Both disappeared inside.

Next day, in a grey dawn, by the time Leonard Joel, the porter at Brook House, arrived to sweep his steps we were already waiting for him, snoozing with coat-collars turned up in a Flying Squad car drawn to the kerb.

'Ah,' he said when we had explained. 'That might account for the little key I found when I swept the stairs yesterday. It didn't belong to any of the people in these offices, for I asked 'em all.'

I took it. 'Try it in the stolen Vauxhall', I said to one of my aides. The squad car whirred away and was back within a few minutes. 'It fits, Chief!'

The Brook House office boy, Brian Cox, was wide-eyed when he came to work that morning to find himself suddenly the most important person in the whole block of offices. For young Brian had been at the doorway just before 3 p.m. on April 29 when two young men brushed past him and hurried into the building. He noticed that the tallest wore a raincoat, and after a while he saw them on the stairs, looking through windows. They asked him if 'a Mr Williams was in', but he said he didn't know any Mr. Williams, and he now noticed the tall man no longer had a raincoat.,

In a disused room on the top floor of Brook House offices, behind a dusty counter, bundled up and shoved out of sight, we found the raincoat with a cap and a pair of gloves in the pocket. Crumpled even further into the unlit corner was a scarf, folded into a triangle with both ends knotted — a murder mask! The maker's name had been carefully picked

Already having been damaged by bombs during the war, Jay's days were numbered. Now the corner is ocupied by the Margaret Pyke Centre.

CALOX Brilliance without injury enamel TOOTH POWDER

WORLD'S LARGEST EVENING NET SALE

The Evening News

LATE EXTRA

NO. 20,350 — LONDON, TUESDAY, APRIL 29, 1947 — ONE PENNY

MURDER BY WEST END GUN GANG

Crowds See Man Shot Dead Trying To Stop Masked Bandits

YARD START BIG KILLER HUNT

2-Gun Gang Leader

"EVENING NEWS" REPORTER

A MAN was shot dead in a West End street this afternoon as he tried to stop three masked gunmen, escaping after a hold-up in a jeweller's shop.

As the bandits dashed, each with a gun in his hand, the leader said to be waving two, from the shop—at the corner of Tottenham Court-road and Charlotte-street—a motor-cyclist slewed his machine across the path of their waiting car. He was shot down and died soon afterwards in Middlesex Hospital.

Street crowds, yelling "Stop thief!" chased the desperadoes, who had beaten up the manager of Jay's, the jewellers. Scotland Yard switched wireless cars to the scene, and a great man hunt swung into operation throughout the whole Metropolitan area.

The dead man had no identity card in his possession, and the hospital did not know who he was.

As he collapsed in the street he groaned: "I have been shot." The gang ran off along Tottenham Court-road and escaped in the crowds.

Men and women ran from the shop, shouting: "Stop thief!" and screaming.

The Chase

Crowds chased the three men, and police whistles shrilled.

A man walking along Charlotte-street at the time of the incident told me: "I suddenly heard a man shout from the open door of Jay's —'Stop, thief!'

"Suddenly three men leaped out ...

BULLETS FLY IN SHOP RAID

JEMMY HURLED AT POLICEMAN

"Evening News" Reporter

ONLOOKERS saw gun-flashes in a darkened West End street during the night when a policeman surprised three men outside a saleroom in Eastcastle-street, off Oxford-street.

The shots shattered glass windows, but none hit the policeman, P.C. Herbert Meredith, of "C" Division. He ducked, too, to avoid a heavy jemmy thrown at him by one of the raiders.

An official of the saleroom's ...

SHOT DOWN IN THE WEST END—A grim picture which emphasises the increase of London's armed criminals.

PARK ATTACK ON LONDON GIRL

LEFT UNCONSCIOUS, TAKEN TO HOSPITAL

'Total Disregard of National Well-Being'—Isaacs

Dock Strike: Stern Warning by Ministers

STRACHEY: SERIOUS IF . . .

Mr. Strachey, Food Minister, said at to-day's food con-...

Lorry Gang Get £5,000 Worth of Cigarettes

"Evening News" Reporter

POLICE throughout the Midlands are hunting for thieves who stole 750,000 cigarettes worth £5,000 from a Walsall warehouse during the night.

The men drove up in a truck, climbed the wall by ladder and let themselves in by a fanlight.

A member of the firm said: "The men were cool. They took about 24 cartons of chocolate wafers, but before they left they sampled them. Police found crumbs of chocolate all over the floor."

£1,100 HAUL
Cat Burglar's Raid

A CAT BURGLAR who broke into the house of Mr. B. Hartstone in Compton-avenue, Highgate, after climbing a drainpipe, entered a bedroom where members of the family were sleeping and escaped with money and furs worth over £1,100. He collected the five fur coats from the hall and then left by the front door.

CAMERAS STOLEN
Thieves Take the Best

MINIATURE cameras worth £1,000 were stolen by another gang from the Charing Cross-road premises of Westminster Photographic Exchange. They broke a window in Cecil-court and then crawled through into the shop. The shop manager, Mr. S. Kay, said: "They selected only the best cameras and lenses."

BUTTER THEFT
Lorry Load Taken

A FIVE-TON motor-lorry loaded with 72 cases of butter was stolen from a garage at Earlham-grove, Forest Hill, in the night. The lorry was the property of Unique Transport.

CHEAP 'SMOKES' FOR PENSIONERS

PRODUCERS TO GET MEAT CUT NEXT MONTH

30,000,000 Eggs From Poland

MR. STRACHEY announced at his Press conference to-day that owing to the restriction in our meat supplies during the next few months it is necessary as from May 5 to make a temporary reduction in allocations of meat to manufacturers of meat products other than general butchers.

On the brighter side he reported the conclusion of an agreement with Poland for the purchase of from 30,000,000 to 50,000,000 eggs, to be shipped here between now and September 30. The first consignment was expected by the end of this week.

He also said the 1947-48 ration book is to come into use on July 20. Issuing to the public will start on June 9, a fortnight later than last year. "The public," he added, "are asked to collect their own books."

Free Choice

"The clothing coupon book will, as usual, be bound into the ration book. There will be general re-registration, with free choice of retailer for meat and groceries, but consumers will not re-register for milk."

The main change in the new ration book is the omission of the six-unit B U coupon—"which is not too popular," said Mr. Strachey.

Mr. Strachey said he would be making an announcement well before the new ration books came into force concerning a slight modification in connection with registration for milk. There was no possibility of returning to free choice of retailers.

YeastVite

LATEST WEATHER FORECAST

CLOSING PRICES PAGE 6

MURDER VICTIM

DOCKS: COMMONS STATEMENT

'QUALIFIED TRAINEES CAN'T GET JOBS'

According to witnesses in the street (and 27 of them were interviewed later by police), as the gunmen ran from the shop they were being chased by a man in shirt-sleeves shouting 'Police!'. He was Abraham Buckner, a salesman from Westcliff-on-Sea. After a few seconds, the three men abandoned the car. Bill Corff, who worked at No. 72 Charlotte Street, had just finished his lunch and had reached the junction with Tottenham Street. 'I was on the east side, watching a motor cyclist try to start his engine. This cyclist moved his machine across the junction of Tottenham Street and Charlotte Street when, looking beyond him at Jay's the jewellers, I saw two men run from the shop and try and get into a car which was standing immediately outside Jay's. They were followed by another man who appeared distressed and calling "Stop! Police!". Within a few seconds three men jumped from the car and ran towards my direction in Charlotte Street. As these men ran in my direction, two went into the road and a third, whom I took most notice of, ran towards the motor cyclist. The motor cyclist appeared to raise his hands as if to stop him, and I heard two muffled reports as the third man almost collided with the cyclist. The cyclist fell on to the road and then I noticed that the man had a gun in either hand. He waved these guns in the air, ran along Charlotte Street, into Chitty Street.'

out from both cap and raincoat but, when I ripped away the lining, I found that inside the seam, near the right-hand pocket, was a cloth stock ticket of a firm of multiple branch tailors. A police car whisked this clue to their factory in Leeds while I took a brief nap in my clothes at Tottenham Court Road Station.

Bad news came after lunch on the phone from Leeds. 'Sorry, Sir. All they can tell us is that the raincoat was delivered to one of three branch shops in London.' Within a few minutes came a teleprint message from the police laboratory at Hendon: 'Regret no identification in raincoat, cap, or gloves.'

Two of the three branch shops to which the raincoat might have been supplied were in fairly high-class suburban districts. The managers hastily turned up their books. 'Ah, yes, here we are . . .' They gave names and addresses of purchasers of coats of the pattern we held.

Sydney Merrick, a chauffeur from Ascot, had driven his employer, Mrs Anson, to London in her Rolls-Royce KYH1 to visit Richards wine merchants in Charlotte Street and was parked nearby. 'I saw two men with handkerchiefs over the lower half of their faces running down the pavement of the side street towards a motor cyclist who was stationary on my side of the street, but the other side of the junction. There was a small crowd of people stood between me and the motor cyclist which partially obscured my view for a second. I saw the leading man of the two masked men with a revolver pointing towards the motor cyclist in a firing position level with his chest. When he was within 3-4 yards I heard the revolver go off which sounded of a small calibre. The moment he fired it seemed to me that he leapt at the motor cyclist and knocked him over, and continued running straight across the crossroads and then turned to his left into a street running parallel with Queen Charlotte Street. The second man turned left at the motor cyclist and was soon lost to sight.'

Alec de Antiquis fell here beside the same GPO inspection chamber (see also front cover). Note how St John's Church further down the street has been replaced by a new office block — Aerial House.

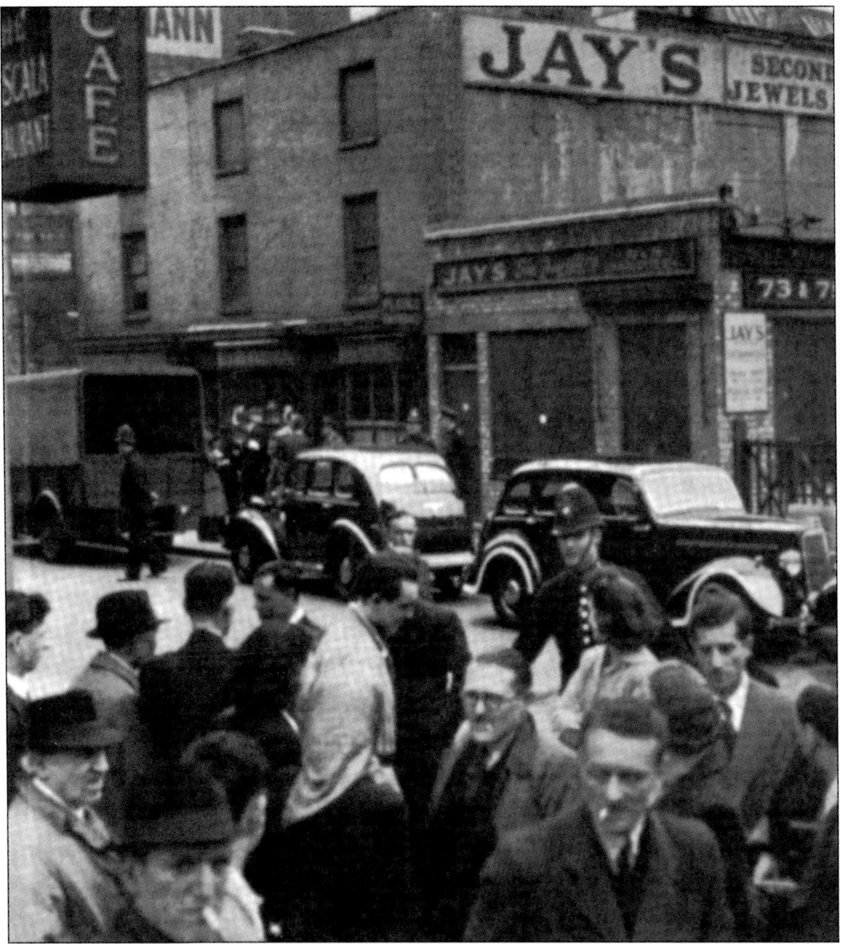

A crowd has quickly gathered on the scene and no doubt some of the bystanders in this photograph later gave statements to the police.

Two astounded suburban householders received calls from detectives and were asked to produce their raincoats . . . then each hurried off to the 'local' to become a hero for the night while we turned the black, polished nose of our high-powered Railton towards the third shop, in High Street, Deptford.

'Why, of course', said Arthur Amos, the manager. We have a record of sale.' He thumbed his books confidently. 'Here we are — sold on 30 December 1946' and he gave me an address in Bermondsey.

It was a block of flats. We saw the man's wife and showed her the raincoat. 'Does this belong to your husband?'

She was agitated. 'Yes. He lost it at a public house about, er, five weeks ago.' I left the flat and shortly afterwards the woman also left. The detective I had placed in hiding to wait for this shadowed her cautiously.

She visited another block of flats then went home again. This was interesting as at that address lived a family named Jenkins. The eldest son was serving eight years for manslaughter during a smash-and-grab raid on a London jeweller's [*see pages 170-173*], while another son, Harry Jenkins, had just been released from Borstal.

I got back to my office to find that the murder gun, fully loaded but with one chamber fired, had been discovered by a schoolboy in the river mud of the Thames at Wapping. The gun expert, Mr. Churchill, examined it and nodded: 'That's the one! It fired the shot that killed Antiquis.' You see, when a bullet leaves a gun, rifling in the gun barrel makes marks on it which are identical on every bullet fired from that gun. All you do is to shoot another bullet from the same gun, match the scratches and it is as sure as a fingerprint!

A few minutes afterwards my other team of detectives, whom I had left to pick up the man at Bermondsey before he got home to his wife, brought him to me at Tottenham Court Road Station, I showed him the raincoat.

'Yes', he said without hesitation. 'That's mine. I lost it in a cinema a few weeks ago.'

'Your wife said you lost it in a public house. Who's making the mistake?'

He hesitated. 'We both are', he said after a pause. 'She lent it to her brother, Harry Jenkins.'

I took a couple of police officers to Bermondsey and arrested Harry Jenkins, a handsome lad of 23, with fair curly hair and a cool confidence in his eyes and smile.

Young Jenkins was not afraid of the police as he had two convictions before he was 20 for assaulting policemen. He broke the jaw of one P.C., and as leader of the lads in the neighbourhood was called 'The King of Borstal'. And when I showed him the fateful raincoat in the quiet of my office, that Sunday afternoon, he simply smiled. 'I understand you borrowed it from your sister,' I said.

The church bells tolled outside. The smile stayed fixed and calmly defiant on Jenkins's handsome young corsair face. 'It looks like Tom's coat, but I'm not saying anything more now as it all looks serious to me,' he said. That was all we could get from him.

He was put in the cells with food, blanket and mattress. From Scotland Yard's Criminal Record Office I got a list of his associates. His best friend was Christopher James Geraghty, aged 21, who had twice escaped from Borstal. Another acquaintance was a boy of 17, Terence Peter Rolt, who had been bound over as a juvenile for shop-breaking.

We went looking for young Rolt and found him just before midnight. His story was that on the day of the Antiquis shooting he had been ill in bed. He was later released. Geraghty was not found that day so we left a message at his home and next morning he came to Tottenham Court Road Police Station. I asked him to account for his movements on April 23. He sat for a few minutes, looked at my calendar on the wall and said: 'As a matter of fact, I was in bed queer. I had some boils and was ill all the week.' Shortly before 11 a.m. I let Geraghty go.

Within an hour we had paraded Jenkins in the main hall of the police station with a row of other fair-haired young men of similar age picked up on Tottenham Court Road. He knew all the tricks, asked for a lunch-edition newspaper to be brought in for him, and stuck it nonchalantly in his pocket so witnesses might think: 'It couldn't be this man — obviously he was out on the street only a few minutes ago!'

One by one, for an hour and ten minutes, the 27 witnesses who claimed they could identify any of the three gunmen they had glimpsed on Charlotte Street filed past, stared thoughtfully and passed on. Nobody identified Jenkins. After it was ended he smirked at me triumphantly, but as I saw the cool challenge of his eyes, the sardonic twist of his confident mouth, I felt certain I was looking into the face of the leader of the gang that had slain Alec de Antiquis.

How the historic scenes of yesteryear have changed . . . but how many remember the man gunned down on this spot.

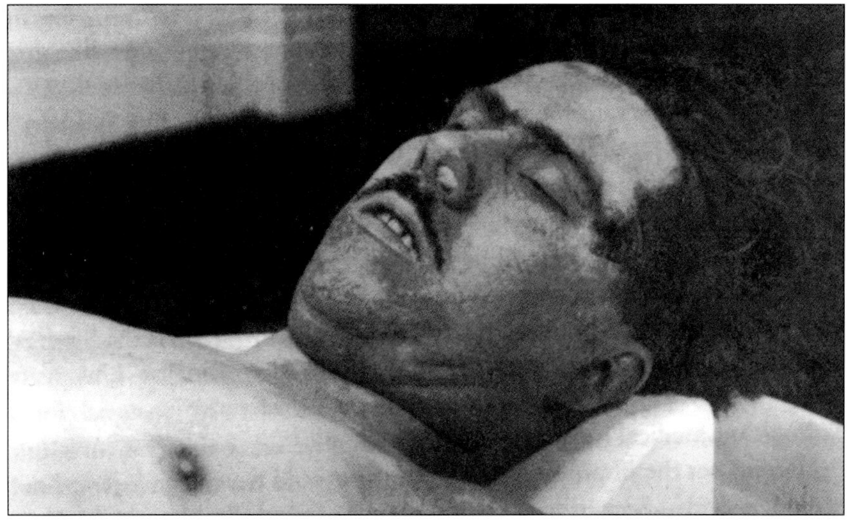

Alec was taken to St Pancras Mortuary for a post-mortem examination — this photograph of the entry wound just beside the tip of the left eyebrow being taken by Detective Sergeant Bill Crumb of the Yard's Photographic Section. His motorbike — which appears to be a Triumph — had been stood upright and was pictured by a newsman in front of the shop.

My clothes were rumpled, dishevelled from days of camping out at the police station; my cheeks were raw from shaving with ordinary soap as I had not even taken time to telephone home for my toilet kit, and my eyes were gritty with need of sleep. I looked again at gang-leader Harry Jenkins; at the pressed suit and crisp silk shirt that friends had fetched in for him. 'All right, Jenkins', I said heavily. 'You can go.'

He smiled, began to walk towards the police station door into Tottenham Court Road. I put a detective on to shadow him.

Two more of my men were also unobtrusively following his gangster pals, Geraghty and Rolt, who after a little while met Jenkins in a public house at Clerkenwell. All three appeared nervous, edgy, apprehensive and talked in whispers.

After Jenkins had been released for a full day and night, I sent a policeman to ask him to come and make a statement about that raincoat. I sent for his sister, too, who had tried to shield Jenkins with the story that the raincoat was one her husband lost in the Green Man tavern. I wanted to study them together. But Jenkins had spent that sleepless night not merely worrying — he had been scheming. The law needed a victim and he would help us find one.

He sat with his sister opposite my desk and said boldly: 'Let us tell Mr Fabian who I lent the coat to.' He lit a cigarette. His fingers were steady and the match-flame did not flicker.

Meanwhile the stolen Vauxhall Fourteen had been taken to the Forensic Science Laboratory at Hendon where it could be examined by Detective Superintendent Fred Cherrill, the Head of the Yard's Fingerprint Branch.

Consulting the sketch plan on page 187, two of the robbers ran through Charlotte Mews ***(left)*** **and then across Whitfield Gardens** ***(right).***

On Tuesday, May 30, the three men charged with the murder appeared in Marlborough Street Magistrates Court. L-R: Terence John Peter Rolt; Christopher James Geraghty and Charles Henry Jenkins. They had been brought to justice by the three men below.

They both began to talk, and out of the statements came a name — Bill Walsh. 'We saw him,' said Jenkins, 'about a week ago in Southend. He's knocking around with a girl who works in a café there.' I was amazed as although Jenkins was a crook, a thief, a gangster, he had never betrayed a comrade. And this was a dangerous betrayal — the man who had that raincoat last was the likely murderer.

Bill Walsh we knew. I sent for his file from the Criminal Record Office. He was a convict on licence and had already broken his parole and failed to report to the police. I took my team, Chief Inspector Higgins and Detective Inspector Hodge, to Southend where we sat drinking tea in the police station while we looked through the bulky pages of the police routine books in which all events of the town were recorded. Did you realise the police always have their eye on you? Each time in your life when you said: 'It's all right, officer, I was only . . . ' and the constable, after listening, touched his helmet and walked on, the constable didn't forget. He put it down in the Occurrences Book.

The Southend Occurrences Book did not disappoint us. It told us that on April 25 at 9.40 p.m., P.C. Frederick Jauncey reported the suspicious behaviour of two young men in a telephone kiosk. He took particulars from the two young men who gave their names as Christopher James Geraghty and Michael Joseph Gillam. There was another entry which said that on April 26 at 7.15 a.m., P.C. James Bunn found a loaded .455 revolver in some shrubbery near the pier.

We searched Southend's cafés for the waitress and went to talk with her parents. Her father told us Bill Walsh had been in Southend on April 25 with Jenkins! 'Suddenly Bill Walsh seemed to disappear. Nobody knew where he'd gone,' said the father. 'Then Jenkins said Walsh had double-crossed him and something about getting his revenge.'

I exchanged quick glances with Chief Inspector Higgins as we had an idea what that might signify. Walsh and Jenkins must have done a robbery together and Walsh run off with the loot!

For the rest of the day we went carefully through every cupboard and loose floorboard in every house in Southend where Walsh was known to have friends. In one house we were lucky. We found two watches stolen in an armed hold-up of a jeweller's shop in Queensway, London, W.2, on April 25, four days before the murder.

Promptly I put out the full hue and cry for Walsh. After three days he was arrested in Plumstead, near his home. As he was brought in to my office I studied him with interest. Was this the murderer I was seeking? He was 37, in appearance not unlike Humphrey Bogart made up for one of his typical parts.

The formidable triumvirate. Divisional Detective Inspector Bob Higgins (left) who, at the time, was the youngest of the DDIs in the Metropolitan Police and had only been in the position for eight months which involved being in charge of the CID in central London. Higgins had recruited Detective Inspector Fred Hodge (centre) as his assistant on the Antiquis case. Detective Chief Inspector Bob Fabian (right) from the C1 Department at the Yard (the CIDs Central Office) was standing in on the investigation as Detective Chief Superintendent Tom Barratt of No. 1 District — which covered all of London north of the Thames — was on holiday. The very mention that 'Fabian of the Yard' had been brought into a case was always a huge measure of confidence as his reputation was fearsome in the eyes of the public.

Today Marlborough Court has been converted into the Courthouse Doubletree Hotel.

Some of the cells have been retained . . . and one can even dine in the original Court No. 1.

'What d'you want me for?' he said boldly. 'Not all this fuss for dodging my ticket-of-leave, surely?' (Ticket-of-leave is the slang phrase for 'convict on licence'.)

I answered him carefully. 'It could be for armed robbery, Walsh — else it could be for murder.' His eyes narrowed. I added, quietly: 'It depends on you and what you know!'

After a while, in which he paced up and down, smoking many cigarettes, Walsh asked for a glass of water. We fetched him the water, and then he began to talk. He denied that he had ever borrowed a raincoat — the fatal raincoat — from Jenkins or his sister. I believed him. He told me that he had discussed the Jay's hold-up before it happened with Harry Jenkins, Christopher Geraghty and somebody else who later withdrew from the scheme. But all he did was to reconnoitre the shop five days before the robbery. He was not one of the three gunmen I was seeking. Then he told me of a robbery at Queensway. With Geraghty, Jenkins and a lad called 'Joe', he had robbed at gun-point a Queensway, Bayswater, jeweller's of £5,000 worth of rings and watches. After the robbery the gang went to Southend where Walsh admitted absconding with all the stolen jewellery. This was why Jenkins had betrayed him. Remembering the Southend Occurrences Book, we identified 'Joe' as Michael Joseph Gillam, an ex-Borstal boy. He and Walsh were tried and sentenced to five years each at the Central Criminal Court for this Queensway robbery.

Meanwhile another schoolboy had found yet another loaded gun in the Thames at Wapping at low tide. The Home Office gun expert examined this latest find, a .45 revolver, and announced: 'This is the revolver that fired the bullet which was extracted from the woodwork of Jay's, the jewellers.' Not the gun that killed Antiquis but one of the guns carried by that same murder gang. Both murder guns had been found at a place less than quarter of a mile from the block of flats where the parents of Jenkins's wife lived. Yet one must break a chain at its weakest point, and clever, cool Jenkins was not weak.

I arrested Geraghty who made a brave show of careless ease, fidgeting with his lank fair hair, and whose eyes became defiant when I casually mentioned Jenkins. I knew that Jenkins and Geraghty were firm friends, and that whatever else may have been sinful and rotten in their young lives, these two ex-Borstal lads would have died for each other. Their sad, doomed underworld friendship was no less sincere for being darkened by blood and theft. So I did not even question him about Jenkins. I asked him about Rolt!

That did it. Geraghty did not mind betraying Rolt. To him, Rolt was insignificant small fry, a new member of the gang, and little more than a child at that. Geraghty damned Rolt in a long and detailed statement, but in that statement, whenever it came to Jenkins, Geraghty paused, then said carefully: 'That other fellow, whose name I don't want to mention.' He told how he and Rolt and 'that other fellow' had broken into a gunsmith's in Union Street near the Borough Tube Station. They stayed in the gunsmith's all Saturday night until nearly noon next Sunday morning when, with guns and bullets in their pockets, they sauntered out and went home.

Two days afterwards, on the Tuesday, they met outside Whitechapel Tube Station at eleven o'clock and went to Goodge Street where they got out and inspected several jewellers' shops around the Tottenham

Left: **Here Jenkins is escorted into the court via the rear yard.** *Above:* **Unfortunately the conversion has meant that the old courtyard has been reduced to a small loading bay but the entrance still remains as it was.**

Two pistols were found on the Thames foreshore by young boys and handed in to police. The first was found by seven-year-old Edward King in the mud at the end of Pelican Steps — the alleyway alongside the famed Prospect of Whitby — in Wapping — a legend of pirates since the earliest days and still complete with hangman's noose. Robert Churchill, the forensic gunsmith, proved that this .320 revolver loaded in five chambers but with the sixth one fired was the weapon used by Geraghty to kill Antiquis.

Court Road. They decided to rob Jay's but as there were too many people about they went to have lunch in a café. Young Rolt was sent to peer into the jeweller's window and 'value' the property. He came back saying it was worth about £2,000 and wondering if it was worth robbing. He did not say this very insistently because he was afraid of being thought a coward. How many times, as that lad of 17 wept below the Old Bailey dock, in one of those little brown brick cells where prisoners wait, must he have wished he had been a coward that day! Then Geraghty went to look at the shop and decided that although the contents of the window were worth nearly £5,000, there were too many people around the shop for it to be safe to rob it.

Meanwhile, Jenkins and Rolt had gone to steal a car. Jenkins walked ahead while Rolt drove the stolen car uncertainly up Charlotte Street. Young Rolt, nerves strung up to a pitch where the fear of seeming afraid was more to be dreaded than the deed itself, halted his car at the kerb and jumped into the shop, pulling out his guns. The others followed. In an instant the shop seethed with struggling bodies. Blows were struck, stools thrown, then a shot boomed out. The three accomplices made their escape, hearts pounding. The brave de Antiquis loomed up and Geraghty shot him down. They were gangsters on the run now — murderers in a hopeless bid to escape.

I arrested Rolt at half-past two in the morning. He said: 'Don't wake my mother,' and crept white-faced into his clothes to come with us. He was told Geraghty had made a statement that involved him so he also made a statement, and since Jenkins was not his heart-sworn comrade he implicated Jenkins. In all details, his statement fitted what we knew.

Next day I completed the job by arresting Jenkins, and at 7.30 on the evening of May 19 all three were lined up before the charge-desk and formally indicted with murder. I went home and, after a while, slept soundly.

All three were found guilty, though Rolt was too young for the death penalty. He was sentenced to be detained during His Majesty's pleasure for a recommended period of not less than five years. On Friday, September 19, exactly four months to the day after they were charged, Geraghty and Jenkins were hanged at Pentonville Prison.

There was a postscript to the Antiquis case. It was spoken by Sir Harold Scott, Metropolitan Police Commissioner, giving evidence before the Royal Commission on Capital Punishment. He said: 'There was a case of shop-breaking at Birchin Lane in 1944. A passer-by, Captain Binney, died from injuries when he tried to stop the thieves' car. Ronald Hedley, the driver, was convicted of murder, and one of his companions, Thomas James Jenkins, of manslaughter. Hedley's death sentence was commuted to penal servitude for life, and Jenkins (brother of the Antiquis murderer) was sentenced to eight years' penal servitude.

'All the persons concerned in this and in the subsequent Antiquis case were associates and lived in the Bermondsey district. After the result of the case against Hedley and Thomas James Jenkins they . . . became actively engaged in crime. Some of them were arrested and sentenced to varying terms of imprisonment, but still they continued living their life of crime.

'Then came . . . the death sentence on Charles Henry Jenkins and Christopher Geraghty. Almost immediately the gang disbanded. They have not been seen in their usual haunts since, and as far as is known are not engaged in criminal pursuits.'

I can add to that, from my own experience. For weeks after the hanging of Jenkins and Geraghty we began to find guns . . . abandoned in parks under bushes, in dustbins, dropped through the floors of bombed houses, fished up by Thames River patrolmen in nets from the low-tide mud. The men of the underworld had decided to think twice about using guns in London. So whenever I think of Antiquis these days it is as one good life lost — but also as a thousand lives saved!

Superintendent Robert Fabian,
Fabian of the Yard, 1955

Reprieve refused. Christopher Geraghty, 20, and Charles Jenkins, 23, the Alec de Antiquis murderers die today.

Daily Mirror, September 19, 1947

Christopher James Gerraghty, 20, and Charles Henry Jenkins, 23, were hanged at Pentonville Prison yesterday for the murder of Alec de Antiquis, who tried to stop them after a London hold-up.

Daily Mirror, September 20, 1947

A second revolver was found on the foreshore at Shadwell Dock Steps just a couple of hundred yards further along Wapping Wall. Both weapons must have been thrown into the river at high tide but not far enough out as a 'beach' of 50 yards appears at low tide. Ten-year-old George Mizon found the .45 here a few days after Edward's discovery and Churchill proved that it was the pistol which had been fired during the scuffle inside the shop, the bullet having been recovered from the wood panelling.

The trial began at the Old Bailey on Monday, July 21, and on the following Monday the judge, Mr Justice Hallett, summed up and the jury retired just after 5 p.m. Within half an hour they were back with a guilty verdict. Because Tony Rolt was under 18 he was removed from the dock while the sentence of death was pronounced on Geraghty and Jenkins. Having been taken down, Rolt returned to be sentenced to be 'detained in custody until His Majesty's pleasure be known' — the euphemistic term used for an indeterminate period of imprisonment, the judge recommending at least five years. Geraghty and Jenkins were executed together on September 19, 1947 at Pentonville by Albert Pierrepoint assisted by Henry Critchell and Harry Allen.

Alec de Antiquis ran L&A Motors at 186 High Street at Collier's Wood, specialising in motorbikes, and their repair, and he had come into town that morning to obtain an exhaust pipe and front wheel and other spare parts. He had set up in business on his demob in December 1945, hoping to benefit from the large number of military machines being sold off by the War Office. He had a wife and six children to support and, exceptionally, the Home Secretary announced that she would be given an ex-gratia sum of £100 per year plus £18 per child each year until they reached the age of 18. Alec was laid to rest at Collier Wood Cemetery in London Road, his cortege slowing as it passed his workshop. His grave, No. 2385 lies in Section 30: 'In Loving Memory of Alec de Antiquis who gave his life in the cause of justice. Devoted husband and a loving father. Aged 34 years.'

John George Haigh was born in Stamford, Lincolnshire, on July 27, 1909. He attended Wakefield Grammar School and was chosen as a chorister for Wakefield Cathedral Choir, also acting as organist for some services. He became a member of the Plymouth Brethren. His first job was as a representative for Shell-Mex in Leeds followed by employment with different firms in the city. He married Beatrice Hamer in July 1934 but in November that year was sentenced at Leeds Assizes to 15 months imprisonment for conspiracy to fraud; aiding and abetting forgery, and obtaining money by false pretences with six similar offences being taken into consideration. All were scams against hire-purchase companies where he obtained finance for non-existant motor cars by forging the documentation. By the time he was released in December 1935 we are told that his wife had left him, having given birth to a child which he denied was his. Early in 1937 he was employed by William McSwan who ran a pin-table business, Mac's Automatics Ltd., and Haigh was taken on as an attendant for an arcade in Shepherds Bush and another at Walham Green. Later that year Haigh was sentenced to four years penal servitude having pleaded guilty to seven cases of obtaining bankers' cheques by false pretences, admitting 28 similar offences. This time he had posed as a solicitor administering an estate disposing of shares. Meanwhile, McSwan kept in touch and paid him visits. He was released in August 1940, becoming a fire-watcher and in February 1941 he registered for military service although this application appears to have been cancelled, possibly because he was already employed in Civil Defence. Haigh was back in prison in June for a spell of 21 months hard labour while posing as a bailee. He was released on September 17, 1943 when he returned to Leeds to live with his parents, later obtaining a job as bookkeeper with the Union Tool & Gauge Company in Crawley, Sussex. While there he lodged with the proprietor. After about a year he moved to London, taking up semi-permanent residence at the Onslow Court Hotel in Queen's Gate from where he conducted his own company Union Group Engineering, his object being to act as a liaison officer between patentees, inventors and engineering firms. The manageress of the hotel stated that Haigh first stayed there on March 28, 1944 and thereafter for two or three nights every week. He also rented a room further up the road at No. 38 Queen's Gate Terrace, although he did not live there.

February 18, 1949 – John Haigh and the Acid Bath Murders

In 1944 I disposed of William Donald McSwan in the basement of 79 Gloucester Road, S.W.7, and Donald McSwan and Amy McSwan in 1946 [*should read 1945*] at the same address. In 1948, Dr. Archibald Henderson and his wife Rosalie Henderson, also in a similar manner at Leopold Road, Crawley.

Going back to the McSwans, William Donald, the son, whose address at that particular time I can't remember, met me at the 'Goat' public-house, Kensington High Street, and from there we went to No. 79 Gloucester Road, where in the basement, which I had rented, I hit him on the head with a cosh, withdrew a glass of blood from his throat as before and drank it. He was dead within five minutes or so. I put him in a forty-gallon tank and disposed of him with acid, disposing of the sludge down a manhole in the basement. I took his watch and odds and ends, including an identity card before putting him into the tank.

About two months or more after the young McSwan, I met a woman of about 35 years of age, 5 ft. 7 in., slim build, dark hair, no hat, wearing a dark cloth coat, and carrying a dark envelope-type blackish handbag, in Hammersmith, somewhere between the Broadway and Hammersmith Bridge. I had never seen her before. We stood chatting by the bridge for about 20 minutes, and then I asked her if she would walk back to Kensington with me. She agreed to do so.

We walked back as far as High Street, Kensington, and then took the Underground to Gloucester Road. From there I invited her round to what I called my flat. That was 79 Gloucester Road (basement). She came with me to this address, where I duly tapped her on the head with a cosh, and tapped her for blood. She had next to nothing in her handbag, and I disposed of her body in the same manner as in the other cases.

Similarly, there was a case of a youngish man, about the autumn of the same year. He was aged about 35, about my own height and build, brownish hair, wavy, wearing a dark double-breasted suit, I believe blue. I met him at the 'Goat' public-house, High Street, Kensington, about 6 or 6.30 in the evening. I had seen him before in the 'Goat,' about a couple of months previously, and had had a drink with him.

On the present occasion we had a drink or two and a snack in the snack bar; I talked to him about pin-tables, and asked him to come down to the basement at 79 Gloucester Road which, on this occasion, I described as a workshop. He came with me and the same thing happened as before. He had no jewellery and no more than a pound in money.

The man I have mentioned called himself 'Max' and I should think he came from the Southern Counties.

Although still retaining the same clasical facade, the Onslow Court Hotel has now been renamed the Kensington Hotel.

By his own admission, Haigh met William McSwan *(left)* at the Goat Tavern public house *(right)* which still stands right opposite the entrance to Kensington Palace on Kensington High Street. McSwan had evaded service in the Armed Forces by registering as a conscientious objector in 1940 but then failing to attend for his medical examination. He acquired a criminal record in 1943-44 from various offences and although put on probation, the officer montioring his behaviour somehow lost track of him.

I had known this McSwan and his mother and father for some time, and on seeing his mother and father, explained that he had gone off to avoid his 'Call-up.' I wrote a number of letters in due course to his mother and father, purporting to come from him and posted in, I think, Glasgow and Edinburgh, explaining various details of the disposition of properties, which were to follow. In the following year, I took separately to the basement the father, Donald, and the mother, Amy, disposing of them in exactly the same way as the son. The files of the McSwans are at my hotel and will give details of the properties which I disposed of after their deaths. I have since got additional ration books by producing their identity cards in the usual way.

On September 9, 1944, Haigh took McSwan to his basement workshop at No. 79 Gloucester Road — the building with the white portico — right opposite Gloucester Road Tube Station where Countess Lubienska was to be fatally stabbed 13 years later (see page 302). Once in the basement, William was coshed and his body dissolved in sulphuric acid. Although Haigh gave the police the date of the subsequent murder of his parents as July 1946, it probably occurred during the first week of July 1945. Haigh said that because the father's corpse did not produce enough blood for him to drink, he killed the mother the same day. Travelling to Glasgow, he then visited a solicitor to take out a Power of Attorney having pretended he was William Donald McSwan. The forged document gave Haigh the ability to deal with McSwan's possessions and specified four freehold properties: 9 Grand Drive, Raynes Park; 104 Kenilworth Avenue, Wimbledon Park; 15 Wimborne Way, Beckenham; and 112 Churchfields Road, Beckenham. Although the first three belonged to W. D. McSwan, the fourth was in fact owned by the mother so Haigh forged a deed purporting to convey this property from the mother to the son, in consideration of £500. Having instructed solicitors in London to lodge the forged Power of Attorney, Haigh dealt with all the properties which enriched him to the extent of about £1,720. In addition, Haigh is known to have obtained, by means of forged transfers, £2,107 of gilt-edged securities held by the McSwan family, and to have profited from the sale of their furniture, household effects and personal belongings.

After Haigh was arrested, the basement became a focus of attention for crowds of people curious to see where the murders had taken place. If we accept Haigh's admission that he also killed an unnamed man and woman there, as well as William, Donald and Amy McSwan, we have a total of five victims for Gloucester Road. Haigh said that 'I had acid and sheet metal for pickling. I found a water butt on a disused site and took it on a cart. I put the body in the tub and poured acid on it. I did it with a bucket. I went to see McSwan's parents and told them he had gone away because of his call up.'

In the 1950s the basement was being used for the manufacture of waterproof coats but in December 1986 a planning application was granted for sealing the access, raising the patio by four steps, and installing a new shopfront for the café on the left. In 1994-96, the premises was re-numbered 77-79 but by 2009 changed to 77A. However, the adjacent Frances King School of English is now 77, which has neatly expunged the notorious No. 79 from the map although the basement still survives!

Left: **This was the doorway to the basement in 1949, since sealed up beneath the raised seating area** *(right).*

Police reported that Mr Albert C. Marshall, who was employed as manager by Messrs. Taylor Lovegrove & Co., estate agents, said that towards the end of August 1944, Haigh negotiated with him for the basement of 79 Gloucester Road, consisting of three rooms, wine cellar, coal cellar and a rear area with a way out at the rear of Stanhope Mews. A monthly tenancy for a minimum period of three months was agreed, £7 being the first month's rent payable in advance. Haigh said that the premises would not be used for any work which would in any way affect insurance premiums, but would be purely for experimental work on Government contract. Mr Marshall described the address as being 'in a terrace with shops on either side. It is a four storied building with basement, which is self-contained as stairs leading to the ground floor have been blocked up.' Mr Marshall said that at the time the ground floor of 79 Gloucester Road was occupied by Messrs. Taylor Lovegrove & Co., the first floor by the League of European Freedom and possibly the Whitehall News, and the second and third floors were occupied by a Mr Lacey, who lived there with his housekeeper, a Mrs. Gordon. It seems that the basement was a very secluded place and even unusual activities there would be unnoticed in the rest of the building. Mr Edward Masek, the manager of the London office and warehouse of Messrs. Canning & Co., Ltd., 77 St John Street, E.C.1. told police that on September 7, 1944, his firm received an order by telephone for one Winchester (6lbs) of muriatic [hydrochloric] acid and two carboys of sulphuric acid (20 gallons, 370lbs). This order was confirmed on September 7, by a letter signed 'J. G. Haigh' and an order, reference SB/C/1001, requesting that the acid was to be handed to the bearer. Today the basement is the downstairs eating area for the Patisserie restaurant!

At Crawley in Sussex, Haigh had the use of this storehouse in Leopold Road as an unpaid director of Hurstlea Products Ltd.

I met the Hendersons by answering an advertisement offering for sale their property at 22 Ladbroke Square. I did not purchase 22 Ladbroke Square. They sold it and moved to 16 Dawes Road, Fulham. This runs in a period from November 1947, to February 1948. In February 1948, the Hendersons were staying at Kingsgate Castle, Kent. I visited them there and went with them to Brighton, where they stayed at the Metropole. From here I took Dr. Henderson to Crawley and disposed of him in the storeroom at Leopold Road by shooting him in the head with his own revolver, which I had taken from his property at Dawes Road. I put him in a tank of acid as in the other cases.

This was in the morning and I went back to Brighton and brought up Mrs. Henderson on the pretext that her husband was ill. I shot her in the store-room and put her in another tank and disposed of her with acid. In each of the last four cases I had my glass of blood as before. In the case of Dr. Henderson, I removed his gold cigarette case, his gold pocket watch and chain and, from his wife, her wedding ring and diamond ring and disposed of all this to Bull's at Horsham for about £300. I paid their bill at the Hotel Metropole, collected their luggage and their red setter and took the luggage to Dawes Road. The dog I kept for a period at the Onslow Court Hotel and later at Gatwick Hall, until I had to send him to Professor Sorsby's Kennels in the country on account of his night blindness. By means of letters purporting to have come from the Hendersons, I kept the relatives quiet, by sending the letters to Mrs. Henderson's brother, Arnold Burlin, who lives in Manchester. His address is in the Index Book in my room. No. 16 Dawes Road, I acquired by forged deeds of transfer and sold it to the present owner, J. B. Clarke. The McSwan properties were also acquired in a similar way and disposed of and the particulars are in the file at the hotel.

Between the late summer and early autumn of last year (1948) I was down in Eastbourne, quite apart from the time when the car was stolen and found over the cliff. On the front, near the Mansion Hotel, I met, in the evening, about 8 p.m. a girl, who later told me her name was Mary. She was shorter than myself, black hair, she was not English— probably Welsh—wearing a white and green summer dress, white beach shoes, carrying a light coloured handbag.

Later the same evening we went to Hastings together, and had a meal at a café on the sea front in the old part of the town. I later took her back to Crawley in my car. We went to the shed at Leopold Road, where I hit her on the head with the cosh, tapped for blood, and put her in a tub, but left her there until the following morning. The tub was one of those I used for the Hendersons which probably explains why one of the tubs you found was almost eaten away.

The following morning, I returned to Crawley, where I pumped sulphuric acid into the tank containing the woman's body. I tipped the sludge out the following morning into the yard. This girl had little or no property, but I do remember a small bottle of scent (in her handbag) about which Inspector Mahon asked me the other morning and for which at the time I could not account.

The Eastbourne girl calling herself Mary said she did not live in Eastbourne, but whether she was there on holiday or for employment I would not know.

John George Haigh,
Statements, February, 1949

The building was demolished in the late 1990s and a new house built on the site of the yard in 1998.

For several years two elderly ladies, a Mrs. Constance Lane and a Mrs. Olive Durand-Deacon, had been living under the same roof in South Kensington at the Onslow Court Hotel. They had become close friends and, while they were in London, saw each other daily. One evening Mrs. Lane happened to notice that the table where her friend was accustomed to dine was unoccupied. The date was Friday, 18th February, 1949.

Next morning another resident, whom Mrs. Lane knew only as a nodding acquaintance, asked her if Mrs. Durand-Deacon was ill. He explained that Mrs. Durand-Deacon had arranged to accompany him to Sussex on the previous day, but that she had not kept the appointment to meet him. Mrs. Lane, mystified, went upstairs and had a word with the chambermaid. It appeared that Mrs. Durand- Deacon had been out all night and had not yet returned.

Mrs. Lane's anxiety was mounting and the following morning, when the same solicitous enquirer came to her breakfast table and again asked her if she had any news, she roundly replied that she intended to report her friend's disappearance to the police. The enquirer appeared to be pondering the remark. Not long after breakfast he resumed the conversation: in the lounge, he approached Mrs. Lane with the suggestion that he himself should drive her to the police station. Had Mrs. Lane known all she subsequently learned about her escort, she would scarcely have accepted his invitation as readily as she did. As it was, she arrived with him that Sunday afternoon at the Chelsea Police Station where they together reported that Mrs. Durand-Deacon had been missing since the afternoon of the preceding Friday.

Following the report, a police sergeant called, as a routine measure, at the Onslow Court Hotel to talk with those who knew Mrs. Durand-Deacon, and who might assist in tracing her. Presumably, because it was a woman who was reported missing, it was a woman police sergeant who performed the duty of instituting enquiries. Among those interviewed was the manageress of the hotel, who gave the sergeant an unfavourable account of the resident who had accompanied Mrs. Lane to the police station. A check was soon made and it was discovered from the Criminal Records Office at the Yard that the man in question, a Mr. John George

The next victims of Leopold Road. Apart from the unidentified girl from Eastbourne called Mary, Dr Archibald Henderson *(left)* and his wife Rosalie *(right)* met their deaths in the storehouse on February 13, 1948.

Haigh, who seemed so plausible, had more than once been convicted for crimes of dishonesty. Could it be that his greed or need for money had induced him to commit a yet more serious crime?

On Monday afternoon he was interviewed by two detective-inspectors at his hotel. 'I will tell you all about it,' he said, and proceeded to make a statement in which he professed to have no notion of Mrs. Durand-Deacon's whereabouts. Three days later, when the police again interviewed him at his hotel, he made a substantially similar statement.

Meanwhile the search was extended. A description and picture of the missing person was issued to the Press, and journalists flocked to the Onslow Court Hotel. They had many questions to ask Haigh, who glibly recounted the same story he had told Mrs. Lane and the police. Far from avoiding publicity, he gave a sort of mass Press conference to some of the leading crime reporters of the country. Haigh stressed his hope that Mrs. Durand-Deacon would be discovered safe and sound. 'I am just as anxious as you or anyone else is on that score,' he said with apparent sincerity.

But crime reporters are blunt and persistent men. Looking Haigh straight in the eye, one of them suddenly remarked: 'I think you ought to know, Mr. Haigh, there are rumours that you have a criminal record.' Thereafter, Haigh could have been left in no doubt that he was under suspicion but he did not end the interview or even protest at the disconcerting innuendo. 'Let us skip that,' he said with a wave of the arm. 'We are talking of Mrs. Durand-Deacon. Now . . .,' and he went on calmly with some fresh graphic observation about the missing widow and her personal characteristics.

Haigh occupied Room 404 at Onslow Court but as the Kensington Hotel has been extensively modified in recent years, one cannot absolutely guarantee that the present 404 is the one from where he ran his business. *Right:* However, the dining room has not been moved so it was here that Haigh targeted his next victim who sat at an adjacent table.

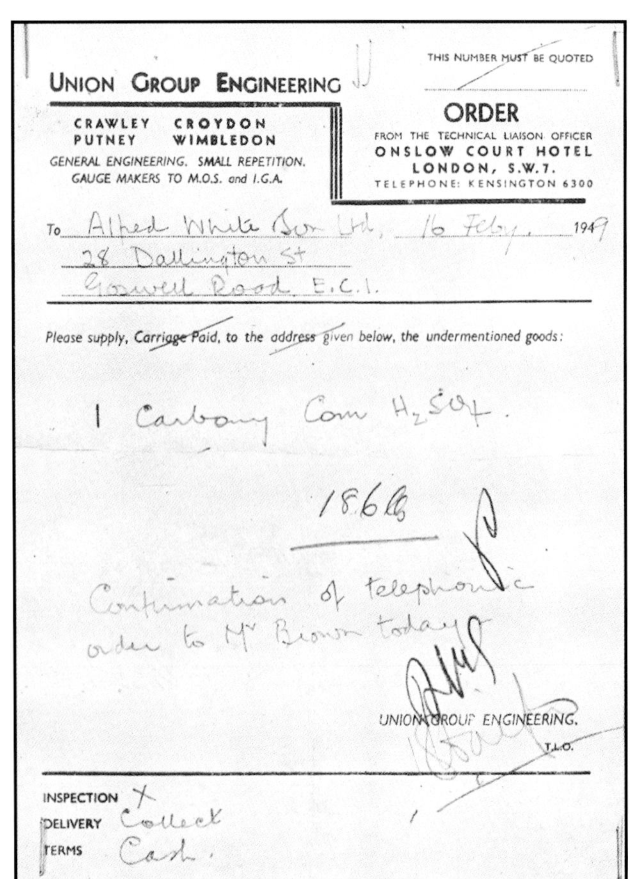

THIS NUMBER MUST BE QUOTED

UNION GROUP ENGINEERING

CRAWLEY CROYDON
PUTNEY WIMBLEDON
GENERAL ENGINEERING, SMALL REPETITION,
GAUGE MAKERS TO M.O.S. and I.G.A.

ORDER

FROM THE TECHNICAL LIAISON OFFICER
ONSLOW COURT HOTEL
LONDON, S.W.7.
TELEPHONE: KENSINGTON 6300

To Alfred White Son Ltd. 16 Feby. 1949
28 Dallington St
Goswell Road E.C.1.

Please supply, ~~Carriage Paid~~, to the ~~address given~~ below, the undermentioned goods:

1 Carboy Com H_2SO_4.

1866

Confirmation of telephonic order to Mr Brown today

UNION GROUP ENGINEERING.
T.L.O.

INSPECTION X
DELIVERY Collect
TERMS Cash.

Haigh must have already planned his next murder as he had already placed his order for another supply of sulphuric acid on February 16.

This was two days before Mrs Olive Henrietta Helen Olivia Robarts Durand-Deacon — who was a permanent resident in Room 115 — met her death at Crawley.

Already the West Sussex Constabulary were on the scent. Their assistance was enlisted, because Haigh, in his statements to the Chelsea Police, described himself as a director of Hurstlea Products Ltd. in Crawley. The representation he volunteered was no doubt calculated to give an impression of respectability. It proved to be not quite true, but it was a signpost to many a clue.

By 23rd February the police had interviewed Mr. Edward Jones, the managing director of Hurstlea Products Ltd. It transpired that Haigh sometimes used the storehouse of the firm, ostensibly for experimental work, and that he had recently told Mr. Jones he was engaged on 'a conversion job' there. The storehouse was a brick-built two-storey shed, situated in Giles Yard, which was surrounded by a six-foot high fence, flanking Leopold Road on the outskirts of Crawley. The firm used it for the purpose of housing steel and other surplus materials which could not conveniently be accommodated at the main business premises in West Street, Crawley. The storehouse was secured by mortice and padlock and, so far as Mr. Jones knew, Haigh still had the keys in his possession. To obtain entry, Detective-Sergeant Heslin, accompanied by Mr. Jones, forced the padlock with a steel bar on 26th February.

Inside were discovered certain articles which, at first sight, might have seemed to have been used for 'the conversion job' to which Haigh had alluded, but a revolver and various papers, including a receipt of a firm of cleaners in Reigate for a Persian lamb coat, were also found. The coat was collected the next day from Reigate by the police and soon identified as Mrs. Durand-Deacon's. Two

Photographed by police, this is the interior of the storehouse in the yard at Crawley where Mrs Durand-Deacon was shot.

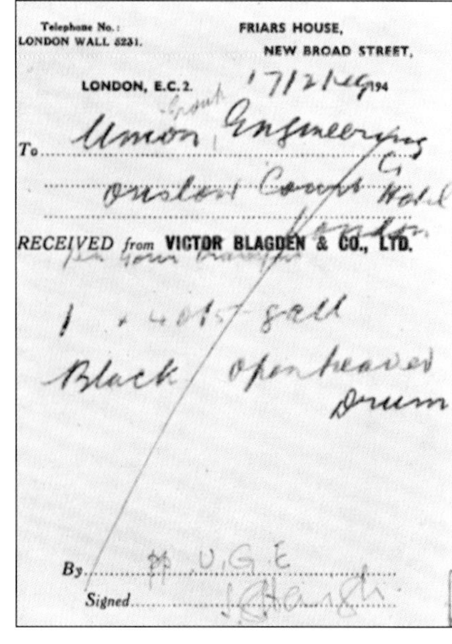

Telephone No.: LONDON WALL 8231.

FRIARS HOUSE,
NEW BROAD STREET,
LONDON, E.C.2. 17/2 Feb 194

To Union Group Engineering Co.
Onslow Court Hotel
London

RECEIVED from VICTOR BLAGDEN & CO., LTD.
per your transport

1 × 40/45 gall
Black / openheaded
Drum

By pp U.G.E.
Signed J Haigh

The carboys of acid can be seen on the left. Haigh had already received delivery of a 40-gallon oil drum on the 17th.

Having stuffed her body in the drum, Haigh was in need of sustenance so he drove to the centre of town for a cup of tea in Ye Olde Ancient Prior's Restaurant, the timbered building on the right.

days later, to crown suspicions, came the news that, on the very day after Mrs. Durand-Deacon had disappeared, her jewellery had been brought by Haigh to Bull's jewellery shop in Horsham for valuation and sale.

Divisional Detective-Inspector Shelley Symes thereupon advised Detective-Inspector Albert Webb by telephone to bring Haigh without delay to the Chelsea Police Station. Consequently, at 4.15 p.m. outside the Onslow Court Hotel, Haigh was waylaid in his car and requested by Inspector Webb to come with him at once. 'Certainly,' replied Haigh obligingly, 'I will do anything to help you, as you know.'

In the police station, where eight days previously he had reported Mrs. Durand-Deacon missing, Haigh continued to affect a detached air. Sitting in an easy chair in the office of the Divisional Detective-Inspector, he nonchalantly smoked, read newspapers and dozed. At 6 p.m. he was given a cup of tea, but no mention was yet made of the nature of the enquiry for which he was required. So prompt had his arrival at the Station been, that two or three hours elapsed before the police were ready to question him.

Although it has changed its name, one can still enjoy a cuppa in the same restaurant, now called Ask.

Returning to Leopold Road, Haigh filled the drum with acid and then went back to the square at Crawley for dinner at the George pub *(right).*

At 7.30 p.m. the fateful interview started, in the course of which Haigh's miscalculated manoeuvres could scarcely have done more than they did to queer any line of defence open to him. His answers to the questions, which were very properly put to him by the police, started with a damning lie about his visits to Horsham. He then shifted his ground. Saying he saw the police knew what they were talking about, he admitted that the Persian lamb coat, which had been recovered from the cleaners in Reigate, was Mrs. Durand-Deacon's, and that he had sold her jewellery in Horsham. Both admissions contradicted his previous explanations.

Then when asked how he had come by the property and where the missing person was, he invented the excuse that it was all a long story of blackmail. Again he prevaricated, asking how he stood about implicating others. 'What you have to say is entirely a matter for you,' said Inspector Symes, who at that point left the room for ten minutes.

I have already made some statements to you about the disappearance of Mrs. Durand-Deacon. I have been worried about the matter and fenced about it, in the hope that you would not find out about it. The truth is, however, that we left the hotel together and went to Crawley together in my car. She was inveigled into going to Crawley by me in view of her interest in artificial fingernails.

Having taken her into the store-room at Leopold Road, I shot her in the back of the head while she was examining some paper for use as fingernails. Then I went out to the car and fetched in a drinking glass and made an incision, I think with a penknife, in the side of her throat, and collected a glass of blood, which I then drank.

Following that, I removed the coat she was wearing, a Persian lamb, and the jewellery, rings, necklace, earrings and cruciform, and put her in a forty-five gallon tank. I then filled the tank up with sulphuric acid, by means of a stirrup pump, from a carboy. I then left it to react. I should have said that in between having her in the tank and pumping in the acid, I went round to the Ancient Prior's for a cup of tea. Having left the tank to react, I brought the jewellery and revolver into the car and left the coat on the bench. I went to the 'George' for dinner and I remember I was late, about nineish. I then came back to town, and returned to the hotel about half-past ten. I put the revolver back into the square hat box.

The following morning I had breakfast, and, as I have already said, discussed the disappearance of Mrs. Durand-Deacon with the waitress and Mrs. Lane. I eventually went back to Crawley, via Putney, where I sold her watch, en route, at a jeweller's shop in the High Street for ten pounds. I look this watch from her at the same time as the other jewellery.

At Crawley I called in to see how the reaction in the tank had gone on. It was not satisfactorily completed so I went on to Horsham, having picked up the coat and put it in the back of the car. I called at Bull's, the jewellers, for a valuation of the jewellery, but Mr. Bull was not in. I returned to town, and on the way dropped in the coat at the 'Cottage Cleaners' at Reigate.

On Monday, I returned to Crawley to find the reaction almost complete, but a piece of fat and bone was still floating on the sludge. I emptied off the sludge with a bucket and tipped it on the ground opposite the shed, and pumped a further quantity of acid into the tank to decompose the remaining fat and bone. I then left that to work until the following day. From there I went to Horsham again and had the jewellery valued, ostensibly for probate. It was valued at just over £130. I called back at the West Street factory and eventually returned to town.

I returned to Horsham on Tuesday and sold the jewellery for what was offered, at a purchase price of £100. Unfortunately the jewellers had not got that amount of money and could only give me £60. I called back for the £40 the next day. I returned to Crawley and found decomposition complete and emptied the tank off. I would add that on the Monday I found that the only thing which the acid had not attacked was the plastic handbag, and I tipped this out with the sludge. On the Tuesday when I completely emptied the tank, I left it outside in the yard.

STATEMENT OF JOHN GEORGE HAIGH, FEBRUARY 28, 1949

Left: **Reigate High Street. Haigh took the Persian lambswool coat to Cottage Cleaners at No. 78-80, but by the time this photo was taken in 1965 the shop (arrowed) had been demolished.** *Right:* **Today it is the Nationwide Building Society.**

On March 2 — the day Haigh was charged with murder — police began their investigation of the yard which has already attracted a crowd of onlookers. The following day the *Daily Mirror* appeared with a sensational headline: 'Vampire Horror in London, S.W.7.' with a follow-up story two days later headed: 'Vampire — a man held'. As Haigh had now been charged, the matter was sub judice and the article could well have seriously prejudiced his trial. Consequently the *Mirror* was taken to court and fined £10,000 and its editor, Silvester Bolam, given a three-month prison sentence.

Alone with Inspector Webb, Haigh turned to him as man to man and asked frankly what were the chances of anyone being released from the criminal lunatic asylum at Broadmoor. As a matter of fact, the chances were about 150 to 1 against being released; but it was an ill-judged question, which might have told heavily against Haigh at his trial, appearing as it did to betray an ulterior motive for what he was about to add. The Inspector correctly declined to discuss the matter at all.

'Well,' continued Haigh, 'if I told you the truth, you would not believe me; it sounds too fantastic for belief.' Presumably in the hope of a comfortable sojourn at Broadmoor, he now decided to make a quite astonishing admission. A second time that evening he was cautioned that he need say nothing, but out came the bombshell.

'I will tell you all about it,' he said. 'Mrs. Durand- Deacon no longer exists. She has disappeared completely and no trace of her can ever be found again. I have destroyed her with acid. You will find the sludge which remains at Leopold Road. Every trace has gone.' An equally revealing afterthought followed: 'How can you prove murder if there is no body?'

No corpse, no conviction. It was a simple maxim and a naive interpretation of the law as to murder. Haigh seems to have clung to the idea tenaciously. It is said to have been the topic of a discussion he had had with his fellow-prisoners when he was serving one of his earlier sentences: after various methods of disposing of the remains of a victim had been discussed, Haigh aired his pet theory that murder could not be proved without a corpse 'because, you see,' he explained, 'there would then be no *corpus delicti*.' His companions chuckled and Haigh was thereafter known in that prison by the nickname of 'Old Corpus Delicti.' The story rings true.

It was Haigh's delight to pose as a cleverjack; but his little learning was a dangerous thing and led him astray more than once. So it had on this occasion.

As soon as Haigh had told Inspector Webb of Mrs. Durand-Deacon's fate, Superintendent Barratt, who was in charge of the

Then . . . and now. The drainpipe on No. 6 on the right is the linking clue.

The police photographs were taken by Detective Sergeant George Brown. These show the rubbish and sludge discovered in the yard and oil drums, one eaten away by acid.

enquiry, and Inspector Symes were called into the room. Haigh was again cautioned and he then dictated to Inspector Symes a statement which, apart from an interval for tea and bread and cheese, took two and a half hours to reduce to writing. In it Haigh announced for the first time that he had shot Mrs. Durand-Deacon. In considerable detail he described not only the circumstances of the crime, but the pecuniary profit of £111, 10s. it had brought him. He went further and, with reference to various documents, bearing the names of McSwan and Henderson, which had been found, he stated that he had killed the five people concerned and on each occasion drunk their blood, as in the case of Mrs. Durand-Deacon.

Haigh did not finish the statement until the small hours of the morning of 1st March. He was thereafter detained in custody where he earned the reputation of being a well-behaved and almost elegant guest. On 2nd March Haigh was taken from London to Horsham Police Station where he was charged by Detective-Superintendent Percy Eagle with the murder of Mrs. Durand-Deacon. He was cautioned and said, 'I have nothing to say.'

On 1st March, the day when Haigh, in the small hours of the morning at the Chelsea Police Station, completed the dramatic statement in which he claimed that no trace of Mrs. Durand-Deacon could ever be found, the Chief Constable of the West Sussex Constabulary applied to New Scotland Yard for the assistance of a chief-inspector and a pathologist.

Chief-Inspector Mahon consequently assumed charge of the investigations and went with Dr. Keith Simpson and Inspector Symes to Giles Yard, the site of the storehouse which Sergeant Patrick Heslin and Mr. Jones had entered three days before.

On the same day he was brought before the Horsham Magistrates' Court on the charge. Local interest in the case was ablaze, and, at the doors of the court, police reinforcements were required to restrain a surge of over two hundred people. Only formal evidence of arrest was given that day and Haigh was remanded in custody. On 4th March, at Haigh's own request, Inspector Webb visited him in Lewes Prison. First satisfying himself that the police were convinced of the truth of his long statement of 28th February, Haigh told the Inspector he considered it 'timely' to mention three other people, a woman from Hammersmith, a youth from Kensington and a girl from Eastbourne, who, he said, completed the list of his victims, totalling nine in all. The statement was taken down and signed by Haigh in the presence of witnesses, but no charge of murdering anyone other than Mrs. Durand-Deacon was ever made against him.

The case of the 'Acid Bath Murder,' as it came to be known, captivated the imagination. All the ingredients of a horrifying mystery were being unearthed, and, to the popular mind, the case was a *cause célèbre* of the first order. In its essentials, the capital charge, formulated against Haigh, was not difficult to appreciate. A financially embarrassed man of apparent charm had ingratiated himself with a widow of some wealth, inveigled her into a death trap, dissolved her body in sulphuric acid and reported her to the police as a missing person. Then, when cornered, the accused heaped horror upon horror, fully describing the crime without any trace of remorse and coolly claiming to have killed eight other human beings and to have drunk their blood.

There was nothing exceptional about a murder for money; most murders are done for money. Nor had Haigh shown particular originality in his method of disposing of his victim's remains. For when Haigh was but a choir-boy in Wakefield, Georges Sarret in France was buying a bath and 100 litres of sulphuric acid, which he thought 'might come in useful sometime'; Sarret's crime conformed to precisely the same pattern as Haigh's: the French acid bath murderer successively shot two people on 19th August, 1925, unquestionably for gain, and decomposed their corpses in an acid bath. The preliminary enquiry in the French case, however, lasted two years, instead of one month. Sarret was tried at Aix-en-Provence in October 1933 and found guilty of the double murder and of another one in addition. There were no extenuating circumstances and therefore, in accordance with the Code Napoléon, he was ordered to be guillotined in public. Haigh may have read of the case and borrowed the Frenchman's ideas; at any rate, Haigh was not the first known acid bath murderer.

Yet, besides hitting the headlines, the case of Haigh possessed features of more durable interest, not confined to the legal profession but spreading to Fleet Street, Scotland Yard and Harley Street.

First, before the trial but not unconnected with it, a national newspaper fell foul of the law. On 4th March, 1949, the *Daily Mirror* published matter relating to a person on a criminal charge, which prompted Haigh's counsel to move in the King's Bench Divisional Court for Writs of Attachment and the contempt of Court was ultimately penalised on an unprecedented scale.

Secondly, unusual difficulties confronted those engaged on the work of detecting the murder. In the previous fifty years, only three other murders in Britain were believed to have presented comparable problems of identifying the remains of the victim.

Thirdly, the case of Haigh evoked a judicial pronouncement on the proper 'venue' of the trial; the case was tried before a great criminal judge, assisted by eminent counsel; and it possibly provided a legal precedent of the recognition of the anomaly of paranoia as a 'mental disease'.

Finally, the mental condition of Haigh was of unusual psychological interest. The notoriety of his trial was justified, not so much by the number he claimed to have killed or by the method he adopted to conceal his crimes, as by his extraordinary claim to have drunk his victims' blood. At the time no other reported case was traceable to suggest that a murderer drank, or claimed to have drunk the blood of the murdered, as an end in itself, unassociated with any sexual perversion.

Lord Dunboyne,
The Trial of John George Haigh, 1953

Chief Inspector Guy Mahon took charge of the case within a few hours of Haigh's confession, and after a few more hours Jean Scott-Dunn, my secretary, and I were being driven in a police car to Leopold Road, Crawley. I did not have any great hope of finding much beyond residual acid sludge but on the way down I pondered on what parts of the body might conceivably have escaped destruction.

The ground outside the storeroom was rough with many small pebbles lying on the earth. Almost immediately, and I suppose rather impressively, I picked one up and examined it through a lens. It was about the size of a cherry and looked very much like the other stones, except that it had polished facets.

'I think that's a gallstone,' I said to Mahon.

Later, when laboratory tests had proved it to be a human gallstone (other mammals also get them), a police officer remarked to me that it was a lucky find.

'I was looking for it,' I told him. Women of Mrs Durand-Deacon's age and habits — 69 and fairly plump — are prone to gallstones which are covered with a fatty substance that would resist the dissolving action of sulphuric acid.

Almost immediately after this first find I made a second. Embedded in a thick, charred, greasy substance I saw several masses of eroded bone. When X-rayed, the largest of these proved to be the greater part of a left foot.

These were exciting discoveries and I was confident that more interesting things might be found in the sludge. But not there. Covering an area of six feet by four feet, and three or four inches deep, this greasy granular mass needed patient sifting and inspection in a laboratory. I asked Mahon to have it all taken to the Metropolitan Police Laboratory, and at once he had his men lifting and packing it into wooden boxes.

Near the sludge we saw the green painted steel drum in which the body had been digested. I looked inside and saw a hairpin stuck in the grease at the bottom.

Inside the storeroom we saw three ten-gallon carboys, two of them partly filled with concentrated sulphuric acid, the third almost empty; also two stirrup pumps, a rubber apron and rubber gloves, and a gas mask. The walls were whitewashed, but I saw there was a patch of finely scattered red spots over the bench. Why should there be blood on that part of the wall? Well, Haigh said he had shot Mrs Durand-Deacon when she was looking at his artificial finger nails. If they were on the bench she would be standing in front of it and looking down, and if he had shot her in the back of the neck her blood could very well have spattered on the wall in just that place. I had the stains photographed and then carefully detached from the plaster. Later, in the laboratory, a precipitin test proved they were human blood.

I spent much of the next three days with Dr Holden and Superintendent Cuthbert in the laboratory at Scotland Yard, where we had the dirty, yellow, greasy, partly charred mass tipped out of the boxes and spread out over steel trays. From it we eventually extracted a mass of about 28lbs of a yellow greasy substance that looked like 'melted' body fat; and when it was examined chemically it was proved to consist of animal fat. But there were other, much more interesting items in the sludge. I picked out two more human gallstones and a number of fragments of eroded bone, eighteen pieces in all. Later, after rigorous cleaning and detailed examination, using X-rays and the microscope, I was able to place eleven of them in the human anatomy. There was nothing about them to suggest they had come from more than one body. Osteoarthritis in certain joints and the fragile state of the uneroded bony tissues were evidence of late adult age. A groove in part of a pelvic (hip-girdle) bone showed it was female, and the sex was confirmed by a handle of a red plastic handbag and the metal cap of a lipstick case. Superintendent Cuthbert made a plaster cast of the piece of left foot I had found and it fitted the dead woman's left shoe. Finally, and most important, we found intact full upper and lower dentures.

So out of the sludge we had reconstructed the body of a person, an elderly woman with gallstones, a little arthritic, with false teeth, a left foot that fitted a particular shoe, carrying a red plastic handbag with a lipstick container in it, and I thought from the amount of body fat recovered that she was probably stoutly built. So much for Haigh's claim that every trace had gone.

Identity was another matter, and once again it was the teeth that did it. 'I could describe them from my notes before I saw them,' Miss Helen Mayo, Mrs Durand-Deacon's dentist, said at Haigh's trial. She had supplied the dentures about a year and a half earlier, and, luckily for us, Mrs Durand-Deacon had been a troublesome patient with inordinate gum shrinkage requiring many visits to Miss Mayo's surgery and, the dentist said, 'an exceptional amount of build-up and padding'. The dentures from the sludge were 'beyond any doubt,' Miss Mayo said firmly, the dentures she had fitted for Mrs Durand-Deacon in September 1947.

Haigh's labours had been in vain. The remains of Mrs Durand-Deacon were identified as surely as if her body had never been given an acid bath.

Dr Keith Simpson and his secretary — later his wife — Jean Scott-Dunn begin sifting through the debris.

If Haigh thought he had carried out a perfect murder in disposing of the body, he was sadly mistaken. Apart from just discarding Mrs Durand-Deacon's plastic handbag in the yard, some 475lbs of grease and earth were transported to New Scotland Yard for examination. Spread into three metal trays, over the next three days 18 fragments of bone were recovered including part of a left foot; three gallstones, intact upper and lower dentures, and 28lbs of melted body fat, a phial of which is now preserved in Guy's Hospital Medical Museum together with the gallstones.

By now the *Mirror* articles had raised the public interest to fever pitch. Here Haigh leaves the Magistrates' Court in Horsham after the first committal hearing on April 1. He was attired in a green Lovat suit and seemed to relish the limelight of infamy, being wholly oblivious to the gravity of his position. At one stage he was highly amused when the prosecution counsel was stung on the hand by a remnant of acid when he handled the stirrup pump presented as Exhibit 40.

Haigh, meanwhile, appeared to be going all out for Broadmoor. After the six murders to which he had already confessed he added three more, perhaps thinking the more the merrier for police inquiries showed they were probably fictitious. He made much of the fact that he had drunk his victims' blood (and his own urine), and to the nine doctors who examined his mental condition before his trial he displayed, in the words of one of them, Dr Henry Yellowlees, a paranoid constitution; although the other eight, and three more who examined him after his trial, had no doubt that he was shamming insanity.

Meanwhile reports of Haigh's confessions had leaked out into Fleet Street, and the editor of the *Daily Mirror*, Silvester Bolam, decided to publish and take the consequences, although he may have miscalculated them. Describing Haigh as the 'Vampire Killer,' although without giving his name, the *Mirror* entertained its readers with vivid accounts of the killing and blood-drinking and 'acid cremations' of the McSwanns and the Hendersons. The editor was charged with contempt of court, and the Lord Chief Justice and two other judges heard the case. Silvester Bolam apologised for his grave error of judgment. 'It is not an error of judgment,' said the Lord Chief Justice, Lord Goddard. 'It is a question of policy.' He ordered the proprietors of the newspaper to be brought before the court. 'Let the directors beware,' he warned. 'If they, for the purpose of increasing the circulation of their paper, should ever again venture to publish such matter as this, the directors themselves may find that the arm of this court is long enough to reach them individually.' The *Daily Mirror* was fined £10,000 and ordered to pay costs, and Silvester Bolam was sentenced to three months in Brixton Prison.

'It isn't everybody who can create more sensation than a film star,' Haigh wrote to his parents: 'Only Princess Margaret or Mr Churchill could command such interest'.

It was indeed a celebrated trial, with the Attorney General himself, Sir Hartley Shawcross, leading for the Crown, and a future Lord Chancellor, Sir David Maxwell Fyfe (later Lord Kilmuir), conducting the defence. ('I'm very glad to see that we have got old Maxy,' Haigh wrote from prison. 'He's no fool.') The judge was Sir Travers Humphreys, 81 years old and known for his inhospitality to any psychiatrist who ventured to appear as an expert witness in his court.

Rex v Haigh was held at the Lewes Assize Court and it was packed inside and besieged outside on 18th July when the case for the prosecution began. It ended the same day, after 33 witnesses were called, because only four were cross-examined. Maxwell Fyfe had no questions for me, and none for Helen Mayo either. As a result there was still time for him, before we went home, to make his opening speech for the defence. He said he was going to call only one witness, Dr Yellowlees, and would ask the jury for a verdict of guilty but insane.

There was, of course, a perfectly rational explanation for all Haigh's murders, including the one for which he was tried. Murder was his business. His profit from killing the McSwanns was more than £4,000, and he had gained perhaps twice as much by wiping out the Hendersons. He had no such expectations from Mrs Durand- Deacon, but he was in debt and would get at least a breathing space with the proceeds of her jewellery (£100) and the Persian lamb coat (worth about £50).

Although it is usual for a trial to take place in the county where the crime has been committed, in this case application was made in Horsham for it to be held at the Old Bailey in London.

However, following legal arguments, the judge ruled that Haigh should be tried by a Sussex jury. Here he is driven from Lewes prison for his appearance at the Assize Court.

The Crown had its own expert witnesses in court, ready to refute Yellowlees, but no refutation was needed. The jury took only 18 minutes to make up its mind that Haigh was guilty and sane, and he was hanged in Wandsworth Prison.

The case had aroused a lot of interest in medical and scientific circles, and considerable doubt had been expressed as to the possibility of completely destroying a body with sulphuric acid. Wouldn't the stouter bones, such as the pelvis and femur, resist destruction? Dr Turfitt, Dr Holden's deputy at the Metropolitan Police Laboratory, performed a number of experiments to clear up the matter. He found that an amputated human foot dissolved completely in four hours, but a fresh leg-bone (of a sheep), stripped of its flesh, took four days. The important factor was the heat generated by the interaction of acid and the water present in a fully hydrated body. The bones all dissolved but the fat was resistant even to hot acid. It was lucky for us that Mrs Durand- Deacon was stout for the preservation of our exhibits was due to the protective action of a film of fat.

But Haigh was too impatient. Another experiment showed that the acrylic resin of which the dentures were made would have disintegrated completely if they had been left immersed for three weeks. Even without longer immersion in the tank, these and other exhibits would have continued to disintegrate in the sludge, which was still strongly acid when we examined it.

Professor Keith Simpson,
Forty Years of Murder, 1978

The tumultuous scene outside Lewes Assizes on July 18, 1949. The following day Haigh was sentenced to death, the jury requiring only 15 minutes to find him guilty. His plea of insanity was rejected as the jury accepted the prosecution argument that he was a ruthless killer who murdered for financial gain. Haigh was executed at Wandsworth on August 10 by Albert Pierrepoint, assisted by Harry Kirk. (The files on his other eight murders were now simply treated as having been cleared up.)

Left: **Miss Elisia Robbie, the manageress of the Onslow Court Hotel, with her book-keeper, Mrs Annie Kirkwood, and Mrs Constance Lane, the long-time friend of Mrs Durand-Deacon and who had first raised the alarm over her disappearance.**

Right: **When the *After the Battle* team visited Lewes in June 2011, a gaggle of photographers were waiting outside what is now the Crown Court for the outcome of the trial of a modern-day serial con artist!**

October 4, 1949 – Donald Hume: 'I Got Away With Murder'

For many years before the Second World War, Warren Street was one of the sights of London. It was not quite comparable with Petticoat Lane or Club Row in the East End, where the traders were more exotic and the goods bought, sold and exchanged more exciting. Warren Street was a cut above these tumultuous bazaars. The cars they dealt in there were not exactly junk, though many unwary buyers would rue the day they ventured into the area with a pocketful of cash. The origin of many of the cars was suspect. But the glib, well-dressed men who thronged the streets and whose duty, so they averred, was to be the benefactors of the car-hungry public, gave the environment an air of prosperity. There might be receivers of stolen cars among them, or ringers and men who knew how to turn a hire purchase agreement inside out, but they were in a minority. Only those in the know, like the astute young detectives from Tottenham Court Road Police Station, knew that all was not as it seemed to be in Warren Street.

Francis Camps, Robert Jackson, 1975

Like most streets there are two sides to Warren Street, London, W.1, but in this case the sunnyside and the shadyside refer to human behaviour, not the position of the sun. For Warren Street is one of the oldest street car-markets in Britain, and though it can claim a long and strictly moral trading history, it has also to face the fact that it is the northernmost boundary of Soho. So because cars are scarce and expensive, it attracts a fair amount of gutter garbage from the hinterland. Lately a man called Stanley Setty was a trader there, and he was found dead and limbless.

I think we got the split personality of this street neatly focused in the first five minutes. We had paused at a street corner which we were told later in a colloquial fashion, is now called 'Setty Corner' because that is where Mr. Setty used to draw up in highly-polished cars and be pestered by small fry who had not the price of a bycicle-bell on them but knew he was about to buy a Rolls-Bentley. Because we were strangers in that street and had a naive look — as of one who would not know a cracked cylinder if we saw it — a man came up to talk to us. He wore an over-tailored coat and a scarf with horses' heads on it but to be completely fair there was a collar underneath.

'Looking for a car?' No. Then perhaps one to sell? Hewitt described his own car and was offered £275 cash for it.

A few minutes later we kept an appointment with Mr Keith Clayton who has a showroom with cars in it, a set of audited accounts, Income Tax receipts, an office and a staff of motor mechanics. It took him no time to establish to us that there were honest traders in the street, for our photographer asked Mr Clayton *his* price for the car. It was £375.

Hilde Marchant, Picture Post, November 1949

Top: **November 1949 — kerbside car dealers loiter in Warren Street, off Tottenham Court Road in the West End of London. This was a well known venue for selling cars in the early post-war years.** *Above:* **We were thrilled to find the old café still standing on 'Setty Corner', even if it had the sad appearance of having served its last customer.**

A number of five-pound notes known to have been in the possession of Stanley Setty at the time of his disappearance have been discovered. Detectives working on the case have traced them to Southend, where several are believed to have been passed. The detectives are now trying to trace who used them and when they were passed.

Supt. Colin MacDougall of Scotland Yard, working with Supt. Totterdell, head of Essex C.I.D., today investigating this latest discovery has also visited a club in Southend known to have been used by men engaged in illicit car deals. Stanley Setty, 44-year-old kerbside car dealer and victim of the murder, was known at the club. Recently Essex C.I.D. men investigating a 'red into white' petrol racket broke into a garage at Little Horkesley, near Colchester, and discovered false registration books and car number plates. Their investigation then led them to the same club in the Southend area, where the murder investigations led them today.

Chief-Inspector S. Glander, head of J Division C.I.D., who with a squad of officers has recently been investigating a large-scale car racket, went to Scotland Yard today with information bearing directly on the Stanley Setty murder. His inquiries indicate that Setty was one of the hitherto unsuspected chiefs of two or three gangs who specialised in stealing new cars, changing their identification, and selling them at vast profits.

Witnesses seen by this squad since the disappearance of Setty on October 4 often mentioned his name when they spoke of illicit car deals they knew something about.

Now, however, these witnesses are terrified to speak because of threats that members of the gang have made since Setty's torso was discovered on the desolate Dengie Flats by chance on Friday.

It is also now regarded as certain in the Yard that he was tortured by members of a rival gang who were either jealous of the power he wielded or who were trying to extract from him some secret about the car-gang operations which he alone knew.

Setty, victim of the Marsh murder, was kept a prisoner — perhaps in a lonely barn or rented garage — for at least four days before he was stabbed to death and his body dismembered.

This vital fact was established during the night when the post-mortem examination, which has taken three days, was completed.

Today, senior detectives are to make a yard-by-yard search of the inlets and creeks on the desolate Dengie Flats.

Evening News Report, October 25, 1949

Stanley Setty was one of the main car dealers who frequented the street, pictured here with a lady friend sometime in the 1940s.

Left: **In June 1958, just after he had been freed from eight years imprisonment for being an accessory to the murder of Setty, the *Sunday Pictorial* took Donald Hume back to Warren Street to retrace his movements back in 1949.** *Right:* **Fast forward to June 2011, Rob Green of *After the Battle* re-enacts the scene in front of the former Fitzroy Café.**

Left: **So the story goes, Hume first spotted his dog — half-Alsation, half-Husky — being walked by a lady in the street. The animal came up to him, wagging its tail and licking his hand. Thinking what a wonderful pal the dog would make, he asked the lady there and then if she would sell him. We are told that she was taken aback but when Hume convinced her that he had been wanting a dog just like hers, and that he could give it a good home, she agreed. One pound changed hands and the dog named Tony was his. In 1947, Hume met Cynthia** ***(right)*** **in the 'M' Club in Welbeck Street. Following a pre-wedding Continental motoring holiday, the couple married at Hendon Registry Office in September 1948, but Hume said later that 'I wanted to get back quickly to be with my dog Tony'. In fact he said, 'Tony meant more to me than my wife or anyone else in the world.'**

One afternoon in September 1949, Donald Hume, accompanied by his inseparable dog Tony, called at Stanley Setty's garage. While Hume and Setty talked the dog sniffed round the familiar premises and approached a Ford Pilot saloon that was standing in a corner, wet from respraying. Suddenly, performing a favourite and well-tried trick of his with cars, Tony sprang in through the window. Unluckily as he did so his scrabbling claws scratched the fresh paintwork, leaving a noticeable mark on the car's side. Setty saw it and turned livid with rage. Using an unprintable epithet he exploded into abuse. 'Look what your blasted dog has done!' he screamed at Hume.

Hume was startled. He had never seen Setty quite so beside himself. With a mumbled apology he reproved the dog and turned away. A moment later he heard Tony yelp and looked round to see Setty delivering a vicious kick at him.

White with suppressed anger, Hume called to Tony and patted him. He said little to Setty, but the venomous look in his eyes told the car dealer clearly what he was thinking. And soon afterwards he drove off from the garage, still raging inwardly. 'It was the worst thing he could possibly have done,' recorded Hume later. 'Tony meant more to me than my wife or anyone else in the world. Nobody could do that to me and expect to get away with it,' he said.

Left: **Setty lived in an expensive second-floor flat in Maitland Court, a large apartment block on the corner of Lancaster and Gloucester Terraces overlooking Hyde Park.**

Right: **His business premises were at No. 20 Cambridge Terrace Mews facing Regent's Park (quite close to where Gladys Hanrahan had been found murdered in 1947 — see page 6).**

Left: **In September 1949, Hume was living in Finchley Road in north London where he occupied the second and third floors of No. 620 — above the greengrocer's shop on the left. The living accommodation was on the second floor with the bedroom overlooking the main road on the top floor and a nursery at the rear for Cynthia and their baby daughter Allison.** *Right:* **The exterior remains virtually unchanged apart from the different commercial use of the shops.**

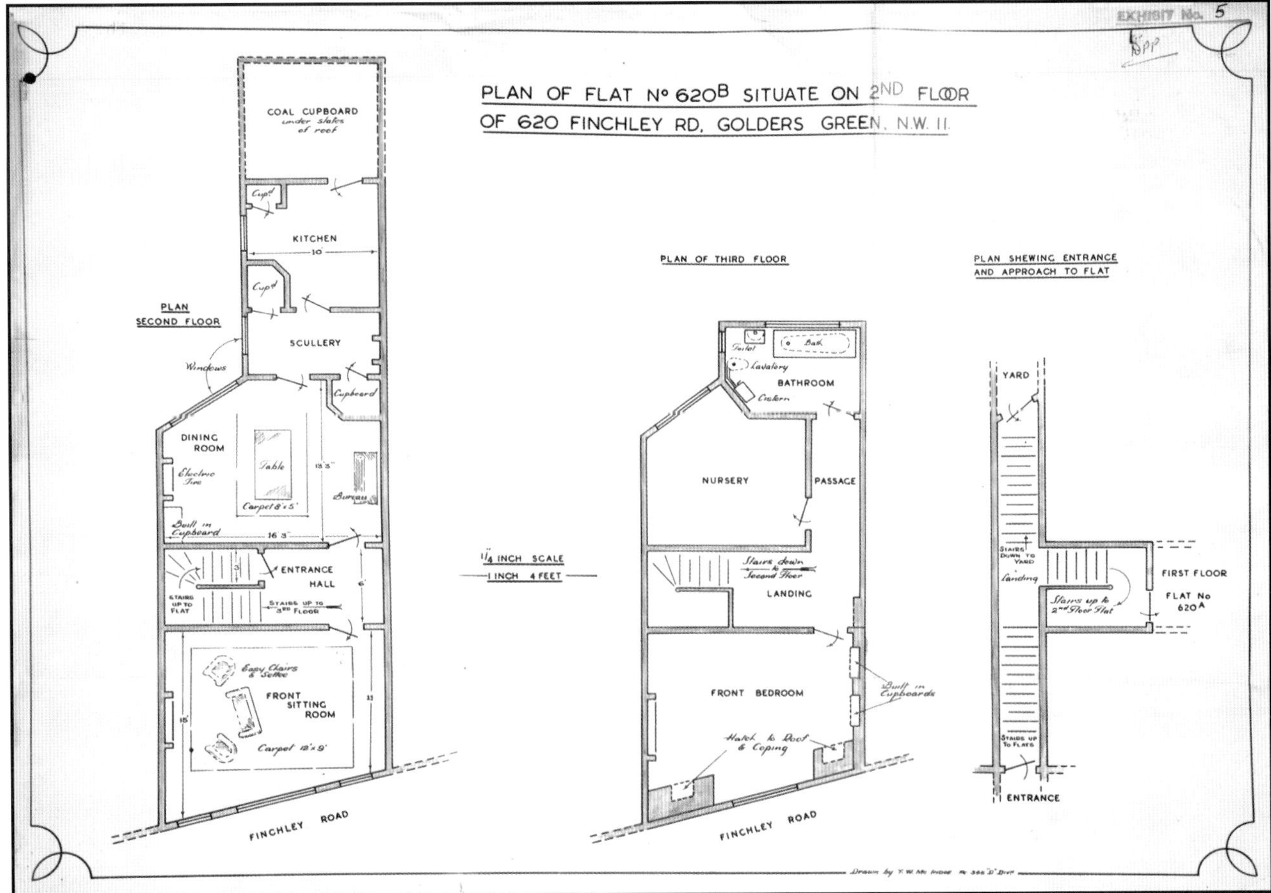

The police plan of No. 620B presented at Hume's trial as Exhibit No. 5.

It has never been reliably explained how Setty gained entry to the flat. Possibly the front door was not latched properly when Cynthia returned from walking her daughter that afternoon. She normally returned by six o'clock for the evening feed and Setty arrived some time before 7.30 p.m. And, of course, there were no electric locks on front doors as there are today.

Thus did the brittle veneer of Hume's friendliness for Setty suddenly crack, to give way to a seething hatred — and all on account of what to most men would have been an action trivial enough to be forgotten in ten minutes. As Hume fondled his unconcerned Tony at home that evening, his anger against Setty welled up anew; and in the ensuing days he brooded over the enormity of the car dealer's offence with a stubborn fury. When Hume said that 'From that moment my relations with Setty deteriorated' he was probably putting it mildly.

He continued to meet and do business with the car dealer, but his old hail-fellow-well-met attitude was replaced by a sour and sullen reserve. As far as he was concerned, their facile intimacy as fellow-racketeers was a thing of the past.

Throughout September the situation built up with growing tenseness, until the fatal evening early in October when Setty, misreading the danger signals once too often, met the full impact of Hume's stored-up fury.

Tuesday, 4 October, was a normal day of business for Stanley Setty. In the morning he was in Warren Street offering for sale an almost new Wolseley Twelve saloon, which he sold after lunch to another dealer for £1,000. The dealer gave him a cheque for this and Setty, explaining that he needed cash in order to buy a Jaguar in which he was interested, arranged for a friend to cash the cheque at a nearby bank for 200 £5 notes, which he pocketed.

Between five and half past he drove off from Warren Street in his cream Citroen car, and an hour or so later telephoned a woman friend, Connie Palfreyman, that he would not be able to see her that evening as arranged, as he had to go to Watford on business. But whether he ever intended to go there or whether he changed his mind on the way is a matter for conjecture. All that is certain is that he called at Hume's home.

When Hume returned home with Tony at about seven-thirty he found Setty in the front room. He had already guessed that he was there for he had seen the Citroen parked near the entrance to the flats. The unexpected sight of the familiar yellow car had given him a shock, set off a sudden surge of anger in him. Furiously he doubled up the stairs. The fact that he had, as he said 'knocked back a few drinks' intensified his fighting mood.

Panting slightly, he burst into the sitting room and saw Setty. The car dealer must have found the door on the latch and walked in: it was typical of the man. Setty heaved himself up, startled, from the sofa where he had been lounging at ease,

'What's up with you?' he asked.

Hume's voice was shaking. 'I'll show you,' he said. 'If you come here again it will be your lot.'

'Who's going to stop me,' sneered Setty. You and who else? If I want to come here, I'll come here.'

Hume moved towards him with fists clenched. 'On your way,' he said, 'or I'll sling you downstairs.'

The threat left Setty unperturbed. Bulky and powerful-looking, he towered solidly over Hume. Hume glared at him, his face working with rage. He knew that physically Setty had the advantage of him and that if it came to a fight his bare fists would be useless against the man's massive thirteen stone. Attacking him would be like a terrier snapping at a bear. Yet, if it was the last thing he did, he had to get the better of this thug who stood deriding and insulting him on his own hearthrug. In a split second it came to him what to do and he ran out of the room and snatched from the wall a knife that hung among a number of treasured war souvenirs a German SS dagger.

He ran back, kicking the door shut behind him. Slowly he advanced towards Setty brandishing the knife in his right hand.

'Next time you come here,' he said, 'you'll get this in you.'

The sight of the knife and Hume's coldly menacing manner broke down Setty's cocky assurance. 'Go away, you silly bastard,' he said. 'What do you think you're doing? Playing at soldiers?'

But now, insults or not, the tables were turned, the advantage was with Hume, and both knew it. 'You can't frighten me,' Setty scoffed as he swung at Hume with the flat of his hand. Hume ducked and closed with him, and they grappled and fell on the floor between the sofa and the fireplace. There was no question now of Hume not using the knife, just as there was no pretence that the issue was anything else but Setty's life. With no holds barred, it was a fight to the death.

Donald Hume had some wartime souvenirs displayed on the wall, one being an SS dagger which he used to stab Stanley Setty to death, ironically he noted the similarity in the initials! This picture was taken on his release from prison but unfortunately the *Pictorial* provided a brown-handled SA dagger for the photo whereas Hitler's Schutzstaffel were given the black SS-Dienstdolch which was first issued in 1933.

Photographed in the 1950s, the sitting room looked much as it did at the time of the murder.

Even while he hacked at Setty's chest in a mad frenzy, one corner of Hume's mind remained detached, coolly observing and commenting on what was happening. 'I was wielding the dagger,' he said afterwards, 'just like our Stone Age ancestors did 20,000 years ago. It seemed to come naturally to me. As we rolled over and over the thought ran through my mind that there is a very thin line of definition between a savage and a civilised man.'

Setty fought in fierce desperation, using his greater weight to try and push Hume's head back and break his neck. But nothing he could do could hold off the knife which Hume plunged repeatedly into his chest and legs. Locked together they edged across the carpet towards the windows, and as first one got on top and then the other, Hume's one aim was to force Setty away from him so that he could go on stabbing. With Hume's knee in his abdomen Setty grunted but would not let go. At one moment Hume raised the knife to see glinting on it in the light the initials of dread significance 'SS' — and it came to him in a flash that the letters now stood, not for 'Schutz-staffel' but Stanley Setty.

Time and again Hume brought the knife down into Setty's ribs until finally he fell back against the sofa and slumped on to the floor, almost under the window. In the ninety seconds of that death-struggle the motive in Hume's hate-maddened mind had been clear enough to him. 'I had to hurt him,' he later explained, 'this man who kicked my dog.'

Outside, to underline the alien horror of Hume's butchery and the macabre incongruity of the primitive ferocity running amok in that room, was the evening bustle of the Finchley Road, the swishing progress of trolley-buses, the array of lighted shops, the orderly pedestrians. And Setty's own parked car, never now to be reclaimed by its owner.

The same room pictured in July 2011. Setty ended up just below the window which overlooks Finchley Road.

Since the murder, the interior of the flat has been extensively altered. Then, as the plan on page 213 shows, one had to pass through each room to reach the kitchen but now a long communicating corridor *(left)* runs from the hall to the coal cupboard, with doors leading off of it into each room. *Right:* Hume's dining room is now a bedroom.

If a further sinister twist of discrepancy were sought, there was the apparent silence with which this death-grapple was carried out. Two men in mortal combat — one of them weighing over thirteen stone and enduring the agonies of a dozen knife-wounds — might have been expected to make a certain amount of noise as they struggled about the room. Yet the nearest neighbours gave no signs of hearing anything.

As with sound, so with sight: that night the sitting-room curtains had not been drawn, and all that had happened since Hume's entry had been veiled by nothing more than the thin lace hangings that covered the three windows looking out on busy Finchley Road. He noticed for the first time the uncovered windows, and he wrenched the curtains across in a new access of terror. Someone, he told himself, *must* have seen or heard the fight! It was inconceivable that it could have gone unnoticed. But the silence above and below him, the absence of footsteps on the stairs or tell-tale hammering on the door, the reassuring normality of the street noises outside, told him that, for the moment, Setty's death was a secret belonging to him alone. Shaking from head to foot he sat down and got to grips with the appalling fact that he was a murderer.

For perhaps five minutes Hume remained dazed, in a paralysed inaction. Striving to get hold of himself and, as he put it, 'to think straight,' he stumbled into the dining-room across the hall. He still could not believe that nobody had heard the struggle, that he was the only one who knew what had happened.

'The thought flashed through my mind,' he said, 'that I could get away with murder.' He could do it — but he would have to move fast, and quietly. There was the body to be hidden, the sitting-room to be tidied up, and Setty's car to be moved from its tell-tale position outside the flat.

Where could he put Setty's body? Casting round frantically for a makeshift hiding-place he hit on the coal cupboard, a small recess at the rear of the flat, on the same floor. That should get rid of it temporarily; he could see about further disposal later. He ran back into the sitting-room, got hold of the prostrate Setty by the legs and dragged him out on his back into the hall, then through the dining-room, kitchen and small breakfast-room, all of which were connected by communicating doors. It was back-breaking work and he had to stop and rest halfway through the dining-room; but heaving and panting he finally got the body to the door of the cupboard and stowed it inside.

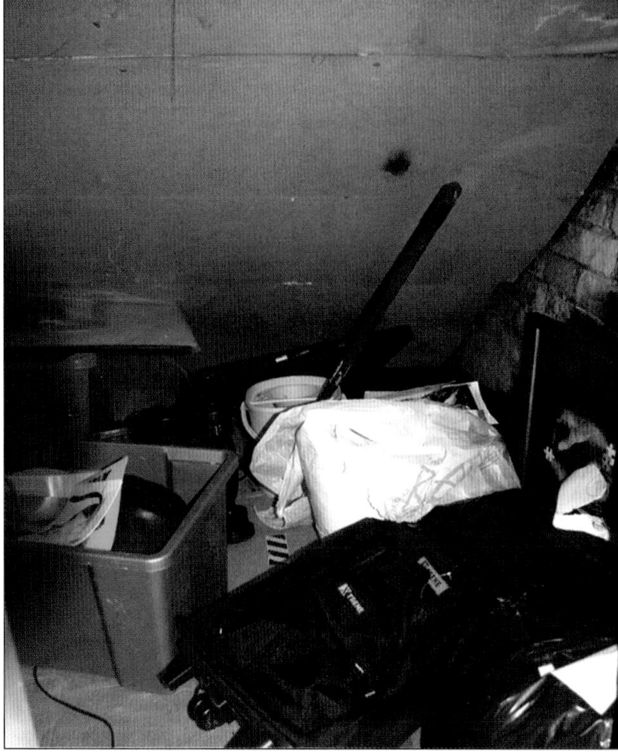

At the far end of the corridor, a cupboard for storing coal was the perfect hiding place for the corpse.

Setty's disappearance was soon notified to police by his sister and his cream Traction-Avant Citroën was discovered parked in Cambridge Terrace Mews, but not secured in his garage as was the norm. One neighbour reported as having heard it being parked on the night of October 4 when Hume drove it back.

The police checked the driving mirror for fingerprints as the first thing any motorist would do on getting into a strange car is to adjust it. Setty was posted as a missing person in the *Police Gazette* of October 8, Interpol notifying the main Paris office on October 20 that they thought Setty may have gone to Palestine.

He wiped his brow: now there was the sitting-room to clean up. The place was in grim disorder; furniture had been displaced and knocked over in the fight, and blood covered the carpet and sofa. It took only a moment to straighten the furniture and then, with a bowl of water and a face flannel he got to work to wipe out the bloodstains. He did not make a very good job of the lightish carpet, but reassured himself with the thought that as this was dirty anyway, the marks would be hard to detect. Finally he cleaned up the trail of blood that led from the sitting-room to the coal cupboard. Superficially, the worst evidences of murder had been expunged. There remained the other immediate task: the removal of Setty's Citroen from the street below.

He crept out of the flat and hurried along to the car. Breathing thanks that the door was unlocked, he got in and reached for the ignition key. Cold panic gripped him again as he found that the key was not there. With a curse he realised that it must be in Setty's pocket. There was nothing for it: he would have to go back for it. So in frantic haste he doubled up to the flat, heaved out Setty's body from the coal cupboard and began to search for the key. By a stroke of luck it was in the first pocket he tried. Within a minute he was back in the car and moving off. Fingerprints on the door or wheel? He had thought of that, and on his way out of the flat had seized a pair of gloves. He turned down Finchley Road with the feeling that there was a fifty-fifty chance of his getting away with murder after all.

It was about nine-thirty as he drove along Finchley Road towards Swiss Cottage. His plan was to return the car to Cambridge Terrace Mews, where Setty normally kept it, and passing down Avenue Road and round Regent's Park he reached the mews in twenty minutes. The cobbled yard was dark and deserted, so he took it in and left it just outside Setty's own lock-up. Then he made off on foot as quickly as possible towards the park.

Hailing a taxi at the bottom of Avenue Road, he got back to the flat about ten forty-five. He realised that he could never get the bulky corpse of Stanley Setty out of the flat whole, so he resolved to cut it up and remove it piecemeal. 'I thought it would be a novel idea,' he said later, 'to dissect him, pack the dismembered remains in convenient sized parcels and drop them over the sea'.

'I congratulated myself on a stroke of genius,' he added proudly. 'What a brilliant way to dispose of him!' His flying knowledge would pay rich dividends but this time the little light blue Auster in which he would take off, as so often before, from Elstree, would hold a more sinister cargo than contraband currency or illicit weapons. It would be exit Mr Stanley Setty for ever. And he would have committed and carried through the perfect murder.

Having got rid of the car, the next job was to clean all traces from the flat. The bloodstains on the carpet needed professional treatment and fortunately there was a cleaners right next door (see photo page 213). Hume enquired of Mrs Frances Hearnden, the manageress *(left)*, if they could dye carpets and when she said they could, he quickly appeared with it rolled up. Hume then cut off the bloodstained edge of the underfelt which initially baffled the police. Dr H. S. Holden of the Metropolitan Police Laboratory made several visits to 620B Finchley Road. First he took possession of the lounge carpet. 'There is a fairly extensive stain on the underside of this carpet,' he reported, 'a human bloodstain but the process of dyeing and cleaning renders it impossible to determine the group.' *Right:* 'I examined the floor of the dining room and numbered the floorboards from 1 to 20 commencing at the door leading to the hall. I found distinct traces of blood in the crevices between the boards numbered 8 to 19. A considerable quantity of dried blood had soaked into the lathes and plaster underlying the floor joists. This was human blood Group O. Further floorboards were lifted and additional bloodstains found on the plaster between 8 and 9 and 17 and 18. Traces of blood were present in the bathroom on the edge of the linoleum covering the floor where it adjoins the bath panel and at the door. I found traces of blood in the small hall between the lounge and dining room and on several of the stairs leading to the top floor where the bathroom is situated. I found a considerable number of small splashes on the wall flanking the staircase between the first and second floors and a small irregular fragment of skin or flesh on the wall above the handrail of the stairs leading to the front door.'

He knew that he was faced with hair-raising risks and that he would have to move fast: do the cutting-up and parcelling after lunch when he would be alone in the apartment before the charwoman arrived, clean up the traces, get at least some of the packages out to Elstree and take them up and drop them at sea before nightfall. It was going to be a busy afternoon.

Before breakfast Hume looked round the downstairs rooms again and saw with dismay that the tell-tale stains were still apparent on the sitting-room floor and carpet and some of the furniture. He fetched a clothes-brush and went over the sofa and chairs with it in an attempt to rub out the marks, used a cloth to clean the floor and then wipe all likely places to remove Setty's fingerprints.

Things looked a little better now, but the carpet still worried him. To his searching eye the stains stood out with an accusing clarity. They would surely be spotted at once. He considered briefly and then had an idea. Soon afterwards he slipped out to the cleaners, which was conveniently next door. Here he asked if they cleaned and dyed carpets. Yes, said the manageress, they did; and she showed him some colour samples. Hume thumbed quickly through these and said he would bring a carpet in and in a few minutes he was back with the rolled-up carpet. He handed it over with instructions to dye it a darker green and left the shop without waiting for it to be unrolled.

While he was out there was something else he had to do: get some varnish to touch up the bare patches on the floor caused by his rubbing. A tin of suitable dark-brown stain was easily obtained, and with it he returned to the flat. Listening for a moment in the hall, he could hear his wife Cynthia upstairs in the baby's room.

When removing the carpet he had noticed that the blood near its edge had soaked through to the underfelt and on to the bare floorboards beneath. How to get rid of the revealing stains on the felt? He scratched his head as he considered the ticklish problem. Obviously, since the stains were near the edge, he could remove them by cutting off a strip of the felt: but that would expose the stains on the boards. Then, a moment's experiment gave him the answer. He found that the loose-woven felt would stretch, and thus, after cutting, would still cover the marks on the floor. Swiftly he snipped off the bloodstained edging and tugged at the felt until the floor was hidden right up to the original line where the border of varnish began.

The tell-tale carpet and floorboards are carried into the Old Bailey on January 14, 1950.

In a few minutes he had re-varnished the bare patches on the borders of the sitting-room and dining-room floors. That was the carpet, the underfelt and the floor — three jobs done. So far things were going well but then the full horror of his situation returned to him as he thought of the body lying grotesquely huddled in the closet. Baby Allison's doctor was coming that morning, and that ruled out any thought of an early start on the horrible work he had to do.

Tense, apprehensive, chain-smoking, he prowled round the flat cursing at his helpless inaction, his eyes drawn again and again to the tell-tale stains on the sofa that defied any further attempts to shift them, and the drying varnish on the floor. Nervously he kept looking at his watch, as its hands crept towards ten o'clock. For ten was the hour at which he had an important rendezvous at the counter of the local bank. This stemmed from the events of the previous evening.

Before moving Setty's body into the cupboard he had gone through the dead man's pockets and discovered the £1,000 in £5 notes that were the proceeds of Setty's car sale in Warren Street that day. It was a rich haul but most of the notes had been so mutilated by his vicious knife-stabs as to be unusable. Many were also bloodstained. However, by trimming the discoloured edges of some of them with scissors he was able to rescue over £100 worth of presentable notes. Most of these he had determined to pay into his local bank to clear an outstanding overdraft. Ten o'clock came and he slipped down to the bank with £90 and paid it in.

Between eleven and twelve the doctor arrived. He wait straight upstairs to the bedroom, and after a while came down to the sitting-room to give some directions about the baby. The doctor wanted her to be taken to the Hospital for Sick Children at Great Ormond Street and explained to Hume how to get there. Those few minutes in the sitting-room were the worst he had had that morning. Here he was, quietly chatting with the doctor about the trivial illness of a child when all the time, a few feet away, lay the body of the man he had murdered.

Setty's body, stiffened by rigor mortis, was difficult to shift from its cramped, wedged-in position in the cupboard but somehow, puffing and panting, Hume heaved it out on to the floor. Looking down at it, he had at that moment about as much compunction as a butcher preparing to cut up a carcase of meat.

Hume had already contrived a plan to get rid of the body by dropping it over the sea. He already had a private pilot's licence and flew with the United Services Flying Club at Elstree so, if he dismembered the body, he could dispose of the pieces over the Channel. The work of cutting off the legs and head using a linoleum knife and hacksaw took place in the kitchen.

'I felt no squeamishness or horror at what I was about to do,' he said,' though I must admit that I didn't eat well that day'.

He struggled to pull off Setty's clothes, the expensive pinstripe suit that now was knife-ripped, blood-stained and fouled with coal dust; and where the corpse's inert bulk hindered this, slit them savagely with his knife, leaving on the shirt and pants, together with the shoes and socks.

Then he set about dismembering the legs. His small half-crown linoleum knife bit deep into the flesh until it pierced the thigh bones. These he thought might prove hard to sever but found that the hacksaw went through than easily. When both legs were severed he tore off a piece of the felt, wrapped them in it, together with the suit, and then tied up the bundle with cord.

Now for parcel number two. The parcel to contain Mr Setty's head. This, he admitted, 'was the worst part of the job'. For one thing, despite his bravado, the staring eyes were still giving him uneasy qualms. 'I didn't want them to look at me,' he confessed, 'so I covered them with a piece of rag.'

With a few quick strokes he severed the head from the body, and looked about for something to put the head in. Among a pile of boxes found a likely one that had contained tins of baked beans. Trying it, he found its size was right, so he placed the head inside and packed round it small pieces of brick and rubble which he had brought in from the back yard that morning as ballast to ensure that the box would sink. The two parcels — all that he was planning to get rid of that day — were ready.

There remained the torso to be tied up and hidden until removal next day, the room to be cleared up.

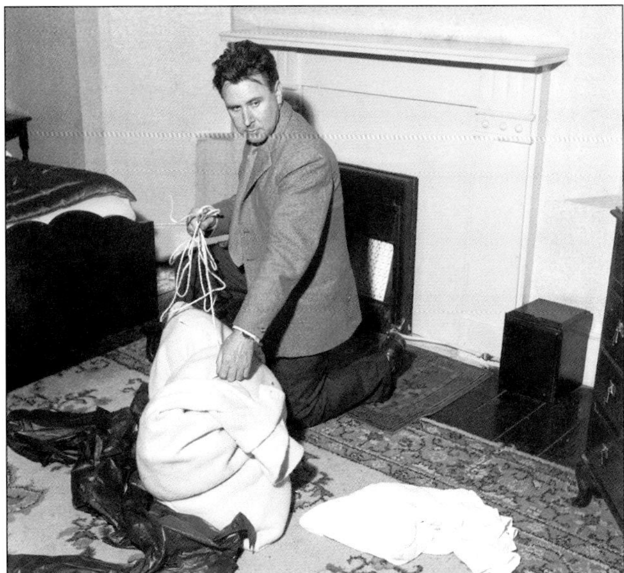

When reporter Victor Sims and photographer Bill Turner of the *Sunday Pictorial* took Hume back to the flat in 1958, they staged their photo *(left)* of him wrapping up the torso in the dining room (instead of the kitchen) but, because of the difficulty of taking a comparison with the double bed in the way, we took our shot in the room where the murder had actually taken place.

Hume had already parked his car — a Singer — at the rear of number 620 and as the cleaner, Mrs Stride, was due to arrive at the front door at any minute, he struggled with the head and legs down the narrow stairs . . . past the flat below *(left)* . . . leading to the back door *(centre)*. He then drove down the alleyway *(right)* leading to Finchley Road.

He was uncertain what to do with the torso. First he tried putting it into a large black cabin trunk which he had handy, but found that the lid would not close. With a curse he pushed the trunk aside, grabbed the felt and bundled the torso into it. Round this he wrapped a blanket, weighted with pieces of lead, and tied the bulky makeshift package securely with cord. He manhandled it into the coal cupboard and shut the door.

Conscious of the speeding minutes, he got down on his knees with a cloth and a bucket of water and cleaned away the traces. He also wiped down the table and the kitchen sink. Then he washed all signs of his bloody work off himself. The felt-wrapped bundle and the cardboard box he put ready by the door.

Casting a last look around the tidied room, he decided that he had left nothing amiss to catch the appraising eyes of Mrs Stride or Cynthia. And now there was only one thing more to do before he was out and away. This was a task that pained him sorely. He had to burn the rest of the £5 notes — nearly £900 worth — that he had taken from Setty's jacket the night before and had found unusable. 'It broke my heart to burn the fivers,' he said, and so that small fortune went up in smoke.

It was now about two-thirty and he knew that Mrs Stride would be arriving any minute. Gathering up his two packages, he sneaked out of the flat, down the stairs past the schoolmaster's door and across to the yard at the back where the hired black Singer, in which he was driving to Elstree, was waiting.

He looked about and, satisfied that no one was watching, quickly stowed the packages on the back seat. Then he drove out into Finchley Road, on the start of perhaps the most bizarre journey a killer had ever undertaken in a bid to dispose of the remains of his murdered victim.

And the weapon and tools with which he had done the killing: the lino knife and the dismantled hacksaw, were wrapped in paper in his raincoat pocket. They were going out of the plane along with the parcels.

Beside Hume on the front seat, as he drove, was Tony. He had no secrets from this

Left: **Inspector Marchant at the rear of 620 Finchley Road when police opened up drains there in 1949.** *Right:* **The characteristic brickwork makes for a good comparison in 2011.**

From Finchley Road Hume drove out of London to the airfield at Elstree. *Left:* The plane he used was Auster J.1 Autocrat G-AGXT. This picture was taken a year or two after Hume's flights, the aircraft still painted blue in the colours of the United Services Flying Club. *Right:* The wooden tower then used for flying control was replaced in 1960.

mongrel pal, closer to him than any human, the only fellow-creature on which he lavished any sentiment. So Tony was with him now, as he had been throughout the gruesome work just finished and perhaps while he had knifed Setty to death the evening before. In the tense hours of suspense and inaction that morning, as Hume had roamed restlessly round the flat, Tony had seemed to know that something was wrong. The dog had kept looking up at him quizzically, even anxiously, as if asking what was bothering his master.

The short drive to Elstree through the crowded roads of north-west London was the most cautious car journey that Hume had ever made. With that grisly freight on the back seat he could afford no mistakes. 'I crept up to each set of traffic lights and carefully signalled every turn,' he said. 'I didn't want the police to pick me up for some trivial traffic offence. My gamble was too big for that.'

Near the airfield he turned down Dagger Lane and a few minutes later he drove through the airfield gates and stopped near the control tower. Hume was well known at Elstree airport, which he had frequently used on his old aerial smuggling journeys — though of course the staff were completely unaware of these illegal activities. So now he confidently approached the controller and explained that he wanted to make a return flight to Southend. This was quickly agreed to and he confirmed that he was to use the Auster G-AGXT which he had often flown before.

He was not taking Tony and, walking back to the car to get the parcels, he gave the dog a final pat of farewell. Then, after looking around to make sure that nobody was particularly interested in his movements, he carried the two parcels over to the Auster and put them in the rear seat. With a last wave to Tony, who was watching him, tail wagging, through the closed windows of the car, Hume climbed into the Auster, put his raincoat on the seat beside him, shut the door and started up the engine. In a few moments the little light blue Auster was airborne and heading eastwards, towards Southend. It was just after three o'clock with about two and a half hours to sunset.

About half-an-hour after leaving Elstree, he turned to starboard and then pulled on to a course of 200 degrees, which took him somewhat west of south and almost into the declining sun, heading for the open sea. He crossed the south coast and headed towards mid-Channel as 'I couldn't afford to be seen dropping suspicious-looking objects near Southend Pier!'

He knew that the Auster had an endurance limit of some three-and-a-half hours on a full tank so he decided to keep going outwards for a total of about ninety minutes and soon he spotted the faint outline of the French coast. This was the spot, he thought; nice and deep, miles from shore and safe from the ebb and flow of tides.

The weapons and tools were going first. He grabbed them from his raincoat pocket, wrenched open the door and threw them out one by one and in a second they had disappeared from sight. Now for the parcels, first one and then the other; the head and the legs, still with their shoes and socks on, plummeted down to the last resting-place. 'I looked for a sign of them on the sea,' said Hume. 'There was none. They must have sunk like stones.'

In a wide sweep he headed for the English coast. It was now about four-thirty and, with the weather thickening, visibility was beginning to get poor. The sooner he made Southend airport the better. It was necessary to call there in order to make his log entries look accurate in case of later inquiries into his movements.

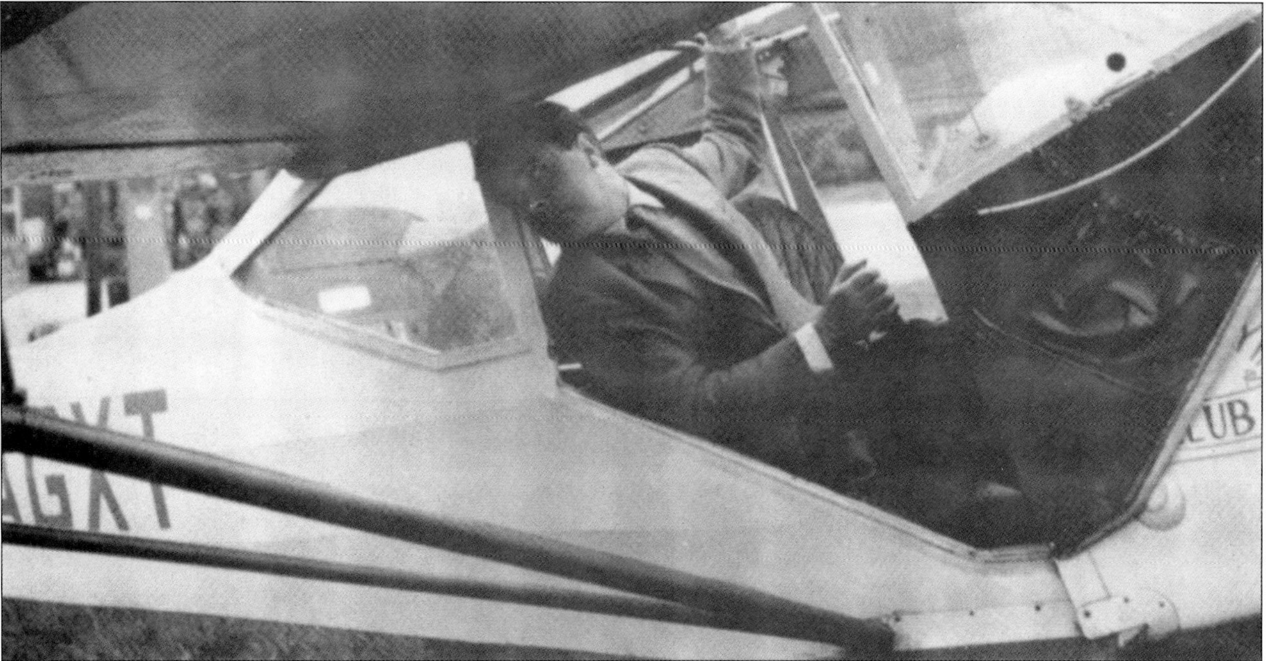

However this recreation picture of Hume in the same Auster by the *Pictorial* photographer Bill Turner appears to have been taken at Southend where he landed after the first sortie over the Channel. However, note that a solo pilot would normally occupy the left-hand seat to be able to operate the overhead lever to adjust the flaps. Pictured ten years after the event, G-AGXT was then on the books of the London School of Flying at Elstree having been repainted silver with their logo on the cowling.

Above: **Having had access to the original aircraft — albeit at Southend — it is difficult to understand why Bill Turner claimed in his caption that G-AGTV was the actual aeroplane used by Hume to dump the body when he had already photographed him in G-AGXT!** *Below:* **He also pictured Hume with yet another Auster Autocrat, G-AIZY, which was parked nearby.**

On the outward trip he had been flying under Visual Flight Rules because visibility had been good. But now the murky weather was blotting out landmarks and he had to depend on his instruments. At last he saw the lights of Southend airfield. It was a welcome sight but as he came in to land two red Verey lights came up towards him. Only after he was down did he discover that he had violated the circuit drill and landed in the path of a four-engined plane!

He was reassured to find that no one at the airport questioned his story that he had come from Elstree. And he went out of his way to be noticed by as many people there as possible. It would all help if inquiries were made later on.

He left the Auster to be refuelled and took a cab into Southend, paying off the driver with one of Setty's fivers. Then, to get some fresh air, he went for a stroll along the pier.

There was no question of his flying back to Elstree that night as he had no night flying experience and no rating on his licence. So after returning to the airport and explaining that he would fetch the Auster next day, he hired another cab to take him home to Finchley Road. 'It cost a lot,' he said, 'but I had fivers to spare that day.'

The maisonette, when he entered it at about eight-thirty, was quiet and the lower floor in darkness. Cynthia was used to his irregular comings-and-goings on affairs about which she never inquired, and was evidently upstairs. Hume went into the breakfast-room and looked quickly around, to note with relief that everything was just as he had left it. But as he got himself some supper there was one thing that did worry him: poor old Tony, awaiting him in the car at Elstree. He rang up the airport and told them he could not fetch the car that night but would come for it the next morning. Meanwhile, he asked, would they let his dog out for a run, and then he could sleep in the car.

Without Tony around, the flat seemed very silent and lonely. And Hume, reacting now to the strain of that nerve-racking, eventful and not unsuccessful day, began to realise to the full the problem that he still had on his hands: the problem of the sinister felt-wrapped bundle that remained in the cupboard off the breakfast-room. His life depended on his disposing of Setty's torso during the coming day. And what he planned to do was to take it up in the Auster from Southend. But first he had two other tasks: fetch his hired car and Tony from Elstree and have the edges of the sitting-room and dining-room floors properly re-stained. His touching-up, he had realised on a further examination, just would not pass muster. The only way to erase the mottled suspicious-looking patches was a new coat of varnish altogether.

Immediately after breakfast on Thursday he hurried out and arranged for a local decorator to come in and do this during the morning. Then he went on to Elstree. It was hard to say whether he or Tony had missed each other most. Hume himself was overjoyed at the reunion and 'Tony, the best pal I ever had, barked with pleasure at seeing me again.'

He got back to the flat soon after eleven, to find the decorator busy on the sitting-room floor, 'unaware', as Hume declared, 'that he was helping to brush away the telltale bloodstains that might have helped to put a noose around my neck'.

Leaving the man at work, he shut himself in the breakfast-room. This was the moment for moving the torso. He tried first to roll out the coal-grimed bundle but found that, dead-weighted with the lumps of lead, it was too heavy to budge. Then he dragged it out by its cord. The problem now was to get it down to the car waiting below. Realising that he could never do this by himself, he decided to ask the decorator to help him. It was just another of those fantastic but calculated risks that Hume had been taking as the only alternative to certain discovery from the moment that he became a murderer. The man agreed at once and went through with Hume into the kitchen. 'It's pretty heavy,' Hume told him as he bent to lift the bulky blanket-wrapped package. 'Don't hold it underneath. You'll find it easier to grip it by the rope.'

So the respectable, law-abiding stranger who was already unwittingly varnishing away the bloodstains of Stanley Setty now, in all innocence, helped Hume further by aiding in the removal of Setty's torso. Together they humped the heavy corded bundle out of the flat and down the awkward, angled staircase. The torso of a thirteen-stone man, supplemented by lead weights, was no light burden, and even the two of them could hardly lift it from the ground. 'It was so heavy,' said Hume, 'that it slid and bumped down the stairs and made peculiar squishy gurgling noises.'

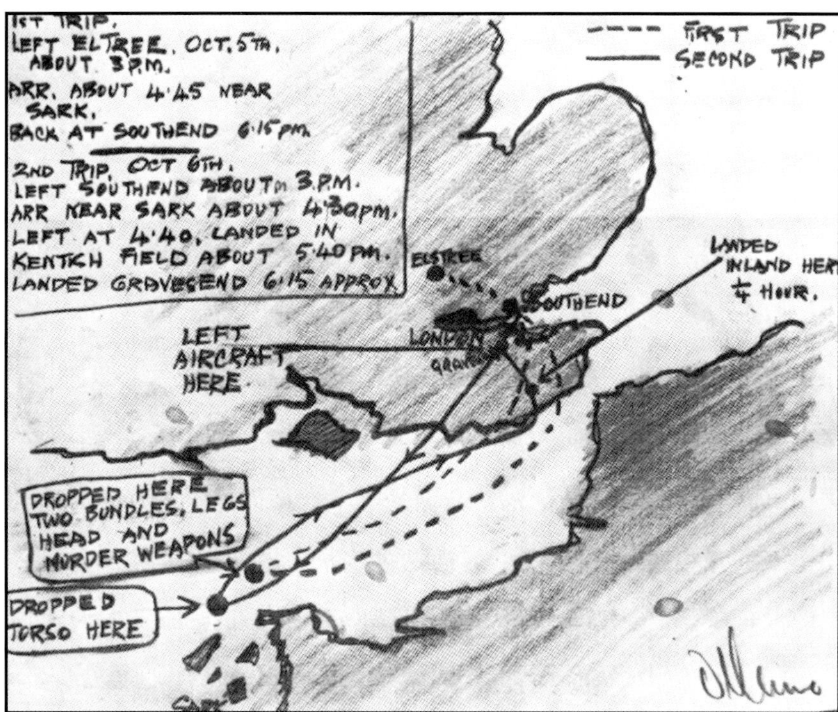

Hume drew this sketch map indicating his two flights while admitting he was a poor navigator. Just look at the map below to see where the torso ended up!

And that was not the worst of the ordeal as he prayed that the man would not handle the under part of the package as blood had begun to seep through the blanket covering. But Hume's helper carried on, miraculously oblivious to the gruesome nature of that bundle, and somehow they got it to the car, parked outside in Finchley Road.

They both returned to the flat, with the sweating Hume registering silent thanks that that terrible experience was over. He marvelled that the man had apparently not suspected a thing. But there it was: the gamble had been taken and had paid off; the last of Setty's body was out of the flat. A few more hours and the torso would follow yesterday's parcels from which recovery was, he assured himself, utterly impossible.

It was now about eleven-thirty, and the coal cupboard had to be cleaned before starting for Southend. And here again Hume seemed to be challenging fate with reckless bravado. 'Fantastic as it may sound,' he boasted afterwards, 'I left the torso in that car, parked in busy Finchley Road outside my flat, for much more than an hour before I drove off with it.'

It was nearly one o'clock when, with Tony, he got into the car and started off. Edging through the traffic as cautiously as the day before, he felt cocky and elated: his sense of triumph was stronger than ever. 'As I headed for Southend,' he said, "it seemed to me that I was getting clear away with murder.'

Some ninety minutes later he drove through the airport gates towards the light-blue Auster which, as he had expected, was standing refuelled and ready. He took the car as near as possible to the plane because getting his cumbersome parcel on to it single-handed was going to be no easy job. And he did not want to be seen doing it. He looked round carefully and then, satisfied that he was unnoticed, struggled to lift the package out of the car. This was going to be the tricky moment, he told himself. The few yards between the car and the Auster looked a long way to him as he staggered, grunting, towards the plane. Then his heart missed a beat when he saw an overalled engineer coming towards him.

'What have you got in there?' the man asked in mild curiosity.

For a second of panic Hume thought it was all up. But somehow he smiled, a quick, knowing, man-to-man smile.

'Fish,' he replied instantly.

The speedy cryptic repartee may have saved the day for Hume. It puzzled the engineer but at the same time — if he had had any suspicions in the first place — totally disarmed him. So all he did now was to ask if he could give Hume a hand. And when Hume politely declined he went off, probably thinking that he was a rum character, but no more.

With heartfelt thanks at this last of many lucky breaks, Hume heaved the bundle on to the front seat of the plane, and set it in an upright position. He got in beside it and then Tony, who was coming with his master this time, jumped into the back seat, wildly excited. They were ready for the take-off. It was about quarter to three.

In some ways this was Hume's most anxious moment of the whole two suspense-ridden days. All he wanted now was to get off the ground quickly, before he was overtaken by some fatal last-minute mischance but perhaps his very eagerness induced a haste that impaired his judgement. 'The take-off was dicey,' as he afterwards confessed. For a few breathless seconds it looked as if the plane would not get airborne in time. And the thing that nearly caused his undoing was the package that bulked awkwardly at his side, its top almost on a level with the top of his head. As the Auster gathered speed along the grass strip and he attempted to pull back the control column, it stuck in the bundle beside him. Quickly Hume reached up to the tail trimmer above his head and began to wind it in order to get the plane's nose up and take the weight off the control column.

Still on the ground, the plane rushed towards the end of the strip, and Hume broke into a cold sweat as it headed straight for a group of tall buildings. Then, by a piece of luck, for which Hume never ceased to be grateful, the machine became airborne, zooming over the roofs with a few feet to spare. 'As I turned out to sea over Southend Pier,' Hume said, 'I thought of the awful mess there would have been if I had crashed!'

His object was to jettison his parcel somewhere in the same area as he had dropped the other two. So, setting a suitable course, he headed south-westwards over the Kent coast and towards mid-Channel. It was hazy over the sea, but below him he picked out some lightships — possibly the Goodwins vessels — and then, through the wispy cloud, he spotted a Bristol freighter and a Viking. He flew on for what he estimated was a total time of about ninety minutes, judging that that should bring him to his chosen deep-water rendezvous. Hume admitted he was an indifferent navigator but a faint blur on the horizon to port suggested the French coast.

He descended from 3,000 to 2,000 feet and, flaps down, throttled back to the Auster's lowest speed, about sixty miles an hour. He tried to open the door against the slipstream, using the weight of the bundle to force it outwards. And in order to free both hands he held the control column clamped between his legs but to his dismay he could not shift the bundle. Upright, massive, ungainly, it was squatting beside him on the seat, an obscene caricature of a living person, a fellow-passenger doggedly resisting his murderous assault. It was as if he was attempting to kill Stanley Setty all over again.

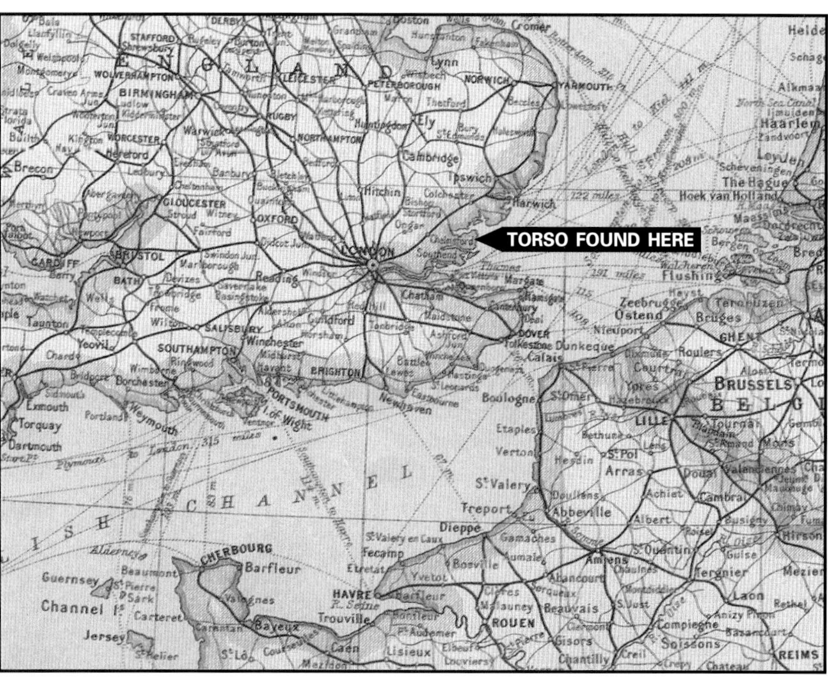

The most famous — or rather infamous — Auster Autocrat continued to operate with the London School of Flying, Richard Riding taking this picture of it over Elstree in 1961. In June 1969 it came a cropper when it hit a hedge near the village of Bickmarsh in Warwickshire after engine failure. The wreckage ended up in Wales.

Hume cursed and swore. It was no good. The weighted torso defied his most strenuous efforts. So with flaps up he tried to gain height for a second attempt. But once again, as in the take-off, there was not room for the control column to come back. Then he tried another tactic, banking the Auster steeply, hoping that the parcel would force the door open with its tremendous weight. But now he had a further problem to contend with. During his struggles with the torso, Tony had got frantically excited; and as the plane banked, the dog had jumped forward, barking fiercely. Hume saw with alarm that if the door burst open suddenly he might easily fall out. So he grabbed hold of the dog and held him back.

With the other hand he pushed and shoved against the bulky package. Nothing happened. Then, as the plane swayed and tilted, half out of control, he summoned all his strength and heaved again. Suddenly there was an enormous bang as the door whipped open and slammed shut. The torso had gone.

Hume righted the Auster and watched the parcel spinning down. He wiped his face, pushed Tony behind him and slumped back momentarily in relief. That, thank God, was the last, the very last, of Stanley Setty. He pulled back the stick to gain height as he circled on to his homeward course. Then he almost fainted with horror when he saw that the outer blanket, with the lead weights trapped inside by the force of the slipstream, was clattering and flapping on his tail elevators. He was still carrying — and perhaps would take back to the airport — evidence that could brand him a murderer.

Hume realised immediately what must have happened. The rope had got slackened by handling and, as the bundle had gone out, the fierce slipstream had whipped off the rope and the loosened blanket, leaving only the felt-wrapped torso to drop. Temporarily stunned by the shock, and half-blinded by the coal-dust from the grimy blanket that had whirled round the cabin while the door was open, for a few seconds Hume let the plane get out of control. It had begun to dive steeply towards the sea before he managed to right it but when he looked again at the tail-plane it was free and the aircraft was trim and level once more. But that afternoon's shocks were not over . . . the worst was yet to come. Circling round the spot where the blanket had dropped, he peered out and saw the felt-covered torso still floating. At that grim discovery Hume nearly lost his grip. This is the end, he thought. Setty's going to get me hanged after all. As Hume flew off northwards it was a loose end in his carefully worked out scheme for committing the perfect murder.

Hume was now far from happy. It was dark and he was running short of fuel. He knew he could never reach Elstree that night so instead made for Gravesend where he landed at about six-thirty having been airborne for more than three hours. After telling the airport control that he had come from Southend, he left the Auster for the night and arranged for a car to take him and Tony back to London. These hire-car journeys were becoming expensive, but he still had a few of Setty's fivers left.

By eight Hume was back home. He was exhausted and without the lift to his spirits that full success in that afternoon's operation would have given him. Certainly, it was good to feel that the coal cupboard no longer held that gruesome secret, that all marks of the bloodstains had been erased from the newly-varnished floors. It was a relief too to be able to talk to Cynthia without, as it were, having to look over his shoulder all the time to make sure that he had missed no glaring clue to what had happened in the flat two nights ago. But even though Setty's body was out of the flat and all immediate danger seemed overcome, the afternoon had been fraught with shocks and mischances and more than once disaster had stared him in the face. And after all the planning, there remained that grim hostage to fortune, somewhere in the waters of mid-Channel. Would the torso sink? Would it float on and be picked up by a passing vessel? Would it be washed ashore? As Hume went to bed that night the queries haunted him. One sure thing was that it had deprived him of getting away with the perfect murder. And nothing short of the perfect murder could guarantee him immunity from the gallows.

John Williams,
Hume, Portrait of a Double Murderer, 1960

Setty's torso washed up on the marshy foreshore of the River Crouch in Essex, and was spotted by Sidney Tiffin while he was out shooting wildfowl on Friday, October 21. Hume said: 'I opened my *Sunday Pictorial* and saw the headline I'd been dreading: "Setty Torso washed up." The report continued: 'The headless dismembered partly decomposed body of Stanley Setty, 46-year-old London car dealer, missing for nearly three weeks, has been found near Burnham-on-Crouch, Essex. It had been washed up by the tide. The head and legs are missing. Identification was carried out yesterday by Scotland Yard fingerprint chief, Superintendent Fred Cherrill".'

Although Setty's disappearance had been reported to the police by his sister Eva, it was also soon noticed by his fellow car dealers in Warren Street, and it was first thought that Setty might have been killed for the £1,000 he had just drawn from his bank. Not realising that the number of the notes had been recorded, Hume had banked those without bloodstains and spent others on the various taxi fares. This was a fatal mistake, as was not removing Setty's hands which made it easy for the police to identify the torso. With the newspapers reporting developments almost daily, Hume must have sweated as the net closed in — his perfect murder turning out to be not so clever after all. By the time he was arrested in a dawn raid on October 27, Scotland Yard had already checked on the movements of the Auster and Dr. Holden had examined the machine at Elstree and found traces of blood behind the left-hand seat. Hume was taken to Albany Street Police Station where he was photographed and charged with murder.

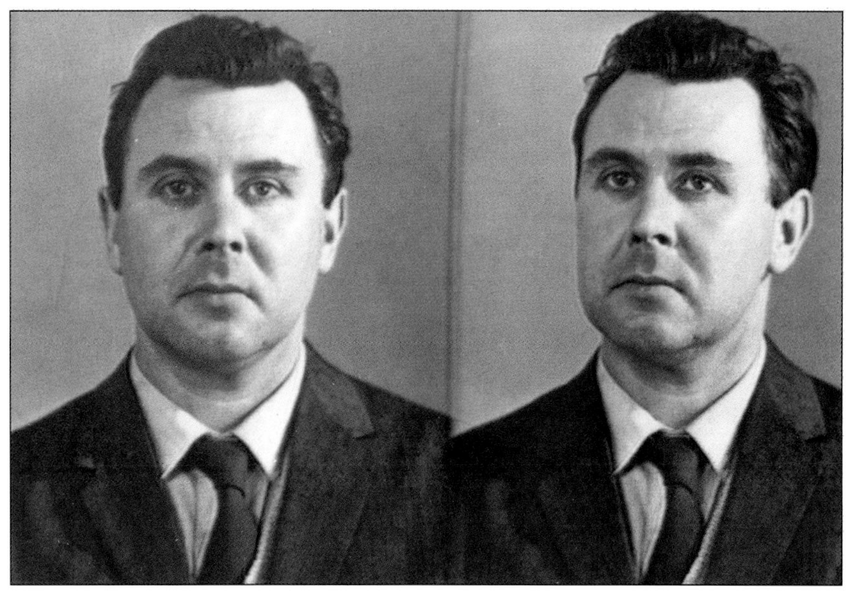

At Albany Street Hume said later that 'I had to be smart. I had to keep my wits about me and stay one jump ahead. Was it any use trying to deny those plane flights with the cut-up body? No, too many people could be found to rip my alibi to shreds. Too many eyes had watched me handle those parcels.' So his fertile brain concocted this explanation: 'Three men, named Mac, Greeny and The Boy, offered me £100 in fivers to drop two parcels from a plane. I needed the money badly and did the job. The parcels could have contained "hot" printing plates for forged petrol coupons for all I knew. But next day the three men came back with a much bigger parcel and offered me £50 to do a second trip. I didn't argue much. One of the men toyed with a gun as he spoke. After they had gone I began to have suspicions about that parcel. But it was too late to draw back because I thought the police would never believe me if I went to them. They would have no time for shady characters like me.'

Brian Donald Hume, 29, a company director, of Finchley Road, N.W., was charged at Bow Street last night with the murder of Stanley Setty, 46, a Warren Street car dealer who disappeared on October 4. Hume will appear before the Court at Bow Street today. A body said to be that of Setty was found on Tillingham mudflats, on the Essex coast marshes, last weekend. The head and legs are still missing. Solicitors for Sidney Tiffin, of Tillingham, who found the body wrapped in a blanket, have claimed on his behalf the £1,000 reward which Setty's family offered for information leading to his discovery.

The Times, October, 29, 1949

Brian Donald Hume appeared at Bow Street Court yesterday and was formally committed for trial at the Central Criminal Court session starting January 10, charged with the murder of Stanley Setty. On October 21, Mr. C. Duveen, for the defence had previously intimated that Hume would plead 'Not Guilty' and would reserve his defence.

The Times, December 7, 1949

The trial of Brian Donald Hume, 29, director, committed from Bow Street Court on a charge of murdering Stanley Setty, will open at the Central Criminal Court next Wednesday.

The Times, January 12, 1950

The trial was concluded at the Central Criminal Court yesterday, before Mr. Justice Sellers, of Brian Donald Hume. When the Judge had completed his summing-up, the jury retired at 12.30 p.m. to consider their verdict. At about 3 p.m. the jury returned to Court and the foreman informed the Judge that they were not agreed, and added that he doubted whether they would be able to reach a unanimous decision. After the jury had failed to agree upon a verdict they were discharged and granted exemption from any further service for a period of five years.

A fresh jury were then sworn and, on the direction of the Judge, returned a verdict of Not Guilty of murder. Hume was then arraigned on another indictment charging him with being an accessory after the fact, by disposing of the body of Setty on October 5 and 6. To that charge he pleaded 'Guilty' and was sentenced to 12 years' imprisonment.

The Times, January 27, 1950

FINAL NIGHT EXTRA

SELF-DRIVE HIRE
£1 per day. Chauffeurs available.
Special facilities for Overseas Visitors.
J. DAVY WESTERN 1225
Logan Place, Earl's Court Road, W.8.

Evening Standard

39,104 THURSDAY, JANUARY 26, 1950 ONE PENNY

everest
TYPEWRITER
PHONE CITY 1107 FOR LEAFLET,
T.S. (OFFICE EQUIPMENT) LTD.
30 NEW BRIDGE STREET, E.C.4.

TEN MEN AND TWO WOMEN TALK 2½ HOURS BUT FAIL TO REACH A VERDICT

HUME GETS 12 YEARS

Murder trial jury disagree and are discharged

THEN HE PLEADS GUILTY TO DUMPING SETTY'S BODY INTO THE SEA

Evening Standard Reporter

There was a sensational end this afternoon to the trial of Brian Donald Hume for the alleged murder of Stanley Setty. The jury of ten men and two women disagreed and were discharged. Hume then pleaded guilty to a charge of being an accessory after the fact and was sent to prison for 12 years.

The murder trial jury retired at 12.30 after a three-hour summing-up by Mr. Justice Sellers. Then at 2.45 the warning

Harriet Cohen

WOMAN IN PLAYFIELD MURDER MYSTERY

Evening Standard Crime Reporter

The body of a woman, believed to be Miss Louisa Frances Bartrip, 44-year-old school teacher missing since December 21, was found this afternoon at the Cardinal Vaughan playing field, Rugby Road, Twickenham, Middlesex.

There were marks of violence on the body and a preliminary investigation suggested that she

£20,000 JEWELS STOLEN

Evening Standard Reporter

Jewellery and furs believed to be worth at least £20,000 were stolen last night from Mrs. Vernon Tate, former Gibson Girl Eva Carrington, and now wife of the chairman of Tate and Lyle's sugar company.

Thieves climbed to a balcony 20ft. up and broke into her suite at the Hyde Park Hotel, Knightsbridge, S.W., while she and her husband were having dinner.

"We went to the grillroom at 9 p.m. and returned at 10," Mr Tate said to-day.

"We were due to leave the hotel this morning after a

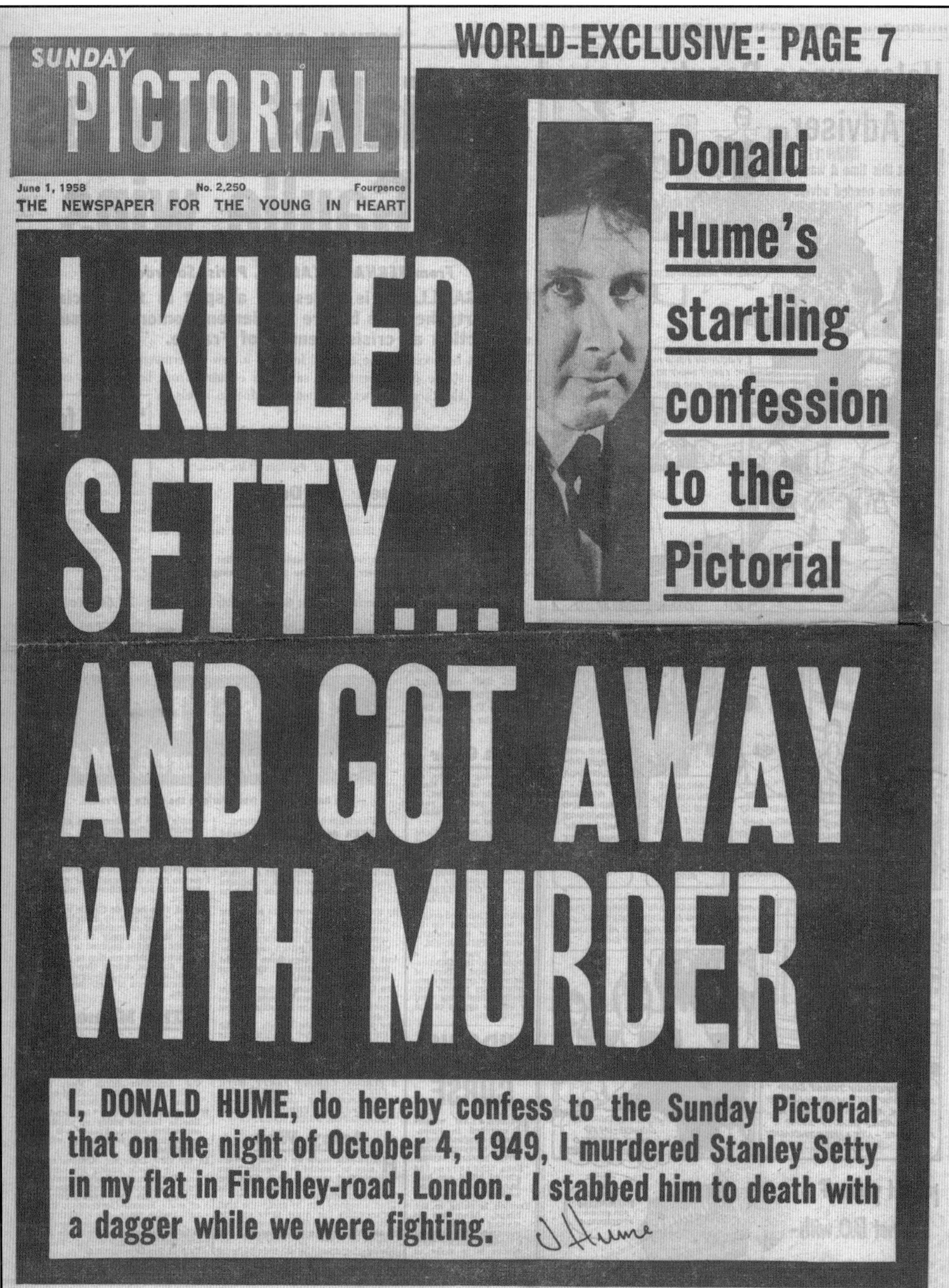

SUNDAY PICTORIAL

June 1, 1958 No. 2,250 Fourpence

THE NEWSPAPER FOR THE YOUNG IN HEART

WORLD-EXCLUSIVE: PAGE 7

Donald Hume's startling confession to the Pictorial

I KILLED SETTY... AND GOT AWAY WITH MURDER

I, DONALD HUME, do hereby confess to the Sunday Pictorial that on the night of October 4, 1949, I murdered Stanley Setty in my flat in Finchley-road, London. I stabbed him to death with a dagger while we were fighting. D Hume

Donald Hume served eight years of his sentence mostly in Dartmoor, and was released with maximum remission on February 1, 1958. With Cynthia having divorced him, it was only then that he discovered that Tony had been put to sleep. Newspapers wanted to buy his story of prison life but he realised he had a much greater story to tell. Although he was concerned as to what might befall him if he revealed the truth, he knew that under the provisions of the double jeopardy rule he could not be tried again for the same offence. The *Sunday Pictorial* offered £2,000 (around £150,000 today) and the paper's special investigator, Victor Sims, was given the job of interviewing Hume. Over three weeks in a hotel at Westcliff-on-Sea, Hume — now having changed his name by deed poll to Donald Brown — recounted the events of October 1949. In June his *'Confession'* was featured over three issues of the *Pictorial*, eagerly lapped up by an astonished British readership.

THE HUME CONFESSION

ON THE FRONT PAGE *of last week's Sunday Pictorial, Donald Hume, who was jailed for twelve years for disposing of the dismembered body of Stanley Setty (left), made this appalling confession that he also murdered the man:—*

❝I, Donald Hume, do hereby confess to the Sunday Pictorial that on the night of October 4, 1949, I murdered Stanley Setty in my flat in Finchley-road, London. I stabbed him to death with a dagger while we were fighting.❞

THE ROOM WHERE I KILLED SETTY

POLICE FIND SETTY'S CITROEN CAR

'I killed Setty . . .'

DONALD HUME'S ADMISSION TO THE PICTORIAL THAT STARTED WORLD CONTROVERSY

I'M HOLDING A DAGGER LIKE THE ONE I USED TO KILL STANLEY SETTY

THERE was a blazing row when car dealer Stanley Setty and I met in my flat at Finchley-road, Golders Green, on the evening of October 4, 1949.

It was 7.35 p.m. I was livid with anger at this man for whom I had been earning money by stealing cars.

The cars I stole on his order had to match the log-books of wrecked vehicles he had already bought.

TREMBLE

BUT, furious as I was, I did not know then that seventeen minutes later I would have his dead body—and his blood—on my hands.

I began to tremble with rage when this black marketeer refused to get out.

I saw red. I yelled at him, then ran out on to the landing and snatched a dagger from the collection of war souvenirs on the wall.

DAGGER

THE handle of the dagger glinted in the light. I could see the initials "S.S."

In war, they stood for Schutz Staffel, the elite army corps of Nazi Germany.

Now those S.S. initials stood for forty-four-year-old Stanley Setty.

I dashed, dagger in hand, through the doorway of my living-room and towards Setty.

I planned to frighten the living daylights out of him. But I reckoned without myself—and my own mad rage.

Back in the living-room, I brandished the blade. Bagdad-born Setty's dusky face seemed to whiten. His forehead looked shiny. For a moment he seemed scared, but then he said:—

"Go away, you silly bastard. What do you think you are doing? Playing at soldiers?"

I looked him straight in the eye.

"I'm not playing," I said earnestly. I took another step forward, the dagger still in my right hand. Setty sneered: "You can't frighten me."

And then he took a swing at me with the flat of his hand. He towered above me, tall and powerful.

We grappled. In a split second—it happened so quickly—we were rolling on the floor.

I was wielding the dagger just like our savage ancestors wielded weapons 20,000 years ago. It seemed to come naturally to me. We rolled over and over and my sweaty hand plunged the weapon frenziedly and repeatedly into his chest and legs.

I had to hurt him.

I aimed my blows anywhere. But Setty continued to struggle. He was as strong as an ox.

The more I stuck the dagger into him, the more he tried to push my head back and break my neck.

I tried to push Setty away from me to keep his blood off my clothes and force a gap between us.

I forced my knee into him. He grunted, but he wouldn't release his grip. It was like a vice.

WRITHE

I HELD the knife up to strike the sixth or seventh blow. I can't remember.

I plunged the blade into his ribs. I know, I heard them crack.

He sank back against the sofa and slumped on the floor. He writhed and rolled over to a spot beneath the window, on his back.

Setty began to cough violently and a trickle of red came from his mouth as he heaved and panted.

I stood over him with the dagger in my hand.

And, with a feeling of triumph at winning the fight, I watched the life run from him.

I looked at the clock. It was 7.52 p.m. The fight had lasted less than two minutes—about the same time as it took you to read about it.

Now Setty lay on his back, his eyes seemed glassily fixed on the ceiling.

When I looked down at him I thought: "The ball has stopped bouncing for you, chum."

PANIC

SUDDENLY, the feeling of elation deserted me. I panicked. I rushed over to the window overlooking the busy street and drew the curtains.

What had I done? Did anybody hear? Did anybody see? Who knew that Setty had come to my flat?

I fought off my daze. My mind started clicking again.

Down in the streets outside, life was going on as usual. Carefree couples strolled arm in arm on their way to the pictures.

But at my feet a man lay dead . . . murdered by me.

I wandered unsteadily into the back room where Tony, my dog, had slept through it all. I wanted time to restore myself to an even balance. I wanted to be able to think straight.

The thought flashed through my mind that perhaps I could get away with murder.

HEAVED

FIRST, I had to get rid of all traces of the killing. Next, I had to get the body out of the way.

I went back into the lounge. Setty still lay on his back, his staring eyes fixed on the ceiling.

I got hold of him by the legs and started to drag him, being careful to keep him on his back, so that blood from his chest did not trail on the floor.

He seemed a ton weight. But I dragged him across the hall, right through the dining room and scullery of my flat, and into the breakfast room.

Then I heaved him into the coal cupboard and covered him with an old piece of felt.

TIDIED

NEXT, I tidied up the lounge and set to rights the furniture that had been knocked over in the fight. I dragged an armchair over to cover a pool of blood in the corner where Setty died.

Luckily the blood had not been enough to seep through into the flat below, where a school headmaster lived.

With a flannel and a bowl of water I wiped blood off the sofa. A wooden lamp standard was

Continued on next page

Donald Hume's Murder Confession

HE KICKED MY PET DOG

Continued from previous page

I played the RAF 'hero' in a £5 uniform

GOSSIP

COMMUNIST

ESCAPE

SPIVVERY

COCKSURE

WEALTHY

I STAND AGAIN ON THE SPOT WHERE I MET SETTY

CYNTHIA—THE GIRL I MARRIED

GAY LIFE

HAGGLED

YELPED

NEXT WEEK HOW I KILLED SETTY

Donald Hume's Confession

MY MURDER

Killer's Calendar

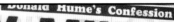

OCTOBER 21, 1949—A headless, legless torso is found on the desolate Essex marshes.

OCTOBER 22, 1949—Fingerprints from the hands still attached to the torso prove that the victim is Stanley Setty, forty-four-year-old street car-trader, who disappeared on October 4.

OCTOBER 28, 1949—Donald Hume, aged 29, is charged with the murder of Setty.

JANUARY 26, 1950—Old Bailey jury fails to agree on a verdict.

THE SAME DAY a fresh jury is directed to find Hume not guilty of murder. He then pleads guilty to being an accessory after the fact of murder by disposing of Setty's body, and is sentenced to twelve years.

FEBRUARY 1, 1958—Hume is released from Dartmoor.

PHOTO-RECONSTRUCTION BY PICTORIAL CAMERAMAN

I, Donald Hume, posed for this Sunday Pictorial photo-reconstruction a few days ago.

I wanted to show readers exactly how I flung the bundled-up torso of car-dealer Stanley Setty into the sea.

The plane is the one I used for the job. It is still flying at Elstree, near London.

A photograph of Tony, the dog I loved, has been pasted into position exactly as he was on the second flight I made to get rid of the sawn-up body.

BAFFLING

I HAVE just been freed after serving eight years of a twelve-year jail sentence for disposing of the body.

I admitted that crime at the Old Bailey. What I did not admit was that I murdered Setty. Now I have confessed it to the *Sunday Pictorial*: I DID MURDER SETTY.

I chose to make my confession to the *Sunday Pictorial*, because I knew this newspaper would demand the real truth from me, and because it has the widest readership.

I am going to tell you how I did it. But, first, please try to understand what makes a man a killer.

To explain that, I want you to know about the fantastic events that led to that night of murder on October 4, 1949 . . . to a crime that they call the most baffling of all unsolved murder mysteries.

This is my story—of my murder:—

DEGRADED

FANTASTIC . . . that's how my life has always been. That's how the stars were stacked for me.

I was born at Swanage, Dorset, with a chip on my shoulder, large as an elephant. I've got a grudge against society.

All my life I've had to fight the shame and degradation of not knowing who my father was.

The only condition that Hume agreed with the *Pictorial* was that they did not go to press before he had left the country. He also decided to take on yet another name but this time duplicating the identity of a real person: John Stephen Bird. Now with the double alias of Brown and Bird, and passports in both names, on May 25, 1958 he flew out of Manchester airport bound for Zürich in Switzerland. Carrying his £2,000, he was already in breach of the law as then there were very strict exchange control regulations and one could only leave the country with £25 sterling. The following week the first instalment of his confession was published causing a huge sensation but at the same time an outcry because he was the first person to publicly declare that he had got away with murder. In Switzerland he quickly made friends with a local girl, boasting that he was a Canadian test pilot. He then travelled to North America where he obtained a Canadian visa and driving licence. Returning to Europe, he hatched a plan to replenish his coffers. He thought that if he based himself in Switzerland, he could fly to London to carry out a bank robbery before fleeing back to the safety of Zürich. *Above:* This is the Midland Bank in Boston Manor Road, Brentford, which he targeted on August 2, 1958 but when one of the cashiers looked as if he was going to resist, Hume callously shot him in the stomach before catching a plane home.

Hume had netted £2,000 but when he learned later that he had been duped as the safe contained £40,000, he decided to pay the bank a return visit. Although he had reservations about robbing the same bank so soon, he returned to London at the beginning of November only to discover that the bank had since moved and the old building was now empty.

Left: He found the new location here on the corner of the Great West Road and Clayponds Road. The robbery on November 12 only provided him with £300 and this time he shot and wounded the branch manager. *Right:* The Midland Bank disappeared with the takeover by HSBC in 1992 and the building is now the west London headquarters of Barratt Homes.

The remains of Stanley Setty were buried in the Jewish Cemetery at Golders Green. This is his grave No. 11 in Row 57, Plot SP-B.

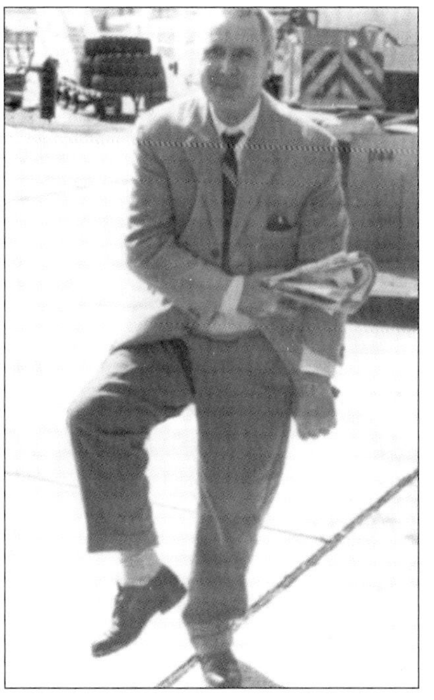

Although Hume successfully returned to Switzerland, police in Britain had already linked both bank robberies and they were now actively looking for a Donald Brown. Then on Friday, January 30, 1959, Hume robbed the Gewerbe Bank in Zürich's Ramistrasse. Without warning he shot and wounded the cashier and when a taxi driver tried to head him off, Hume shot him dead. He was found guilty of murder in September 1959 but, as Switzerland had abolished the death penalty in 1942, Hume was sentenced to life imprisonment with hard labour. He was a troublesome prisoner, becoming so truculent that the Swiss attempted to have their most recalcitrant prisoner transferred to Britain. Hume was released with remission after serving 16 years in Regensdorf prison but on his arrival at Heathrow in 1976 *(left)*, he was promptly taken to Broadmoor, the hospital for the criminally insane. A period of trial leave to St Bernards Hospital, Ealing, began in 1988, Hume spending his last days in Thompson House in Wornington Road, Kensal Town, west London. He died in North Hampshire Hospital on July 9, 1998 and was buried in an unmarked grave *(right)* in Basingstoke Cemetery. With Tony no longer with us, Miss Daisy pays her respects at Grave F720.

WORLD'S LARGEST EVENING NET SALE

The Evening News

B NO. 21,623 LONDON, WEDNESDAY, JUNE 6, 1951 THREE-HALFPENCE

P.C.'s KILLER IS SHOT DEAD IN 'SIDNEY-STREET' SIEGE

Bullets and Tear Gas Used in Chatham House Battle

GUNMAN'S LAST STAND IN TINY ATTIC

"EVENING NEWS" REPORTER

A 20-YEAR-OLD GUNMAN, KILLER OF A CHATHAM POLICEMAN, DIED TO-DAY AT THE POINT OF HIS OWN GUN. FOR 105 MINUTES INSIDE A CHATHAM HOUSE HE WITHSTOOD A SIEGE BY ARMED POLICE AND TROOPS, ANSWERING THEIR BULLETS AND TEAR GAS BOMBS WITH BURSTS FROM HIS STEN GUN.

Then in the little council house that was his home in Symons-avenue, there was a long silence. The 200 men outside moved closer. The long axes of the firemen broke down the door and a small group went in.

They tramped up the stairs to the tiny, raftered loft, still and quiet, yet hung with fumes from the smoke-bombs. On the floor lay Alan Derek Poole, Army deserter, dead.

Lying across his chest was the Sten gun. Beside his legs was a heavy dagger.

Later a preliminary medical examination was to show that almost certainly he died from a bullet from his own gun.

They carried him down to the street, out of the house where he had been brought up and where he had lived with his father, mother, brothers and sisters, and where, unknown to them, he had taken refuge after his Sten gun shot down P.C. Alan Baxter, aged 33, of Ernest-road, Chatham, when the constable challenged him on Monday night beside a rubbish tip.

That was the start of the manhunt which ended in the new Siege of Sidney-street—the Siege of Symons-avenue.

Troops and police who had been searching for Poole assembled at Chatham police station waiting to move off to renew the hunt. Then came an urgent message.

A uniformed superintendent shouted: "Where are the armed police? There's shooting up there."

Police and troops were rushed by car and coach to Symons-avenue—not far from All Saints' Hospital, where Mrs. Baxter, wife of the dead constable, is a patient after giving birth on Friday to a baby which died later.

The house was surrounded by armed police and steel-helmeted troops with rifles. Members of the family, including a child in arms, came out of the back door.

The house is one of a block on the corner of Symons-avenue and Haig-avenue. Police officers cleared the occupants from nearly 50 council houses around the area, and warned the occupants of those who were not moved to close their windows in case tear gas seeped in.

From behind the houses and from several of the bedroom windows police officers took up their positions to cover this house in case Poole should try to make a break.

And so, with the bright June sunshine pouring down, drama and tragedy came closer to the normally quiet corner of Chatham.

Once members of the family were out of the house police crawled nearer the house on their stomachs. A burst of gunfire came from the trapped man. Then four shots were fired by police into the front of the house. Again came a silence.

A senior police officer shouted an appeal to the hidden man. "Surrender now! You are surrounded by 200 armed men."

At 10 a.m. ex-Scots Guardsman Police-Sergeant Walter Iveson, of the Rochester Traffic Division, covered by Assistant Chief Constable Horwood, and a constable, both of whom had Sten-guns, crept round an angle of the house and dropped a teargas bomb through the letterbox.

For two hours more the police ringed the area with riflemen and officers carrying Sten-guns and threw tear-gas bombs at the front door in an effort to smoke Poole out. Then the Chief Constable of Kent, Major J. F. Ferguson, decided that the time had come to close in.

Det.-Insp. E. G. Everett and a Sten-gun man began the search of the ground floor, still chokingly thick with tear gas, and Det.-Sgt. Sam Potter and another officer, P.C. G. Stevens, wearing gas masks, crept up the stairs to the bedrooms.

The man on the run had reached the end.

As the police carried him down his father watched. Then, hands in pockets, he walked slowly down the street.

SIDNEY-STREET SIEGE RECALLED.—SEE PAGE 5.

Two armed ... with his rifle ... house in Symons ... wait for the gunman to ... an appearance.

... and his ... to-day ... Bevan.

The father of the dead gunman walking with police officers and armed constable during the siege.

105 Minutes In Symons-ave.

THIS was the timetable for to-day's siege of Symons-avenue:

9.15: First shots heard from house. Neighbours phoned for police.

9.18.—Council of war at police headquarters breaks up as armed men race by car to scene.

9.35.—Police throw cordon round block of houses.

9.50.—Police Sergt. Iveson and dropped tear gas bombs through letter-box.

10.4.—Child in arms was among six people who came out into street.

10.26.—Police fired four shots into front of house.

10.30.—Short burst of fire from a Sten gun in house.

10.37.—Senior officer shouted surrender appeal. There was no response.

10.38. — Police crept round walls and threw tear-gas bombs into windows at front and rear.

10.53: Further heavy tear-gas attacks.

10.59: Police rushed the house covered by rifles.

11.6: Gunman was carried out dead.

THEY CALLED HIM 'THE TERROR'

THREATS TO POLICE

"Evening News" Reporter

DEREK ALAN POOLE had been the terror of Chatham's Symons-avenue area, in which he lived for a long time.

He was known as a youth of quick temper, who was willing to use violence at any time he was crossed.

He first came under the notice of the police in his early teens, when he was sent to an approved school by the Juvenile Court.

On the way to the school he absconded. His whereabouts were unknown for days.

Three Convictions

He had three convictions for housebreaking. The last resulted in him being sent to Borstal for three years.

On his release he joined the Royal Corps of Signals. He deserted last October, and has been on the run ever since.

He has threatened the police with violence several times. Once, when a policeman went to apprehend him at Chatham football ground, he drew a sheath-knife, and said: "If you come any nearer you'll get this."

Two other policemen appeared, and he dropped the knife.

500 POLICE SEEK STOLEN GUNS

Five hundred Ulster police were searching to-day over a wide area for the machine-guns, rifles, and ammunition which were stolen from Ebrington Naval Barracks, Londonderry, where they were stored for the Territorial Army.

Houses are being searched, cars stopped and the drivers questioned, while lonely out-of-the-way places are being investigated for arms dumps.

The authorities, fearing a repetition of the raid, are planning the transfer of other arms and equipment to military barracks.

IT MAY GET COLDER

Chance of Showers

With temperatures approaching the 70s in many places colder air was moving towards England from Scandinavia to-day. To-morrow temperatures are expected to drop ten degrees and there is a chance of some showers, but the break in the fine spell may only last 36 hours.

JAIL FOR FRAUD

Cork, Wednesday. — Michael Judge, 30-year-old accountant, whose wife lives in Broadway, Hendon, was jailed for a year in Cork for fraud.

JAPS TO VISIT B.B.C.

Tokio, Wednesday. — Tetsuro Furuaki, president of the Japan Broadcasting Corporation, and two officials will leave for London at the end of this month at the invitation of the B.B.C.—Reuter.

HIGHWAY HINT

Beware of the sun in your eyes in the long evenings. In addition to the sunshade in the car, glare can be reduced by wearing coloured glasses. But do not get them too dark, otherwise it may be difficult to judge distances accurately.

Police officers armed with automatics extending and taking up their positions in a field to cover the rear of the house held by Alan Poole.

OIL—TALKS TEAM NAMED

ARRIVING NEXT WEEK

THE Anglo-Iranian Oil Co. announced to-day that the directors to take part in talks with the Persian Government were: Mr. B. R. Jackson, deputy chairman, Sir Thomas Gardiner, one of the Government directors, Mr. N. A. Gass, and Mr. E. H. O. Elkington.

"The talks were foreshadowed in ... company's representative in Teheran on June 3. It is hoped that the directors will arrive in Teheran early next week.

ALLIES BREAK INTO 'LITTLE MAGINOT'

Tokio, Wednesday.—Troops of the United Nations to-day broke through the tough outer shell of the Communist defence line in Central Korea — the so-called "Little Maginot Line"—to drive two miles nearer to Chorwon and Kumhwa, southern anchors of the enemy's "Iron Triangle."

In 48 hours, in bitter fighting in worsening weather, the Allied infantry have battled on another five miles, advancing along mountain trails turned into running streams by heavy rain and across fields churned into mud.—B.U.P.

Food Ships Held Up By Dock Clerks' Strike

THE London tally clerks' strike spread to-day to Tilbury Dock where all the clerks stopped work. Strikers now total more than 1,000.

With the stoppage affecting the Royal group, Surrey Commercial and West India Docks normal work was possible only in the London Dock and the Upper Pool.

Thousands of dockers and stevedores ... the clerks.

Food cargoes are held up and about 50 ships are idle.

ADELAIDE HALL ROBBED OF FURS

£3,000 LONDON RAID

"Evening News" Reporter

WHILE coloured singer Adelaide Hall was entertaining guests at the opening of her new club, the Calypso Club, in Regent-street last night, thieves broke into her house in Drayton-gardens, Kensington, and stole £3,000-worth of furs.

MEAT PACT HOPES

Montevideo, Wednesday. — Differences between Britain and Uruguay on the projected meat pact have been settled, say Montevideo reports.—B.U.P.

WEATHERALL TELLS OF QUARREL

MR. EDWARD CHRISTOPHER WEATHERALL said at a Hucknall, Nottingham, inquest to-day that he had quarrelled with his wife after she returned from a week-end in London.

The inquiry was being continued into the death of Mrs. Florence ... found in a ditch not far from her home, The Forest Lane, near Hucknall, Notts.

Mr. Weatherall told the coroner that in May, 1950, while they were living at Grantham, his wife told him that she was going to London to stay with friends for the week-end, but would not say who they were. On her return, she said that she had had a very miserable time.

DUKE OF WINDSOR

Visit to Palace

The Duke of Windsor, who arrived in London on Monday on a private visit, and is staying with friends in London, will call at Buckingham Palace late this afternoon. There he will probably see the King who has been advised by his doctors to have a period of complete rest. Later the Duke will visit his mother, Queen Mary, at Marlborough House.

Gunman Said: 'Goodbye, Mother'

IT was just before nine o'clock this morning that Alan Derek Poole's mother, Mrs. Dorothy May Poole, aged 47, found that he was in the house in Symons-avenue, Chatham.

Red-eyed and trembling, Mrs. Poole, who has ten children altogether, told me:

"We did not know a thing until after the others had gone to work and I had seen the children off to school.

The five foot 11 in. deserter, with sleek brown hair, a Clark Gable moustache and "sideboards," suddenly walked downstairs.

"He said he had been up in the attic since the night before last. He had to come down because he was thirsty.

"He said, 'I'm going to shoot anybody who comes here.'"

Said Goodbye

"He told us to get out and Mr. Poole and I went."

Mrs. Poole said her son said good-bye before she left.

"He said: 'I am going and someone's going with me.' Then he turned to little Doreen and said: 'Good-bye. You won't see me any more.'"

Her husband, Albert William Poole, aged 57, said: "We have a space up in the roof which we can reach through a trap-door. He must have been hidden there all the time. I don't know how he got into the house.

"He had a mad look in his eyes. I am sure he had gone mad. He shot twice at something out of the back of the house. I could not see what it was, but I suppose it was one of the policemen. Before I left he said: 'When I have shot all those — I'll shoot myself.'"

Father Went Back

Twenty minutes after he left the house and after conferring with senior police officers, Mr. Poole decided to go back to try to make his son give himself up.

"It was a bit nerve-racking, but I didn't really think he would shoot his father," said Mr. Poole.

"I went into the house, but I could not hear a sound, so I went upstairs towards the room leading to the attic.

"As I got to the top I found that a big single bed had been pushed to the head of the stairs as a barricade. It reached almost to the ceiling.

"I could not get through. I shouted to him to come out, but I got no reply, so I came out again. Then the police closed in."

WEATHER FORECAST

UNTIL NOON TO-MORROW: Light or moderate north to north-west wind, perhaps fresh at times to-morrow; sunny and warm today, cloudy and cooler to-morrow. **OUTLOOK:** Cooler and mainly cloudy with chance of showers. **CHANNEL:** Sea moderate. **BAROMETER:** 30.05in., falling slowly.

Lighting-up time 10.12 p.m. Sun sets 9.12 p.m., rises to-morrow 4.45 a.m. Moon sets 11.50 p.m., rises 0.20 a.m. to-morrow. First quarter next Tuesday. High water London Bridge 3.47 a.m., 4.4 p.m.

WHAT IT DID

June 6, 1944. "D" Day: The invasion had been postponed for 24 hours on account of the weather, and when the vast fleet approached the beaches at last, it bore an army that fought a battle against seasickness.—Stephen Bone, "British Weather."

HAGUE WILL HEAR OIL CASE

The Hague, Wednesday.—International Court of Justice have accepted lodgement of Britain's case in dispute with Persia over oil nationalisation.—Reuter.

1,189 DOCK MEN ON STRIKE

With spread of London tally clerks' strike to Tilbury, number of strikers rose to 1,189, affecting 66 ships, 55 of them being completely idle. In Royal group alone thousands of tons of foodstuff held up.

PETAIN'S DOCTOR IS OPTIMISTIC

Paris.—Prof. Coumel, French ... Petain, said that lung trouble from which the aged Marshal had been suffering had been overcome and he was optimistic about his chances of survival.

PAPAGOS AGAIN SAYS 'NO'

Athens, Wednesday.—The U.S. Ambassador here, Mr. John Peurifoy, has dropped his attempts to persuade Field-Marshal Papagos to resume as Greek C.-in-C. "There is nothing I can do to be of further help at this time," Mr. Peurifoy said in a statement.—Reuter.

WOMEN'S GOLF

Fifth Round results: Miss Blazood beat Miss Beverly ... Donald beat ... Miss M Paterson at 19th.

RACING RESULTS

BRIGHTON

2.0.—CREAM CRACKER 7—2 A. Harvey
First Shot 8—1 What Fun 3—1
RNRS-Cream Cracker, Gold Sandal, What Fun, First Shot, Myrina, Abracadabra, Gas Chance.
2.30.—GOLDEN EVE 3—1 K. Gethin
Vectis 7—4f My Word 100—8
RNRS-Vectis, Medal Lass, My Word, Political Broadcast, Golden Eve, Princess Tiana.
3.0.—DEERSLAYER 15—2 T. Gosling
Jill Again 7—1 Deputy Lieutenant 5—1
RNRS-Belinda Fair, Deerslayer, Keyhaven, Fancy Ian, Aspirant, Deputy Lieutenant, Jill Again, Kim, Clem, Stagestruck, London Wall, Night Train, Kiss me Kate, Black Secole.
3.30.—COUNTRY LIFE 3—1 G. Richards
Sporting Offer 2—1f St. Paul 5—2
ALSO RAN-Pee-Wee.

YORK

2.0.—DENOUNCE 5—1 C. Pike
Harvest Maid 15—8f Downland Darkie 11—2
2.30.—ROYAL VALE 8—1 G. Littlewood 7 ran
Cascadeur 4—11f Thorn 4—1
3.0.—BOISEL 4—1 J. Bruce 6 ran
Torchlite 2—1f Ortolan 9—4
3.30.—ORDERLY ANN 20—1 A Carson 8 ran
High Forest 8—11f Copernitus 9—2

CRICKET LATEST

SURREY
• GLOUCESTER ...122—2
DERBY ...103—2
• HANTS ...
GLAMORGAN ...
• NORTHANTS ...163—6
SOMERSET ...116—6
• YORKS ...
SUSSEX ...
• NOTTS ...123—6
WARWICK ...
• ESSEX ...93—2
CAMBS. U. ...101—1
• MIDDLESEX
KENT ...133—5
• MINOR COUNT'S.
WORCESTER ...129—3

Alan Poole was the third eldest of eight brothers and two sisters living at 114 Symons Avenue, Chatham, in Kent. His mother described him as a 'quiet boy, sometimes moody' but was known in the neighbourhood to have a quick temper, and that he was easily aroused to violence. Poole's life of crime began at the age of 15. In 1947 he appeared in Chatham Magistrates Court for the first time with his brother Frederick to face three charges of breaking into commercial premises. Then at the West Kent Quarter Sessions at Maidstone when 19 other offences were taken into consideration, he was sent to an Approved School. At 16 he again appeared before magistrates at Chatham but now as an escapee and was consequently sent to Borstal Institution for three years. Just four months later he was in the South East London Juvenile Court for further breaking and entering offences, being sentenced to seven days imprisonment before being returned to the Borstal. He absconded again in April 1949 and when a police constable tracked him down at Chatham Sports Ground, Poole threatened the officer with a knife before surrendering. He was again returned to Borstal and on his release on licence in 1950 joined the Army, enlisting in the Royal Corps of Signals but deserted in November having taken with him a Sten and 1,000 rounds of ammunition stolen from the armoury. On June 4, 1951, he was spotted using the gun on Sharsted Farm, a couple of miles from his home in the company of two girls — later both established as being a pair of absentees on the run from an Approved School.

June 4, 1951 – Gun-battle at Chatham

It was shortly after ten o'clock on Monday night that the shooting of Police Constable Alan Baxter occurred.

The affair started when four boys saw a man with a woman's scarf round his face and a Sten gun in his hand talking to two girls, aged about seventeen, in a field at Sharsted. The boys shouted at him, but he raised his gun and ordered them away.

The boys immediately ran to Sharsted Farm and told 27-years-old Mr. Norman Attwood what they had seen. Mr Attwood went into the field and saw the man with the girls, but as he drew near them the man shouted threateningly.

Mr Attwood then hurried back to his house and made a '999' call to the Chatham Police Station.

PC Baxter was the patrol car driver that night and with Police-sergeant William Langford, they set off in the car to Sharsted to investigate, and picked up Mr. Attwood on the way.

Near a shed on Chatham Council's refuse tip at Sharsted the patrol car stopped and Police-sergeant Langford and Mr. Attwood got out and approached the man, who was standing in the door of the shed.

Left: **Poole had built himself this makeshift hide in the woodland above the farm. When four boys approached they were chased away, running to the farm where the young Norman Attwood** ***(right)*** **was working in his garden.**

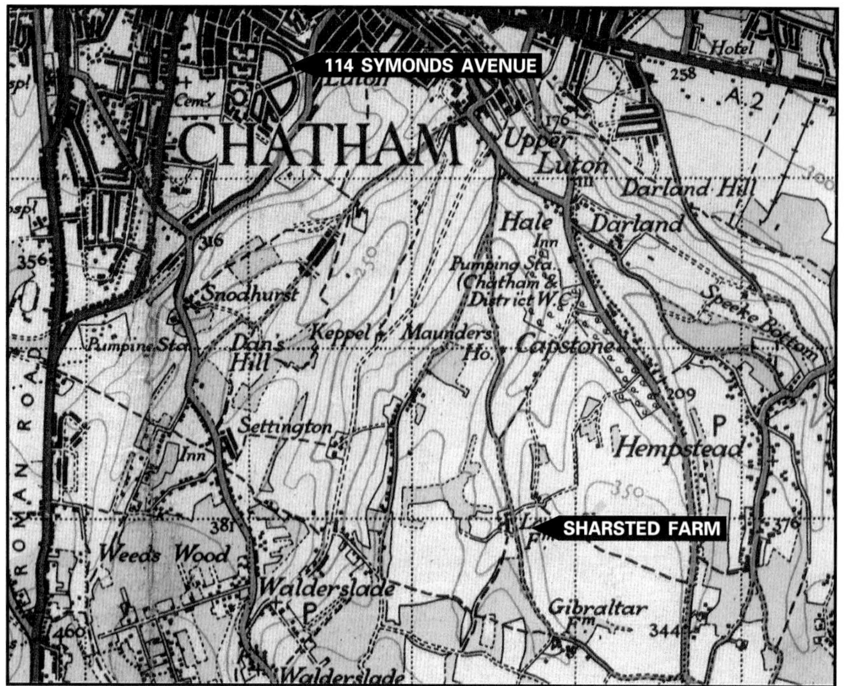

The Press report is not quite correct for when Norman tried to dial 999 his telephone was dead so instead he had to cycle to the nearest phone box nearly two miles away in the High Street at Luton to raise the alarm. He then cycled back to the farm to await the police. When the van arrived, Police Constable Alan Baxter drove on to the refuse tip while Norman walked with Sergeant Bill Langford across the fields to where the man and the girls were loitering.

At one time detectives hurried to Chatham railway station after a report had been received that a man had been seen acting suspiciously there.

Bus stops were watched and conductors received a warning that the wanted man might try to board their vehicles. A police watch on lorries was kept.

Police-constable Baxter still lay unconscious in hospital, with the doctors and nurses doing everything they could for him.

All through the day further reinforcements arrived from different parts of the county to try to swell the search parties.

Every squad car in the district was sent to the scene of the shooting. All cars on main roads in the area were stopped and their drivers questioned. Chatham, Rochester and Gillingham were cordoned off.

Eventually the two girls were traced and taken to Chatham police station, where they gave a description of the man who was talking to them. As a result of what they said, the search was concentrated in the 15 square mile area between Luton, near Chatham, Rochester airport and Bluebell Hill.

During the night some of the searching police officers who had been called from their beds had carried arms, but when daylight came these were discarded.

More servicemen were called in and they were divided into three main groups which began to beat the district towards a junction in the centre of the area. The parties kept in touch with each other by means of Army walkie-talkie sets.

Recently Sten guns and ammunition were reported stolen from a local cadet store. 1,000 rounds of ammunition then disappeared.

Describing the incident, Mr Attwood said: 'We went down to the tip and we saw the man and the two girls at the entrance to the shed. As the sergeant and I approached the man swung up a gun and we started to dodge. He fired and the sergeant fell. I thought he had been shot but he had only tripped, and we went into the cover of the side of the shed. The man ran towards the police car and as the constable began to get out he fired again, hitting him in the chest and stomach. The windows of the police car were shattered. The man ran off up over the bank and disappeared. The girls vanished too.

Picking up his unconscious and badly wounded colleague, Sgt. Langford drove him back to Chatham in the patrol car and a general alarm was raised.

Immediately the grave news was communicated to headquarters at Chatham, uniformed and plain-clothes police were sent out to search the area and a message was flashed to all police stations in the county telling them to be on the lookout for a man aged about twenty years, dressed in dark clothes with a roll-neck jersey and armed with a Sten gun and sheath knife.

All through the early hours of the morning the search went on, most of the officers taking part having been up all the previous day and night.

As dawn broke, some police dogs, which had been brought from Guildford, were used but they were unable to pick up the scent.

In the morning, arms were issued to the searching police and they were ordered to take no chances.

About 30 ratings of the Naval Patrol were called in to help and after a conference had been held with Army officers from local units, including the Royal Engineers from Kitchener Barracks, soldiers, too, joined in the hunt.

As the day wore on the search spread over the North Downs, in an area stretching from Watling Street, through the miles of dense woods at Walderslade, down to the Chatham-Maidstone road. Relentlessly the search went on through the trees and undergrowth and across fields.

The council yard of 1951 has been closed and moved a few hundred yards to the north.

This was the yard set up by the council to deal with waste paper. Poole came down along the tree line from his hide in the wood top right, and was already hiding behind straw bales when the police arrived.

Just before the death of Police-constable Baxter was announced the following statement was issued by the police: 'In connection with this incident: the police are anxious to trace a twenty-years-old absentee from the Royal Corps of Signals named Alan Derek Poole, whose home is at Chatham, as it is thought that he can assist enquiries.'

This was the first time that Poole's name had been divulged in connection with the shooting.

The search continued until darkness fell and then the search parties were withdrawn, but pickets were left to prevent Poole from breaking through the cordon.

All through the night Poole's home in Symons Avenue had remained surrounded by police.

Sixty years later we took this photograph from the same hillside showing the old council yard turned back to nature.

Norman Attwood came with us to describe and show us exactly what had happened. ***Left:*** **As the police van arrived here at the entrance to the yard, Poole was ready and his first shot holed the windscreen** ***(right).*** **PC Baxter then emerged from the driver's door and stumbled onto the road whereupon Poole fired again as he lay on the ground. The later post-mortem confirmed that he had been struck by four bullets. Poole then disappeared. Norman helped lift the stricken PC into the back of the vehicle and travelled with him to hospital.** ***Below:*** **The exact spot where the officer was gunned down.**

The first intimation that Poole was hiding in his parents' home came just before nine o'clock on Wednesday morning when a shot was fired from the bedroom window at police officers who were in the field behind the house. This was a signal for reinforcements to be called to Symons Avenue.

Troops and police who had been searching the woods since dawn assembled at Chatham Police Station and a senior police officer was heard to call from the door of the Police Station: 'Where are the armed police? There is a shooting up there.'

Gas respirators were distributed among the police and tear gas bombs were provided by the naval authorities. In police vans the reinforcements moved off to Symons Avenue where the siege had already begun in the Council house, one of six in a row.

And it was so in the brilliant June sunshine that one of the greatest dramas in police history unfolded itself in a normally quiet suburban street.

Poole's father went through the cordon to the house and called out for his son to surrender but there was no reply.

It was now ascertained that Poole was in an upstairs room and the police had the knowledge that he had plenty of ammunition and meant to fight it out.

Stand-off in Symons Avenue. Army and Navy personnel join the police on the corner of Haig Avenue. Although Poole's house was surrounded, initially the police were not sure that he was inside. Mrs Dorothy Poole explained: 'My daughter Maureen, who is eleven, came back from school before nine o'clock [Wednesday morning]. She was crying and said she did not want to go to school because the other children were laughing at her. I sat down to write a note when Alan appeared at the door of the room and said, "I'm going to shoot anyone who comes here." He said he had been in the attic since the night before last. He had changed into his best clothes and had a mad look in his eyes. He ordered us out of the house but before we went he said goodbye to us.' Mr Albert Poole described how he came home from work feeling that something was wrong and went into the house to find that his son had barricaded himself behind a single bed at the top of the stairs. His son told him to go and as Mr Poole left the house, he fired his Sten gun at the police. This was the shot which raised the alarm.

Kent Police were in no mood to allow a long siege to continue and after the first shots came from the house, within the hour Major J. F. Ferguson, ex-Durham Light Infantry, the Chief Constable, decided it was time for action. Tear gas was thrown through the front window to which Poole responded with a burst from his Sten. The police returned fire, and offered Poole the chance to surrender, but when there was no response more tear gas was used before officers stormed the house. They found Poole dead in the front bedroom. *Left:* The windows have been thrown open to disperse the gas. *Right:* In August 2011, the current occupant, Robert Blackburn, kindly allowed us to inspect his house.

At ten o'clock Police-sergeant Walter Iveson, of the Rochester Traffic Department and an ex-Scots Guardsman, ran the gauntlet across the front of the house, covered by Assistant Chief Constable Horwood and constables with Sten guns. As he passed Poole's house he lobbed tear gas bombs in through the front window and letter box. Almost immediately clouds of blue smoke curled from the doors and windows.

All was quiet for about half-an-hour and then came a burst of Sten gun fire from the house. The police replied with a volley from opposite.

Another surrender appeal was made by the police and by Poole's brother Bert, but again there was no response.

There was a grim silence among the hundreds of people who watched the drama from a distance.

While a further tear gas attack was made on the house, the Chief Constable, Major J. F. Ferguson called together other senior officers and it was decided that the time to close in had arrived.

A ladder was procured in case it was needed and covered by Sten guns and rifles, the police made their first moves towards the house. With them was Poole's brother Bert.

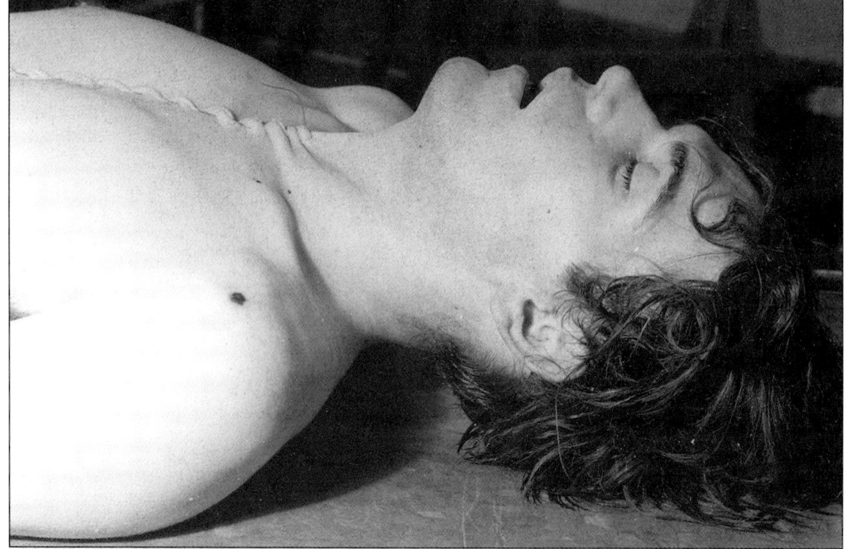

A neighbour told reporters: 'Poole looked like a gangster, he walked like a gangster and talked out of the side of his mouth. And he died like a gangster.'

With Poole's body having been carried into the roadway, an ambulance draws up to take it to the mortuary.

Stand down! No. 114 is on the left with the open windows . . . but inside the house there was a surprise in store.

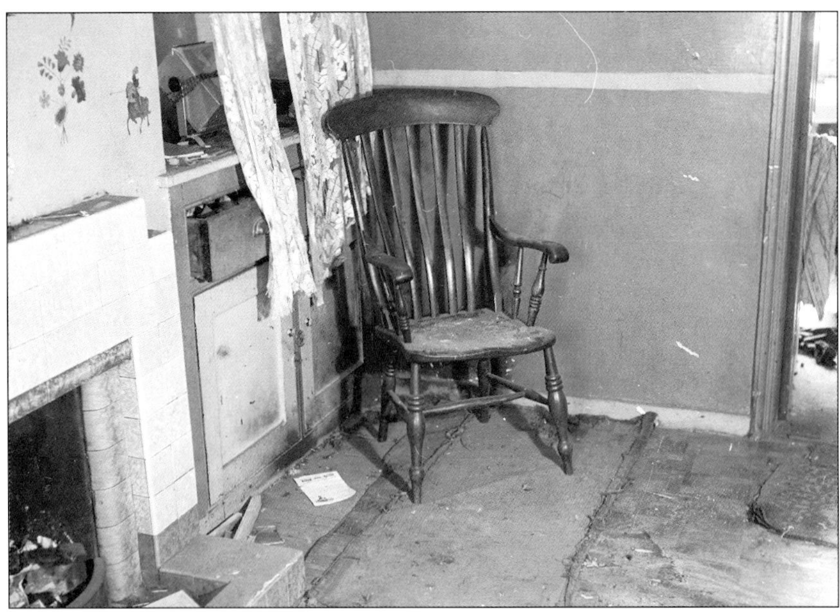

What appeared to be a normal front room . . .

The clothes on the body were not those which Poole had been wearing at the time of his attack on Police-constable Baxter. It was obvious that during his period of hiding he had changed from the dark jacket, flannels and roll-neck sweater into a brown suit.

Dr. C. S. Grosmark, of Chatham, the police surgeon, who had been standing by throughout the battle of Symons Avenue, walked through the crowd of police and soldiers and examined the body. He confirmed that Poole was dead.

He had died not like the heroes of the cheap American comics which he was known to read, but like a rat in a trap.

Although the Army and Navy played a large part in bringing to an end this tragic affair, at all times the police went to the fore.

Chatham Observer, June 8, 1951

An inquest was opened yesteday at All Saints' Hospital, Chatham, on the body of Alan Derek Poole, aged 20, who was found dead in an upper room at his parents' house in Symons Avenue, Chatham, on Wednesday morning after he had defied armed police and troops with a Sten gun.

The Times, June 9, 1951

Sergeant Iveson, who had been throwing the bombs, led the party through the front door of the house with a Sten gun after the door had been broken by Sergeant Baker of Gravesend. Others in the party of officers were Mr. Horwood, Chief Superintendent C. J. Broughton, Detective Inspector E. G. Everett, Detective-sergeant L. T. Potter, Detective-constable T. Bodell, and Detective-constables Blackman and Dixon from Gravesend.

While Detective-Inspector Everett, covered by a Sten gun, searched the ground floor rooms, Sergeant Potter with other officers went upstairs and found Poole's body.

It lay on its back beneath the window in the front bedroom with a Sten gun across it. Near by lay a sheath knife and a Ghurka's knife. Poole had plenty of ammunition left.

Through a back window of the house Detective-sergeant Potter waved a white handkerchief to show that the siege was over.

Poole's limp body was carried downstairs and out of the front door and was laid in the road. A second or two later a police officer came out of the house with a brown blanket and covered it.

. . . turned out to be a hiding place for a secret trapdoor!

The jury at the resumed Rochester inquest to-day on Police-constable Alan Baxter returned a verdict of Wilful Murder against Alan Poole, aged 20, who was shot dead after a two-hour siege of his home in Chatham.

Police-sergeant S. J. Langford told the court how he went with Police-constable Baxter and another policeman to Sharsted Farm, near Luton, Chatham, in answer to a 999 call at about 9.45 p.m. on June 4. When he attempted to stop a man and two women leaving a shed, the man fired at him with a Sten gun and he took cover. There was a pause for a few seconds and then the firing started again and he heard a scream and a groan from the direction of the truck. He found Police-constable Baxter lying at the near side front wheel of the truck in the road. With the help of Mr. Norman Attwood he took Police-constable Baxter to St. Bartholomew's Hospital, Rochester.

Jean Violet Smith, aged 17, of Fosterhill Road, Bedford, one of the two girls who were with Poole, said she heard Poole shout to the police-sergeant: 'I will shoot my way through.' As she and the other girl were running away she saw Poole near the truck. 'I saw a policeman start to get out of the truck,' she said. 'He was just out when I heard a shot and saw him stumble and fall down on to his knees.'

The Times, June 15, 1951

Left: **And in the back garden Alan Poole was in the process of digging another secret hideaway.** *Right:* **The two Roberts discuss the events of another age as Roxy the Rottweiler searches for the long-lost tunnel!**

A verdict of justifiable homicide by means of a gunshot wound fired by a police officer in the course of his duty was returned by the jury at the resumed inquest at All Saints' Hospital, Chatham, to-day, on the body of Alan Derek Poole, 20, of Symons Avenue, Chatham. Poole, who had previously shot and killed a policeman, died after a two-hour siege.

The jury commended the courageous way the police had acted in the case. The Coroner, Mr. W. J. Harris, congratulating the police, said: 'It was due to their careful planning that no further injury or loss of life was sustained.'

Dr. J. L. Dales, pathologist at All Saints' Hospital, Chatham said that a post-mortem examination revealed a bullet wound in the left shoulder. It had the appearance of a wound inflicted by a gun fired at some distance from the body.

In his summing up the Coroner said that the weight of evidence was against Poole's having taken his own life.

The Times, June 16, 1951

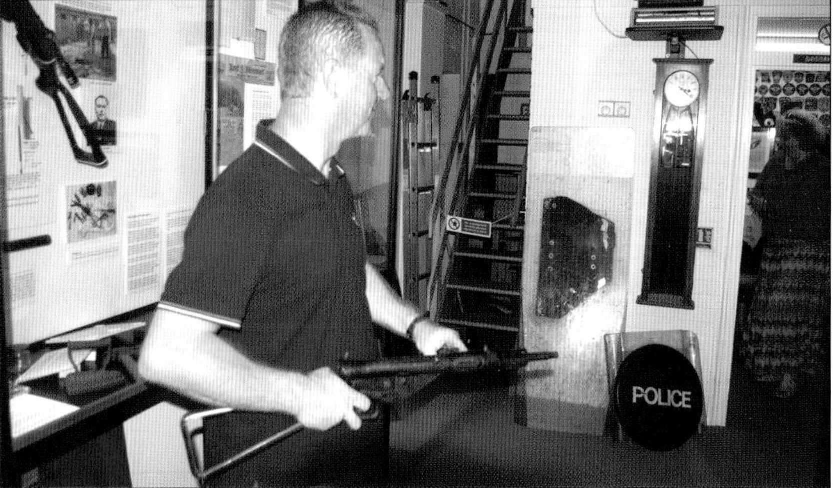

Rob Green inspects Poole's 9mm Sten, now in the Kent Police Museum at Chatham. It is a Mk II fitted with a mid to late war cheaper two-piece stock.

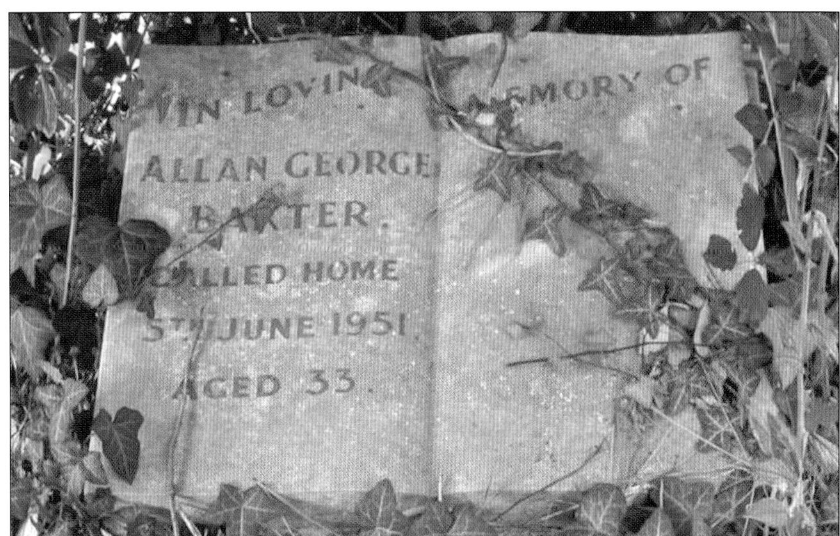

Alan Baxter was born at Tovil, near Maidstone, where his father worked in the nearby paper mills. His parents moved to Hayling Island near Portsmouth, and upon leaving school he joined the Merchant Navy. At 21 he returned to Kent to join the Kent Police and served at Sittingbourne for several years before being recalled to the merchant service during the war, attaining the rank of Second Officer. While serving at Sittingbourne he met Miss Peggy Harmon of Milton and they were married at Tunstall Parish Church in August 1943 while he was still in the Navy. Mrs Nelly Harmon, Peggy's mother, described the couple as 'madly in love and living only for each other. They were the happiest pair one could meet. Alan was a brave and happy man.' Yet his death was compounded when Peggy lost her baby on the Friday before Alan was killed, the same misfortune she had with their first child. She was still in hospital when her husband was shot. The following Monday, June 11, Alan Baxter was cremated at Charing Crematorium following which his ashes were taken to Hayling Island to be interred in St Mary's Churchyard.

1943-1953 – No. 10 Rillington Place, London, W11

You will not find Rillington Place in any street map of London now, for it has long been demolished. It was a mean shabby cul-de-sac of ten houses on either side. Although the houses had three floors, they were small, almost miniature houses, and their most striking characteristic was peeling paint and rotting stucco. The street was bounded at one end by St Mark's Road and at the other by the wall of Rickard's Transport Depot for coaches and vans. Originally Rickard's was Bartlett's Iron Foundry, and the foundry chimney still stands. It rises, as it were from the centre of the boundary wall, and its squat pear-shaped form seemed to dominate the street.

Just beyond the houses on the north side lay the Metropolitan Railway Line, and the sounds of the trains coming and going were part of the lives of the people who lived there. Many of them lived two and three to a room. On summer evenings the children played in the street and on the pavements, and the parents sat at the open windows watching the world go by. No. 10 was the last house on the south side hard up against Rickard's wall and beneath the shadow of the foundry chimney.

10 Rillington Place was a house of three floors. It was quite small, almost a doll's house; and if there had been soft earth outside the front instead of concrete, it would have been possible to jump from the top-floor window without doing oneself much damage. The house was divided for letting purposes into three flats, one to each floor, and it was the ground-floor flat that was taken over by the Christies. As the plan shows, this consisted of a living-room facing the street, a bedroom behind it looking out into the yard, and at the end of the passage a kitchen, also facing the yard, but beyond and at right angles to the bedroom. Between these two rooms was the back door opening into the yard. The stairs to the upper floors were directly facing the front door, and only two or three feet away from the bedroom and living-room doors.

At the far end of the kitchen was a recess or alcove, which was used for storing coal, and in front of this a small wash-house, separated from the alcove by a brick wall and accessible only from the yard. The wash-house measured fifty-four inches by fifty-two inches. There was a copper in it and a sink, but the copper was out of use, and the place was mainly used for emptying slops and storing things. Beyond the wash-house was a lavatory, the only one on the premises and used by the tenants of all three floors. Beyond the lavatory was a tiny piece of wasteland, some twenty feet square, and euphemistically called the garden.

The first-floor flat also consisted of three rooms, a living- room above Christie's living-room, a bedroom above Christie's bedroom, and a kitchen, approached from a half-landing on the stairs, above Christie's kitchen. The tenant of this flat when the Christies arrived was a Mr Charles Kitchener, a man of over sixty whose sight was beginning to fail him. Mr Kitchener had spent his life on the railways. He had been in that flat since some time in the nineteen-twenties when he and his wife had parted.

The top-floor flat was smaller than the other two. It consisted of a bed-sitting room at the front and a kitchen at the back.

Ludovic Kennedy,
10 Rillington Place, 1961

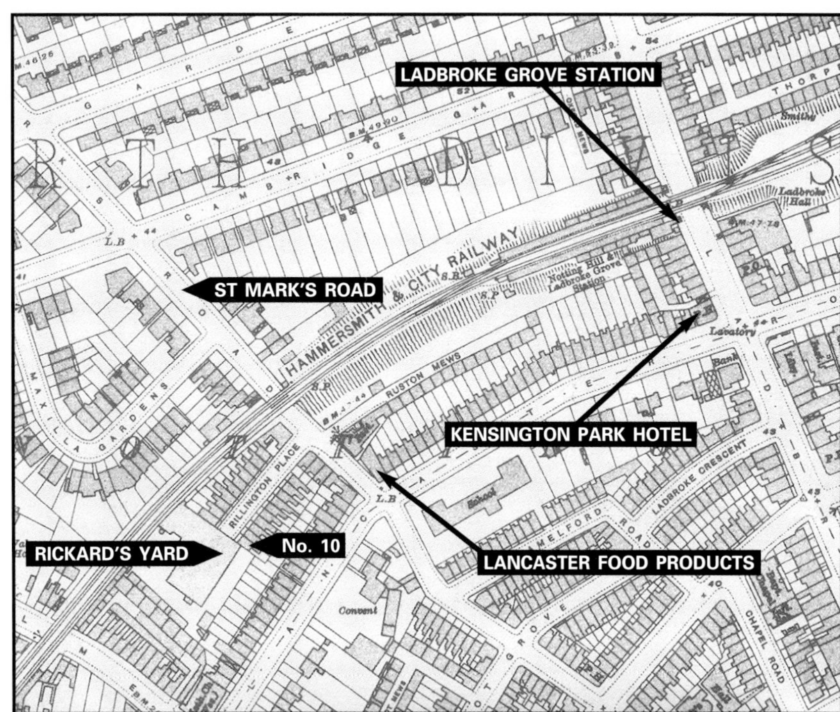

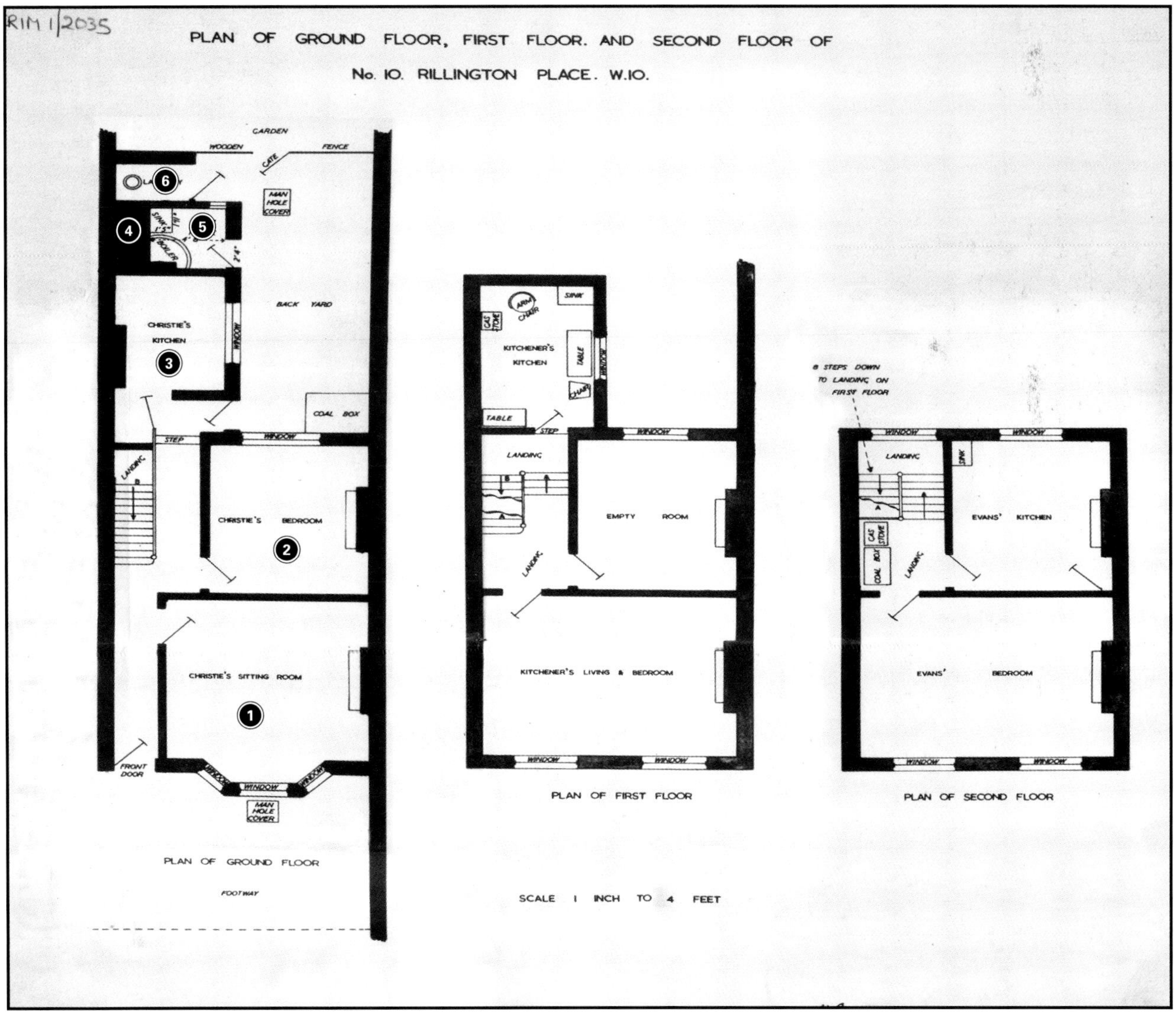

Opposite: **No. 10 Rillington Place photographed by the Metropolitan Police.** *Above:* **PC William Rogers drew up this plan to which we have added the following detail. The ground floor had been occupied since December 1938 by Mr and Mrs John Christie: [1] Sitting room. [2] Bedroom. [3] Kitchen. [4] Coal cupboard. [5] Wash-house. [6] WC. A retired railway worker Charles Kitchener lived on the first floor and the top flat was home for Mr and Mrs Timothy Evans.**

Rillington Place will forever be one of the most notorious streets in Britain. Here spectators gather on March 25, 1953 when the enormity of the murders committed in No. 10 became known. On the right the Rainbow Café, often frequented by John Christie.

Just as we have seen with the 'Ripper' crimes of the 1880s — where Buck's Row was renamed Durward Street (see page 20) and Berner Street changed to Henriques Street (page 26) — so Rillington Place became Ruston Place in May 1954. The London County Council had directed the move in an attempt to cut down the number of visitors who were causing annoyance to the residents who had petitioned the Royal Borough of Kensington for the name to be changed. However, it did little to expunge the memory and it was not until the area was scheduled for redevelopment that the new Bartle Road was laid down on a completely new alignment some 25 yards to the north of the original road — basically right through the Rainbow Café!

John Reginald Christie was born in Halifax, Yorkshire, on April 8, 1898. He saw service in the First World War and was invalided out in March 1919. His criminal career began two years later when he was caught stealing mail while working as a postman for which he received three months' imprisonment. In 1923 he was put on probation for violence and the following year was given nine months' with hard labour for theft. Then in 1929 he served a further six months' hard labour for malicious wounding and another three months in 1933 for stealing a motor car. *Left:* Although he had married Ethel Simpson Waddington in May 1920, following Christie's imprisonment in 1923 she left him for some ten years until a reconciliation was agreed during a visit to see Christie in prison in 1933. *Right:* In spite of his dubious record, in 1939 he was accepted as a Special Constable in the War Reserve Police, receiving two commendations.

Christie's poor health dated back to 1918 when he suffered a mustard gas attack and was injured by shell-blast, claiming as a result to have lost the power of speech for over three years. Then he was knocked down by a motor vehicle and had to have operations on his shoulder and knee. From 1934 he made frequent visits to his doctor, Dr Matthew Odess, at his surgery, originally located on this corner at No. 30 Colville Square *(left)* for a variety of complaints including back-pain, insomnia, enteritis, diarrhoea, fibrositis, memory loss, headaches, giddiness and depression. Finally in 1949 Dr Odess recommended him to be added to the Register of Disabled Persons and for re-housing due to his ill health. Later, when Christie was being held on remand at Brixton, Dr John Matheson, the Principal Medical Officer, said that he considered Christie had a weak character and a hysterical personality, and was immature in his sex life which had given him a feeling of inferiority. He considered Christie very abnormal but not legally insane at the time of the murders.

John Christie, statement to police: 'When I was in the Police War Reserve I met an Austrian girl in the snack bar at the junction of Lancaster Road and Ladbroke Grove *(above right)*. It was in the summer of 1943. I was living in the ground-floor flat at No. 10 Rillington Place, and my wife was away in Sheffield. The only other person living in the house was a Mr. Kitchener who lived on the first floor. The Austrian girl told me she used to go out with American soldiers and one of them was responsible for a baby she had previously. I got friendly with her and she went to Rillington Place with me for two or three times. I have seen a photograph in a newspaper recently of a girl named Ruth Fuerst *(above left)*. I could not recognize the photograph, but I remembered that her name was Fuerst. She was about 24. She told me she lived in Oxford Gardens. One day when this Austrian girl was with me in the flat at No. 10 Rillington Place, she undressed and wanted me to have intercourse with her. I got a telegram while she was there, saying that my wife was on her way home. The girl wanted us to team up together and go right away somewhere together. I would not do that. I got on to the bed and had intercourse with her. While I was having intercourse with her, I strangled her with a piece of rope. I remember urine and excreta coming away from her. She was completely naked. I tried to put some of her clothes back on her. She had a leopard skin coat and I wrapped this round her. I took her from the bedroom into the front room and put her under the floorboards. I had to do that because of my wife coming back. I put the remainder of her clothing under the floorboards too. My wife came home in the evening; my brother-in-law, Mr. Waddington, came with her. Mr. Waddington went back home the next day and during the afternoon my wife went out. While she was out I pulled the body up from under the floorboards and took it into the outhouse [the wash-house]. Later in the day I dug a hole in the garden *(right)* and in the evening, when it was dark, I put the body down in the hole and covered it up quickly with earth. It was the right-hand side of the garden, about half-way along towards the rockery. My wife never knew. I told her I was going to the lavatory. I buried all the clothing in the garden. The next day I straightened the garden up and raked it over. There was an old dustbin in the garden with holes in it which I used for burning garden refuse. When I was burning some rubbish I got the idea into my head to burn the clothing, and what I could pull out I put into the dustbin and burnt it. Months later I was digging in the garden, and I probably misjudged where it was, or something like that. I found the skull and put it in the dustbin and covered it up. I dug a hole in the corner of the garden and put the dustbin in the hole about 18 inches down. The top of the dustbin was open, and I still used it to burn any rubbish.'

Christie continued: 'I was released from the War Reserve in December 1943, and started work at Ultra Radio, Park Royal. I got friendly with a woman named [Muriel] Eady *(right)*, who was about thirty. She used to live at Putney. I took this woman and her man friend to Rillington Place and introduced them to my wife. They came several times together and had tea, and on one occasion we all went to the pictures together. On one occasion she came alone. I believe she complained of catarrh, and I said I thought I could help her. She came by appointment when my wife was out. I believe my wife was on holiday. I think I mixed some stuff up, some inhalants, Friar's Balsam was one. She was in the kitchen, and at the time she was inhaling with a square scarf over her head. I remember now, it was in the bedroom. The liquid (inhalant) was in a square glass jar with a metal screw-top lid. I had made two holes in the lid and through one of the holes I put a rubber tube from the gas into the liquid. Through the other hole I put another rubber tube, about two feet long. This tube didn't touch the liquid. The idea was to stop what was coming from smelling of gas. She inhaled the stuff from the tube. I did it to make her dopey. She became sort of unconscious and I have a vague recollection of getting a stocking and tying it round her neck. I am not too clear about this. I have got them confused. It may have been the Austrian girl that I used the gas on. I don't think it was both. I believe I had intercourse with her at the time I strangled her. I think I put her in the wash-house. That night I buried her in the garden on the right-hand side nearest the yard. She was still wearing her clothing. Several years afterwards I was digging the garden and came across a bone which was broken in half. I knocked one piece into the ground next to a post in the garden.'

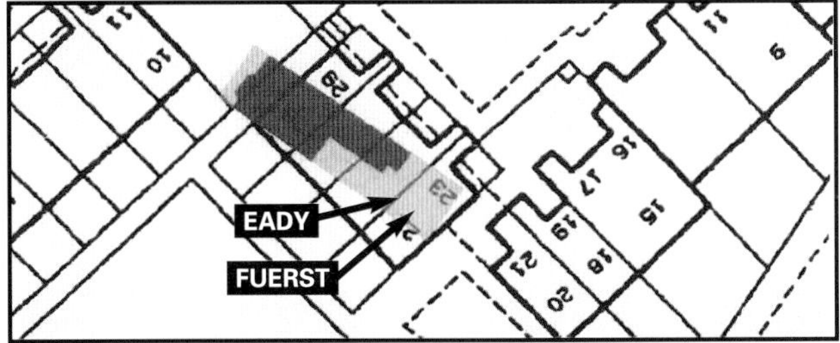

The site of the original garden now lies under the building on the right, the house having been expunged from the map.

Timothy John Evans, left, was born in Merthyr Vale in south Wales on November 20, 1924. He was a backward child and had never learned to read and write. He also missed much schooling due to constant hospitalisation due to a poisoned cut in his leg that refused to heal. Due to the Depression, in 1935 his parents decided to seek work in London, renting accommodation in the Notting Hill area. In 1947, Timothy was introduced to Beryl Thorley, right, and on September 20 that year they were married. When in early 1948 Beryl found she was pregnant, the Evans's looked around for a place of their own and spotted that the top floor of No. 10 was available to rent. They moved into the two rooms around Easter time and Geraldine was born on October 10. In this picture, the baby is being held by Timothy's half-sister, Mrs Mary Westlake.

At the time, Evans worked as a van driver for Lancaster Food Products located not far away on this corner *(left)* of St Mark's Road and Lancaster Road. Beryl proved to be a poor housekeeper, often not providing a hot meal when her husband arrived home from work. Finances were also strained, arguments became more frequent, some quite violent, and when in the late summer of 1949 Beryl again fell pregnant, matters came to a head. There was no way Evans's wage could support four mouths, plus paying the rent, let alone the repayments on their furniture. Having tried to abort herself, Beryl turned to Christie who had claimed — or lied — to Timothy that he had carried out several successful abortions in the past. At first Evans would not hear of it but during a conversation with his wife at the beginning of November, Beryl declared she was going ahead regardless. This led to further arguments, which culminated on Sunday, November 6 with Evans storming off to spend the day at his 'local' — the Kensington Palace Hotel, or 'KPH' *(right)* — on the corner of Ladbroke Grove. On Monday morning Beryl told Tim that she would be leaving to go to her father in Brighton, and that she had asked Mr Christie to carry out the abortion the following morning.

About the beginning of October my wife, Beryl Susan Evans, told me that she was expecting a baby. She told me that she was about three months gone. I said, 'If you are having a baby, well, you've had one, another won't make any difference.' She then told me she was going to try and get rid of it. I turned round and told her not to be silly, that she'd make herself ill. Then she bought herself a syringe and started syringing herself. Then she said that didn't work, and I said 'I am glad it won't work'. Then she said she was going to buy some tablets. I don't know what tablets she bought because she was always hiding them from me. She started to look very ill, and I told her to go and see a doctor, and she said she'd go when I was in work, but when I'd come home and ask her if she'd been, she'd always say that she hadn't.

On the Sunday morning, that would be the sixth of November, she told me that if she couldn't get rid of the baby, she'd kill herself and our other baby Geraldine. I told her she was talking silly. She never said no more about it then, but when I got up Monday morning to go to work she said she was going to see some woman to see if she could help her. Who the woman was she didn't tell me, and that if she wasn't in when I came home, she'd be up at her grandmother's.

Then I went to work. I loaded up my van and went on my journey. About nine o'clock that morning I pulled up at a Transport cafe between Ipswich and Colchester. I can't say exactly where it is, that's the nearest I can give. I went up to the counter and ordered a cup of tea and breakfast, and I sat down by the table with my cup of tea waiting for my breakfast to come up, and there was a man sitting by the table opposite to me. He asked me if I had a cigarette I could give him. I gave him one and he started talking about married life. He said to me, 'You are looking pretty worried, is there anything on your mind?' Then I told him all about it. So he said, 'Don't let that worry you, I can give you something that can fix it'. So he said, 'Wait there a minute, I'll be back,' and he went outside. When he came back he handed me a little bottle that was wrapped in brown paper. He said, 'Tell your wife to take it first thing in the morning before she has any tea, then to lay down on the bed for a couple of hours (on the bed) and that should do the job'. He never asked no money for it. I went up to the counter and paid my bill and carried on with my journey.

After I finished my work I went home, that would be between seven and eight. When I got in the house I took off my overcoat and hung it on the peg behind the kitchen door. My wife asked me for a cigarette and I told her that there was one in my pocket, then she found this bottle in my pocket, and I told her all about it.

I got up in the morning as usual at six o'clock to go to work. I made myself a cup of tea and made a feed for the baby. I told her then not to take that stuff when I went in and said 'Good morning' to her, and I went to work, that would be about half past six. I finished work and got home about half past six in the evening. I then noticed that there was no lights in the place. I lit the gas and it started to go out, and I went into the bedroom to get a penny and I noticed my baby in the cot. I put the penny in the gas and went back in the bedroom and lit the gas in the bedroom. Then I saw my wife laying in the bed. I spoke to her but she never answered me, so I went over and shook her, then I could see she wasn't breathing. Then I went and made some food for my baby. I fed my baby and I sat up all night.

Between about one and two in the morning I got my wife downstairs through the front door. I opened the drain outside my front door, that is No. 10 Rillington Place, and pushed her body head first into the drain. I closed the drain, then I went back in the house. I sat down by the fire smoking a cigarette. I never went to work the following day. I went and got my baby looked after. Then I went and told my governor where I worked that I was leaving. He asked me the reason, and I told him I had a better job elsewhere. I had my cards and money that afternoon, then I went to see a man about selling my furniture. The man came down and had a look at my furniture and he offered me £40 for it. So I accepted the £40. He told me he wouldn't be able to collect the furniture until Monday morning. In the meanwhile I went and told my mother that my wife and baby had gone for a holiday. I stopped in the flat till Monday. The van came Monday afternoon and cleared the stuff out. He paid me the money. Then I caught the five to one train from Paddington and I come down to Merthyr Vale and I've been down here ever since. That's the lot.

Timothy John Evans,
Statement, November 30, 1949

Beryl's body was not found for another month, police discovering it trussed up and hidden under the sink *(left)* in the wash-house on Friday, December 2. The police removed the door so the photographer, Chief Inspector Percy Law, could take a closer picture *(right)* to show how the body had been hidden behind planks of wood and painter's kettles. These items had possibly been left behind by contractors sent in by the landlord's agents to carry out repairs to the roof of the wash-house and toilet. So until the workmen had departed on Tuesday, November 8, Beryl's body was temporarily hidden in Mr Kitchener's second floor flat as fortunately he was away in hospital,. The body was most probably moved down to the wash-house on Friday, November 12 as Christie went to Dr Odess the following day complaining of severe back pain.

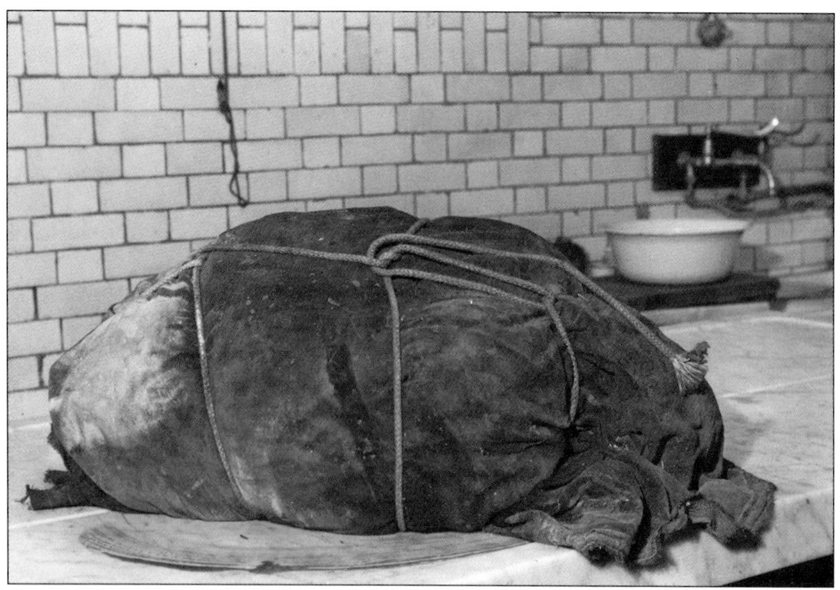

The bundle was taken unopened to Kensington Mortuary before being unwrapped. Although there is another photograph in this series it is too awful to publish.

In August 1949, there was a terrific row upstairs on the top floor between Mr. and Mrs. Evans and a blonde who was living with them. My wife told me afterwards that a woman who lives in Lancaster Road, overlooking the back of 10 Rillington Place, had told her that she had seen Mr. and Mrs. Evans fighting at their open kitchen window and that Mr. Evans appeared to be trying to push his wife out of the window. I think it was Mrs. Hyde who told my wife this. I think Mrs. Swan saw it from her garden next door. Mr. Evans's mother called while the fight was in progress. After the row had quietened down, Evans's mother told the blonde to pack up and clear out. I was in my front room when I heard this shouted. I also heard Evans say that if she (the blonde) went he would go with her. Evans, his mother and the blonde were at the first floor coming down the stairs, when I heard this said. The mother went out and Evans and the blonde went back upstairs. As the mother went out she said to us, me and my wife, that she was going to throw the blonde out there and then.

That evening Evans went out with the blonde and he was carrying a suitcase. He came back alone later. The next day Mrs. Evans told my wife that she was going down to the Police Court to get a separation from her husband. My wife and I had a chat and we agreed between us that if they did separate we would adopt the baby, but Mrs. Evans told my wife that if they did separate his mother would take the baby. At a later period Mrs. Evans told me that her husband was knocking her about and that she was going to make an end of it, meaning that she was going to commit suicide.

One morning shortly after this, it would be early in November, I went upstairs and found Mrs. Evans lying on a quilt in front of the fireplace in the kitchen. She had made an attempt to gas herself, and I opened the door and window wide because there was a lot of gas in the room. There was a gas pipe at the left-hand side of the fireplace with a tap about 2 feet 6 inches from the floor at about the level of the top of the kitchen fireplace. There was a piece of rubber tubing from the tap to near her head. She was lying with her head towards the window. She was fully dressed and was not covered over with anything. When I opened the door and window she started coming round. I gave her a drink of water. I do not know what she said, but a little while after she complained of a headache, and I made her a cup of tea. My wife was downstairs but I did not call her or tell her. Mrs. Evans asked me not to tell anyone. Mr. Evans was out and I don't know if there was anyone else in the house. I had a cup of tea too, because my head was thumping as I had got the effect of it (the gas) too. After a little while I went downstairs.

The next day I went upstairs again, I couldn't say if it was the morning or afternoon. I think it was about lunch-time. She still said she intended to do away with herself. I am certain that there was a small fire in the grate in the kitchen when I found Mrs. Evans the day before, and that's why I rushed to open the window.

When I went up to Mrs. Evans at lunch-time the next day she begged of me to help her to go through with it, meaning to help her to commit suicide. She said she would do anything if I would help her. I think she was referring to letting me be intimate with her. She brought the quilt from the front room and put it down in front of the fireplace. I am not sure whether there was a fire in the grate. She lay on the quilt. She was fully dressed. I got on my knees but found I was not physically capable of having intercourse with her owing to the fact that I had fibrositis in my back and enteritis. We were both fully dressed. I turned the gas tap on and as near as I can make out, I held it close to her face. When she became unconscious I turned the tap off. I was going to try again to have intercourse with her but it was impossible, I couldn't bend over. I think that's when I strangled her. I think it was with a stocking I found in the room. The gas wasn't on very long, not much over a minute, I think. Perhaps one or two minutes. I then left her where she was and went downstairs. I think my wife was downstairs. She didn't know anything about it.

Evans came home in the evening about six o'clock. It was dark when I heard him come in. I went to my kitchen door and called him. I spoke to him in the passage and told him that his wife had committed suicide, that she had gassed herself. I went upstairs with him. We went into the kitchen, and Evans touched his wife's hand, then picked her up and carried her into the bedroom and put her on the bed. It was dark, there were no lights on in the kitchen or the bedroom. I feel certain it was a stocking I strangled her with. I didn't tie it round the neck. I just wound it round the neck. Before I went downstairs, I think I took the stocking off and threw it in the fireplace. I think there was a fire in the grate. I did not feel any effects of the gas.

After Evans lay his wife on the bed, he fetched the quilt from the kitchen and put it over her. I then lit the gas in the centre of the room, the front room which is used as the bedroom. I told Evans that no doubt he would be suspected of having done it because of the rows and fights he had had with his wife. He seemed to think the same. He said he would bring the van down that he was driving and take her away and leave her somewhere. I left him and went downstairs. I think this was on a Tuesday and on the following Friday Evans sold his furniture, and after my wife had given him some dinner he left saying he was going to Bristol.

At that time I was under the impression that he had taken his wife away in his van. I didn't go into the bedroom that day until Evans came home in the evening. I can't recollect seeing the baby there. I think Evans told me the next day that he had fed the baby.

At the same time, Percy Law photographed the body of Geraldine, half hidden behind the door.

In Evans's first statement to police in Wales (see page 247), he claimed to have put his wife's body down the drain outside the house so a phone call was put through to Notting Hill to check. The fact that it took three men to lift the heavy manhole in the roadway soon put paid to that explanation, Evans having simply repeated what Christie had told him. ***Left:*** **The scene was re-enacted in the 1971 film *10 Rillington Place* although the police plan on page 241 puts its position incorrectly close to the bay window.** ***Above:*** **This is the comparison today of Christie's view from his front room window.**

Early in December police called at the house and said they were making inquiries about Mrs. Evans. There were three officers — Detective-Sergeant Corfield, Detective Byers, and, I think, Inspector Black. They told me that they had got Evans in Wales and that he had made a statement that he had put his wife down a drain. They said they had already had the drain up before they came to the door. They asked me to go to Notting Hill Police Station to make a statement, and I went with them in a car. I stayed there from 11 p.m. till five in the morning. When I got back I found they had taken a statement from my wife. They left a policeman there all night and came again the next day and made a search. They found something in the outhouse and asked my wife to go to the outhouse (wash-house). She told me afterwards that they pointed to a bundle and asked her if she knew anything about it. She said she did not and they asked her to touch it to see if she knew what it was. She said she touched it but didn't know what it was and she had never seen it there before. An officer told us soon after that they had found a body.

When I left Evans in the bedroom on that Tuesday evening he did not know that his wife had been strangled. He thought she had gassed herself. I don't know when he first found out that his wife had been strangled. I never mentioned it to him. I never had intercourse with Mrs. Evans at any time. We were just friendly acquaintances nothing more. I went up that first afternoon to have a cup of tea as she had previously asked me once or twice. I believe it was a couple of days previously that she had asked me to go up and get some sugar she had saved up for me. When I was up there she said she had just made a cup of tea and asked me to have one. I had a cup of tea with her then and she told me to come up any time I wanted a cup of tea.

The wash-house was a communal one, but actually it was only used for keeping rubbish and junk in. There was no key to it and the lock was rusted and broken and not usable. It could be opened and shut by turning the handle but could not be locked. The wash-house was only used for getting water to rinse out pails or put down the lavatory.

I had some shoring timber and old floorboards from my front room which had been left behind by the work people and I asked Evans to take it to the yard for me as I could not carry it owing to my fibrositis. He took it to the yard and I suggested he put it in the wash-house out of the way. I saw it in the wash-house afterwards and some of it was stacked in front of the sink. I don't think it was possible to get to the tap after the timber was put in there.

I feel certain I strangled Mrs. Evans and I think it was with a stocking. I did it because she appealed to me to help her to commit suicide. I have got in the back of my mind there was some other motive, but I am not clear about it. I don't know anything about what happened to the Evans's baby. I don't recollect seeing the baby on the Tuesday or at any time afterwards.

John Reginald Christie,
Statement, June 8, 1953

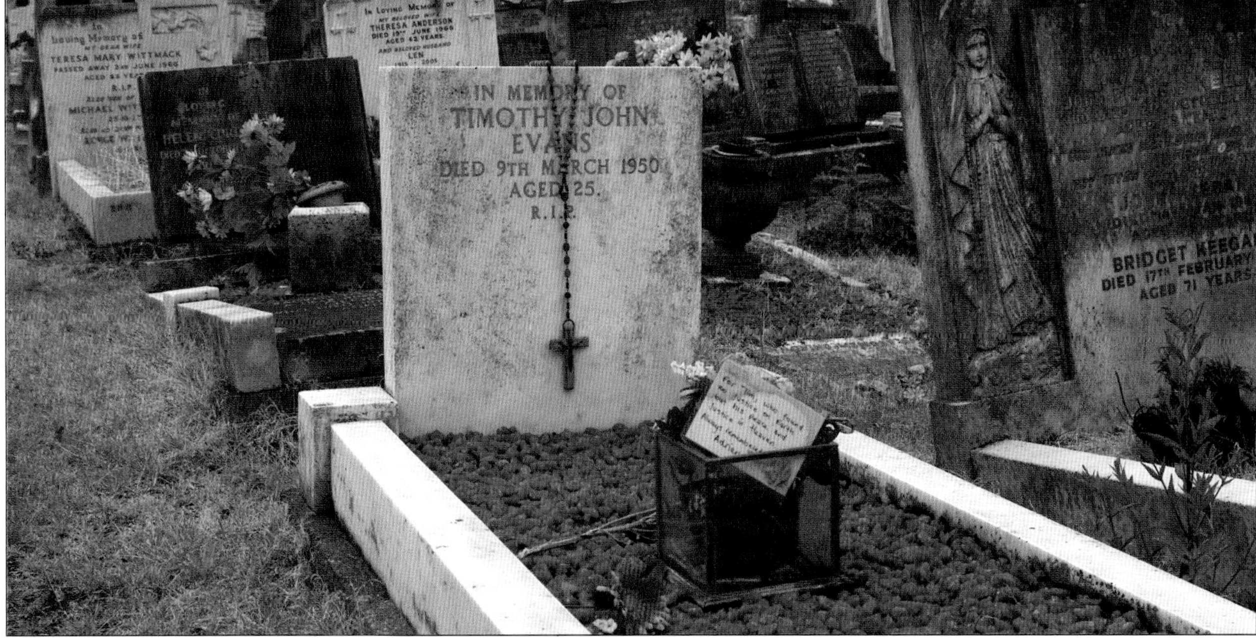

Christie's statement — in which he admitted killing Beryl although not Geraldine — was only obtained after he was arrested in March 1953 . . . but that was three years too late to save Evans from the gallows. His trial lasted three days, the jury only retiring for 40 minutes before returning with a guilty verdict. Timothy Evans was refused a reprieve and was hanged by Albert Pierrepoint and Syd Dernley on March 9, 1950. At the time, Evans's trial and execution was overshadowed by the more gory revelations in the Setty murder (see page 210), Evans actually meeting Donald Hume while remanded in Brixton prison. Christie had broken down in the court when the guilty verdict was given and Timothy had already told his mother that 'I never done it Mum. Christie done it. Tell Christie I want to see him. He is the only one who can help me now.' Unfortunately Evans had given police four statements, all of which conflicted, and only went to show the jury that he was a liar. Exhumed from Pentonville in November 1966, he now lies buried in St Patrick's Roman Catholic cemetery in Leytonstone.

Beryl and Geraldine had been buried on December 7, 1949 in a single coffin in Kensington Cemetery which lies in Gunnesbury Park, on Gunnersbury Avenue. This particular grave (No. 179 in Plot G) already contained several previous burials. Also it is somewhat unusual for common graves to be marked with named headstones.

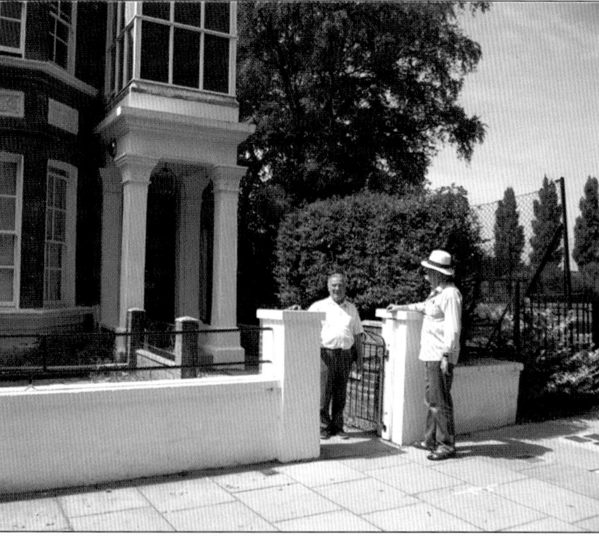

It is always so easy to be wise after the event but if the police had taken more notice of Evans's plea to his mother — which she relayed to them — they might have looked further and discovered the bones of Christie's wartime victims, thus sparing the lives of four more women. As it was, Christie explained that 'it was about this time that my dog had been digging in the garden and I found the skull from the body of the woman Eady that I had buried in the nearest corner of the garden. I just covered it up with earth and later in the evening, when it was dark, I put my raincoat on. I went into the garden and got the skull and put it under my raincoat. I went out and put it in a bombed house, the last standing bombed house *(above)* next to the tennis courts in St Mark's Road. There was corrugated iron covering some bay windows and I dropped the skull through the window where the iron had been bent back. I heard it drop with a dull thud as though there were no floorboards.'

Christie's next victim was his wife Ethel, strangled while she lay in bed on December 14, 1952. He hid her body beneath the floorboards in the front room, no doubt still loose since Ruth Fuerst was put there during the war. It would appear from these sequential police photographs that Christie must also have removed a floor joist to be able to squeeze the body below as the police had to remove it to extract Mrs Christie.

I have been told that I am not obliged to say anything unless I wish, but whatever I do say will be taken down in writing and may be given in evidence. (Signed) J. R. Christie.

I'll tell you as much as I can remember. I have not been well for a long while, about eighteen months. I have been suffering from fibrositis and enteritis. I had a breakdown in the hospital. I got better by September 1952, but kept having attacks after.

My wife had been suffering a great deal from persecution and assaults from the black people in the house No. 10 Rillington Place and had to undergo treatment at the Doctor for her nerves. In December she was becoming very frightened from these blacks and was afraid to go about the house when they were about and she got very depressed.

On December 14th, I was awakened at about 8.15 a.m. I think it was by my wife moving about in bed. I sat up and saw that she appeared to be convulsive, her face was blue and she was choking. I did what I could to try and restore breathing but it was hopeless. It appeared too late to call for assistance. That's when I couldn't bear to see her, so I got a stocking and tied it round her neck to put her to sleep. Then I got out of bed and saw a small bottle and a cup half full of water on a small table near the bed. I noticed that the bottle contained 2 Phenal Barbitone tablets and it originally contained 25. I then knew that she must have taken the remainder. I got them from the Hospital because I couldn't sleep.

I left her in bed for two or three days and didn't know what to do. Then I remembered some loose floorboards in the front room. I had to move a table and some chairs to roll the lino back about half way. Those boards had been up previously because of the drainage system. There were several of these depressions under the floorboards. Then I believe I went back and put her in a blanket or a sheet or something and tried to carry her, but she was too heavy so I had to sort of half carry and half drag her and put her in that depression and cover her up with earth. I thought that was the best way to lay her to rest. I then put the boards and lino back.

John Reginald Christie, Statement, March 31, 1953

I am a Chief Inspector, 'F' Division, Hammersmith Police Station. On the evening of 24th March, 1953, I visited 10 Rillington Place, Notting Hill, and examined the front room. Several floorboards were loose. They were lifted, and underneath the floorboards, buried in earth and rubble, there was a body. It was left there till the following day. I was present when photographs were taken. I saw the body unearthed and removed. Exhibit 3 are the photographs of what I found. On 24th March I was present when Mr. Waddington identified the body as that of his sister Ethel.

On 31st March, I saw Christie at Putney Police Station with Inspector Kelly. I told him who we were and asked him if he was John Reginald Halliday Christie. He said he was. I told him I had found the body of a woman, later identified as his wife, buried under the floor in the front room, and asked him if he wished to say anything about it. Christie began to weep, and then he said: 'She woke me up. She was choking. I couldn't stand it any longer. I couldn't bear to see her suffer. You know what I did.'

CHIEF INSPECTOR ALBERT GRIFFIN, OLD BAILEY, JUNE 22, 1953

Christie went on to say that 'I was in a state and didn't know what to do and after Christmas I sold all my furniture. I made a bed on some bedding on the floor in the back room. I had about four blankets there. I kept my kitchen table, two chairs, some crockery and cutlery. These were just enough for my immediate needs because I was going away. I wasn't working and had a meagre existence. I was getting money from the Unemployment Exchange. This was £2.14.0. I got £11 for the furniture and £2 for some other bits that I sold. I got thirty-seven shillings for my wife's ring. I took it off her finger as a keepsake, but sold it to a jeweller's at Shepherds Bush when I was hard up and hadn't enough money to get food.' It was on January 6 that Christie sold his furniture to Robert Hookway, trading at No. 319 Portobello Road, the same man who had purchased Evans's furniture for £40 back in November 1949. Two of our ATB team know the Notting Hill area well and they soon found Mr Hookway's old shop somewhat modernised! (Roger Morgan, left, discovered the name of 'Major Martin', the spoof corpse used in Operation 'Mincemeat' (see *After the Battle* No. 94), and Barry Cheese was featured in *The Ace Café Then and Now*.)

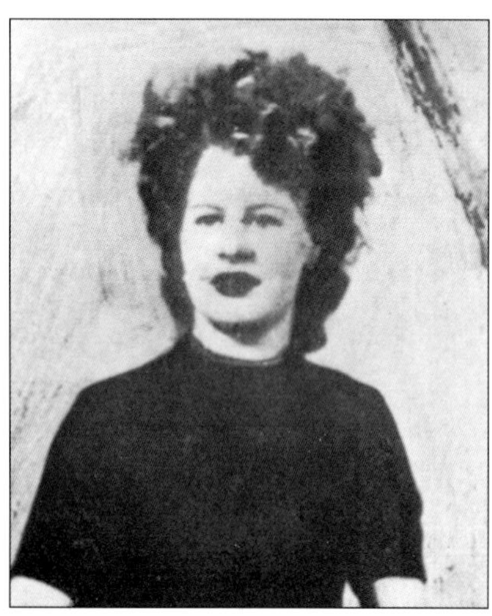

Some time after this, I suppose it was February, I went into a cafe at Notting Hill Gate for a cup of tea and a sandwich. The cafe was pretty full, there wasn't much space. Two girls sat at a table and I sat opposite at the same table. They were talking about rooms, where they had been looking to get accommodation. Then one of them spoke to me. She asked me for a cigarette and then started conversation. During the conversation I mentioned about leaving my flat and that it would be vacant very soon and they suggested coming down to see it together in the evening. Only one came down. She looked over the flat. She said it would be suitable subject to the landlord's permission. It was then that she made suggestions that she would visit me for a few days. She said this so that I would use my influence with the landlord as a sort of payment in kind. I was rather annoyed and told her that it didn't interest me. I think she started saying I was making accusations against her when she saw there was nothing doing. She said that she would bring somebody down to me. I thought she meant she was going to bring some of the boys down to do me. I believe it was then that she mentioned something about Irish blood. She was in a violent temper. I remember she started fighting. I am very quiet and avoid fighting. I know there was something, it's in the back of my mind. She was on the floor. I must have put her in the alcove straight away.

This is Christie's grotty little kitchen where he killed his next three victims as he described in his June 8 statement: 'I gassed the three women whose bodies were found in the alcove, by getting them to sit in the deck chair in the kitchen between the table and the door. There is a gas pipe on the wall next to the window, that at one time had been used for a gas bracket. The pipe had been plugged. I took the plug out and pushed a piece of rubber tubing over the pipe and let it hang down nearly to the floor. There was no tap on it so I put a kink in the tube with a bulldog clip to stop the gas escaping. When they sat in the deck chair with the tube behind them I just took the clip off and let the fumes rise from the back of the deck chair. When they started getting overcome that's when I must have strangled them.' One can accept that Christie was confused as to the order that his victims were despatched but the sequence in which the bodies were secreted in the coal cupboard, seen just beyond the range, confirm that Rita Nelson *(above left)* was first. We have included extracts from Christie's statement but re-arranged them in the correct order.

On the third day of the trial, the judge, Mr Justice Finnemore, questioned Christie about the kitchen murders but even the judge was confused as to which woman was killed first — rather surprisingly bearing in mind that he had these same photographs in front of him as evidence! ***Left:*** **The empty coal cupboard and** ***(right)*** **with the wrapped up body of Rita Nelson.**

I lived in the flat and one evening I went up Ladbroke Grove to get some fish and chips for the animals. I had a dog and a cat. On the way back, in Ladbroke Grove, a drunken woman stood in front of me and demanded a pound for me to take her round the corner. I said 'I am not interested and I haven't got money to throw away.' I'm not like that. I haven't had intercourse with any woman for over two years, my doctor will tell you that. He is Dr. Odess, Colville Square. She then demanded thirty shillings and said she would scream and say I had interfered with her if I didn't give it to her. I walked away as I am so well known round there and she obviously would have created a scene.

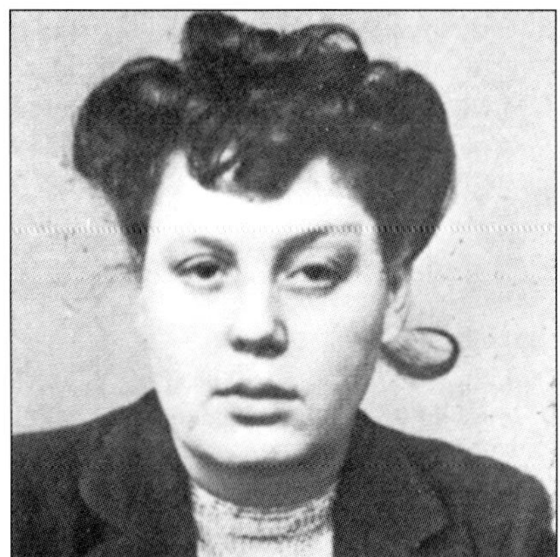

She came along. She wouldn't go, and she came right to the door still demanding thirty shillings. When I opened the door she forced her way in. I went to the kitchen, and she was still on about this thirty shillings. I tried to get her out and she picked up a frying pan to hit me. I closed with her and there was a struggle and she fell back on the chair. It was a deck chair. There was a piece of rope hanging from the chair. I don't remember what happened but I must have gone haywire. The next thing I remember she was lying still in the chair with the rope round her neck. I don't remember taking it off. It couldn't have been tied. I left her there and went into the front room. After that I believe I had a cup of tea and went to bed.

The body of Kathleen Moloney, Christie's next victim, was wrapped and stacked in front of Rita, both having been killed in late January.

I got up in the morning and went to the kitchen and washed and shaved. She was still in the chair. I believe I made some tea then. I pulled away a small cupboard in the corner and gained access to a small alcove. I knew it was there because a pipe burst during the frosty weather and a plumber opened it up to mend the pipe. I must have put her in there. I don't remember doing it, but I remember pulling away the cupboard because it came away in two pieces. I slung her clothes in the bedroom. She started to undress before she picked up the frying pan. I put the small cupboard back. It wasn't a fixture.

Not very long after this I met a man and woman coming out of a cafe at Hammersmith. If I remember rightly, I had been to sign on that day. It was in the morning. The man went across the road to talk to a friend and while he was away she said they had to give up their diggings at the weekend. He was out of work. Then I told her that if they hadn't found anywhere I could put them up for a few days. They both came up together and stayed a few days. They said they had been thrown out of their digs. I told them they would have to go as he was being very unpleasant. He told me that police were looking for her for some offence. When they left the man said that if they couldn't find anywhere could they come back for that night.

The girl came back alone. She asked if he had called and I said 'No,' but I was expecting him. She said she would wait, but I advised her not to. She insisted on staying in case he came. I told her she couldn't and that he may be looking for her, and that she must go, and that she couldn't stay there alone. She was very funny about it. I got hold of her arm to try and lead her out. I pushed her out of the kitchen. She started struggling like anything and some of her clothing got torn. She then sort of fell limp as I had hold of her. She sank to the ground and I think some of her clothes must have got caught round her neck in the struggle. She was just out of the kitchen in the passageway. I tried to lift her up, but couldn't. I then pulled her into the kitchen on to a chair. I felt her pulse, but it wasn't beating. I pulled the cupboard away again and I must have put her in there.

John Reginald Christie,
Statement, March 31, 1953

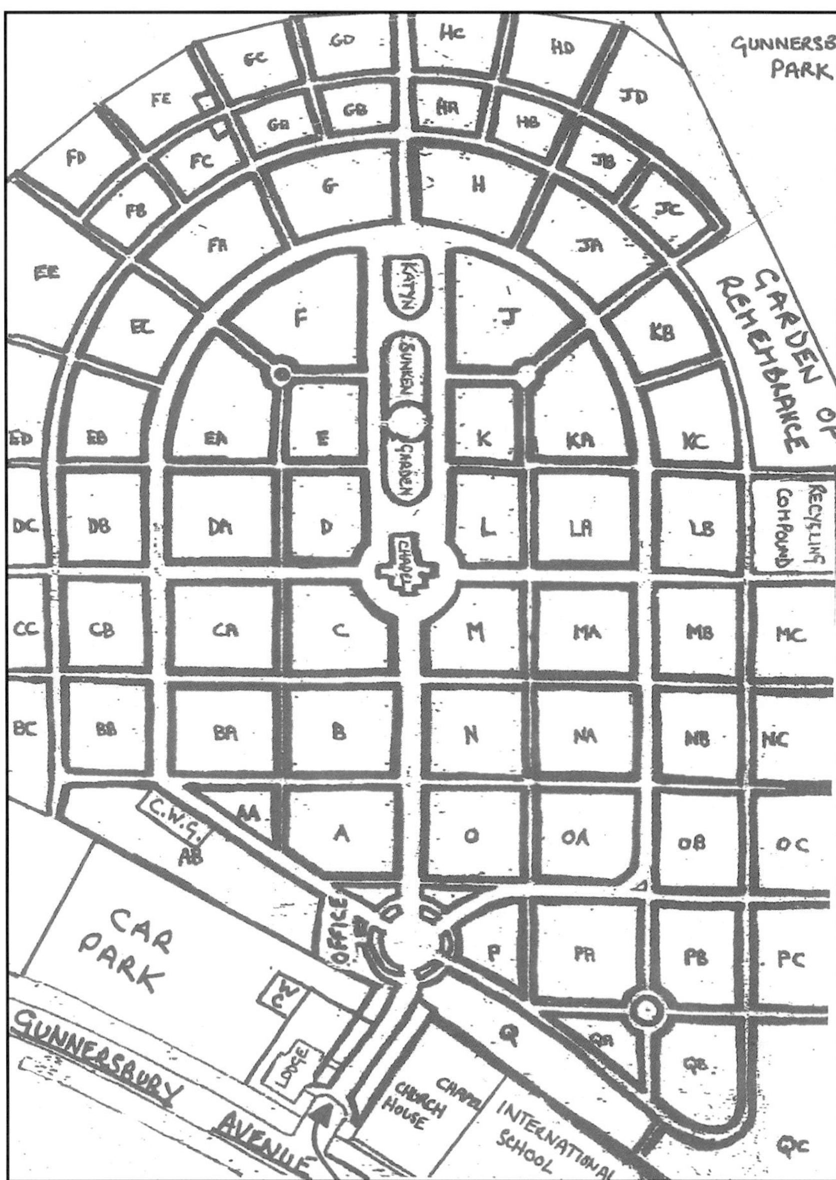

Rita and Kathleen were both interred in common graves in Plot JB in Gunnersbury Cemetery where Beryl and Geraldine are also buried. However, with no headstones to mark these graves, Barry Cheese stands in the background beside Rita's grave (No. 104) while Rob Green marks Grave No. 49 where Kathleen lies buried.

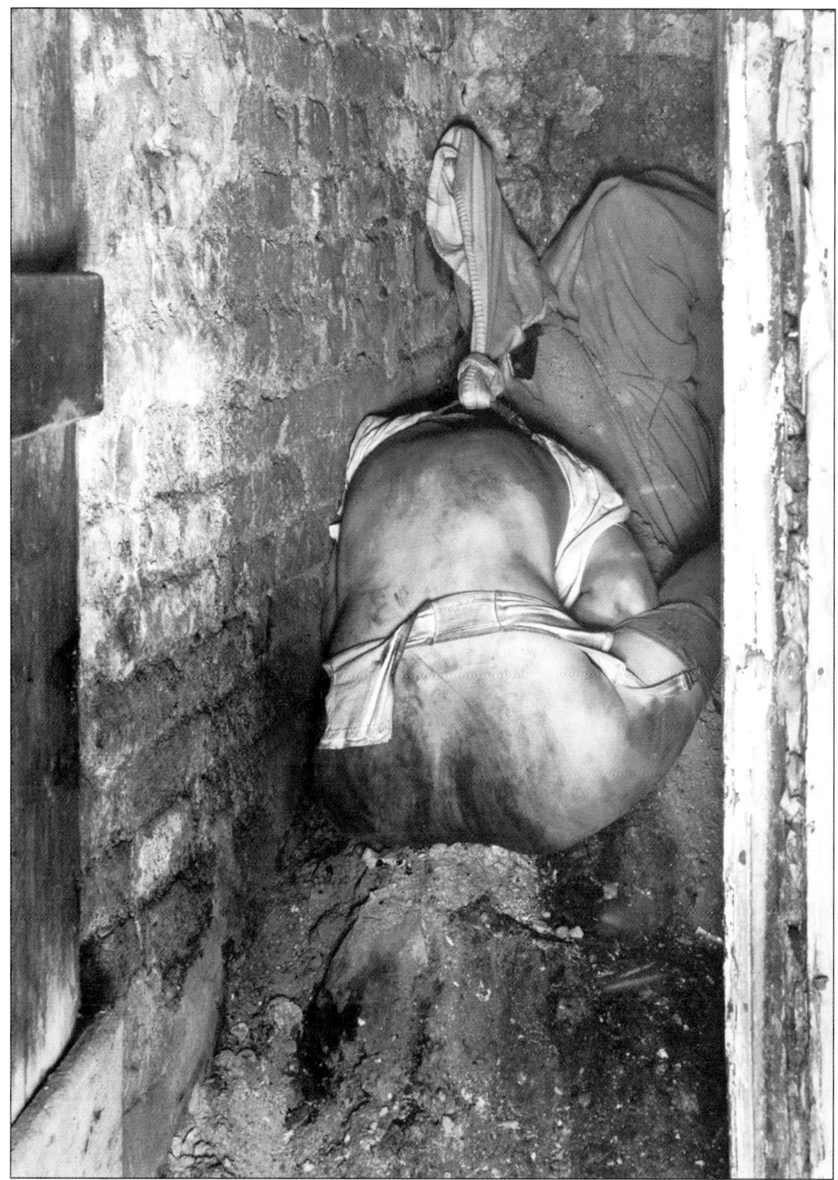

Hectorina was also buried at Gunnersbury but in her case her common grave, No. 298 in Plot HD, is marked.

As far as can be established, Hectorina MacLennan *(top right)*, the third victim, died on Friday, March 6 after which Christie papered over the cupboard door. Although the flat was not his to sub-let, a week later he rented it out to a Mr and Mrs John Reilly, obtaining three months' rent in advance, before leaving to book into a homeless refuge: Rowton House near King's Cross. When the Reillys moved in on March 21, they immediately noticed an unpleasant smell in the kitchen but when Charles Brown, the landlord, called to collect Christie's rent, he promptly evicted them. The upper floors were already let out and the landlord told Beresford Brown, who was occupying Evans's old bedroom, that he could meanwhile use Christie's kitchen. On March 24, while fixing up brackets for his wireless, he found that the wall was hollow and peeling away a corner of the wallpaper was horrified at what he saw inside. The police were called, Chief Inspector Albert Griffin of 'F' Division breaking down the cupboard door. 'I also examined the front room [where] several floorboards were loose. They were lifted and underneath the floorboards, buried in earth and rubble, there was a body. It was left there until the following day. A complete search was then made of the house and garden and a quantity of bones were uncovered from the garden *(right)*.

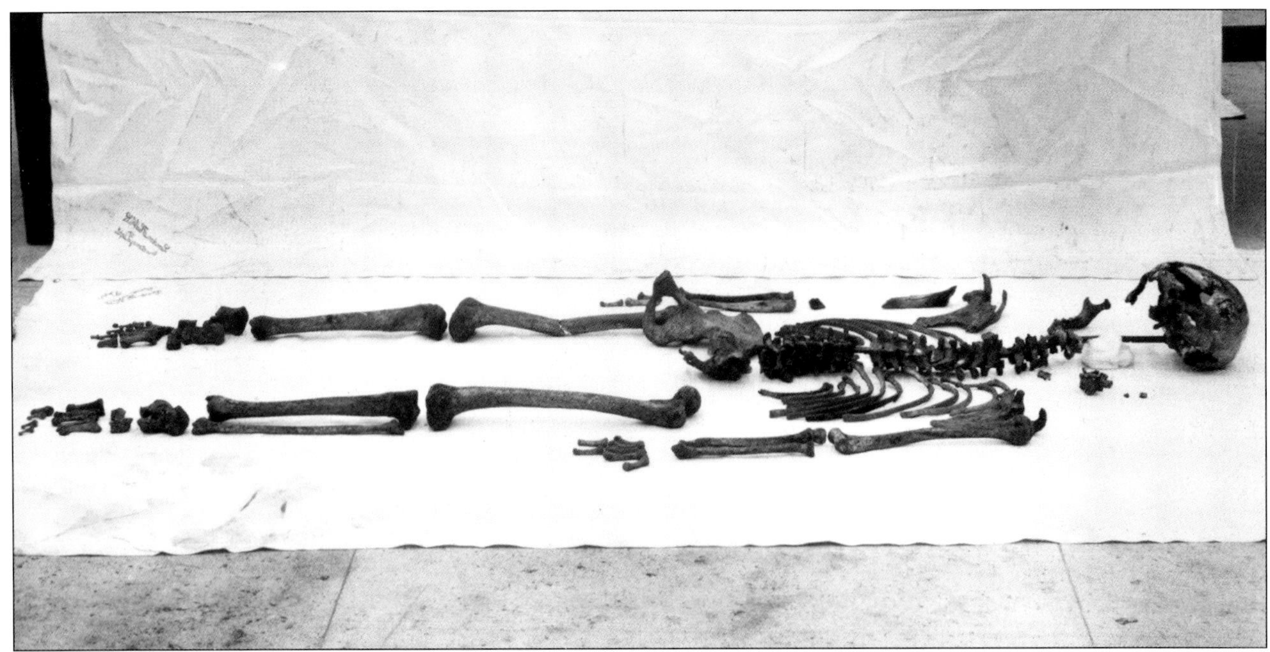

Christie: 'I have been told that human bones comprising almost two complete skeletons have been found in the garden at No. 10 Rillington Place, Notting Hill. I cannot remember whether it was the Austrian girl Ruth Fuerst or the woman Eady who inhaled the gas. I can't remember whether the gas was inhaled in the bedroom or in the kitchen.' The bones were taken to the London Hospital *(right)* in the Mile End Road in east London where Dr Francis Camps painstakingly assembled them into two skeletons, minus of course Muriel Eady's skull. That had been found by children in the bombed house and handed in to police. They assumed it had come from a Blitz victim and had it destroyed. Ruth Fuerst's skull was charred where Christie had attempted to burn it in his dustbin. More disturbingly, Dr Keith Simpson revealed that four teeth found in the garden had not been proven to belong to either woman. When he was later questioned about any other killings he might have committed, he said: 'At times I have got something in my mind. I have had it there for years.' Could it be that he was also guilty of another unsolved murder in nearby Maida Vale: that of Dora Lloyd in February 1932?

The two victims recovered from the garden had been notified to police as missing persons during the war. Ruth Margarete Christine Fuerst *(above)* was born in Voeslau, Vienna, on March 29, 1922 and was the daughter of Ludwig Fuerst, a Viennese painter who had escaped from Austria with his family in 1939. Although the skull was very charred, a dental cap of Continental origin helped Dr Camps identify this skeleton as hers. Her death was not registered until August 1953.

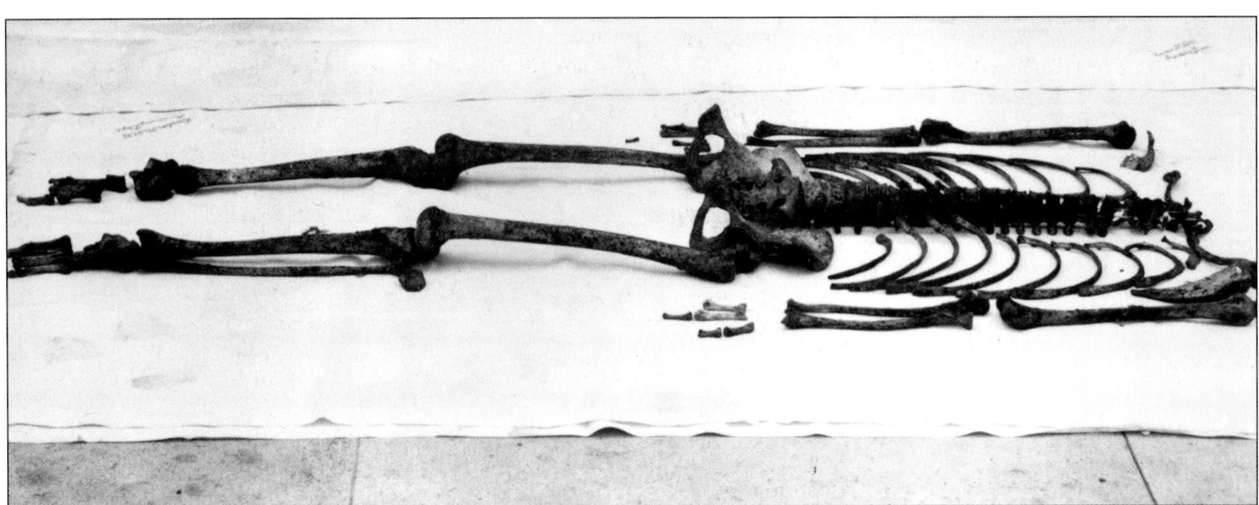

Muriel was born to Fanny Eady on October 14, 1912 at No. 20 Baron Road in West Ham, a street since lost in post-war redevelopment. Her father was a merchant seaman at Brightlingsea, Essex. When she was murdered she was living at 12 Roskell Road, Putney, her death certificate was also issued by the Coroner in August 1953.

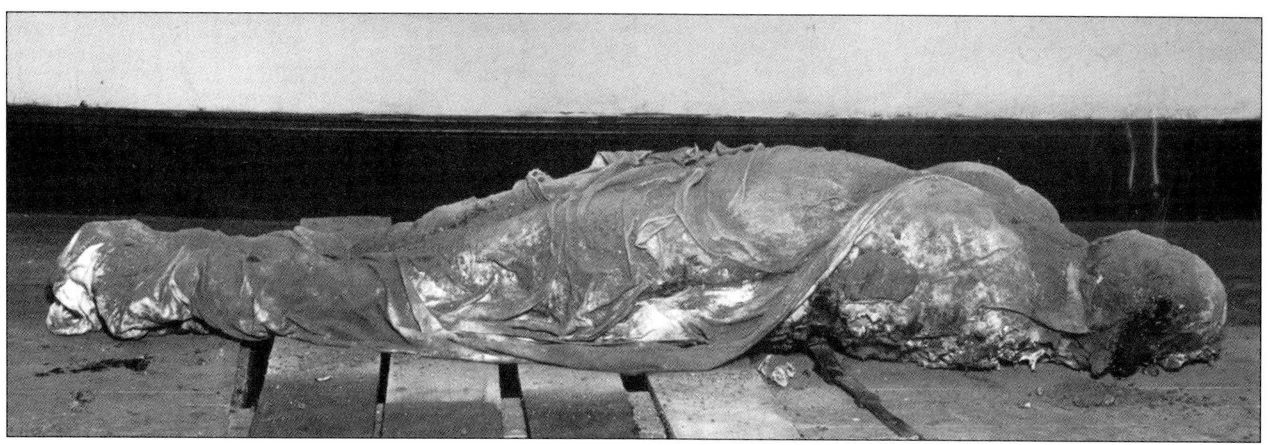

Each body was photographed by Chief Inspector Law before being removed from the building. *Top to bottom:* Ethel Christie, Rita Nelson, Kathleen Moloney and Hectorina MacLennan. Mrs Christie was later cremated at Kensal Green Crematorium.

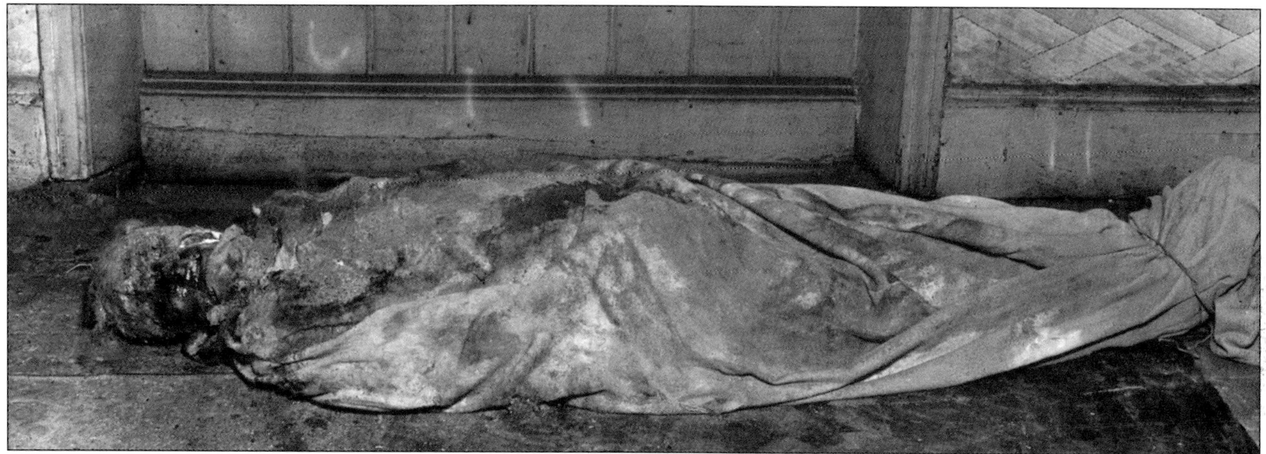

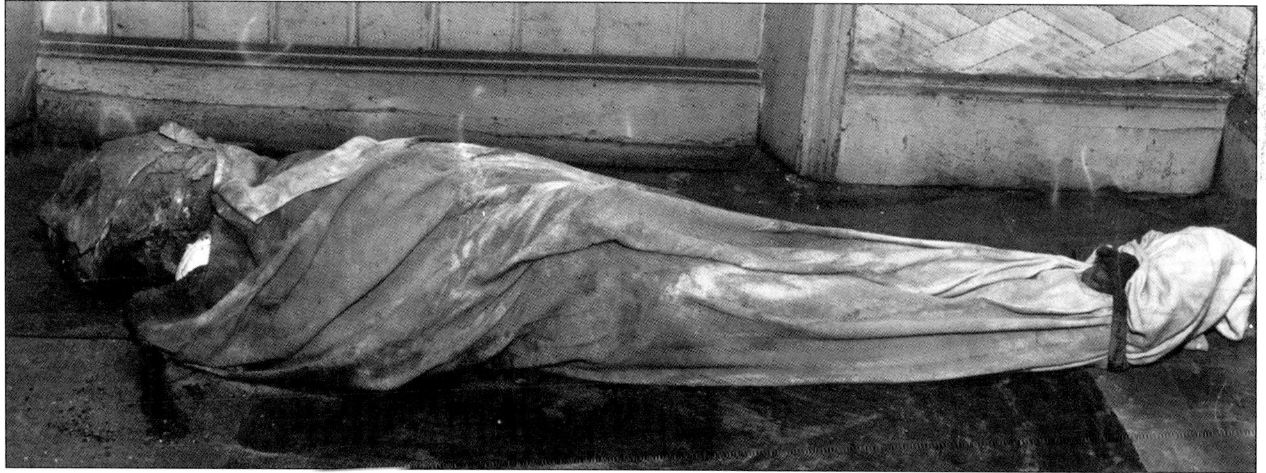

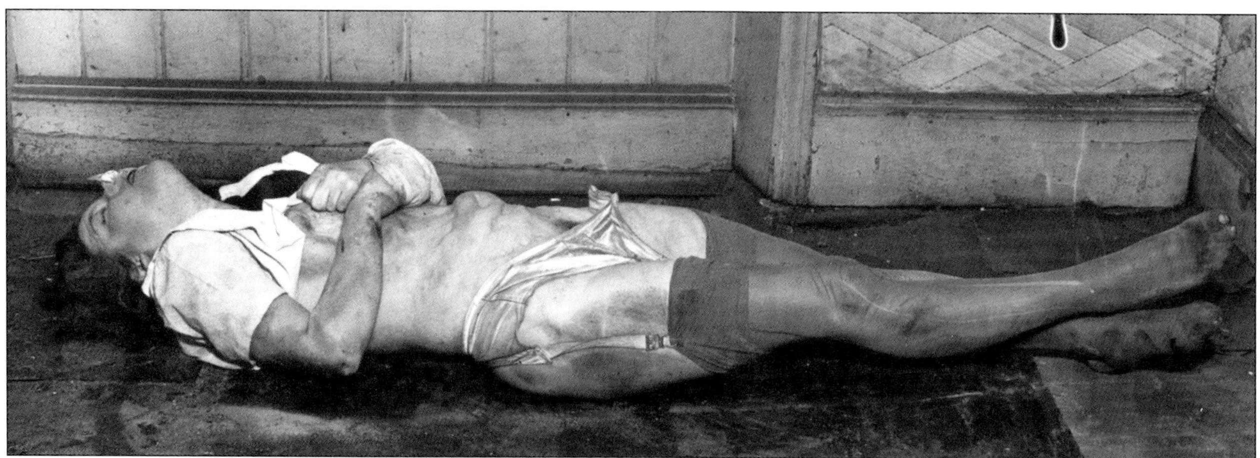

Right: The bodies were removed by J. H. Kenyon, the London funeral directors, and taken to Kensington Mortuary just off Kensington High Street. On the evening of March 24 Dr Camps was called to Rillington Place but as it was late, it was decided to leave the body in the front room overnight. Next morning he carried out a post-mortem examination of Mrs Christie in the presence of Chief Inspector Albert Griffin. The body was wrapped in a flannelette blanket, secured with a safety pin at the top. There appeared to be a silk dress which was wrapped around the body and a flowered cotton garment lay beneath it. There were stockings on both legs but no other clothes. The head was wrapped in a pillow case — on the right side it was dry and covered with mould but the left side was wet and decomposing. Lying between the legs, in the position of a diaper, was a silk/wool/cotton mixture vest. Dr Camps took a blood sample and swabs from the vagina and the liver and intestines. The stomach was empty with no sign of pheno-barbitone. He told the court that her cause of death was asphyxia with no evidence of coal-gas poisoning or suggestion of it.'

Dr Camps continued to explain that he was present when the bodies of the three females were removed from the cupboard. Hectorina MacLennan had been strangled and subsequent analysis of her blood showed relatively high saturation of carbon monoxide which gave the appearance of having been gassed while she was alive. There was material emerging from the front passage which turned out to be semen, consistent with intercourse having been had with the girl just before, or during, or after death. Kathleen Moloney was wrapped in a blanket and tied round the ankles with a sock. A silk-mixture vest was placed between her legs in the position of a diaper. The cause of death was consistent with her having been strangled and carbon monoxide poisoning. A swab from the front passage later revealed positive for semen. Rita Nelson had a piece of material between her legs and symptoms of carbon monoxide poisoning with the cause of death being pressure on the neck. She was 24 weeks pregnant but the pregnancy had not been interfered with.

On March 24, Barry Cheese was standing on this very spot in front of the Rainbow Café and vividly remembers the cries from the crowd as each of the four coffins was brought out: 'And another one!'

The murders in Rillington Place captivated public attention for weeks in 1953, people flocking to the street just to stand and stare at the end house guarded by a constable. This photo was taken on April 18 by the *Picture Post* photographer Ronald Startup.

Fifty-eight years later, Bartle Road still sees curious visitors yet it is only the cognoscente like Roger on the right who knew exactly where to look. The line of new tarmac marks the position of Rickard's boundary wall from which point the road visibly drops down as the ground level in the old yard was several feet lower than the road.

When on April 27 Christie admitted being responsible for the death of Beryl Evans (although not of baby Geraldine), instructions were given to exhume her body for further examination. From a pathology point of view it was a unique occasion as Dr Donald Teare was present, having carried out the original post-mortem in 1949, together with Dr Keith Simpson who had been appointed by John Christie's defence counsel, while the Attorney-General had detailed Dr Camps to carry out the second autopsy. ***Left:*** **Dr Camps's landmark cases included in this book were Harry Hailstone, the taxi-driver killed at Colchester, Stanley Setty, John Christie and PC Ray Summers, while Dr (later Professor) Simpson** ***(centre)*** **did Leonard Moules, Joan Wolfe, Neville Heath, John Haigh and Michael Gregsten.** ***Right:*** **Dr Teare worked on the so-called 'Cleft-Chin' murder of George Heath, the stabbing of John Beckley, and the shooting of Detective Sergeant Raymond Purdy.**

Once, and only once, we three — Dr F. E. Camps, Dr Donald Teare and I — were 'on the job' together. It was a famous case, probably the most famous for all of us. The occasion was an exhumation, and the disinterment was unusually well attended in spite of the unsocial hour.

We met in the Roman Catholic cemetery of the Royal Borough of Kensington at Gunnersbury Lane on 18th May 1953, at the usual exhumation hour of 5.30 a.m. Those who arrange these affairs, and doubtless sleep through them, have always assumed that if timed at the crack of dawn an exhumation will be a quiet, private affair. To make doubly sure, and because this was a cause célèbre, the authorities had erected barricades, closed the cemetery to unauthorized persons, and sent a patrol of thirty constables to keep out the public and the Press. In spite of these precautions hordes of newspaper reporters and photographers with telescopic cameras lined the raised Bath Road embankment as the coffin was lifted; and, as usual, many early risers found time to stop and stare on their way past the cemetery railings in the hope of a glimpse of what was, admittedly, no ordinary exhumation.

It had been asked for by the defence lawyers, not the prosecution; the prisoner protested his guilt, not his innocence; and another man had already been hanged for the double murder three years before.

I represented the accused, and the Attorney-General had nominated Camps to carry out the post-mortem examination. Teare was with us because he had carried out the original autopsies in December 1949. A fourth doctor, not a pathologist but a psychiatrist, Dr Jack Abbott Hobson, was present in the background for the defence.

We looked down into a pit nearly five feet deep, for the headstone had been lifted and most of the earth removed before we arrived, the coffin was the top of six in a common grave. The lid was cleaned and the plate exposed and photographed by the police. Then the coffin was freed at the sides and lifted out. The undertaker, the mortuary superintendent, and the gravedigger solemnly identified the plate. It said there were two bodies in the coffin: 'Beryl Evans, aged 19 years' and her daughter, mis-spelt 'Jeraldine', of 14 months. We were pleased to see that the

May 18, 1953, Kensington Cemetery. A screen has been erected around the grave in Plot G while the Press has been kept at a respectful distance for the exhumation of Beryl and Geraldine. With Christie's trial at the Old Bailey due to start in just over a months' time, it was deemed necessary to try to establish if an innocent man had been hanged.

Left: **The coffin is lifted from the grave.** *Right:* **The wording on the headstone has now faded.**

wood, which was one-inch elm boarding and kerfed, was in good condition, with the lid only slightly warped. I consented to a slight raising of the lid to allow the escape of gases before the coffin was removed from the cemetery.

At Kensington Mortuary we were joined by L. C. Nickolls, Director of the Metropolitan Police Laboratory, and two Chief Inspectors: George Salter, the Scotland Yard liaison officer, and George Jennings, who had identified the bodies at the original autopsies and was going to try to do the same again. Jennings was the officer who had taken down Timothy John Evans's confession and charged him with murdering his wife and daughter.

Evans was convicted only of the murder of his daughter, though most of the evidence was directed to prove that he had murdered his wife. The reason for this paradox is that English criminal law procedure does not allow a person to be tried for more than one murder at a time but may allow evidence of murders other than the one for which he is tried. When there are two or more indictments, the prosecution chooses which to take first. The case against Evans was much stronger for the murder of Beryl, and she had been killed first; but the prosecution chose to proceed with the murder of the child because it carried no danger of a provocation-and-manslaughter defence. The two crimes were considered a single transaction and, after a legal wrangle, the judge allowed all the evidence concerning the murder of the wife. Everyone involved — prosecution, defence, the judge, and later the three learned judges of the Court of Criminal Appeal — accepted that both murders had been committed by the same person, and it seemed indisputable at the time; but another judge, Brabin, reviewing the evidence sixteen years later, was to conclude this assumption was probably false. There is a common belief that the Brabin Inquiry found that Evans did not kill his wife. As a matter of fact it found that he probably did.

Evans had been convicted of the murder of his daughter Geraldine on 13th January 1950, after a trial at which he refuted his confession to the murder of both Beryl and Geraldine and accused the chief witness against him, John Christie, of having committed both murders himself. Christie had had opportunities as he lived in the same house, but as he had no apparent motive the Crown counsel dismissed the accusation as 'bosh'. The jury concurred and Evans was executed.

Three years later the remains of six more female bodies were found in the same house. Two had died several years before Beryl and Geraldine, the other four afterwards. When Christie was caught, wandering on the Thames Embankment near Putney Bridge, he admitted he had killed them all. Later he confessed also to the murder of Beryl Evans, and that was where I came in.

There was no mystery about Christie's motive for murder, which had been thought non-existent at the trial of Evans. Camps and Nickolls discovered this before his arrest. Two of the bodies were only skeletons that had been buried in the garden about ten years before; but the other four had been dead only a few months and, by chance, had been stored in cool dry surroundings

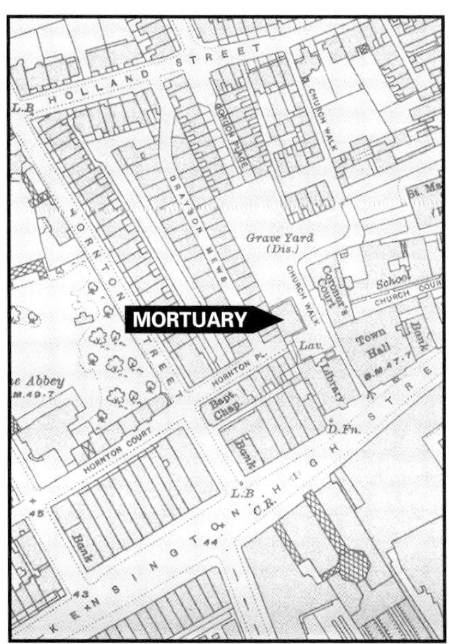

In the 1950s the mortuary at Kensington was tucked away at the end of Hornton Place, a cul-de-sac bordering the church. It was a very old building which had been built in 1883 and Dr Simpson later explained that 'it was typical of the kind of premises that all three of us had been campaigning to have scrapped.'

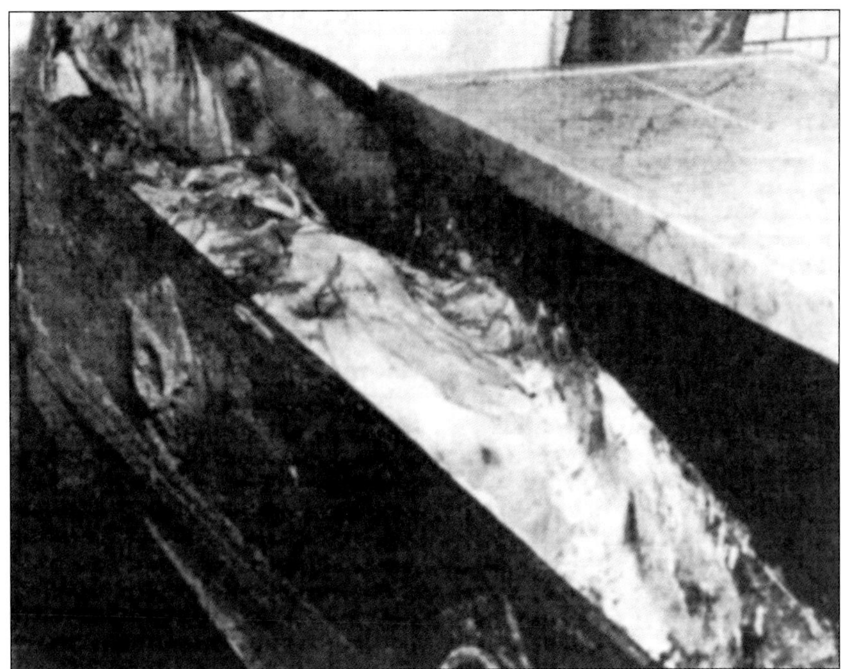

Dr Simpson: 'The post-mortem room was walled with glazed white tiles and had two operating tables, each lighted by a 500-watt bulb overhead. The lighting was adequate: a detail of some importance, as it was in this room, with exactly the same lighting, that Teare had performed the original Evans autopsies and that Camps had examined the bodies of Christie's last four victims.'

(Christie's kitchen alcove) with some air movement, almost perfect conditions for preservation. All were more or less clothed, but none wore knickers. In the most recently dead (about twenty days) Camps found whitish material exuding from the vulva and inside the vagina. He took vaginal swabs from all four bodies, and under the microscope three of these showed the presence of spermatozoa. The exception was Christie's wife.

The exhumation of Beryl and Geraldine Evans had as yet nothing to do with the Evans case, which was officially filed as solved. Christie's lawyers had decided his only possible defence was insanity, and they thought seven murders might seem slightly madder than six. Christie was sane enough to appreciate this opinion, which he paraphrased for the prison chaplain: 'the more the merrier' was the way he put it to that shocked clergyman.

It seemed hardly likely that a relatively small addition to Christie's score could make any difference to the verdict at his forthcoming trial, but the reason for the extraordinary public interest in the exhumation had little to do with Christie. If he had killed Beryl, Evans had not, and therefore might well not have killed Geraldine either. (Christie had not confessed to the murder of the child, but reticence would be understandable: there could be no extra merriment in the destruction of a girl so far from nubility.) So we knew, when the lid came off that coffin, that we were looking for evidence that might prove an innocent man had been hanged.

Christie's four most recent victims had all been killed by strangling with a ligature, and he said he had used the same method on the two that time had reduced to skeletons. In three of the four bodies Camps had examined (Mrs Christie was the exception) he had observed clear signs of carbon monoxide poisoning which had been confirmed by examination of the blood with a spectroscope. Vaginal swabs from the same three bodies proved that sexual intercourse had taken place at about — one can never be sure whether it was before, during, or after — the time of death.

Christie's first confession to the murder of Beryl Evans, made to his solicitor, Roy Arthur of Clifton's, in Brixton Prison, followed the same pattern: gassing to unconsciousness, followed by strangling with a ligature and sexual intercourse. When he repeated his confession to Dr Hobson, Christie said he was not sure which of the latter occurred first. Clifton's had supplied me with a copy of Teare's original autopsy reports and asked me if I thought there was anything in the medical evidence that supported his confession.

The strongest item was that Beryl (and Geraldine too) had been strangled with a ligature, Christie's invariable technique. Most stranglers use their bare hands. On the other hand Teare's report showed that Beryl had been beaten up before death: a black eye and a bruised upper lip suggested punches on the face, and there were more bruises on her thigh and leg. These injuries were alien to Christie's style of murder. Teare had also noted two marks on the posterior wall of the vagina — one an old scar, and beside it a small bruise which, Teare said at the magistrate's court, 'could have been caused by an attempt at forced intercourse or in a struggle'. Later he thought it had more probably been a self-inflicted injury caused by a syringe that Beryl seemed to have been using to try to abort herself (she was four months pregnant). Her body was found fully clothed except that she wore no knickers, but Teare did not take a vaginal swab for examination.

Teare's report was most revealing in something it did not say. If Christie had gassed Beryl, her skin and tissues would have been cherry-pink. This characteristic sign of carbon-monoxide poisoning could not possibly have been overlooked by a pathologist of Teare's care and experience in a case of obvious murder. Camps had observed it very clearly on three other bodies, two of which had then been dead about two months. Beryl's body, almost equally preserved, had been dead less than a month at Teare's autopsy. Moreover, with characteristic thoroughness, Teare had made a routine laboratory test for carbon monoxide and found none.

I would not in any case have expected to be able to find a residue of carbon monoxide in a body that had been buried more than three years, but there was another reason for the exhumation. When the police searched that notorious house where Evans and Christie had lived they found a two-ounce tobacco tin containing four separate tufts of human pubic hair. They had been teased out, forming ringlets, each of which occupied a corner of the tin. They were all interlocking so that they were held in what Mr Justice Brabin described as an 'artistic display'. Clifton's gave me to understand that Christie acknowledged ownership of these trophies and had said he had taken one from the body of Beryl Evans.

A whitish mould hung down in stalactites from the inside of the coffin lid. The shroud was overgrown with the same mould, but the bodies were clearly outlined underneath. The child lay on top of the mother, who was on a bed of brown damp sawdust. We waited for Chief Inspector Jennings to see if he could identify the bodies for the second time in the same mortuary. This proved unexpect-

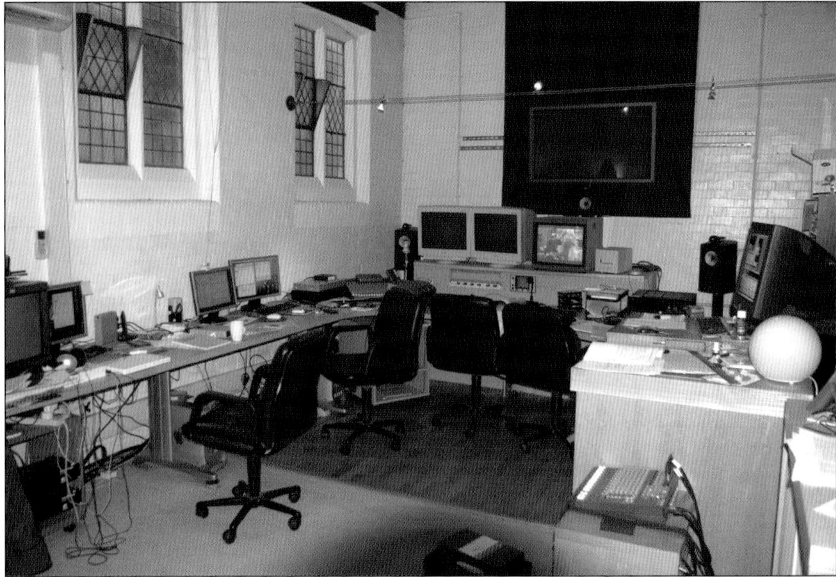

The mortuary for the Royal Borough of Kensington and Chelsea is now combined with Westminster in modern facilities in Horseferry Road. The old building fell into disrepair and was in a derelict state when Carl Forbes found it while searching for premises for a design studio. Now it is occupied by his company, N2K Publishing.

Christie stayed at Rowton House for two or three days before he began to wander the streets of London, ending up at one point as far away as the Barking Road in East Ham! He was arrested outside the Welcome Cafe on the south bank of the Thames at Putney where perhaps he had just enjoyed an early morning cup of tea . . . his last as a free man.

edly easy, for, to everyone's surprise, both bodies had been marvellously well preserved for identification purposes, by the formation of adipocere.

Adipocere is seldom well developed in bodies buried in coffins, which seem to decompose more rapidly than those without, but it had been favoured by some unusual conditions: the cold weather at the time of death, the position of the bodies in the outside wash-house, and the effect of the rather wet common grave and the well-drained sandy soil.

At the first autopsy the child's body had been described as almost black with post-mortem changes: now it was whitish-yellow. Camps lifted out the little body and stripped off a second thin shroud, and we saw that the mother's body was equally well preserved, and of the same whitish-yellow colour, except for an area on both thighs, which was pink. Cherry-pink!

'I want specimens of the thigh tissue for carbon-monoxide analysis,' I told Camps.

'Yes, of course I'd like you to do that,' Teare said to me immediately.

He was cool and unflurried, and clearly confident that my tests would prove negative. It was a tense moment, but the only person flustered was Camps.

That was nearly 60 years ago and time moves on . . . as do tastes to more exotic eateries from the Far East.

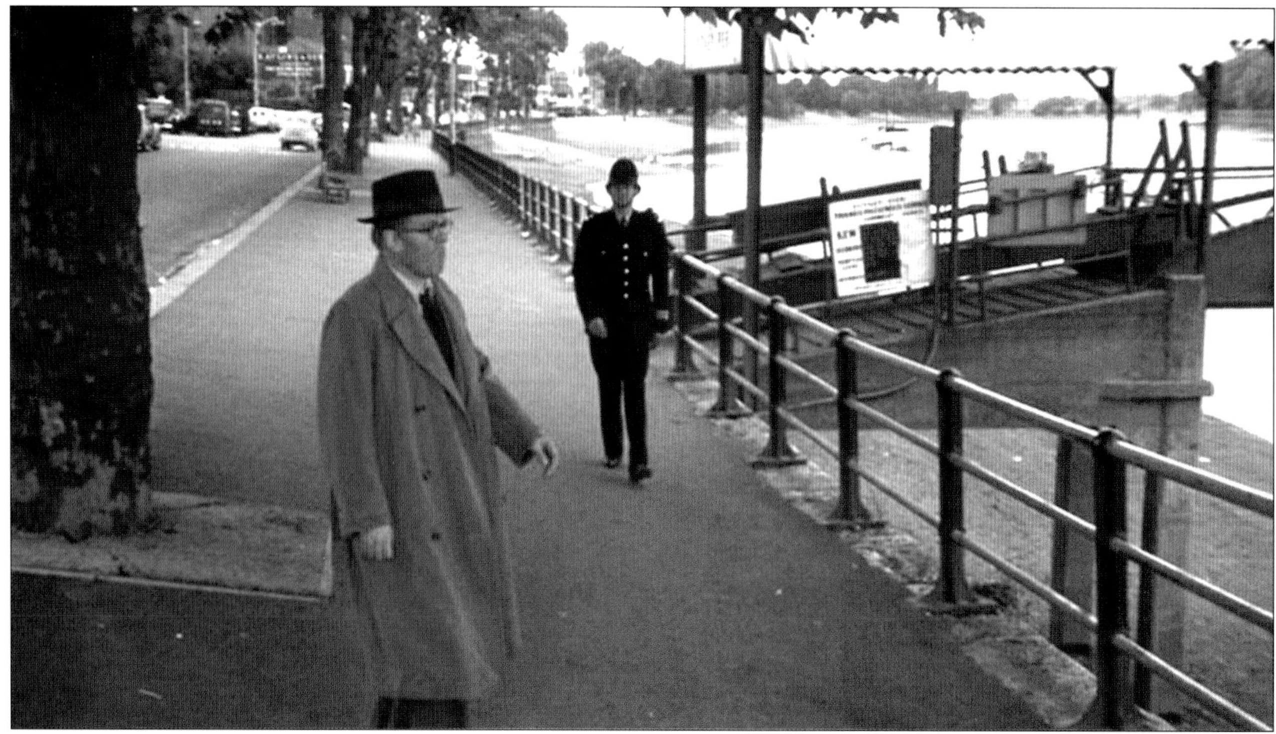

The arrest was re-staged where it took place for the film *10 Rillington Place* based on Ludovic Kennedy's book of the same name. Here Richard Attenborough, looking very down and out after supposedly walking the streets for ten days, stands where Police Constable Tom Ledger *(left)* apprehended Christie on March 31, 1953.

Below: In the reverse shot we see the road bridge at Putney. PC Ledger was played by the late Richard Coleman, our comparisons *(above and below)* being taken in August 2011.

Left: **Christie was taken to Putney police station on Upper Richmond Road where a large crowd soon gathered.**

Right: **The site is now occupied by Percy Laurie House next to the pillared entrance to Putney's old burial ground.**

'I'm in charge here,' he said tersely. 'I'm going to do this my way.' It was pure bluster, and I could only think he was irritated by our agreeing on the matter before he could say a word. He would have preferred us to argue and ask him for a ruling. 'I'll deliver all the specimens to Nickolls, and you can examine them at Scotland Yard,' he added in a truculent tone.

I had, of course, a right to examine anything I wished for the defence, but I said nothing, and the moment of tension passed. As Camps continued the autopsy I noticed that the cherry-pink colour was beginning to fade. It had evidently been preserved by the contact with the body of the child and was disappearing on exposure to the air. I thought Teare probably had good reason not to worry: it looked like nothing more sinister than 'post-mortem pink'. The tests would show.

The hair on Beryl's abdomen and pubis was in a normal condition, and appeared complete except for a small portion that had adhered to the shroud. I could not see any sign of a tuft having been cut out but there was no trace either of the removal of a sample by Teare at the first autopsy. I asked him how much he had taken. 'Just a pinch': he held a few hairs between his thumb and forefinger to demonstrate. I showed Camps the area of abdominal wall I wanted for further examination, and asked also for a sample of the debris containing hairs that had sloughed out of the skin.

The following day he appeared at West London Magistrates' Court *(above)* charged with murdering his wife. Five further appearances took place — at West London and Clerkenwell — and on May 6 he was committed for trial at the Central Criminal Court, now accused of four murders.

Although the main court building in North End Road still stands, it is now used for commercial offices and the rear yard *(left)* in Vernon Street has been demolished. *Above:* This is the comparison looking across the road at Nos. 6 and 7.

While the pathologists were carrying out their investigations in Kensington, a couple of miles away in Rillington Place preparations were underway for the next big event: the Coronation of Queen Elizabeth II to be held at Westminster Abbey on Tuesday, June 2. With the houses, including No. 10 *(left)*, gaily decorated, a street party *(right)* was held on the following Saturday.

Camps reopened the body by cutting Teare's sutures. The organs were remarkably well preserved. The lungs, although dehydrated, were easily recognizable. They were pink, cherry-pink, just like the area over the thighs. Again the colour disappeared on exposure to air.

The heart and other organs gave clear evidence that Beryl had died, as Teare had said, of asphyxia. Then, most remarkable of all, came the uterus, vagina, and vulva all in one piece, complete with pubic hair, just as Teare had removed it for examination three years before. We could measure the uterus and see that it had been in a pregnant state. I inspected the vagina and cervical canal and saw the two small marks on the posterior vaginal wall which Teare identified as the scar and the bruise he had noted at the original autopsy. The pubic hair gave no evidence that a tuft had been cut away.

We had first gone over the material from the autopsy again with a hand lens to see if the pubic hair had been defaced in any way. I concluded that while Teare could well have plucked a few hairs, in the way he had shown me, without it being evident even at the time, a specimen the size of Christie's trophies could not have been removed without leaving a visible mark. The cut ends of hair would still be showing if it had been cut, and if it had been plucked (to be trimmed afterwards) the area would show on the skin.

Taking a representative sample of Beryl's pubic hair, we compared it with each of the four tufts in Christie's tobacco tin. Three of these were entirely different. The fourth, however, was identical in colour, thickness, and general microscopic structure. The hair was mid-brown and of a very common type, and equally identical specimens could have been found on about 15 to 20 per cent of the population.

We examined each of the identical specimens in greater detail, to see if there was perhaps an unsuspected difference; and we found that most of the hairs in Christie's trophy had been cut at both ends. In each case one cut was recent, and had presumably been made by Christie when he took the hairs from the body; the cut at the other end had rounded off and was about six months old. The hairs in the sample from Beryl's body were uncut.

The conclusion was inescapable: the hairs in the tobacco tin could not have been taken from Beryl's body at the time of her death.

Christie was tried for the murder of his wife only, and the prosecution did not lead any evidence about his other ghastly crimes. The defence made up for this, and in the witness box Christie repeated his confession to killing Beryl Evans. I was in court, at his solicitor's request, but I was not called to give evidence. If I had gone into the box I

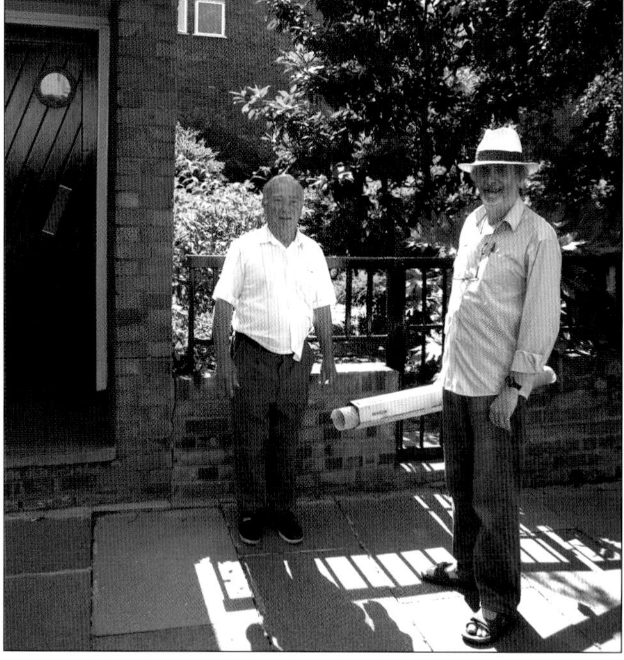

Left: **The house soon became a magnet for sightseers such as these two American tourists in 1954.** *Right:* **Although attempts have been made to eliminate the past, visitors — some on a mission like Barry and Roger — still seek out Rillington Place, much to the annoyance of the residents. This is the exact comparison we took on our visit in July 2011.**

Early in the investigation, the police stated that there was no connection between the Evans killings and the Christie murders, and certainly in the 1950s no one wanted to believe in the infallibility of British justice. Five years earlier Sir David Maxwell Fyfe had said that there was no practical possibility of a miscarriage of justice in a murder trial in Britain, and as Home Secretary he later refused clemency to Derek Bentley (see page 268). However, the probability of two mass murderers living in the same house was too much of a coincidence, consequently there were demands from many directions — the Press, Members of Parliament, and Timothy Evans's mother — for an inquiry. Bowing to the inevitable, on July 6 Sir David appointed the Recorder for Portsmouth, John Scott Henderson, Q.C., with the almost impossible task of completing the inquiry before Christie was hanged, a matter of just ten days. The 70-page report was presented to Parliament on July 14 and Christie was executed the next day by Albert Pierrepoint and Harry Smith. The report, which stated that there had been no miscarriage in the conviction of Evans for the murder of his daughter, was highly criticised with the inference that Henderson 'had reached his conclusion before he had started'.

Movie-making in the street in 1969. Depending which source one believes, the interior scenes in *10 Rillington Place* were shot in No. 6 or 8. Richard Attenborough, portraying Christie, says that he believed that No. 10 was pulled down the day after the filming ended. With him are Judy Geeson and John Hurt playing Mr and Mrs Evans.

could only have supported Nickolls's opinion that none of the tufts in the tobacco tin could have been taken from Beryl Evans's body at the time of her death.

Whether Christie had killed Beryl was of such little importance in this trial. Pinning a seventh murder on Christie would not affect the answer to the only question at issue, which was whether or not he had been insane according to the M'Naghten Rules. The jury decided Christie had not been insane, and he was found guilty of murder and sentenced to death.

But had he killed Beryl Evans? The question that mattered so little at Christie's trial assumed immense importance outside the court. Suddenly British justice itself was put on trial. Members of Parliament, the public, and the Press demanded an official investigation. The Home Secretary appointed a senior Q.C., John Scott Henderson, to carry out an inquiry in private.

Scott Henderson preferred the opinion of three pathologists to that of a psychiatrist on both the pubic hair and the carbon monoxide.

After interviewing Christie himself in prison he concluded that his confession to the murder of Beryl was false and that there could be no doubt that Evans had killed both his wife and his child. He published his report on the day set for Christie's execution, on which date Christie was duly hanged.

That was still not the end of the affair. Fifteen years later, after continued pressure, the case was reheard in public, at the Royal Courts of Justice, by Mr Justice Brabin, a quiet scholarly man of great patience. The main hearings took place on a total of thirty-two days, spread over several months. His final conclusion was, however, quite unexpected: 'More probably than not,' he said, 'Evans had killed Beryl but Christie had killed Geraldine.'

If so, Evans had been executed for the wrong murder. He was thereupon given a posthumous free pardon and his body was exhumed, not for a second autopsy but for reburial outside Pentonville Prison.

A Member of Parliament who objected to the free pardon pointed out that Mr Justice Brabin had confirmed Evans's guilt in the murder of his wife. The Home Secretary replied that Evans had been pardoned because it was for the murder of the child that he had been tried and hanged. If the prosecution had chosen to proceed with the charge of killing his wife, as Evans' defenders thought it should have done, and if he had then been convicted and executed, as was likely, presumably no pardon would have been forthcoming, and his remains would still lie under a prison yard.

Professor Keith Simpson, Forty Years of Murder, 1978

In refuting the allegations, Mr Henderson provided a supplementary report in August but this still failed to satisfy his critics and so the campaign for a further unhurried inquiry continued for the next ten years until a new Home Secretary, Sir Frank Soskice, finally agreed in July 1965 to authorise another one under the direction of a High Court judge, Sir Daniel Brabin. This was the year that capital punishment ended, following which next-of-kin could apply to have the remains of executed dead returned to them, Evans being exhumed that November (see page 249). However, when the Brabin report was published in October 1966 it proved to be another bomb-shell as Sir David now stated that 'while Evans had probably not murdered the baby [for which he was executed], he probably had killed his wife! As a result, Roy Jenkins, the current Home Secretary, had little option and quickly advised the Queen to grant Evans a posthumous Royal Pardon. ***Left:*** **Five years later the end came to No. 10 when the whole street was earmarked for slum clearance. In this photo we can see Mr Kitchener's first floor flat where Beryl's body was hidden prior to its removal to the wash house.** ***Right:*** **The comparison today looking across Christie's front room.**

On the night of Friday, March 14, 1952, a gang led by Niven Craig *(above)* drove to Waltham Abbey on the outskirts of Epping Forest in Essex bent on house-breaking and robbery. Parking their Buick in Tennyson Avenue *(right)* so it was just out of sight, the five masked men walked some 100 yards down the main road — Honey Lane — to No. 55 on the opposite side where the Whiten family were asleep. Shortly after 2 a.m. Mrs Whiten was woken up by someone speaking to her and poking a pistol in her face. Leaving one man to keep watch on her, the others went to the other bedrooms and did the same to her husband and sister. All were then tied up, the men demanding the keys to the safe.

November 2, 1952 – Derek Bentley and Christopher Craig

In the early hours of March 15, 1952, a big noisy car drove into Tennyson Avenue, Waltham Abbey and woke one of the residents. Wondering quite what was afoot the woman got up and saw five men get out of the strange car and walk around the corner into Honey Lane. A few minutes later Mrs Beryl Whiten of 55 Honey Lane, Waltham Abbey, was shaken awake from her sleep into the glare of torches in her eyes as she lay in bed with her two children. She soon became aware of no fewer than five men, each wearing a gangster style trilby hat and a scarf as a mask. One of the five pointed a Luger automatic pistol, and demanded the keys to the safe. It was not very long before the rest of the household was awoken, firstly her husband, Herbert Whiten, in the adjoining room, and then her sister, Miss Betty Freeman.

As the keys were not at home, they were unable to give the gunman the items he sought. The Whitens, their young children and sister, spent a terrorised half hour as the five intruders tied them up and searched for alternative items to steal. In the end the robbers made do with taking £4 in cash, a cigarette lighter and some 'Scroll' brand ball-point pens, the whole lot costing less than £6. 10s. (£6.50p)

The five then left the house and drove off in their American Buick but the car crashed and turned over shortly after the robbers left. A police area car crew found it at 3.15 a.m., three miles from Waltham Abbey in a ditch adjoining a notoriously fierce double bend on the borders of Chingford.

Another police car travelling down South Street, Enfield, disturbed three men walking from the direction of the Lea Valley Road (and the car crash). All three ran into the shadows. One of these, local villain George King, 28, was picked up and linked by fingerprints to the Buick and, by possession of one of the still-rare ball-point pens from the Honey Lane robbery. He was also already wanted for a £6,651 mailbag robbery in Bruce Grove, Tottenham, on February 29th, and had eight previous convictions. Considered by some of the policemen who knew him as 'London's No. 1 Gunman', he had only been released from a seven-year term for shop breaking in January 1951.

Having got the car and linked it to King, it was a natural progression to try and contact the registered keeper and then the new owner and question them about the crime. The first was 27-year-old Cyril Burney and

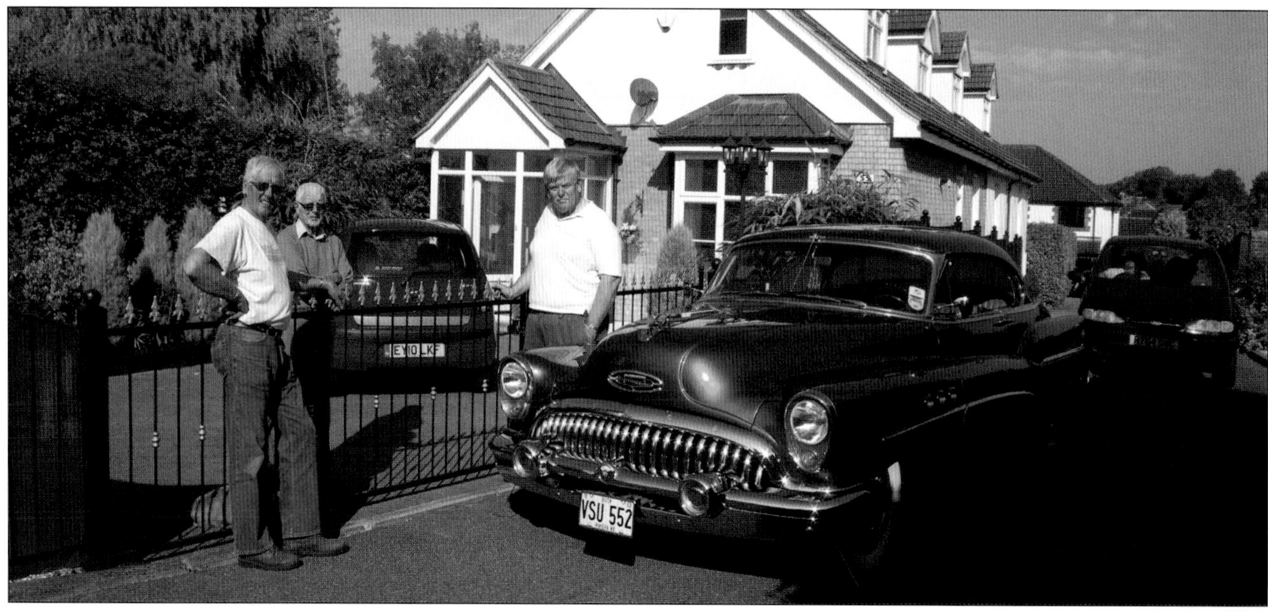

According to the report in the Press the following day, the robbers had backed the car into the drive of No. 55 to enable one of the men to climb on the roof to cut the telephone wire. Malcolm Springham, left, brought down his 1953 Buick Riviera for us to recreate the scene. Bryn Elliott, right, explains what took place 60 years ago to James Norton who now resides in No. 55.

The keys were not in the house so, after having cut the telephone wire, the robbers departed having taken £4 from Mrs Whiten's wallet, a Ronson cigarette lighter and several of the then-new ball-point pens. Later that night Police Constable Leonard McCartney found the black Buick overturned in the ditch *(right)* alongside a tricky double bend, some 120 yards north of the Fox pub on the Sewardstone Road, some three miles from Honey Lane. At the same time another police car was driving along South Street in Ponders End near Enfield, when its headlights revealed three men walking along the road. When the policemen stopped to question them, two of the men ran off but George King was caught. He appeared in court in June and was sentenced to 12 years' although he died three months later.

The tree is badly scarred from many accidents on this notorious bend on the Sewardstone Road.

the second was 26-year-old Niven Craig. Both of them were known in police circles and they both went on the run.

George King, who was identified at Waltham Abbey by Betty Freeman, was dealt with alone for both of the crimes some time before the other two were traced. After being committed for trial at the Essex Assizes from Chingford Magistrates' Court, he was found guilty and sent away for 12 years on June 18, 1952. George King only served three months of his term as he died in Pentonville Prison on September 11, 1952.

Three days later, on September 14, Craig and Burney were arrested in Bayswater. Craig was found in possession of a loaded gun and extra loose ammunition. Dealt with at the Central Criminal Court, Niven Craig received a sentence of 12 years' imprisonment on October 30. In the court at the time was Niven's mother and younger brother, 16-year-old Christopher. It is said that Christopher was deeply shocked at the treatment his brother received and harboured a deep hatred for all policemen, and particularly for the Waltham Abbey police after this second run in with them. It was said that the first brush with the law in the town had resulted in the arrest of one of the gang for a raid on the premises of Betser's, a wholesale tobacconist and confectioner in Rue de St Lawrence. Niven Craig's defence had included both a denial of involvement and a veiled suggestion that Christopher was one of the untraced robbers in Honey Lane.

Bryn Elliott, Police Historian, Waltham Abbey, 2011

When he sentenced two men to twelve years' imprisonment for armed robbery and robbery with violence yesterday, Mr Justice Hilbery told one of them, Niven Scott Craig, 28:

'You are a young man determined to indulge in desperate crime. I do not remember in the course of some seventeen years on the bench a young man your age who struck me as being so dangerous as you.'

The judge had been told at the Old Bailey that when police went to arrest Craig and the other man, Cyril Burney, 27, in Kensington Gardens Square, London, Craig put his hand under his pillow where he had a fully-loaded automatic pistol. Detective-Sergeant William Lewis jumped for the bed and took the pistol from Craig's hand.

Craig and Burney were said by the prosecution to have been in a gang of five men, masked and wearing trilby hats, who broke into a house at Waltham Abbey, Essex, where they robbed Herbert Whiten of £4 and a lighter after using violence.

Speaking of Mrs Beryl Whiten, wife of the victim of the robbery, the judge said to the jury: 'You may think it enough to frighten the life out of any woman being awakened in the middle of the night by a torch shining in her face, and finding a man with a gun in his hand and five men in all in the room in masks and hats pulled down — and she a lone, defenceless woman.

'But that is the way today,' Mr. Justice Hilbery went on, 'and almost every day we read in the papers of men in the country behaving this way. The cowardice of it revolts any decent person.

'But we must not, in deciding a case, allow our anger and horror and contempt for that sort of thing to weigh our judgment in a particular case,' the judge said.

Craig, who was also charged with possessing the pistol, had said he got it in Italy with 200 rounds of live ammunition. Commenting on this the Judge said:

'For a mere souvenir one would not require live rounds, and Craig had said that he kept it because he was interested in shooting.' Of Craig's excuse that he had no chance to unload the gun before he returned to the room of his girlfriend, the judge said:

'To unload it is a demonstrative way of making the thing harmless, but he said out of consideration for her nervousness and sensitiveness he did not unload it in her presence.'

The jury might think that Craig when in the witness box answered some questions with 'impudent indifference' the judge said.

When the jury had found Craig and Burney both guilty of armed robbery and robbery with violence and Craig also of possessing the gun with intent to endanger life, the judge told Craig: 'You are cool and cold-blooded. I believe that if you had the opportunity to do so you would shoot any police officer who was attempting to arrest you or any lawful citizen who tried to prevent you from doing some felony.

'I think you would do it absolutely coldly and utterly regardless of the pain you were inflicting' said the judge. Craig smiled when sentenced and appeared absolutely unconcerned. He cried out loudly before being sentenced: 'I am definitely not guilty of this charge and I shall appeal.' The judge quietly told him he would find all the necessary papers for an appeal in his cell.

To Burney the judge said, 'You, too, are dangerous.'

Detective-Inspector Garrod put before the court a long record of Craig's criminal career from 1940. A field general court-martial sentenced him to five years penal servitude in 1947 for holding up drivers of Army vehicles at pistol point and stealing their vehicles in Austria. His Army character was described as very bad.

Inspector Garrod said Burney was sentenced to five years' in 1948 for store breaking, when eighteen similar cases were taken into consideration. He had been released two months before the robbery at Waltham Abbey.

Daily Mirror, October 31, 1952

Niven Craig and his accomplice Cyril Burney were traced to a room in one of the cheap hotels in Kensington Gardens Square in Bayswater. Craig attempted to pull out his gun but was overpowered and on October 30 received a sentence of 12 years. The fourth Honey Lane robber was never caught although it has been speculated that it was Craig's younger brother Christopher. In any event, it was the catalyst to what took place four days later in Croydon.

Sixteen-year-old Christopher Craig had left Norbury Manor School but was without a job, normally living with his parents at 9 Norbury Court Road *(right)*. He was fascinated with guns — which were easy to acquire in the early post-war years — and captivated by gangster films, picturing himself in the role of his screen idols. Having just seen his brother put away for a long stretch on Thursday, by the weekend he was full of anger against the police in general. Carrying a .455 Service revolver with a shortened barrel, loaded with .45 rounds, and with a home-made knuckle duster, he was armed and ready for action.

The London crime wave reached a new peak last night. A detective was shot dead and another seriously wounded in a second 'Battle of Sidney Street'. They had seen the flash of a torchlight in the warehouse of Barlow and Parker, wholesale confectioners, in Tamworth Road, Croydon, just after 10 o'clock. They entered the building. They cautiously edged their way in. Inside, the raiders were so far undisturbed. Ambulances and fire brigades had been summoned. Then as the bandits realized they had been trapped by a police cordon, shooting began.

The gangsters armed with a Sten-gun hit one of the officers as he climbed the fire escape towards the bandits. He was Police Constable Miles, in plain clothes, of Z Division, a married man with two children and with 22 years' service. He was killed.

His colleague, PC Frederick Fairfax, who was in a police patrol car, dashed into an alleyway leading to another fire escape up which the gunmen had climbed. As he went to help Miles, there was another shot and people coming out of the Sunday cinemas heard one of gunmen cry 'You won't get me'.

Five streets away lived 18-year-old Derek Bentley at No. 1 Fairview Road *(left)*. This picture of him *(centre)* was taken in the back garden but Mr Pirzada, the current owner, has knocked out the original sash window and installed French doors.

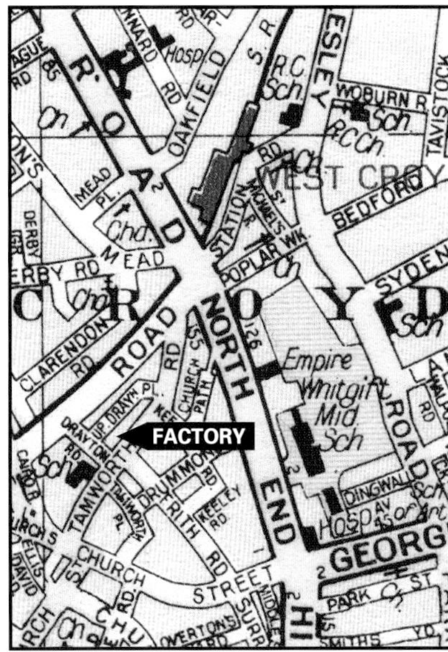

Derek Bentley described what happened that evening in the statement which he later gave to police: 'I was watching television tonight and between 8 p.m. and 9 p.m. Craig called for me. My mother answered the door and I heard her say that I was out. I had been out earlier to the pictures and got home just after 7 p.m. A little later Norman Parsley and Frank Fazey called. I did not answer the door or speak to them. My mother told me that they had called and I then ran out after them. I walked up the road with them to the paper shop where I saw Craig standing. We all talked together then Norman Parsley and Frank Fazey left. Chris Craig and I then caught a bus to Croydon. We got off at West Croydon *(left)* and then we walked down the road where the toilets are — I think it is Tamworth Road.'

PC Fairfax fell wounded in the shoulder. By this time 200 police were there, 30 of them armed with revolvers. Shots were exchanged. The gunmen dodged from vantage point to vantage point, firing at everything — police, ambulances, fire brigade officers. Scotland Yard sent reinforcements. In a few minutes an area a quarter of a mile round the buildings was sealed off. The bullets still flew. The police dodged and ducked.

For nearly an hour the gunmen fired to prevent any attempt at their capture. They seemed to have an unlimited supply of ammunition as bursts from the Sten-gun hit the streets. Then the end came. As three officers, crouching low, sprung on to the rooftop the Sten-gun was flung into their faces. The ammunition had run out.

Then began a chase over the roofs after the gunmen. They dodged behind chimney-pots. One of them attempted to lower himself by a stackpipe at the rear of the premises. By this time more police were on the roofs, and there were hand-to-hand battles before the two gunmen were finally overpowered, handcuffed and brought to street level.

Here one of the gunmen was found to be injured, and was taken to Croydon General Hospital. When the shooting began Scotland Yard mobilized all police officers and C.I.D. men from Kent and the Metropolitan area. 'Get them at all costs', was the order to the 200 police officers in the battle.

Daily Mail, November 3, 1952

Although this account is completely incorrect, we have deliberately included this fanciful newspaper report from the *Daily Mail* as a good example of what not to believe, for in no way does it accurately describe the events of that Sunday night. Their initial plan was to break into a butcher's shop here at 57 and 59 Tamworth Road *(above right)* but when they got there the lights were still on so they continued to the premises of Barlow & Parker, a wholesale confectioner, which then lay on the opposite side of the road at Nos. 27-29. Today it has been replaced by the new housing seen in the far distance on the left-hand side of the road *(right)*.

WHOLESALE
CROYDON HOUSE
BARLOW & PARKER LTD
Multi storey car park

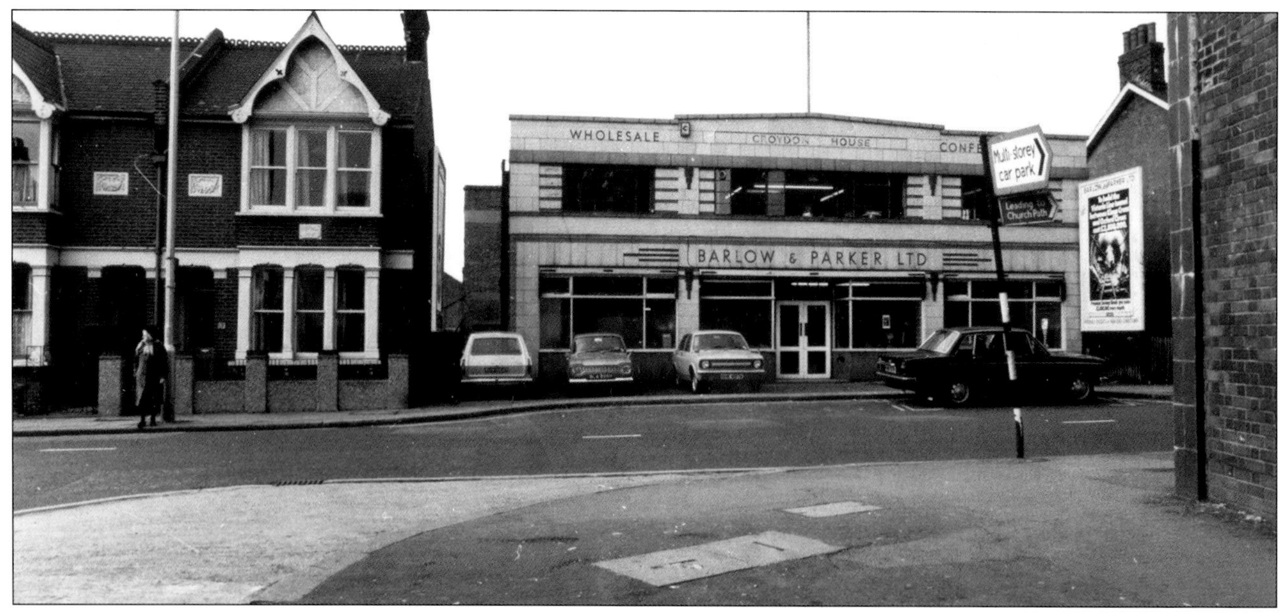

This is the confectionery warehouse of Barlow & Parker as photographed by the police. The plan below shows No. 74 on the opposite side of the road where nine-year-old Pearl Ware spotted two youths climbing the gate behind where the white car is parked.

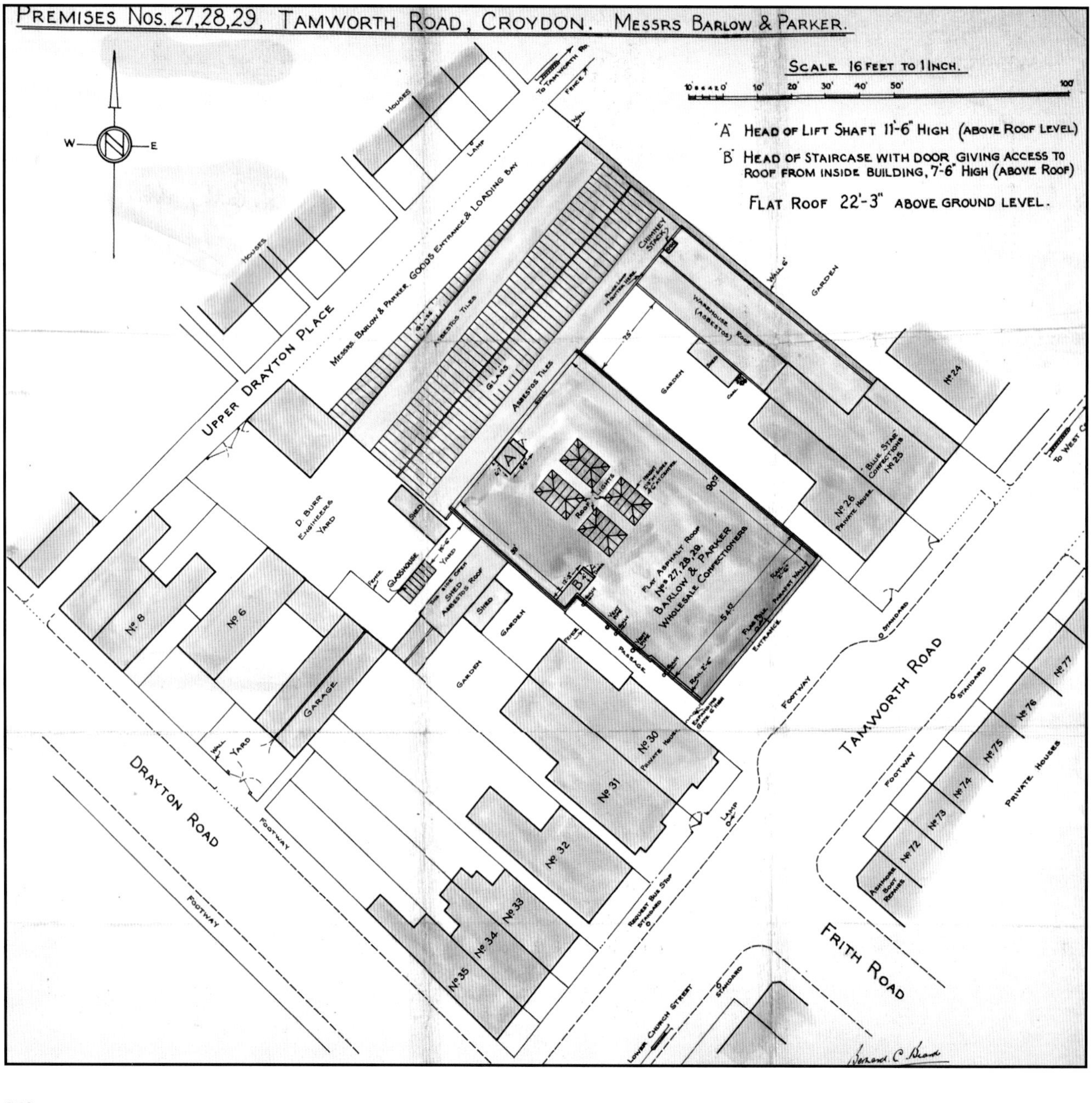

PREMISES Nos. 27,28,29, TAMWORTH ROAD, CROYDON. MESSRS BARLOW & PARKER.
SCALE 16 FEET TO 1 INCH.
'A' HEAD OF LIFT SHAFT 11'-6" HIGH (ABOVE ROOF LEVEL)
'B' HEAD OF STAIRCASE WITH DOOR GIVING ACCESS TO ROOF FROM INSIDE BUILDING, 7'-6" HIGH (ABOVE ROOF)
FLAT ROOF 22'-3" ABOVE GROUND LEVEL.
W
E
HOUSES
UPPER DRAYTON PLACE
MESSRS BARLOW & PARKER. GOODS ENTRANCE & LOADING BAY
ASBESTOS TILES
GLASS
D BURR ENGINEERS YARD
FLAT ASPHALT ROOF
Nos 27, 28, 29.
BARLOW & PARKER
WHOLESALE CONFECTIONERS
ROOF LIGHTS
GARDEN
GARAGE
YARD
PASSAGE
ENTRANCE
Nº 8
Nº 6
Nº 24
Nº 25
Nº 26
Nº 30
Nº 31
Nº 32
Nº 33
Nº 34
Nº 35
Nº 72
Nº 73
Nº 74
Nº 75
Nº 76
Nº 77
PRIVATE HOUSES
DRAYTON ROAD
FOOTWAY
TAMWORTH ROAD
FRITH ROAD
LOWER CHURCH STREET

The warehouse was demolished in September 1977; this is exactly the same view, the tell-tale concrete manhole in the foreground being the clue. The present-day Ordnance Survey plan covers exactly the same area as on the police drawing.

As the two boys scaled the gate to the yard, John Ware ran from his house to telephone the police. Scotland Yard relayed the message to Croydon Police Station: 'Suspects on premises, Tamworth Road, Croydon'. It was around 9.25 p.m. that Detective Constable Frederick Fairfax left the station with three other officers, heading for Tamworth Road. They arrived just as another wireless car pulled up. The driver was Police Constable Sidney Miles with PC James McDonald as his radio operator. After a quick word with Mr and Mrs Ware, Fairfax and McDonald climbed the gate and surveyed the drainpipes by which Craig and Bentley had reached the roof. 'I then climbed up a drainpipe at the western wall of the premises,' stated Fairfax later. 'The pipe — which had already borne the strain of two climbers — felt none too safe. I didn't know whether to pray to God or curse the plumber who'd put it there'. Once he reached the flat roof, he saw two men standing to the left about 15 yards away between the roof lights and the stairhead. Fairfax called to them; 'I am a police officer; come out from behind that stack', whereupon Craig replied: 'If you want us, fucking well come and get us.' At that Fairfax dashed forward and caught hold of Bentley and pulled him behind the stairwell. He was then technically in custody, if not under close arrest. Fairfax then started to approach Craig at which point Bentley was alleged to have shouted: 'Let him have it Chris!' Craig fired from a distance of six feet and the bullet, somewhat underpowered due to the wrong calibre rounds and shortened barrel, hit him in the shoulder without penetrating his body but knocking him to the ground. By now PCs McDonald and Harrison had reached the roof although none of the police were armed. At this point reinforcements were heard coming up the stairway. *Below:* The sequence of events on the roof was re-enacted for a BBC documentary before the building was demolished.

Derek Bentley: 'There was a little iron gate at the side. Chris then jumped over and I followed. Chris then climbed up the drainpipe to the roof and I followed. Up to then Chris had not said anything. We both got out on to the flat roof at the top. Then someone in a garden on the opposite side shone a torch towards us. Chris said, "It's a copper, hide behind here." We hid behind a shelter arrangement on the roof. We were there waiting for about ten minutes. I did not know he was going to use the gun. A plain clothes man climbed up the drainpipe and on to the roof. The man said, "I am a police officer — the place is surrounded." He caught hold of me and as we walked away Chris fired. There was nobody else there at the time. The policeman and I then went round a corner by a door.'

'A little later the door opened and a policeman in uniform came out. Chris fired again then and this policeman fell down. I could see that he was hurt as a lot of blood came from his forehead just above his nose. The policeman dragged him round the corner behind the brickwork entrance to the door. I remember I shouted something but I forgot what it was. I could not see Chris when I shouted to him — he was behind a wall. I heard some more policemen behind the door and the policeman with me said, "I don't think he has many more bullets left." Chris shouted, "Oh yes I have," and he fired again. I think I heard him fire three times altogether. The policeman then pushed me down the stairs and I did not see any more. I should have mentioned that after the plain clothes policeman got up the drainpipe and arrested me, another policeman in uniform followed and I heard someone call him "Mac". He was with us when the other policeman was killed.'

Christopher Craig, aged 16, and Derek Bentley, aged 19, were convicted before me yesterday. In Craig's case the defence endeavoured to obtain a verdict of manslaughter.

Had the jury returned such a verdict I should have passed a sentence of detention for 15 years as I am convinced that he is a most dangerous young criminal. In Bentley's case the jury added a recommendation to mercy. I have no doubt that the reason for their recommendation was that they realised a capital sentence could not be passed on to Craig.

So far as merits are concerned, I regret to say I could find no mitigating circumstances in Bentley's case. He was armed with a knuckle-duster of the most formidable type that I have ever seen and also with a sharp pointed knife and he called out to Craig when he was arrested to start the shooting.

Lord Justice Goddard writing to Home Secretary, December 12, 1952.

This is a very difficult case and I have given prolonged and anxious consideration to it.

As I see it, the following are the most important considerations to be urged in mitigation. Bentley did not himself use any violence. He made no attempt to escape after the shooting started. Craig would probably have fired at the police anyway, whether or not Bentley had encouraged him to do so. There is no doubt that Craig was the worst offender of the two.

The jury recommended Bentley to mercy no doubt on the grounds that Bentley did not fire the fatal shot and indeed at the time the shot that killed the policeman was fired, Bentley was in police custody. There are precedents for reprieving one offender where for some reason the principal offender cannot be executed.

If in these circumstances Bentley is executed it is possible that public sympathy would be felt for him outweighing the horror which was felt for the crime. On the other hand, it is clear that Bentley knew that Craig had a gun and ammunition, and incited Craig to use his gun.

It was a very bad murder, involving the death of a police officer, committed at a time when there is much public anxiety about the numbers of crimes of violence.

Many of these crimes of violence are committed by young persons and I must pay regard to the deterrent effect which the carrying out of the sentence in this case would be likely to have.

If Craig had been of an age when he could have been executed, the sentence would have been carried out in his case and there would have been no grounds for interfering with the sentence against Bentley.

It would be dangerous to give the impression that an older adolescent could escape the full penalty by using an accomplice of less than 18 years of age. I feel also that it is important to protect the unarmed police.

David Maxwell Fyfe, Home Secretary, Memorandum, January 22, 1953

As Police Constable Sidney Miles emerged from the stairwell door, Craig fired at him from nearly 40 feet away. Bearing in mind the condition of the weapon, it was an extremely lucky — or unlucky as the case may be — for the bullet struck the policeman straight between the eyes. It was such a fluke shot that as armed police were now on the scene, some authors have even speculated that it could have been a bullet from a police revolver that killed him. Craig then called out: 'I'm Craig. You have given my brother 12 years. Come on you coppers. I'm only 16.' At this, it was decided to remove Bentley from the roof. As he was being escorted, he called out: 'Chris, they're taking me down.'

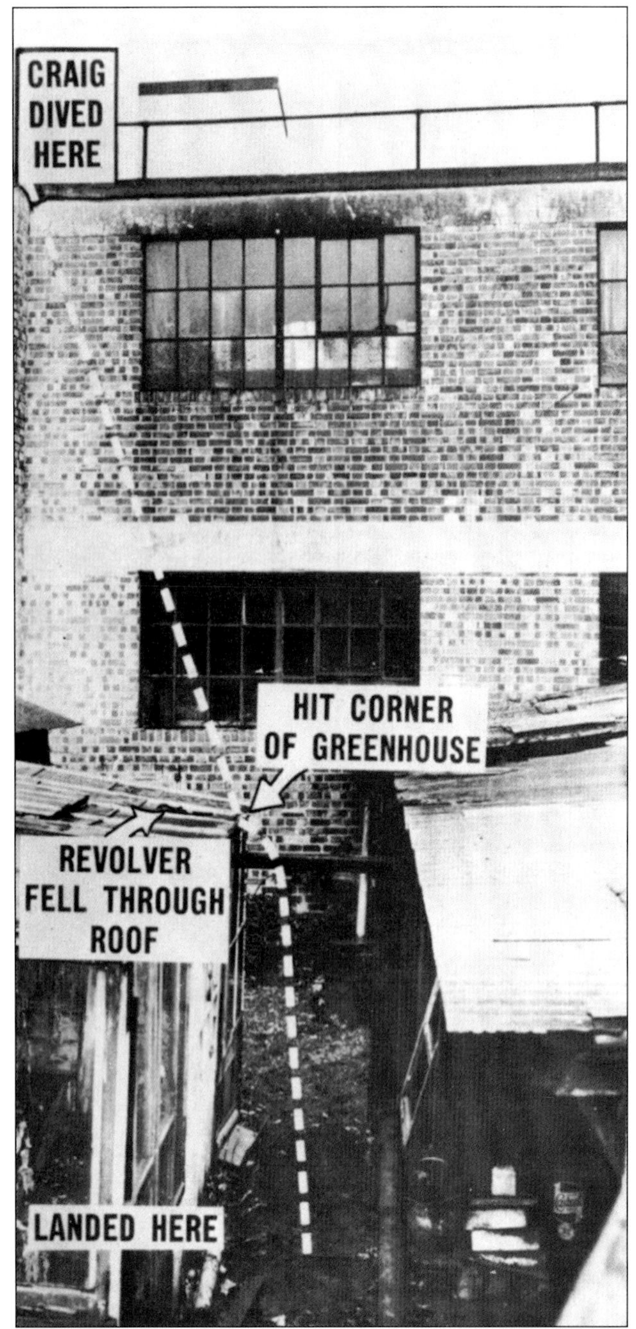

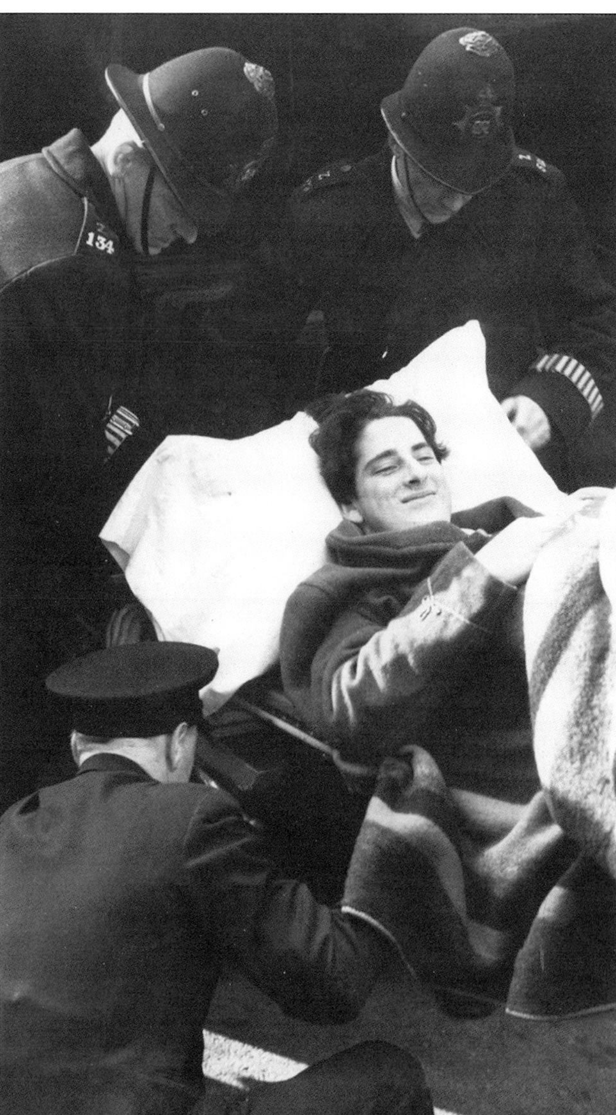

Fairfax took Bentley down and collected a pistol to return to the roof on equal terms. After firing a couple of shots, Craig shouted: 'You are going to make a shooting match of it are you? Come on then copper, lets have it out then.' But Craig's revolver suffered a mis-fire and, realising the game was up, he jumped from the roof. Falling over 20 feet, he fractured his spine, dislocated his breastbone and broke his left wrist. His final words as he was being stretchered off: 'I wish I was fucking dead. I hope I've killed the fucking lot.'

Although the warehouse has gone, Rob Green pinpointed the exact spot where Craig landed beside the greenhouse (see plan page 272).

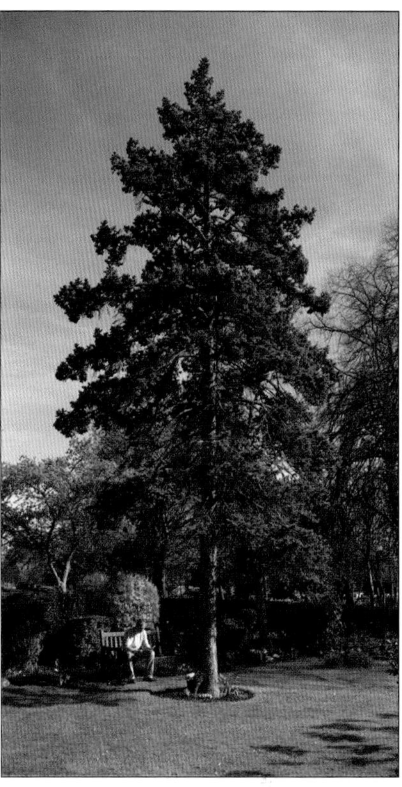

Four days later, Mrs Catherine Miles *(left)* led her husband's funeral attended by over a thousand mourners including the Home Secretary, Sir David Maxwell Fyfe. *Right:* Sidney Miles's ashes were scattered in the Crematorium Gardens of Croydon Cemetery. This fir tree marks the spot. Later Craig's mother Edith wrote to Catherine: 'Dear Mrs Miles, I have taken my pen so many times to write to you and put it down again feeling that I did not dare intrude upon your grief. Yet as the days go by I feel I cannot remain silent. Believe me when I say that when I was first told of this horrible tragedy, my thoughts flew first to you. What could I do? Nothing. What can I say? So little. I speak for my family when I try to say we are so terribly sorry. Long after the papers, the public, and the world in general will have forgotten your husband and my boy, this unhappy family will still mourn your husband and grieve with you. Yours very sincerely, Edith Craig.'

Christopher Craig, aged 16, of Norbury Court Road, Norbury, and Derek William Bentley, aged 19, of Fairview Road, Norbury, at the Central Criminal Court yesterday, were found Guilty of the murder of Police-constable Sidney George Miles. The jury added a recommendation for mercy in the case of Bentley, who was sentenced to death. Craig was ordered to be kept in strict custody until the pleasure of Her Majesty be known.

In passing sentence, the Lord Chief Justice (Lord Goddard) told Craig that he was the more guilty of the two and that his heart had been filled with hate. His Lordship said that he would tell the Home Secretary, when passing on the jury's recommendation with regard to Bentley, that in his opinion Craig was one of the most dangerous young criminals that had ever stood in the dock. In his summing up, which lasted about 45 minutes, the Lord Chief Justice said that this was in many respects a very terrible case, and one which they should approach in as calm a frame of mind as they could.

The Times, December 10, 1952

Bentley must hang. That was the final, the ultimate, the irrevocable decision by Sir David Maxwell Fyfe at ten o'clock last night after a last desperate bid by 200 M.P.s to save the youth's life. The Home Secretary's decision was delivered by his private secretary to the House of Commons after six M.P.s led by Aneurin Bevan pleaded with him in his room in Whitehall. As the message arrived, young people were demonstrating outside the Commons, shouting: 'Bentley must not die.'

Daily Express, January 28, 1953

The trial before the Lord Chief Justice Goddard — nicknamed the 'Hanging Judge' — began on Tuesday, December 9 at the Old Bailey and lasted three days. Its outcome was a foregone conclusion . . . a policeman had been killed and someone must pay . . . only in this case it was the man who had not fired the gun and who was notionally under arrest when the fatal shot was fired. Christopher Craig was too young to hang as the passing of the Children and Young Persons Act in 1933 removed the death penalty for anyone under the age of 18 years. However, under the principle that both the accused were equally guilty, Derek Bentley was sentenced to death although the jury gave a reccomendation for mercy, i.e. a reprieve. It was now Thursday, December 11, 1952 and three clear Sundays now had to pass before the execution would be put into effect if there was no reprieve. With Bentley's application before the court of Criminal Appeal set for January 13, this had the automatic effect of postponing the execution. Here William and Lilian Bentley with their daughter, Iris, and son, Denis, are on their way to the Law Courts in the Strand.

Where at first there had been public outrage at the two boys for killing a policeman, this attitude changed dramatically when it became known that the appeal had failed and that Derek Bentley would face the gallows on January 28. William Bentley now told his son that he would mount a public petition which resulted in a deluge of letters of support, and letters were sent to the Queen, the Prime Minister and the Home Secretary. Support for a reprieve was given by over 200 Members of Parliament with more than 11,000 names being gathered on the petition which was delivered to the Home Secretary. *Left:* Monday, January 26 — father and daughter are pictured on their way to see their MP, Fred Harris, at the House of Commons carrying more piles of correspondence. *Right:* Tuesday, January 27 — a last-minute visit to the Home Office.

Daily Mirror

WED JAN. 28 1953

FORWARD WITH THE PEOPLE

No. 15,305

Registered at G.P.O. as a Newspaper.

Bentley dies today

NO LAST-MINUTE REPRIEVE

Their grief became nation's problem

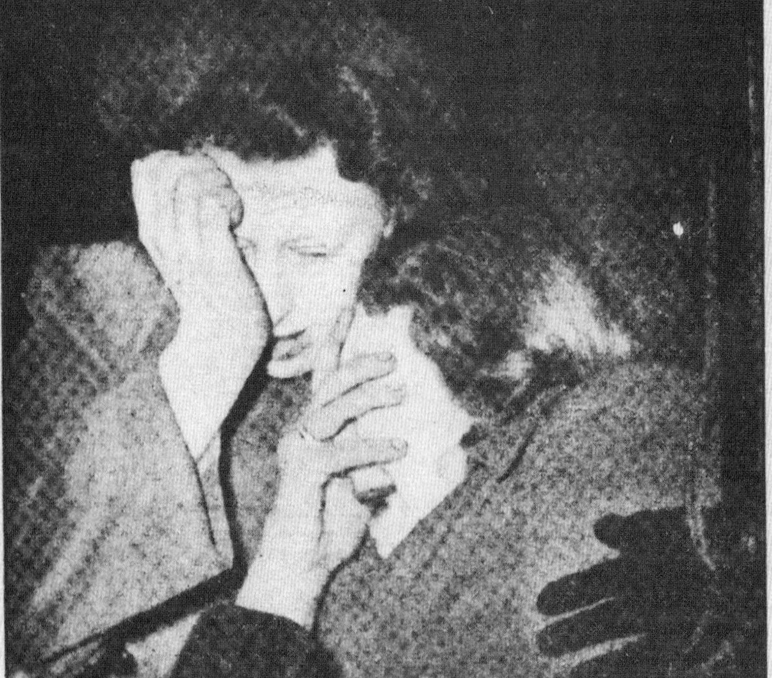

200 M.P.s SIGN PLEA —'DON'T HANG HIM'

Police are called to Home Office crowd

'Daily Mirror' Reporters

THERE is to be no last-minute reprieve for Derek Bentley. The execution, fixed for 9 a.m. today at Wandsworth, will be carried out.

The final decision was sent over to the Commons from the Home Office late last night, in a letter which the man with the power of life or death, Home Secretary Sir David Maxwell Fyfe, wrote in his own hand.

IT WAS THE REPLY TO A DRAMATIC LAST-DITCH PETITION BY MORE THAN 200 M.P.s

'Cheerio,' he told them

A MOTHER weeps for her son a sister for her brother. Mrs. Bentley and Iris Bentley, 21, leave Wandsworth Prison yesterday afternoon after a last family visit to see condemned nineteen-year-old Derek Bentley.

But it had not all been tears. Mr. Bentley, who was also there, said: "Derek was cheerful, even under the shadow of the gallows.

"He fired questions at us and asked: 'How are we getting on outside?'

"I told him we were putting up a

to their Norbury (London) home a Home Office messenger called. He bore a letter saying that Sir David Maxwell Fyfe, Home Secretary, had considered "representations" made by Mr. Bentley that morning, but that he was unable to find grounds for changing the "No reprieve" decision.

The "representations" concerned points arising from conversations between Mrs. Craig and her son Christopher, 16, Bentley's accomplice. It was Craig who shot Police-Constable Miles

When Derek arrived at Wandsworth he became one of four convicted men there due to be hanged. On December 17 John Livesey was executed by Albert Pierrepoint and Syd Dernley for killing his mother-in-law, and on January 2 Pierrepoint, assisted by Harry Smith, hanged James Alcott. He had stabbed to death a railway porter having previously killed a night watchman while serving in the Army in Germany in 1949. Another prisoner awaiting execution was Albert Curtis but he was reprieved on January 19 leaving just Bentley in the condemned cell. This is how it looks today having been converted into a staff rest room following the dismantling of the execution suite.

The day before his execution he walked about the condemned cell, stumbling for words while the warder sat with pencil to write a letter for him.

That night in my room at Wandsworth Prison — after checking Bentley's weight, height and physical structure, making my calculation for length of drop and the routine test of all the apparatus — I sat drinking a bottle of beer and listened to the radio.

Parliament was at a late session and 200 members had signed a petition demanding mercy for Bentley. The motion for a debate had been rejected, but the possibility of a last-minute reprieve still hung in the air, stronger than I have ever known it on any other execution eve.

I must say that my own thoughts were not concerned with any private sympathies for Bentley. I was occupied with the thought that he was 6ft tall, a weightlifter and boxer with a brain younger than his body.

As one grey-haired prison officer mumbled to me: 'If that boy does blow his top tomorrow Albert, you're going to see the toughest five minutes you've ever had. Next day, I woke early, did my morning test of the apparatus and found all in order.

I ate my usual Wandsworth breakfast of fried plaice and potatoes and studied the newspapers for any last minute news of a reprieve — just as Bentley's friends and family were presumably studying theirs. But the morning papers carried headlines only that there was to be 'No Reprieve for Bentley' and I knew I would have my job to do.

With my assistant Harry Kirk, I reported to the governor. He was pale and obviously forcing himself to be very calm. He spoke in a low voice. 'Good morning Albert, I see that it has got to be done.'

'That's all right sir,' I told him. He led the way to the condemned cell, and we waited half-a-minute until the governor gave the signal at 60 seconds to 9 a.m., January 28, 1953. The door was hastily opened. I went in as quickly as I could without seeming to hurry.

Bentley had jumped at the sudden opening of the door. Now he slowly rose. The prison officers on each side of him came quickly to their feet.

I went round the table after Bentley, took his arm without a word and very carefully so there was no jerk that might trigger off his resistance. I put the pinioning-loop upon his wrists and suddenly made it tight.

I am sure he still had not properly weighed up the situation. He was still uncertain what was happening. He moved his shoulders wonderingly, but did not say anything.

I whispered: 'Just follow me lad,' and added soothingly 'It's all right Derek, just follow me.'

He started to move and his body caught the edge of the table. He appeared not to feel this, although the table shook.

He followed me unaided into the adjoining execution chamber and stood on the chalk-marks upon the wooden floor.

I put the white cap over his head, and noose with it, and heard the familiar click of belt and buckle as Harry Allen swiftly pinioned his legs, then flung his arms back.

The controversy from that instant became purposeless, for Derek Bentley was dead.

Albert Pierrepoint, Unpublished Memoirs, 1998

The account by Pierrepoint reproduced above, which appeared in several newspapers in 1998, is claimed to have been written for his memoirs but omitted from the final draft of his book *Executioner Pierrepoint*, published in 1974. Its authenticity has been disputed. This picture was taken shortly after 9 a.m. on Wednesday, January 28, 1953. As an officer posts the official notice of Bentley's death, the crowd surges forward throwing coins and stones to smash the glass. At the execution, carried out by Pierrepoint and Harry Allen, it was reported that such was its speed that one of the supporting officers standing on the scaffold boards was unable to grab hold of the rope support, and when the trap opened he lost his balance and fell into the pit.

Above: **Bentley was buried within the prison alongside this wall on the south-eastern corner (see page 93) in Grave No. 79, his being the second burial in that grave. With the passing of the Abolition Bill in 1965, the Home Office made it known that applications would be considered for the exhumation of the bodies of executed dead and we have already seen on page 62 that the remains of the two IRA killers of Sir Henry Wilson were repatriated to Ireland in July 1967. (The section of repaired tarmac in the picture** *above right* **marks the former grave of John Amery, hanged for treason in December 1945.)** *Right:* **Derek Bentley was exhumed on March 3, 1966 and buried in Grave 38038** *(below)* **in Plot NN of Croydon Cemetery, within a short distance of where the ashes of PC Miles had been scattered. However, the local council refuse to allow the family to erect a headstone including the words 'A Victim of British Justice'. Meanwhile, by then, Christopher Craig had served his sentence of ten and a half years and had been released from Wakefield Prison.**

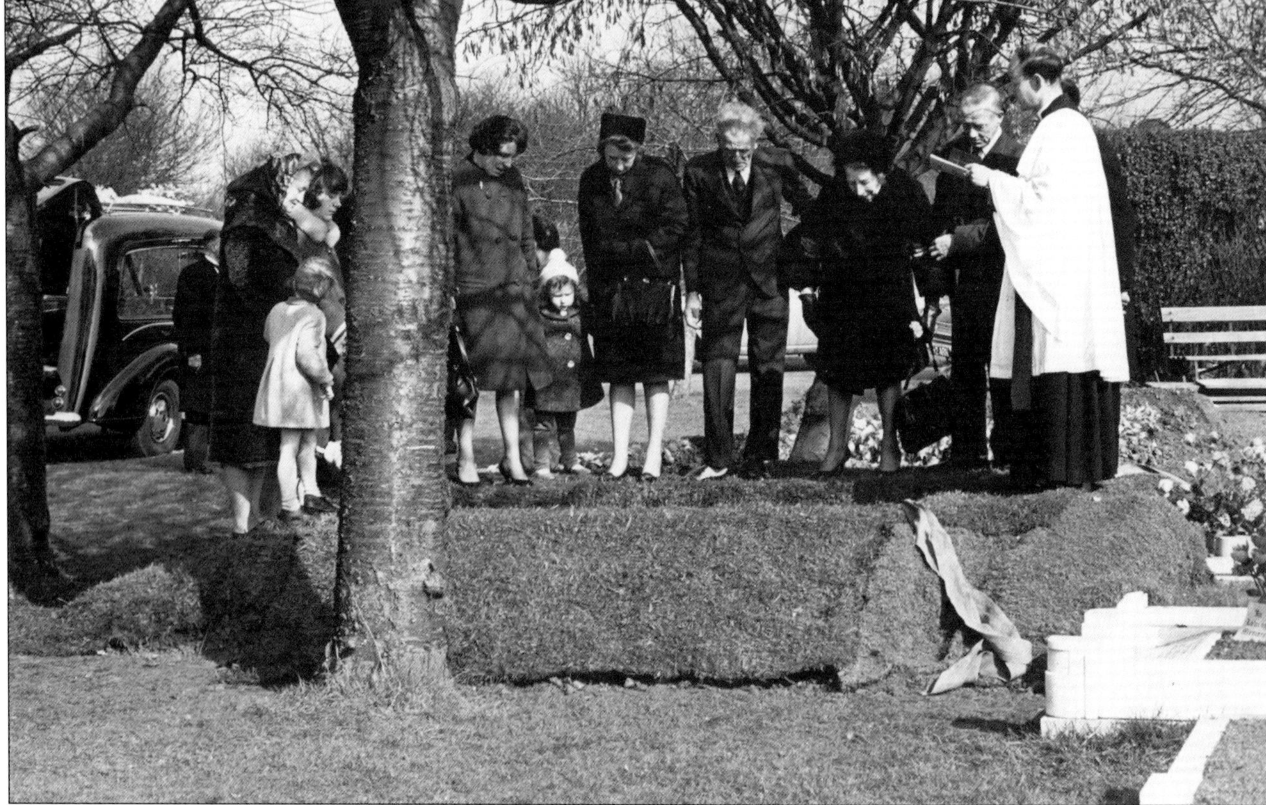

And at Wandsworth, Niven Craig had made an early bid for freedom when he and ten other prisoners mounted an escape attempt on June 24, 1961. Breaking out of the laundry store, four men climbed over the back wall, one breaking his legs as he dropped down. At the time it was the biggest jailbreak in British history, earning an entry into the *Guinness Book of Records*.

The sister of Derek Bentley, hanged 37 years ago for murdering a south London policeman, will today urge the Home Secretary David Waddington to order a public enquiry into the case.

Iris Bentley, who is seeking a posthumous royal pardon for her brother, will present Mr Waddington with an updated edition of a book first published in 1971 which claims that the bullet that killed PC Sidney Miles could have been fired accidentally by a fellow police officer.

The book, *To Encourage the Others*, by David Yallop, says vital evidence was ignored at the Old Bailey trial, crucial witnesses were not called, and that Bentley's mental state was totally overlooked. The book also contains an open letter to the Home Secretary urging him to reopen the case.

Miss Bentley said: 'We want a full public inquiry so that the facts can be fully known. My brother was innocent and the whole affair prematurely killed my parents and has devastated our family.

The Guardian, July 23, 1990

New evidence to be put to the Home Secretary today casts further doubt on the conviction of Derek Bentley, hanged in 1953 as an accomplice to the murder of a policeman.

A former police constable, Claude Pain, aged 82, claims to have been within inches of PC Sidney Miles when he was shot dead on top of a warehouse in Croydon, south London. He was not called to give evidence at Mr Bentley's trial at the Old Bailey and has not spoken out before.

Mr Pain says he never heard Mr Bentley shout to his friend, as alleged by police witnesses at the trial: 'Let him have it Chris'. Another witness said she heard a shout of 'Let him have it,' but only after shots had been fired.

Mr Bentley, who was 19 with a mental aged of nine, was hanged for those words, which have been interpreted by some not as urging his friend, Christopher Craig, to shoot PC Miles — as the prosecution alleged — but to hand over the gun.

The Guardian, September 11, 1990

John Patten, a Home Office minister, said in a written reply that he has now received the police report on the Derek Bentley case and hoped to decide soon whether any action was appropriate.

The Times, January 24, 1992

Home Office officials are studying a Scotland Yard report which could lead to a posthumous pardon for Derek Bentley, hanged on January 28, 1953, for the murder of a policeman during a burglary. A decision by Kenneth Baker, the Home Secretary may be taken within weeks.

The Times, January 27, 1992

The Home Secretary was legally wrong to refuse a posthumous free pardon to Derek Bentley who was hanged 40 years ago for the murder of a policeman, the High Court was told yesterday.

Kenneth Clarke claimed last October he could not allow the pardon because it had not been established that Mr Bentley was morally and technically innocent of murdering PC Sidney Miles.

But during a judicial review of Mr Clarke's decision, prompted by Derek Bentley's sister Iris, three High Court judges were told the Home Secretary had considered the wrong issues.

The Guardian, May 25, 1993

William Bentley pursued a relentless course to have his son pardoned and on the anniversary of Derek's death each year, the family would place a wreath outside the prison, this picture being taken in 1973. After Mr Bentley died in July the following year, and his wife in October 1976, the campaign was taken up by Iris (right) who, for the following 25 years, fought to clear her brother's name.

Iris at the graveside in January 1997, still unmarked with no formal headstone.

Iris died in January 1997 having achieved a conditional pardon as the Home Secretary, Michael Howard, agreed with the High Court that Derek should not have been executed, although not conceding the full pardon that she wanted. So the campaign continued, led now by her daughter Maria Dingwell-Bentley. A significant event along the way took place in 1991 when Thames Television asked Christopher Craig to take a lie detector test. Bentley's alleged — and ambiguous — cry 'Let him have it Chris!' had always been central to the argument about Derek's culpability. Back in 1940 a similar phrase had sent two men to the gallows when Appleby and Ostler were caught breaking into a store in County Durham. As they were apprehended by a policeman, one of them had said: 'All right, let him have it!' ***Right:*** **The two principal witnesses, who claimed that they heard Bentley call out on the rooftop, were Detective-Constable Fairfax, left, and PC Harrison, right.**

The Home Secretary's refusal last October to grant a posthumous pardon to Derek Bentley — hanged 40 years ago for murder — should not be subjected to a judicial review because the discretion he employed is outside the court's jurisdiction, three High Court judges were told yesterday.

Kenneth Clarke's decision has been challenged as a legal error by Bentley's sister Iris, who prompted the review.

Defending Mr Clarke's decision, Stephen Richards said Parliament was the proper forum to question the Home Secretary's use of discretionary powers under the Royal Prerogative. 'The whole essence of the prerogative is that it is a purely discretionary decision entrusted to the Home Secretary,' he said.

Lord Justice Watkins replied: 'I don't see why he should not be called to account here. The Home Secretary acts for all of us. There is no magic in the discretion.'

The Guardian, May 26, 1993

The British judiciary yesterday owned up to a 40-year wrong. Derek Bentley, aged 19, who was hanged in 1953 for killing a police constable, should have been reprieved, said the High Court. It urged Michael Howard, the Home Secretary, to pardon him.

Kenneth Clarke, Mr Howard's predecessor, refused a pardon nine months ago. That decision was challenged in the High Court by Iris Bentley, aged 61, Derek's sister.

Lord Justice Watkins delivered an unprecedented judgement yesterday. It was the first time any member of the judiciary conceded that Derek Bentley, who would have been 60 last week, should have lived.

Lord Justice Watkins at the end of an hour-long judgement said: 'We would invite the Home Secretary to look at the matter again, and to examine whether it would be just to exercise the prerogative of mercy in such a way as to give full recognition to the now generally accepted view that this young man should have been reprieved.

The High Court was recommending a conditional pardon. That would mean Mr Bentley was still guilty of murder, but there would be recognition of mitigating factors, which would have seen his sentence commuted to life imprisonment.

The Guardian, July 8, 1993

Derek Bentley today won a conditional posthumous pardon — 40 years after being hanged for his part in the murder of a London policeman.

Home Secretary Michael Howard's decision is official recognition that the death penalty should never have been carried out against Bentley.

Three judges ruled last month that former Home Secretary Kenneth Clarke 'erred in law' when he refused to grant any form of pardon last October and said Mr Howard should look at it again. Mr Howard said a free pardon remained inappropriate, but, had he been Home Secretary at the time, he would not have let Bentley die.

Evening Standard, July 30, 1993

Iris Bentley died yesterday without seeing a successful end to her 44-year campaign for a free pardon for her brother Derek, hanged in 1953 for the murder of a policeman.

Miss Bentley, 64, who had fought cancer for 20 years, had been hoping to hear her brother's case considered by the newly-established Criminal Cases Review Commission. It was due to be dealt with in April.

Daily Telegraph, January 23, 1997

Christopher Craig, now 61, is ready to tell the Appeal Court that Bentley tried to STOP him firing the fatal shot.

The gunman, who was 16 at the time, was too young to be executed but Bentley, then 19, went to the gallows on the basis that it was a 'joint enterprise' — even though he had no weapon.

Lawyers have told the Lord Chief Justice, Lord Bingham, that Craig did not give the evidence at Bentley's trial because he was advised it would harm his plea that the killing of PC Sidney Miles was accidental.

Now Craig is set to reveal that when he and Bentley were confronted by police on the roof a Croydon warehouse during a 1952 break-in, his accomplice attempted to stop him using the gun and said: 'What the bloody hell's got into you?'

Craig, who is now a plumber in Bedfordshire, shot dead PC Miles after the officer began to move towards him.

Bentley's conviction and execution hinged on five words he is alleged to have shouted just before the shooting.

Three police officers claimed he yelled: 'Let him have it Chris.'

But during the Old Bailey trial Craig — who was detained at Her Majesty's pleasure and served 10 years — denied the words were ever uttered and has stood by his testimony ever since.

It has also been claimed that if Bentley did say the words it could have meant he was asking Craig to hand over his weapon.

Mr Edward Fitzgerald, QC, is appealing to Lord Bingham and two other senior judges to quash the murder conviction.

He says the words were invented by the officers determined to seal the case.

The Mirror, July 21, 1998

Craig's insistence that Bentley never uttered the words was borne out in the lie detector test.

Derek Bentley's conviction for the murder of a policeman was finally overturned by the Court of Appeal yesterday — with scathing criticism of the Lord Chief Justice who condemned him to hang 45 years ago.

In an unprecedented attack on his predecessor, Lord Bingham of Cornhill said that Lord Goddard had denied Bentley his birthright as a British citizen — a fair trial.

He had behaved more like an advocate than a judge and far from encouraging the jury to approach the case calmly, his summing-up had been 'a highly rhetorical and strongly worded denunciation' of the defence and that left the jury with little choice but to convict.

'It is with genuine diffidence that the members of this court direct criticism towards a trial judge widely recognised as one of the outstanding criminal judges of this century. But we cannot escape the duty of decision. In our judgement the summing-up in this case was such as to deny the appellant that fair trial which is the birthright of every British citizen.'

The Times, July 31, 1998

Left: **Lord Chief Justice Rayner Goddard trumped by Lord Bingham of Cornhill** *(right)* **who presided over the Court of Appeal.**

The end of a long road. Maria rejoices in the quashing of her uncle's conviction outside the High Court. She later celebrated by opening a bottle of champagne brought by Derek's father for this express purpose 40 years previously.

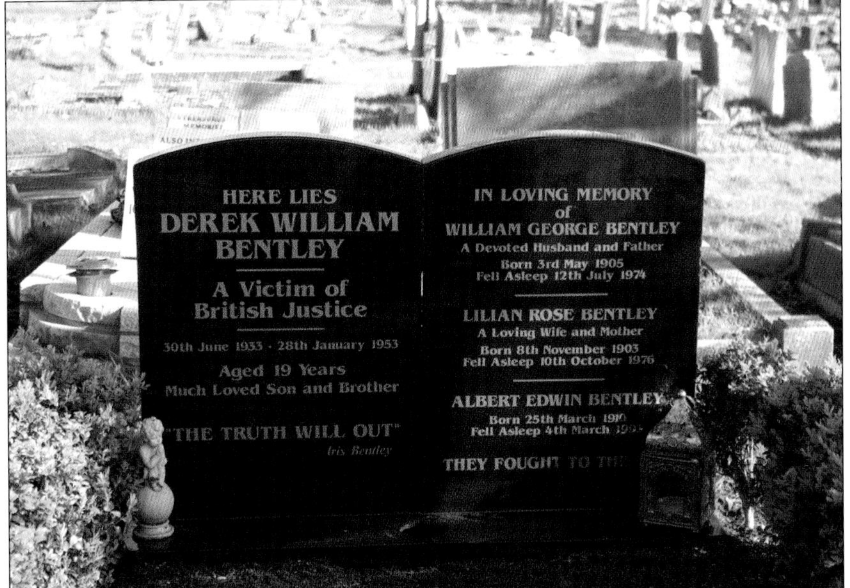

Celebrities are being invited to a memorial service dedicating a gravestone to Derek Bentley as 'a victim of British justice'.

The ceremony is likely to attract more attention than the unveiling of a plaque at Croydon police station in November 1994 to PC Sidney Miles, who was shot in November 1952 by Bentley's accomplice Christopher Craig.

Bentley was hanged for murder. His remains were reinterred in an unmarked piece of unconsecrated ground in the municipal cemetery in 1966. His parents have since been buried in the same plot.

In 1973, Bentley's father asked for a memorial bearing the words: 'Lest we forget Derek Bentley — a victim of English injustice.' Croydon's Conservative-controlled council refused permission but implied that it supported the sentiment of the epitaph. Efforts to change the wording to indicate that Bentley's family had faith in his innocence were rejected by relatives.

When Labour won control of the authority for the first time, it approved the gravestone. Saturday's memorial service marks the 42nd anniversary of Bentley's hanging.

The Times, January 25, 1995

THE CREEP

Dancers stand a foot apart; each places hand on partner's shoulder; the other hand, fingers intertwined with partner's, is dropped toward floor.

1. Man steps back on left foot, then back on right —

2.— then to the side with left foot, then closes with right. Girl does counterpart.

All counts are slow counts—each step requires two beats of the music.

July 2, 1953 – The 'Teddy Boy' Murder

Five youths accused of being concerned in the murder of seventeen-year-old John Ernest Beckley, were remanded to prison yesterday.

Two of the youths, one aged fifteen and the other sixteen, would normally have been sent to a remand home, but a police chief said he did not think it would be safe 'because of their unruly disposition.'

Beckley, who lived in Amelia Street, Walworth, London, was stabbed to death on Clapham Common last Thursday night.

The five accused youths are Ronald Coleman, 15, Shop assistant of Chessington House, Union Road, Clapham; Terence Power, 17, unemployed of Somerleyton Road, Brixton; Allan Albert Lawson, 18, carpenter, of Newlyn House, East Hill Estate, Wandsworth; Michael John Davies, 20, labourer of Turret Grove, Clapham; and Terence David Woodman, 16, street trader, of St Lukes Avenue, Clapham.

The public gallery at the South-West London Magistrates' Court was crowded as the youths entered the court. They smiled at several of the people they knew, among whom were three young women.

When the inquest on Beckley, an apprentice electrical engineer, was opened at Battersea yesterday, Dr Donald Teare, pathologist, said death was caused by stab wounds in the chest and stomach. The inquest was adjourned until July 23.

Daily Mirror, July 7, 1953

At about 9.30 p.m. on Thursday, July 2, 1953, an evening session of open air dancing was about to finish at the bandstand on Clapham Common in south London. This was the era of the Teddy Boy — youths dressed fashionably in Edwardian drape jackets, bootlace ties, drainpipe trousers and thick crepe-soled shoes dubbed 'brothel-creepers'. The Ted's favourite dance was Ken Mackintosh's *The Creep*. John Beckley with three friends Brian Carter, Matthew Chandler and John Ryan were sitting on two free-standing seats on the grass, just off the tarmac surround on the northern side of the bandstand. They had pulled up the second seat so two of the youths sat on each side with their feet resting on the opposite seat. Another Teddy Boy, Ronald Coleman with his girlfriend in tow, for no apparent reason tried to pass between the seats — an action which was resented by Beckley and friends. Although Coleman walked away, he was joined by other Teds.

Sensing that there was trouble brewing, John Beckley ***(left)*** **and his three companions deemed it prudent to walk away. The police report explains that: 'When they had walked a distance of approximately 249 yards to a point near a water fountain, they were assaulted by Coleman and a number of other youths, in the course of which Ryan (who is referred to as the "tall blonde fellow") received a superficial stab wound.' (Davies admitted in his statement that he took part in this assault on the 'blonde'.)** ***Right:*** **The path leading to the drinking fountain.**

There is a colossal amount of work to be done in the case concerning five youths accused of being concerned in the murder of John Ernest Beckley, 17, said a police officer yesterday.

Daily Mirror, July 14, 1953

Four more youths were charged last night with being concerned in the murder of seventeen-year-old John Beckley, who was found dying from stab wounds on Clapham Common, London, on Thursday.

The youths are Terence Power, 17, unemployed, of Somerleyton Road, Brixton; Allan Albert Lawson, 18, of Newlyn House, East Hill Estate, Wandsworth; Michael John Davies, 20, labourer of Turret Grove, Clapham, and a sixteen-year-old youth who lives in Clapham.

They will appear at the South-Western Magistrates' Court, London, today with sev-

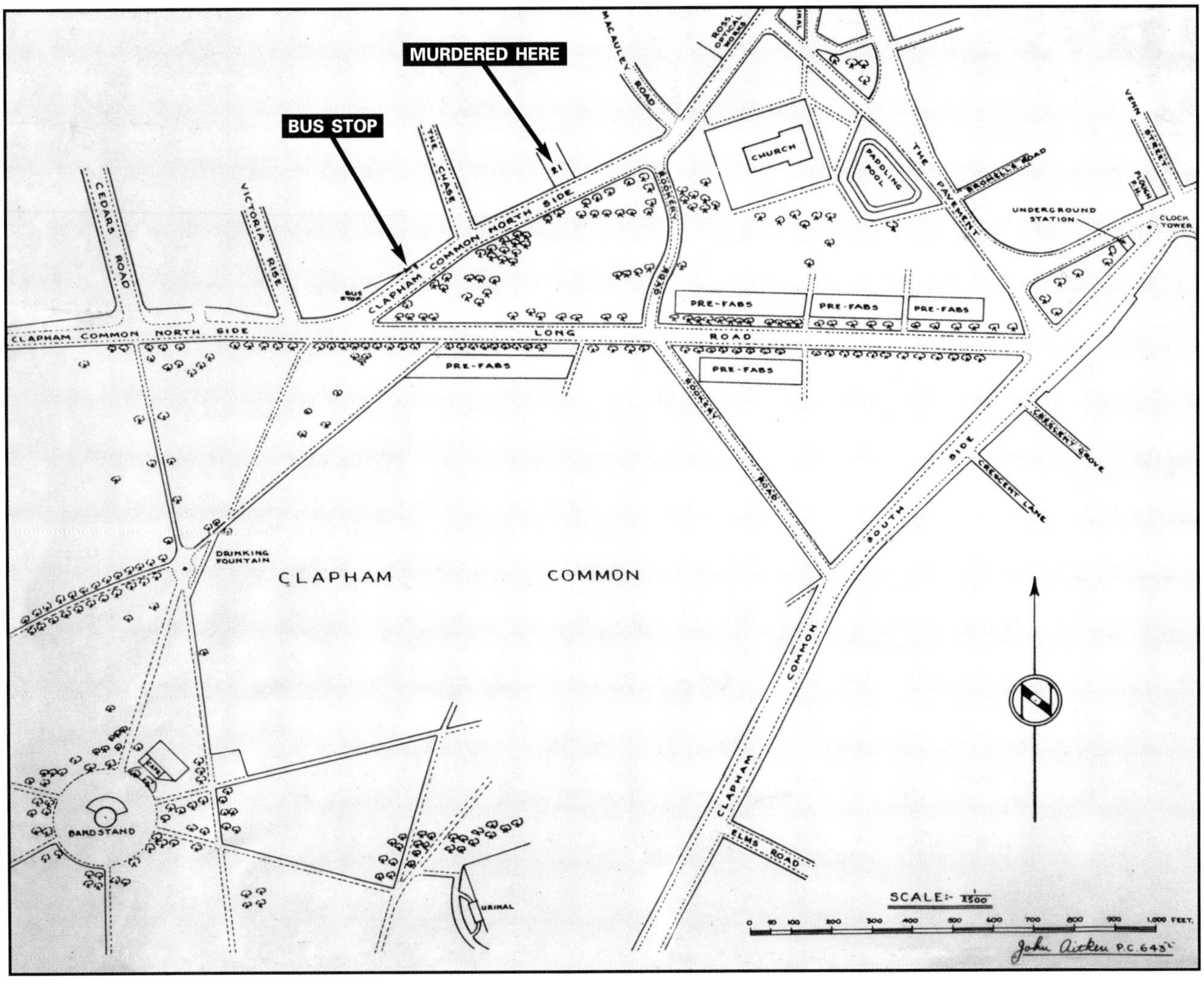

One witness described how he saw a youth on the ground by the fountain being kicked by six youths with about the same number of girls. This is where Ryan suffered a stab wound before running down the north-easterly path (on the right). Meanwhile Beckley and Chandler ran straight ahead towards Cedars Road. Only the base of the fountain remains today.

enteen-year-old Ronald Coleman, a shop assistant, of Chessington House, Clapham, who on Saturday night was charged with murdering Beckley.

Detectives are still looking for a dark-haired heavily made-up girl of about seventeen who, it is believed, was with a gang of youths in the Clapham Common district at the time Beckley was stabbed. Beckley lived at Amelia Street, Walworth.

Daily Mirror, July 6, 1953

Reaching the main road, they ran across to where a bus was waiting at the traffic lights. Jumping aboard it pulled away towards the next stop which lay just a couple of hundred yards away down North Side.

Buses on the Route 137 were of the RT type with an open platform. A passenger on the bus said both youths were out of breath and appeared bewildered when asked for their fares. They remained on the platform continuously looking around.

'The assailants started to chase Beckley and Chandler but when they lost sight of them, turned in the direction in which Ryan was running. Ryan was a fair distance away so the pursuers diverted their chase towards Long Road with the intention of intercepting the bus. As they reached it at the request stop in North Side, they found Beckley and Chandler still on the platform about to enter the lower deck. They pulled both boys off the bus and a violent and brutal assault followed. One passenger on the bus told the police that one of the youths was hurled violently across the pavement, crashing with a loud noise against the side of the bus which had just begun to move off. The driver then stopped. At first Beckley appeared to have the upper hand but then was kicked in the chest while being attacked by another boy. He made to run away . . .

. . . but slumped to the ground outside Okeover Manor.

Although Michael Davies and Ronald Coleman were charged with murder, at the first trial the jury failed to reach a verdict. Davies faced a second trial on October 19 and having been found guilty, was sentenced to death on October 22 with the date for his execution fixed for November 11. However, when Davies appealed, the execution was postponed and on December 10 he was given permission to appeal to the House of Lords.

John Beckley was buried in Nunhead Cemetery but see page 4.

As this would not be heard until January 12, 1954, consequently Davies had to be removed from the condemned cell at Wandsworth to make way for the hangings of John Wilkinson on the 18th and Alfred Whiteway on the 22nd. Davies's appeal was dismissed on January 15 and he was returned to the death cell but finally reprieved on January 21 whereupon he was transferred to Wormwood Scrubs to begin a life sentence.

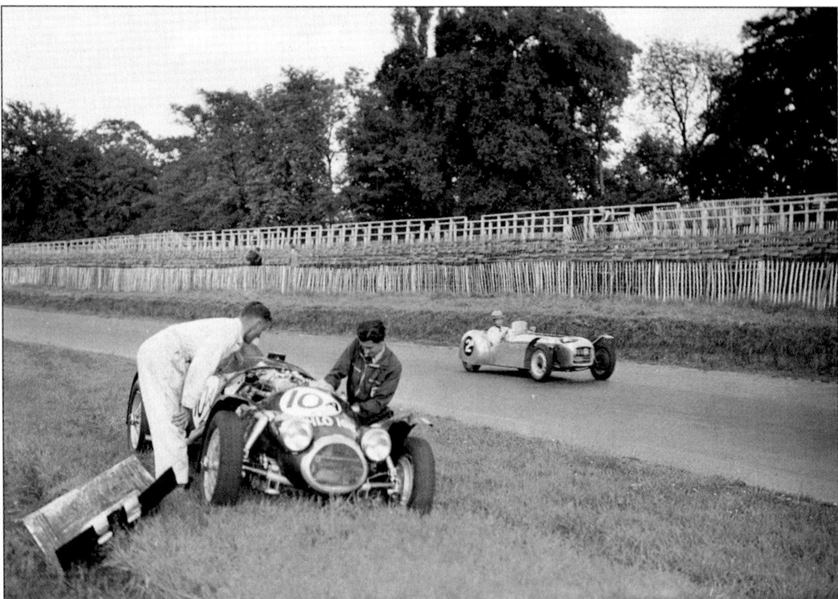

David Blakely's motor racing career began in 1951, the picture *(right)* being taken in September 1953 when his HRG Lightweight came third at Crystal Palace. The circuit in south London had only been reopened that year, the park having been taken over by the War Office on the outbreak of the Second World War. It had originally been laid down in 1927 when speeds in the order of 50-60 mph were achieved but by the 1950s average speeds exceeded 100 mph. The final meeting was held on September 23, 1972 with Mike Hailwood having set the lap record at 103.39 mph earlier that year.

April 10, 1955 – Ruth Ellis: The Last Woman to be Hanged

On December 27th the British Racing and Sports Car Club took a chance on the winter weather and held a mixed race meeting on the popular Kentish circuit. An excellent entry, 'ranging from 500-c.c. cars, through assorted sports cars to out-and-out racing cars, gathered in the paddock for the first Christmas meeting in the British Isles, the weather mercifully being anything but wintry, with a pale sun and intermittent blue skies above. In fact, as good as most of the summer meetings had been during 1954.

As a 'cadet-drivers' circuit, Brands Hatch fills an excellent position, providing just the right sort of meeting for those who eventually aspire to stardom at Goodwood, Oulton Park and, later, the Continental circuits, and while the Boxing Day entry was almost wholly of an amateur status, some close and hard-fought racing resulted, the efficiency of the running of the meeting being of a very high standard.

The sports cars were divided into two races, the first for those up to 1,500 c.c., and in this Lotus cars dominated the scene, they being 1-2-3 at one point in the race. Coombs showed greatly improved driving skill and kept his Connaught-engined streamlined Lotus in front to the end, though he was hard pressed by Naylor driving a similar car powered by an M.G. engine, the third car of this type being driven by Allen.

Among the cars that followed was Blakeley's new one, called Emperor, using his twin-cam Singer/H.R.G. engine in a tubular chassis with trailing link VW independent front suspension and a de Dion rear-axle layout, the whole enshrouded by a bulbous body that looked rather like a Mondial Ferrari that had been pressurised. On this, its maiden voyage, it ran extremely well and eventually beat Allen's Lotus-M.G. and finished second after Naylor's Abingdon motor went sick.

Hard on the tails of these cars came the pretty little R.W.G.-Ford, driven by Lund, who was showing as much skill and polish as he had in the 500-c.c. event. Though he could not pass the bigger cars he lost no ground to them at all, and his consistency of line on some of the bends was very good.

THE MOTOR RACING CAREER OF DAVID BLAKELY

Date	*Race*	*Car*	*Result*
July 28, 1951	National Silverstone Heat 1	HRG Lightweight	1st
July 28, 1951	National Silverstone Final	HRG Lightweight	1st
July 28, 1951	National Silverstone	HRG Lightweight	1st
August 25, 1951	Six Hour Relay Silverstone	HRG Lightweight	3rd
March 22, 1952	National Goodwood	HRG Lightweight	3rd
May 17, 1952	National Goodwood (Handicap)	HRG Lightweight	4th
May 17, 1952	National Goodwood	HRG Lightweight	4th
June 2, 1952	Goodwood Whitsun	HRG Lightweight	16th
June 7, 1952	National Silverstone	HRG Lightweight	1st
July 10, 1952	Jersey International	HRG Lightweight	22nd
July 26, 1952	National Silverstone	HRG Lightweight	4th
August 16, 1952	Nine-Hour Goodwood	HRG Lightweight	11th
August 30, 1952	Six-Hour Relay Silverstone	HRG Lightweight	6th
March 21, 1953	National Goodwood	HRG	6th
April 4, 1953	National Castle Combe	HRG	1st
July 25, 1953	National Goodwood	Leonard	6th
August 2, 1953	Rheinland Nürburgring	Kieft	*
August 15, 1953	Charterhall International	Leonard	*
August 15, 1953	Charterhall International	Leonard	NK
August 22, 1953	Nine-Hour Goodwood	HRG Lightweight	‡
August 30, 1953	1000 km Nürburgring	Leonard	‡
Sept. 19, 1953	Crystal Palace International	HRG Lightweight	3rd
Oct. 17, 1953	National Snetterton	HRG Lightweight	2nd
Oct. 17, 1953	National Snetterton	HRG Lightweight	3rd
June 5, 1954	National Snetterton	Leonard	3rd
June 5, 1954	National Snetterton (Handicap)	Leonard	3rd
July 10, 1954	National Oulton Park	Leonard	NK
July 17, 1954	British GP	Leonard	11th
August 2, 1954	Brands Hatch Int. (S1.5 Heat 2)	Leonard	NK
August 2, 1954	Brands Hatch Int. (S1.5)	Leonard	NK
August 2, 1954	Brands Hatch Int.	Leonard	5th
August 15, 1954	Zandvoort International	Leonard	†
August 21, 1954	National Silverstone	Leonard	5th
Oct. 2, 1954	Aintree International	Emperor	*
Dec. 26, 1954	National Brands Hatch	Emperor	2nd
April 2, 1955	British Empire Trophy	Emperor	†
April 12, 1955	Goodwood Easter	Emperor	¶
June 12, 1955	24-Hour Le Mans	Bristol 450	¶

** Did Not Attend   † Did Not Start   ‡ Did Not Finish   ¶ Entered but Deceased*

By 1955 one could say that 28-year-old David Blakely was at the pinnacle of his racing career having poured all his money into a new car — the HRG-Emperor. This had been built specially for him by Anthony Findlater, a former Aston Martin engineer. He had managed to obtain HRG's twin-cam version of the 1500cc Singer engine which gave 108bhp in road trim so it was the most promising engine that could be bought in 1954. For the technically minded, the Emperor had a tubular chrome-steel chassis, a VW front suspension, a de Dion rear end and a full-width aluminium body reminiscent of a Ferrari Mondial which is believed to have been made at Aston Martins without the knowledge of the management. The car had its first race at Brands Hatch on Boxing Day 1954, Blakely finishing second, *Autosport* reporting that it was a 'splendid debut for the promising new Emperor'. From then on, Blakely and Findlater worked non-stop on the car to make it ready for the new season.

At the back of the field there was a pleasant standard-car battle going on between Aley (H.R.G.) and Shove (M.G. TF), their roadholding showing just how outstanding that of the leading cars was. At the end of this 15-laps event one felt that either the Coombs/Lotus combination had been going extremely well or else the others had been going very slowly, but in the unlimited sports-car event Coombs ran again, being an addition to the programme, and he proved that C./L. had been going very well indeed.

For the whole of the 15 laps of the big sports-car race he clung on to the tail of Crook's Cooper-Bristol, and their free-for-all battle was the highlight of the meeting. Crook was out to win and his Bristol engine was sounding superb as he howled his way along the top straight, his gear ratio for the circuit being as perfect as one could wish for, and he never gave Coombs the slightest chance to nip by, for the Lotus-Connaught was almost touching his tail at times and the two drivers gave a fine display of concentrated driving skill in a battle where one missed gear-change, or a mistake of only a yard on cut-off or braking point, would have spelt disaster. Crook was the rousing winner, with the worthy Coombs right behind him.

Motorsport, February 1955

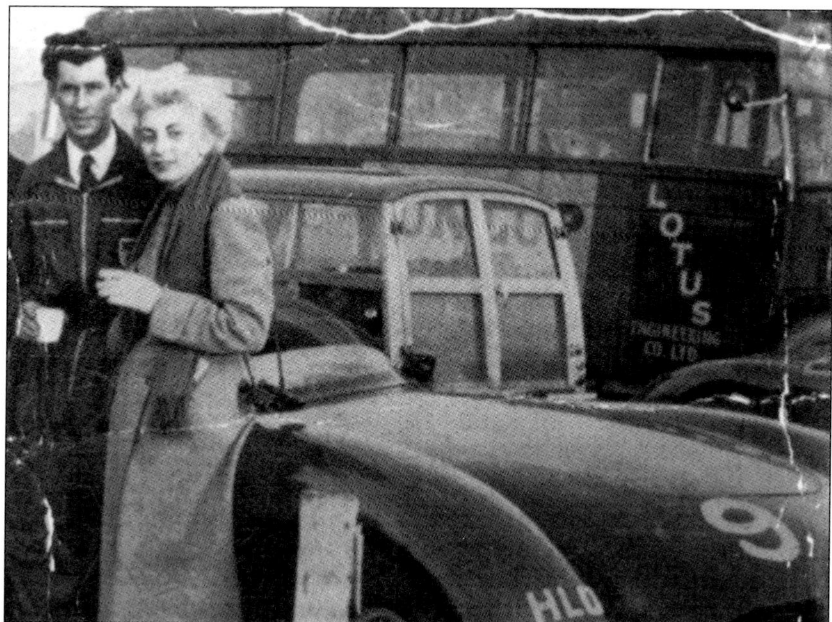

We are told that he first met Ruth Ellis in 1953, this snapshot being taken at the Boxing Day meeting at Brands Hatch when the Emperor bore number 9.

Ruth Ellis's career had been given a kick-start in 1951 when she was chosen to appear as an extra in *Lady Godiva Rides Again* — a story about a waitress (played by Pauline Stroud, standing to the left of Diana Dors in this line up), who wins a local beauty contest and becomes a charm school starlet and later a strip-tease artist. This particular scene was filmed in Folkestone, the Press report stating that 11 beauty queens took part. Ruth, still a brunette, is fourth from the left; Kay Kendall, second right and Joan Collins fifth from the right. See how many more you can identify? Jane Hart appears at the end of the line-up and at the time of the filming her boyfriend was the osteopath and pimp, Dr Stephen Ward, who, we are told, supplied many of the models for the film.

My mother had nine children, four dying from scarlet fever. I was born Irma Muriel Hornby in Chorlton-upon-Medlock near Manchester in November 1920, and my sister, Ruth Nielson, came along in 1926 after we had moved to Rhyl in North Wales by which time, for some reason, my father had changed his surname to Nielson.

Having moved to Monk Sherborne, Ruth, my brother Granville, and I started school together in September 1932. I was still only a little girl, not twelve, when Father started interfering with me. When mother was out he forced me to do things. Ruth was subjected to Father's abuse when she got to eleven. I heard her scream the way I did. I knew what he was doing. She'd go into the new bathroom and wash herself when he'd finished saying: 'Muriel, he's doing those dirty things to me.'

By the time Ruth was a young teenager she was determined he wouldn't ruin her life. But it didn't stop him trying. One occasion stands out. I was hanging out the washing and heard Ruth's screams coming from the house. He'd forced her, just like he did me. It was the same brutal treatment she'd have to endure later in life from her husband George Ellis and her lover, David Blakely. I'm sure the way we were treated, the viciousness and abuse, affected our personalities. She may have been six years younger, but acted ten years older than me: 'I'm not letting him do to me what he's done to you. You've got to promise one thing Muriel, never talk about Father's filthy behaviour to anyone.' I kept that promise — till now.

Father had turned into a bully. If Ruth and I didn't get home from school early to get his tuppeny Woodbine he'd hit and kick us. Sometimes he'd pull me downstairs by my hair, threatening to kill me if he didn't have his cigarettes. On one occasion he took all the photos of Ruth and me off the walls and they all went in the fire. When he'd bashed the hell out of us, he'd show no remorse. He'd go out of the room whistling, pleased with himself because he'd upset my mother. Ruth got out of the way as much as she could

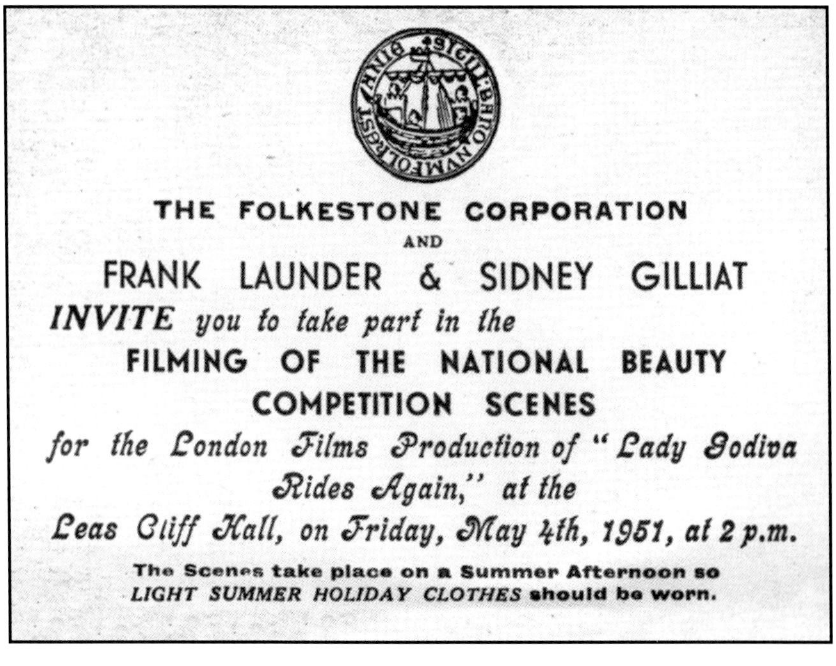

THE FOLKESTONE CORPORATION

AND

FRANK LAUNDER & SIDNEY GILLIAT

INVITE you to take part in the

FILMING OF THE NATIONAL BEAUTY COMPETITION SCENES

for the London Films Production of "Lady Godiva Rides Again," at the Leas Cliff Hall, on Friday, May 4th, 1951, at 2 p.m.

The Scenes take place on a Summer Afternoon so *LIGHT SUMMER HOLIDAY CLOTHES* should be worn.

In 1953 Ruth was appointed manageress of the Little Club, located on the first floor of No. 37 Brompton Road in Kensington. Then, the shop on the ground floor sold jewellery and umbrellas; today the premises is owned by Hobbs Ltd, the fashion people, who refused to give us permission to take comparison photos, claiming 'high levels of confidentiality'.

and in years to come she learned how to give him some of his own medicine, throwing anything at him that was in sight.

Within a few years, as Ruth started growing up, it seemed strange that Father would proudly say: 'There's not a better-looking girl than either of you two in the village.' It didn't stop him beating us though.

Ruth was turning into a lovely looking girl with high cheek-bones and rosy cheeks. She'd hardly ever worn make-up but as soon as she left school she started wearing lipstick. We hadn't discovered the eyes in those days, no mascara, liner or anything. She didn't dye her hair either. She had thick auburn hair and she didn't peroxide her hair till she was about twenty-four, four years before she died.

During the Second World War, Ruth had fallen in love with a French-Canadian soldier, Clare Andrea McCallum. She became pregnant, giving birth to his child Andrea Clare McCallum in September 1944. Clare promised to marry her but at the end of the war he returned to Quebec to his wife and children.

She became a photographer's model and met vice-boss Maurice Conley who persuaded her to work as a hostess at his Mayfair club, the Court Club, where in 1950 she met George Ellis. He was forty-one, she was twenty-three. He was a dentist, an alcoholic and violent. They married in November

Left: Ruth was given the flat on the second floor, the one above that being used by girls on the game. _Right:_ However, after she lost her job in December 1954 through David Blakely causing a scene, her friend and devoted admirer Desmond Cussen came to her rescue and she moved into his flat, No. 20, in Goodwood Court in Devonshire Street, Marylebone.

Ruth stayed with Cussen from December 7 until February 9, 1955 when she moved to No. 44 Egerton Gardens just off the Brompton Road with Blakely. It was an odd move for on February 6 Ruth said that 'David started beating and kicking me so severely that I was a mass of bruises from head to toe.' The argument would appear to have been caused by his jealousy over the fact that she had been living with Cussen although why she would then choose to stay with Blakely after being so ill-treated is difficult to understand. It was Cussen though who took her to Middlesex Hospital the following day and even paid the rent on her flat for two months in advance.

1950. In October 1951 she gave birth to a baby, Georgina, but Ruth and George parted before she was born.

David Blakely, a racing driver and ex-public schoolboy, came on the scene in 1953 at the Little Club in Knightsbridge, where Ruth had been promoted to manageress by Conley. Blakely and Ruth became lovers and he moved into her flat above the club. While Blakely was racing at Le Mans in 1954, Ruth began an affair with Desmond Cussen, a thirty-two-year-old wealthy businessman, an ex-bomber pilot and described as her sugar daddy. He wanted to marry Ruth but she refused him.

Blakely, like Ellis, drove Ruth to the edge of sanity. He beat her up, pleaded poverty, had affairs with other women, but she still wanted him. He convinced her he loved her. Because of money problems and Blakely's bad behaviour before Christmas 1954, Ruth lost her job and flat at the Little Club. He had smashed the place up because Ruth wouldn't give him money to finance his racing car obsession. Ruth, now homeless, moved in with Cussen at Goodwood Court, a smart address in Marylebone.

Later she moved into a bedsitter in Egerton Gardens, Kensington, with Blakely, because he was jealous of her staying with Cussen. But Cussen wouldn't let go. In March 1955 Ruth miscarried Blakely's child after being kicked in the stomach by him. She was emotionally disturbed, drinking heavily and taking tranquillisers. The situation was made worse by Blakely's friendship with Anthony and Carole Findlater who turned David against Ruth. Anthony worked as Blakely's mechanic on the Emperor racing car they were constructing together.

Muriel Jakubait,
Ruth Ellis, My Sister's Secret Life, 2005

Ruth had married George Ellis in November 1950 and their daughter Georgina was born in October 1951 (in fact Ruth was pregnant with her in the photo on page 290). At first the baby was looked after by Ruth's sister Muriel but later Ruth's parents took the young child into their care. George Ellis finally obtained custody just before Ruth was executed. Her son, nine-year-old Clare Andrea, had been born following a wartime liaison with a French-Canadian soldier Clare McCallum but he had returned home to Quebec. As a result, young Andrea had always moved around with her. It was in January, while staying with Desmond Cussen, that the boy showed Ruth's French language teacher, Mrs Marie Thérèse Harris, two pistols that were kept in a drawer. One was this .38 Smith & Wesson revolver, the Military & Police Model of 1905, now in the Crime Museum at New Scotland Yard. This model, when supplied to the British Commonwealth, was specially chambered for the shorter .38 S&W cartridge which was loaded with a 200 grain bullet — hence the model was nicknamed the .38/200 British Service Revolver. Over 570,000 were supplied to Britain and the Commonwealth, between 1940 and 1945 but Cusson's pistol, No. 719575, was part of a contract ordered by the Union of South Africa where, we are told, he served in the RAF. It was shipped from the Springfield factory to Cape Town on December 2, 1940. Andrea later told Muriel that Uncle Desmond had taken him with mummy to Epping Forest to teach her to shoot.

I reside at 29 Tanza Road, Hampstead, N.W.3, with my wife Carole and our daughter Francesca aged one year. We have lived at this address for the past two years.

For about the past five years my wife and I have known David Moffat Drummond Blakely who, so far as I know, is aged twenty-five. We have a common interest in motor racing and this is how I believe I first met him. I know his mother and step-father and his brothers and sister. He was an engineer by profession. He also was a professional motor racing driver.

About two years ago David Blakely met a woman named Ruth Ellis at the Little Club in Knightsbridge where she was then the manageress. He was a member of that club. From that time an association started between these two. Ruth Ellis was, I believe, at the time that David met her, married and the mother of two children. I gathered that she was separated from her husband. One child, a boy of about nine years at the time, was living with her. Recently, a matter of a few months ago, I heard from David that Ruth had got a divorce from her husband. I do not know the facts of the divorce.

David had entered the Emperor in two races in 1955, the first being the British Empire Trophy at Oulton Park on April 2. Anthony Findlater, pictured here with his wife Carole, helped David build the car and travelled with the couple to Chester on Friday, April 1. However the car blew up in practice and had to be towed back to London on the Sunday.

During the early part of the association between David Blakely and Ruth Ellis, she was living in a flat above the Little Club. I know on various occasions he spent the night there with her. He did not live there permanently.

From the start of the association between these two people there were frequent rows. David often told me of having had rows with her. He would leave her and after a time start seeing her again.

About six months ago David told me that Ruth had had a row with the man who owned the Little Club, Morri Conley, and had left the flat she had been living in. She had gone, so I understood, to live in the flat of a man whose Christian name was Desmond. I cannot remember his surname. He had apparently frequented the Little Club and was a friend of hers. I know that David visited her at this flat on occasions. I cannot now remember the address but if necessary could take police to it.

During this period David and I were working on building a new racing car. The car was built at some works we rented at Islington, and when the car was completed, we gave up the works and I now keep it at a garage at 12 Rex Place, W.1. As a result of the work on this car I saw David Blakely almost every evening. He was working at Penn in the daytime and came to help me with the car in the evenings. As a result of this I heard a lot from him about his troubles with Ruth Ellis. It was obvious that he wanted to break off his association with her but apparently every time he left her she created a scene and he would go back.

On one occasion, about three months ago, I received a telephone call at home from David. He asked me to come to the flat at which Ruth Ellis was living 'to get him out of trouble'. He gave me the address, it was somewhere in Marylebone. It was the flat of the man Desmond. Mr Clive Gunnell was with me and we went along together. On

In his police statement, Anthony Findlater explained how Clive Gunnell, a car salesman, *(left)* gave them the use of his large double garage, situated at No. 12 Rex Place which lies just off of Park Lane in the West End of London, to repair the car.

arriving at the flat I found David and Ruth there together. He told me he wanted to leave and break off with her and that she would not let him go. I said: 'Come on David, let's go'. We left the flat with Ruth following. The conversation was sarcastic, but not threatening. He had scratches on his face and it was obvious they had been fighting.

When we got outside, Ruth got into David's car. David, Clive and I got into the car I was driving. Ruth got out of David's car and leaned in through the window of our car so that I could not drive away. We all got out of the car and Clive started to try and reason with her. Whilst he was doing this I told David to drive off in his car and we would keep her occupied. This was successful, he got away, but Ruth Ellis was very hysterical. Clive and I took her for a coffee and later dropped her back at her flat.

On another occasion David showed me a scratch on his arm and said that this had been caused by Ruth when she had drawn a knife on him.

During the time that Ruth Ellis was living in the man Desmond's flat, she was pestering David Blakely whenever he was away from her. I know she 'phoned him at home and at his work at Penn and visited Penn by car. On these occasions she was accompanied by the man Desmond, so far as I know.

On Friday, 1st April, 1955, David and I took our racing car and his own to Chester for a race at Oulton Park, Cheshire. Ruth came with us. I know that by this time Ruth Ellis had changed her address and was living in a flat in Egerton Gardens. Whilst we were in Chester we stopped at an hotel, the name of which I can supply. Later Ruth and David stayed as man and wife. During practice on Friday the car blew up. However we stayed and watched the racing on Saturday, spent Saturday night at the same hotel, and towed the car back to London on Sunday.

From Monday, 4th April, until Good Friday, 8th April, 1955, I only saw very little of David but on Good Friday, he came up to my address in the late afternoon to see me and discuss what we should do about the racing car. In the evening we went to the Magdala Public House for a drink. Whilst we were there David said he had to get away at about 8 p.m. or 8.30 p.m. to meet Ruth. My wife was with us. I suggested to him that this was foolish, continuing to see this woman, as he wanted to break off with her. He said: 'If I don't she will go to Penn again.' By this he meant she would go to his home and cause a scene. I suggested he should stay with my wife and I for the weekend and that if she came along I would cope with her. He agreed to this.

We went home together and before we went to bed Ruth Ellis 'phoned and I spoke to her. She asked me if I knew where David was. I said I did not.

After we had gone to bed and I had gone to sleep David woke me up and told me that she was outside our house banging on his car and that she had previously been telephoning and ringing the doorbell. I looked out of the window and saw Ruth Ellis outside. She was banging with something on David's car windows. I immediately telephoned the police. Whilst I was waiting for them she went up the steps outside the door and pressed our doorbell continuously. The police arrived. I went down and asked the police to stop Ruth Ellis ringing the doorbell and banging on the door. I then went back to bed. This was about 2 a.m. on Saturday morning.

About half an hour later David came in to me again and told me that Ruth was outside again banging on the car. I again 'phoned the police. When the police arrived I went and spoke to them, but Ruth Ellis had disappeared. We did not hear or see Ruth Ellis again that night.

On another occasion a heated argument between Ruth and David took place here in the road outside Desmond Cussen's flat in Devonshire Street.

Left: **David gave this signed photograph to Ruth shortly before the end.** *Right:* **After being lost for many years, his beloved Emperor came up for auction at Coys International Historic Festival at Silverstone in July 1999, being purchased by Julian Messent of LMB Racing for £30,000 on behalf of his principal in Belgium. It was later rebodied by Rod Jolly Coachbuilding, this picture being taken for us in June 2011. It appears that the registration number HLO 168 was switched by David Blakely between cars, possibly because it was a new design and not road registered.**

The Findlater's flat was located at No. 29 Tanza Road, Hampstead (beside the Ford Fiesta) and it was here on the night of April 8/9 that a further altercation with Ruth took place in the road outside.

At about 8.30 a.m. on Saturday, 9th April, 1955, Ruth Ellis telephoned again. I recognised her voice and hung up. Later in the morning Ruth Ellis telephoned 12 Rex Place where David and I were working repairing the windows of his car which she had pushed in during the night. Clive Gunnell was with us. He answered the 'phone and told me that a Mrs Roberts wanted to speak to me. I went to the telephone and immediately recognised Ruth Ellis's voice. She said: 'Thank you for calling the Black Maria last night. If I had known I would have waited for it.' I did not answer but hung up. Later at 12 Rex Place the 'phone went again. A man, whose voice I think I recognised as Desmond's, asked for David. I asked who was speaking and he said: 'Lionel Leonard.' I know Lionel Leonard. I knew it was not his voice but said 'Anthony here, how are you?' There was a pause and the 'phone was hung up. We then returned to Hampstead and David stayed with us on Saturday night.

On Sunday afternoon, at between two and three o'clock, David offered to drive our children's nurse to Victoria Station. He returned about an hour and a half to two hours later. He said he had been into a film for an hour on the way back.

Just before seven o'clock on Sunday evening, 10th April, 1955, David and my wife went in my car to pick up Clive and his gramophone. They returned to my flat and had also bought some beer on the way home. About two hours later David said 'I think I'll go down the road and get some more beer.' Clive went with him. That was the last time I saw him.

Statement to police by Anthony Findlater, April 10, 1955

It was Easter and David was staying over with Anthony to thrash out what could be done with the Emperor when they were faced with another repair job — this time to David's Standard Vanguard estate. After the household had retired for the night, Ruth had turned up and attacked the car, pushing in three windows which were only held in place by rubber seals. Anthony called the police (this is their photograph *(right)* taken later) but . . .

About two years ago I met David Blakely when I was manageress of the Little Club, Knightsbridge; my flat was above that. I had known him for about a fortnight when he started to live with me, and has done so continuously until last year, when he went away to Le Mans for about three weeks, motor racing. He came back to me and remained living with me until Good Friday morning.

. . . we were amazed when a police car pulled up just as we were taking the photographs, although this time on an enquiry regarding a burglary not vandalism to a car!

He left me about ten o'clock a.m. and promised to be back by 8 p.m. to take me out. I waited until half-past nine and he had not 'phoned, although he always had done in the past. I was rather worried at that stage as he had had trouble with his racing car and had been drinking.

I rang some friends of his named Findlater at Hampstead, but they told me he was not there, although David had told me he was visiting them. I was speaking to Findlater, and I asked if David was all right. He laughed and said: 'Oh, yes, he's all right.' I did not believe he was not there, and I took a taxi to Hampstead where I saw David's car outside Findlater's flat at 28 [*sic*] Tanza Road. I then telephoned from nearby, and when my voice was recognised they hung up on me.

I went to the flat and continually rang the door-bell, but they would not answer. I became very furious and went to David's car, which was still standing there, and pushed in three of the side windows. The noise I made must have aroused the Findlaters, as the police came along and spoke to me. Mr Findlater came out of his flat, and the police also spoke to him.

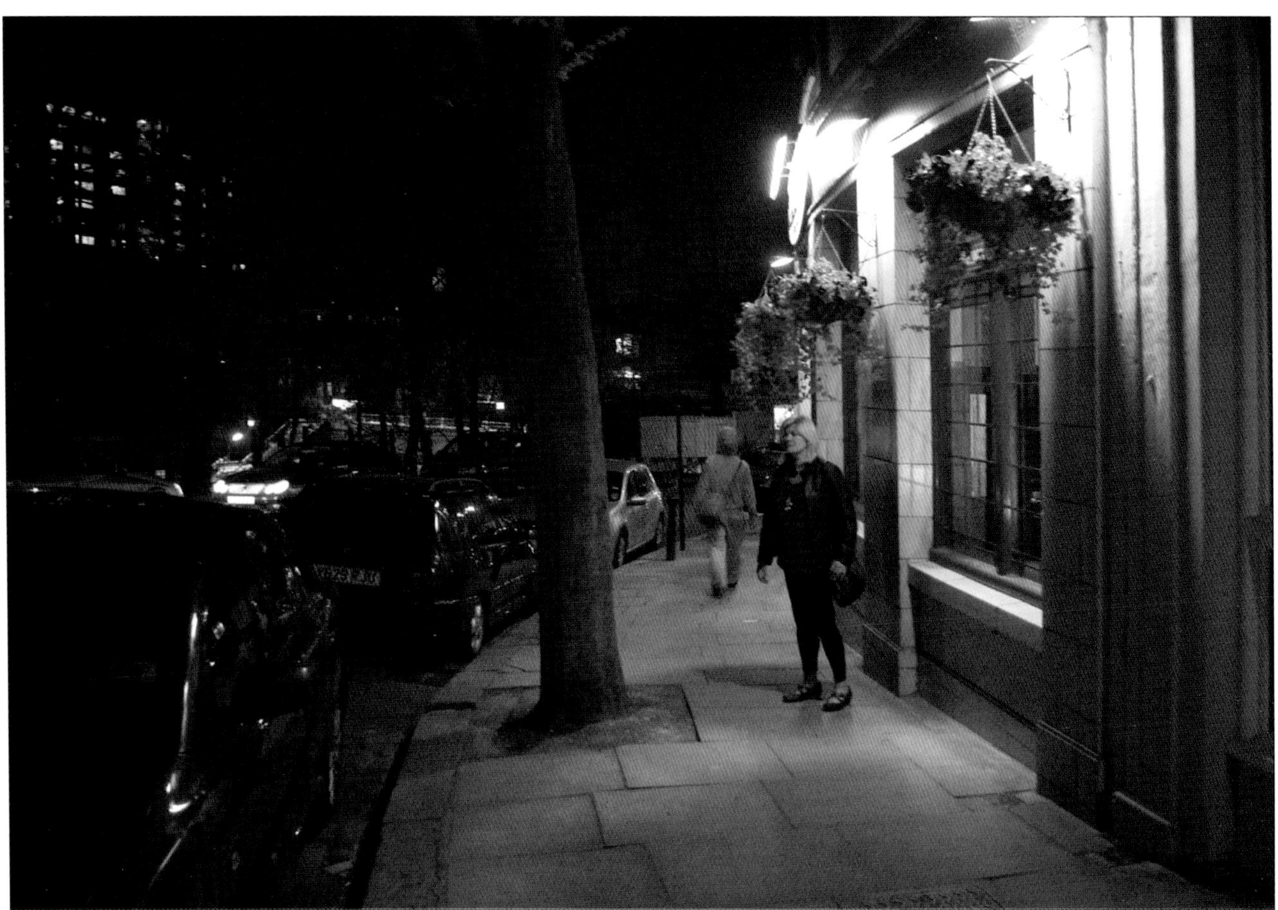

David Blakely was shot on the evening of Sunday, April 10 . . . and when we looked at the calendar for 2011 we could not believe that April 10 again fell on a Sunday! So we just *had* to take this photo at the exact time — 9.20 p.m. Gail stands in for Ruth.

David did not come home on Saturday, and at nine o'clock this morning (Sunday) I 'phoned the Findlaters again, and Mr Findlater answered. I said to him: 'I hope you are having an enjoyable holiday,' and was about to say: 'because you have ruined mine,' and he banged the receiver down.

I waited all day today (Sunday) for David to 'phone, but he did not do so. About eight o'clock this evening (Sunday) I put my son Andrea to bed. I then took a gun which I had hidden, and put it in my handbag. This gun was given to me about three years ago in a club by a man whose name I do not remember. It was security for money, but I accepted it as a curiosity. I did not know it was loaded when it was given to me, but I knew next morning when I looked at it. When I put the gun in my bag I intended to find David and shoot him.

I took a taxi to Tanza Road, and as I arrived, David's car drove away from Findlater's address. I dismissed the taxi and walked back down the road to the nearest pub, where I saw David's car outside. I waited outside until he came out with a friend I know as Clive. David went to his car door to open it. I was a little way away from him. He turned and saw me and then turned away from me, and I took the gun from my bag and I shot him. He turned round and ran a few steps round the car. I thought I had missed him, so I fired again. He was still running, and I fired the third shot. I don't remember firing any more, but I must have done. I remember then he was lying on the footway and I was standing beside him. He was bleeding badly, and it seemed ages before an ambulance came.

I remember a man came up, and I said: 'Will you call the police and an ambulance?' He said: 'I am a policeman.' I said: 'Please take this gun and arrest me.'

This statement has been read over to me, and it is true.

Ruth Ellis, Statement, April 10, 1955

The police took their photograph the following day in daylight but by then the Vanguard had been taken to Hampstead Police Station. It had been parked facing downhill i.e. facing to the left. Ruth was standing with her back to the pub so the claims that bullet holes can be seen in its walls are spurious! PC Alan Thompson, 'L' Division, was off duty and in plain clothes in the saloon bar, and he testified that he saw a blonde woman wearing spectacles looking into the bar through the rippled glass window near the door. About five minutes later he said he heard several explosions close at hand. 'I ran out into the street and saw a man lying on his left cheek; he was moaning and bleeding from the mouth. The accused was standing with her back to the wall of the public house. She was holding a revolver. I said that I was a police officer and took the firearm from her and said that I was detaining her.'

Clive Gunnell said that 'it was arranged that we would meet at lunchtime on Sunday to have a drink at the Magdala and I met them there as arranged. Anthony's wife was with him. David was alone and I brought a friend named Osmond with me. We had drinks and it was arranged for me to take my gramophone and records to Tanza Road at seven o'clock. The same party as we had at lunchtime was to be there. Everybody arrived as arranged and we had a party until about nine o'clock. David and I left to get some more beer and went to the Magdala. We went into the Saloon bar and David cashed a cheque for £5. The time then was roughly ten past nine. David had a gin and I had a bitter. We collected three quarts of bitter and left about twenty past nine. We had a motor car when going to the public house — a Vanguard converted van. I went to the passenger side round the front of the van and tried to get in but the door was locked. I heard two bangs but took no notice as I thought it was adjustable bangers David had fixed on his car. Then I heard David scream "Clive" and I rushed round the back of the van and saw the woman Ruth with a gun in her hand. David was lying on the pavement face downwards and I saw her fire several more shots into David's back. I ran over and picked his head up and the blood was spurting out of his mouth. David said nothing and I stood up. The woman Ruth said to me: "Go and call the Police." I asked the landlord to call the police and an ambulance. I accompanied David to the New End Hospital, Hampstead.'

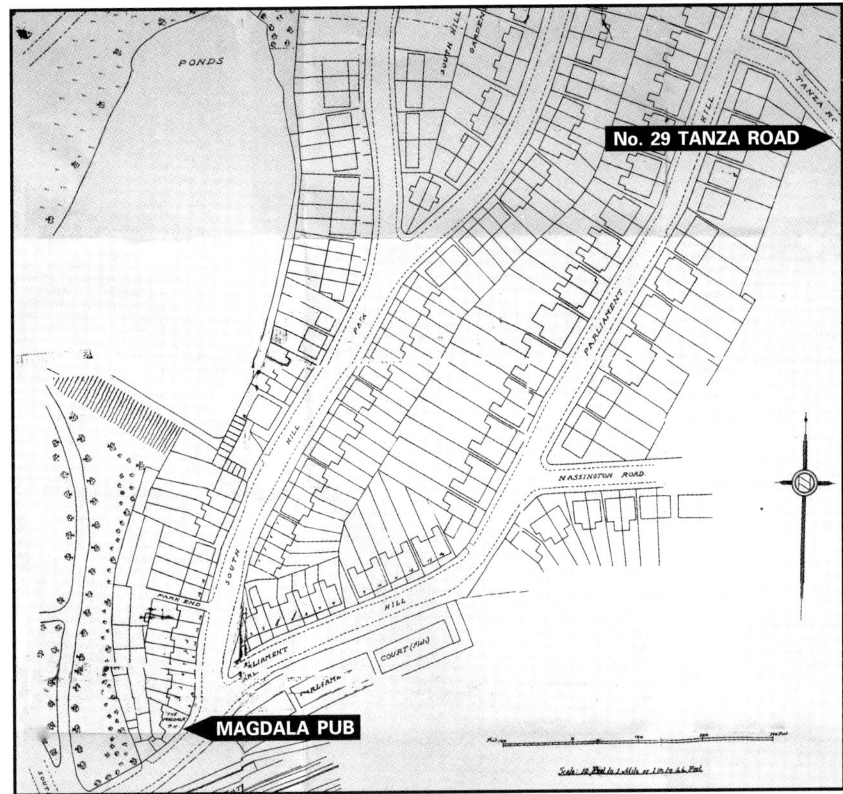

Police scene of crime plan produced by PC Philip Banyard of 'S' Division.

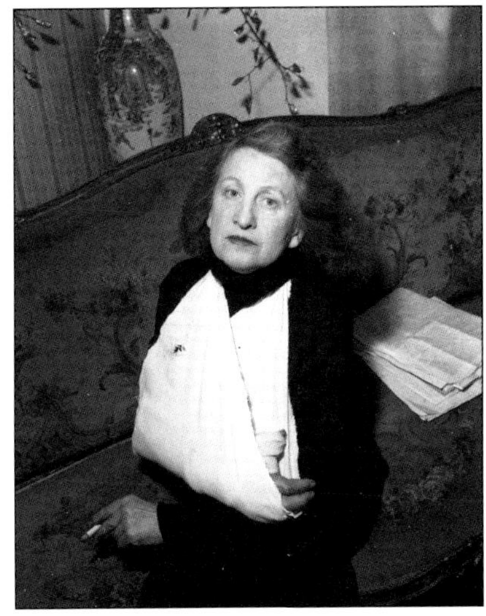

Mr and Mrs Donald Yule, who lived at 24 Parliament Hill, had decided that evening to go for a drink at the Magdala. They were walking down their road on the right-hand pavement. 'Just before we reached the junction of South Hill Park and Parliament Hill,' Mr Yule told police later, 'I noticed a blonde, hatless, woman, wearing a light grey suit and horn-rimmed glasses, walking slowly up and down on the pavement outside the pub. I also noticed a large motor car outside the pub. The woman seemed to be waiting for somebody. As we reached the junction I saw a man try the nearside door of the car which was facing downhill. Then I saw another man trying the offside door of the car, that is, the driver's door. This man was wearing a dark suit, appeared to be dark-haired, and had what appeared to be a beer bottle in his hand. I then turned toward my wife and was speaking to her when I heard the sound of a shot from the direction of the pub. I looked in that direction and saw the dark-haired man running along the nearside of the car, chased by the woman. His back was toward me and I heard the sound of another shot. The man was chased in a clockwise direction round the car and when they both reached the pavement again, almost opposite the Saloon bar of the public house, he seemed to face her. She fired at least a couple more shots and he fell to the footway. Almost immediately my wife cried out that she had been hit in the hand. I looked and saw that her right hand was bleeding profusely. At that moment a taxi-cab came down Parliament Hill and passed us. I shouted at the driver and he stopped almost immediately opposite the Magdala. We ran up to it and after a little argument, I persuaded him to take my wife and I to the Hampstead General Hospital. Just as I was helping my wife into the taxi, I recollect that I saw the blonde woman standing rigid on the pavement at the foot of the man lying there. I do not remember seeing a gun.' *Right:* Gladys Yule's account was similar: 'When we were about twenty-five yards from the public house, I saw a youngish man, dark-haired, run out of the Saloon bar door, followed, almost on his heels, by a blonde woman. I heard a shot fired and the man ran round a car which was parked outside the Magdala and ducked down by the side of it. He went round the car and backed on to the pavement again. I then heard more shots and the man collapsed to the pavement. She was shouting something at him when she was running after him but I couldn't make out what she said. When the man went down she continued firing the gun. By that time my husband and I were about twenty yards away, when I felt a searing pain in my right hand and I knew I had been shot. The woman was still standing between the man and the car, waving the gun. A taxi cab came along the road from Parliament Hill, and I shouted and ran after it. I got into it and was taken by my husband to Hampstead General Hospital and was detained for treatment for a bullet wound through the base of the thumb. The bullet appears to have passed completely through it.'

Dear Mrs Cook,

No doubt these last few days have been a shock to you. Please try to believe me when I say how deeply sorry I am to have caused you this unpleasantness.

No doubt you will hear all kinds of stories regarding David and I. Please do forgive him for deceiving you as regarding myself. David and I have spent many happy times together.

Thursday 7th April. David arrived home at 7.15 p.m. He gave me the latest photograph he had, a few days hence had taken, he told me he had given you one.

Friday morning at 10 o'clock he left and promised to return at 8 o'clock but never did. The two people I blame for David's death, and my own, are the Finlayters [*sic*]. No doubt you will not understand this but perhaps before I hang you will know what I mean.

Please excuse my writing but the pen is shocking.

I implore you to try to forgive David for living with me, but we were very much in love with one and other. Unfortunately David was not satisfied with one woman in his life.

I have forgiven David, I only wish I could have found it in my heart to have forgiven when he was alive.

Once again I say I am very sorry to have caused you this misery and heartache.

I shall die loving your son. And you should feel content that his death has been repaid.

Goodbye

Ruth Ellis

LETTER TO DAVID BLAKELY'S MOTHER, HOLLOWAY PRISON, APRIL 12, 1955

Mrs Ruth Ellis, aged 28, model of Egerton Gardens, Kensington, appeared on remand at Hampstead yesterday, charged with the murder of David Blakely, aged 25, racing driver, who was found outside a public house in South Hill Park, London N.W., on Easter Sunday night.

Mr J. Claxton, for the prosecution, said that Mrs Ellis and Blakely had been living together. On Easter Sunday Blakely and a Mr. Gunnell had gone to the public house to get beer for a party at a flat in Hampstead where Blakely was spending the weekend with friends. As they left Mr. Gunnell heard two bangs and saw Mrs. Ellis standing with a revolver in her hand. Blakely was lying face downwards on the pavement, and he (Mr. Gunnell) saw Mrs Ellis fire more shots into Blakely's back as he lay, Counsel alleged that when seen by police officers Mrs. Ellis said 'I am guilty.'

Through Mr Sebag Shaw, Mrs. Ellis pleaded Not Guilty to murder and reserved her defence. She was committed for trial at the Central Criminal Court.

The Times, April 29, 1955

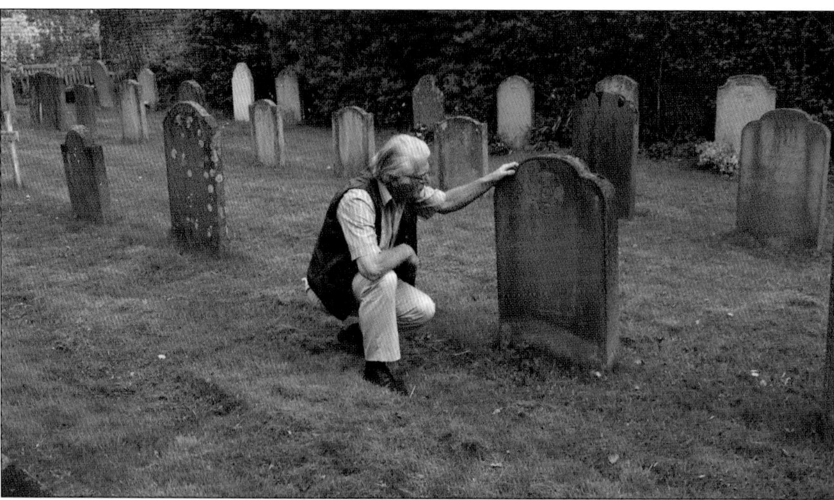

David Blakely was buried in the churchyard of Holy Trinity in Penn, the insignia on his headstone reflecting his National Service with the Highland Light Infantry. His brother John, who died in 1965, is buried beside him.

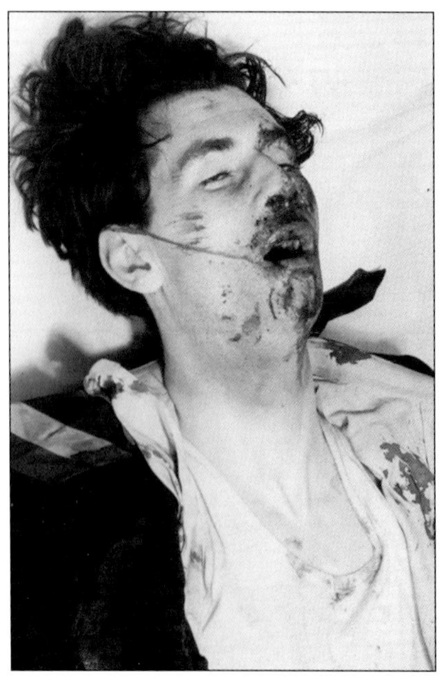

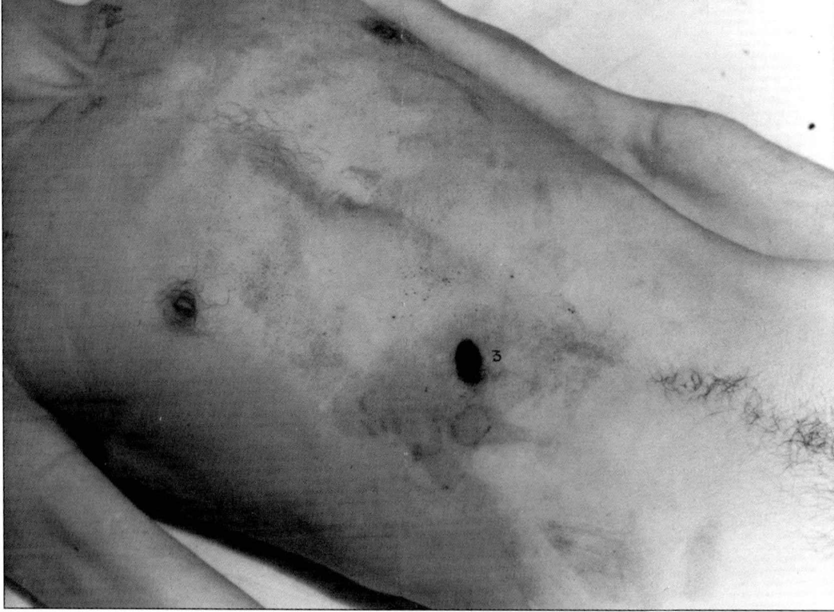

As happens with all murders, the body of the victim is photographed by the police and Detective Constable Thomas MacMacken of New Scotland Yard's Photographic Department attended Hampstead Mortuary where David had been taken. The post-mortem carried out at 9.30 a.m. on Monday morning revealed that while one or two of the shots out of the six fired had just grazed his skin, two had caused the fatal injuries. Detective Chief Inspector Leslie Davies and Detective Constable George Claiden took possession of one bullet recovered from the body. Later, at Holloway Prison, Ruth told her solicitor John Bickford that she wanted to see the police photographs. The prison report notes that the female officer found Ruth very 'upset on return from solicitor's visit — had been crying. Said she had insisted on seeing the photographs of David. They were worse than she imagined. States it is the first time she has cried since she has been here.'

On July 13 Ruth Ellis is due to be taken to a place of execution and there to suffer death by hanging and her body buried in the precincts of the prison where she has been confined.

The jury in this case swiftly pronounced her guilty within twenty-three minutes.

They made no recommendation to mercy.

The judge said that no other verdict was possible.

Her lawyers decided to make no appeal.

Death at the hands of the public hangman is very near and only the Home Secretary, left with the last agonising decision, can save her from a shameful doom in a prison yard.

It is unlikely that he will do so.

What sort of a killing was this?

It was a fierce, white-hot murder. Ruth Ellis fired six shots at her lover. Four of them hit him. She had to pull back the trigger for every shot she aimed at him.

It was not one continuous burst of fire but six separate, deliberate operations. One deadly wound resulted from the muzzle of the gun being held within three inches of the dying man's body.

Pity comes hard after such dreadful deeds. Compassion weeps but is silent.

Yet had I the power I would save her. This was a murder of love and hate. The one as fierce as the other—the storm of tenderness matching the fury of revenge.

In human nature, where passion is involved, love and hate walk hand in hand and side by side.

The difference between them is a hair's-breadth. The one can change to the other in a trice. Infinite sweetness and affection become infinite wickedness and black insensate cruelty.

This was no slow poisoning. But a sudden explosion of the forces of evil that are latent in the hearts of more men and women than would care to admit it—terrible, senseless, evil, and all too human.

There are thirteen more days to go.

The trial was held in No. 1 Court at the Old Bailey on Monday, June 20, before Mr Justice Havers. Ruth's answers from the dock (in the foreground) helped seal her fate: 'I had an idea I wanted to kill him and it is obvious that when I shot him I intended to kill him'. The jury were only out for 23 minutes, returning with a guilty verdict and no recommendation for mercy.

By the nature of her crime, by the nature of her appearance, by the ingrained horror that most people have at the prospect of a woman shortly to be dragged to the scaffold, it is inevitable that millions of people will be increasingly drawn towards the shortening shadow of the hideous event to come.

Some will be fascinated—morbidly so. Others will be horrified and haunted.

But there will be an almost tribal unanimity in the interest of the case. It is part of the degrading price that capital punishment demands—and always gets.

Justice not only has to be done, but it also has to be seen to be done. And so have the barbaric penalties of execution. They, too, have to be seen to be done.

This ghastly business, this obscene ritual which we, who claim to be the most civilised people in the world, have never succeeded in getting rid of, is witnessed by many people—most of whom have the decency to want to vomit.

Cassandra (William Connor),
Daily Mirror, June 30, 1955

Ruth refused to appeal, or to implicate Cusson, and her execution by Albert Pierrepoint and Royston Rickard was set for July 13. This was the tumultuous scene outside Holloway prison on that Wednesday morning.

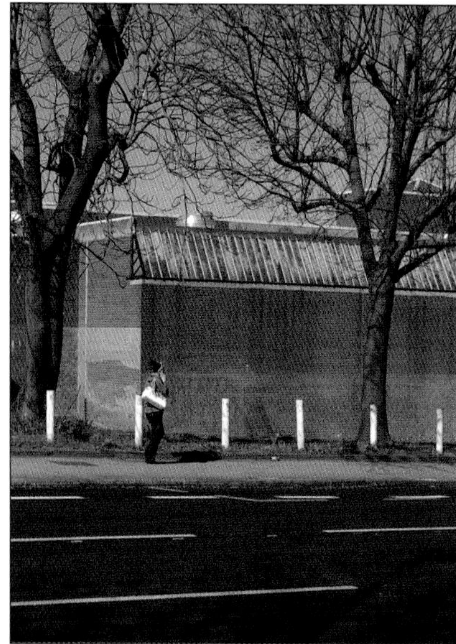

Left: **The sad figure of Mrs van der Elst (see page 7) in her lonely vigil long after the crowds had dispersed.** ***Right:*** **Holloway opened in 1852 as a mixed prison but became female only in 1903. It was demolished and rebuilt in 1968 at which point the bodies of all of the five executed women buried there were exhumed. The present day entrance to the prison is further down Camden Road (really now on Parkhurst Road) but the trees which lay on either side of the old main gate still stand.**

As she awaited the death sentence Ruth Ellis only cried once, when an MP tried to cajole her into seeking clemency, according to Home Office files in the National Archives. It was only hours before her execution that she admitted that she had got the gun that killed David Blakely from her other lover, Desmond Cussen.

Even then, she did so with great reluctance, and that seems to have played a part in the decision of Gwilym Lloyd George, the Home Secretary, not to grant a reprieve.

He noted on a plain sheet of A4 paper: 'Our law takes no account of the so-called *crime passionel*, and I am not prepared to differentiate between the sexes on the grounds that one sex is more susceptible to jealousy than the other. 'In the present circumstance, the woman was as unfaithful to her lover as he was to her. 'If a reprieve were to be granted in this case, I think that we should have seriously to consider whether capital punishment should be retained as a penalty.'

The Daily Telegraph, September 17, 2003

The last woman to be hanged in Britain was given an extra minute of life because of a hoax telephone call to the governor of Holloway prison.

Ruth Ellis was hanged at 9.01 a.m. on 13 July 1955 after the caller, claiming to be the private secretary to the Home Secretary, Major Gwilym Lloyd-George, said there had been a stay of execution.

Governor Dr Charity Taylor spent the next six minutes trying to establish whether the call was genuine. Having failed to do so, she ordered the execution to go ahead, one minute late.

Evening Standard, May 26, 2000

The sister of Ruth Ellis, the last woman to be hanged in Britain, has begun an appeal to have her conviction for murder overturned.

Muriel Jakubait, 77, now says it is her 'dying wish' to see her younger sister's conviction for murder reduced to manslaughter. The case is due to go before the Criminal Cases Review Commission later this month. It will be argued that the jury was not told that Ellis had been receiving psychiatric treatment and had suffered a miscarriage after being beaten by Blakely.

The Times, Wednesday August 12, 1998

The sister of Ruth Ellis, the last woman to be executed in Britain, is to seek a pardon from the Home Secretary after the Court of Appeal upheld her conviction for murder nearly half a century ago.

Muriel Jakubait, 81, said yesterday that she would not stop campaigning until she won justice for Ellis, who was hanged in 1955 for shooting David Blakely, a racing driver with whom she was having an affair.

'I feel absolutely stunned. I cannot believe it,' Mrs Jakubait said after the hearing. 'I am not going to stop now. Until I am taken from this Earth I shall go on.' Two years after Ellis's execution, Parliament changed the law to allow a defence of diminished responsibility. Yesterday, the judges said such a defence was not available at the time of Ellis's trial.

The Daily Telegraph, December 9, 2003

At her trial, Ruth maintained her silence about Desmond Cussen who had not only provided the pistol but driven her to Hampstead in the taxi he used for personal transport. On April 18, officers Davies and Claiden interviewed him having been told by the French teacher, Mrs Harrris, about the guns in his desk drawer, and they took possession of a Webley air pistol and Emge starting pistol. In the end Ruth's best friend, Jacqueline Dyer (seen here taking flowers to the prison), managed to get her to admit that Cussen had given the gun to her, but she then tried to backtrack. The day before she was executed, Ruth gave a statement to Victor Mishcon (who was representing her following her sacking of Mr Bickford): 'I Ruth Ellis, have been advised by Mr Victor Mishcon to tell the whole truth in regard to the circumstances leading up to the killing of David Blakely and it is only with the greatest reluctance that I have decided to tell how it was that I got the gun with which I shot Blakely. I did not do so before because I felt that I was needlessly getting someone into possible trouble. I had been drinking Pernod in Desmond's flat and Desmond had been drinking too. This was about 8.30 p.m. We had been drinking for some time. I had been telling Desmond about Blakely's treatment of me. I was in a terribly depressed state. All I remember is that Desmond gave me a loaded gun. I was in such a dazed state that I cannot remember what he said. He drove me to Hampstead and left me at the top of Tanza Road.' Desmond Cussen went to Australia in 1964 and kept silent until 1977 when Peter Williams, a British TV producer, tracked him down to a flower shop in Perth. However, he protested that he had not given Ruth the gun or driven her to Hampstead. He died in May 1991 and was cremated at Karrakatta Cemetery in Claremont, Western Australia.

After Ruth was exhumed on April 1, 1971, Andrea wanted her buried close to David but the vicar of Holy Trinity at Penn refused so instead he approached the nearby parish in Amersham. The London Necropolis Company, which had interred the other Holloway dead at Brookwood (see page 69), carried out the burial in the far corner of St Mary's Churchyard. Andrea later had a headstone erected on the grave, the surname 'Hornby' being her father's name before he later changed it to Nielson. His aunt Muriel, remonstrated with him saying that he should have had the stone engraved 'Ruth Ellis'. Andrea committed suicide in June 1982, the Coroner announcing that he had taken a drug overdose while depressed to end a life devastated by his mother's death when he was ten. Shortly before he died he smashed the headstone.

Surely the most amazing photograph in this entire book — the executioner pictured beside the grave of the woman he hanged. Albert Pierrepoint had written to Ruth's sister in May 1979 asking if he could have his photograph taken at the graveside. Muriel never replied but she claims that two months later reporters waylaid her while out shopping and introduced her to the hangman in a nearby restaurant. She and Pierrepoint were driven to Amersham, a two-page article appearing in the *Sun* on July 17, 1979 including this picture. In his will, Andrea requested that he be laid to rest with his mother but, because his body was so decomposed, he had to be cremated. His ashes were then buried in his mother's grave. As a final irony, the undertaker's bill was settled by Christmas Humphreys — the advocate who had prosecuted Ruth back in 1955!

Then . . . and Now. The Ravensbrück concentration camp, located 50 miles north of Berlin, was set up in May 1939 specifically for women prisoners. Here the camp is being inspected in 1941 by Reichsführer-SS Heinrich Himmler. By the time the war ended when he died by his own hand, over 90,000 had lost their lives in the camp through both starvation and execution.

May 24, 1957 – The Slaying of Countess Teresa Lubienska

Scotland Yard were continuing yesterday their efforts to trace the murderer of Countess Teresa Lubienska, aged 73, who was stabbed to death at Gloucester Road Underground station late on Friday night.

The Countess, head of an old Polish family, was a tireless worker for various Polish exile organisations in London. She was returning to her furnished room in Cornwall Gardens, Kensington, from a birthday party at a friend's house at Ealing. After she had left the train at Gloucester Road she was struck several times in the chest with a knife. No one appears to have seen her assailant. The Countess was seen staggering towards the ticket barrier, where she collapsed. She died in hospital soon afterwards.

Scotland Yard last night issued the description of two people they are trying to trace who left the lift at the station just before the Countess entered. The lift was operated by a coloured employee. The police say that the two people may have seen the Countess attacked or seen someone running from the stairs leading from the lift to the platforms. One is a man aged about 27, height about 5ft. 8in., of medium build, clean shaven, with fair hair, possibly a foreigner, dressed in a light brown check suit. The other is a woman aged about 20, about 5ft. in height, with short black hair, black handbag, red high-heel shoes, and of smart appearance. They were not together. No one else was in the lift at the time.

Some men were seen talking together on the platform shortly before the train entered the station at 10.20 p.m. About the same time some youths were indulging in some rather rough horseplay.

Many of the Countess's Polish friends have told the police that they do not think a Pole would have committed the murder because she was so well loved. She was founder and chairman of the Association of Polish ex-Political Prisoners in Germany and carried with her a reminder of her days in Ravensbrück concentration camp — a number stencilled on her forearm.

The view that a political motive was behind the murder is one of the lines of enquiry being made by the police.

Three thousand Poles who attended Mass at Brompton Oratory yesterday afternoon for the patronal feast of St. Philip Neri offered special prayers for the Countess.

The Times, May 27, 1957

Most of the inmates came from the Soviet Union and Poland, Countess Teresa Lubienska being transported to Ravensbrück in August 1944. The Lubienska family were among the leading Roman Catholic landowners in eastern Europe. They played a prominent part in the development of agriculture and adopted progressive methods on their estates in eastern Poland. They also played a leading part, especially after the First Wold War, in shaping their country's foreign policy. Countess Lubienska was president of the Polish Red Cross before the war and was associated with many welfare organisations. Her son was killed on September 19, 1939. The Countess was first arrested by the Germans in November 11, 1942 and held in the Pawiak political prison in Warsaw before being sent to Auschwitz in May 1943, when she was branded '44747' on her left arm, being made to wear the red triangle to denote she was a political prisoner. She was transported to Ravensbrück in August 1944 (becoming prisoner No. 50850) until the camp was liberated in April 1945 when she was taken to Sweden by the Swedish Red Cross. She was also an accomplished film producer and artist.

The search for the murderer of Countess Teresa Lubienska has now been confined to the Kensington area. The police investigations have produced evidence which convinces them that her assailant was one of a gang of youths who had probably been reproved by her for their unruly behaviour on previous occasions.

Seventeen passengers left the train the Countess had travelled in but, being elderly, she lingered behind and when attacked was probably alone on the platform.

The detectives are satisfied that the murderer could have made his escape up the emergency stairs, but the two people who used the down lift at the time, for whom the police have appealed, may be in a position to substantiate information already obtained that 'scampering noises' were heard on the stairs.

About half the people who travelled on the same train as the Countess have come forward, but the police think there must be someone who may have noticed a group of youths leaving the station in a hurry. They hold the view that the youths did not intend murder but may have accosted the Countess with a view to discouraging her from any further interference with their behaviour.

The examination of correspondence found in the room occupied by the Countess has not produced anything to support suspicions of a political motive.

The Times, May 29, 1957

In London the Countess was known among Polish refugees as a devout Roman Catholic and, a few days before her death, it was reported that she was about to go to Rome to meet the Polish Primate, Cardinal Wyszynski. On Friday, May 24, 1957 she had spent the evening with friends before returning home to Kensington. She alighted on the westbound platform at Gloucester Road underground station.

Police believed that she possibly remonstrated with roudy youths on the platform — she called them 'Bandits' — or perhaps they tried to rob her. Either way, she was stabbed several times although she managed to somehow stagger to the lift.

Left: **Nowadays the lifts are operated automatically but 60 years ago they were worked by an attendant. Mr Akinyemi saw that she had been wounded but she made it to the surface before collapsing in the booking hall.**

It is almost certain that her assailants escaped by running up the emergency stairs which emerge into the booking hall to the right of the lifts. In fact the attendant told police that he heard scurrying footsteps while the lift ascended.

Left: **This picture was issued by Scotland Yard of Countess Lubienska following the attack. Mortally wounded, she was unable to help police with a description of her killer before she died.** *Above:* **On May 31 her body lay in state in the undertaker's chapel on Brompton Road.**

The inquest on the body of Countess Teresa Lubienska, aged 73, who was stabbed to death at Gloucester Road Underground station, S.W., on Friday night, was opened at Hammersmith yesterday and adjourned at the request of the police until June 24. Medical evidence was that she died from a haemorrhage caused by stab wounds to the chest.

General Anders, head of the Free Polish community in Britain, yesterday made a posthumous award of the Golden Cross of Merit with Swords to Countess Lubienska.

The police now believe that the Countess was probably attacked by a hooligan, angered at being rebuked for perhaps a jostling incident. Youths are known to have been shouting and scuffling as the Countess left the train.

The Times, May 28, 1957

A verdict of Murder by some person or persons unknown was returned by a jury at the resumed inquest at Hammersmith, W., yesterday on Countess Teresa Lubienska, aged 73, a Pole, who died after being found with five stab wounds at Gloucester Road underground station on May 24.

Detective Chief Inspector John Du Rose said: 'It has been necessary to interview something like 18,000 people. Many of these people are abroad, and inquiries are still coming in. The person responsible has not yet been traced. Neither have certain people, who, the police believe, know this person, come forward to assist.'

Mr Emanuel Olu Akinyemi, a foreman ticket collector at Gloucester Road station, said that 'on the night of May 24 a woman came into the lift from the platform. She kept saying 'Bandits, Bandits.' Going up in the lift he noticed blood streaming from her chest. 'I asked her what was wrong, and she kept saying Bandits, he said. 'She said nothing else.'

About five minutes before he saw the Countess a lot of people had arrived at the station on a west-bound train from Piccadilly Circus, but he had noticed nothing strange about any of them. While going up in the lift with the Countess he heard footsteps on the spiral staircase leading to the street. Usually the only people who left the station that way were people without tickets. The only way to the street from the platforms was by the lift or the staircase.

Police-constable R. Sherfield said that the Countess told him: 'I was on the platform and I was stabbed.'

Mr. Adam Antony Bielinski, a builder and decorator of Kensington Gate, S.W., who said that Countess Lubienska was his wife's cousin, was asked by the Coroner, Mr. Gavin Thurston: Can you tell me whether the word 'Bandit' as used by the Countess would have any special meaning?

She used to say that word very often describing some hooligans. I remember it very well. Was it a word she would use rather generally?

Speaking about some people who are drinking too much, making a noise, she used it very often.

Dr. Donald Teare, pathologist, said that there were five stab wounds, three on the left side of the front of the chest, one on the left side of the back of the chest, and one in the abdomen. One of the stabs on the front of the chest had reached the heart, piercing it in two places.

Countess Lubienska, who lived alone in Cornwall Gardens, Kensington, had been in Britain since 1946 or 1947.

The Times, August 20, 1957

The following day a Requiem Mass was held at the Brompton Oratory. Second on the right is General Wladyslav Anders, the leader of the free Poles (in 1957 Poland was under Communist rule), who posthumously awarded the Countess the Golden Cross of Merit with Swords.

Having been privileged to be associated with Countess Lubienska in her work for ex-victims of Nazi concentration camps, I should like to pay tribute to this brave and noble Polish lady. She was herself in Auschwitz and Ravensbrück, and bore the branded prisoner's number on her arm. Like so many of her heroic fellow-countrymen, she lived in great poverty, giving everything she had, including all her time and strength to helping her fellow-victims.

Today, when the horrors of the Nazi camps are well-nigh forgotten, and it is in vain that some form of compensation for the survivors is sought from the German Federal Government, in spite of solemn undertakings on paper, perhaps Countess Lubienska's tragic and violent death will once more stir the consciences of the civilised world to do something for these people who bear the brandmarks in their souls as well as on their bodies. Were this so, Countess Lubienska would surely gladly have laid down her life for the lives of her friends. May she rest in peace, at last, her task well and truly done.

THE HON. MRS DOUGLAS WOODRUFF,
JUNE 5, 1957

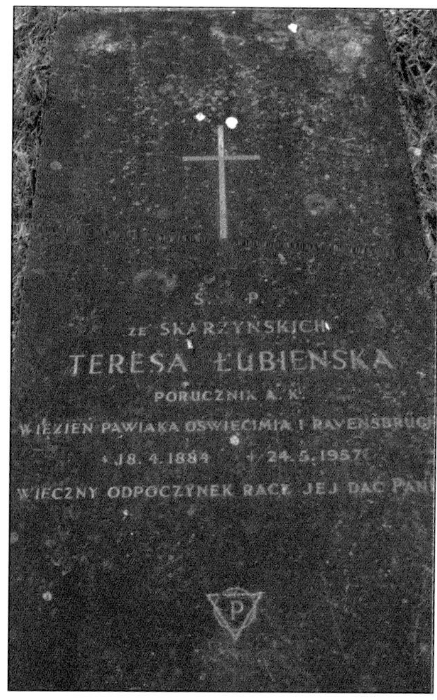

The Countess was taken to Brompton Cemetery and laid to rest in a common grave in the front row of Compartment F.

Left: **Pictured on his wedding day, December 14, 1957, Ronald Marwood, aged 25, lived at No. 37 Huntingdon Street** ***(right)*****, a turning off the Caledonian Road in North London. It was ironic that it was barely a stone's throw from Pentonville prison where he met his end at the hands of the hangman Harry Allen assisted by Harry Robinson in May 1959.**

December 14, 1958 – The Murder of Police Constable Ray Summers

Police Constable Raymond Henry Summers, aged 23, of Highbury Vale Section House, died at the Royal Northern Hospital after being involved in a fight with a number of men in Seven Sisters Road, Highbury, late last night. A police spokesman said that there were no wounds on the body; a post-mortem examination was being made.

The Times, December 15, 1958

Police Constable Raymond Summers was stabbed in the back as he dispersed a crowd watching a fight between youths on Sunday night. A post-mortem examination disclosed that he died from the stab wound.

The Times, December 16, 1958

Lights beamed out from the dance-hall, cutting a swathe through the December dark. The noise of the music ebbed and flowed in throbbing waves that Sunday night in London's Seven Sisters Road, but in the shadows beyond the sight and sound of frenzied revelry, PC Reg Summers, pounding a more familiar beat of his own, saw another kind of latent fury: a group of youngsters were arguing on the pavement near the dance-hall and the situation looked ugly enough to investigate.

Incidents like these were common enough in the winter of 1958 and they held no particular fear for Reg Summers, who, in his two years' service as a police officer in one of the city's toughest divisions, had acquired the experience and tact necessary to handle trouble when it came.

You could call it a psychological knack that had not only made him popular among the other bachelors in his section house near the Arsenal football ground, but would surely mark him out for promotion before long. Furthermore he was a big man, broad-shouldered, all of six feet four inches in his regulation boots and, at twenty-three, as near the peak of physical fitness as it is possible to get.

No one was prepared to say with any accuracy what happened when the young officer approached the youths. There was a brief scuffle and within seconds Reg Summers slumped to the pavement. He was dying when a passer-by dialled 999 and before an ambulance could get him to hospital he was dead.

On the evening of his first wedding anniversary, he left his wife at home to go drinking with his mates. *Left:* **He started out at the Spanish Patriots pub which stood here on the corner of White Conduit Street and Mantell Street, where he downed five pints.**

Then, with four friends, they drove over to Stratford to carry on at the Kray's Double R Club in the Bow Road. Both venues have since been demolished; the Double R being located behind the blue railings in the picture *(above)***.**

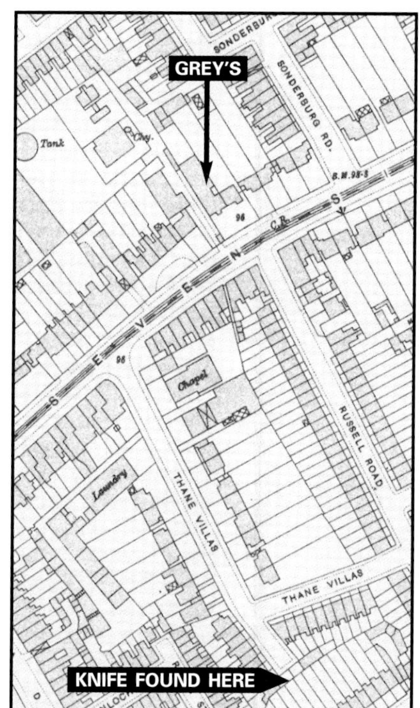

Having drunk a similar amount at the Double R, Marwood and four boys set off by car for Grey's Dancing Academy on the Seven Sisters Road at Holloway. All were tooled up with a variety of weapons including knives, bayonets, choppers and razors, Marwood being armed with a diver's knife. There had been a gang fight the previous Thursday at Barry's Dancing Academy at Highbury Corner and this was to be a return match. On a Sunday evening, Grey's was open from 7.30 p.m. to 11 p.m. with an admission price of half a crown (12½p). It was not licensed but light refreshments were available.

My telephone rang late that night. Would I attend a post-mortem to be conducted by Professor Francis Camps the following morning? I asked how the constable had died and was told that preliminary investigation indicated a heart attack. A heart attack? How old was he? Twenty-three? Surely it would be better if we held the post-mortem that night? I could get there from my home in Surrey in thirty minutes if they could summon Professor Camps. No, they said. There was no great urgency. In the circumstances, the morning would be more suitable. Besides Professor Camps was at his home in the country. A few hours' delay wouldn't make any difference in this case.

The next morning I saw PC Summers for the first time. He was lying on a stretcher in the St Pancras mortuary still fully dressed from his helmet to his boots. I don't know what made me ask, but after looking at the dead constable I said to one of the attendants: 'Help me turn him over, will you?'

When we did I could have wept with anger and frustration. For there in his back, hidden in a rucked up fold of his blue raincoat, was a thin slit little more than an inch long and clearly a stab hole. As I got to my feet Professor Camps walked into the room. 'This chap's been murdered,' I said.

Now most of the time I am a reasonably placid man, but to understand my feelings on that shivery morning in the late fifties you would have had to be a policeman too. Twelve hours had been lost. Twelve hours in which the murderer had had time to get away, flee the country, set up an alibi, go to ground — anything. But it was more than the sum of all these things put together. This was the murder of a police officer. A constable stabbed to death in the performance of his duty. All the resources of police forces throughout Britain could, and should, have been alerted and a nationwide murder hunt put under way hours before.

To a policeman, the murder of a colleague takes on a special significance and urgency of its own. There is a personal sense of loss, a private agony that brings us all that much closer as comrades. And here — I could scarcely believe it — was a police murder that had gone unnoticed for twelve hours, a precious long time.

What distressed me was that the valuable, even crucial, time lost was entirely due to the fact that whoever examined the young constable in the first place did not know what to look for because he had not been sufficiently trained. In the absence of an obvious wound whoever was responsible had presumed his death to be heart failure.

To be fair to those involved, I must say that preliminary police inquiries had been made during the night before I saw the body in the mortuary. The trouble was that the detectives did not know they were investigating a murder. Police officers had hurried to the homes of known youngsters who might have been outside the dance-hall when the fracas started; after all there had been rumours for some days of a pending gang fight in the area. Among those interviewed was Ronald Marwood who was known to 'run' with a particularly violent crowd in North London. He gave them an account of his movements that night and he was allowed to go. Would he, I wonder, have been allowed his freedom quite so quickly if the officers concerned had known that they were investigating not just the unfortunate death of a colleague but his murder? As it happened Marwood disappeared the following day and it was not until six weeks after the murder that he was seen again. That was when he surrendered to the police in response to an appeal for his help.

It was established at the trial that the constable collapsed as he tried to reach the police station and died from a wound inflicted with a knife used by underwater swimmers. The blade of the murder weapon, ten inches long, had penetrated the officer's mackintosh, his uniform tunic, cardigan, shirt and vest, piercing his body to a depth of four to five inches.

Detective Superintendent John McCafferty, Mac, I've got a Murder, 1975

Although much of Seven Sisters Road remains unchanged, unfortunately the buildings on this stretch of the road have all been demolished. Grey's dance hall stood here.

That Sunday, Police Constable Ray Summers was on the 10 p.m. to 6 a.m. 'Night Duty Relief' on No. 2 Crime Patrol, from Holloway Road Police Station.

The incident in which Police Constable Raymond Summers received a fatal stab wound arose from two rival factions meeting outside a dance hall at Seven Sisters Road, Holloway on December 14, it was stated at North London Magistrates' Court on Saturday when 11 youths and young men appeared on remand accused of unlawfully making an affray 'in a public place and highway'.

The defendants are Brian Robert Murray, aged 21; Ronald Bergonzi, aged 19; Ronald James Jackman, aged 21; Frederick John Jackman, aged 23; Frederick Robert Newbolt, aged 20; George William Fletcher, aged 21; John Budd, aged 19; David Henry Bailey, aged 18; Michael David Bloom. aged 24; Brian John Thwaithes, aged 21, and Peter Sydney Dean, aged 19. All the accused except Bloom were on Saturday further charged with having in their possession, without lawful authority or reasonable excuse, an offensive weapon. The weapons were said to be a weighted stick, choppers, a hammer, an air pistol and a knife.

The Times, December 29, 1958

Opening the case yesterday at the North London Magistrates' Court, Mr M. J. Palmes for the Director of Public Prosecutions said: 'The whole of the affray was sparked off originally by a very trivial incident which happened on Thursday, December 11, the affray taking place on Sunday, December 14. On December 11, Budd, Murray and Fletcher were in a place known as Barry's Dancing Academy. It appeared that a man named Flanagan insulted Budd. It was suggested he flicked a piece of paper at him. Budd, Murray and Fletcher went out,

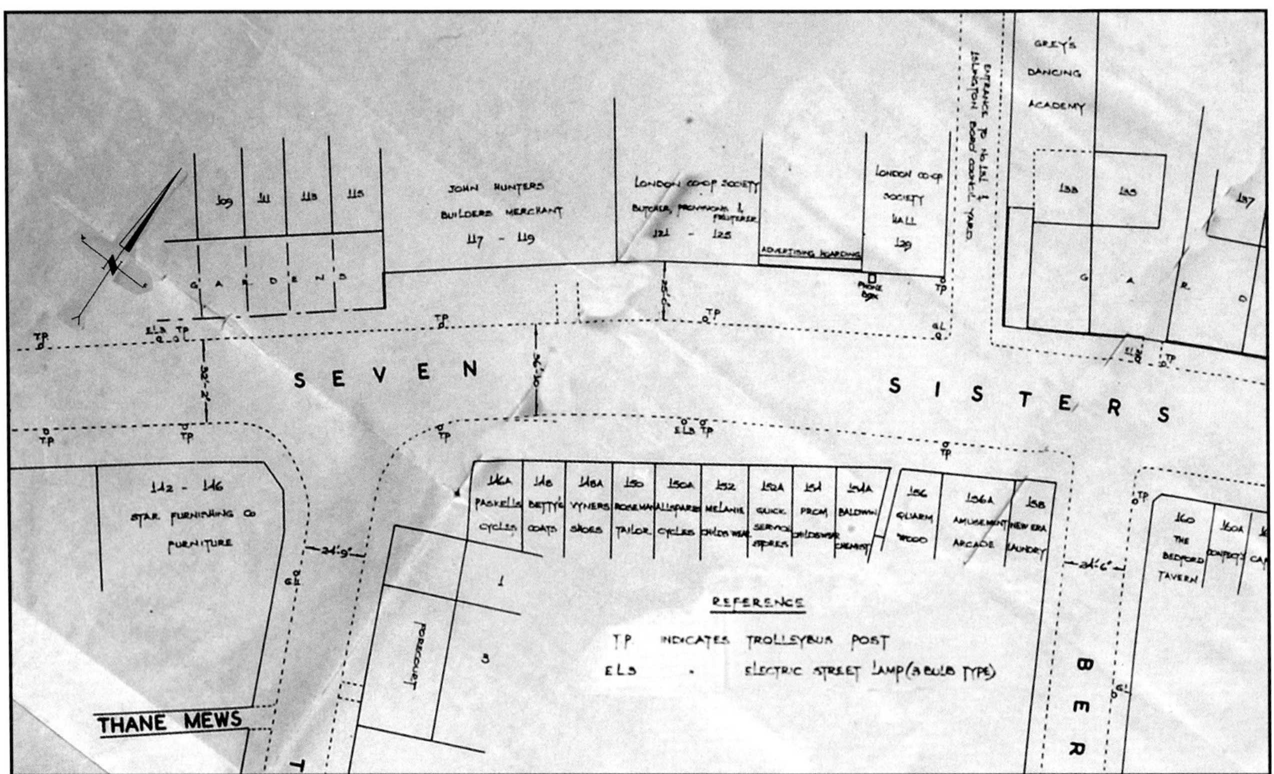

He was patrolling on the south side of Seven Sisters Road when he saw a disturbance taking place outside Grey's so crossed the road to deal with it. Witnesses stated that there were 40-50 youths, many armed with offensive weapons, but some ran away at the sight of the policeman. When Summers told the group to move on, some pushing and shoving followed outside the Co-op, culminating in Marwood stabbing the officer in his back. The policeman fell to the ground beside the pole supporting the trolleybus wires. This is the scene of crime plan prepared by the police.

Trolleybuses were phased out in London in the 1960s and the corresponding supports for the wires removed. According to Marwood, he then ran across the road and suddenly realised he still held the knife in his hand. At the bottom of this road (Thane Villas), he threw the knife over a garden wall, then jumped into the garden after it and crouched down, trying to collect his thoughts. He was joined by a youth named Bailey, and after about five minutes they decided to leave. Marwood later maintained that some other 'bloke' gave him the knife earlier in the evening during one of the car journeys and had said to him at the time, 'Here you are, you might need this.' He claimed that he had forgotten all about it until he struck the policeman with it! While they were walking away from the garden in which he and Bailey concealed themselves, they arranged the 'story' about being in a fight at Manor House in case they were stopped by police that night. After changing his clothes at home the next day, Marwood said he went to 'some friends' who put him up in one or two different places.

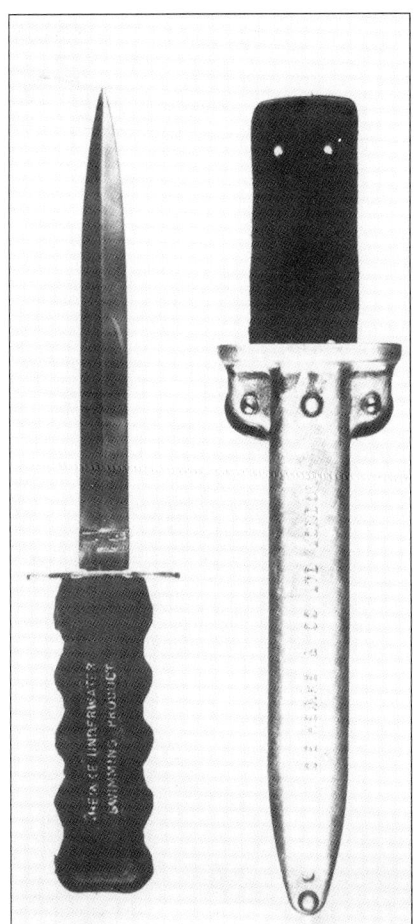

Above: The police found the knife *(left)* amongst this rubbish in a garden at the end of Thane Villas. *Below:* The site has now been redeveloped with the Sobel Leisure Centre.

Marwood remained in hiding for three weeks but on January 27, 1959 he walked into Caledonian Road Police Station asking to make a statement. He admitted to being at Grey's that night and said: 'I did stab the copper. I have been puzzling over in my mind during the last few weeks why I did it but there seems to be no answer.' After being questioned for 17 hours he was charged with the murder of PC Summers and taken to Holloway Road Police Station. Here he is being driven to the North London Magistrates' Court on the morning of the 28th.

collected some supporters and returned. There was a minor brawl and Dean apparently entered it on the side of Flanagan. Budd and his friends set upon Dean who was "knocked about a bit". Dean then threatened Budd, and it seems to have preyed on Budd's mind,' said Mr. Palmes. 'According to his own statement, he thought the most advisable thing would be to take the offensive. There you have the picture of the gradual build-up of gang war.

'On the following Saturday and Sunday there was some talk of seeking out Dean, and from the statements it would appear that ten of the defendants with others went in three cars to Grey's Dancing Academy. They gathered outside,' he said. 'Budd and Bloom, on their own admissions, went up to the door of the dance hall and tried to get in, but were refused admission.'

In his statement, Dean had said that he had heard there was a gang of people outside and he went out "to meet the trouble half way". Budd and Dean met in the dance hall forecourt. Dean was armed with a long knife and Budd with a chopper. Someone separated the men and pulled Dean back into the hall.

'Simultaneously with this, a 16-year-old youth comes out of the dance hall, crosses the road and runs into a number of Budd's associates. There was an altercation and two or three of Budd's men set upon the youth, who was struck in the back with an axe. A policeman came on the scene and someone shouted, "The law is coming". The majority of the people scattered. The policeman tried to arrest one man and, although it has nothing to do with this case, the officer was stabbed and subsequently died.'

The Times, January 3, 1959

Ronald Henry Marwood, aged 25, scaffolder, whom police wished to interview in connection with an affray in Seven Sisters Road, Holloway, N., on December 14, called at Caledonian Road police station last night. He was interviewed by Detective Superintendent R. G. Fenwick.

The Times, January 28, 1959

Ronald Marwood, was remanded in custody for a week at North London Magistrates' Court yesterday when charged with the murder of Police Constable Raymond Henry Summers on December 14, 1958 at Seven Sisters Road, Holloway. Detective Superintendent R. Fenwick said that he was asking for a remand in order that the matter could be reported to the Director of Public Prosecutions. Giving evidence of arrest, he said that he saw Marwood at Holloway Road Police Station. When cautioned, Marwood said: 'I have already told you the truth, how it happened, in my statement.'

The Times, January 29, 1959

Three youths who took part in a gang fight in Seven Sisters Road were sentenced at the Central Criminal Court yesterday. David Henry Bailey, aged 18, window cleaner, of Margery Street, W.C., was sent to a detention centre for five months for possessing an offensive weapon and unlawful assembly with intent to break the peace; Brian Robert Murray, aged 21, newspaper packer, of Phoenix Road, Camden Town, was fined £20 or sent to prison for three months on the same charges; and Peter Sidney Dean, aged 19, warehouseman, of Essex Road, Islington, was sent to a detention centre for three months for having an offensive weapon. Passing sentence, the Common Serjeant, Sir Anthony Hawke, recalled that eight other youths involved had been sent to prison.

The Times, February 18, 1959

After considering their verdict for two and three-quarter hours, the jury at the Central Criminal Court yesterday found Ronald Henry Marwood, guilty of the capital murder of Police Constable Raymond Summers on December 14. He was sentenced to death.

The Times, March 20, 1959

The execution of Ronald Henry Marwood has been fixed for Friday, May 8, at Pentonville Prison, London. Marwood, aged 25, of Huntingdon Street, Islington, was convicted at the Central Criminal Court last month of the capital murder of Police Constable Raymond Henry Summers.

The Times, April 23, 1959

Two petitions seeking a reprieve for Ronald Marwood were handed in to the Home Secretary's office at the House of Commons yesterday by Mr Albert Evans, Labour M.P. for Islington, South-West. Marwood's family live in Mr. Evans's constituency. One petition bore the names of 150 M.P.s — six Conservative, one Liberal, and the remainder Labour. The second petition was a public one for which signatures were collected by the Rev. W. J. Fenner, vicar of St Silas, Penton Street.

The Times, May 2, 1959

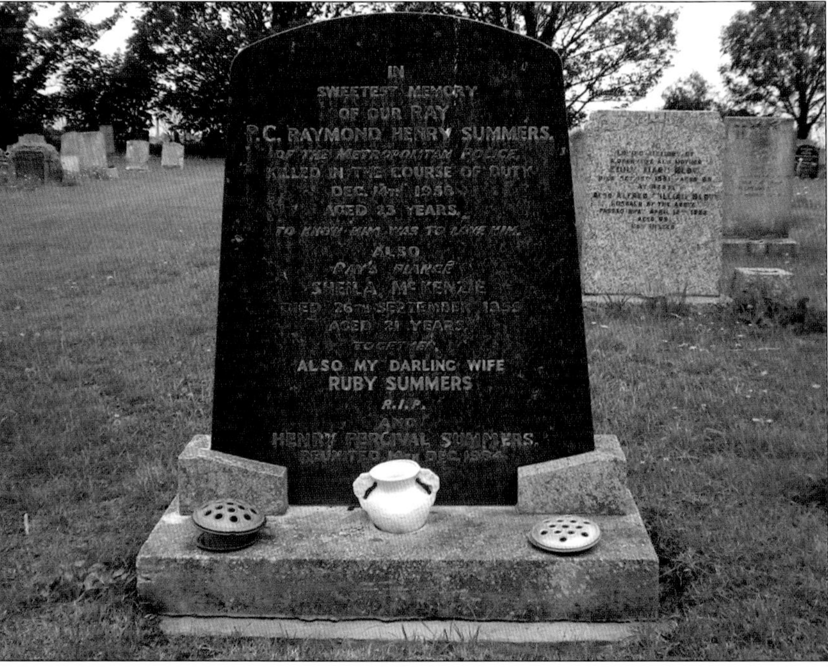

Ray Summers was buried in the churchyard of St Peter-in-Thanet, Broadstairs. He was a single man but engaged to Sheila McKenzie who sadly died ten months later aged 21. She was laid to rest with him.

A large crowd gathered outside Pentonville on the morning of May 8, 1959 to await the execution of Marwood, the first person to be hanged for murdering a police officer since Derek Bentley in 1953. The executioners in this case were Harry Allen (who had been promoted to chief executioner in October 1955 following Albert Pierrepoint's resignation) assisted by Harry Robinson.

The Home Secretary has been unable to find any sufficient grounds to justify him in recommending a reprieve for Ronald Marwood who will be hanged tomorrow at Pentonville. In a letter to Mr Albert Evans, Mr Butler says: 'Marwood was convicted, after a very full trial, of the capital murder of a police officer acting in the execution of his duty, and an appeal against his conviction was dismissed. I have examined the case in the light of all the available information and all the relevant circumstances; and I have failed to discover a sufficient ground to justify me in recommending Her Majesty to exercise the royal prerogative of mercy. I have regretfully come to the conclusion, therefore, that the law must take its course.'

The Times, May 7, 1959

A crowd of nearly 1,000 people yesterday demonstrated outside Pentonville Prison when Ronald Marwood was executed for the capital murder of a London policeman. The incidents started as 9 a.m. approached, when police, hearing a disturbance in the crowd, made their way to the spot and carried a young man across the road and inside the prison gates. He struggled and five policemen lifted him off the ground as the crowd booed and jeered. There were shouts of 'Savages', 'Beasts' and 'Murderers'.

Mounted police were called in and the crowd scattered. The foot police then joined hands in a line in front of the gates and pushed the crowd back. Quickly, the crowd re-formed opposite the gates, but the mounted police continually prevented them from moving over. The noisy scenes stopped at 9 a.m.

All through the night men were outside the prison with banners which said 'Save Marwood' and 'Hanging is no deterrent'. At dawn more people had gathered and several joined in prayers. On Thursday night, after attempts to save Marwood had failed, prisoners staged a 30-minute demonstration, and burning material was pushed through a cell window.

The Times, May 9, 1959

The grim sequence of events that ended, yesterday, with the hanging of a murderer must give us all grave cause to think. It is possible for citizens, equally free from emotional bias, to hold diametrically opposing views on capital punishment. It is no less possible to disagree on the merits and shortcomings of the Homicide Act.

The anomalies that flow from present law, and the consequential state of confusion created in the public mind on particular occasions, are evidence that the Act is far from perfect. It does not convince laymen that justice — absolute or relative — is always done and, to that extent, it fails one of the tests of socially healthy legislation. Against this background of confusion and, perhaps, of transition, the case of Marwood must be considered as a cautionary lesson. His name was on all our lips in the past few days, although that of the other young man, who lost his life when he was doing his duty, had relatively been forgotten.

The Times, May 9, 1959

The events leading up to the murder of Detective Sergeant Raymond Purdy began here at South Kensington Underground Station.

July 13, 1959 – The Death of Detective Sergeant Raymond Purdy

On July 13th, 1959 Deputy Commander Spooner came into my room and said, 'You'll be sorry to hear, Sir, that one of our sergeants has been shot. He's dead.' The story, as I soon learned, had actually begun five days earlier. Detective Sergeant Purdy was on duty at Chelsea Police Station when a message came in from an American lady, named Mrs Schieffman, saying that she had a blackmailer on the phone.

The call had been expected. Mrs Schieffman's flat in South Kensington had been broken into about ten days before while she was away. As well as a mink stole and some jewellery, the burglar had taken her passport. Two days later she received an express letter signed 'R. M. Lavine, Detective, U.S.A.' The writer said he had been hired to check on her activities; had amassed photographs and tape recordings, and was now prepared to sell them to her for $500. In consideration of this sum he would also send a favourable report to his employer. He gave her a few days to think it over. Like a sensible woman, and having done nothing to be blackmailed about anyway, she immediately showed the letter to the police.

On July 12 the blackmailer rang, asking for her decision. Following a plan which had been agreed with the police, she said she would pay. The blackmailer promised to ring back later with instructions about the method of payment. Mrs Schieffman told the police, who arranged for any further calls to be traced.

Next morning the man phoned again. He instructed Mrs Schieffman to draw $500 from the bank and then wait for another call. It came in the afternoon. She kept him talking while a neighbour notified Chelsea Police Station. Quickly the Post Office engineers traced the call. It came from Knightsbridge 2355, a public phone-box at South Kensington Underground Station. Sergeant Purdy and Sergeant Sandford raced to the scene in a police car. They saw a man in the call-box, speaking into the telephone and holding a small black notebook. They burst in, seized the man, and took the notebook. Purdy identified himself to Mrs Schieffman over the phone, and then told the man he was being arrested for demanding money with menaces. They started marching him towards the police car, but before they reached it he broke away.

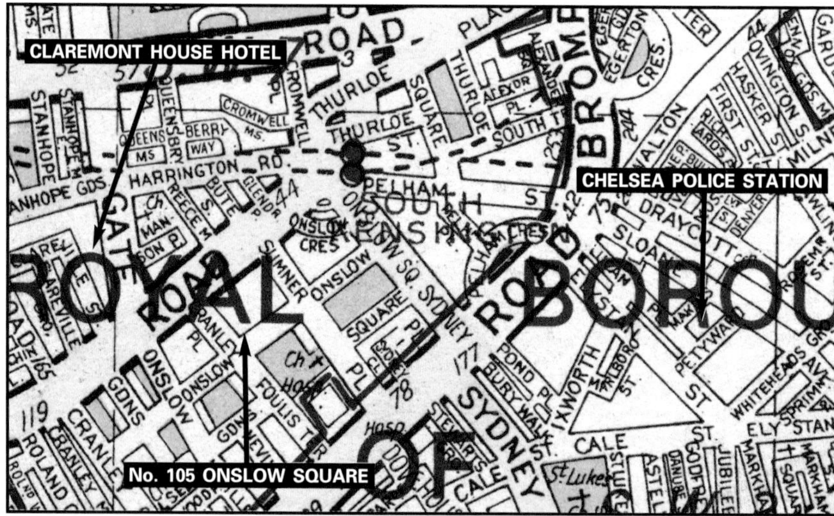

Left: **In the days before mobile telephones, all underground stations had individual phone booths like these pictured at South Harrow on the Piccadilly Line. Nowadays they have all been removed but it was from a similar booth in the booking hall at South Kensington *(right)* that Mrs Schieffman received a call on the morning of July 13, 1959. She had already informed the police of blackmail threats she had received and they were standing by ready for action at Chelsea Police Station.**

Responding to the call were Detectives Ray Purdy *(left)* and John Sandford *(right)*. They apprehended the caller in the end booth but as he was being brought up to the street he broke away and ran to Onslow Square. The officers gave chase and saw him enter No. 105 *(below)* where he was found trying to hide behind the right-hand pillar in the lobby *(bottom)*. Sergeant Purdy said to the man: 'We are police officers, we are detaining you and taking you to Chelsea police station,' ordering him to sit on the window sill behind the door, which he did by putting his hands on either side of his body and easing himself onto the sill with his back to the window. Sergeant Sandford walked across the hall to the bell to call the porter but there was no reply. 'As I said "the porter must be out," Sergeant Purdy turned his head towards me. As he did so I saw the prisoner get off the window sill and put his right hand inside the left side of his jacket. I shouted: "Watch out, he may have a gun!" the words were no sooner out of my mouth when I saw the prisoner produce a large black automatic pistol. He pointed it at Sergeant Purdy and fired at point-blank range.'

Purdy stumbled. Sandford commandeered a taxi-cab. They piled in, and swung after their quarry into Onslow Square. They saw him dart into the entrance of a block of flats. They raced in pursuit and caught him hiding behind a pillar in the hall.

Purdy made the man sit on a window-sill and told him to behave himself while Sandford crossed the hall and rang for the porter. There was no reply. 'The porter must be out,' he called to Purdy. For a moment Purdy turned his head towards him. Sandford saw the man begin to slide off the window-sill and his hand going inside his jacket. He shouted a warning, but, before Purdy could react, the man had pulled out a gun and fired point-blank at Purdy's chest.

Purdy fell, gasping. The man ran out of the door Sandford started after him and then, realizing he couldn't catch him, returned to see what he could do for Purdy A couple who had heard the shot came and helped while Sandford phoned Scotland Yard and Chelsea Police Station. The two senior detective officers from Chelsea, Superintendent David Hislop and Chief Inspector Robert Acott, arrived just in time to see Purdy die.

Then began the grimmest and most serious of all man-hunts: the hunt for an armed and ruthless criminal who had already murdered a policeman and had now vanished into the great maze of London. He had left us with only two clues, his palm-prints on the window-

The lobby has remained unchanged from when the police photographed it in 1959.

sill and his thumb-prints on the little black notebook. The contents of the notebook, which might have provided further clues, were so cryptic that they defied our powers of detection. Pages were headed with single words such as HORSES, TRAINS, LAUGHS, WATER, CRASHES. Under CRASHES came these four entries:

CAR: Paul Temple etc and suitable other crashes 1903

TRAIN: Good with steam 20B49

WOOD-SPLINTERING: 3B23/25

COW: 1B68

Sherlock Holmes or Lord Peter Wimsey would no doubt have solved the puzzle very quickly but it mystified my officers who consoled themselves with the thought that, even if they could decode it, they weren't likely to be helped much in their search for Purdy's murderer. The mystery wasn't, in fact, solved until much later when the ownership of the notebook was traced to a studio manager at Broadcasting House who had lost it in a burglary. The notes were references to items in the BBC's library of sound-effects.

Meanwhile we did at least know what the murderer looked like: aged about thirty; height—five foot nine or ten; clean-shaven; thin build; brown hair, crew-cut; American-style green-blue tinted sunglasses; soft-spoken, American or Canadian accent; light sports coat, light grey trousers, light brown suede shoes. Sergeant Sandford supplied all these details, and, for once, we could be quite sure that the description was accurate. It went out immediately on the teleprinter to all stations in the Metropolitan Police district, and then to all other police forces throughout the United Kingdom. Just two hours after the murder it was also put out on radio and television news bulletins.

Sergeant Sandford: 'The prisoner then ran between the hall door and Sergeant Purdy's falling body and out into the street. I went over to Sergeant Purdy, then straight out into the street after the man and chased him for a short distance down Cranley Place. Realising I couldn't catch him I returned to 105.' Mr. David Bruce, a 39-year-old stock-broker, said that he was in his flat on the ground floor when there was a bang and he heard running and shouting. He immediately went out and he saw a man on the floor apparently shot through the heart. 'I put a pillow under his head and did what I could for him but he died in about seven minutes.'

Sergeant Purdy fell here, obviously very seriously injured.

It didn't take long for newsmen to arrive on the scene, one of the doors clearly showing a bullet hole in the glass.

At that stage the public was very much on our side. Everyone wanted to help. Messages of sympathy and encouragement — as well as the usual crop of well-intentioned but false sightings — poured into Scotland Yard.

Naturally both the Commissioner and I were very concerned about the progress of the hunt. Both of us visited Chelsea Police Station, but we followed the cardinal principle of never interfering with the men on the job. I returned to my office to await further news.

The police worked late into the night. Hundreds of reports from the public were investigated, and at the same time a great comb-out was taking place through all the coverts of the underworld. Whispers began to come in, whispers about a man calling himself Mike Galento or Colato, who had recently appeared in Soho. He had come to England, the rumours said, for the first time in his life, but had quickly bought a gun and scraped acquaintance with some well-known rogues. His description fitted.

Superintendent Hislop and Chief Inspector Acott were piecing these hints together in the early hours of the following day, when they received another item of information. Hislop went to a hotel near West London Air Terminal and took possession of the register. What interested him was an entry dated May 21st. The signature, in a Continental script, appeared to be 'G. Jodola', the address was 'Montreal' The description given by the hotel staff matched 'Galento' and matched the man who killed Purdy.

An inquiry was radioed to the Royal Canadian Mounted Police. A few hours later, the reply came from Ottawa:

'Our records disclose person named Guenther Fritz Erwin Podola. We are forwarding airmail today fingerprints, criminal record and photograph.'

Podola, we learned, was a German citizen, who had been deported from Canada a year before. We therefore radioed to Interpol at Wiesbaden asking for Podola's fingerprints and photograph from their files.

Detective Superintendent David Hislop was put in charge of the investigation.

Fifty-odd years have gone by yet Onslow Square remains a timeless corner of Kensington.

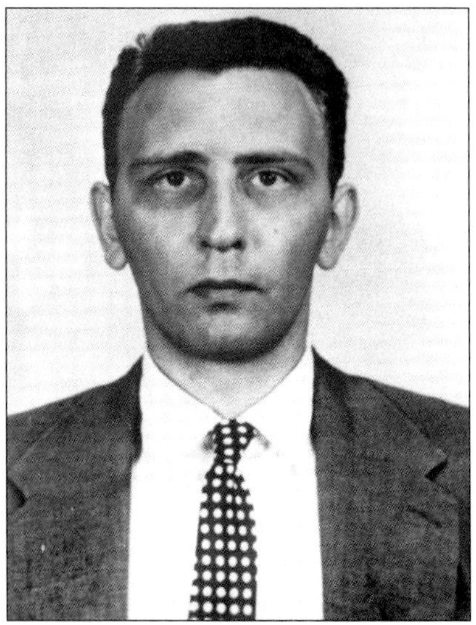

When Superintendent Hislop discovered that a possible suspect from Montreal had stayed at a hotel near the West London Air Terminal in Cromwell Road, the Royal Canadian Mounted Police were asked if they had any record on file for a 'G. Jodola'. They replied that this was probably a mis-spelling for 'G. Podola' and full details with fingerprint records and photographs were being flown to Britain. ***Left:*** **Here a detective meets the Trans-Canada Airlines station manager who is handing over the package.** ***Right:*** **This was the photo supplied by the Mounties of Guenther Podola.**

Now we knew whom we were looking for. He was born in Berlin in 1929, had emigrated to Canada in 1952, and had been deported in 1958 after serving a prison term for housebreaking and theft. He had gone back to Germany, then came here. We picked up his trail at London Airport. He had been directed to the nearby hotel, after ten days he had moved to a guest-house in the Cromwell Road, from which he had been ejected on June 23rd for not paying his rent. And there the trail ended until Sergeant Purdy saw him in the phone-box.

Before releasing Podola's photograph to the Press, Hislop showed it to Sergeant Sandford, together with photographs of eleven other men, and asked him which, if any, of these twelve had shot Purdy. Without a moment's hesitation Sandford pointed at Podola.

Around noon on the same day Acott heard that a man answering to Podola's description was staying at a hotel in Queensgate. A raiding party was assembled and given pistols. Acott and another senior officer from Chelsea, Inspector Vibart, entered the hotel first. They examined the register and found that a Canadian from Montreal had signed himself in as 'Paul Camay'. The writing was unmistakably Podola's. Acott showed Podola's picture to the manager's wife, and she identified him as 'Camay'. He was in Room 15, she said.

When police received information that a man fitting the description was staying at the Claremont House Hotel at 95 Queensgate (see map page 312), the detectives made discreet enquiries and found that a Canadian photographer, Paul Camay, was occupying Room 15 located on the top floor. ***Left:*** **The open window marks his room on the second floor.** ***Right:*** **No longer a hotel, the building is now split into separate rented rooms.**

While Vibart stood guard in the hotel, Acott went to fetch the others who were waiting nearby. They followed him back into the hotel at discreet intervals — Hislop first, unarmed, because, like many British policemen of the old school, he preferred, even then, not to carry a gun; Detective Sergeant Chambers and two others, all with pistols; and finally a dog-handler with a police dog called Flame.

At Hislop's request the hotel manager went upstairs to check that 'Camay' was still in Room 15 and reported that he was. The officers took up their positions round the door. Vibart handed his gun to one of the others and charged the door. It didn't give. He stepped back and shouted: 'Open. Police. Open this door.'

For about fifteen seconds there was silence. Then they heard a slight metallic click inside the room. It sounded like a gun being cocked. Sergeant Chambers hurled his sixteen-and-a-half stone against the door. This time it flew open. It hit Podola in the face and sent him staggering back across the room. Chambers hurtled in after him. Podola cannoned into a chair and finished up on the floor, face uppermost, with his head in the fireplace. Chambers fell on top of him.

The dog Flame was brought into the room, but kept under control near the window. Podola was struggling violently while Chambers held his arm down to stop him getting at a gun. The others crowded in, seized Podola's arms and furiously kicking legs, and he suddenly went limp. They searched him where he lay. He had no gun. The click they heard had been Podola unlocking the Yale lock on the door.

The manageress, Mrs Bridget Harding, pictured with detectives outside Room 15 on July 16. When Detective Sergeant Albert Chambers (left) charged the door, it flew open. 'There was no resistance from the door as it burst open,' said Chambers later. 'I caught a glimpse of Podola just as the door hit him in the face, and the force of it hitting him made him stagger back across the room. He went over the arm of a chair and he finished up lying on the floor face uppermost with his head in the fireplace. I let myself go forward and fell on top of him.'

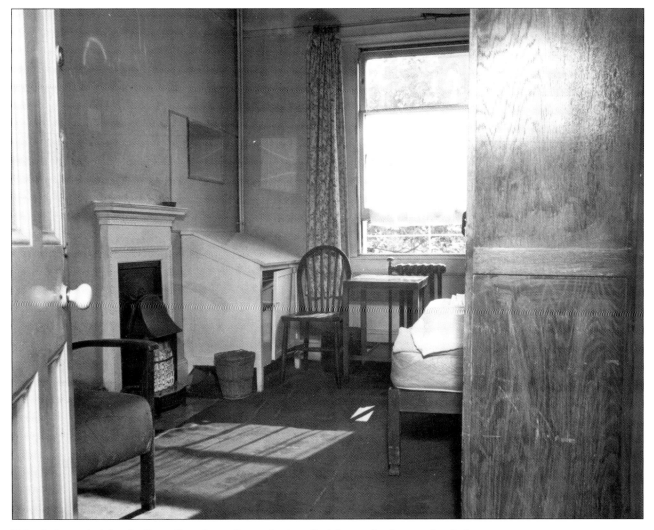

This photograph, taken by the police, shows the spot where Podola was finally apprehended.

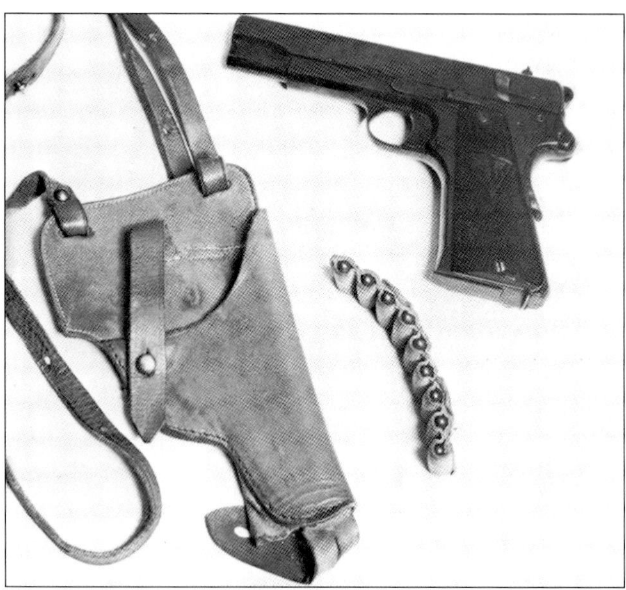

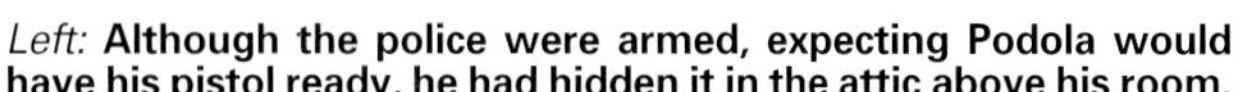
Left: **Although the police were armed, expecting Podola would have his pistol ready, he had hidden it in the attic above his room.**

Right: **The automatic, a 9mm Radom Viz, No. D8017, with 40 rounds, is now held in the Crime Museum at New Scotland Yard.**

They put Podola on the bed. He seemed to have been knocked out; he had a cut eye and blood was flowing down his face. They washed his wound and staunched the bleeding. A few minutes later he sat up, watching them with his right eye; his left eye was now completely closed. He drank several cups of water. In case he was shamming, they handcuffed his hands behind his back, and then let him stand up and walk round the room. From time to time he broke into violent shaking. When he seemed fit to be taken to the police station they helped him down the three flights of stairs to the ground floor

Summoned by some mysterious jungle telegraph, reporters, photographers, and sightseers had gathered outside. Since the only witness to the murder had already identified a photograph of Podola, the routine precaution was not strictly necessary, but routine is routine, and not lightly to be departed from, so Acott ordered Podola's head to be covered. Then he was put in a car and driven straight to Chelsea Police Station.

The Divisional police surgeon, Dr Shanahan, was summoned at once. He examined Podola carefully and found no injuries apart from an abrasion over the left eye, which he cleaned and dressed. Podola refused to talk and appeared to be in a state of collapse; he was suffering from a withdrawal syndrome, the doctor thought, and possibly recovering from concussion. Dr Shanahan ruled that Podola was not yet fit to be charged, but was fit to be detained at the police station.

Podola is brought down to the street where alert photographers were already on hand to picture the arrest.

The grapevine was quickly at work, the high-profile killing leading to sightseers congregating, both at the hotel on Queensgate . . .

. . . and at Chelsea Police Station off Sloane Avenue, where the injured Podola had been taken . . .

After the doctor had left at about 5.30 p.m. Podola was kept under continuous observation. He slept, or seemed to sleep, most of the time, but at one point he managed to smoke a cigarette and drink a cup of tea. His condition was still far from normal, however, and at 11.30 p.m. Dr Shanahan was summoned again. He made another examination, found that Podola was not recovering as he had expected, and recommended admission to hospital.

Podola was taken on a stretcher to St Stephen's, where he was examined by the Consultant Physician, Dr Philip Harvey, who suspected there might be a brain injury. Podola's skull was X-rayed, but showed no fracture. A lumbar puncture was performed. Dr Harvey decided that Podola had suffered concussion and some mild contusion of the brain, nothing worse. Three days later Podola was pronounced fit, taken back to Chelsea Police Station, and charged, in the presence of his solicitor, with the murder of Sergeant Purdy. He was then taken to West London Magistrates' Court, remanded in custody for a week, and driven to Brixton prison.

These are the simple facts of the arrest and detention of Guenther Fritz Podola. I am quite certain that they are as I have given them. All the officers concerned acted properly and with considerable courage. But, within a very short time, public anger against

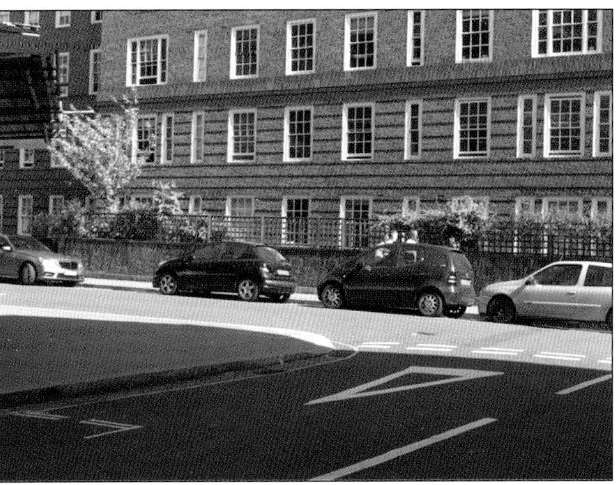

. . . and where officers were pictured carrying in his effects removed from room No. 15.

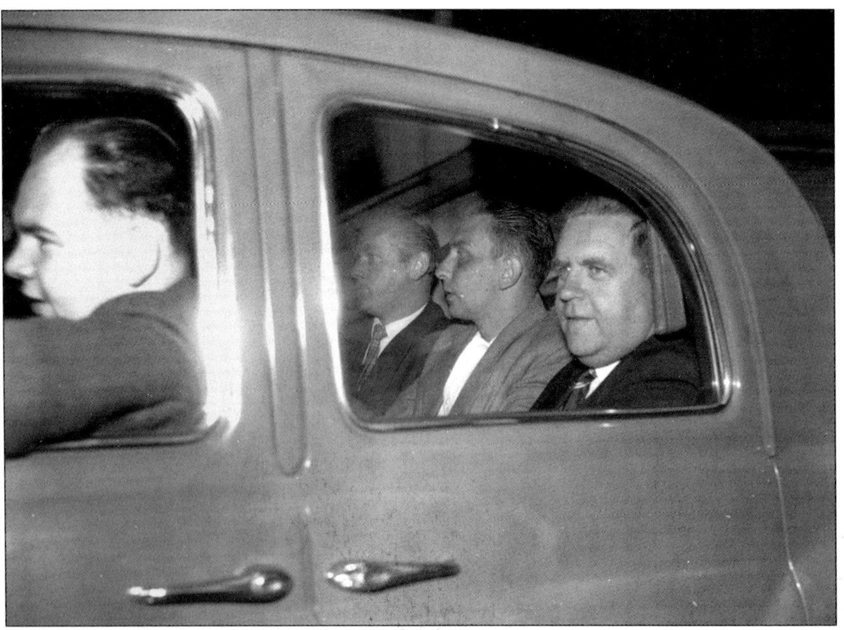

When Podola made his first court appearance at West London Magistrates' Court sporting a black eye and after a stay in hospital of four days (due to his mental health, not his physical injuries), people jumped to the conclusion that he had been beaten up by police. This aspect, plus the fact that Podola claimed loss of memory, led to much argument and debate as to whether he was fit to plead.

Purdy's murderer had been converted into an extraordinary storm against the police. This change was precipitated by accounts of the affair which appeared in certain newspapers. One, for example, told how 'police dog Flame was slipped into Room 15 and, snarling, went like an arrow for the man on the bed. The powerful brindle Alsatian caught him on the cheek.' Another described the dog as going for Podola's arm. Both versions were wholly fictitious; the dog never went near Podola. Such inaccuracies were harmless enough, however, compared with the other tales which began to spread. These tales would not have been believed if a lot of people hadn't wanted to believe them, nor would they have spread if some people hadn't wanted to propagate them.

On July 20th Mr R. T. Paget, Labour Member of Parliament for Northampton, asked a question of the Home Secretary, Mr R. A. Butler: 'What happened to Guenther Podola during the six hours at Chelsea Police Station which necessitated his removal to hospital on a stretcher?' Mr Butler replied that Podola had been allowed to leave hospital, and that as he was being charged with murder it wouldn't be proper to say more.

'I am not concerned about the charge against Guenther Podola,' said Mr Paget. 'I am concerned about the people who beat him unconscious. Have charges been preferred against them?'

Later in this exchange, Mr Paget said, 'I gather from the Home Secretary that no charge has been brought as to an attack on Mr Podola, in which, according to some accounts, he received injuries to his skull and jaw. Surely the attack on him when in police custody cannot possibly have any bearing on whether or not he committed a murder previously.' He added that people should be safe in British police stations, and the idea that either vengeance or beatings up should occur there was utterly unacceptable.

Hard-pressed, Mr Butler finally said, 'I am absolutely satisfied that this man was not beaten up in the police station.' This ambiguous reply failed to allay the anger and suspicion which had been aroused by the Home Secretary's earlier answers.

Inevitably, the rumours about what the police had done to Podola proliferated; one version said that every police officer in the station had been invited to hit Podola once. The messages of sympathy we had received after the murder were replaced by a torrent of angry letters. A thick file of them was brought to me each morning, but in the end I simply gave up reading them. Voluble members of the lunatic fringe write to the police about every sensational crime; the letters about Podola were all the more sad and irritating because quite a lot of them came from ordinary citizens who were filled with righteous anger about what they thought had happened. Some people, of course, took a different view. They said that the police were fully justified in beating Podola up; he deserved it. The police forces of other countries with which I was in touch couldn't understand what the fuss was about. They thought Podola was lucky not to have been shot. All in vain did I insist that Podola had not only not been shot, he hadn't been beaten up either; nothing had happened in Chelsea Police Station. Everyone was quite sure it had.

Podola's trial took place in September, about five months after Marwood's [*see page 306*]. Interest really centred on the preliminary issue of whether he was fit to plead. His counsel, F. H. Lawton, Q.C., maintained that Podola had no memory of anything which occurred before July 17th, the day after his arrest. 'In all fairness,' Lawton added, 'I should state specifically that there is no evidence of any kind that any violence was done to Podola at Chelsea Police Station. Indeed, such evidence as exists points the other way. His shock is the shock of his arrest and the circumstances of it.'

The prosecution replied that Podola's amnesia was a fake. Nine doctors were called to give evidence on one side or the other. Dr Shanahan said that Podola had shown 'a withdrawal reaction', and agreed that there had been no physical injury except the cut above his eye and the swelling round it, and no additional marks in the evening which hadn't been there in the afternoon. Dr Harvey recalled his diagnosis of concussion and mild contusion of the brain. Dr Colin Edwards, a neurologist who had examined Podola while he was on remand in Brixton, disagreed about the concussion and said he thought Podola's amnesia was hysterical and of purely psychological origin. Another neurologist, Dr Michael Ashby, took much the same view.

The jury decided that Podola was not suffering from genuine loss of memory and was fit to stand trial.

The trial at the Old Bailey attracted a large crowd, seen here queuing to gain entry to the public gallery on September 10. The defence submitted that Podola was suffering from amnesia and so could not be tried, and lengthy pre-trial arguments — the first in British legal history — continued until September 22 when it was decided Podola should stand trial. Two days later the jury only required a recess for 30 minutes to find him guilty as charged.

Efforts to obtain a reprieve included claims that Podola had a double and/or another policeman had shot Purdy. *Left:* All this was to no avail and the usual large crowd gathered outside the front entrance to Wandsworth prison on November 5 when Podola was executed by Harry Allen assisted by Royston Rickard. *Right:* In the late 1970s, a wall was built in front of the main gate to the height of the main prison wall but this was reduced to its current level in 2007.

The trial itself was much shorter than the hearing of this preliminary issue. On September 24th Podola was found guilty and sentenced to death. After the rejection of his appeal, three weeks later, he suddenly recovered his memory and tried to establish an alibi. He now said that at the time of the murder he had been breaking into a flat in Sloane Avenue. The police duly investigated and found that the flat had indeed been broken into on the day of the murder and that the thief had not been caught. The address of the flat, written in Podola's hand, appeared in the black notebook, so Podola probably was the housebreaker but, as he could have entered at any time between 8.30 a.m. and 2.30 p.m., this hardly constituted an alibi.

Podola now remembered something else. He had a double named Bob Lavine, he said, whom he'd known both in Canada and in Germany. They were alike as two peas. He and Bob had arranged to meet at 105 Onslow Square, the place where Sergeant Purdy was killed. Podola hadn't kept the rendezvous, but his prints were there because they had previously cased the joint together. Dutifully we asked the Canadian and German police if they could find any record or trace of Bob Lavine. They found none. Podola was hanged.

Of course policemen do sometimes behave with less than perfect propriety. Dealing with violent men, they are sometimes rough. The party which went to arrest Podola was no doubt nervous, as, indeed, they had every reason to be, and might well not have been gentle in taking him. But the story about his being beaten up in the police station was intrinsically implausible. They wanted Podola hanged, not beaten up. Their instinct would have been to behave towards him with scrupulous correctness, careful to give the defence no excuse for distracting attention from Podola's crime by attacking them.

Most people, I am sure, still think of Podola as the man who was beaten up at Chelsea Police Station, and will continue to do so as long as his name is remembered at all. The truth of the matter can only run limping and panting behind.

Sir Richard Jackson, Assistant Commissioner CID, New Scotland Yard, Occupied with Crime

All this time people lost sight of the fact that an officer of the law had been shot down in cold blood. On Tuesday, July 21, Sergeant Purdy's funeral took place at St Matthew's Church, Surbiton, Surrey, with Detective Sergeant Sandford (left front) the leading pallbearer. A thousand policemen lined the route on the mile-long procession with Mrs Irene Purdy and her son Alan following the coffin.

Ray Purdy had joined the force in 1939 and became a detective in 1947, being promoted to sergeant in 1955. His grave (XXIX 7294) lies in Surbiton Cemetery.

Metropolitan Police Statement of Witness, June 3, 1961: 'I am married to John Hall *(left)* and was married on 1st April, 1961, at the Methodist Church, Forest Gate, E.7. After our honeymoon we went to live at 88 Balfour Road, Ilford, in two furnished rooms. We have lived there about six weeks, and he worked for Wells of Manor Park. Since our marriage we have had differences but nothing serious. He did not go to work last Thursday and Friday and at about 3 p.m., we had a row and he hit me with his fists. I decided to go home to Mother, and after he had left the house I went to my Mother's at 35 Tavistock Road *(right)* where I waited for them to come home. About 7 p.m., my Mother and sister came home and I told them what had happened. About 15 minutes later the 'phone rang, my sister answered it. Shortly after there was a knock on the door, and Mother and Eileen answered it. I heard a fight in the hall and went up there and saw my husband struggling with them. He was hitting them with his fists. My sister went to 'phone Police.'

June 3, 1961 – Police murders at West Ham

Shortly after 1 p.m., on Saturday, 3rd June, 1961, John Hall, age 30, of no fixed abode, escaped from West Ham Police Station whilst being detained on charges of causing grievous bodily harm to his wife, her mother and his sister-in-law.

The escape was effected by Hall producing a Walther automatic pistol, directing it at C.I.D. officers, and leaving the Police Station by the main entrance.

An immediate hue and cry was raised and several Police Officers chased Hall across the Recreation Grounds, opposite the Police Station, in West Ham Lane.

Hall finally made his escape but before doing so shot and fatally wounded Inspector 'K'/129523 Philip Pawsey Wt. and Police Sergeant 80 'K'/122805 Frederick George Hutchins. Police Constable 607 'K'/132059 Charles Edward Cox was also shot, but fortunately his injuries, although serious, did not prove fatal. Another officer, Police Constable 168 'K'/139637 Leslie Charles England was also fired upon by Hall, but the bullet missed and the officer was unhurt.

The circumstances under which these officers were shot prove they were doing their duty with the full knowledge of the danger they were facing. They were not deterred, however, and their actions are therefore brought to notice for the highest possible recognition.

This tragic affair arose out of a domestic dispute between John Hall and his wife, Sylvia. In her statement Mrs. Sylvia June Hall, age 22, now residing with her parents at 35 Tavistock Road, West Ham, E.15, states she was married to John Hall on 1st April, 1961, and lived with him in furnished rooms at 88 Balfour Road, Ilford. On 2nd June, 1961 (the day before the shootings) the couple quarrelled and Hall struck his wife with his fists.

As a result of this assault Mrs. Hall decided to leave her husband and return to her parents. Shortly after 7 p.m., that evening Hall arrived at the address, apparently with a view to collecting his wife. When he found he was being thwarted he went berserk with a chair, causing extensive injuries to his wife, her mother and the sister-in-law, all of whom were taken to hospital with wounds necessitating many sutures. Although not mentioned in this statement, Mrs. Hall reported that the first beating she received from her husband was whilst honeymooning in Spain immediately after they were married.

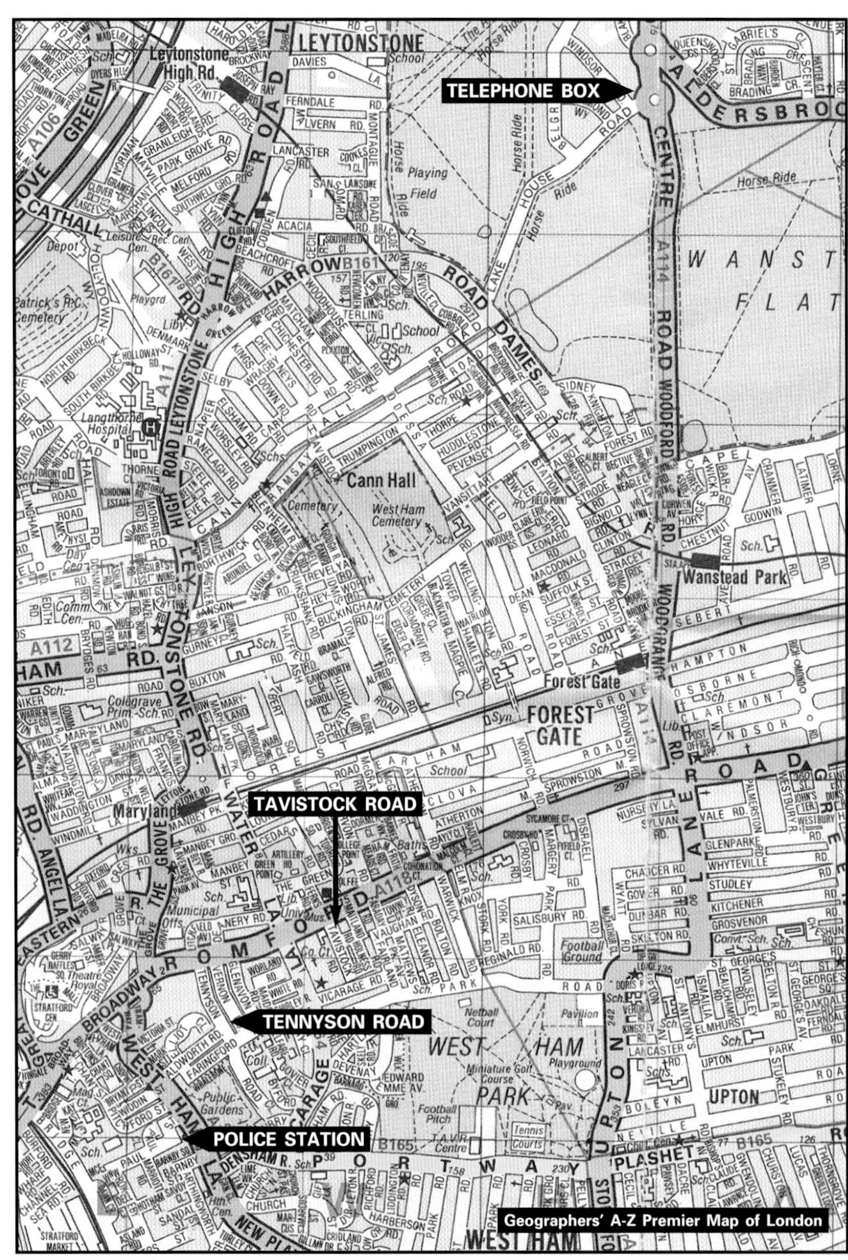

Police photographs taken on July 3 of West Ham Lane looking north-west with the station on the left. After pulling out a Walther, John Hall ran out of the front door and across the road into the recreation ground.

Statements by Mrs. Agnes Alice Roberts, age 57, mother of Mrs. Hall and Eileen Constance Roberts, age 20, a sister. These witnesses merely support the story of the attack made upon them and indicate the savage brutality of John Hall.

A further indication of Hall's mentality is given in a statement made by Mrs. Joy Hall, of 817 Romford Road, Manor Park, E12, the former wife of John Hall, who obtained a Decree Absolute against him on 21st March 1961.

This lady describes how she was visited on the evening of 2nd June 1961, by Hall after the assaults. There is no doubt Hall was extremely scared of the consequences and expected his ex-wife to smooth matters over as she has undoubtedly done on numerous occasions in the past.

Apparently Joy Hall did her best in this direction, but without success. Hall, at this time, had two pistols in his possession and said repeatedly he would not be taken.

Mrs. Joy Hall again saw Hall on the morning of 3rd June, 1961, when he said he was going to the Police Station. Before he left he was asked by her if he had any guns and he assured her he had not.

On the evening of 2nd June 1961, the allegations of bodily harm were made at West Ham Police Station and the injured persons were interviewed by Detective Sergeant Russell Lewis of that Station.

At about 12.05 p.m. Saturday, 3rd June, 1961, Detective Inspector George Jones received a telephone call at West Ham Station and spoke to a man who announced himself as John Hall. The caller was asked to come to the Station. At about 12.45 p.m. Hall arrived and was seen by Detective Inspector Jones in the Charge Room, adjoining the main entrance of the Station.

Whilst talking to Inspector Jones, Detective Sergeant Lewis entered and was introduced. Hall then accompanied both officers upstairs to the C.I.D. office, where he was told he would be detained, and was asked to empty his pockets.

At this stage Hall was perfectly rational, and seemed genuinely upset over the injuries he had inflicted upon his wife.

From his left-hand trouser pocket Hall produced six bullets and placed them on the desk. He then produced an automatic pistol from his right-hand trouser pocket and covered both officers, saying 'You're not keeping me here'. Hall then backed out of the C.I.D. office and ran down the stairs into the Charge Room and a hue and cry was raised.

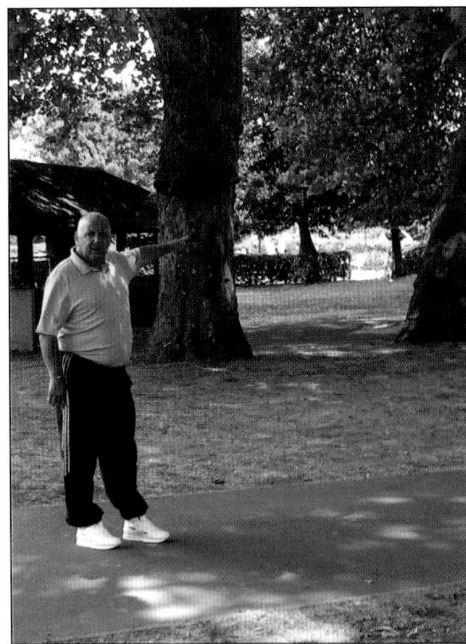

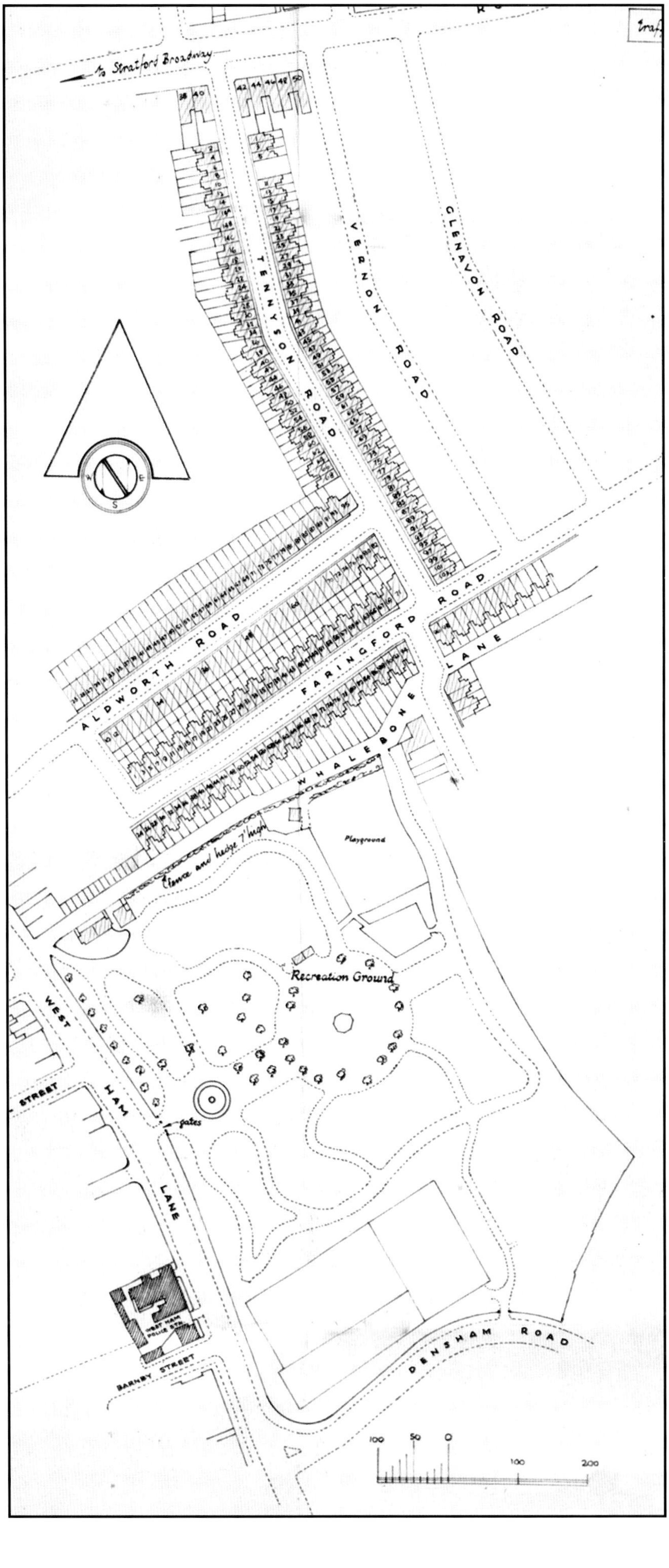

As Hall ran across the recreation ground, 10-year-old Barry Noakes was playing on the putting green. In June 2011, exactly 50 years later, we took him back to the park. Barry saying that he thought the man had a Luger.

Detective Inspector Jones followed other officers out of the Station across West Ham Lane into the park opposite the Police Station. He saw Hall climb over a chestnut paling, fence, closely followed by P.C. Cox into Whalebone Lane.

As Detective Inspector Jones was leaving through nearby exit gates he heard two shots and on entering Tennyson Road, saw Sergeant Hutchins and P.C. Cox lying on the footway, both obviously injured.

Hall was 150 yards down the road, being closely followed by P.C. England on his light-weight motorcycle. After getting a lift in a motor van, Inspector Jones again saw Hall walking towards him in Deanery Road. The wanted man was reloading the firearm with bullets from his pocket. On seeing the Inspector, Hall scaled a low wall at the rear of some houses and disappeared.

Detective Sergeant Russell Lewis supports the story told by Inspector Jones and also describes finding the police car containing Inspector Pawsey in Tennyson Road near Romford Road. He saw the Inspector was seriously hurt and summoned assistance on the car's radio.

Police Constable Cox 607'K' is still detained in Hospital suffering from a bullet wound in the lower abdomen. There is now every hope of a complete recovery.

On 3rd June, 1961, at about 1 p.m. P.C. Cox was in the passageway from the Charge Room to the Canteen, and was in uniform. He saw a man run down the stairs from the C.I.D. office and heard shouts of 'Stop that man!' As Hall reached the main entrance of the Station he turned and pointed a gun at P.C. Cox and P.C. England, then ran across the road into the park. As Hall scaled the fence on the other side of the Park, P.C. Cox was joined by Police Sergeant Hutchins, who was in plain clothes. After losing sight of Hall for about a minute he was seen walking towards Tennyson Road and Sergeant Hutchins said 'That's him' and both officers ran towards him. Sergeant Hutchins reached the wanted man first and jumped on his back. Hall, who was a powerful man over 6 ft tall, threw the Sergeant off and fired one shot at point-blank range. Sergeant Hutchins said 'He's shot me' and with that Hall, who was facing P.C. Cox walking away backwards, fired at the officer from a range of about 3 feet. Both officers collapsed and P.C. Cox remembers very little of what happened.

Whalebone Lane today looking towards West Ham Lane. Hall ran out of the park on the left towards the camera position, leading into the southern end of Tennyson Road, chased at this stage by a posse of policemen.

Police Constable 168'K' Leslie Charles England was on duty in uniform at West Ham Station at about 1 p.m. on 3rd June, 1961. He was performing duty on a lightweight motorcycle, had just entered the Station and was talking to P.C. Cox and another officer in the passage leading to the Canteen and Charge Room. This officer heard a banging from upstairs but paid little attention to it until he heard shouts of 'Stop him!'. He then saw Hall descend the stairs and as the other officers approached, Hall pointed a gun at them and they wisely stopped where they were. As soon as Hall left the Station by the main entrance the officers followed and P.C. England saw him cross the road and enter the park. Whilst other officers followed the escapee, P.C. England returned to the Station and collected his motorcycle.

He then drove through the Park and several officers were able to direct him as to the direction taken by Hall. P.C. England drove into Whalebone Lane from the park, spoke to P.C. Cox and then drove down Farringford Road and saw Hall arrive at the junction of Farringford Road and Tennyson Road. He states he saw the man tackled by Sergeant Hutchins and P.C. Cox and saw him shoot both officers who fell to the ground. Hall then ran down Tennyson Road in the direction of Romford Road. P.C. England went to the two injured officers and Sergeant Hutchins said 'Get him Les, he's got us'. After shouting to bystanders to call an ambulance, P.C. England set off on his machine after Hall. When he got to within 20 feet of Hall the latter turned and fired a shot at the officer, which fortunately missed.

Roy Norcott, aged 13 (nearest the camera), and 11-year-old Keith Pearman point in the direction in Tennyson Road where Sergeant Frederick Hutchins *(below left)* was mortally wounded and Police Constable Charles Cox was shot. This Press Association photo was taken later in the day after Hall had made his escape.

Right: **This photo from the police file shows the car, in which Inspector Philip Pawsey *(above)* arrived, still standing beside the spot where he was shot dead.**

As Hall almost reached the main Romford Road, Inspector Pawsey arrived in a police car. P.C. England saw the car turn into Tennyson Road. The officer signalled to the Inspector to keep away, but the car stopped alongside Hall and Inspector Pawsey opened the driving door. P.C. England saw Hall point the weapon at the Inspector, who immediately closed the door. The door then opened again and Inspector Pawsey was about to get out of the car when Hall shot him again at point-blank range. The wanted man then ran off into Romford Road.

P.C. England went to the car and Inspector Pawsey said something to the effect of 'Get after him' and appeared to reach over to the radio set. The P.C. did not realise the Inspector was fatally injured and left him to follow Hall. It was then believed that the escapee had boarded a lorry and the officer followed it and caused it to be stopped when nearing Ilford only to find he was not on board.

Mrs. Doris May Bethell age 37, of 71 Farringford Road, West Ham, E.15, a greengrocer, witnessed the shooting of Sergeant Hutchins and P.C. Cox. At least she saw him shoot Sergeant Hutchins and as she turned to run into her shop to call Police she heard the second shot which felled P.C. Cox.

The shooting of these two officers was also witnessed by Mrs. Winifred Norcott, age 47, of 91 Tennyson Road, West Ham, E.15, a housewife, who saw Hall shoot the two officers then fire upon the officer on the motorcycle, P.C. England.

A Mr. Colin Frederick Addis, age 17, of 36 Burrard Road, Custom House, E.16, saw Hall being chased by Police Officers and as they just about caught up with him, he heard two shots and on looking round again saw a uniformed officer and one in plain clothes lying together on the footway. He saw Hall point the gun at the two officers as they were on the ground. Mr. Addis then rode his motor scooter to Queen Mary's Hospital and escorted a doctor back to the scene.

Mrs. Florence Beatrice Smith, age 61, of 13 Caister Park Road, Stratford, E.15, was sitting in a parked car in Tennyson Road at about 1.30 p.m. on 3rd June 1961.

She saw a large black car turn in from Romford Road and after travelling a few yards in Tennyson Road stop dead. Mrs. Smith saw the driver start to get out of the car and at the same time saw a man running along Tennyson Road towards Romford Road. As this man passed the car she saw he had a gun in his hand and at about two yards from the car he turned and fired deliberately at the driver.

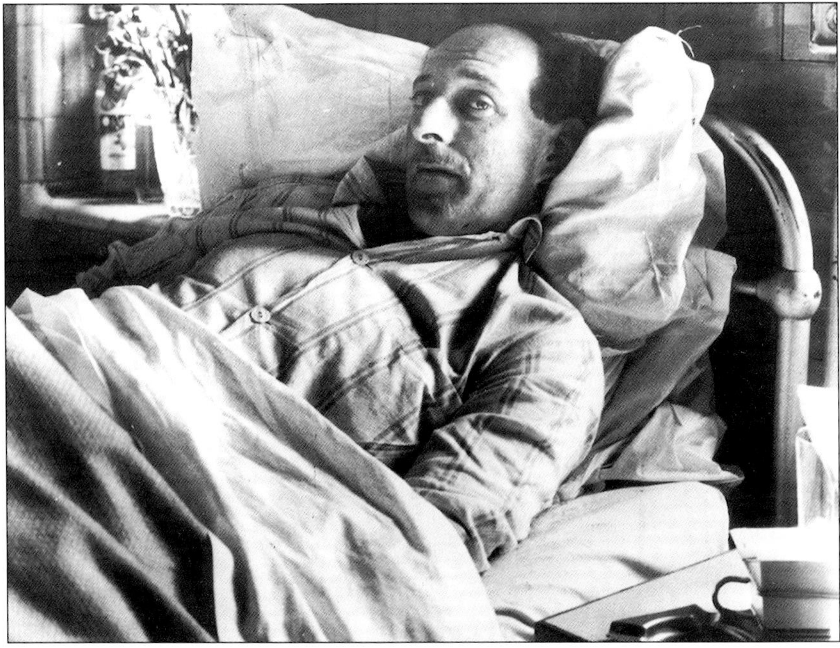

Police Constable Cox was taken to Queen Mary's Hospital in West Ham Lane suffering from a bullet wound in his lower abdomen. He was awarded the George Medal and retired from the force in December 1977.

As Hall disappeared towards Romford Road, a massive manhunt was put into operation and the photograph of him (reproduced on page 322) was distributed to the Press and broadcast by the BBC and the first ITV station for the London area, Associated Rediffusion. Then, inexplicably, at 8.30 p.m. that Saturday evening, Hall telephoned the *Sunday Express*. Ernest Sullivan took the call in the news room and heard the caller say: 'I am the killer. I am the man who killed a policeman.' Sullivan kept the man talking and persuaded him to give him the telephone number of the kiosk from where he was speaking: WANstead 4199. A colleague listening in immediately passed the information to Scotland Yard and within 14 minutes of Hall beginning the call, police had traced the location to this box on the northern side of Wanstead flats and cars converged on Lakehouse Road. As officers closed in, Hall shot himself using the same Walther pistol (No. 3571) which he had used earlier. He was taken to Queen Mary's Hospital where he lingered for a week.

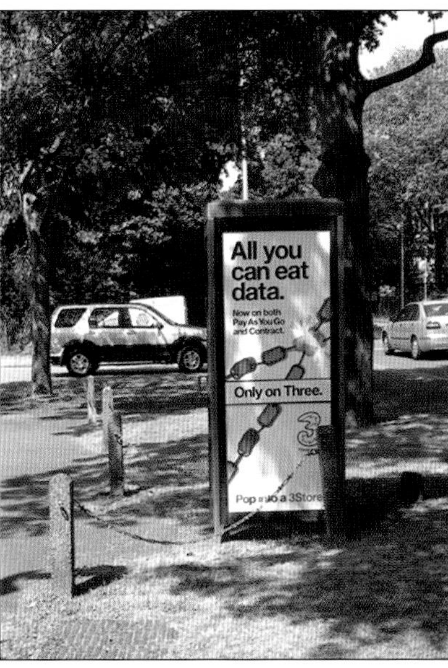

Statements were given by Dr. John George Fagler, Casualty Registrar, and Dr. David John Burne, Senior House Surgeon, both of Queen Mary's Hospital, Stratford, E.15, who attended the injured Police Officers on their arrival at hospital and certified life extinct in the case of Inspector Pawsey.

As will be seen, Inspector Pawsey was dead on arrival and Sergeant Hutchins 'died' shortly after admission. After heart massage was applied and artificial respiration with oxygen, Sergeant Hutchins was brought back to life, but after two hours hard work by the doctors, they were unable to maintain the improvement and he died at 4.30 p.m.

Dr Alan Grant, Pathologist of Guy's Hospital, performed post mortem examinations on Inspector Pawsey and Sergeant Hutchins.

After identity of the killer had been firmly established, photographs of him were copied at C.O.C.3. Department and passed to the Press Bureau, with the result that many evening newspapers and television authorities, published the picture and name of John Hall, and all provincial forces and sea and air ports were informed. Observation was kept on all places and persons with whom it was thought he might visit or contact.

At about 8.30 p.m. that evening Hall telephoned the offices of the *Sunday Express* and spoke to Mr. Ernest Horatio Nelson Sullivan, a journalist, who was on duty at the news desk.

As a result of the conversation the telephone kiosk was located at Lakehouse Road, Wanstead, and police were informed. Within a matter of minutes all available wireless cars on 'K' and 'J' Divisions converged upon the kiosk and surrounded it. A few of the officers were armed and Hall was trapped in the kiosk and knew it.

He then shot himself through the chest and was taken by ambulance to Whipps Cross Hospital where a kidney and his spleen were removed. He died a week later owing to the failure of the remaining kidney.

On the morning he died, Hall insisted on talking to Detective Jones, the officer at his bedside. This officer recorded the conversation which is similar to that which passed between Hall and the *Sunday Express* reporter Mr. Sullivan.

Detective Superintendent
E. Williams, 'K' Division, June 30, 1961

On Friday, June 9, the day before Hall died, the funeral of Inspector Philip Pawsey and Sergeant Frederick Hutchins was held at the nearby City of London Cemetery. Both officers were cremated and their ashes scattered in the Garden of Remembrance. They were posthumously awarded the Queen's Police Medal for Gallantry, PC Leslie England receiving the British Empire Medal.

The following week, a low-key memorial service was held for John Hall in Forest Gate Methodist Church where he and Sylvia Roberts had been married nine weeks before. Sylvia placed her wedding dress in his coffin before it was taken to the City of London Cemetery for cremation. His ashes were also scattered in the same memorial garden.

The murder of Michael Gregsten, and the rape and wounding of his mistress, Valerie Storie, is one of those crimes which — even 50 years later — still has so many unanswered questions. It all began here at the Traffic and Accident Division of the Road Research Laboratory on the Bath Road (the A4) at Langley, Buckinghamshire. In its varied history, Langley Hall had been a boys' school, an actors' orphanage, and, during the Second World War, the headquarters for No. 26 Group (which controlled an assortment of RAF units) before it was taken over by the Ministry of Transport in 1955. Buckinghamshire County Council purchased it in a derelict state in 1970 for incorporation into the campus of East Berkshire College.

August 22, 1961 – Rape and Murder on the A6

Hanratty. For over forty years his name has been associated with murder, not only because of the crime he allegedly committed, but also the relentless campaign to prove his innocence, and that his conviction was a miscarriage of justice. Which is ironic as the name derives from the Irish meaning 'descendant of the lawyer'.

The crimes were brutal: the death of an innocent man and a woman raped and shot five times and left for dead at the roadside. It was never going to be an easy case for the police to crack but crack it they did, in terms of arrest and conviction of the alleged killer. However this case does not reflect well on the police — even if they got the right man — because the case against Hanratty was built on an amazing coincidence, and a few others besides.

These crimes followed a series of events that began in Buckinghamshire, traversed other regions and ended up in Bedfordshire. So it was the Bedfordshire Constabulary which had responsibility, at first, for the investigation. In those days, however, when a murder was committed in the provinces, it was normal to call in 'the Yard', which had greater expertise and resources, not necessarily because they were better detectives.

Events began on a summer's evening, Tuesday, August 22, 1961 at Taplow, a small village in south Buckinghamshire. Michael Gregsten, 36, who lived with his wife and two sons at Abbots Langley, near Watford, was having an affair with Valerie Storie, 22. They had met in the canteen of the Road Research Laboratory at Langley, near Slough, where they both worked and had been seeing one another for some time. It had been a typical day: Gregsten had taken his sons to play in Cassiobury Park, Watford, and after taking them home he told his wife, Janet, who was aware of the relationship, that he was off to see Valerie.

Gregsten had the use of his aunt's grey Morris Minor, registration 847 BHN. He and Storie went to their regular haunt, the Old Station Inn at Taplow, leaving after nine o'clock. They then drove to Dorney Reach and parked in a cornfield overlooking the Thames. It was dusk. As they sat talking a man tapped on the driver's window and when Gregsten wound it down he said: 'This is a hold-up. I am a desperate man.' The individual then got into the back seat, behind Gregsten, and pointed a gun, which he said was loaded, at his head. The man wore a handkerchief around the bottom half of his face.

Michael Gregsten *(left)* was born in December 1924 and served from 1943-46 as an RAF navigator. He joined the civil service in 1949 being transferred to the laboratory as a research assistant in 1956. He was living with his wife Janet at Abbots Langley which was some 20 miles from his place of work. He was attracted to Valerie Storie *(right)*, some 14 years his junior, who also worked there, both having a mutual interest in car rallies. Janet Gregsten knew about their affair but would appear to have been tolerant of the liaison which, depending on which of the women one believes, had been going on from one to four years. With the Gregsten's marriage already falling apart due to earlier affairs, we are informed that he was also suffering from mental health problems exacerbated by him being in financial difficulties so much so that he had to sell his car. Temporarily he was using a Morris Minor belonging to his aunt. Valerie had lodgings in Slough and Michael had planned to move to Maidenhead on August 27, 1961.

In August 1961, Gregsten took his family on holiday to Devon, returning on Saturday the 19th. Spending the Sunday with Valerie, he was due back at work on the following Wednesday. On Tuesday (22nd) he left Abbots Langley to pick up Valerie from work, driving to the Old Station Inn *(left)* for a drink. *Right:* Formerly located here on the A4 just across the railway line at Taplow, the pub closed in 1997 and was demolished three years later. Today this car dealership stands on the site.

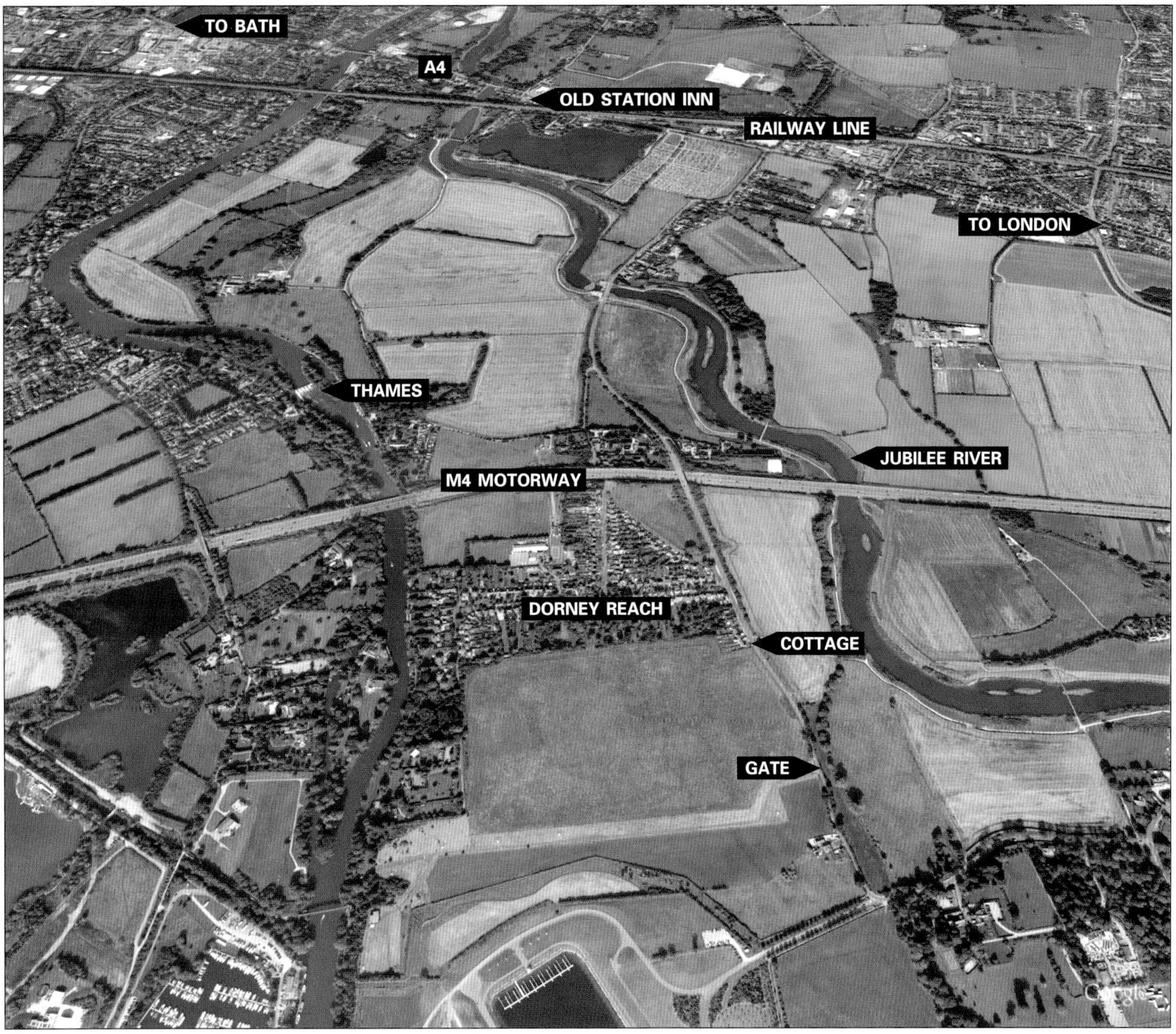

Michael and Valerie had a regular courting spot in a field which bordered the River Thames, a mile and a half from the Old Station Inn. The landlady later told police that the couple left the pub around 9.30 p.m. which in August would have meant that it was just getting dark. This oblique from 2011 also shows the man-made Jubilee River which was constructed in the late 1990s to alleviate flooding in the towns of Maidenhead, Windsor and Eton. The end of the rowing course, specially dug for Eton College, can be seen at the bottom of the photograph.

That evening 19-year-old David Henderson left his girlfriend's home around 9.45 p.m. to travel home on his motorbike and, passing Dorney Reach, he spotted a car parked in this field: 'It was definitely a Morris, a Morris 1000 I think. It was facing into the field and about eight yards from the road. It was dark and I had the headlights of my motor-cycle on. I can only say that the car was a lightish colour. There was a light on inside the car, I think it was a fitted interior light. I could not see into the car because the rear window was misted. I did not think anything unusual and continued on my way home.'

The man robbed the couple of their watches and made Gregsten hand over his wallet, which contained £3, and Storie her purse which had contained £7 although she had sneaked the notes into her bra without the man noticing. There was much conversation between the parties until finally the man said he wanted something to eat. He told Gregsten to start driving.

Valerie Storie later explained that they usually parked just inside the gate, and that while they were talking a man — who they presumed was the farmer — tapped on the driver's window. Gregsten wound it down whereupon a masked stranger poked the barrel of a revolver through, exclaiming: 'This is a hold-up. I am a desperate man.' Having taken the ignition key, he then got in the back of the car instructing them to 'keep facing the front and don't turn around. This is a real gun and I haven't had it very long. It's like a cowboy gun, I feel like a cowboy,' and they could see that he actually had an outlaw-style handkerchief covering the lower part of his face. After a while the gunman told Gregsten to drive further into the field and then swing round facing the gate. Valerie said that 'when he got in the back of the car we had some conversation. He said he had been living rough for two days and had been woken up the previous morning wet through because it had been raining, but I wondered how he had got himself so clean and tidy. One would never believe he had been sleeping out in the open the previous night for as far as we could see he was immaculately dressed with clean shoes.' Today, although old wooden gateposts still stand, Thames Water have installed a new security fence to the Dorney pumping station, but Michael Collins found that the house (circled) on the far side still remains as a reference point. No explanation has ever been given as to how the man had reached the field as it was a fair walking distance from the nearest public transport. No parked car was found yet the police refused to consider the possibility that he could have been dropped there by an accomplice.

One can imagine the scene: the three of them in the little Morris Minor on quiet roads as they were then, driving through the night. They went through Slough, called for petrol near Heathrow airport, then continued through Greenford, Harrow, Watford and St Albans. At one point Gregsten flashed his reversing lights to try and attract attention. This caused a car to pull up alongside, the occupants making gestures towards the rear, whereupon Gregsten and the man (presumably now minus his mask) got out to check the rear lights. Valerie Storie could have fled but would not leave her lover to the mercy of the gunman.

Eventually, they drove up the A6 into Bedfordshire. At Deadman's Hill, south of Bedford, the man told Gregsten to pull off into a layby and turn off the lights. It was well after midnight. The man said he wanted to 'kip' (a word that would feature later when Hanratty was interviewed by police) so he decided to tie up his captives. There was a duffel bag by Storie's feet so the man told Gregsten to give it to him, possibly hoping to find something suitable. Gregsten picked it up and thrust it over his shoulder towards the man, too forcefully perhaps, for the man then shot Gregsten twice through the head. 'He moved too quick,' he said. The murderer then sat there for twenty minutes with Gregsten lying dead in the driving seat next to Valerie.

A little later the man asked Storie to kiss him. She refused but he forced her at gunpoint into the back of the car where she succumbed to sexual intercourse, which in these circumstances amounted to rape. Later still she was made to help the man drag Gregsten's body from the vehicle, after which he asked her how to start the car and to show him how it worked. He then fired at her several times, reloading his pistol between shots, before driving off leaving her for dead.

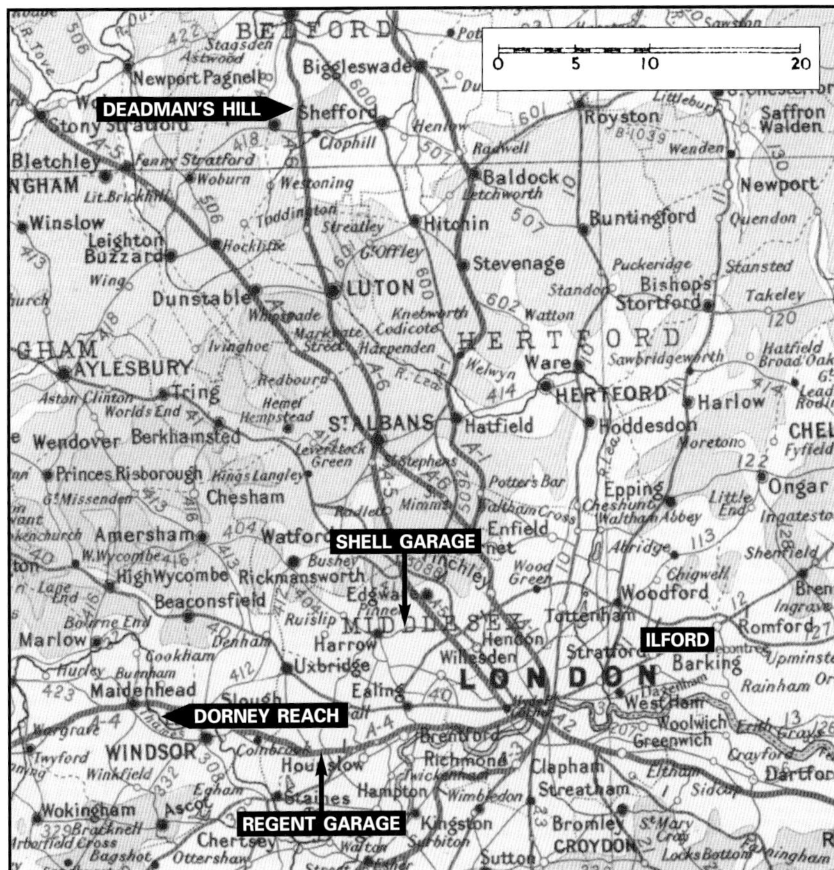

The map shows the road network prior to the introduction of motorways, the distance to Deadman's Hill being at least 60 miles.

Some time after 10.30 p.m. the lights were turned out in the cottage beside the field (see aerial photo page 329) and they heard the occupier putting his bicycle away in his shed. The man then expressed a desire to get something to eat and wanted to put Gregsten in the boot while they returned to the field. Valerie said that because there was a crack in the exhaust, this would be dangerous so the man ordered Gregsten to take the wheel and drive up to the A4 at which point he told him to turn right to Slough. Passing through the high street, the clock on the post office showed 11.45 p.m. Valerie Storie: 'He asked us how much petrol there was. There were a couple of gallons in the car and Mike said there was only one gallon, mainly to sort of say we can't go far, and he said, "How far will it go?" I said about thirty miles. In fact, it was going about forty to the gallon but he wasn't to know that, and he said, "Well, we'd better get some petrol then." We went through Slough, we stopped opposite Neville and Griffins and we said, "Let's get some milk if you want something," but we discovered that none of us had got any sixpences and we said, "Shall we go and ask?" thinking that we could get an opportunity of doing something. He replied: "No, it doesn't matter, I know a cafe near Northolt airport." I think he said "On Western Avenue." Just past London airport, on the left-hand side there is a Regent garage, the first one after the Colnbrook bypass opposite the airport. He said: "Go in there and get two gallons. Don't forget, don't get out and don't say anything to the man at all. Don't pass him any notes. Just say what you want." We drove in. The garage attendant came up to Mike. Mike opened the window and asked for two gallons. When the car had been filled Mike handed him a £1 note. The attendant brought back a 10 shilling note and a 3d piece. After leaving the petrol pump we carried on towards London.' *Left:* The Regent brand was taken over by Texaco in 1965 but this is the garage, since modernised, she described. However, when the police followed this up, for some unexplained reason they completely ignored what Valerie said and instead interviewed a pump attendant at a Shell garage *(right)* some 12 miles away near Harrow. Harry Hirons at the 584 garage at Kingsbury Circle gave three statements, and attended two identity parades, although was not called to testify at the trial.

Valerie Storie goes on to describe what happened next: 'From then onwards he gave us various other directions such as "turn left" and "turn right" and "go straight on" until we came to the Western Avenue at Greenford. There was a roundabout there and we said: "If you want to go to Northolt you will have to go left" but he said, "no, go straight on over Western Avenue" which we did. He then gave us other instructions and we went in a north-easterly direction around the Harrow area. I remember going past the turning which is Kenton Road northwards towards Stanmore. It was here that he suddenly told Mike to be careful because there were some roadworks round the corner and sure enough, when we got round the bend there were some roadworks, but he hastily added, "I do not know this area." Mike then said to the man: "I must get some cigarettes" so he said that when we saw a machine in a suitable place we would stop and get some. I believe it was in the Stanmore region he saw a cigarette machine on the left-hand side of the road. The man said, "You can stop and get some there, but don't do anything silly, because I am pointing the gun at the girl." When Mike returned to the car, he opened a packet of cigarettes and said to the man, "Do you want one?" so he said, "Yes, go on driving." So Mike gave the packet of cigarettes to me and the matches. I lit two cigarettes myself and gave one to Mike and held one out for the man to take. It was at this time that I noticed he was wearing black gloves. Whether or not he smoked the cigarette or not I do not know but he had told us earlier on that he did not usually smoke as he did not like smoking. He seemed a very nervous passenger; he was forever saying, "Mind that crossing in front, Be careful of those traffic lights, Mind the corner." We continued driving northwards, going through Radlett and St Albans. After we passed Silsoe, he saw a turning off to the left. He appeared to be looking out of the car on the left-hand side and he saw this turning. He said to Mike: "Turn down there" and we turned down this little lane. I saw a post with a notice on it which said "Private, no parking". I said to the man, "We cannot stop here. This is a private road and we shall only draw attention to ourselves." So he agreed we should turn round and continue northwards on the A6. A little while after he saw another little turning off to the left and he said "Go down there." After 50 or 100 yards down this little turning there were some houses. Mike stopped by the houses and I again said, "We cannot stop here, someone will see us." And so, for the second time he agreed we should turn round and continue going north.' By now they had been driving for over four hours the time was approaching 2 a.m. on the 23rd. Gregsten had been trying to call the attention of other drivers by flashing his rear light and, although one car overtook them with the passenger pointing to the rear of the car, the driver failed to stop. Just after the turning to Clophill another opening appeared on the left, actually an old section of the A6, since straightened and bypassed. They pulled in and drove to the far end. Valerie continued: 'The man said, "I want to kip, but first I must tie you up. What about cutting that rug up?" We told him we had nothing to cut it up with so he said to Mike, "Let me look in the boot of the car to see if you have any rope." He made Mike get out of the car, go with him to the boot, and there was a small piece of rope in the tool-kit which he took.

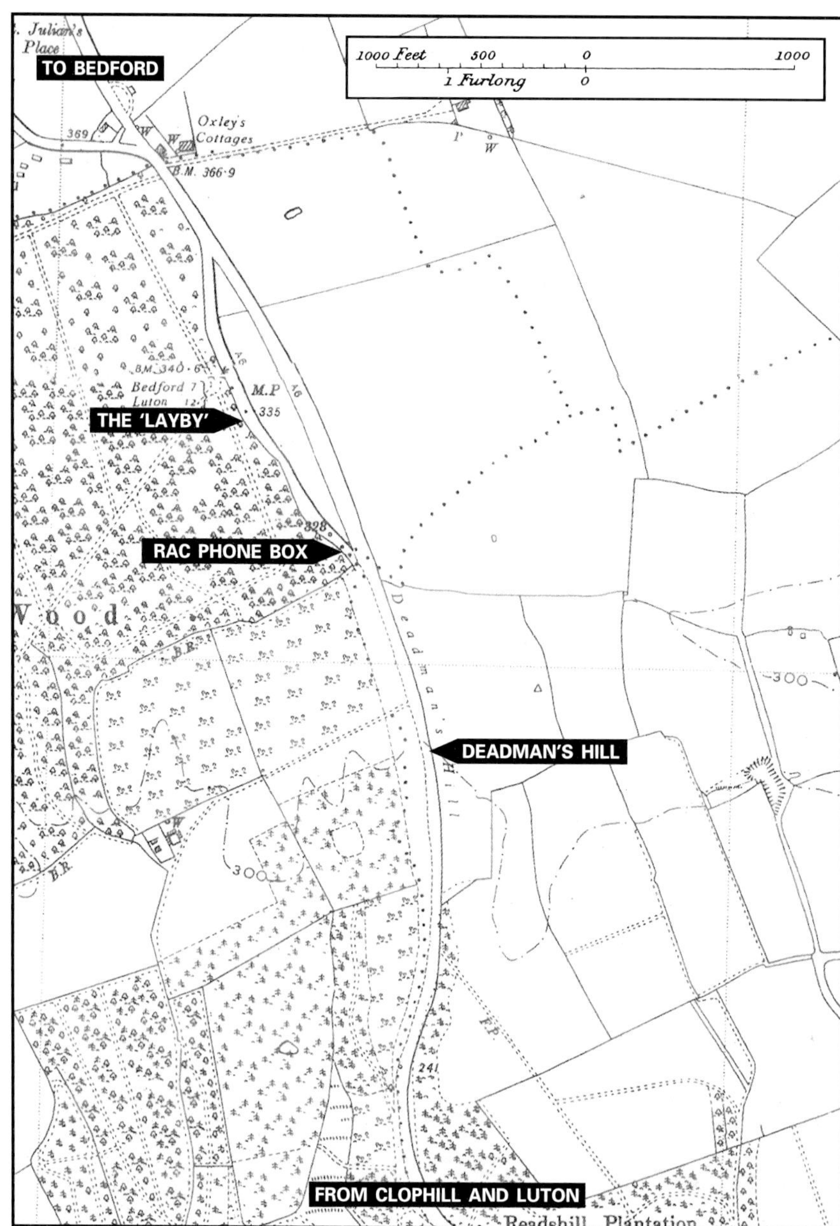

'They got back into the car again, Mike in the driving seat and the man in the back still pointing the gun at us. He told Mike to hand over his tie, which Mike did and he told me to turn round and face him and put my hands together in front of my body so that he could tie my wrists. As he put the tie against my wrists I held them apart so that although he thought he was tying them up very tightly, it was in fact loose when I did put my arms together. Having tied my wrists with the tie, he then proceeded to do the same with the piece of rope, tying one end of it to the car door handle. When he had finished tying me up he said to Mike, "I have got to find something to tie you up with" and I said, Why do you not tie us up together, just leave us outside and tie us up, and then you can go? Somehow or other the duffle bag containing the washing had got into the front of the car. I cannot remember at exactly what stage it was moved from the back into the front, but it was done by Mike. He turned to Mike and said, "Give me that bag up." Mike picked the bag up with both hands, turned towards the centre of the car, that is to his left, and just as he was lifting it over the back of the seats the man fired two shots in very quick succession at Mike's head. The gun could not have been more than an inch or two inches from Mike's head. Mike fell forward over the steering wheel and I could hear the blood pouring out of his head. For the first time that evening I screamed. He said, "Stop screaming" and I did and turned to him and said, You shot him, you bastard. Why did you do that? and he said, "He frightened me. He moved too quick, I got frightened." My hands were at this time free of the tie and the rope, although I was still holding them together as if they were secure. Mike moved and flopped back against the seat and his head fell back. I said to the man, For God's sake, let me get Mike to a doctor quick. I will do anything you want if you will let me take the car and get Mike to a doctor. He said, "Be quiet, I'm finking." I said, Let me move Mike. I will take the car. I will take you anywhere you want to go but let me try and find help for Mike. He said, "No, he's dead" so I said, Let me take Mike somewhere. I must try and get help. Then he said, "Yes, all right, he is not dead." I said, If I see a car coming I will stop them and ask them to give you a lift. I will not say anything about what has happened as long as we can get help. Again he said, "Be quiet, will you, I'm finking".'

With Gregsten lying dead in the driver's seat, the murderer ordered Valerie: 'Kiss me!' Just as she refused, a vehicle came up the road from Clophill and its headlights revealed the man's face no longer hidden by his mask. She said he had 'very large, pale blue, staring eyes and brown hair combed back with no parting. The light was only on his face for a few seconds as the vehicle went past and then we were in complete darkness again.' As soon as the car had passed and they were in darkness again, he asked Valerie to kiss him at gunpoint. 'I leaned across and with my left hand tried to grab the gun. He was too strong, and he said: "That was a silly thing to do. I thought you were sensible. I cannot trust you now." I said no. Several times he asked me. Several times I refused. Then he said, "Get out and come and sit in the back with me. will count five and if you have not got in I will shoot." I got out of the car slowly, trying to play for time, hoping that someone would come by. He was still sitting in the car and he opened his rear door and with the gun on me, pointing towards me all the time, he said, "Come on, get in." I said no. So he got out and, with the gun almost touching me, said, "Get in!" I got in the back of the car. He followed me and shut the door. Between me and the side of the car was the bag of washing. I was sitting behind Mike. The gun was resting on the murderer's lap. He tried to kiss me again. He tried to touch me and I managed to remove the £7 which were still in my bra and put the notes into the pocket of the mac which I was wearing. He tried to touch me and he tried to kiss me. Then he said, "Take off your knickers!" I said no. Again he threatened to shoot me if I did not agree. So I was forced to take them off. He then put the gun on the back window shelf of the car. He was still wearing these black gloves. He started to take one off. I cannot remember now which one it was. I think it was the right one. I am not certain. He seemed to be having difficulty in getting them off. When he got them half off, he held out his hand and he said, "Pull!" and I could feel that these gloves were of a very thin, nylon-type texture. Having got the one glove off, he put it into a pocket. He undid the zip of the fly of his trousers, pushed me back into a half-lying, half-sitting position, leaning against the bag of washing, and without removing any more of his own clothing, he raped me. This only lasted for a very short time, a minute or so. Then he sat back and he said, "You have not had much sex have you?" I said, Can I put my knickers back on? He said, "yes". He did up the fly of his trousers and put his glove back on and got the gun off the back window sill. I said, For goodness' sake, go, take the car, it is almost daybreak. He sat back and again said, "Be quiet will you; I am finking." He said, looking at Mike, "We will have to get him out." He said, "I will leave you here and take the car." 'He told me to get out of the car and followed me out. We opened the driver's door of the car and the man turned to me and said, "You will have to get him out; I must not get blood on me." Mike's hands were gripping the steering wheel. When I touched them, they were stone cold. I managed to get the top of Mike out of the car. His legs seemed to be caught round the pedals and he was too heavy for me to lift out. So I said to the man, You will have to help me and he managed to get Mike's legs out of the car I dragged Mike to the back of the car, across the back of the car and to the edge of the concrete strip and laid him down. I said, Let me have my things out of the car. I must have my basket; it has some rally things in for work. I must have it. He said, "I do not want your things. You can have them." He said, "There is no hurry." So I said, You must go quickly or it will be daybreak and someone will see you. So I got my basket out of the front of the car, and the bag of washing, and I tried to grab a few things out of the glove pocket, stuffing it all into my basket. I grabbed it all and put it down on the ground beside Mike. I said, Go on, take the car. He asked me to start the car for him and show him where the gears were. I started the car and showed him the positions of the gears. He asked how you got reverse gear. I showed him. He wanted to know how the lights worked, and I showed him and, leaving the car running, I walked back towards Mike. He came back with me. He seemed rather undecided as to what to do. He said, "You will go for help." I said, No, I won't. Just go hurry. The car suddenly stopped. I said, I will start the car again for you. You must go quickly. I re-started the car and showed him how the gears worked yet again. He said yes, he understood and sat in the driver's seat, I went back and sat down on the ground beside Mike with my legs tucked up underneath me, almost with my back towards the car. The man got out of the car again, came up to where I was sitting and said, "I think I had better hit you on the head or something to knock you out, or else you will go for help." I said, No, I won't. I won't move. Just go. I put my hand in my mack pocket and took out a pound note. I held it out to him. I said, Here you are. You can have that if you will go quickly. He said, "Where did you get that from?" I said. Oh, it was just in my pocket. He never asked me if I had got any more. He took the pound and started to walk away. When he was about six or ten feet away from me he suddenly turned round and he started to shoot. I felt one bullet hit me. When the second bullet hit me I felt the use of my legs go and I fell over. He then fired another two or three bullets at me while I was lying on the ground. There was a pause and I heard a clicking sound as if he was reloading the gun, and then he fired another three shots. I do not think these hit me. They seemed to go over my head. I lay perfectly still. I heard him walk towards me and I tried to stop breathing and pretend I was dead. I felt him touch me, whether it was with his hand or whether he kicked me, I do not know. He stood looking at me for a few seconds. I heard him walk back to the car. I heard him get in. I heard him slam the door. I saw him put the headlights on, and he started to drive off. He drove off in the direction of Luton.'

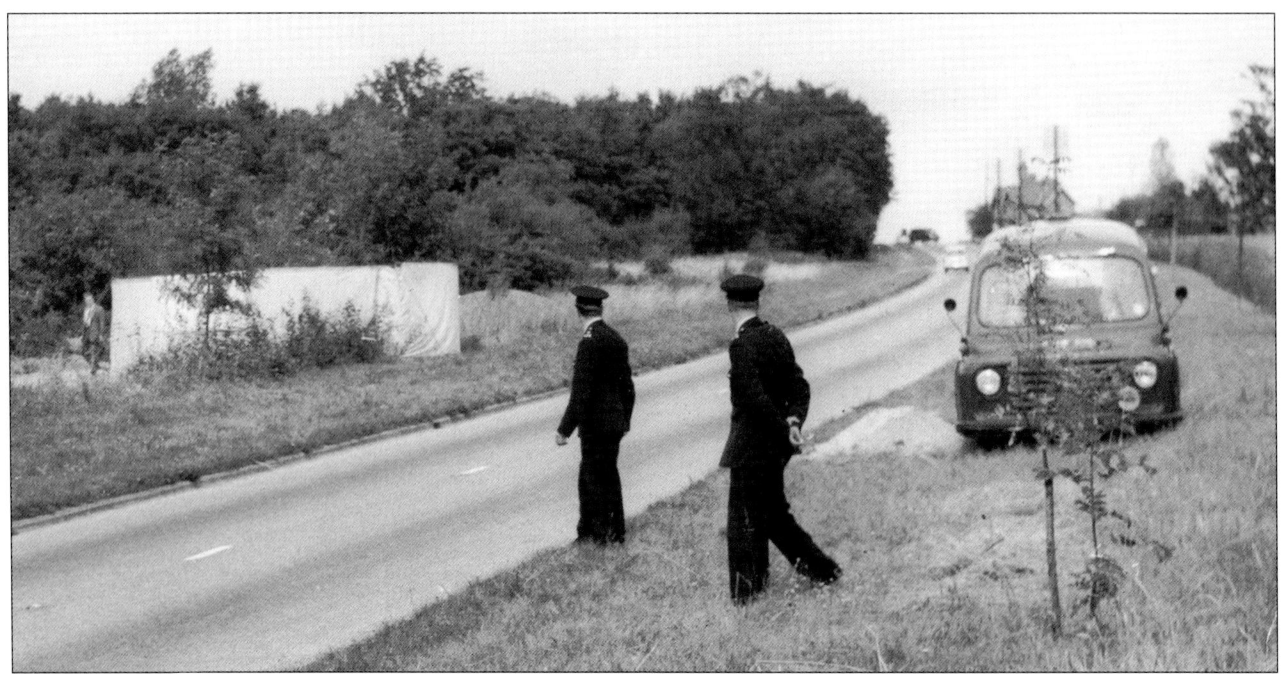

Although Valerie was paralysed, having been shot through her spine, she tried shouting for help and Sydney Burton found her at 6.30 a.m. 'As I was passing the layby I heard a groan — it was a young lady.' At the far end of the layby John Kerr was conducting a traffic survey and Burton told him that 'there's some woman up there in a terrible state.' Kerr said later, 'It was a woman, with somebody else lying beside her. I said, Are you alright? She replied: "No, I've been shot." So I ran across the road and flagged down a car and asked them to go and get the police.' The driver, Thomas Reay, stopped at the RAC box *(right)* at the southern end of the loop and dialled 999. The time was 6.55 a.m. Meanwhile John Kerr had returned to Valerie to ask her what happened. 'She gave me certain details which I wrote down. I had a clipboard with various pages of the census form so I turned one over. I wrote down the number of the car and her name. I asked her what the man was like and she said: "He had big staring eyes, fairish brown hair, slightly taller than I am." Kerr handed the sheet of paper to a police officer but this vital piece of evidence was lost — another unexplained episode.

Sixty years later, the old bypassed carriageway — called a 'layby' in all the published literature although it is a road nearly half-a-mile long — is now hidden from the A6 which has since been upgraded to a dual carriageway.

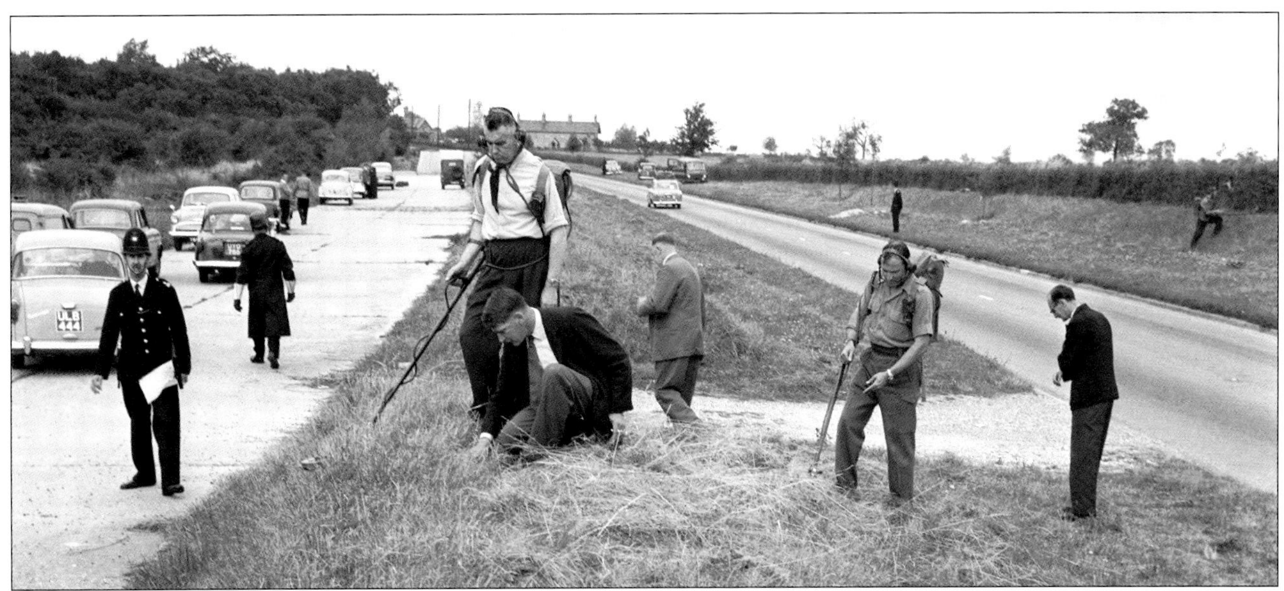

Just before nine, Janet Gregsten telephoned the laboratory to see if her husband had arrived as she had been worried that he had not returned home but it was not until midday that police arrived to break the news. Yet there was worse to come. Although someone always has to confirm the identity of a body at the mortuary, in this case Janet was driven to the A6 to identify Michael where he lay. By now the Bedfordshire police had called in Scotland Yard and men of the Royal Engineers were drafted in with mine detectors to search for the weapon. *Above:* A screen shields the body at the far end of the layby. Dr Keith Simpson was the designated pathologist: 'I went first to the scene, as I always did, to join the police team in their initial survey, then later drove on to Bedford Mortuary. From the fall in temperature, rigor mortis, and other conditions I estimated that Gregsten had died between 3 and 4 a.m. He had two .32 [*sic*] calibre bullet wounds of the head, shot 'through and through' from left ear to right cheek. The skin was tattooed round the entry wounds, and the range could not have been more than an inch or two; the shots had evidently been fired in rapid succession, before the head had moved.'

Above and below: The murder scene . . . then and now.

In those days, if a police force asked Scotland Yard for help, the next available detective on a roster held by the Murder Squad would be assigned to the case. On August 23, this duty fell to Detective Superintendent Basil 'Bob' Acott, recently on the investigation into the murder of Detective Sergeant Purdy (see page 313). He is seen here (left) with Superintendent Charles Barron of the Bedfordshire CID.

At 6.30 a.m. she was found by a farm labourer, who heard her groaning. He went down the road and found John Kerr, 18, who was conducting a traffic survey, and Kerr flagged down a passing motorist. Storie survived but she had been shot through the spine and was paralysed from the neck down and would never walk again. Police took possession of her clothing in keeping with the rape allegation.

Valerie Storie gave police a description of the attacker but one might question how accurate it would have been given that the events took place in the dark with the gunman in the back seat of the car. She did say that at one point in the layby she saw his face lit up by the headlights of a passing car. He had staring eyes, she said. And she had heard him speak. He had a London accent.

At 7.10 a.m. that morning the Morris Minor was seen being driven erratically in Ilford on the other side of London. (Remember, the gunman had asked Valerie Storie to show him how the car worked, suggesting he could not drive.) Witnesses saw the driver's face. The car was found abandoned that evening, just off the Eastern Avenue and close to Redbridge Tube Station. The Yard was called in and Detective Superintendent Bob Acott put in charge.

At 8.45 p.m. the next day, a revolver and sixty rounds of ammunition, wrapped in a white handkerchief, were found hidden behind the back seat on the top deck of a number 36A bus in the depot at Peckham in south London. The pistol was confirmed as the murder weapon but there were no fingerprints.

I went to the scene of that dreadful crime with Superintendent Bob Acott and his team and had examined the whole area round the body. Obviously there were unusual circumstances for a shooting crime. A revolver had been used and there was one feature I had not seen before - the culprit had emptied a full cylinder of fired cartridge cases on to the ground at the scene and, judging by the number of fired shots, had obviously reloaded and fired others. Normally when a revolver is used no fired cases are found at the scene, as they are with a self-loading pistol, which automatically ejects the cases. That circumstance was extremely fortunate for me and a bad slip on the part of the criminal.

The gun that had been used is heartily disliked by firearms examiners as it presents extreme difficulty in matching the bullets but it is comparatively easy to match the fired cartridge cases. After an examination at the laboratory I was able to tell Bob Acott that if the weapon was found, it could be positively connected with the fired cases. As it turned out, the clue of the fired ammunition was the only really worthwhile material found at the scene.

After weeks of exhaustive inquiries the investigators were no nearer to identifying the culprit than they had been at the beginning. Then came the breakthrough. Two cartridge cases discovered in a hotel room in West London had been sent to the laboratory for us to check them against the bullets and cases I had taken from the murder scene. They were just two of hundreds sent to us for comparison from all parts of the country, but these two hit the jackpot. Whoever had left them in that hotel room had a positive connection with the murder.

DETECTIVE SUPERINTENDENT
JOHN McCAFFERTY, 1975

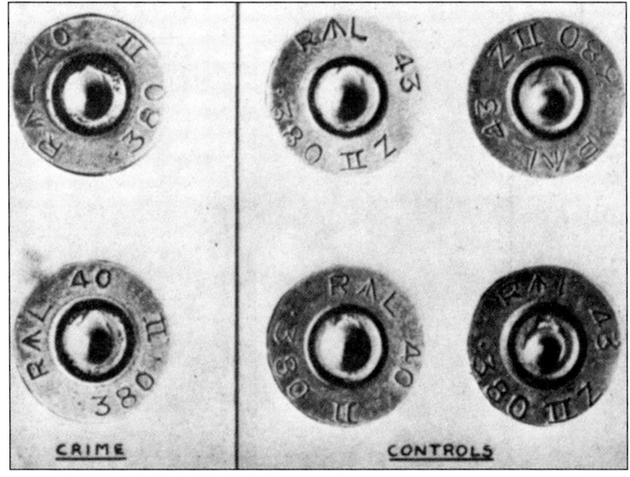

Left: **This picture was issued by Scotland Yard on Saturday, September 2 of the .380 Enfield used in the crime although they did not state where it had been found. The police hoped that anyone knowing about it and the boxes of ammunition found with it — or their theft or loss — would come forward. The pistol was serial number 8839 and the ammunition all manufactured during the war.** *Right:* **Superintendent McCafferty's photograph of two of the fired cases found at the scene (left) matched four test rounds fired from the pistol which had been found on a 36A bus in the depot at Rye Lane, Peckham on Thursday evening (24th).**

On the evening before the revolver was found, Gregsten's Morris Minor was discovered on the other side of London. It was found parked on the pavement in Avondale Crescent, Ilford, just yards from Redbridge underground station — the obvious route that the murderer had taken to make his escape. There was damage to both the front and rear of the car.

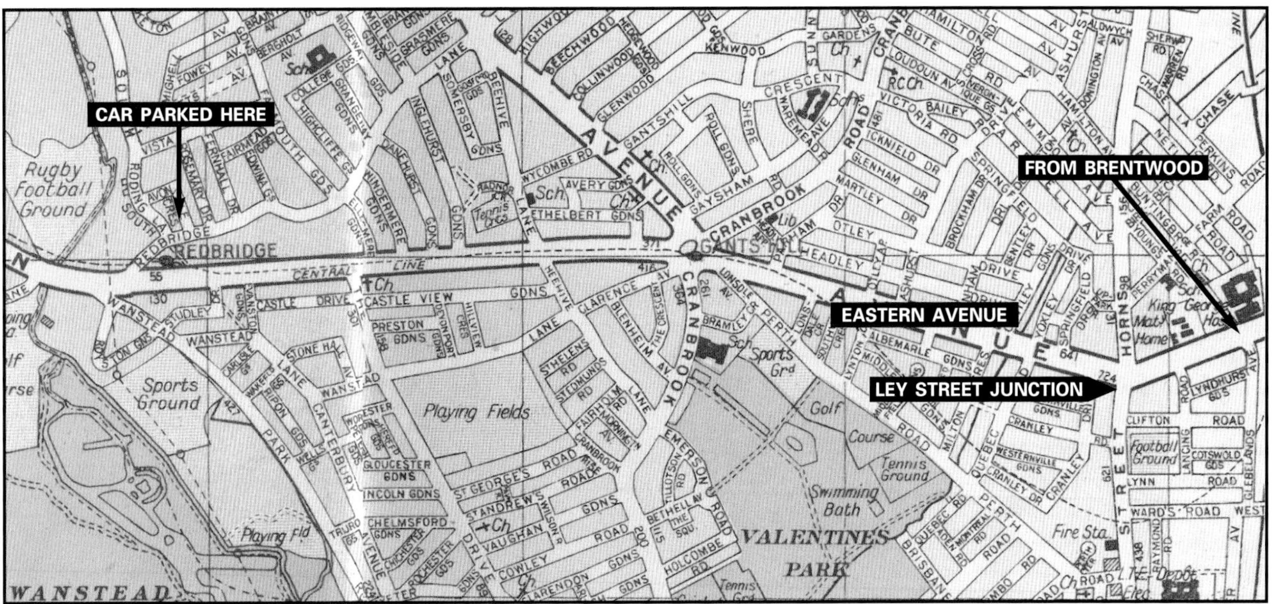

When news of the discovery was published in the Press on Thursday morning, Edward Blackhall immediately phoned the police to say that he had seen the vehicle being driven dangerously on nearby Eastern Avenue. It was around 7 a.m. that his work colleague John Skillett was driving along the A12 from Brentwood. They pulled up behind an A40 at the junction with Ley Street as the lights were on red: 'A grey Morris Minor suddenly came speeding on the inside of us, swerved in front of our car and practically hit us. He put his brakes on and did a back skid. He pulled up between us and the A40. The lights turned green. The Morris Minor shot off in the nearside lane, but got wedged in behind a Greenline bus. By the time we reached Gants Hill roundabout he came out from behind the bus and shot in front of us again. The car was being driven very erratically. He was swerving in his own lane and kept trying to come into our lane as if he was in a hurry.' As they pulled alongside the other driver to deliver a few choice words, they saw that 'the man just had a horrible smile on his face'. Another witness, James Trower, standing in Redbridge Lane just after seven also told police that as the car came past the driver clashed the gears as if he was having considerable difficulty driving the car.

When the car was examined there was found to be a considerable amount of blood in it. Although Valerie said the driver had draped their car rug over the driver's seat, saying that he didn't want to get Michael's blood on him, police still believed that the killer must have still had some traces on his clothing. However, in spite of the fact that the man had spent several hours in the car, no other forensic evidence like fibres or hair was found.

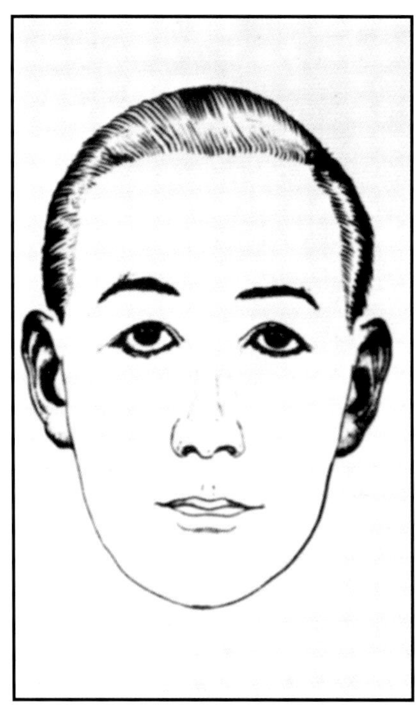

Police did not arrive at Bedford General Hospital to interview Valerie until late on Wednesday by which time the killer had nearly a 12-hour start. As one nurse said: 'The patient wasn't expected to live so why leave it to late afternoon to interview her?' From Valerie's recollection, the following description was issued of the wanted man: 'Man aged about 30, height 5'6", proportionate build, dark brown hair, clean-shaven, brown eyes, fairly pale face, has a distinct East End of London accent. Wearing dark lounge suit and believed dark tie and shirt.' Back in the 1940s, Hugh Macdonald of the Los Angeles Police Department had developed sets of facial features on transparencies to save time sketching descriptions of criminals and Detective Sergeant Ray Dagg had adopted the system in Britain earlier in the year so Acott used the 'Identikit' to try to identify the killer. On Saturday (August 26), Detective Sergeant Jock Mackle, the Met's photofit expert, spent the afternoon with Valerie in hospital producing the composite *(left)*. Then he put together a second impression *(right)* from details given by Edward Blackhall and James Trower, the Redbridge witnesses. Both images were broadcast by the BBC and ITN on Tuesday, August 29 and they were published in newspapers the following day.

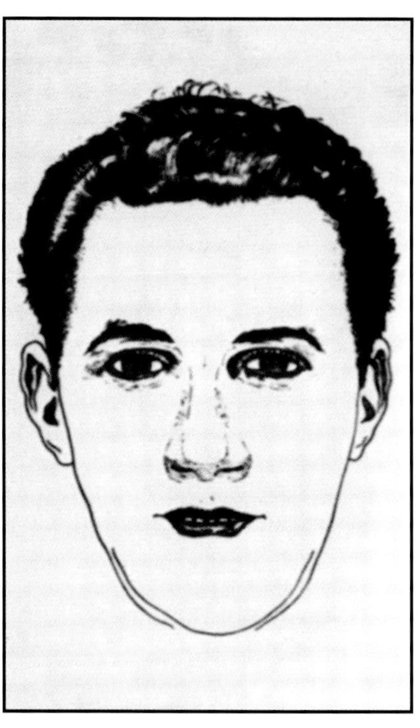

Police made a routine appeal to hotels and guest-houses and they received an interesting reply from the Alexander Court Hotel in Finsbury Park. Guests were suspicious of a man called Frederick Durrant from Sussex. The name and address proved to be false so the police took him in. He admitted he was Peter Louis Alphon of Streatham, south London. He said he used a false name because he sometimes left hotels without paying his bill. The police found a newspaper cutting of the A6 murder in his case. On the day of the murder he had stayed in Room 6 at the Vienna Hotel in Maida Vale, north London. Alphon was released 'pending enquiries'. Then on September 11 two fired cartridge cases were discovered in Room 24 of the same hotel, both confirmed as having been fired by the murder weapon.

This turn of events — a chance call following an appeal concerning Peter Alphon and subsequently the discovery of the two cartridges — was to lead directly to the arrest of James Hanratty. According to the hotel register, Room 24, where the cartridges were found, had been occupied on August 21 — the day before the murder — by one 'J. Ryan' who, as the police would discover, was an alias for Hanratty.

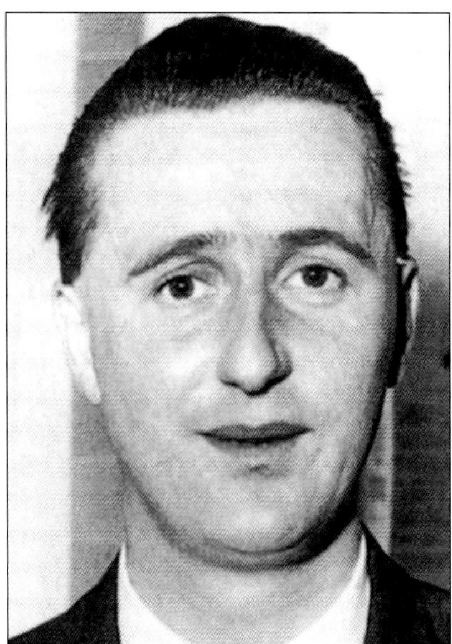

The two suspects. Peter Louis Alphon, alias Frederick Durrant, began his criminal record by taking and driving away a motor car in 1953.

First, though, we must deal with Peter Alphon who was already known to police and had a criminal record. The hotel manager, a dubious character called William Nudds, and his equally dubious 'wife', Florence Snell, had originally provided Alphon with an alibi saying he was at the Vienna at 11 p.m. on the day of the murder. The police, convinced he was the killer, took new statements, in which Nudds and Snell rescinded their first statements and now stated that Alphon had not returned to the hotel by 2 a.m. They also said that he had visited Room 24 before taking Room 6. Alphon was placed on an identification parade at which Valerie Storie picked out another man, not him, as the murderer. When the case against Alphon collapsed, the police took a third statement from Nudds and Snell in which they changed their statements once again, saying now that the first ones were true after all; that Alphon *was* at the hotel and therefore had an alibi. In fact, checking Alphon's alibi proved to be impossible. Nudds had at least eight or nine (or more) other names and he and Snell were utterly unreliable.

So now, having had their prime suspect apparently eliminated, the police had to find someone else. They turned their attention to 'J. Ryan' but how they ever discovered that he was James Hanratty was never established.

James Francis Hanratty was born in London on October 4, 1936. His father was Irish and his mother came from Durham. He first got into trouble with the law at 17 when he stole a motorcycle. He graduated to burglary and stealing cars and inevitably ended up in prison. He had no 'form' for violence. As it happened, he was currently wanted by the police for housebreaking having been identified by his fingerprints at the scene of a crime.

On September 7, just over two weeks after the murder, Hanratty was in Ireland. When he got wind that he was a suspect for the A6 murder through his father who had been told by the Press, he telephoned Superintendent Acott and told him he did not commit the crime. In another call he confirmed that he had stayed at the Vienna Hotel on the 21st (the day before the murder) for one night. Then, he said, he went to Liverpool to stay with friends but he would not tell Acott who they were.

On October 11 two policemen in Blackpool had suspicions about a young man drinking coffee in a café. They waited for him outside and when he emerged said he was Peter Bates but the officers were not fooled. They had just detained Britain's most wanted man: James Hanratty. He was put on an identity parade at Bedfordshire police headquarters where he was picked out by the two witnesses who had seen the man driving the car in Redbridge. However two others failed to identify him.

Then the police put him on another parade, this time in the ward at Stoke Mandeville Hospital, where Valerie Storie was being treated in the spinal injuries unit.

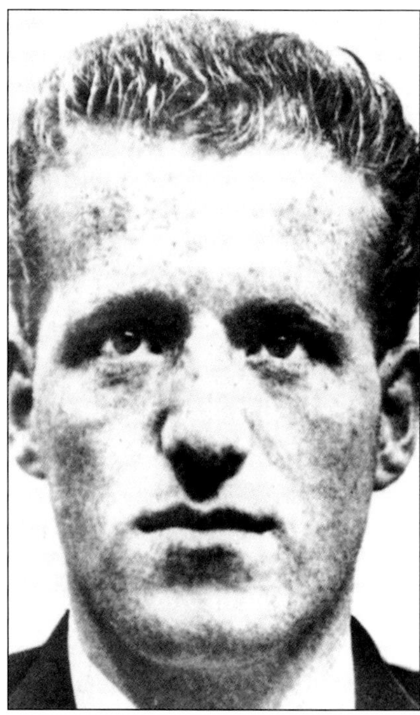

James Hanratty, alias James Ryan, began his long criminal career for housebreaking including car theft and burglary in 1954.

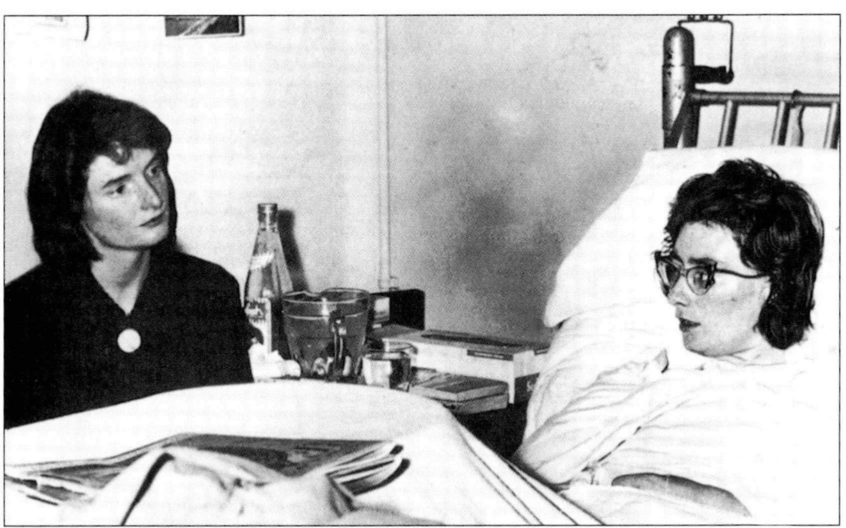

Valerie's wounds were first examined by Dr Andrew Pollen, the consultant orthopaedic surgeon at Bedford Hospital: 'My examination revealed a bullet entry wound on the left side of the neck, and an exit wound on the right side of the neck at a slightly higher angle. I next saw five bullet holes in the region of the left shoulder, of which four were in a vertical line from the tip of the shoulder downwards, the fifth was situated high up on the left side of the chest. I was unable at this stage to say which were entry or exit wounds.' So that she could receive appropriate medical attention, Valerie was transferred to Guy's Hospital in London (where Dr Simpson was the pathologist) and it was there that Janet Gregsten was pictured at her bedside.

Propped up in her hospital bed, she was pushed back and forth along the line of men. She picked out Hanratty as the man who had murdered her lover and who had raped and tried to kill her by asking every person to say, 'Be quiet, will you, I am thinking,' just as the man had done that night. Every man on the parade said it and she chose Hanratty.

Critics will point out she was bound to choose him bearing in mind that the line-up comprised servicemen, all from different parts of country, all with different accents. Taking into account that at the first identification parade she had picked out the wrong man, and the conditions on the night of the crime, it must be assumed that Valerie's identification, through no fault of her own, was very suspect. The police would need more than this evidence of identification, such as it was, to prove the case against Hanratty. Yet they charged him that night, even as they learned that none of the fingerprints found in the Morris Minor were his.

If Hanratty could prove he was elsewhere at the time of the murder, then obviously he was not the killer. Given that it was now about six weeks later, this was to prove difficult. In any event, he claimed that on the morning of August 22 he left the Vienna Hotel and took a bus to Liverpool, arriving there between 4 and 6 p.m. He persisted with this account, even into his trial. He was lying, as he later admitted, probably to protect criminal friends or maybe because lying was a fact of life with him.

James Hanratty was put on trial at the Shire Hall, Bedford, in January 1962 before Mr Justice Gorman. The case was prosecuted by Graham Stanwick and defended by Michael Sherrard. Hanratty was indicted with the murder charge only to which he pleaded not guilty.

Valerie Storie, testifying, said she had known Michael Gregsten since 1958. They went motor rallying together. She said the man in the dock, Hanratty, was the gunman. He had staring eyes. She had no doubt, she said.

However the evidence of identification was scant to say the least. Of the witnesses, Storie had attended two identification parades, in the first picking out an innocent man, in the second picking out Hanratty by his London accent. Two men had identified him as the driver of the car on the morning after the crime, but two others had failed. The only forensic evidence was that the gunman's blood was Group O, as was Hanratty, but so are 40 per cent of the male population, including Alphon. The blood grouping was determined from semen taken from Valerie Storie which ruled out Gregsten as the man who had intercourse with her that night as he was of another blood group. There was no forensic evidence and no fingerprints to link Hanratty to the crime. The recovered gun and ammunition could not be connected with him. The spent cartridges were recovered from the room in which he slept at the Vienna Hotel, but how long had they been there, hidden in the upholstery? How many others had slept in the room, and over what period?

Would 'J. Ryan', alias Hanratty, have come into the picture in the first place if the police had not called at the Vienna Hotel to make enquiries about another person entirely? Or, could Alphon really be the killer? A serving prisoner, Roy Langdale, gave evidence to say Hanratty had confessed to him when they had been on remand in Brixton. However he was discredited after he admitted he had approached newspapers for payment for his story, and it seems much of what he alleged Hanratty had told him was either incorrect or could have been read in newspapers.

At the beginning of the second week of the trial, Hanratty said he had lied about his alibi. He had not been in Liverpool on the day of the murder: he had been in Rhyl, North Wales. Lying to one's own side, especially when your life is on the line, may seem a strange thing, but if he was innocent he may have thought that no jury would believe he could be guilty, certainly not in England where you get a fair trial. Or maybe, having lied about Liverpool, he felt he could not change his story, and that to do so would make things worse. Or maybe he thought that even if he was in Rhyl there was no one to back him up.

What a tangled web Hanratty weaved! Now his defence team had to dispatch someone to Rhyl to try and find someone who could support him, and be quick about it. Meanwhile, it was the turn of Superintendent Acott to take the stand. Apart from the usual

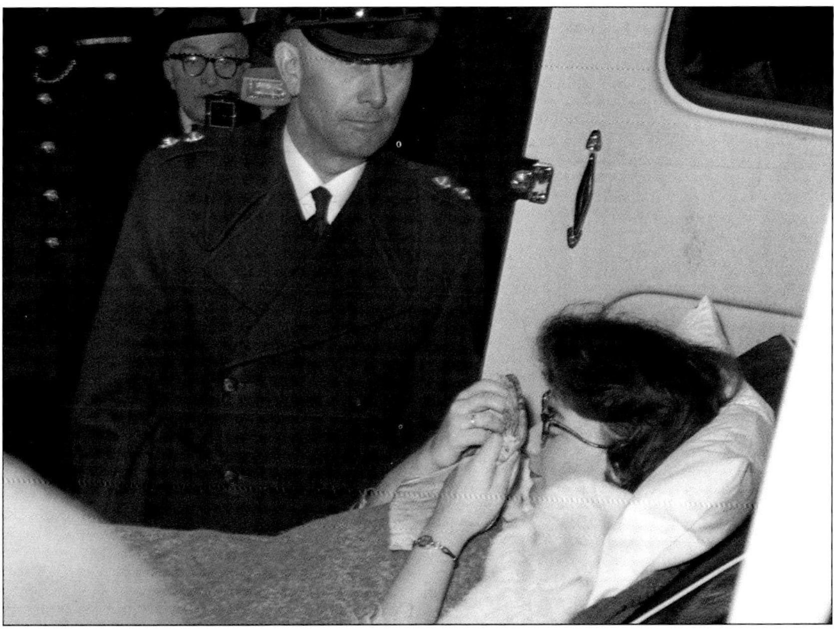

It was following Janet's visit that police issued an appeal in the Press that they wished to interview Peter Alphon to help them in their enquiries and, as a result, Alphon walked into Scotland Yard. Having taken his statement, Superintendent Acott put him on three different identity parades, the third in front of Valerie at Guy's. Although she had just undergone an operation to remove two bullets, and Dr Simpson thought it too early to subject her to the ordeal of possibly coming face to face with her assailant, nevertheless the parade took place on Sunday, September 10. However, after spending five minutes looking at the line up, instead of picking out Alphon, she selected another man. Later, after she had been transferred to Stoke Mandeville Hospital for specialist treatment for her spinal injury, she picked out Hanratty at another parade at which point he was charged with the murder. There had been legal arguments in favour of holding the trial at the Old Bailey rather than Bedford — where the crime was a very emotive issue — but permission had been refused and the trial was scheduled to be held at Bedford Winter Assizes on January 22, 1962. This picture was taken on the second day when Valerie appeared to give her testimony.

Left: **Michael with Janet and his son Simon pictured in happier days in 1953. Like most of the victims of murder their name so often gets overshadowed by that of the murderer. Thus Michael Gregsten's body remained in the mortuary at Bedford for four months before being cremated at the old crematorium in Fosterhill Road** ***(above)*** **on December 18, 1961. Janet died suddenly of a heart attack in January 1995 while recounting to a friend the tragic events surrounding the death of her husband.**

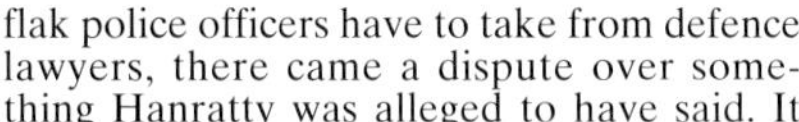

flak police officers have to take from defence lawyers, there came a dispute over something Hanratty was alleged to have said. It concerned the work 'kip', meaning sleep. Acott said Hanratty had said 'sleep'. Hanratty said he had used the word 'kip' but the relevance of this would not be discovered until the case was reviewed nearly forty years later.

Found guilty, James Hanratty was executed by Harry Allen and Royston Rickard on April 4, 1962. At the time, his trial at 19 days was the longest for murder in British legal history.

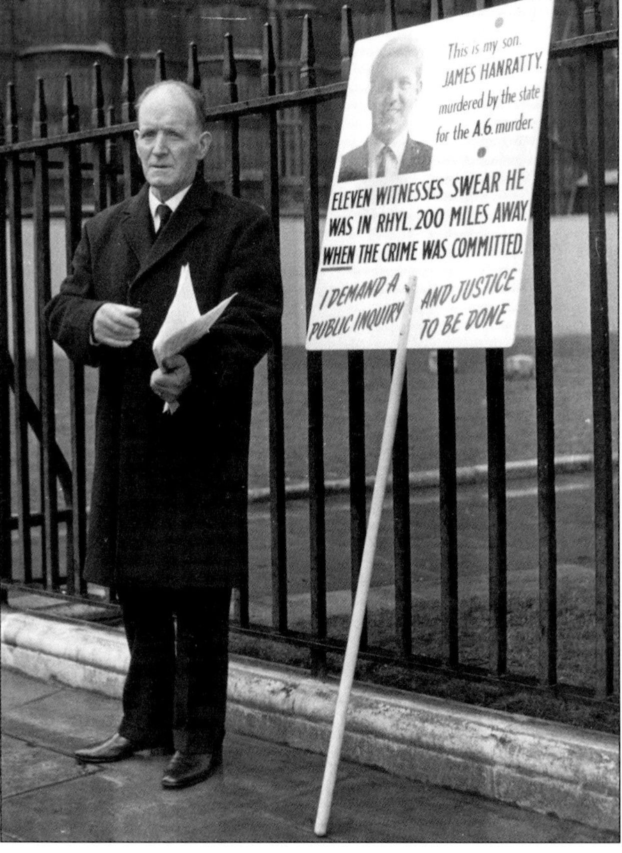

Widespread campaigning began immediately to try to clear his name, spearheaded by his father who conducted many lonely vigils. James Hanratty Senior died in 1978, his mission unfulfilled.

The prosecution alluded to part of Valerie Storie's statement in which she had said the gunman had said: 'Call me Jim', suggesting this meant Jim as in James (Hanratty). However the defence argued that the phrase meant that Jim was anything but his real name. Sherrard described the prosecution case as 'weak and shameful'.

Although Hanratty took the stand he didn't have to; he could have said nothing at all. In this case, the judge would have been obliged to comment on this to the jury along the lines: 'Would you believe someone is innocent if they say nothing?' Hanratty told the court that if he had wanted to do a 'stick up' he would not have gone to a cornfield, but to a bank or a shop. He accused Acott of omitting much of what he had said during interview, and adding things he had not said. His alibi in Rhyl did not stand up, but that would not mean it was untrue, it simply could not be satisfactorily established.

The jury retired to consider their verdict and at 9.10 p.m., ten hours later, they gave their verdict: 'Guilty'. Asked if he had anything to say, Hanratty declared, 'I am innocent'.

Hanratty's mother protested her son's innocence, as all mothers do, but she was not with her son on that fateful night and neither were any of his family or supporters. His last hope was a reprieve by the Home Secretary to whom a petition of 23,000 signatures and 300 letters were submitted. But there was to be no reprieve. On April 3, 1962, Hanratty wrote to his parents, praising their courage. He said, 'I am going to face up to it. I am going to be the son you can be proud of. Many a man would be glad to have the home you and dad gave to me.'

At 8 a.m. the following morning James Hanratty was hanged in Bedford prison by Harry Allen and Royston Rickard. He never confessed to the crime but someone else did. On August 22, on the first anniversary of the murder, Peter Alphon visited Hanratty's parents, told them he had committed the crime, and offered to pay them compensation. He confessed again, to a group of journalists in France and yet again on British television. He wrote to the Home Secretary, saying, 'I killed Gregsten, the establishment murdered Hanratty.'

In 1999, over thirty-five years after Hanratty was hanged, the case was referred by the Criminal Cases Review Commission (CCRC) to the Court of Appeal. The defence, and indeed the public at large, had been ill at ease with his conviction, so it was

Both suspects had admitted to the crime, Hanratty to a fellow prisoner while on remand at Brixton and Alphon soon after the execution, and again in 1967 at a Press conference in Paris *(above)*. He provided a further admission of his guilt to film producer Bob Woffinden for his 1991 documentary *Hanratty — The Mystery of Deadman's Hill*.

right to refer the case providing there was another ingredient to add to the many that had been trawled through over the years. That ingredient was now DNA.

There were two material exhibits. The first was Valerie Storie's knickers, the second the white handkerchief which was wrapped around the murder weapon found on the number 36A bus. But DNA wasn't the only matter. The CCRC had discovered 'serious flaws' in the case. First there was the ESDA test (Electro-Static Document Apparatus). This works like an ordinary photocopier, except that where a photocopier makes an image of a document, ESDA detects impressions of, say, handwriting from the overlying page.

In two of the police interviews with Hanratty, part of what he said had been changed — just as Hanratty alleged in court. The police had discarded part of their original notes and substituted others, and now the pages below betrayed them. If that was what the police were up to, one has to question the veracity of everything else they said or did, 'Kip' to 'sleep' being one example.

There were also many undisclosed documents that the prosecution had not made the defence or the court aware of. The police had chosen to submit only those that supported the prosecution case; those that did not were withheld. They included statements regarding the alleged sighting of the Morris Minor and other important evidence. This was not an uncommon practice in the 1960s when the police were the prosecutors and so selected documentary evidence to support their case. (Today the Crown Prosecution Service must be served with all documents, and they in turn must serve them all on the defence.)

These factors played a major part in the appeal to have the conviction quashed. The defence maintained that had the jury been allowed to hear the 'hidden' evidence at the time of the trial, then an already tenuous case would have been thrown out. A crime has to be proved 'beyond reasonable doubt' but would there have been reasonable doubt if other witnesses, who did not support the prosecution case, had testified?

Back in the 1960s DNA identification did not exist. Polymerase Chain Reaction (PCR) is a laboratory process since developed to copy parts of DNA in order to generate a DNA profile. When the semen on Valerie Storie's knickers and the mucus on the handkerchief were examined, the DNA profiles indicated that the man who raped her also handled the gun used to shoot her and Michael Gregsten. But who was he? The Crown Prosecution Service sought the only means left to settle things once and for all: the authority to obtain DNA from James Hanratty's remains. The court agreed, and in 2001 Hanratty's body was exhumed. Scientists were able to obtain a DNA profile which was compared to the DNA from the knickers and handkerchief and got a match. There was no doubt, the scientists said.

The Hanratty team may yet succeed in having the conviction quashed on the grounds that he should not have been convicted in the first place. That does not mean he didn't commit the crime; it means he should not have been convicted in 1962. All arguments aside, there has always been, and will always remain, doubt about his role in the murder.

Detective Inspector Paul Heslop, 2011

Finally, with the advances in DNA testing, on March 22, 2001, Hanratty's body was exhumed from Carpenders Park Cemetery at Watford (Plot D, Grave 873) to obtain a sample for testing. The scientists reported that 'we were able to obtain DNA from the remains and when we compare that DNA, point by point, with the DNA that we'd found on the handkerchief [in which the pistol had been wrapped] and on the knickers, we found no discrepancies. We had a match there and therefore this considerably strengthened the evidence that we were looking at DNA from James Hanratty rather than anybody else in the population.' Nevertheless, our author, Detective Inspector Heslop, explains that in those days, before anyone knew about DNA, cross-contamination was possible as clothes from both Hanratty and Storie were carried back and forth, from the police station to the court room. So one is left to wonder if the truth will ever be known?

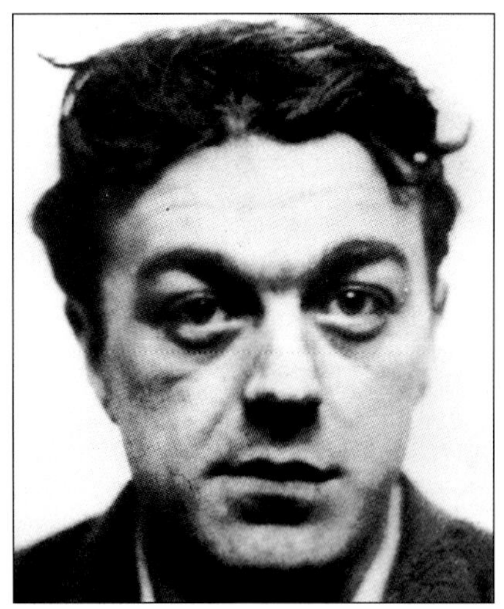
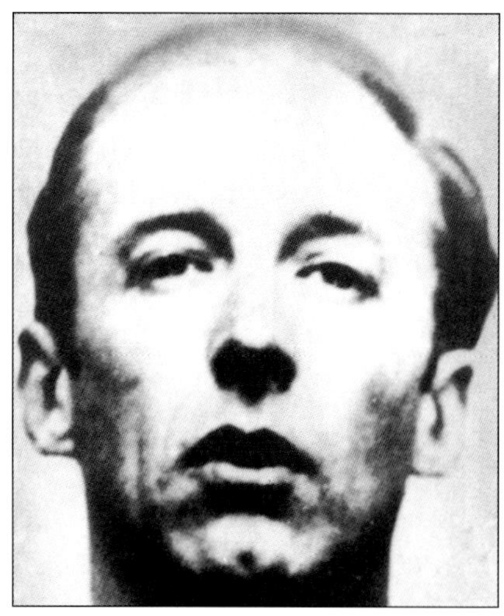
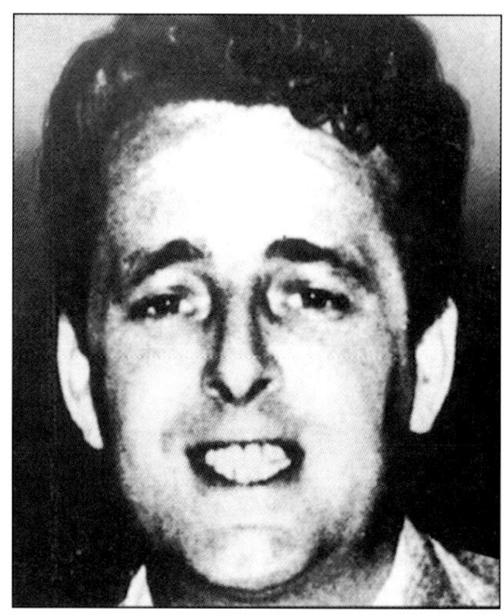

The three criminals who set out to steal getaway cars for a robbery: L-R: Harry Roberts, John or Jack Witney and John Duddy.

August 12, 1966 – The Shepherd's Bush Murders

Friday 12 August 1966 was the first day of the shooting season. The glorious twelfth! And it was a glorious day too — hot and sunny. Me and two mates — Jack Witney and John Duddy — were planning a robbery at the local engineering works and we needed cars. We'd decided on three for the job and they had to be good. High performance. Two Jags and a Ford Executive would be ideal. So we got into Jack's van and went looking for them. We drove to Regent's Park and cruised around the outer circle. We normally went down there to nick our cars because we knew the commuters parked there all day while they were working and it was common knowledge that no one would notice the missing cars until about 5 p.m. By that time we were long gone and, nine times out of ten, we would have done the robbery.

We spotted the two Jags we needed but couldn't find the Ford Executive and the day was wasting away. We ended up driving to Harrow and found a Ford Executive parked down a side street next to the tube station. Me and Jack got out of the van and sneaked across the road to nick it. Jack crouched down, pushed a small piece of wire in the lock and jiggled it up and down and then, much to my annoyance, he broke the 'jiggler'. I got the right hump and stormed back to the van. It was all a waste of time. Jack jumped in the driver's seat and we drove off to Northolt to look at the engineering factory.

We drove around for a while and I was getting right pissed off. The morning had gone and we had not done a thing. So we decided to go to the pub and have some lunch. After a pint and a game of darts, we thought we'd better go back to work.

We were driving down Erconwald Street when we spotted a Triumph 2000 following us. There were three men in the car. I turned to Jack. 'That's the Old Bill. I bet they're going to nick us.' He looked worried and carried on driving. We drove into Braybrook Street. It was 2.45 p.m.

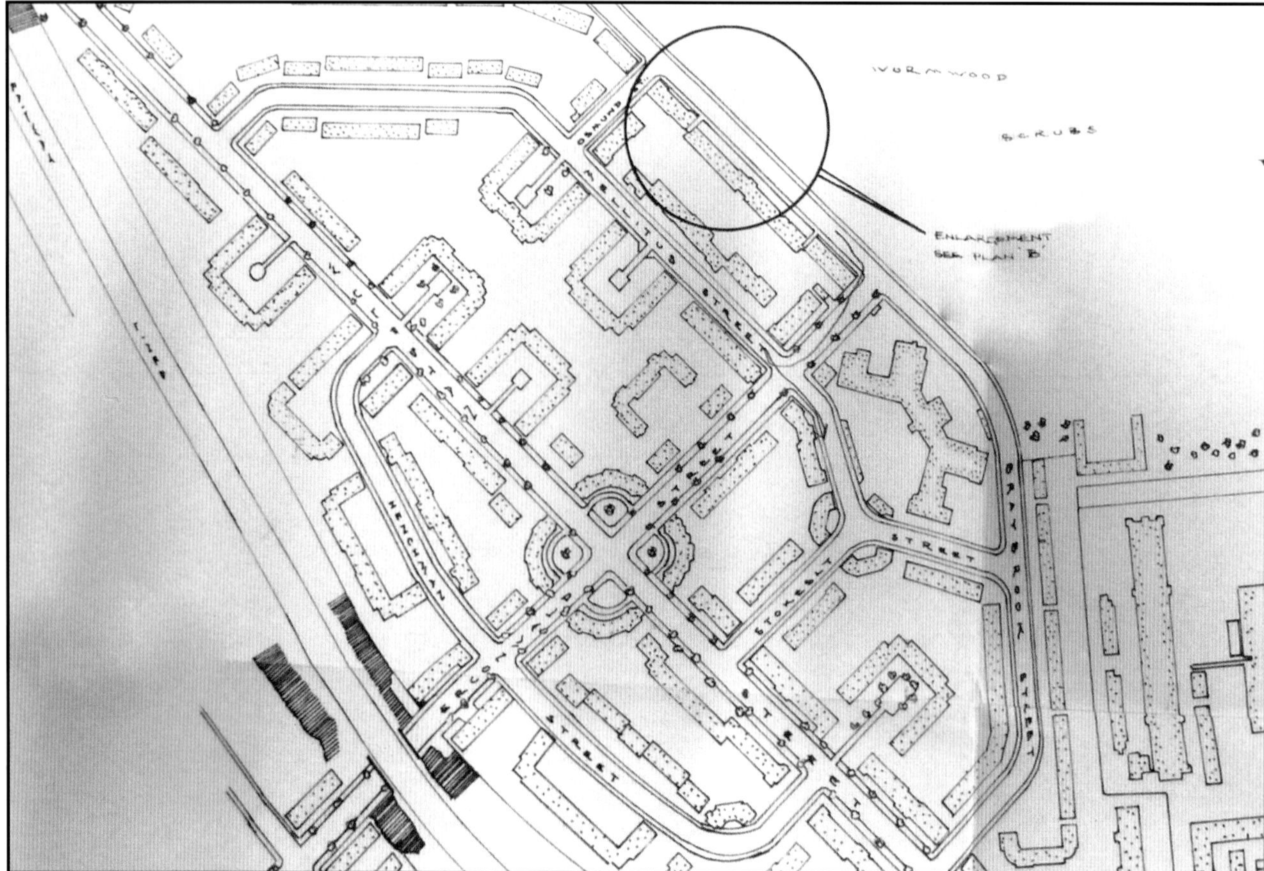

Scene of crime plan drawn up by Police Constable 501 Terence Robertson, based at Hammersmith Police Station.

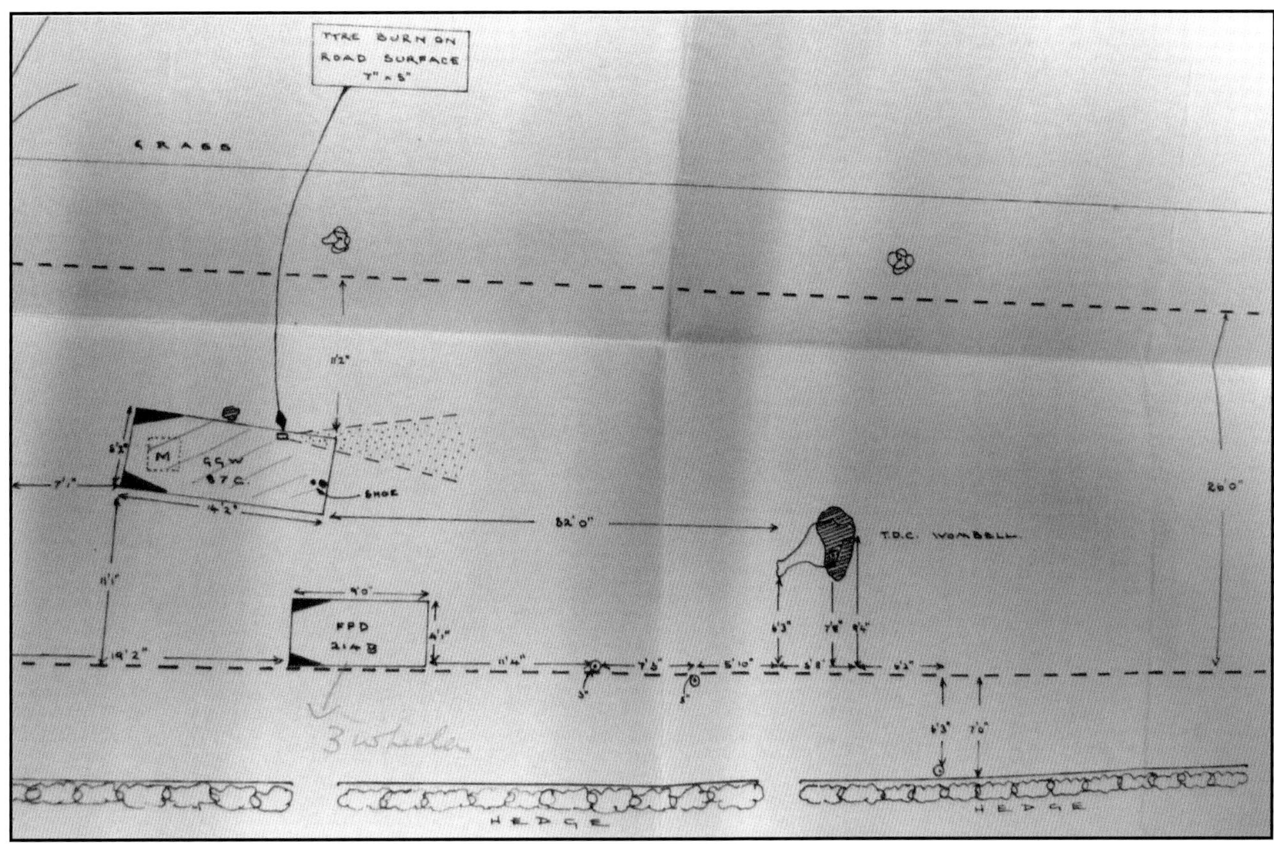

The file containing the police photographs is closed until 2051 but press photographers rushed to Shepherd's Bush, arriving in Braybrook Street even before the bodies could be covered. This is Detective Constable David Wombwell shot in the head by Roberts.

The car overtook us and stopped about 130 feet ahead. One of the men got out of the car and started to come towards the van. We were panicking trying to hide all our tools including the shooters. The man, who turned out to be PC Wombwell, came around to Jack's side of the van and Jack wound down the window.

'I'd like to see your driving licence and insurance certificate,' he snapped. Jack reached into the glove compartment and gave them to him. Wombwell walked back to the police car and we could see him talking to the other officer, Sergeant Head.

Jack handed me the 9mm Luger that he had under the dashboard. PC Wombwell returned to Jack's side of the van. Now he wanted to see what was in the back. 'Fuck off,' said Jack and a violent row erupted. Sergeant Head came around to my side of the van and, with my elbow, I quickly flicked the switch down so he couldn't open my door. That annoyed him and he started shaking the van, grabbing hold of the door handle and screaming, 'Open the fucking door!' Me and Jack looked at each other. By this time PC Wombwell had his head through the open window, screaming at Jack.

With half a smile, Jack said quietly, 'Let the slag have it, Harry.' Instantly, I raised my arm and, with the Luger Jack had just handed me, I shot Wombwell point-blank. The bullet whizzed past Jack's nose and hit Wombwell just below the eye. He slumped to the ground. I could hear my heart thumping. The air was electric.

In 1984 the Police Memorial Trust was founded to mark the locations where officers had lost their lives. The memorial in Braybrook Street was unveiled on June 29, 1988.

At 3.15 p.m. that afternoon, the 'Q' Car (an unmarked police car with the crew in plain clothes), a Triumph 2000 GGW 87C, call-sign 'Foxtrot One-One', was being driven by PC Geoffrey Fox. Detective Sergeant Christopher Head sat alongside him as the wireless operator with Detective Constable Wombwell in the rear seat. When he was shot, Head apparently started to run back towards the 'Q' car when Roberts got out of their Standard Vanguard van and gunned him down. He fell in front of the police car.

I turned towards Sergeant Head. My elbow caught the door knob and the door flew open while he was still pulling on it. I could see the shock and disbelief in his eyes. I jumped out of the car still holding the gun. Sergeant Head turned and started running back towards the police car.

I aimed my gun and fired. I got him right in the middle of his back. He went down like a sack of shit. I ran up to him. He was lashing out with his legs. I held his legs, aimed my gun at his head and pulled the trigger. Click. It was a dud. I took a step back and ejected the blank from the chamber. Then I tried to grab his legs again but he kicked me in the face, making my nose bleed and splitting my lip.

Again, I aimed the gun at his head but, to my horror, it was another dud. I couldn't fucking believe it. He was struggling like fuck and managed to get to his feet and he started to run again. But he only made it to the front of the police car and fell in front of it.

At that moment, Duddy got out of the van and ran towards the police car firing at PC Fox. As the constable fell forward with a shot through the head, his foot jammed the accelerator of the automatic gearbox and the car shot forward, running over the dead body of DS Head. In this Press photo, Wombwell's body has now been covered. In the background the massive bulk of Wormwood Scrubs prison.

At that moment there seemed to be a slight lull. I heard Jack shout, 'Get the driver!' I looked towards the van and saw John Duddy standing in the road like some kind of cowboy. He was holding his gun out in front of him and 'fanning' the trigger. I hadn't noticed the police car starting up. PC Fox, the third man in the car, had been sitting there, watching. Now he crunched the car into reverse gear. Suddenly Duddy shot all the windows out and there was glass flying everywhere. PC Fox was in total panic and rammed the gear lever into first in a vain attempt to get away. But as the car shot forward he ran over Sergeant Head who was lying in front of the police car, wedging him under the back wheels. At that moment I turned to face the driver, only to see him take a bullet in the head from Duddy. I saw him slump down over the steering wheel. It was as if he just went to sleep. In less than 30 seconds all three police officers were dead.

Jack had already jumped out of the van and taken all his papers from PC Wombwell's body and was now back in the driver's seat with Duddy in the back. The van had started and was beginning to move. I ran towards it and for a moment I thought that they were going without me. I shouted, 'Wait for me, you bastards!' and I dived into the passenger's seat, and screamed, 'Go! Go! Go!'

We screeched backwards out of Braybrook Street. Jack was driving like a madman. We drove backwards all the way down Erconwald Street and we were reversing down a third street when we cut across a geezer in a Ford. He took down the number of the van. Jack spun the van around and we drove away at top speed into Oak Common Lane. At that moment a police motorbike came alongside us. Jack said, 'Give it to him as well' but the copper must have realised he was in danger because he quickly veered off.

Because the press were using telephoto lenses from outside the police cordon, the view appears foreshortened compared with our comparison. It was after policewoman Yvonne Fletcher was killed outside the Libyan Embassy in St James's Square in 1984, that Michael Winner, the film director, wrote to *The Times* suggesting that a memorial should be erected to her. 'It would serve to indicate that not everyone in this country takes seeming pleasure in attacking the police in the execution of their difficult duties, but that most of us regard their conduct and bravery under a whole series of endless and varied provocations, as demonstrably noble and worthy of our thanks.' Thus began the tradition of now placing memorials at the locations where police officers have been killed in the course of their duty.

The Standard Vanguard was registered in Witney's name so it didn't take the police long to trace him to his flat in Fernhead Road, Paddington. *Left:* The following day the vehicle was found in this railway arch off Tinworth Street in Vauxhall. *Right:* Today No. 105 is a bonded warehouse with no chance of taking a comparison inside.

We carried on across Hammersmith Bridge, continuing down the South Bank side of the river towards Vauxhall. As we approached Battersea Bridge roundabout, I couldn't believe it when the van started to pink and slow down!

'What the fuck's happening, Jack?'

He slapped the steering wheel in frustration and said, 'Jesus Christ! We're out of petrol!' He kept his finger on the starter motor button and, like a kangaroo, we jumped down the hill to where we could see a garage.

We pulled in behind a Triumph Vitesse. An old lady in a tweed suit was sitting at the wheel. There was only one attendant and, just our luck, the old dear had decided to have the works: 'Can you check my oil?' she said. 'What about the water?' It seemed to take forever. We were all trying to act normal.

In the distance, we could hear the sound of the police bells ringing. Duddy yelled at Jack to hurry up. But the old dear wasn't going to be rushed. We had to stay calm. At last we got some petrol and sped off to the lock-up garage in Tinworth Street where Duddy and I got out. The lock-up was by the railway arch and Jack crunched the wing as he pulled into the garage. He then joined me and Duddy down on the Embankment, but then he declared: 'I'm off!' and he ran down the street.

Duddy's flat at Euston was on the eighth floor and he always used to look out of his toilet window to see who was approaching and he saw me and Jack walking up the path. We sat talking about what we were going to do and thought it was a good idea to split up. So Jack went home and I went back home to Lilly. As I walked in, Lilly said, 'Have you heard the news? Three policemen are dead!'

'Have I heard it? We *fucking did it!*'

Me and Lilly stuck to the telly and were watching the news when the newsreader announced that Jack had been arrested and taken to Harrow Road police station. The van registration number had been traced back to him.

The first thing I thought of in the morning was that we had to get rid of the van. We had to burn it. I went round to Duddy's flat. He said he felt trapped eight floors up so I got him to come round to the flat at Maida Vale. He wouldn't ride in my car so we walked. As we were walking down the Portobello Road, all of a sudden we heard the sound of a police car coming towards us with its bells ringing. I froze but Duddy took off like a shot. I found him in the newsagents, hiding in the corner pretending to read *The Times*.

When we finally got back to the flat, Duddy collapsed on the couch. He was in a terrible mess. He couldn't eat or drink; at any little noise he leapt to his feet. I knew the only thing that could tie us in with the shooting was the van. I had to get rid of it. I had to find a way. As time was going by I was getting more and more paranoid. I couldn't think straight. Duddy was making me uneasy. By the afternoon, I just had to get out of that flat. I suggested that we all go to the park with June's two kids. As we were walking through the park, two police officers were walking towards us.

My heart was in my mouth as they got closer. I said to Duddy, 'I think this is it, I think it's all come on top.' Duddy panicked. He picked up one of June's kids, put him on his shoulders and tore off through the park. I put my arm around Lilly and took a deep breath. As the police officers walked passed us, they both said, 'Afternoon'. I nearly died. We went back to the flat and decided we had better stay put until dark then we had better go and torch that van.

Duddy was no use at all so it was down to me and Lilly. We waited until 10 p.m. Lilly drove a car that she had hired earlier in the day. We drove slowly towards the railway arches. It was really quiet and nobody was around. I didn't like the look of it. I kept thinking it was an ambush. We decided to park the car in the next street. Lilly stood guard at the top of the road.

I tried to keep in the shadows. I squeezed the handle of my gun tight. The only sound I could hear as I got closer to the lock-up was the thumping of my heart. I was scared stiff. The closer I got the more I was convinced it was an ambush. I couldn't do it — my bottle went. I turned and hurriedly made my way back to where Lilly was waiting for me. I grabbed her hand and said, 'Let's get the fuck away from here.'

Early on Sunday morning [August 14] we went to bury the guns — a Luger, a Smith and Wesson and a Webley — up at Ken Wood on Hampstead Heath. Duddy was still in a right state. He wanted to go to Scotland and promised he would go to Dundee. He thought he'd be safe there. I was becoming increasingly paranoid and Duddy was becoming a burden so I gave him £30 and told him to fuck off.

I knew I couldn't stay at the flat any longer so I packed a bag and arranged to meet Lilly under the clock at Paddington Station at 3 p.m. It was a lovely sunny day so I decided to kill time in Hyde Park. I wandered around for a while and lay on the grass to do a bit of sunbathing. But I felt as if there was a huge neon sign on my head with a big arrow pointing at me saying, 'Here I am, I'm the murderer.'

Kate Kray, Lifers, 1994

Hiding the van there was rather stupid as the arch was rented in Witney's name. Three fired cartridge cases were found behind the passenger seat.

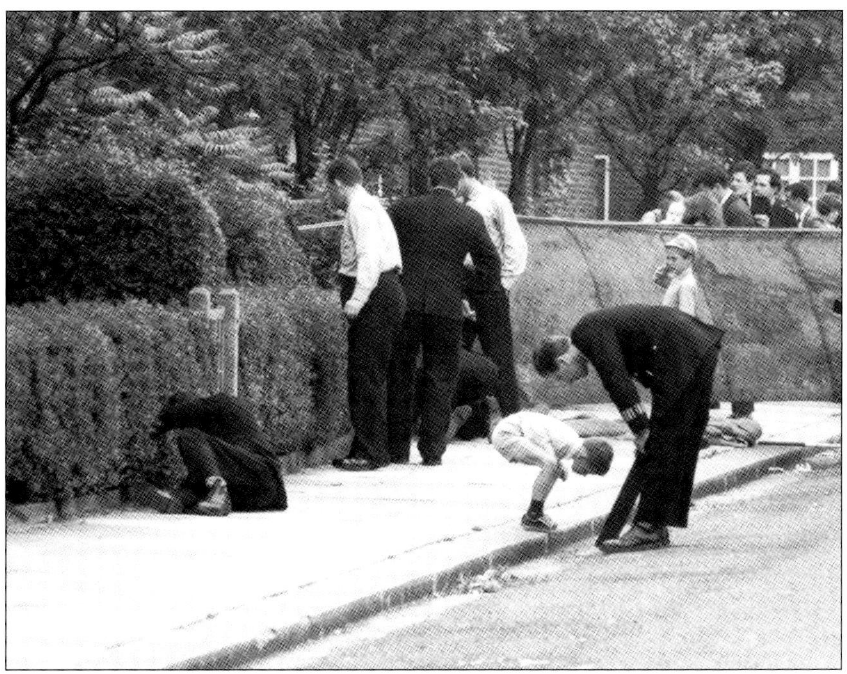

Midst the tragedy, a spot of humour as a small boy helps in the search for clues. Note how the murder scene has now been screened off.

Armed police joined the hunt last night for gunmen who killed three policemen in a London street.

They were issued with .38 revolvers at Shepherd's Bush police station in West London. Other officers with tear-gas guns were held ready.

A police officer said: 'More guns will be issued if these men are cornered.'

Nearly 200 policemen from all parts of London were sent to Shepherd's Bush police station, headquarters of the hunt for the killers. Most were volunteers — men on leave or away on holiday hurried back to help the hunt.

Drivers of all London's radio-controlled taxis were asked to look out for the gunmen's getaway car — a blue 1955 Standard Vanguard, believed to be a van converted into an estate car. Its number is PGT 726.

Scotland Yard started a street by street search of garages and yards for the car. Meanwhile they issued descriptions of three men they wish to interview:

One: Aged about 30, 5ft. 7in. to 5ft. 9in., dark and sun-tanned, wearing dark jacket and trousers.

Two: Aged 30 to 35, longish hair brushed straight back, pointed face, nose and chin.

Three: Aged 20 to 23, with thick wavy hair, wearing a light coloured sweater with a red and blue pattern and blue-grey jacket.

Death came to the three policemen on routine patrol in just four seconds — the time it took to fire a few rounds from one or more revolvers in quiet, sunny Braybrook Street, bordering Wormwood Scrubs Common.

As the crew of Foxtrot One lay dead the radio on their dashboard gave out a report of the shooting.

The Yard, alerted by a 999 call, had radioed to the car believing it to be the nearest to the scene.

For a few seconds Braybrook Street, a long crescent lined on one side by council houses, was silent. Gunsmoke drifted in the air. The children had to run clear.

But soon dozens of policemen were on the spot. A senior Scotland Yard officer said: 'It was the most callous crime I have known.'

So callous that PC Wombwell was believed to be holding his hands above his head to prove he was unarmed when he was gunned down.

A man's name scribbled on a pad beside the gear lever of the Q car may help the hunt. It was written by Sergeant Head shortly before the shooting.

Police think he may have recognised a suspect in the parked Vanguard and had time to write down his name before he was shot.

Police are anxious to trace the driver of a green Minivan who sped away from the scene within seconds of the shootings.

Daily Mail, August 13, 1966

The phone rings. Three policemen shot dead at Shepherd's Bush. Their bodies still lay where they had fallen in the roadway. I knew all three well but this was a time when personal feelings had to be kept in the background in case one's mind was distracted from the job in hand. I had to reconstruct exactly what happened in order that any bullets and cartridge cases found could tell the whole story. There is a live round in the roadway that has been through a pistol. A faulty gun? Two different types of ammunition. A pistol and a revolver used? One officer appears to have been facing in that direction when he was shot clean through the head, so the bullet must have gone in the direction of that distant bank over the large field.

A posse of police has to be engaged to search the area but first show them the type of bullet to look for. I am surprised by the number of fired cases and bullets found which are unconnected as they have evidently been there for months or years. Careful examination of the police car and arrangements made to have it removed for further examination. Then to the mortuary where again remember the necessity not to become affected by circumstances but to keep the material facts of a major investigation.

Back to the laboratory and a detailed examination of the bullets and cartridge cases. Probably an Enfield .380 revolver and a 9mm Luger. Bullets and cases carefully preserved until the receipt of the weapons.

Detective Superintendent John McCafferty, Mac, I've got a Murder, 1975

Duddy had done a runner to Scotland but Glasgow police traced his brother who said that John was hiding in a tenement in Stevenson Street, Bridgeton *(left)*. He was arrested without a fight and flown to London the same day *(right)*. That left only Roberts on the run. A reward of £1,000 is probably the equivalent of around £11,000 today.

I got to Paddington Station to meet Lilly and I stood at the top of the ramp and looked down. I could see her standing under the clock. I was nervous as I made my way towards her. I felt sure everyone was looking at me but they weren't. It was just me being paranoid. I hugged Lilly. It was good to see her. It seemed she was the only friend I had in the world. We decided to stay in a hotel and found a reasonably priced one, called The Russell Hotel, in Russell Square. We went in, trying all the time to act normal but I knew it was getting time for me to leave her. It was getting too dangerous to keep Lilly with me. I knew that when the police did finally catch up with me they would probably kill me.

We booked out of the hotel early on Monday 15th. I had it in my mind what I was going to do. I was going to drop Lilly off then go and hide in the woods. First, though, I had to get some supplies so we made our way to Camden Town and bought some camping equipment, a sleeping bag, a small stove, heavy boots, a camouflage jacket and a small radio. Then we got some food: a loaf of bread, three tins of baked beans, Oxo cubes, a packet of tea and some dried milk. I stocked up on Old Holborn tobacco and green papers. I stuffed everything into a large rucksack and we caught a number 720 Greenline bus out of Camden Town to Epping Forest.

We got off the bus at a small country pub called the Wake Arms. Lilly was wearing her best coat and high-heeled shoes and she held my hand tight as we made our way deep into the forest. She never spoke a word, not even when she snagged her coat on a bramble.

When we stopped, I changed into my new boots, lacing them up slowly. We both knew the time had come to split up. I turned to Lilly and said, 'It's time I was on my own, Lilly.'

She started to cry and said, 'But I can help you. Please let me stay with you.' I was choked up and tried to explain that it was me they wanted, not her, and I would have a better chance on my own. She had been so good, so loyal and I loved her so much. I couldn't put her life in danger any longer. I promised that I would phone her at a phone box in Maida Vale every Tuesday afternoon at 2 p.m.

As we made our way back to the edge of the forest, she held my hand tight and tried not to let me see her crying. It nearly broke my heart as I waved her goodbye on the bus. I don't think I have ever felt as lonely as I did at that moment. I got myself together and made my way back into the forest. I pulled my heavy rucksack on my back and started to make my way along the A11. I wanted to get out of Epping Forest as I reckoned the police would look for me there. I knew exactly where I was heading — Thorley Woods near Bishop's Stortford.

METROPOLITAN POLICE

£1,000 REWARD

MURDER

A reward or rewards up to a total of £1,000 will be paid for information leading to the arrest of HARRY MAURICE ROBERTS, b. Wanstead, Essex, on 21-7-36, 5ft. 10in., photo. above, wanted for questioning in connection with the murder of three police officers on the 12th August, 1966, at Braybrook Street, Shepherds Bush.

Information to be given to New Scotland Yard, S.W.1, or at any police station.

The amount of any payment will be in the discretion of the Commissioner of Police for the Metropolis.

J. SIMPSON,
Commissioner of Police.

Police discovered that Roberts had caught a bus to Epping Forest on the north-western outskirts of London and a manhunt was set in operation, conducted by up to 500 officers, many armed like this man with a .303 No. 4 Lee-Enfield.

By November I'd been on the run for three months. Wherever I made a camp I tried to put myself between a town and a gypsy camp, so if the town people saw me they would think I was a gypsy, and if a gypsy saw me he would think I was a townie. It had been a good cover for me until then. On Friday the 11th a policeman who'd been chasing me made his way to the edge of the gypsy camp where his dog had cornered a young gypsy as I watched from a distance. I saw the policeman lead the young man away. I knew the gypsy would protest his innocence and would be sure to mention the geezer living in the woods nearby, meaning me. This was going to be enough to bring half the London police force down on me. I couldn't risk going back to my camp. I wandered around and found a barn about a mile away. It was full of straw and I decided to stay there. It was, I thought, as good a place as any.

Early the next morning, I went back to the woods. I needed some of my stuff from my camp. I crept through the woods and it was eerily quiet. I waded down a small stream so that any police dogs around wouldn't pick up my scent and made my way around the back of my camp, peering gingerly through the bushes. It was deserted. The soft muddy ground had only dog paw prints. I could see no boot prints. But it was too quiet. Something wasn't right. Then I noticed the flap of my tent was open and I was sure I wouldn't have left it like that.

I was just about to stand up and approach my camp when a policeman came out of my tent. He was heavily armed. I stopped dead in my tracks. He hadn't seen me. I tried to turn slowly without making a sound. As I took a step back, *crack*, I stood on a twig. I didn't hang about to see if the policeman had seen or heard me. I took off and made my way back to the barn.

I was cold and hungry but I was too scared to leave the barn. I had made myself a good hide-out among the bales of straw and had completely buried myself in the middle of a giant stack. At night, the only sound was the rustling and creaking of many animals scurrying about on the cold hard floor of the barn. The bales were infested with rats. I stayed huddled in the barn all Sunday, too scared to move.

On Monday I woke up early with a start. I tried to move my legs but they were stiff with the cold. I made a little hole in the straw and peered out. There was no one around. I squeezed through the gap and stretched my aching joints. I thought to myself, 'I could murder a cup of tea'. I was starving hungry, cold and thoroughly pissed off and I knew I couldn't carry on much longer. I thought, 'Fuck it, I'm going into town and going to buy myself some fish and chips.' Once I was in the town, I could see the whole area was rotten with police but I didn't care. All I could think of right now was getting something hot inside me. I walked out of the chip shop, leant against a wall and scoffed it down. It was the best fish and chips I've ever eaten. I popped into a shop and bought a few bits and pieces, tobacco and a bit of grub. After eating, getting caught didn't seem such a good idea so I made my way back to the barn as quickly as I could.

In the morning I woke to the sound of tractors and men shouting. At first I thought it was just farm workers. I peered through a little hole that I had made in the straw. I could see a tractor pulling a trailer full of men. They weren't farm workers, they were the London Murder Squad. They looked out of place posing as farmers in their country tweed suits and green wellies. I snuggled down in the straw, not moving a muscle. They came into the barn laughing and joking, and started climbing all over the bales, poking and prodding with their sticks. I didn't move. My heart was pounding so loud I thought they would hear it. Then, much to

Roberts says that he got off the bus at the Wake Arms. There are two roundabouts on the A11 (now the A104) which runs through the forest. Coming from the direction of London, this is the one before at the Robin Hood pub, the photograph being taken on August 18.

Roberts had two hideaways. *Left:* **This is his tented camp found by police on the edge of Thorley Wood near Bishop's Stortford.** *Above:* **The 'barn' that Roberts keeps referring to in his account given to Kate Kray, wife of the late East End gangster Ronnie Kray, was actually this blister hangar just off the north-eastern perimeter track of Sawbridgeworth aerodrome.**

my surprise, they left. I looked through the hole again to see them climbing back on the trailer and starting off down the lane.

Four times they searched the barn and each time they missed me. From where I was I had a clear view over the fields and woods. I could see the police combing the whole area. For most of the morning I watched them. The whole place was cordoned off. Then I saw two officers, apart from the rest, making their way around the edge of the woods. I watched them getting closer and closer. One of them suddenly left the other and started to make his way towards the barn. I covered my face with straw and laid still. He was a uniformed officer and had just slipped away for a fag.

I felt him climb the bales of straw right beside me. Much to my horror, he sat down and lit a cigarette and, as he put his hand down, he put it straight on my face. I sat bolt upright.

'Who are you?' he said.

I knew there was no sense in trying to lie. The whole place was surrounded and if I started fucking with them I would probably end up getting myself shot. So I said, 'I'm the geezer you're looking for. I'm Harry Roberts.'

He looked at me in disbelief and, dragging on his fag, he said, 'Don't fuck me about, give me your real name'.

'It's Harry Roberts,' I said.

All of a sudden his face changed to one of horror. He panicked and fell straight off the bale of straw. He crashed to the ground and was fumbling to get the gun out of his holster. 'Don't move! Don't move!' He was shaking so much I thought his gun was going to go off.

I told him: 'Take it easy pal, I ain't got a gun on me' and pointed to my Luger in my hideout. He reached out and got my gun then started shouting to his mate, 'I've got him! I've got him.'

I climbed down from the straw and put my hands in the air. I could see the other copper running towards the barn. I turned to look at my captor. Still in a panic, he had fallen arse over head backwards and got tangled in some barbed wire. I went to help him up. 'Keep back! Keep back!' he yelled.

As I looked around, the other copper had his rifle aimed at my head. The first copper untangled himself from the barbed wire and was up on his feet now. Waving his gun towards the entrance, he said, 'Come on, out!' Slowly I walked out with him right behind me. When we reached the other officer, he was calling and waving his arms to a Land-Rover that was parked just down the lane with two farmers in it.

The Land-Rover pulled up and I was bundled in the back with the two officers. We drove to the edge of the woods. In those days the police didn't have radios so the two officers needed to inform their colleagues personally that they had me. As we got there, the police were just coming out of the trees. I was shocked by how many there were.

In seconds the Land-Rover was surrounded by the Old Bill. Hearing I was inside, all hell broke loose and a policewoman started spitting and screaming at me through the open back of the Land-Rover. This seemed to whip the rest of the police into a frenzy and they started beating the soft top of the Land-Rover with their sticks. They didn't only hit me, they were also hitting the two coppers who had caught me. At one point I thought they were going to drag me out and lynch me. The two coppers in the Land-Rover with me screamed to the farmers to drive on and we screeched off leaving the mob of mad coppers behind. I was quickly moved to the local nick at Bishop's Stortford.

Kate Kray, Lifers, 1994

Roberts was apprehended there by Police Sergeants Peter Smith and Oswald Thorne.

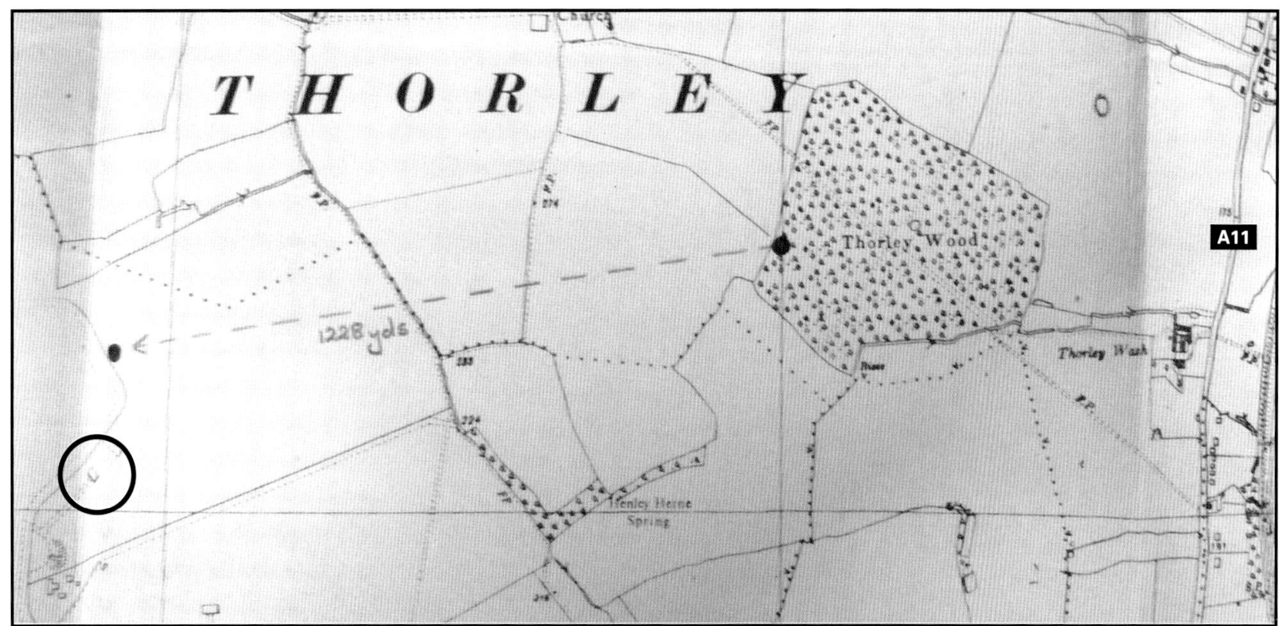

The police plan is marked showing where Roberts's tent camp was located (red dot), and where he was captured on the edge of Sawbridgeworth airfield (blue dot). However, the latter position is incorrect as the hangar was not on the approach to runway 24 but further to the south. We have circled the correct position where Extended Over Blister 82/5 was located.

The massive police hunt for Harry Roberts, the man wanted for questioning about the police murders continued in the Epping Forest area all day yesterday (Thursday). By noon the search had moved near Epping, and the man was reported seen in Theydon Bois and Theydon Mount. Police — there were 500 of them — were certain the wanted man was in the area.

The hunt, one of the largest ever in the forest, was started at 8.30 p.m. on Wednesday after the murder squad had received a reliable tip-off that Roberts was sleeping rough in the forest. He is known to have kitted himself out with camping equipment. At 10 o'clock Chief Superintendent G. Evans of 'J' Division called off the hunt, but all roads were patrolled through the night.

Yesterday the hunt moved towards Epping and four schoolboys phoned the police after they heard someone 'moving furniture around' in the Epping Foresters Cricket Club pavilion. Within minutes scores of police had raced to the spot. Eventually they got into the pavilion, but Roberts, if he had been there, had gone. Some of the police searches were in the vicinity of the King's Oak public house at High Beech.

West Essex Gazette, August 19, 1966

On Friday the number of police officers searching the forest for Roberts had swelled to 700. Some of them were armed with guns.

The searches were concentrated at High Beech and Connaught Waters.

During Friday morning some of the police searchers had rushed from the forest to Loughton railway station after a report that a man answering Roberts' description had been seen on a Central Line train.

Police with dogs, boarded a number of trains stopping at Loughton and closely checked the passengers. Their dogs failed to pick up any scent of Roberts in the compartments.

Loughton and West Essex Gazette, August 26, 1966

Both locations have since been expunged; the wood having largely been cut down and the blister hangar demolished.

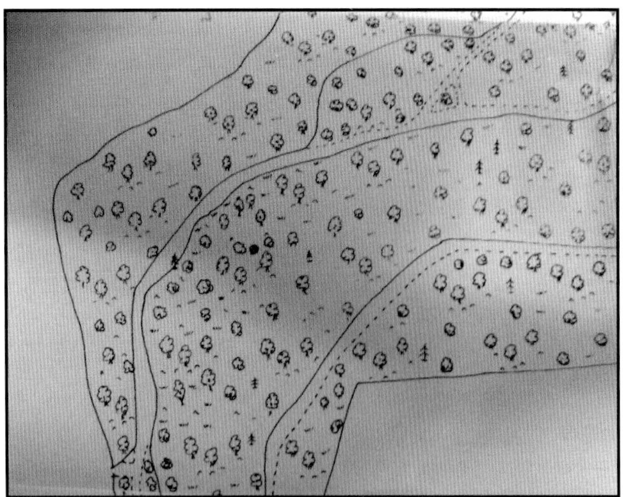

The trial of Duddy and Witney had begun at the Old Bailey on November 14 but when Roberts was caught later the same day, it was halted and the Crown immediately proffered a Bill of Indictment against Roberts. This meant that he could be taken straight to the Central Criminal Court to join the other two in the dock rather than being processed first through the magistrates' court system. The firearms that had been used were all recovered, a 9mm Luger (serial 206) and a .380 Colt (17515) being found in Roberts's belongings in the hangar. *Above:* **These illustrations taken from the police file show the location (red dot on plan) where the third pistol, a .38 Enfield revolver (19210), was dug up from where Roberts and Duddy had first hidden their weapons in Ken Wood on Hampstead Heath. The trial began again on December 6, all three men being sentenced to life imprisonment with a recommendation that they serve a minimum of 30 years.**

A decision by Mr Baker, the Home Secretary, to release a man jailed for life 25 years ago for murdering three police officers was condemned by police representatives yesterday.

John Witney, 61 was one of three men sentenced for shooting a 'Q' car crew near Wormwood Scrubs, west London, in August 1966. The crime sparked one of Britain's largest murder hunts.

Witney's release makes him the first adult murderer of a policeman to be set free since the abolition of hanging in 1965. The killer, who was transferred to Leyhill open prison near Bristol in 1985, was freed last week, a Home Office spokesman said.

Roberts is still serving his sentence and Duddy died in Prison in 1981.

The Daily Telegraph, June 19, 1991

Harry Roberts, who shot dead three police officers near Wormwood Scrubs prison, could be released this year after serving the recommended 30 years of a life sentence imposed in 1966.

Roberts is now 59 and reports are being compiled for a committee to consider his parole application.

Sentencing Roberts, Mr Justice Glyn-Jones said: 'I think it likely that no Home Secretary, regarding the enormity of your crime, will ever think fit to show mercy by releasing you on licence.'

The Daily Telegraph, April 1, 1996

Britain's most evil police killer, Harry Roberts, is poised to be freed from jail after serving almost 34 years of a life sentence.

The 63-year-old triple murderer has been moved to an open prison prior to being granted parole and can expect to be free within two years.

Three weeks ago, Roberts was suddenly moved from the Category C jail at Ashwell, Leicestershire, to Sudbury open prison in Derbyshire. Over the years, he has tried and failed to break out of prison 22 times. Four years ago, when he had completed 30 years, he was refused parole and declared that he wanted to die in jail, but he has since changed his mind and has recently been pressing for his freedom.

Duddy died in jail and Witney died last year, after being released on licence.

The Mail on Sunday, April 23, 2000

Police and victims groups demanded yesterday that Harry Roberts, the triple police killer, remain in jail for the rest of his life.

Roberts, 67 has started a legally aided High court challenge to a decision to stop him and his lawyer seeing secret documents that could determine whether he wins his freedom.

Yesterday, as police groups called for him to remain in jail, Jo Dobry, spokeswoman for the Parole Board, said: 'We welcome the judicial review because it gives the opportunity for the courts to clarify what is a difficult and sensitive issue relating to disclosure.'

Jan Berry, chairwoman of the Police Federation which represents rank-and-file police officers, said 'It is our view that life should mean life for anyone who murders a police officer.'

The Times, July 31, 2003

The funeral of the murdered officers was held on August 31 with a formal service at St Stephen's Uxbridge. This was the same day that Scotland Yard issued the wanted poster for Roberts. Later a larger memorial service was held in Westminster Abbey on September 6 with many calls from the 1000-strong crowd outside for the restoration of capital punishment which had only recently been abolished. Since 1965, 75 police officers have lost their lives in the line of duty as a result of criminal acts, adjudged to be either murder or manslaughter.

Geoffrey Fox was buried in Mortlake Cemetery, Section C12, Grave 20.

Britain's most notorious police killer hopes to be freed from prison within months, having served 42 years in jail. Harry Roberts, who was jailed for life for the murder of three policemen, has already completed the first stage of a Parole Board hearing, which he believes will clear the way for his release.

He hopes that a final hearing will find that at the age of 72, he is no longer a risk to the public. He has already served 12 years more than the minimum recommended by the judge.

A detailed plan to resettle Roberts in the community will have to be drawn up by the prison and Probation Service, including providing him with housing and benefits. Ministers will be concerned that his release could provoke public fury and put him at risk, but will be powerless to halt it.

The Times, February 28, 2009

IN
TREASURED MEMORY OF
CHRISTOPHER TIPPETT HEAD,
(CHRIS)
DETECTIVE SERGEANT
METROPOLITAN POLICE
WHO DIED ON DUTY 12TH AUGUST 1966,
AGED 30 YEARS.
ALSO HIS MOTHER
PHYLIA HILDA HEAD
DIED 21ST SEPT. 1978.

Christopher Head was taken to Torquay Cemetery where his remains were interred in Grave 2259 in Section LX.

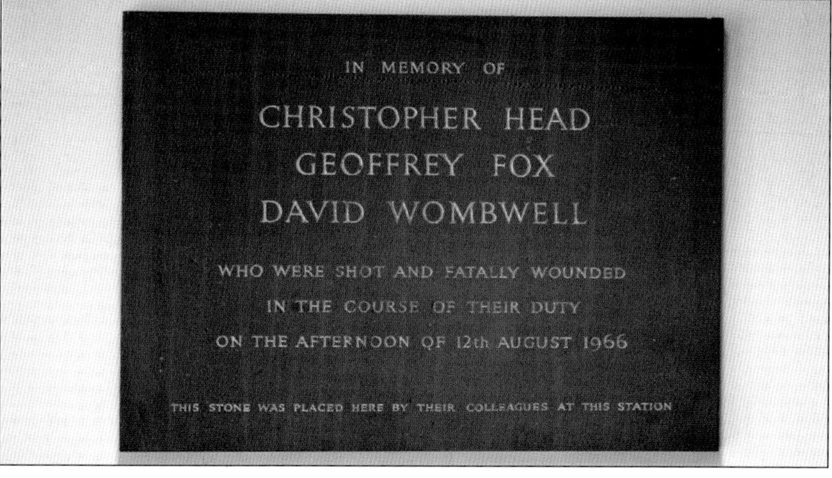

David Wombwell was cremated and his ashes scattered in St Thomas's Church at Acton (which has since been destroyed by fire). This plaque was erected in the entrance to Shepherd's Bush police station.

DAILY MAIL, Wednesday, February 21, 1968 PAGE 5

Violence in the rush hour

'I never thought I would see this in a London street'

February 20, 1968 — Death in a London Street

This picture was taken in a London street yesterday morning. The rush-hour was tailing off. The night workers had reached home. Jorgy Koka was a night worker. But he did not reach home yesterday. Shots were fired and Mr Koka, Albanian-born factory worker, lay dead. This picture may seem to some shocking.

The *Daily Mail* was shocked too that on February 20, 1968 a man could be lifted from the pavement in a London street and into a coffin. A woman passer-by, who knew Mr Koka, said: 'Seeing him lying there made me think I was at a film.

'It seems crazy to walk into this. I never thought I would see this in a London street.'

Mr Koka was shot at 7.59 a.m. and died almost instantly.

For the next two hours he lay on the pavement in Burlington Gardens, Acton, London, while detectives, fingerprint men, the police surgeon and the official photographers got to work.

Housewives, children going to school, a milkman on his rounds, all stopped to watch.

Some of them knew Mr Koka, for the big black-moustached Albanian was a popular figure. He would give sweets to the local children, who called him 'Uncle Jorgy'.

Neighbour Mr Patrick English, 25, said: 'He spoke only a little English and was a favourite with the local children. He used to tap my two-year-old son on the head, give him sweets and call him 'butchka.'

The Daily Mail, February 21, 1968

And so we end this book as we began . . . with the death of Jorgy Koka. He lived in the Albanian hostel near the scene of the shooting. His Italian wife, Sarah, worked day shifts at the same factory as her husband. She was there when police called to tell her of his death. The wall has since been rebuilt losing the stone buttresses. The car is emerging from the entrance where the second police Jaguar was parked (see Frontispiece pages 2-3).

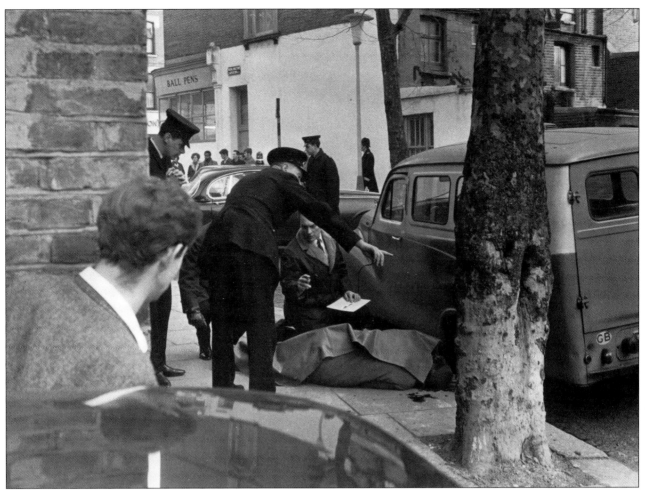

There are two Burlington Gardens in West London — this is the one close by Acton Central station.

During the war, the Americans had a temporary burial ground in front of their First World War cemetery at Brookwood (see plan page 134). After the graves were disinterred in 1948 for permanent burial at Cambridge or in the United States, this area was used by the Commonwealth War Graves Commission for the erection of the Memorial to the Missing.

Murderers commemorated on the Brookwood Memorial in 1958

As we have described earlier (see page 134), the American Graves Registration Service established a separate Plot 'X' at Brookwood, hidded away behind the service area, to bury their executed dead. After the war, the US Quartermaster General of the Army asked the American Battle Monuments Commission if they had any space suitable to inter all those executed in the European Theater of Operations (some 96 in total) in one location. As a result, in 1949, General of the Army George C. Marshall, the Commission's Chairman who had also been Chief-of-Staff during the war, together with the Commissioners, chose a plot of land adjacent to but outside the American First World War Cemetery at Oise-Aisne in France (see also page 149). The intention was not only to establish a special 'dishonoured' plot, which would be secure from public view, but also to ensure that 'no stigma, either actual, imagined, or implied, could become attached to the soldiers buried nearby who died honourably in battle'.

Executed murderers serving with US forces in Britain were exhumed from Brookwood and reburied in a 'dishonoured' Plot 'E' at the First World War American Military Cemetery at Oise-Aisne, 14 miles north-east of Chateau-Thierry in France.

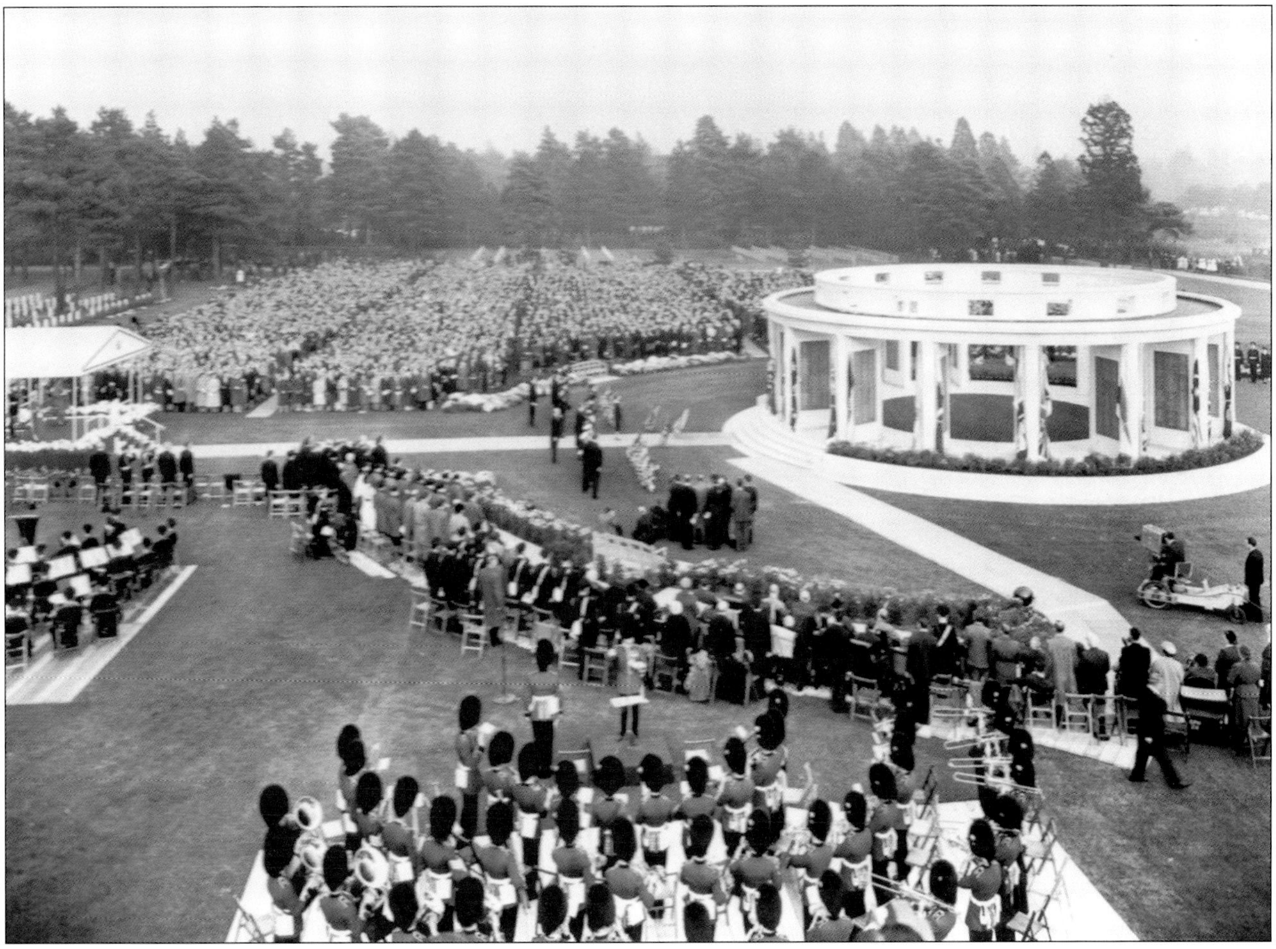

The Brookwood Memorial was opened by Her Majesty Queen Elizabeth II and HRH The Duke of Edinburgh on October 25, 1958.

Contrast this view with the decision by the British War Office in 1946. A memorandum dated May 30 states that 'the question of the commemoration of personnel of the Army who have been judicially executed has been under review and it has been agreed that in the cases of those who were buried at the place of execution, and all traces of the graves were removed at the time of execution, the Imperial War Graves Commission will include their names in the list of missing which will be commemorated by the Imperial War Graves Commission in a manner which has not yet been decided but which will probably follow the policy of the War 1914-1918.' (It must be emphasised that the Commission plays no part in the decision as to who or who will not be commemorated as they act solely under instructions issued by the military authorities.)

As we have seen, crimes of murder (and manslaughter, treason and rape), when committed by service personnel in the United Kingdom, are always tried by civil court. Clearly Parliament regarded these crimes as the most serious offences in the criminal calendar and felt it appropriate to require that if they were committed within the area of jurisdiction of the British criminal courts, they should always be tried by those courts, rather than by military court-martial. For example, although Gunner Kemp (see page 150) was convicted of killing a servicewoman, this still did not alter the criteria, and all those so executed were immediately buried in recorded, although unmarked, graves within the prison walls, Kemp's burial being the second one in Grave No. 68.

His victim Miriam Deeley was buried on February 18, 1944 in a plot chosen by her father in the City of London Cemetery at Manor Park in East London and after the war the Imperial War Graves Commission (the name was changed to Commonwealth in March 1960) erected a headstone of white Portland stone on the grave (see page 157).

Two years earlier the Brookwood Memorial was inaugurated in Brookwood Military Cemetery, near Woking, Surrey, to commemorate those members of the land forces of the British Commonwealth and Empire whose circumstances of death were such that their names could not appropriately be assigned to any of the campaign memorials. Dedicated to those 'to whom the fortune of war denied a known and honoured grave', similar Memorials to the Missing were provided for the Royal Navy at Chatham, Plymouth and Portsmouth, and the Royal Air Force at Runnymede. However, no convicted sailors or airmen are listed on those memorials as the individuals concerned (like Cummins on page 98) were discharged before being executed. On the other hand, among the 3,555 names inscribed at Brookwood are 18 soldiers who were hanged in civil prisons for their crimes. Their names can be found inscribed alongside those who died honourably in battle, or perhaps were murdered by the Gestapo, and have no known grave.

However, these particular criminals do have known graves which are located withn the prisons.

Private David Jennings of the 1st Battalion, South Lancashire Regiment, who shot Albert Farley, a night-watchman. Convicted at Dorset Assizes, he was executed at Dorchester Prison on July 24, 1941 where he is buried. His name appears at Brookwood on Panel 12 of Column 1.

Private Arthur Peach of the 11th Battalion, South Staffordshire Regiment, shot and killed 18-year-old Kitty Lyon at Walsall. He was found guilty at Stafford Assizes and executed and buried in Birmingham Prison on January 30, 1942. Now also commemorated on Panel 12 of Column 1.

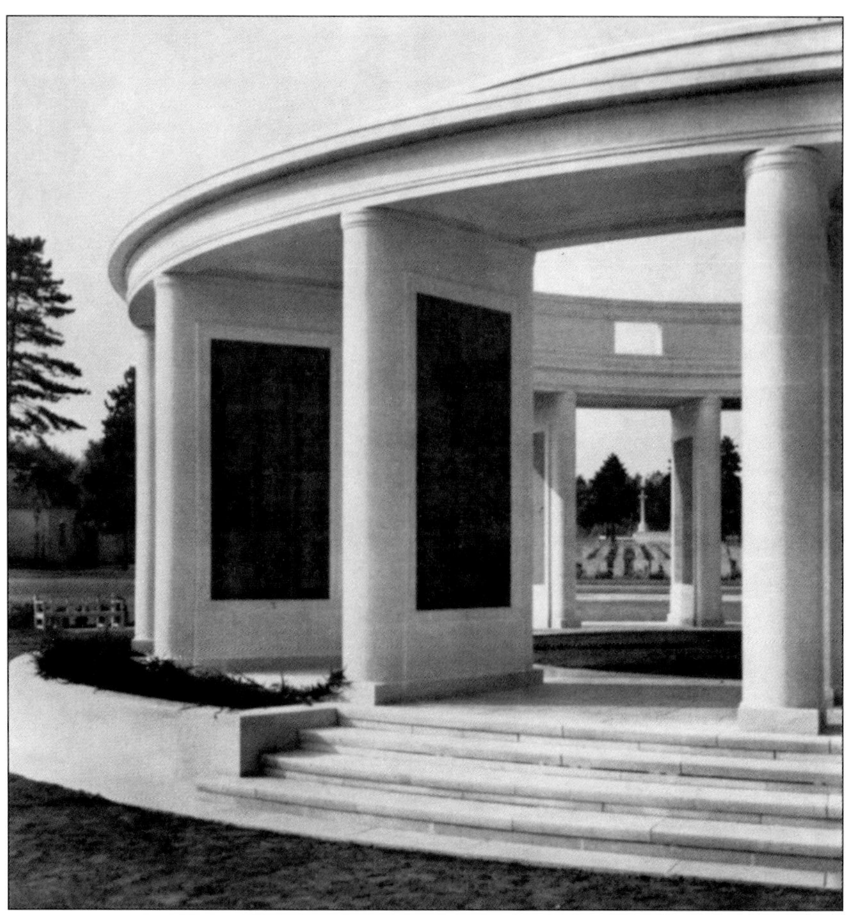

In her address, Her Majesty stated that 'this memorial has been built in honour of 3,500 soldiers of the land forces of the Commonwealth' adding that 'all upheld the proud tradition of their country and the Commonwealth.' Panels of green slate were provided to record the names of those who have no known grave . . . but the convicted murderers *do* have known graves in the cemeteries within the prisons where they were executed, so in no way did *all* on the memorial die with honour.

Private Cyril Johnson, 2/5th Battalion, West Yorkshire Regiment, strangled his girlfriend Maggie Smail. Convicted at the Old Bailey, he was hanged at Wandsworth on April 15, 1942 and is now commemorated on Panel 10 of Column 1.

Lance-Corporal Frederick Austin, Royal Army Service Corps, shot his wife Lillian. He was convicted at Hampshire Assizes and executed in Bristol Jail on April 30, 1942. Now on Panel 16 of Column 1.

Corporal Dudley Rayner, serving with the Pioneer Corps, kicked his wife to death on February 8, 1943. Josephine Rayner was a private in the Auxiliary Territorial Service and her grave (No. 18916) can be found in Beckenham Cemetery. After being found guilty at the Old Bailey, Corporal Rayner was executed at Wandsworth on March 31, 1943 and his name appears on Panel 20 of Column 3.

Private August Sangret, Royal Canadian Infantry Corps — see page 116. His name is inscribed on Panel 23 of Column 3.

Private Charles Raymond, 5th Infantry Brigade Company, Royal Canadian Army Service Corps, On January 31, 1943, he battered to death Aircraftwoman 1st Class Marguerite Burge of the Women's Auxiliary Air Force. He was tried at the Old Bailey and hanged at Wandsworth on July 10, 1943. He is commemorated on Panel 25 of Column 1 while Marguerite is buried in Havant Cemetery (Grave 105).

Private Charles Gauthier of Le Régiment de Quebec, Royal Canadian Infantry Corps. He was having an affair with Annette Pepper at Portslade and shot her in a jealous rage with his Bren gun. He was hanged at Wandsworth and buried in the prison graveyard on September 24, 1943 after being convicted at the Old Bailey. Now he is listed on Panel 24 of Column 2.

Private Terence Casey of the Royal Army Medical Corps raped and strangled Mrs Bridget Milton at Putney. Found guilty at the Old Bailey, he was executed at Wandsworth on November 19, 1943 and is now commemorated on Panel 18 of Column 2.

Private Mervin McEwan, a deserter from the Royal Canadian Ordnance Corps, killed a postman, Mark Turner, in Halifax. After his trial at Leeds Assizes, he was hanged at Leeds Prison on February 3, 1944 where he was buried. His name appears on Panel 25 of Column 1.

Sergeant Ernest Digby, serving in the Royal Artillery, battered his baby daughter to death. He was jointly charged with his common law wife (who was acquitted), and on being found guilty at Taunton Assizes, admitted to killing another child the previous year. He was hanged at Bristol Jail on March 16, 1944 and is commemorated on Panel 2 of Column 3.

Gunner Ernest Kemp of the Royal Artillery – see page 150. Now on Panel 3 of Column 2.

The travesty caused by the War Office not treating convicted murderers the same as the Air Ministry or Admiralty is clearly indicated by these two victims, both from the Women's Auxiliary Air Force. ***Left:*** **ACW1 Marguerite Burge lies in Havant and Waterloo (Havant) Cemetery (Grave 105). She was murdered by Private Charles Raymond, buried in Wandsworth Prison, but now he is memorialised on Panel 25 at Brookwood.** ***Right:*** **ACW1 Winifred Evans was buried in Grave 19 of Section B in Willesden New Cemetery after her death at the hands of LAC Arthur Heys, a member of the RAF, but he was not commemorated on their Memorial to the Missing at Runnymede.**

Private John Davidson, absent without leave from the Royal Army Ordnance Corps, strangled Gladys Appleton in a drunken rage after she resisted his advances. Convicted at Manchester Assizes, despite a recommendation for mercy, he was hanged at Liverpool on July 12, 1944. His name is inscribed on Panel 19 of Column 1.

Private Horace Gordon of the Royal Canadian Ordnance Corps, stabbed to death Mrs Dorothy Hillman, who was heavily pregnant at the time. Although the Canadian government pleaded that the Jamaican-born soldier had a previous good record, he was executed at Wandsworth on January 9, 1945. His name now appears on Panel 25 of Column 1.

Private Arthur Thompson, at the time an absentee from the General Service Corps, strangled Mrs Jane Coulson, the licensee of a Bradford public house. He was convicted at Leeds Assizes and hanged on January 31, 1945 at Leeds Prison. Now his name is listed on Panel 21 of Column 2.

Although hostilities against Germany ended in May 1945, and against Japan in August, the charter of the Imperial War Graves Commission was extended until December 31, 1947 to account for those servicemen dying of wounds or on mine-clearance duties, etc. Thus the following three names are also included on the Brookwood Memorial.

Bombardier Joseph Grossley of the Royal Canadian Artillery was a married man with a wife in Canada. He shot Lily Griffiths, the woman he was living with in Wales, supposedly during his botched attempt to commit suicide. The defence at Swansea Assizes claimed it was an accident, or at worst manslaughter, but the jury disagreed and he was convicted. Hanged in Cardiff Prison on September 5, 1945, his name appears on Panel 23 of Column 2.

Theodore Schurch, a private in the Royal Service Corps, was a former member of the British Union of Fascists who had been 'captured' at Tobruk to volunteer his services to the Italians. He was court-martialled in September 1945 and found guilty of nine charges of treachery and one of desertion. He was hanged on January 4, 1946 at Pentonville but the War Office still saw fit to commemorate his name at Brookwood on Panel 17 of Column 3.

Lance-Corporal Walter Clayton, serving with the 9th Battalion of the Cameronians, strangled Joyce Jacques at Morecambe on April 12, 1946. He was found guilty and executed in Liverpool Prison on August 7. His name now appears on Panel 11 of Column 1.

Back in 1984, when I first found that Gunner Kemp had so been commemorated for his awful murder, I asked the Ministry of Defence, the present-day successor to the War Office, the reason why. Their spokesman replied that the criteria set out at the end of the war for the commemoration of British war dead stated that any serviceman or woman who died between September 3, 1939 and December 31, 1947, from whatever cause, would automatically be referred to the Imperial War Graves Commission for commemoration. The spokesman went on to say that this decision was made so that servicemen and women who died from natural causes or from road or other accidents, or even were murdered, while in the service of their country, would still be commemorated, either in name or by a known grave, alongside those who had lost their lives in battle. Also, because of the enormous numbers involved, and the inevitable degree of uncertainty in many cases of the circumstances of death, this dictated that the qualification was not *how* but *when* a person died.

However this explanation is flawed because the RAF and Royal Navy simply avoided the problem by discharging individuals sentenced to death so that they were executed as civilians, whereas the Army failed to do so.

The Ministry also stated that they were just following the policy adopted in the First World War, i.e. referring to those executed by firing squad on the field of battle (see *After the Battle* No. 114). However, execution following a court-martial for a military crime, like cowardice or desertion, is totally different to that of a conviction for murder in a civil court in Britain, and no Army murderers in 1914-18 were ever commemorated.

Including the names of known criminals, tried, found guilty and executed for horrendous murders or treason, on any memorial alongside brave war dead, can no longer be excused as something that has simply slipped through the administrative net. This is not only an insult to the other servicemen and women whose names justifiably appear on the Brookwood Memorial; it is an added insult to the victims of those criminals as well as their families.

Furthermore, it is a contradiction to the very purpose of the memorial which is 'dedicated to those whom the fortune of war denied a *known and honoured grave*'. In every case of those listed above, the burial place is known and clearly recorded, and with crimes including murder, rape and treason, their actions certainly do not deserve to be honoured.

WINSTON RAMSEY, EDITOR, 2011

Photographs

Superintendent Percy Savage of New Scotland Yard describes how Frederick Browne and William Kennedy were brought to justice for the murder of Police Constable George Gutteridge in 1927 on pages 73 to 80.

The copyright is indicated for all original illustrations where known. All present-day photographs are the copyright of After the Battle unless stated otherwise.

Akomos Photography: 294 bottom right.
Barry Cheese: 269 bottom.
Bill Quill: 150 top left and right, 151 bottom right.
Bourne Hall Museum: 55 bottom left.
British Film Institute: 290 top.
Cambridge City Council: 131 bottom.
Commonwealth War Graves Commission: 358 top.
Essex Police: 70 centre and bottom left, 71 top left, 74 bottom, 75 top, 77 top left, 78 top left and right, 79 top left and right, bottom left and right, 82 top left, 145 bottom.
Francis Frith: 203 top, 204 bottom left.
Getty Images: 39 top, 45 bottom left, 52 top, 58 bottom, 62 bottom left and right, 67 centre, 100 top, 101 top left, 107 bottom, 192 centre, 193 bottom left, 198 top, 199 top left, 205 top, 207 top, 208 top, 210 top, 220 bottom left, 225 top, 237 top, 242 top, 244 bottom, 258 top, 259 top, 263 top, 265 top left, 266 top left, bottom left, 275 bottom left, 276 top right, 277 top left, bottom, 280 bottom, 282 top, 289 top, 292 top right, 299 bottom, 301 top, 309 bottom left, 311 top, 321 centre, 334 top, 335 centre, 336 bottom left, 340 bottom left, 343 centre, 344 top, 345 top, 347 both, 349 top and centre.
Godalming Library: 116 top.
Greater London County Council: 26 top.
Imperial War Museum: 160 bottom right, 170 top.
John Frost Newspapers: 225 bottom, 226, 227.
John Gallehawk: 288 top left.
JS Crime Library: 117 top, 118 top and bottom, 120 top, 123 centre, 124 top left, 125 bottom, 153 top left, 161 centre, 163 both, 217 top left, 318 bottom left, 342 bottom, 343 top, 351 top, 352 top left.
Kathy Taylor: 88 top.
Kent Police: 231 top and bottom left, 233 top, 234 top, 235 top, and bottom right, 236 top left, centre and bottom, 238 top and bottom, 239 top left, bottom left.
Kevin Lamberth: 87 centre and bottom, 128 bottom, 129 bottom.
London Transport Museum: 151 top right, 187 top right, 286 bottom left and right, 312 top left, bottom.
Mirrorpix: 155 bottom, 156 top left, centre and bottom left and right, 211 top and bottom left, 214 bottom, 219 bottom left, 221 bottom, 222 top left and right, 285 top left, 297 bottom right.
National Archives: 90 top, 91 top and bottom left, 96 bottom, 99 top right, 101 top right, 102 top left and right, 104 top left and right, 108 both, 113 both, 119 top, 122 bottom, 125 top and centre, 126 all, 154 top, 155 top, 213 bottom, 218 top right, 224 bottom, 240, 241 bottom, 247 both, 248 both, 250 bottom left, 251 all, 252 bottom right, 253 top left and right, bottom right, 255 top left, 256 both, 257 all, 272 both, 274 top, 275 bottom right, 285 bottom, 295 centre, 296 bottom, 297 top, 298 bottom left and right, 307 top right, 308 top right and bottom, 309 centre, 313 centre and bottom left, 314 top, 317 bottom, 323 top, 324 right, 325 top left, 326 top, 346 top left, bottom, 350 top right, 352 top right.
Norman Attwood: 231 bottom right.
Northamptonshire Police: 128 top, 129 centre, 130 bottom.
Ordnance Survey: 117 centre, 166 bottom, 258 centre, 273 bottom.
Police Roll of Honour Trust: 308 top left, 313 top left, 353 top left, centre left, bottom left.
Press Association: 7 bottom, 44 top left and bottom, 68 bottom, 69 top, 99 top left, 165 top right, 173 bottom right, 185 top, 188 top, 192 top left, centre and right, 209 top left, bottom left, 218 top left and bottom, 225 bottom, 255 bottom, 265 bottom left, 266 top right, 267 top, 268 bottom left, 278 top left and right, 279 bottom, 283 top left and right and centre right, 288 top right, 292 bottom, 300 top left and bottom, 304 top right and bottom, 305 top, 306 top left, 310 top, 313 top right, 316 top left and right, bottom left, 317 top, 319 top left, centre left, bottom left, 320 top and bottom left, 321 top left, 322 top left, 325 centre, bottom left, 326 top left, 335 top, 336 top, 337 top left, bottom left, 339 bottom, 341 top, bottom left, 348 top left and right, 350 bottom left and right, 352 bottom.
Rex Features: 195 top.
Richard Riding: 221 top left, 224 top.
Robert W. Gould/Michael J. Waldren: 61 centre.
Roger Morgan: 244 top right.
Royal Artillery Museum: 157 centre.
Steve Casely: 132 top, 136 top right, bottom right, 139 bottom, 146 top left and right, bottom, 147 bottom, 353 centre right.
Steve Fielding: 89 top, 90 bottom, 114 top, 115 bottom.
Stuart McLaughlin, Wandsworth Prison Museum: 83 top left and right, 92 all, 279 top, 280 top left and right.
Surrey Police: 121 top.
***The Sun*:** 301 centre.
Topfoto: 212 top right, 213 top left.
US Judge Advocate General: 129 top, 137 both, 138, 139 top, 140 top, 141 all, 142, 144 top right, 158 top, 159 top, 166 top right, 167 centre and bottom, 168 both, 169 top left and right.
US Signal Corps: 356 top.
The Wardrobe (Berkshire and Wiltshire Regiments) 357 top.

INDEX

COMPILED BY PETER B. GUNN

Page numbers in *italics* refer to illustrations. There may also be textual references on these pages.

In Memory of
Wren DOREEN MARGARET MARSHALL
51177, H.M.S. PRESIDENT, Women's Royal Naval Service
who died age 21 on 04 July 1946
Remembered with honour HARROW (PINNER) NEW CEMETERY

Commemorated in perpetuity by the Commonwealth War Graves Commission

Any communication on this subject should quote the date and number on the reverse of this form.

Postage must be prepaid.

METRO

C.I. DIVISIO

REPORT for the information of the Regis
Somers

respecting letter Ref.No. NE/49/1767 c

Corres.No. 201/49/47. CONFID

(The information given is supplied on the clea
the source from which it is obtain

On 10th August, 19
murder of Mrs. Olive Durand
into this case it was estab
persons on or about or betw

William Donald McSWAN
22, Kempsford Gardens

Donald McSWAN, N.R.I.
Sarah McSWAN, N.R.I.C
S.W.1, between 2nd an

Dr. Archibald HENDERS
Mrs. Rose M. HENDERSO
Dawes Road, Fulham, S

Amongst the proper
identity cards relating to
books for the period 1948/4
the three ration books, Hai,

dent.

udent

cretary

her on her ret